ALSO BY GARY LACHMAN

the SECRET TEACHERS of the WESTERN WORLD

GARY LACHMAN

JEREMY P. TARCHER / PENGUIN
an imprint of Penguin Random House
New York

JEREMY P. TARCHER/PENGUIN
An imprint of Penguin Random House LLC
375 Hudson Street
New York, New York 10014

Most Tarcher/Penguin books are available at special quantity discounts for bulk purchase
for sales promotions, premiums, fund-raising, and educational needs. Special books or
book excerpts also can be created to fit specific needs. For details,
write: SpecialMarkets@penguinrandomhouse.com.

Library of Congress Cataloging-in-Publication Data

Lachman, Gary, 1955–
The secret teachers of the western world / by Gary Lachman.
pages cm
ISBN 978-0-399-16680-8
1. Occultism—History.   2. Occultists.   I. Title.
BF1411.L235   2015
130—dc23
2015021615

Printed in the United States of America
1   3   5   7   9   10   8   6   4   2

Book design by Gretchen Achilles

For Jean Gebser (1905–1973)

Only someone who has overcome himself

is truly able to overcome.

CHAPTER TWO   57
OUT OF THE MYSTERIES

CHAPTER THREE   86
THE SECRET GNOSIS

stand of paganism • The cult of Mithras • Military mysteries • Soothsayers and Wonderworkers • The Sibyls • The Juliani and the Chaldean Oracles • Apollonius of Tyana • "The Lamia" • Jesus Christ, the Secret Teacher • Similarities between Apollonius and Jesus • A pagan Christ • *The Jesus Mysteries* • Was Jesus a mushroom? • A Secret Christianity? • Morton Smith and the secret Gospel • The Gospel of Thomas • *Thunder, Perfect Mind* • The Gnostics • Early Christian critics • A False World • The demiurge and the left brain • Emanations and archons • A cosmic prison: Heidegger and Gurdjieff • Hylics, psychics, and pneumatics • Conspiracy theories and the "hermeneutics of suspicion" • Gnostics at Work • Mani, Valentinus, Basilides of Alexandria, Carpocrates, Simon Magus and Sophia • Antinomianism • Marcion • The Roots of Gnosticism • Merkabah mysticism • The Essenes and the retreat to the desert • Zoroastrianism • "Platonism run wild"

Alexander the Great and the founding of Alexandria • Aristotle's' student • No worlds left to conquer • Rise of the Ptolemies • A City of Sects and Gospels • Death of Cleopatra • The religious mysteries of Egypt • Fusion of Greek and Egyptian religious ideas • Syncretism • Serapis • The spiritual marketplace • The library of Alexandria • Amr ibn al'Aas: burn the books to heat the baths • *Episteme* and *gnosis* • The Other Gnostics • Clement of Alexandria • The Need for Symbols • Philo of Alexandria • The Great Chain of Being • Origen • A eunuch for God • A posthumous heretic • *Against Celsus* • A Gnostic Trinity • *Apocatastasis* • Thrice Greatest Hermes • Who were the Hermetists? • When Thoth met Hermes • The *Book of Thoth* • The *Asclepius* • Bad days for Egypt • The Creation According to Hermes • G. R. S. Mead and the doubting mind • *Nous* • A creature of two worlds • The Journey Through the Planets • A pre-Christian Christianity • The ladder of consciousness • Cosmic Consciousness • "If you do not make yourself equal to God you cannot understand him" • Hermetic participation • Drawing Down the Gods • Theurgy • Plotinus and the Man He Was Looking For • Disdain for the body • No pictures, please • Ammonius

CHAPTER FIVE   155
GREAT PAN IS DEAD

things" • Alchemical Changes • Transformations • The quest and the mystic marriage • Alchemical "self-made men" • Imaginal Medicine • A healthy correspondence • "Direct knowledge" • Jeremy Narby and ayahuasca • The Inner Firmament • Imagination and the Philosopher's Stone • Mary Anne South and the Mysteries • *A Suggestive Inquiry* • The Mystic Cobbler • Jacob Boehme • Boehme's pewter dish • Learning more in one quarter of an hour • The Signature of Things • A Christian theosopher • War of the worlds • A dramatic universe

"counterculture" • Eranos • Psychic Societies • The Society for Psychical Research • F. W. H. Myers and *Human Personality and Its Survival of Bodily Death* • William James and *The Varieties of Religious Experience* • Golden Dawns • The Hermetic Order of the Golden Dawn • MacGregor Mathers • Fräulein Sprengel and the cipher manuscript • Aleister Crowley • The Old New Age • A. R. Orage, a "desperado of genius" • *The New Age* • Theosophists and socialists • Superman consciousness • Annie Besant • From secularist to mystic • C. W. Leadbeater and Krishnamurti's Aura • Talking with the Masters • *Occult Chemistry* • Home Rule • Indian independence • Ouspensky's Fourth Dimension • A "time-haunted man" • *Tertium Organum* • Seeking God at the Stray Dog Café • Dr. Steiner, I Presume? • Geometry and visions • From Active Seeing to Supersensible Perception • Goethe • Steiner and Theosophy • Cosmic evolution • The End of Old Europe • World War I • The golden age of modern esotericism • Meeting a Remarkable Man • Mr. Gurdjieff • Mechanical man • Remember Your Self • Gurdjieff and Heidegger • Food for the Moon • Seekers of Truth • A Miraculous Escape • The Madness of C. G. Jung • Descent into the Unconscious • Jung the Gnostic • Schools of Wisdom • Count Keyserling • *The Threefold Commonwealth* • The Abbey of Thelema • The Institute for the Harmonious Development of Man • Reconstructing Europe • The end of the system • A new morning ahead?

Flying saucers • A hunger for *something more* • Jung and the mandalas from outer space • *Aion* and the age of Aquarius • Magical Mornings and Mushrooms • *The Morning of the Magicians* • The occult revival of the 1960s • Albert Hofmann and LSD • Timothy Leary and the new mysteries • John Lennon turns off his mind • The Return of the Beast • Crowley and the Beatles • Pop esotericism • The New New Age • Dark side of the Aquarian Age • Domesticated occultism • The New Humanism • Maslow • Human potential at Esalen • "Forced spontaneity" • Transpersonal Psychology • Roberto Assagioli • Alice Bailey • Spiritual Summer Schools •

Olga Fröbe-Kapteyn and Casa Gabriella • Psychosynthesis • Aquarian Conspiracies • Marilyn Ferguson and *The Aquarian Conspiracy* • The *Brain/ Mind Bulletin* • H. G. Wells and *The Open Conspiracy* • Channels, Crystals, and Other Accessories • Here comes the New Age • Shirley MacLaine is out on a limb • Spiritual consumerism • The Lindisfarne Association • On the Way to 2012 • The Harmonic Convergence • My Part in All This • Esoteric Internet • Too much of a good thing? • "The secrets once imparted only to initiates are there on the bookshelves" • *Meditations on the Tarot* • Valentin Tomberg, a modern esotericist • Gebser's Breakdown • The last days of the mental-rational structure of consciousness • A World Gone Mad? • Uncertain particles • A Different Perspective • The end of things • A Last Stand • The New Consciousness • Babies and bathwater • The "irruption of time" • The Integral Brain • The importance of language • On the brink of the integral consciousness structure • Completing the Partial Mind • Goldilocks and beyond

REJECTED KNOWLEDGE

For some time now I have been involved in a study of what is known as the "western esoteric tradition." I've written biographies of some of its major figures, looked at its impact on politics, literature, popular culture, and society, and tried to understand its place and importance in the evolution of the western mind. "Esoteric" means "inner" and "secret," and although its exact roots are unclear—some place its origin in lost Atlantis, others in ancient Egypt—the western esoteric tradition has its source in several mystical and occult teachings of the past: Hermeticism, Gnosticism, Kabbalah, and the Neoplatonism that arose in Alexandria in the early centuries of our era.

Accounts of these and other esoteric philosophies will be found in the pages that follow, but one thing they all share is that they are for the most part rejected by our accepted intellectual tradition, the standard "official" story of the history of the western mind. They form, as the historian of the occult James Webb called it, a body of "rejected knowledge," the intellectual refuse we have discarded as we abandoned the superstitions of the past in order to embrace the science of the modern day.

In some ways this is an accurate if incomplete assessment. Yet as I have tried to show in earlier books, this "other" tradition, however disparaged, refuses to disappear, and it remains in different forms available to us today. Why is this other knowledge rejected and why does it refuse to go away?

The central reason this knowledge is rejected is that it fails to meet the criteria of "real" knowledge set by modern science. Since its beginnings in the seventeenth century, modern science has focused on the kind of "facts" that can be grasped by the senses and proven by measurement. It abandoned the religious explanations for the world, which posited an unseen God behind the universe; accepted only that which it could see and touch; and brought an acute analysis to the phenomena of the physical world. Gradually, and with increasing certainty, it came to the conclusion that the only knowledge worth knowing was the kind that could be quantified. Physical laws that could be observed and measured would, it believed, account for everything, and the belief that anything else was needed or that anything could escape the necessities imposed by these laws was abandoned. The results of this belief we see around us everywhere, from the computer I am using to write this book to the probes we have sent out into space in order to explore the mysteries of the universe.

To say that this kind of knowledge is good and useful is an understatement. As more than one historian has pointed out, because of it the world has advanced more in the last few centuries than in the millennia that preceded them. This knowledge is absolutely indispensable, and because of it we today, who profit by it, live lives undreamed of by our ancestors. But is it the only kind of knowledge?

The esoteric tradition says no. There is another kind of knowledge. It is not one of physical facts, nor can it be quantified and measured. It is a knowledge of our inner world, not the outer one, a knowledge of what we used to call the spirit or the soul, that invisible, intangible something that animates us and leads us to ask questions about who we are and what our place in this mysterious world can be. It is essentially concerned with the meaning of our existence, a question that the other kind of knowledge cannot answer or rejects as nonsense. For our scientific kind of knowledge, the spirit or soul are superstitions, delusions, as neither can be detected by the senses. Who has seen the soul or spirit? For the esoteric tradition, the physical world available to the senses that science affirms as the only reality is only a small part of a much greater reality, an invisible, inner reality, that informs the outer world and gives it life and meaning.

For those who have a sense of this invisible, other reality, the answers to life's mysteries offered by modern science are inadequate and unsatisfying. They are unable to accept them and they find themselves seeking something else.

For most of our history, mankind in some way believed in the existence of this other, invisible world, inaccessible to the senses. It is only in relatively recent times that we have rejected it as unreal and placed all our faith in the truths of modern science. Yet not everyone has been happy with this conclusion; traces of this other knowledge remain and many persist in trying to understand it and what it can tell us about ourselves. The proponents of modern science insist this is a mistake and assure us that we must reject this false knowledge in order to gain the truth. Yet the feeling that this other knowledge has something to tell us persists, and despite all the attempts by modern science to eradicate it, it stubbornly remains.

For different people in different ways there is a nagging, insistent sense that something is missing, and that for all its undeniable achievements and advances in understanding the physical world, the explanations for themselves and the universe offered by modern science lack something important. There is the feeling that somewhere, in the background, there is something that would help make sense of it all, but that we can't quite put our finger on it. The knowledge offered by the esoteric tradition may be rejected, but the feeling that without it we are somehow incomplete is something that simply won't go away. Whether we like it or not, we seem to be stuck with it.

In 2011, I came across a book that led me to see this rejected knowledge in a new and very suggestive light. It was *The Master and His Emissary* (2009) by the psychiatrist and literary scholar Iain McGilchrist. *The Master and His Emissary* is about our two cerebral hemispheres, the right and left sides of the brain, and the differences between them. What exactly our having two brains has to do with the western esoteric tradition may not seem immediately clear. But if the reader will bear with me, the connection—a very important one—should become less obscure as we go along.

OUR OTHER SELF

As everyone today knows, the cliché idea about the left and right brain is that the left is a scientist while the right is an artist. In the nineteenth century, this neat dichotomy was summed up in a handy formula: "left for language, right for recognition." The fact that we have two brains has been recognized for millennia—Greek physicians in the third century B.C. speculated about it—although exactly why we do has never been clearly understood.[1] The left, the story goes, deals with language, logic, and sequential thought and has an acute sense of time, while the right is attuned to patterns, intuition, sees wholes simultaneously, and seems to reside in a kind of eternal present—at any rate it has a poor sense of time. The left cerebral hemisphere deals with language, it is the home of our ego, the verbal "I" with which we identify. Next door to it—or "us"— separated by a bundle of neural fibers called the corpus callosum or com- missure, resides, for all intents and purposes, a stranger. This stranger does not speak but communicates in symbols, images, intuitions, hunches, even physical sensations, and may, as some theorists have speculated, be involved in paranormal phenomena.

One of the most bizarre findings of split-brain research is that when, for some reason, the corpus callosum, which facilitates communication between the hemispheres, is severed—sometimes in order to inhibit epi- leptic fits, which are a kind of "electrical storm" within the brain—the result is that the patient literally becomes two people. For some unknown reason, the right side of the body is controlled by the left brain, and the left side by the right. When the connection between the hemispheres is broken, the oddity about this arrangement becomes clear. Experiments with patients with severed commissures produced extraordinary results.

For example, our right visual field is controlled by the left brain, and our left visual field by the right (each eye has a right and left field, but for convenience's sake I will speak of the left and right eye). A patient whose commissure was severed was shown an apple with his right eye, connected to the left, verbal brain, and an orange with his left eye, connected to his speechless right brain. When asked what he had seen, he replied "apple"; when asked to write with his left hand—connected to his right brain— what he had seen, he wrote "orange." Shown two different symbols—a circle and a square—with each eye, when asked what he had seen, he replied "square." When asked to draw with his left hand what he was just shown, he drew a circle. When asked what he had just drawn, he replied "a square." A patient might bump into something with his left side, connected to his right brain, *but not notice it*. He didn't notice it because "he" lives in his left brain and so really did not bump into anything; it was the stranger in his right brain who did. One woman was shown a sexy picture with her left eye and blushed; asked why she was blushing, she replied quite accurately, "I don't know."[2]

Some split-brain patients find that they have become a divided self, literally battling with their other half. One patient complained that doing grocery shopping became an ordeal. "I'd reach with my right hand for the thing I wanted, but the left would come in and they'd kind of fight." Even dressing became a struggle: the two sides had different tastes and a patient might wind up wearing three outfits at once.[3] Yet there are times when the right brain comes to the aid of the left. The neuropsychologist Roger Sperry tested split-brain patients by flashing red and green lights randomly at their left eye and asking them to guess which color they had just seen. As the patient couldn't have seen anything—"he" lives in the left, verbal hemisphere—the results should have been fifty-fifty. Yet more times than not, a patient would say "red," then suddenly start, change his mind, and answer "green"; his right brain had heard the incorrect answer and metaphorically kicked his other half under the table. We all have had the experience of having a name or word on "the tip of the tongue," but not quite being able to remember it; the French have a term for this, *presque vu*, "almost seen." What may be at work here is that the right brain somehow knows what we want to say, but can't tell the left. Yet we are right to think that we do know it, as our other half does, and it may try to give us clues.[4] Goethe famously wrote in *Faust* that *"Zwei Seelen wohnen, ach! In meiner Brust"* ("Two souls, alas, live in my breast"). It seems that Goethe was right.

Yet with all this fascinating material, neuroscientists soon began to lose interest in studying the split brain. One reason was that, with increasing research, the neat localization of functions in either side of the brain did not hold up. Scientists soon realized that although one hemisphere may be more dominant in some processes—as the left is with language— both sides of the brain do the same things and are involved in practically all our activities.[5] The neat separation into localized functions unraveled and scientists began to wonder if there really was anything interesting in the fact that we have two brains. Some even joked that we have a second one as a kind of spare, in case the other is damaged.

Another reason research into our two hemispheres dwindled is that most "hard" scientists disapproved of the popularizing of split-brain theory by "soft" self-help psychology and New Age gurus, and understandably wanted to back away from it. Peer pressure, professional prudence, and the recognition that there were no significant functional differences between the hemispheres meant that most serious neuroscientists made a discreet exodus from our twin brains. The one legacy from the early days of split-brain theory that remained enshrined in mainstream neuroscience is that the left "logical" brain is dominant. The right, it believed, was "minor," a kind of slightly helpful sidekick who tags along while the boss deals with serious matters. The right brain was the "spare," it seemed, while the left was the main set of equipment, something that McGilchrist, with a daunting amount of research, set out to disprove.

DUAL REALITIES

The Master and His Emissary is important because it revamps the split-brain discussion, and it does it in a way that opens up whole new areas of investigation, some of which, I believe, throw new light on our rejected, esoteric tradition. There is an important difference between our two cerebral hemispheres, McGilchrist argues, but it is not a difference in *what* they do, but in *how* they do it.[6] Both sides of our brain may do the same things, and be involved in the same functions, but each side performs these functions differently—very differently, in fact. Our two brains have radically different approaches to our experience and the world; indeed, McGilchrist even suggests that they are different *personalities,* something split-brain patients have discovered for themselves, with their "other" brain having different tastes in food and clothing. McGilchrist argues that the differences between our cerebral hemispheres are so great that "for us as human beings there are two fundamentally opposed realities," an insight that, in different ways, is shared by our rejected esoteric tradition.[7]

The right brain, which, McGilchrist tells us, is older and more fundamental—it is the "master" of his title—presents reality as a unified whole. It provides the "big picture" of a living, breathing Other, that strange, ambiguous world that exists outside our minds. It is geared toward the new, the unfamiliar, and with what we can call the immediate "is-ness" of things, the *Istigkeit* of the medieval Rhineland mystic Meister Eckhart. It is concerned with *implicit* meanings that can be felt but not pinned down exactly; it is partial to what the philosopher Michael Polanyi called "the tacit dimension," the implied, intuited meanings of which, as Polanyi says, "we can know more than we can tell."[8] Poetry, metaphor, images, and symbols are some ways in which we try to communicate what the right brain shows us, and the meanings these forms of expression convey share in this implicitness. Good poetry has an aura of *suggestiveness* around it, a sense that it reaches out beyond the dictionary meanings of the words it uses; it alludes to a significance that we cannot express specifically, but which nonetheless *touches* us.

The right brain is geared toward engaging with living things, McGilchrist says, and with recognizing overall patterns, meanings, and relations. It is attuned to the network of connections that links everything with everything else. Its fundamental attention is to the "whole," which it takes in simultaneously. It is more geared to perceiving the forest, we might say, and not the individual trees.

The left brain, on the other hand—literally—is geared, McGilchrist argues, toward breaking up the whole that the right presents. It turns the right brain's unity into bits and pieces, which it can then manipulate. Its job is to analyze the big picture presented by the right and reduce it to easily manageable parts, which it can control and arrange to suit its purposes. These are generally geared toward survival. Where the right is open to "newness" and appreciates the "being" of things-in-themselves, the left is geared to representing reality as something familiar and sees things in terms of their *use*. The left brain has a utilitarian approach to reality, whereas the right just accepts things as they are. The left brain "stands apart" from experience, it *distances* itself from it in order to master it, while the right brain is *in* it. We use the left brain to "cope" with the world, as it were, while it is through the right that we *appreciate* it.

McGilchrist explains that the right brain needs the left because its picture, while of the whole, is fuzzy and imprecise. The left brain "unpacks" the whole that the right brain presents, and brings its details into sharper focus. The left, on the other hand, needs the right because while it can focus with dazzling clarity on discreet bits, it loses the connections between things and can find itself stranded in a fragmented world. One brain can lose itself in a vague, hazy perception of the whole; the Other, in a narrow obsession with the part. One brain gives us context, the other detail. One looks at a panorama, the other through a microscope. One brain presents everything "allatonce"; the other in bits and pieces "one-at-a-time." If we think of a camera and how its lens can be focused on either the background or the foreground, we can see how these two opposing perceptions of things complement each other. In life, we need to see the forest *and* the trees, often at the same time, and this can prove difficult. It would be impossible for one brain to do this, McGilchrist contends, and so we have two.[9]

WHO'S THE BOSS?

Probably the most controversial argument in *The Master and His Emissary* is McGilchrist's contention that the right brain, rather than a superfluous sidekick, is really the boss, although the left brain generally refuses to recognize this. As mentioned earlier, the right brain is older; its form of perceiving and interacting with the world is primary. We would not, McGilchrist argues, have a "world" for the left brain to carve up and manipulate if it were not for the right brain's "presencing" of it in its unadulterated wholeness.

In fact, McGilchrist sees the relation between the two hemispheres as a friendly but serious rivalry. Throughout our history, he argues, they have been engaged in a system of cerebral checks and balances, with each inhibiting the other's excesses in a neurological embodiment of William Blake's dictum that "Opposition is true friendship." As we have seen with split-brain patients, this friendly opposition can get out of hand, with the two sides canceling each other out. But for the most part, McGilchrist says, our two brains have complemented each other amiably.

Until recently, that is.

McGilchrist argues that since the Industrial Revolution, this power-sharing agreement has broken down, with the left brain assuming an increasingly dominant position. It was at this point that the "Emissary" usurped power from the "Master." The situation is rather like that of the Gnostic creation myth, in which the demiurge, or craftsman, employed by the "true God" to create the world, comes to believe that *it* is really in control, that it is the supreme deity, and enacts a coup d'état, with disastrous consequences. The left brain likes to deal with what is familiar, with what it knows, and in modern times it has been busy turning the world around it into what it knows best: a machine. Its demand for precision, clarity, definiteness, and parts has created a world that is more and more *like itself*. This means, McGilchrist argues, that there is less and less of an "other" for the right brain to "presence," because increasingly all it can reflect back is the world the left brain has created. Modern cities, vast industrialized areas, the seemingly unstoppable digitizing of experience—think of our growing demand for the "lifelike" presentation of entertainment, of HD television and 3-D films, that represent to us in electronically enhanced detail a "natural world" that is itself steadily diminishing: all of this points to an increasingly left-brain world. According to McGilchrist, for the last two centuries, the left brain has been busy creating a mechanical environment, a world of parts, bits, and pieces that it can manipulate and through which it can fulfil its utilitarian aims and goals, at the expense of the whole.

One result of this left-brain takeover is that the materialist, reductionist science which it informs increasingly diminishes the right brain's contribution to our understanding of the world. One example of this is mainstream neuroscience's contention that the right brain is "minor," "secondary," and, ultimately, unimportant. On a wider scale, the overarching belief that we live in a purposeless, meaningless universe, within which we ourselves are equally purposeless and meaningless, has come to dominate our consciousness. The only kind of "meaning" the left brain can grasp is explicit; it is the kind involved in a "how-to" kind of question, not the "why" variety, or the kind provided by measuring devices, graphs, and figures (as you might expect, the right brain is a music lover; the left has a tin ear). And it can only assimilate it in an "either/or" context—the binary 0 and 1 of our computers. This being so, it can see no meaning to our existence, and that seems to be the general assessment. As the astro-physicist Steven Weinberg famously remarked, "The more the universe seems comprehensible, the more it also seems pointless."[10] Comprehensi-ble to the left brain, that is.

LEfT-BRAIN AGGRESSION

There was much in what McGilchrist said that interested me, but here I want to make one point. There is a fundamental *aggressive* character to the left brain's recent bid for power. To be sure, there is a fundamental aggres-sive character to left-brain consciousness to begin with. This is clear in its propensity for analysis, for breaking up the whole into separate pieces, for manipulating reality. It is, as it were, our tool for *attacking* reality, for shap-ing it to our needs. In *The Alphabet Versus the Goddess,* Leonard Shlain argues that left-brain consciousness developed in male hunters because of their need to focus their attention tightly on their prey, excluding every-thing else; right brain "field awareness" developed in female gatherers/nurturers, who needed to be more aware of their surroundings.[11] As the poet Wordsworth wrote, "We murder to dissect." All of this is necessary. The left brain is our indispensable tool for surviving in the world, and it is because of it that we have become the dominant species on the planet. McGilchrist is certainly not saying that we should get rid of the left brain and return to a right-brain–dominated world. We need both in order to, as the poet W. B. Yeats says in "Under Ben Bulben," complete our partial mind, as well as our "partial reality." But if, as McGilchrist says, our cere-bral hemispheres have distinct temperaments and personalities—something split-brain patients experience at first hand—then it makes perfect sense to wonder if the left brain would *purposely* try to undermine the right. If it is involved in a competition with its rival, we can assume that it would go out of its way to diminish the right brain's input, or to eradicate it completely.

With this in mind, I began to wonder: is there some expression of right-brain thinking, of a right-brain view of the world, that would be a prime target for the expansionist aims of the left brain? Is there a body of "right-brain knowledge," so to speak, that the left brain would certainly want to topple, or at least to cast aspersions on? Is there some right-brain tradition, the reputation of which the left brain would like to undermine?

McGilchrist was not the first to suggest that the left brain had aggressive tendencies toward the right. In *The Alphabet Versus the Goddess*, Leonard Shlain argued that the rise of literacy—a left-brain development—and its focus on linear, sequential thinking led to the decline of the earlier, right-brain, image-oriented goddess religions, as well as to the rise of monotheism and patriarchal forms of society. Left-brain literacy, Shlain contends, is male friendly, while right-brain imagery is more feminine. The subtitle of Shlain's book is *The Conflict Between Word and Image,* and as we've seen, the left brain works with language and logic while the right is more at home with symbols and imagery. Shlain makes a strong case that, since the rise of literacy in the second millennium B.C., the left brain has increasingly gained greater and greater dominance, and has, at times, fought a highly aggressive campaign against its opposite hemisphere. "Speech," Shlain writes, "gave the left brain the edge to usurp the sovereignty of the mind from its elder twin"; Shlain agrees with McGilchrist that the right-brain form of consciousness is primary.[12] Whatever we may think of Shlain's argument—in *A Secret History of Consciousness*, I point out some of its drawbacks—he does show that at different times in history, "left-brain consciousness" seems to have waged an often ruthless war against its right-brain counterpart.[13]

If the left brain has waged a smear campaign against the right, would it take other forms than Shlain's "conflict between word and image"? Would it, as it were, open up other fronts? One target of left-brain aggression, it seems to me, would certainly be the western esoteric tradition.

ESOTERICISM AND THE RIGHT BRAIN

The more I thought about this, the more obvious it became. For one thing, the esoteric tradition deals in imagery and symbols, the meanings of which are often complex and multiple, and which elude the left brain's demand for clarity and definiteness; they are more attuned to what McGilchrist calls the right brain's "both/and" approach, rather than the left brain's "either/or." Indeed, imagination, linked to the right brain, is one of the central pillars of the esoteric tradition. As the historian of esotericism Antoine Faivre writes, imagination is "a kind of organ of the soul, thanks to which humanity can establish a cognitive and visionary relationship with an intermediary world," what Faivre's fellow esoteric scholar Henry Corbin called the "*Mundus Imaginalis*," the "Imaginal World," an *inner* yet nonetheless *objective* symbolic territory, having its own rules and inhabitants. Imagination, Faivre argues, is an indispensable "tool for knowledge of self, world, Myth," and he makes imagination one of the "four fundamental elements" of esotericism.[14] In the same sense, the poet and essayist Kathleen Raine, who has written about poetry and its links to esotericism, speaks of a "learning of the imagination." The esoteric tradition is also intuitive, focusing on our subtle, inner worlds, rather than our obvious outer one. It believes in a living, organic, spiritual, even conscious universe, rather than a dead, mechanical, oblivious one. It is also concerned more with the whole than with the part, with the "correspondences" between things—the "network of connections that links everything with everything else"—than with what separates them. It is also more attuned to the kind of simultaneity associated with the right brain than with the sequential thought associated with the left.

It is also rooted in what it calls "ancient wisdom" and is less concerned with the future. As mentioned, McGilchrist believes the right brain predates the left—it is older—while the left, he argues, has an often manic self-confidence and "forward-looking" fixation. The esoteric tradition is more focused on *being* rather than *doing,* on inner change rather than controlling the world. And it is less keen on maintaining the strict subject/object, "I" and "not-I" relation to the world than the left is. A key insight, in some form or another, in the esoteric tradition is that "all is one," and that the usual sharp distinction between inner and outer worlds that the left brain is at pains to uphold is not as secure as it seems. Lastly, the esoteric tradition is concerned with the timeless, the eternal; it is involved with the mythic character of our consciousness and even speaks of a "perennial philosophy." The left brain, we know, is obsessed with time.

There are other characteristics of the western esoteric tradition that would suggest that if the left brain was planning an assault on the reputation of the right, it would turn its sights in its direction. We know that with the rise of modern science in the seventeenth century—a development clearly linked to the temperament of the left brain—the esoteric tradition lost much of its prestige and that, in order to maintain itself, it had to go "underground" and become, as it remains today, a kind of "counterculture." In my book *The Quest for Hermes Trismegistus* (2011), I speculate that Hermeticism's loss of prestige in the seventeenth century was related to what philosopher Jean Gebser calls the "deficient mode of the mental-rational consciousness structure."[15] There are some important similarities between Gebser's ideas and McGilchrist's and, if the reader will allow, it is necessary to touch on some of them here.

STRUCTURES Of CONSCIOUSNESS

The German-born Swiss philosopher Jean Gebser is little known to English-speaking readers; this is unfortunate, as he is one of the most important thinkers of the last century. His life reads like an intellectual adventure story. He was a child during World War I, saw the rise of the Nazis, just missed being killed in the Spanish Civil War, escaped Paris on the eve of the German occupation, and finally settled in Switzerland, where he became friends with C. G. Jung and took part in the famous Eranos Conferences over which Jung presided. In 1932, while working on a book about the Austrian poet Rainer Maria Rilke, Gebser had an insight whose implications were stunning and which he devoted the rest of his life to grasping. In Rilke's poetry, Gebser seemed to see evidence that a change was taking place in western consciousness, that it was somehow becoming *different*. A new kind of consciousness seemed to be appearing in the West, Gebser believed, and he began to see evidence for this in a variety of fields: in science, art, literature, philosophy, as well as other disciplines. Gebser spent the next decade and a half collecting material supporting his insight and collating his data; in 1949, his magnum opus, *The Ever-Present Origin*, appeared; it would not be translated into English until 1985.

The central argument of *The Ever-Present Origin* is that human consciousness is not static. Throughout its history, it has gone through several changes—what Gebser calls "mutations"—before arriving at our own form of consciousness. These mutations transform consciousness from one "structure" to another. There have been four such structures so far, what Gebser calls "the archaic," "the magical," "the mythic," and the "the mental-rational," ranging from our prehistoric ancestors to modern times. Gebser also posits a fifth "structure of consciousness," what he calls "the integral," which is an integration of the previous four structures, and he believed that we, in the late modern world, were beginning to experience the effects of the shift from the mental-rational to the integral structure. These effects, Gebser believed, had to do with our experience of time. Gebser offers a sometimes daunting amount of evidence for his structures of consciousness and for our current passage into the integral structure, and in *A Secret History of Consciousness,* the reader can find my extended account of his ideas.[16]

The basic idea behind Gebser's structures of consciousness is that they are characterized by an increasing separation and distinction from what he calls "Origin," an atemporal, nonspatial ontological source, which is "before all time," yet which is also "the entirety of the very beginning."[17] "Origin," Gebser tells us, is a "preforming and primal paradigm of Being," a kind of timeless "matrix" out of which all things come into existence.[18] If the reader finds this a bit confusing, he is not alone. Readers of Gebser soon become aware of a frequent difficulty with his terminology; this is because he is forced to use our everyday language in order to express insights that transcend the everyday. Georg Feuerstein, in his book on Gebser, speaks of "Origin" as "the ever-present reality . . . by nature divine and spiritual" out of which our different consciousness structures emerge, and that seems a workable enough definition.[19] One thing to note about Gebser's "Origin" is that it is very similar to Gnostic ideas about "the Pleroma," as well as to Neoplatonic and Hermetic notions about "the One" or the Kabbalistic *"En-Sof"*: all are a kind of nonmanifest source of the manifest universe, but at the same time are posited as a goal for those pursuing the spiritual path. While the left brain has difficulty comprehending ideas about a "nonmanifest source" and "ever-present reality," the right brain, it seems, is quite at home with them.

Each structure of consciousness goes through a period of development, at the end of which it enters what Gebser calls its "deficient mode." This is when what initially was an asset becomes a handicap, when the potentials of a structure have been exhausted, and when the characteristics associated with a consciousness structure atrophy and harden into exaggerations of themselves. They become, as it were, a kind of caricature. This development is necessary in order for the next consciousness structure to emerge. The previous one needs to break up so it can make space for the new structure and the process is not always easy. The history of our consciousness, Gebser maintains, is littered with psychic catastrophes, a reflection McGilchrist agrees with. According to Gebser, who died in 1973, we are living through the last stages of the deficient mode of the mental-rational structure, and he believed that within a few decades, a "global catastrophe" was, if not imminent, certainly very likely.

THE MENTAL-RATIONAL STRUCTURE
AND THE LEFT BRAIN

As its name suggests, the mental-rational structure, which Gebser believed began circa 1225 B.C., is characterized by rational, discursive thought, the kind of logical, sequential thinking associated with the left brain. Whereas the previous structure of consciousness, the mythic, is characterized by "a shaping or designing of images"—a right-brain activity—the mental-rational structure is focused on words. Gebser's dating for the beginning of the mental-rational structure falls within suggestive reach of the dating of the first alphabets, thus aligning his "mutations" of consciousness fairly closely with Leonard Shlain's ideas about the rise of literacy.

What sets the mental-rational structure apart from the previous three structures is that it is the most separated from "Origin." In it, human consciousness, which had previously felt a fundamental connection to the world around it, was now unattached and "free." The subject/object divide became firm. Consciousness and the world were clearly experienced as different, radically opposed realities. In the mental-rational structure, for the first time man learned how to think about the world as something separate from himself, and this also meant the growing dominance of the ego, the verbal "I" which, we've seen, inhabits the left brain. As Feuerstein writes, in the mental-rational structure we find for the first time "the individual who could brave life, more or less, on his or her own, who did not feel particularly bound by, or even beholden to, the past, but who looked ahead to the possibilities of the future."[20] It was with the rise of the mental-rational structure that, Gebser argues, our idea of a linear time arose, and with it "the future." The previous mythic structure, he argues, saw time as cyclical, as a kind of "eternal recurrence," a coupling that the historian of religion Mircea Eliade also recognized in his book *The Myth of the Eternal Return* (1954). We've seen that the left brain is partial to both time and the future.

The similarities between Gebser's and McGilchrist's ideas suggest that there is good reason to link Gebser's mental-rational structure with the kind of consciousness McGilchrist associates with the left brain. For all intents and purposes, Gebser and McGilchrist are, I believe, speaking about the same thing. There are important differences between their ideas, but in a broad and significant sense they are fellow travelers.

HERMETIC RENAISSANCE

Gebser believed that the mental-rational structure entered its deficient mode around the early fourteenth century; his evidence for this is the rise of perspective painting during the first stirrings of the Renaissance.[21] Medieval man felt himself to be a part of nature; he was *in* it, in a way that we are not. With perspective, consciousness withdrew from the tapestry of nature and stood apart from it; perspective was a radical break with earlier painting because it aimed to be "lifelike," to present the world as we "really" see it. The Renaissance was one of the periods in history when, according to McGilchrist, the two sides of the brain briefly worked together, producing an enormously creative time. It was also a time of a large-scale "Hermetic revival," and some scholars have even suggested that the Renaissance owes more to Hermes Trismegistus than it does to Plato.[22] Yet within two centuries of Hermes' return, the entente cordiale between the left and right brain that McGilchrist associates with the Renaissance had clearly broken down.

In 1471, the Florentine philosopher Marsilio Ficino published his translation of the *Corpus Hermeticum*, the collection of magical and philosophical writings attributed to the legendary Hermes Trismegistus, which had been lost for a millennium. For roughly the next century and a half, the prestige of Hermes and his teaching were secure, and he was even considered of equal stature with Jesus and Moses.[23] Even figures associated with the rise of modern science and the modern world—Copernicus, Johannes Kepler, Isaac Newton—were profoundly influenced by Hermetic ideas. Kepler, who discovered the laws of planetary motion, made a living as an astrologer, and Newton wrote more about alchemy than he did about gravity—which, if nothing else, is a very "occult" force, given that no one has ever seen it.[24] Yet by 1614, something had changed. Rising critical scholarship revealed that the *Corpus Hermeticum*, believed to have been written by Hermes Trismegistus before the Flood and to be the fount of the "ancient wisdom" at the heart of Hermeticism, could not have been written then. The texts were more likely the product of the Egyptian-Greek syncretism of first- and second-century Alexandria, and could not have been, as they had been believed to be, the source of Plato and other ancient philosophers' wisdom. From being revered as one of the most important spiritual, philosophical, and magical teachers of all time, Hermes Trismegistus was now seen to be a fraud—he had, in fact, most likely never existed. His teaching was a joke and his followers fools and laughingstocks.

It was of course precisely this dethroning of Hermes and his teachings that paved the way for the rise of modern science and for the kind of knowledge associated with it. To grasp the laws of planetary motion, we had to abandon the idea that the planets were moved, in Dante's words, by "the love that moves the sun and the other stars." In order to understand the world intellectually, the left brain has to distance itself from it and turn it into an object. But when reading accounts of the transition from a magical way of seeing the world to our scientific one, I was struck by the aggressiveness of much of the anti-Hermes rhetoric.[25] It was not simply a case of recognizing a mistake, which, certainly, would have caused some embarrassment, and then carrying on. On the contrary, what took place seems to have been more like an all-out war on the Hermetic view of the world.

ANTI-HERMES

This campaign was led chiefly by the Catholic monk, theologian, philosopher, and mathematician Marin Mersenne, who was a close friend of René Descartes, the thinker who, more than anyone else, is associated with the strict separation of consciousness and the world.[26] In 1623, Mersenne published a mammoth work, *Quaestiones Celeberrimae in Genesim*. This is ostensibly an unwieldy commentary on the book of Genesis, but in actuality it is an extended attack on the Hermetic tradition. Mersenne denounced magic, divination, Kabbalah, pantheism, astrology, the *Anima mundi* or "soul of the world," and, most crucially, animism, the idea, central to esotericism, that the universe is in some way a living, sentient being with which man can communicate. Yet Mersenne did not merely argue that such beliefs were wrong or blasphemous—he was, strange for our time, fighting in the service of both the church and the new, mechanical view of the world. Mersenne went further and insisted that such beliefs were clearly insane, that is, pathological.[27] If, as the esoteric scholar Joscelyn Godwin writes, the Hermetic view "combines the practical examination of nature with a spiritual view of the universe as an intelligent hierarchy of beings," and "draws its wisdom from all possible sources," while seeing "the proper end of man as the direct knowledge of God," Mersenne would have none of it.[28] As the historian Frances Yates wrote, Mersenne was "actively combating Renaissance animism and magical conceptions in order to clear the way for the new times."[29] In other words, he was doing his utmost to ensure the triumph of the new mechanical way of seeing the world, and he had no reservations about fair play to achieve his goal. As we've seen, according to McGilchrist, the left brain is much more at home with machines than it is with living things, and René Descartes, friend of Mersenne, argued persuasively that animals were, in a sense, really only a kind of machine, or, as we would say today, robots. And the kind of mechanical way of seeing the world, denuded of all interiority and value, that Mersenne and Descartes trumpeted, is, according to Gebser, a quintessential expression of the deficient mode of the mental-rational structure of consciousness.

INTEGRATION

Mersenne's attack on the Hermetic view of things, as well as the many others that followed in its wake and continue today, was, it seems to me, nothing less than an all-out attempt at character assassination. It was an effort not only to point out that such a view was wrong, from the rising scientific perspective, but to defame it and its adherents. In our context here it was, I submit, a left-brain assault on a right-brain body of thought, much like the kind of "word versus image" campaign Leonard Shlain describes in *The Alphabet Versus the Goddess*. But we could just as equally say that it was an attack by the deficient mental-rational structure on the remnants of the mythical structure that resided in the esoteric, Hermetic view, as well as on the hints of the integral structure this view embodied. As McGilchrist argues, the Renaissance was a time when the two rival hemispheres came together briefly, that is, they "integrated," and formed a creative union that produced remarkable works of art and architecture. This was something different from the *embeddedness* in the world of an overly right-brain consciousness—a characteristic of Gebser's mythic structure of consciousness—or the *objectification* of the world to which the left brain is prone—exemplified in Gebser's mental-rational structure—but a creative combination of the two, something along the lines of the "practical examination of nature" combined with the "spiritual view of the universe as an intelligent hierarchy of beings" Joscelyn Godwin mentions above.

CONSCIOUSNESS WARS

The esoteric, Hermetic tradition, forced underground by the rise of material, mechanical science, has suffered, I believe, a full-scale, no-holds-barred assault by the left brain and the deficient mode of the mental-rational structure. Its right-brain worldview, with its sense of a living, intelligent universe with which we can participate through our imagination, was targeted for attack by its left-brain antagonist. It is not the case, as it is generally accepted, that the Hermetic/esoteric view, anchored in what it erroneously believed was a profound "ancient wisdom," was, with the rise of reason, rationality, and the Enlightenment, simply superseded by a more correct view. It was not simply a case of "superstition" giving way to "science," or of dogma dissolving in the face of free thought. That "more correct view," informed by the proselytizing zeal of a *competing form of consciousness*, seems to have purposely and ruthlessly set out to consciously obliterate its rival. This was, indeed, a real war, one carried out on the fields of consciousness.

In the early stages of its campaign, the antiesoteric view enjoyed many victories, and it eventually established itself as the sole arbiter of what is true, what is "real" knowledge, and what is not. But now, some four hundred years after Hermes Trismegistus, the thrice-great sage of magic and the ancient wisdom, was dethroned, his usurper's position seems threatened—or at least the foundations on which it established its supremacy seem somewhat less secure. In our time, the deficient mode of Gebser's mental-rational consciousness structure has reached its peak, as it were. Developments like deconstructionism and postmodernism suggest that the western intellectual tradition has begun to take itself apart, with the left brain's obsession with analysis turning on itself.[30] Even earlier than these, the rise of the "new physics" of quantum theory and related fields in the early part of the last century has shown that the neat nineteenth-century vision of a perfectly explainable mechanical universe is no longer tenable. But there are more pressing concerns. We've seen that Gebser in his last days believed that we were heading toward a "global catastrophe," and the various crises—ecological, environmental, economic, social, political, religious, and cultural—that fill our daily news reports suggest he was not far wrong. Our era has had no shortage of Cassandras, and it would be easy to lump Gebser's concerns together with other, less eloquent—not to mention less researched—jeremiads. But there is a tension, an anxiety about our time that somehow seems to suggest that *something* will happen, that some dike will burst, and that we will have a flood. As the philosopher Richard Tarnas remarked, "late modern man"—that is, ourselves—is "the incongruously sensitive denizen of an implacable vastness devoid of meaning," living in a world in which "gigantism and turmoil, excessive noise, speed and complexity dominate the human environment."[31] Things, many believe, cannot stay this way much longer. As Yeats said long ago, "the centre cannot hold."

Gebser was hopeful that with awareness and will, catastrophe can be avoided, and the shift from our decaying mental-rational structure into the new integral one could be achieved without the world collapsing. McGilchrist is hopeful too. Although he believes that left-brain dominance is increasing and that this is resulting in a world that is more and more like that familiar to people suffering from schizophrenia, McGilchrist also believes that the very crisis induced by left-brain dominance will—or at least may—trigger a reversal.[32] He points out that in the past, similar periods of left-brain dominance have, in a sense, set off an alarm that resulted in a shift toward right-brain values. In what Jung called an *"enantiodromia"*—that is, a reversal of values when one's conscious attitude becomes lopsided and the unconscious steps in to restore the balance—our hyper left-brain view may trigger a resurgence of the right.

Yet the idea is not merely to jettison the left brain and return to an earlier, right-brain mode of consciousness. That would merely push the pendulum back to the other side. Our left-brain consciousness was not a mistake, or "fall," but an experiment on the part of the right, out of which it emerged. It is, as McGilchrist says, the right brain's emissary. It is needed, absolutely necessary, and has a job to do; the problem is, it does it too well. The point is to educate our left brain—that is, ourselves—so we can achieve the kind of psychic integration that both McGilchrist and Gebser suggest is our salvation.

BRINGING IT ALL TOGETHER

They were not the only ones to see this. A reader of *The Master and His Emissary* familiar with the esoteric tradition could not be criticized for experiencing a distinct feeling of déjà vu. One of the central themes informing the western esoteric tradition, as well as that of the eastern, is the union of opposites. We see this in the ancient Chinese *yin-yang* symbol, in the *mysterium coniunctionis* or *coincidentia oppositorum* of alchemy, in the pillars of Mercy and Severity that border the Middle Pillar of

Harmony in Kabbalah, in the union of microcosm (man) and macrocosm (universe) in Hermeticism and in its central dictum "as above, so below." The idea that by bringing opposites together, some new, third element, not given, is produced, or that a third element is necessary in order to bring about the union, also has a long history in esotericism, as well as in more mainstream forms of thought.

In alchemy, for example, the Great Work of transmutation requires the union of sulfur and mercury—the Sun and the Moon—brought about through the medium of salt (Earth). Hindu philosophy speaks of the three *gunas*, which are characteristics or tendencies of being. Left to themselves, *tamas*, the *guna* of inertia, and *rajas*, the *guna* of agitation, lead to ill health and disturbances, unless they are balanced by *sattva*, the middle *guna* of bliss. We have already mentioned Blake ("Without contraries is no progression," again from *The Marriage of Heaven and Hell*). The philosopher Hegel's dialectic, the three-step dance of thesis, antithesis, and synthesis, is another expression of this threefold arrangement, as is Nietzsche's pairing of Apollo and Dionysus, the Greek gods of order and madness, whose union, Nietzsche believed, was behind the beauty of Greek drama. Rudolf Steiner's "spiritual science" offers a similar tripartite arrangement. For Steiner, the spirits of Ahriman, associated with deadening materialism, and Lucifer, the source of pride and hubris, are united and transcended by Christ, the mediator of these opposing spiritual forces. Gurdjieff spoke of a "law of three," a "fundamental law" responsible for all phenomena in existence.[33] And Jung spoke of the "transcendent function," brought about by the union of the conscious and unconscious mind, which produces some new, unexpected development that can help an individual break free of a psychic deadlock.[34]

The psychologist and paranormal investigator Stan Gooch argued, much like McGilchrist, that humans inhabit two different and-opposed realities, which he called Reality O (the objective world) and Reality S (our inner, subjective world), and that these are reconciled in what he called Reality U, or "universal reality."[35] One of the best guides to understanding these opposed realities, Gooch believed, were the *Letters on the Aesthetic Education of Man* by the German Romantic poet Friedrich Schiller. In these Schiller writes that "Freedom arises only when a man is a complete being, when both his fundamental drives [of imagination and intellect, or right and left brain] are fully developed; it will, therefore, be lacking as long as he is incomplete, as long as one of the two drives is excluded."[36] Schiller was a contemporary and friend of Goethe, whose own thinking focused on the tension between two forces, what he called "polarity" and "intensification," the work of dividing unities and unifying divisions, the "systole" and "diastole" of the eternal heartbeat. Goethe shared this insight with his younger English contemporary, Samuel Taylor Coleridge, who spoke of the "universal law of polarity" which was "first promulgated by Heraclitus," the pre-Socratic philosopher who argued that the "way up and the way down are one and the same."[37] More than a century after Coleridge, Arthur Koestler proposed what he called a "holoarchy," a hierarchy comprising what he calls "holons," which are simultaneously both "parts" and "wholes." Holons are "parts" of the level of the holoarchy that is above them, and "wholes" to the part that is below. In this they display what Koestler sees as fundamental characteristics of all "holons," whether physical, organic, or social: what he calls their "self-transcending" and their "self-assertive" tendency; that is, their tendency to merge into a larger whole, and their tendency to affirm their independence. It is suggestive that Koestler speaks of this as a "Janus principle," taking the name from the two-faced Roman god.[38]

A DOUBLE-TRUTH UNIVERSE

This list could go on. When I began to see what Richard Tarnas calls our "double-truth universe" in light of our twin hemispheres, I experienced a kind of "double-truth" myself.[39] Was this a profound insight, or a numbing platitude? When you begin to look for these oppositions, they seem obvious. And yet, they are so obvious that we overlook them, or feel they are not important. I do not know whether our "dualities"—those mentioned above as well as the many I have not mentioned—originate in the fact that we have two brains, or rather if our having two brains is a neurological expression of some fundamental law of being, some irreducible cosmic *yin-yang* that runs through everything. In one sense this doesn't matter. What is important is that the central idea running through all of these philosophies of "polarity," "opposition," and "duality" is the need for the creative tension between them to be maintained. This means that any imbalance between them, with one side dominating the other, must be rectified. This is not in order to achieve some bland equilibrium, but to keep the creative interchange between them going.

From the perspective of Jung's psychology, if the conscious, rational mind ignores or obscures the input from the unconscious, the situation can be corrected in two different ways. The individual can consciously attempt to open up a dialogue with his or her other half and actively try to absorb and assimilate what it has to say—Jung developed a method of doing this, "active imagination," the aim of which was to stimulate the "transcendent function" mentioned above.[40] Failing this, the unconscious would do it itself, and this can be calamitous. The unconscious contents are not always polite; they can burst into our conscious life in sometimes terrifying ways. They are willing to work with us if we are open to them, but they will make themselves felt, whether we want them to or not. The first route is preferable but harder, and demands discipline and determination. The second route is easier: you just let yourself go mad.

I don't want to put too Freudian a point on this, but I think we can say that with the rise of left-brain dominance and the deficient mode of the mental-rational structure, our culture has swung into a dangerous imbalance, by repressing the contribution of our other self, our other mode of consciousness. And one sign of this, I suggest, is the wholesale rejection of what we call "the western esoteric tradition." For the last four centuries we have pushed this aside, made it a laughingstock, diminished its importance, and ignored it—when we haven't made determined attempts to eradicate it once and for all. Scientists periodically announce that they have finally and categorically debunked "the occult," the paranormal, mysticism, and everything related to it, but as anyone familiar with the history of our defamed inner tradition knows, it will not go away. We can't get rid of it for the simple reason that it is literally part of us; if I am correct it has its roots there, a few millimeters across from "us," next door in our right brain.[41] Whether we like it or not, we have to make an attempt to get to know our neighbor, our other self, or suffer the consequences.

OUR SECRET TEACHERS

What follows is a kind of history of our "other" mode of consciousness, our "other" mind, and a look at what we can learn from its rejected knowledge. This knowledge has been subject to abuse by both the church and science, been driven underground and parodied in popular culture, but its influence has always been felt, if not acknowledged, and it has produced a remarkable canon of ideas, insights, and speculation about ourselves and our place in the cosmos. There is the standard history of who we are, how we got here, and what the outlook for our future may be. But there is another history, a "secret history" of our consciousness, as I have argued in an earlier book. That history is not as easily accessible as the official one, although, to be sure, it has become more available to us in recent years through the Internet and other sources on our "information highway." The standard history teaches us that the actors in this secret history were a muddled, superstitious lot, gullible and credulous, when they were not simply madmen or fools. The western inner tradition has certainly had its fair share of eccentric types, but this wholesale low assessment of its members is merely propaganda, and the western world owes much to its "secret teachers," to the men and women who devoted themselves to understanding and expressing the vision of our other mode of consciousness.

Some of these teachers we know and in a sense are not secret at all. Yet in many cases what they have to teach remains so. Some are not so well known, indeed, are hardly known at all. One can be a secret teacher in the sense of being unknown, but one can also be a secret teacher in the sense that what you teach is secret, hidden, obscured, or perhaps in some cases, even purposely disguised. Esoteric means "inner," that which resides within, as opposed to the exoteric, which relates to the outer surface of things. It also means something aimed at a small group, those who share an interest in and have a familiarity with concerns to which the majority is oblivious. The western inner tradition has always faced criticism about elitism, about select groups who pride themselves on being different, if not superior to the masses. A smug spiritual self-satisfaction can arise with those who enjoy the distinction between "us" and "them." But this is true of any group; esotericism has no monopoly on egos and the false sense of superiority to which they are prone. The message of our secret teachers is open to everyone. To understand it requires the same degree of intelligence, discipline, and determination needed to master a musical instrument or gain proficiency in quantum mechanics. But perhaps the most important thing is that you must want to learn.

What makes an esoteric education different from learning to play a musical instrument or grasping quantum physics is that its subject and the person pursuing it are one and the same. In studying esotericism, we are in reality studying and exploring ourselves, our being, our consciousness, and this is not a study from which we can remain "scientifically" detached. As the historian of esotericism Arthur Versluis remarks, within its different branches, western esotericism displays a "consistently recurring theme of transmuting consciousness, which is to say, of awakening latent, profound connections between humanity, nature and the divine, and of restoring a paradisal union between them."[42] We should, Versluis argues, view "esoteric traditions as written maps of and means toward the exploration of consciousness," and see the initiations that make up much of the esoteric tradition as ways of "awakening . . . higher degrees of consciousness."[43]

I agree. What draws most people to the study of esoteric ideas and philosophies is a profound felt need for this change, this transmutation of consciousness. Something is missing, there is some lack that the usual sources of satisfaction cannot meet. There is a vague, obscure sense that one must change oneself in order to meet this need, and the different insights and philosophies making up the varied strands of the western inner tradition suggest a way of doing this. I would add to this that we have good reason to believe that at least some of what is missing is the contribution to our self-understanding offered by our much maligned yet infinitely patient, wise, and silent neighbor living in the brain next door.

So let us take a look at the sources of our rejected knowledge and what lessons we can learn from the secret teachers of the western world.

CHAPTER ONE

AN ANCIENT WISDOM

The western inner or esoteric tradition often speaks of an "ancient wisdom." We find this in the Hermetic tradition, with the idea that its founder, the legendary Hermes Trismegistus, received a divine revelation at the dawn of time, which he subsequently passed on to his disciples. Today we know that the *Corpus Hermeticum* was not written "before the Flood," as some of its earliest readers believed, but is most likely a product of the religious and philosophical syncretism characteristic of Roman Alexandria. But in esoteric circles, the idea of an initiatic descent, a *Aurea Catena*, or "Golden Chain" of adepts, reaching back into the dim vaults of antiquity and beyond, persists. The Renaissance, which saw a powerful Hermetic revival, was of course informed by the retrieval of ancient philosophy, namely Plato, which was lost during the so-called Dark Ages. But it was precisely the belief that the *Corpus Hermeticum* was written by Hermes Trismegistus in very ancient times—indeed, well before Plato—that made its rediscovery in 1463 so spectacular.[1]

For the philosophers and scholars of the Renaissance, the older an idea or a teaching was, the better, and the very old was the best of all. This is in sharp contrast with much of our own sensibilities, which see the new, the novel, the "breakthrough," and the "cutting edge" as more worthy of our attention. Scholars of the Renaissance believed that the ancient texts that had been lost for centuries were closer to the source of knowledge, and hence were more pure, much as a mountain stream is clearer nearer its source, unlike the muddy waters of the lowlands. Renaissance scholars were indeed excited by Plato. But the wisdom that Plato had to offer, so the story went, was given to him by earlier sages, who themselves received it from even earlier adepts, who, as Frances Yates writes, "walked more closely with the gods."[2]

As the historian Christopher McIntosh remarked, it was the fifteenth-century Florentine philosopher Marsilio Ficino, translator of the *Corpus Hermeticum,* who "started the habit of talking in terms of a special wisdom handed down from sage to sage."[3] This special wisdom was indeed very old, and Ficino himself heard about it from his patron, Cosimo de' Medici, the great power broker of Florence. Cosimo himself had heard about this ancient wisdom from the Byzantine Neoplatonic philosopher George Gemistos Plethon. Suffice it to say here that it was Plethon's conversation with Cosimo about a "primal theology," a *prisca theologia,* received by the Persian mage Zoroaster and other adepts at the dawn of time, and which informed all the world's religions, that eventually led to the rediscovery of the *Corpus Hermeticum* and, through this, much of what we know as the Renaissance.

Plethon's idea of an ancient wisdom, intermittently lost and rediscovered, has become a mainstay of esoteric thought. Practically every esoteric thinker has recourse to it. Some speak of it more than others, but in general all refer in some sense to a knowledge that was available to mankind in earlier times, but which has, over the centuries, become obscure, if not completely forgotten. In his sometimes unreliable but still very readable account of the philosophy of the occult, *Dogme et rituel de la haute magie,* translated into English by the occultist A. E. Waite as *Transcendental Magic,* the nineteenth-century French magician Eliphas Levi presents a moving, if highly romantic, expression of the idea:

> Behind the veil of all the hieratic and mystical allegories of ancient doctrines, behind the darkness and strange ordeals of all initiations, under the seal of all sacred writings, in the ruins of old Nineveh or Thebes, on the crumbling stones of old temples and on the blackened visage of the Assyrian or Egyptian sphinx, in the monstrous or marvelous paintings which interpret to the faithful of India the inspired pages of the Vedas, in the cryptic emblems of our old books on alchemy, in the ceremonies practiced at reception by all secret societies, there are

found indications of a doctrine which is everywhere the same and everywhere carefully concealed.[4]

That what is said in this passage is not strictly true does not take away from its romantic and imaginative power. It is clear to most critical students of esotericism that there is not a single "doctrine" shared by the various groups associated with the esoteric, nor is there the kind of historical continuity between different esoteric movements that less historically minded readers may imagine. (Although having said this, there is, I believe, what Arthur Versluis calls an "ahistorical continuity," a continuity of shared ideas, some which we will encounter as we go along.[5]) It is, in fact, a mistake to speak of "esotericism" as if it were a single, monolithic teaching, like communism or socialism. As I discovered while researching for this book, there are almost as many definitions of "esotericism" as there are esotericists or historians of esotericism writing about it.[6] In fact, much of the "academic esotericism" of recent years is taken up with refining the definition of its subject—applying, we might say, left-brain explicitness to a right-brain implicit understanding—a common enough practice in academia, but which may be a stumbling block for the average reader.

"Esotericism" is a wide umbrella term covering a variety of ideas, beliefs, and practices which, while not necessarily sharing a single common element, do seem to share what the philosopher Wittgenstein called a "family resemblance."[7] This is a collection of overlapping similarities, which link different members of a group together, but which can easily dissolve if we attempt to make their connection too explicit.[8] It is, in a sense, more concerned with *recognition*, which is a right-brain affair, than *definition*, which is much more the business of the left.[9] Even among professing esotericists, there are different ideas of what esotericism is. Gurdjieff's esotericism is not the same as, say, Rudolf Steiner's, and both of their ideas about it may differ significantly from that of some other teacher's. But unless we are sectarians, we would not say that Gurdjieff or Steiner's ideas were not "esoteric," even if we could not define the term in a way acceptable to academics. For our purposes here, I will follow Joscelyn Godwin, who writes that "the word *esoteric* refers to the inner aspect of a religion or philosophy, of which the outer aspect is *exoteric*," and repeat what I said previously, that such *inner* teachings are fundamentally concerned with the "transmutation of consciousness."[10]

In the esoteric tradition, this "transmutation of consciousness" is commonly known as *gnosis,* a Greek word meaning "knowledge," but not knowledge in our everyday sense of the word, knowledge of "facts" or concepts. It is a kind of *experiential* knowledge, a knowledge that is also an "experience." It is a kind of "knowledge in italics." When you know something in the sense of *gnosis,* you *really know* it. In *The Quest for Hermes Trismegistus,* I write at length about *gnosis*; here I will repeat my own definition of it: "immediate, direct, non-discursive cognition of reality," a reality, that is, that includes the spiritual.[11] This is the knowledge of "the hidden or invisible realms or aspects of existence."[12] I will hazard the statement that the essence of esotericism is the attainment of such knowledge, and that this is its central contrast with orthodox religions, which are based on faith and belief. Without such a focus, the study of esotericism, it seems to me, would be concerned solely with what is *exoteric,* that is nonessential, about it.

It was passages like Eliphas Levi's above that led Madame Blavatsky, one of the founders of the Theosophical Society and herself an important "secret teacher," to title her first major work of esoteric philosophy, *Isis Unveiled: A Master-Key to the Mysteries of Ancient and Modern Science and Theology* (1877). Indeed, it was a lecture on "The Lost Canon of Proportion of the Egyptians, Greeks and Romans" given to her earlier "Miracle Club" that led to the formation, in 1875, of the Theosophical Society itself, one of whose aims is "the study of ancient religions, philosophies, and sciences."[13] Some years later, Annie Besant, successor to Madame Blavatsky as head of the Theosophical Society, wrote a book called *The Ancient Wisdom* (1897). Even esotericists who have no truck with Blavatsky or the Theosophical Society still look to the ancient past as the source of their study. One of the major esoteric movements in the twentieth century, Traditionalism, takes as its central belief the existence of a primordial spiritual tradition, which was revealed by a divine source and flourished in the ancient past, but which has been subsequently lost. The founder of Traditionalism is generally considered to be the French metaphysician René Guénon, but other Traditionalists include the art historian Ananda Coomaraswamy, the philosopher Huston

Smith, and the far-right Italian esotericist Julius Evola. All, in different ways, share the idea of a *philosophia perennis*, a "perennial philosophy," the belief that "all religions shared a common origin in a single perennial (or primeval or primordial) religion that had subsequently taken on a variety of forms," an idea, we've seen, that it shares with Hermeticism.[14] Gurdjieff is another target for the Traditionalists, who consider his "Fourth Way" teaching "counter-initiatic," that is, a kind of esoteric "black magic."[15] Yet Gurdjieff, like the Traditionalists, also spoke of an ancient teaching, and his discovery of this, in the monastery of the Sarmoung Brotherhood in Central Asia, forms the climax to his spiritual adventure story *Meetings with Remarkable Men*.[16]

Mention of the Sarmoung Brotherhood brings us to another mainstay of esoteric thought: the belief that throughout history there have been "schools" informed with this ancient wisdom, secretly at work "behind the scenes" of civilization, helping humanity in its struggle to evolve. These secret schools, so the story goes, are the real agents of our development, and at crucial points in history, they inject esoteric ideas into the mainstream, in order to help mankind in its slow growth toward spiritual maturity.

THE OLD WORLD

We have seen that Iain McGilchrist believes that the right brain is older than its upstart emissary, the left, a belief he shares with Leonard Shlain and other "split-brain" theorists. This would suggest that the kind of consciousness associated with the right brain would also be older than that associated with the left.[17] We have also seen that Jean Gebser believes that before the rise of the mental-rational consciousness structure—which we have linked to the left brain—humankind lived in the mythic consciousness structure, one more attuned to images, feelings, and intuitions, all elements of right-brain consciousness. Our own consciousness is slanted more to the left than to the right. We see the world as something firmly outside us; there is a clear distinction between our inner world of thoughts, feelings, impressions, and the outer one of physical things. We see things in sharp detail and perceive them as separate, independent objects, and although we know that nature is "alive" in the sense of being "organic," we do not believe that it, like ourselves, has an "inside," and we certainly don't believe that inorganic things, like stars and stones, are alive in any way at all. There is good reason to suspect that our earlier form of consciousness saw things differently. In *A Secret History of Consciousness*, I look at a number of different philosophies of consciousness, some esoteric, some more mainstream. I try to show that all, in different ways, suggest that at an earlier time, human beings had a more "participatory" kind of consciousness, a kind of consciousness more in line with what we know about right-brain consciousness than the left; that is, a consciousness that was more permeable, less rigid in its distinction between "inside" and "out." This is a kind of consciousness that, except in certain circumstances, we only experience now as children.

For example, the philosopher of language, and great friend of C. S. Lewis, Owen Barfield—one of our secret teachers—believed that the history of language revealed what he called the "evolution of consciousness," and he argued this point in his first book, *History in English Words*. Put briefly, Barfield believed that as we look back into the history of language, we see that it becomes more figurative, more metaphorical, more, in a sense, alive and poetic; our own age is, as the literary philosopher Erich Heller said, much more one of prose. This is because, Barfield believed, at an earlier time the world was more "alive," had more, as we would say, "soul," and that when earlier people—and modern-day poets—said that the world *spoke* to them, they were speaking the truth.[18] To say that the world "back then" was more alive is another way of saying that our consciousness then perceived it as such; it was a kind of consciousness that, as Barfield says, could see the inside of things, rather than, as we do, only their surface. It was a kind of consciousness that participated in the world around it, rather than one, like our own, that only, as it were, bumps up against it.

Barfield came to his insights independently, but when he became aware of the work of Rudolf Steiner, he saw that Steiner, on a larger scale, was saying the same thing. Steiner, one of our most important secret teachers, also believed in an evolution of consciousness, but his outline of it included not only human history, but that of the cosmos as well. In fact, for Steiner, the evolution of consciousness goes hand in hand with that of the cosmos because for him, fundamentally, our consciousness and the cosmos are two sides of the same thing. In other words, for Steiner, the kind of world we perceive depends on the kind of consciousness perceiving it, an insight he shares, in a different way, with McGilchrist.[19]

Steiner's system is vast, like a huge cathedral, and in some aspects it shares much with that of Gebser.[20] In his reading of the evolution of consciousness, Steiner spoke of "epochs" rather than "structures of consciousness," and he also spoke of earlier stages of our evolution that preceded our own Earth stage in the somewhat awkward terms of "Old Saturn," "Old Sun," and "Old Moon." In the "Old Moon" stage before our current Earth stage, consciousness perceived things in terms of images; it was, as Steiner called it, a "picture thinking," something more akin to our own experience of dreams.[21] We would not then, he claimed, see a discreet, definite object and then have a "concept" or idea about it "in our heads," but would respond to the "picture" as a symbol that would elicit the appropriate *feeling*. Steiner's picture thinking seems very close to how Gebser describes the mythical structure of consciousness, a key part of which was the *reflection* of the inner world in the outer. Gebser sees the myth of Narcissus, the youth who fell in love with his reflection in a pool, as emblematic of the mythic structure.

Both Steiner's "picture thinking" and Gebser's "reflection" strike me as in line with what we know of how the right brain interacts with the world. Both would be open to the kind of "both/and" approach associated with the right brain, as opposed to the left brain's "either/or." In his account of Steiner's teaching, Stewart C. Easton remarks that "In the age before autonomous thinking"—the age, that is, before the rise of the left brain—"men perceived and interpreted . . . the world through their feeling. Thus to the ancient Egyptian there was no contradiction when his literature provided him with different stories of creation and assigned the deed to various gods." "No contradiction was present to the Egyptians," Easton says, "because contradiction belongs to thinking, not to the feelings."[22] Contradiction, we've seen, is something troubling to the left brain, but not the right, which is open to metaphor and multiple meanings, as is the case in its appreciation of symbols.

HOW OLD IS THE SPHINX?

Mention of the Egyptians brings me to another connection between the right brain, esotericism, and the kind of consciousness that may be the source of "ancient wisdom"—or that at least may point us in its direction. In *The Caretakers of the Cosmos*, I make a connection between what we understand about right-brain consciousness and some of the ideas of another secret teacher, the French alchemist and maverick Egyptologist René Schwaller de Lubicz.

The work of René Schwaller de Lubicz became widely known in the 1990s through popular books such as Graham Hancock's *Fingerprints of the Gods* and Robert Bauval and Adrian Gilbert's *The Orion Mystery*, as well as Bauval and Hancock's *The Message of the Sphinx*. The title "de Lubicz" was given to Schwaller by the esoteric Lithuanian poet O. V. de Lubicz Milosz in 1919, when both were members of a secret occult society.[23] Bauval and Hancock argue that an unknown but highly advanced ancient civilization preceded the historically known civilizations, and both drew on Schwaller de Lubicz's contention that the Great Sphinx of Giza was much older than the official accounts declared. The official account says that the Sphinx was built around 2500 B.C. during the reign of the pharaoh Khafra, but in one of this last books, *Sacred Science*, Schwaller remarked that it had in fact been built much earlier, at around 10,500 B.C. The reason for this dating, Schwaller argued, is that the body of the Sphinx showed clear signs of water erosion. Schwaller originally believed this was caused by flooding, but it was later determined that rainfall was responsible. The last time enough rain fell in Egypt to cause such erosion was some twelve thousand years ago—when, that is, it was not yet a desert.[24]

As a maverick Egyptologist, who also dabbled in alchemy and had a penchant for secret societies and right-wing politics, Schwaller did not reach a wide audience, and the mainstream Egyptologists who knew of his work considered him a crank. But in 1979, John Anthony West's *The Serpent in the Sky*—an extensive study of Schwaller's ideas—brought Schwaller's work to a wider, more appreciative readership, the budding New Age movement. It was through West's book that Hancock came across Schwaller's remarks about the Sphinx. Schwaller's dating of the construction of the Sphinx gained strong support in 1989 when West convinced the geologist and paleontologist Robert Schoch, a professor at Boston University, to test Schwaller's theory. Schoch was an expert on soft stone, like the limestone of which the Sphinx is made, and to his surprise, Schoch discovered that Schwaller was right, at least about the erosion marks. They were caused by water, not wind and sand, as the official accounts stated.

Understandably, Schoch's results caused consternation among orthodox Egyptologists, but their ire was raised even more by Bauval's argument that the entire plan of the Giza complex, including the Sphinx, the great pyramids, and the Nile, was laid out in Schwaller's date of 10,500 B.C. It was originally designed, Bauval argued, to mirror the night sky over Giza at that time, specifically the constellation Leo, the belt of Orion, and the Milky Way. In order to provide a picture of the night sky over Egypt circa 10,500 B.C., Bauval and Hancock used a computer to simulate the "precession of the equinoxes," the apparent backward movement of the sun through the zodiac.[25] They discovered that the Giza complex did indeed reflect with surprising accuracy the heavens directly above it, and they argued that this arrangement was designed to commemorate what in Egyptian mythology was known as Zep Tepi, the "First Time."

This "First Time," i.e., the beginning of Egyptian civilization, occurred during the age of Leo, some twelve thousand years ago. The official account of human history tells us that twelve thousand years ago, we were incapable of the kind of engineering skills needed to construct the Sphinx, or practically anything else, and that we certainly didn't have the tools for the job. At best, the only implements available to our Neolithic ancestors then were some flint and sticks. Even the construction of the pyramids, which Bauval and Hancock agree took place later, poses problems. The engineering ability necessary to build the pyramids alone baffles us, but what is even more baffling is the kind of *knowledge* that seems to be embodied in the stone.[26]

As dozens of books have pointed out, the Great Pyramid of Giza is a compendium of mathematical and astronomical knowledge far in excess of what we believe the people responsible for them should have possessed. As early as 1864, an amateur Egyptologist, the London publisher John Taylor, argued that whoever built the Great Pyramid had included π (pi) in their measurements, a number that was supposed to have been first discovered by the Greek mathematician Archimedes in 250 B.C.—that is, centuries later.[27] (For those who have forgotten, π is the ratio of a circle's circumference to its diameter.) Much nonsense has been written about the pyramids, linking them to everything from biblical prophecy to UFOs, and giving rise to what some skeptics call a subgenre of junk literature written by "pyramidiots." But to the unbiased reader it is clear that whoever was responsible for the pyramids and other Egyptian mysteries, such as the temples at Karnak and Luxor, knew a great deal more than what our official accounts suggest. Since 1894, when the British astronomer Norman Lockyer demonstrated in *The Dawn of Astronomy* that Egyptian temples, as well as the pyramids, were most likely, if not exclusively, used for astronomical purposes, many researchers have come to see that the kind of knowledge involved in their construction—as well as in other ancient structures, like Stonehenge (Lockyer was the first to suggest it was a kind of observatory)—was vastly different from what our official accounts allow.[28]

Schwaller too recognized that whoever built the Sphinx, the Great Pyramid, and the temples at Luxor and Karnak was mathematically and cosmologically astute. From 1936 to 1951, Schwaller and his wife, Isha, herself the author of a series of novels about ancient Egypt (*Her-Bak: Egyptian Initiate* is the best known), studied the ancient Egyptian monuments. Schwaller found evidence in them for pi, but also for much more: a knowledge of the precession of the equinoxes, of the Pythagorean theorem centuries in advance of Pythagoras, of the circumference of the globe, as well as evidence of φ (phi), known as the Golden Section, a mathematical proportion that was again supposedly unknown until it was discovered by the Greeks. As John Anthony West makes clear, the Golden Section is more than an important item in classical architecture. It is, according to Schwaller, the mathematical archetype of the universe, the reason why we have an "asymmetrical" "lumpy" world of galaxies and planets, and not a flattened-out, homogenous one, a question that today occupies contemporary cosmologists.[29] In his writings, Schwaller linked phi to planetary orbits, to the architecture of Gothic cathedrals, and to plant and animal forms. It is, he argued, a "form constant," that is, a kind of blueprint for reality or "law" of creation. Through his research, Schwaller came to believe that all of Egyptian life—from mundane, everyday items to their religious sites—was centered around what he saw as a central metaphysical vision about "cosmic harmony" and "the forces that bring about the becoming of things."[30]

THE INTELLIGENCE OF THE HEART

The mathematical and cosmological knowledge that Schwaller discovered embedded in the ancient Egyptian monuments was indeed astounding, but what was perhaps even more astounding was the fact that this knowledge was the product of a form of consciousness radically different from our own. Schwaller came to believe that Luxor, Karnak, and other Egyptian monuments were living organisms of a kind; they were, he saw, compendia of esoteric knowledge, whose central purpose was a kind of transmutation of consciousness. This knowledge, he believed, was rooted in a form of consciousness that he called "the intelligence of the heart." This was essentially a way of looking into the *insides* of things, much as Owen Barfield, discussed above, believed was true of human consciousness at an earlier stage. Our own modern consciousness—what Schwaller called "cerebral consciousness" or "the Set mind," named after the Egyptian god of chaos, storms, and the desert—was limited, Schwaller believed, to the *outside* of things. "Cerebral consciousness," Schwaller argued, "granulates" reality into bits and pieces; it severs the ties in the "network of connections that links everything with everything else" which, we've seen, is associated with a right-brain form of consciousness. "All in the universe," Schwaller wrote, "is in interdependent connection with all," a version of the "all is one" perception of the world common to esotericism.[31] Schwaller's "intelligence of the heart" is essentially a participatory form of consciousness. This is made clear in Schwaller's enigmatic posthumous work *Nature Word*. With the "intelligence of the heart," Schwaller tells us, we can "tumble with the rock that falls from the mountain/Seek light and rejoice with the rosebud about to open" and "expand in space with the ripening fruit."[32] In other words, with the "intelligence of the heart," we can experience all of these things—and more—from the *inside*.

It was this ability to perceive the "inside" of reality that, Schwaller argued, allowed the ancient Egyptians a kind of immediate access to the type of mathematical and cosmological knowledge that our "cerebral consciousness" has acquired slowly only after much labor and many years. The ancient Egyptians, Schwaller believed, saw the world *symbolically*, much as Stewart Easton above says our "Old Moon" consciousness did. Nature was a kind of text—hence Schwaller's title *Nature Word*—that conveyed truths about the forces behind it. The Egyptians called these forces "Neters," which we translate as "gods," and they portrayed these forces in different symbolic forms. This "symbolic perception" allowed the ancient Egyptians a greater leeway in interpreting reality. For one thing, it allowed them to experience what Schwaller called "the simultaneity of opposite states."

Schwaller first came upon this kind of "double-thinking" through his study of quantum physics, especially the work of Werner Heisenberg and Niels Bohr. Heisenberg, we know, developed what he called "the uncertainty principle," the recognition that at the level of elementary particles, we can know either a particle's position or its speed, but not both; securing one obscures the other. Bohr is famous for what he called "the principle of complementarity," the idea that light can act as a wave or a particle depending on the context, giving rise to the portmanteau term "wavicle." Before this, physicists banged their heads on the question of whether it acted as one or the other, as it gave conflicting evidence of both.[33]

The "intelligence of the heart," Schwaller argued, was what allowed the Egyptians to develop what he called "*symbolique*," that is, the ability to hold mutually exclusive ideas together simultaneously. For example, when an ancient Egyptian saw the hieroglyph of a bird, he knew it *denoted* the actual, living creature, but he was also aware of its *connotations*, that it was a symbol of the "cosmic function" embodied in the bird, that is, of flight. For Schwaller, hieroglyphics not only *designated*, they *evoked*. That is, they served dual purposes simultaneously. As we've seen, this is something the right brain ("both/and") is partial to, but which gives the left brain ("either/or") much grief.

HENRI BERGSON'S BRAIN

Another link between Schwaller's ideas about the consciousness of the ancient Egyptians and the right brain came from Schwaller's background in the work of the French philosopher Henri Bergson, a secret teacher of the mainstream. For a time in the early part of the last century, Bergson was the most famous philosopher on the planet, but he is little read today, although there has been renewed interest in his work in some areas.[34] In his early days, Schwaller was a student of the artist Henri Matisse, and Matisse himself had been a student of Bergson, so it is not unreasonable to think that Schwaller absorbed some of Bergson's ideas (indeed, given Bergson's popularity, it would have been almost impossible for him not to). Bergson believed that the human brain and nervous system serve an essentially *eliminative* function. That is to say, their purpose is to keep stimuli and information *out* of conscious awareness—not to bring it in— and to allow only as much of reality into consciousness as, in Aldous Huxley's words, "will help us to stay alive on the surface of this particular planet."[35] Huxley made this remark in the context of his famous experiment with mescaline, which, he said, allowed him to see "what Adam had seen on the morning of his creation—the miracle, moment by moment, of naked existence."[36] (Interestingly, Huxley speaks of experiencing the *Istigkeit* ["is-ness"] of Meister Eckhart, mentioned in the Introduction.)

Huxley believed mescaline—as well as other psychedelic drugs— achieved their effects by turning off the brain's "reducing valve" and, as it were, allowing the "taps of reality" to run full blast. When this happened to Huxley, he was flooded with what he calls "Mind at Large." Huxley quotes the philosopher C. D. Broad, who had paraphrased Bergson's ideas about the eliminative function of the brain. Broad had written that "Each person is at each moment capable of remembering all that has ever happened to him and of perceiving everything that is happening everywhere in the universe." Were the brain not to reduce or "edit" this universal awareness—or "cosmic consciousness," as the psychologist R. M. Bucke, a little known secret teacher, called it—we would be swamped, Broad said, with a "mass of largely useless and irrelevant knowledge." As it is, our inner editor does a very good job of providing us with only that very small selection of reality "which is likely to be practically useful."[37]

Bergson, Broad, and Huxley did not have the material on split-brain theory that is available to us, but if they did, I believe they would have recognized its importance. We have seen that the right brain is aware of the "network of connections linking everything with everything else," which seems in line with our remarks about "universal awareness" and "cosmic consciousness" above. And we have also seen that the left brain is geared toward focusing tightly on its objectives, and ignoring everything else. We can, I think, see Bergson's cerebral "reducing valve" and "eliminative function" as operations involving the left brain, and that what it reduces is the broader, wider awareness of the right.

A SUCCESSFUL ADAPTATION

The brain's eliminative function is, as Bergson and Huxley saw, a highly successful evolutionary adaptation. Were we not able to edit out most of the "interdependent connections" everything has with everything else, we would not have become such a successful species. Huxley recognized this when he remarked that if everyone took mescaline, there would be no wars, but there would be no civilization either, because no one would bother to create it. We would be too happy enjoying our sense of "cosmic consciousness" to do anything so boring. In order to function effectively— and to spur our creative efforts—consciousness needs to be *limited*. We need, in effect, to be dissatisfied enough with our situation in order to improve it. (The advice to "be here now," offered by many spiritual teachers is valuable and salutary, but it can also lead to us "remaining there then.") Yet, as we've seen, our highly efficient editor does his job too well. Much of the "irrelevant knowledge" it leaves out of our awareness has to do with what makes life worth living, its beauty and meaning. Huxley understood this when, as mentioned, he felt that under mescaline, he saw existence in its pristine form. In *The Doors of Perception*, his account of his drug experience, Huxley writes that he saw everything shining with an inner light that reflected its infinite significance; looking at the bamboo legs of a chair, Huxley felt that he had *become* them. This is a common experience within the western—and eastern—inner tradition. That is, Huxley saw into the inside of the chair, and everything else around him. The seventeenth-century Bohemian visionary Jacob Boehme spoke of seeing into what he called "the signature of things," and this seems to be what Huxley saw too.

This ability to see into the interior of reality Bergson called "intuition." This was, he said, a "kind of intellectual sympathy by which one places oneself within an object in order to coincide with what is unique in it and consequently inexpressible." Anyone who has read Boehme will know his accounts of his mystical vision are not easy to grasp, and we remember what was said in the Introduction about the difficulty in conveying implicit meanings. On the other hand, our everyday consciousness, Bergson said, "reduces the object to elements already known, that is, to elements common both to it and other objects."[38] As we have seen, the left brain likes to turn everything it encounters into something familiar.

THE NINEVEH NUMBER

There is good reason then, I think, to equate Schwaller de Lubicz's "intelligence of the heart" with a kind of right-brain awareness. Robert Lawlor, one of Schwaller's translators and an authority on "sacred geometry," said as much when he wrote that "localization in the right hemisphere of the highly intuitive aspects of thought, together with the capacity for non-verbal pattern recognition, is consistent with the dominant quality of mind which, in Schwaller de Lubicz's view, could have produced the temple architecture and hieroglyphic writings of the ancient Egyptians."[39] If the kind of knowing associated with a right-brain awareness was familiar to the ancient Egyptians, can we also find it in other ancient people? The answer seems to be yes.

One of the most curious mysteries of the ancient world is what is known as the "Nineveh number." In 1843, Paul Emile Botta, French consul at Mosul in what was then Mesopotamia (today Iraq), made a remarkable discovery. Digging at a mound known as Kuyunjik, near the upper

Tigris, he came upon the library of the ancient Assyrian king Assurbanipal, who reigned in the sixth century B.C. Looking through the many clay tablets he unearthed, Botta came upon one that contained an unusually long number, running to fifteen places: 195,955,200,000,000. The mound in which the tablet was discovered was at the site of the ancient city of Nineveh, so it became known as the "Nineveh number." What struck Botta and others at the time as strange was what ancient people would *do* with such a number? What could they use it for? Although fairly common today, people in the nineteenth century rarely used the idea of a million. What possible function could a number just short of two hundred *trillion* serve the ancient Assyrians?

In his book *Our Cosmic Ancestors* (1988), Maurice Chatelain, a French space scientist and former NASA communications systems chief, writes of using a computer to investigate the Nineveh number. He came up with some curious results. One was that the number was not arbitrary. It is 60 times 70, brought to the power of 7. Chatelain then remembered that the Sumerians, credited with inventing writing, calculated using base sixty rather than base ten; we have inherited our sixty-second minute and sixty-minute hour from them. The Assyrians inherited their culture from the Babylonians, who inherited theirs from the Sumerians, so Chatelain wondered if the number 60 could offer any clue to the meaning of the Nineveh number. He discovered it did, and that the vast number could be seen as equaling 2,268 million days—just over six million years—worked out in *seconds*. Other surprises followed. Chatelain wondered if the Sumerians, who were obsessive astronomers, had known about the precession of the equinoxes. A complete precessional cycle takes roughly twenty-six thousand years. Chatelain divided this into the Nineveh number and discovered that it worked out to precisely 240 cycles, or "Big Years." Chatelain then recalled the idea of "the great constant of the solar system," a kind of astronomical "highest common factor," into which all other cosmic numbers—planetary orbits, as well as those of satellites—will divide. Again using a computer, Chatelain calculated the length of the planetary and satellite orbits in seconds and found that they too divided into the Nineveh number equally. Whoever had calculated this figure, Chatelain concluded, seemed to know a lot about the stars.

But the Nineveh number had even more surprises. Chatelain computed the period of the Earth's rotation against the Nineveh number and was surprised to find it produced a slight discrepancy: it was off by one twelve-millionths of a day per year. This troubled him. The error was indeed slight, but so far he had not come across any inaccuracies and he wondered why he should do so now. Then Chatelain realized something that the ancient Sumerians—or whoever the Nineveh number originated from— would not have known: that the Earth's rotation has been slowing down at an infinitesimal rate, and that in twelve million years, a year will be a day shorter. Factoring this into his equation, Chatelain discovered that if the Nineveh number was a correct figure for the Earth's rotation, it must have been computed some 64,800 years ago. But beings intelligent enough to compute such a figure were simply not around then—or were they?

THE BIRD'S-EYE VIEW

Chatelain's own suggestion was that the knowledge contained in the Nineveh number came from extraterrestrials. His book is in the Erich von Däniken school of thought, that sees human evolution as a result of experiment and intervention carried out by "ancient astronauts." This may suggest a shaky provenance, but Colin Wilson has suggested that the kind of knowledge responsible for the Nineveh number—and other ancient astronomical mysteries—may be similar to that displayed by "calculating prodigies."[40] In 1826, a six-year-old boy named Benjamin Blyth was out walking with his father when he asked what time it was. His father told him and a few moments later Benjamin replied, "In that case I have been alive for . . ." and went on to give the exact figure in seconds, around 160 million. His father jotted the answer down and when they returned home he worked out the calculations. He told Benjamin he was off by 172,800 seconds. But Benjamin corrected him, saying he left out two leap years.

Zerah Colburn, the nineteenth-century "lightning calculator," was asked whether 4,294,967,297 was a "prime number" or not. Prime numbers cannot be divided exactly by any numbers other than one or themselves. We know the easy ones: 5, 7, 11, 13, 17; but past a certain point they are no longer obvious and need to be worked out. The trouble with primes is that there is no easy method of doing this: you simply have to divide all the smaller numbers into it. Even a computer has to do it "the hard way," and with large numbers this takes time. Yet Zerah was able to do it "in his head" and almost immediately say that this ten-digit number wasn't prime, but could be divided by 641. Similarly, the psychiatrist Oliver Sacks has written about "idiot savants" who entertain each other by swapping twenty-four-digit primes.[41] These individuals are otherwise severely mentally handicapped, but in this one instance they display powers that strike us as miraculous.

There is no logical way for these people to have arrived at their calculations. As Wilson suggests, it is as if they can somehow simply "see" the correct answer. In a sense there is no "calculating" at all, at least not in the usual way. Rather, it is as if their minds could somehow "hover in the air, like a hawk, over the whole number field, and pounce on prime numbers [or any other correct answer] as if they were rabbits."[42] They had a "bird's-eye view" of the problem and, rising above it, seemed to use some form of "pattern recognition" to "see" which number would "fit." Wilson remarks that Keith Critchlow, the architect and authority on sacred geometry, suggests that a similar "method" was used by the Babylonians when working out right angles that ran into thousands of feet, and Wilson suggests that something similar may have been at work with the Nineveh number. Other ancient architects may have been privy to a similar insight. Studying the standing stones at Callanish, in Scotland, and at other megalithic sites, the aeronautical engineer Alexander Thom declared that the people responsible for them were "prehistoric Einsteins."[43] Thom noticed that the main north-south axis at Callanish was aligned directly with the Pole Star. But he also knew that when Callanish was erected—some estimates are as early as 3000 B.C.—the Pole Star was not in its current position. For the builders of Callanish to have aligned the site to geographic north without the Pole Star as a guide would have required highly sophisticated engineering ability—the kind, again, that should not have been capable then.

This seems bizarre. But then, as we've seen, the philosopher C. D. Broad maintained that "each person is at each moment capable of remembering all that has ever happened to him and of perceiving everything that is happening everywhere in the universe." The fact that we do not experience this kind of awareness—or only rarely, in "mystical experiences"—is because of our left brain's highly efficient editing abilities. Perhaps someone with a less efficient cerebral editor would, in some way we can't yet understand, be able to tap into the knowledge necessary to erect Callanish and other sites of "archeoastronomy," or "know" immediately whether a ten-digit number was prime or not.

HOW OLD IS MAN?

Needless to say, Maurice Chatelain's suggestion that the Nineveh number dates from nearly sixty-five thousand years ago will no doubt raise several eyebrows, but in *A Secret History of Consciousness,* I write about some speculation that "anatomically modern human beings" have existed in time periods when, according to the standard accounts, they should not have been there.[44] Some of the material I looked at came from a controversial book, *Forbidden Archaeology* by Michael A. Cremo and Richard L. Thompson, published in 1993. Its nine-hundred-plus pages are filled with what, from the standard account, are disturbing archaeological anomalies, but the fact that Cremo was a follower of Swami Prabhupada's "Krishna Consciousness" movement was enough to suggest to most orthodox archaeologists that they could ignore his and Thompson's findings with good conscience. But perhaps even more disturbing and certainly more difficult to ignore is an account by the respected anthropologist Mary Leakey. In 1978, at Laetoli, twenty miles south of the famous Olduvai Gorge, Mary Leakey, her son Philip, and another member of their party discovered what seemed to be typically human footprints preserved in volcanic ash that dated from 3.5 to 3.8 million years ago. The prints were left by hominids that walked upright, and Mary Leakey spoke of "unique evidence, of an unimpeachable nature" which argued that "our hominid ancestors were fully bipedal a little before 3.5 million years ago." This went against all the standard accounts of human development. According to the accepted view, humans like ourselves only came on the scene some forty thousand years ago. Yet, as Mary Leakey wrote, "the essentially human nature and modern appearance of the footprints were quite extraordinary."[45] This, of course, does not prove that Chatelain's dating of the Nineveh number is correct, or that the number itself is of any importance. But it does suggest the possibility that humans like ourselves may have walked the earth much earlier than we believe.

NEANDERTHAL MAN

One group of humans rather unlike ourselves who seem to have had a surprising astronomical knowledge were the Neanderthals, who flourished from 100,000 to 40,000 B.C. The clichéd picture of Neanderthal is of a stocky, beetle-browed, club-bearing subhuman, dragging his mate along behind him; but increasingly we see that this is little more than an ignorant caricature. In a series of brilliant books written in the 1970s and '80s, the psychologist and paranormal investigator Stan Gooch argued that, in fact, Neanderthal was not the brutish caveman we believe him to be, but was in truth responsible for a "civilization" millennia before our own. A pioneer of "Neanderthal studies," Gooch was laughed at when he first presented his ideas, but in recent years many of them—including the notion that Neanderthal and Cro-Magnon, our direct ancestor, mated and produced us— have been vindicated, without, sadly, Gooch receiving any credit.[46]

One of Gooch's suggestions is that Neanderthal's large brain capacity— 1,400 cubic centimeters compared with our 1,300—was due to his larger cerebellum. The cerebellum ("little brain") is located at the back of the skull, next to the brain stem and below the occipital and temporal lobes. It is a kind of early cerebrum, the part of the brain that contains the cerebral cortex, and like the right brain, the cerebellum is older. Gradually, the cerebrum increased in size until it covered over the cerebellum, much as a tree may grow around a stone; the cerebellum is now almost completely obscured by the cerebrum. Gooch argues that Neanderthal's larger cerebellum made him "psychic" and allowed for a greater sensitivity to natural forces, like magnetic fields, but also to phenomena we would call "paranormal." He also suggested that modern "psychics" would have larger, or at least more active, cerebella than nonpsychics.[47] The eighteenth-century philosopher Emanuel Swedenborg—one of our secret teachers—who studied the brain extensively, also paid especial attention to the cerebellum and, in his later religious writings, said that it was through it that the "influx from the Divine" reaches the soul. (That is why in heaven, Swedenborg says, no angel stands behind another, so as not to block the flow.) Swedenborg also believed that in an earlier time, man had greater contact with the Divine, unlike today, when we are separated from it by our rational intellect.[48] In Frances Yates's words quoted earlier, for Swedenborg, early man "walked more closely with the gods." In his book *The Paranormal,* Gooch points out that Swedenborg, who, like Gooch, was psychic, reported that he had felt "actual conscious experience of the cerebellum during . . . paranormal activity," and Swedenborg often spoke of being visited by angels and taking trips with them to heaven and hell. So Gooch's ideas about the cerebellum may be significant.[49]

Among other surprises Gooch uncovered was that Neanderthals were very religious. They took care of their elderly and sick, and their dead were ritually buried, usually decorated with flowers and often with food and other offerings, suggesting a belief in an afterlife, an idea first proposed by the archaeologist Ralph Solecki in 1972 in *Shanidar, the Humanity of Neanderthal Man.* The dead were also painted in red ochre, a name for the iron ore hematite. In one mine discovered in southern Africa dating to a hundred thousand years ago, it is estimated that a million kilograms of the ore had been removed. This suggests a large coordinated effort involving many individuals motivated by deep religious convictions over many years—although perhaps "convictions" is the wrong word for something that would have been much more "intuitive." Red ochre was important to Neanderthal, Gooch argues, because its color linked it to menstrual blood; the menstrual cycle, Gooch believes, was central to the Neanderthal "religion."

TWO REALITIES

In the Introduction, I mentioned that Gooch argued that modern humans lived under two different "realities," what he called Reality O and Reality S.

This "duo-consciousness" is the result of our Cro-Magnon/Neanderthal ancestry. Reality O is the "objective" approach to the world that we have inherited from our Cro-Magnon ancestors, the tightly focused and highly edited awareness of the physical world that Leonard Shlain argued started with early hunters. Reality S is the "subjective" approach to life, the broader, more psychically sensitive awareness that Gooch believes we have inherited from Neanderthal. Gooch believes that Neanderthal were a devotee of a Goddess-based religion, which they associated with the moon. Cro-Magnon, on the other hand, were more attuned to a solar, masculine deity.

Eventually, the highly efficient Cro-Magnon eradicated his laid-back but more intuitive cousin, but not before he mated with her, and in our own psyches we continue the battle between them, much as McGilchrist argues goes on between our two brains. It should be mentioned that Gooch did not see the struggle going on between the cerebral hemispheres, but between the cerebrum and the cerebellum.[50] But although he disagrees on its location and participants, on all other accounts his version of the battle is practically the same.[51] Our inheritance from Neanderthal, Gooch argues, is behind what, in *Total Man* and other books, he calls our "ancient adversary" and "other self" with whom our rational ego is in constant conflict. According to Gooch, this "adversary" has given rise to our myths and legends of vampires, werewolves, goblins, centaurs, to fairy tales and other fables, as well as to works of literature such as Robert Louis Stevenson's *The Strange Case of Dr. Jekyll and Mr. Hyde.*

Cro-Magnon's "solar" consciousness worked best in the bright light of day, and it revealed useful knowledge about the hard, physical world. Neanderthal's intuitive approach was more suited to the night—he was nocturnal—and he was attuned, as Schwaller believed the later Egyptians were, to cosmic forces. Also like Schwaller's Egyptians, Neanderthal most likely experienced a kind of "group consciousness."[52] In *Cities of Dreams*, Gooch argues that an entire Goddess-based Neanderthal "Moon civilization" once stretched across Europe, but was eventually lost with the rise of Cro-Magnon and his descendants, much as the cerebellum was eclipsed by the rise of the cerebrum. (We are reminded of Steiner's "Old Moon" consciousness, and of Leonard Shlain's Goddess civilization, eclipsed by aggressive left-brainers. In *The White Goddess,* the poet Robert Graves proposed a similar idea.) This civilization, however, was not like ours, made of technology, massive cities, machines, and an indiscriminate exploitation of the natural world, but was one more attuned to natural rhythms, to Schwaller de Lubicz's "intelligence of the heart" and the "forces that bring about the becoming of things." It would be a much more "inner"-based civilization than an "outer" one; as Gooch says, it would be a "civilization more of the mind than of buildings."[53] Hence Gooch's title *Cities of Dreams.* Such a "civilization" would not necessarily leave many physical remains—think of the "civilization" of Native American Indians, all but wiped out by white settlers—but its cultural traces could be uncovered. In *The Guardians of the Ancient Wisdom,* Gooch argues that much of the western esoteric tradition is, like our fairy tales and legends, a garbled account of the Neanderthal Moon religion, and he argues that many of our superstitions and holy days are too. In this sense we can certainly see our Neanderthal ancestors as collectively making up one of our secret teachers.

THE SEVEN SISTERS

One need not agree with Gooch completely to appreciate his main idea: that prior to the rise of historical times, there existed an ancient people who had a "wisdom"—and consciousness—different from our own, and which may indeed, as Gooch suggests, have in some way informed the western inner tradition. One apparently universal myth which, according to Gooch, was bequeathed to us by Neanderthal involves a faint group of stars called the Pleiades, also known as the Seven Sisters.

As a nocturnal being, Neanderthal would spend a great deal of time looking at the night sky. Neanderthal charted the movement and phases of the moon, and he seemed to have created ritual objects as part of his worship. At a Neanderthal site at La Quina in the Dordogne region of France, seventy-six perfect stone spheres were discovered, along with a flat flint disk some twenty centimeters in diameter. No obvious utilitarian use for these objects could be discovered and it seems they are a kind of religious artifact, related to Neanderthal's moon worship.[54] But while we can accept that Neanderthal was obsessed by the moon—it is, after all, the largest and brightest object in the night sky—the attention he paid to the Pleiades seems less obvious. In *Cities of Dreams*, Gooch relates the strange fact that myths surrounding the Pleiades, also known as the Seven Sisters, can be found around the world, in places as far apart as ancient Greece, aboriginal Australia, North America, and Siberia. In fact, the Pleiades are the only constellation noted and named by every culture on the planet, past or present. They are always known as the Seven Sisters and they are always being hunted by the constellation Orion. The myths all tell the same story. But the Pleiades are not a bright constellation— they are made up of fourth magnitude stars—and to the naked eye seem rather faint. There are much brighter objects in the sky to attract the attention of early stargazers and mythmakers.

Yet Gooch argues persuasively that some thirty thousand years ago, late Neanderthal charted the movement of the Pleiades. He did this because, back then, the rise of the Seven Sisters marked the arrival of spring. As moon worshipers, Neanderthal would be interested in all heavenly activity, and as Goddess worshipers, the arrival of spring and its procreative powers would be important to them. Because of the precession of the equinoxes, however, the rise of the Pleiades and the arrival of the vernal equinox no longer happen at the same time, but Gooch argues that the significance the Seven Sisters had for Neanderthal was inherited by his Cro-Magnon competitor, who was just about to squeeze his starry-eyed cousin out of existence. Neanderthal's astronomical knowledge was gradually transformed into myth, something, Gooch maintains, that happened to all of Neanderthal's "wisdom," and was diffused across the globe.

Gooch was not the only one to notice this strange status of the Seven Sisters. In *Lost Civilizations of the Stone Age*, the Oxford anthropologist Richard Rudgley notes that the Russian prehistorian Boris Frolov also remarked on the curious ubiquity of the Pleiades in world mythology. Frolov was convinced that such acute parallels—even to exact names—across such distances could not be coincidental, and that they can only be explained by a "common heritage." Yet Rudgley comments that such a common heritage would point to a "tradition of communicable knowledge of the heavens that has existed for over 40,000 years." That is, since the "beginning of the Upper Paleolithic," and before both the New World and Australia were inhabited. It would also mean that the people of that time had a language. Rudgley recognizes that most authorities will not accept this—it would be "extremely awkward for most widely accepted views of the history and knowledge of science"—yet he does suggest that such a "knowledge" could help account for "certain objects of early Upper Paleolithic" that seem like "advanced examples of calendars based on both solar and lunar observations."[55] One such calendar was a piece of bone the prehistorian Alexander Marshack discovered in an Upper Paleolithic site. It dated from thirty-five thousand years ago yet had markings charting the phases of the moon, a finding he announced in his book *The Roots of Civilization.*[56]

DIRECT PERCEPTION

Rudgley is no occultist or esotericist, and his interest in ancient astronomers is strictly scientific, but as the title of his book suggests, he does believe that people of an earlier time knew more than we suspect. How did they know? We have seen that Schwaller de Lubicz believed it was through "the intelligence of the heart." Gooch believed that Neanderthal and the humans that followed him experienced what he called "direct perceiving," a form of intuition in which "you get things right straightaway—'just like that.'" This is opposed to our more common "indirect perceiving," in which you have to work things out.[57] The difference between the two, Gooch points out, is that with "direct perceiving," you don't know how you know, you just do. The knowledge just "pops into your head" and you have no idea how it got there. With the more laborious and time-consuming "indirect perceiving," you do know how you know, and what's more, you can show someone else how to know it too. This is our usual kind of knowledge, what the Greeks called *episteme,* and we arrive at it through the boring methods of trial, error, memory, and rote, what in general terms we call "education." Our other kind of knowledge is something different, and because our usual ideas about reality—based on our left-brain accounts—can't explain it, we either dismiss it as impossible, or ignore it. Nevertheless, it is real.

The dark magician Aleister Crowley said that "even the crudest Magick eludes consciousness altogether, so that when one is able to do it, one does it without conscious comprehension, very much as one makes a good stroke at cricket or billiards."[58] Crowley's remark echoes that of the Austrian novelist and occultist Gustav Meyrink, who said that magic is "doing without knowing." Jean Gebser believed that all magic required "a sacrifice of consciousness."[59] Zerah Colburn, the "lightning calculator" whose talents certainly seemed magical, could not give an account of how he arrived at his answers, although they were correct. Neither could Oliver Sacks's "idiot savants." As Gooch writes, "It seems to me that the ancients, in particular, of course, Neanderthal and then those who came after him who were close to him, did gain real understanding intuitively, a real knowledge of aspects of human life and human biology, of some of the functions of the planet's geology and perhaps some knowledge even of atomic and molecular structure." They acquired this knowledge, Gooch suggests, through dreams and clairvoyance or "simply by looking and saying 'this is so.'" And the strange thing is, as Gooch points out, "they were right."

Gooch's "direct perceiving," like Schwaller de Lubicz's "intelligence of the heart," seems to be a form of knowing very similar to *gnosis*, discussed earlier in this chapter. All three suggest the kind of "participatory" character that Owen Barfield argued was typical of human consciousness at an earlier time. Again, we needn't agree with all of Schwaller de Lubicz's or Gooch's arguments to recognize their basic idea: that at some point in our history, we seemed to possess a way of knowing that was different from our more familiar one, and that this way of knowing allowed us a kind of "wisdom" that we have lost touch with, or at least have less access to than we once did. "Lightning calculators" still seem to have some access to it, and in the annals of parapsychology and mysticism there are innumerable examples of an inexplicable knowledge coming to many individuals. We have also seen that drugs like mescaline can open our "doors of perception," allowing us an experience of this older form of consciousness. In one form or another, these examples—and there are others—suggest that they are in some way related to the ancient wisdom we are in search of.

Where did it go?

WHAT HAPPENED?

No one knows exactly when or how we lost our ancient wisdom and arrived at the kind of consciousness we now possess. Rudolf Steiner speaks about the change from our "Old Moon" picture-based consciousness to our more logical, rational "Earth" consciousness, and Gebser of the transition from the mythic structure of consciousness to the mental-rational; but the actual mechanism involved remains unclear, although each gives plenty of evidence that the change did take place. Stan Gooch sees the cerebrum as the culprit, and McGilchrist puts the blame on only one half of it. Undoubtedly something happened that made things different, but no one knows exactly what triggered it. There have, however, been some suggestions.

In *The Origin of Consciousness in the Breakdown of the Bicameral Mind*, Julian Jaynes argues that at around 1250 B.C. a series of crises involving wars, massive migrations, pirate raids on the coastal towns of the Mediterranean carried out by the mysterious Sea People, natural disasters like the terrific volcanic eruption on the island of Santorini, and other disturbances led to the rise of our own ego-based consciousness.[60] Prior to this, Jaynes argues, consciousness was "bicameral," two-chambered, which, in effect, means that before the "breakdown" of the "bicameral mind," humans were more or less like the split-brain patients mentioned in the Introduction. (Gebser believed that the mental-rational structure began around 1225 B.C., so his and Jaynes's dates seem to line up too.) Jaynes believed that prior to the end of the Bronze Age, humans did not experience an interior "self-consciousness" in the way that we do, but heard voices in their head which they believed came from the gods but were really issuing from the right brain. Much of Jaynes's evidence comes from Homer's *Iliad*, which was written down in the eighth or ninth century B.C., but which speaks of events—the Trojan War—taking place during the Mycenaean civilization some six or seven centuries earlier.

The *Iliad*, Jaynes argues, contains no words that describe inner states of mind. "The picture then is one of strangeness and heartlessness and emptiness," Jaynes writes. "We cannot approach these heroes by inventing mind-spaces behind their fierce eyes as we do each other."[61] "Bicameral man" would not ask himself what he should do or what he thought about something, but would wait for a "message" from the gods—or, as Jaynes, argues, the right brain. (Jaynes's own "inspiration" for his theory came when he experienced an "auditory hallucination" while pondering the problem of knowledge.[62]) When he received his answer, he would go on with whatever he was doing. Jaynes even says that "bicameral man" might have had to ask the same question several times. On his way to build a dam across a river, he might forget where he was going and what he was supposed to do when he got there, and would have to petition the god again.

This kind of dreamy, absentminded approach to life worked fine for a long time—and it still does for many people. Life followed well-grooved routines and little happened to upset them. But when these routines were broken by wars, famine, or natural catastrophes, the older, more leisurely way of life collapsed and man had to learn how to react to things more quickly. Those who didn't fell by the wayside. Jaynes points out that the "bicameral men" who went against instinct and had the presence of mind—the phrase is instructive—to allow their wives and daughters to be raped by invaders would survive; those who followed the old edicts of the gods and tried to defend them would more than likely be cut down. Artifacts from after the time of Jaynes's proposed breakdown seem to corroborate his thesis. In 1230 B.C., a stone altar made by Tukulti-Ninurta I, a tyrant of Assyria, shows Tukulti kneeling before the *empty* throne of his god. A tablet from the same time reads, "One who has no god, as he walks along the street, headache envelopes him like a garment." Again, we don't need to accept all of Jaynes's argument to grasp the basic idea: that at some point toward the end of the Bronze Age, something happened to human consciousness that put it on its road to us.

Leonard Shlain places the "split" between the old consciousness and the new a bit further back, to the rise of the alphabet circa 1700 to 1500 B.C. The Phoenicians are generally credited with the invention of the alphabet, but there is reason to believe that an earlier alphabet preceded the Phoenician, and more than likely the credit for this revolutionary development should be shared among several peoples who lived in the region between Egypt and Mesopotamia in the second millennium B.C.

Whoever invented it, for Shlain the rise of literacy and its linear means of communication was, as we've seen, not an unalloyed benefit. For all its advantages, it has led, he argues, to a left-brain–dominated culture that diminished and degraded the earlier holistic, right-brain, image-based Goddess civilization.

One of the disturbing insights that Shlain shares with Jaynes is that for both, the rise of a left-brain ego-based consciousness seems to have gone hand in hand with the rise of violence and cruelty. The Phoenicians, according to Shlain, were a cruel people, given to child sacrifice, and they left no literary or cultural remains.[63] The Assyrian Tiglath-Pileser I (1115–1077 B.C.), who came a century after Tukulti-Ninurta, inaugurated one of the bloodiest reigns in history. Laws made by Tiglath-Pileser carried inordinately severe penalties, even for minor infringements. Bas-reliefs of Assyrian campaigns depict whole populations being impaled. "The Assyrians," Jaynes writes, "fell like butchers upon harmless villagers."[64] We have seen that the left brain has a fundamentally aggressive approach to experience, and Jaynes's and Shlain's accounts seem to corroborate this. As the left brain is geared toward dealing with the world, this makes a strange, disturbing kind of sense. Faced with a world thrown into chaos, and increasingly losing touch with the gods (or goddesses), the "old ways" no longer worked and our ancestors had to make snap decisions and achieve their aims as quickly as possible. As we all know, the quickest way to get something we want is to simply take it. "Smash and grab" is the shortest route to fulfilling desires. Pain is a good persuader. Although in the long run they are self-defeating, violence and cruelty, then, may be a kind of "shortcut" taken by a consciousness suddenly confronted by a dangerous world, and driven by a need to deal with things swiftly.[65]

A NECESSARY LOSS

Yet no matter how the shift from the old consciousness to the new was engineered—and it more than likely took place at different tempos over a long time—that it needed to be accomplished is clear. As I remarked earlier, in order to operate effectively, consciousness needs to be limited. We need challenges, resistance, and obstacles in order to evolve. A perpetual Golden Age would be a curse, as would an indefinite stay in the Garden of Eden. As Aldous Huxley saw, if everyone took mescaline, no one would do the dishes, and they would soon pile up. We need to come up against some barrier in order to get the best out of us. As Nietzsche wrote, "What is happiness?—The feeling that power *increases*—that a resistance is over-come."[66] Bicameral man, Neanderthal, the ancient Egyptians most likely felt little resistance; closely connected to nature and the cosmos, how could they? In order to get things going, evolution, or the intelligence behind it, purposely put a damper on human consciousness, and over time drew it back from its awareness of "the network of connections linking everything to everything else" and fixed it firmly on what was right in front of it. The ancient Egyptians may have enjoyed, as Schwaller de Lubicz believed, "an unreflective grasp of the fundamental laws of existence," but they didn't necessarily know *how* they knew these laws, nor did they feel that they should. At home in the cosmos, they did not feel the need to explore it, in the way that our limited left-brain consciousness does. If you have a strong intuitive knowledge of something, you rarely make the effort to try to explain it, and, as we've seen, most times you can't. For all its undeniable mystery and magic, Egyptian civilization remained static for millennia.

Evolution or the force behind it does not want us to remain static. It pushed us out of the cosmic nest, into the cold and difficult regions of left-brain consciousness, because it is in those unwieldy climes that we can best actualize our capabilities.

CHAPTER TWO

OUT OF THE MYSTERIES

In the *Way to Wisdom*, the German existential philosopher Karl Jaspers proposed the idea of an "axial age." This was a kind of "axis of history," when new ways of thinking emerged that fundamentally shaped human development.[1] This age lasted, Jaspers believed, from 800 to 200 B.C., and it was during this time that "the man with whom we live today came into being."[2] This was because it was during this time that "the basic categories in which we still think" and "the world religions out of which men still live" made their first appearance. In more recent times, Karen Armstrong proposed a similar idea in her book *The Great Transformation*; and in *Order and History*, the philosopher Eric Voegelin echoed Jaspers in speaking of this period as encompassing a "Great Leap of Being."

The few centuries of his axial age produced, Jaspers tells us, an extraordinarily creative growth in human consciousness, and this surge of the human spirit was worldwide. "In the years centering around 500 B.C.," Jaspers wrote, "the spiritual foundations of humanity were laid, simultaneously and independently in China, India, Persia, Palestine, and Greece."[3] In China during this time, we find Confucius and Lao-Tzu, the founder of Taoism. In India, it was the age of the Upanishads and of the Buddha. Zoroaster emerged in Persia and laid the foundations of Zoroastrianism, and in Palestine the Hebrew prophets Elijah, Isaiah, and Jeremiah arose, announcing a new relationship between man and God. And in Greece we have the beginning of philosophy itself.

In Greece, Jasper's axial age saw the arrival of a new kind of individual, the "thinker," whose appearance we can see as the result of "bicameral man's" nervous breakdown, and the development of Gebser's mental-rational consciousness structure. Thales, Anaximander, Anaximenes, Heraclitus, Parmenides, Empedocles, down to Socrates, Plato, and Aristotle, represent a break in how human consciousness perceived the world, as well as a radically new way of understanding it.

QUESTION TIME

Although the transition from our earlier mode of consciousness into our more familiar one was not quite as sudden or complete as this notion of a "break" might suggest, it is clear that with the rise of these "thinkers," something new had appeared on the scene. Whether it was the breakdown of the bicameral mind, the rise of literacy, Gebser's mental-rational consciousness structure, an uppity cerebrum, or some other unknown or unsuspected reason, it is clear that by the middle of the first millennium B.C. something different was coming into play, at least in that part of the planet that would later be seen as the birthplace of the "western world." At this point "the mythical age with its peace of mind and self-evident truths was ended," Jaspers wrote. "The opinions, customs, conditions, which had hitherto enjoyed unconscious acceptance came to be questioned." "The world," Jaspers said, "was thrown into turmoil," and men and women had to find a new way to live in it.[4]

One sign of this new development was that, rather than accept the time-worn mythical answers about the fundamental mysteries, people starting asking questions. People had, of course, asked questions before, but the kinds of questions being asked now were different. "Bicameral man" may have asked the gods—or his right brain—"Where can I find good hunting?" or "Where is a fresh stream?" or "What sacrifice should I offer to ensure a good harvest?" The questions now being asked by a few eccentric characters had nothing to do with useful things like these, but were *ends in themselves*. The people asking them wanted to know, not because it would help them in some way, but because they were curious. They were infected with what the literary philosopher George Steiner calls a taste for "the sovereignly useless," and had acquired the bizarre habit of being "interested in something for its own enigmatic sake," which Steiner suggests "may be the best excuse there is for man."[5] "All philosophy begins in wonder," Socrates, through his scribe Plato, said in the *Theaetetus*, a dialogue about knowledge and wisdom. Aristotle and many others would soon echo him. And from the accounts that have come down to us, it seems that the Greeks of the axial age began to wonder about quite a few things.

The myths about the creation of the world that can be found in Homer and Hesiod, and later in Ovid, give a narrative, poetic account of how it came into being, that is, a story. The first thinkers of the axial age asked a different sort of question and looked for a different kind of answer. They did not ask how the world came into being, how, that is, the gods created it, but of *what* it was made. What one of Jaspers's axial-age Greeks, pointing to the ground, or a star, or a cloud, wanted to know was, "What is this *made of* ?" What is its essence? That was the question.

LOST IN THE STARS

What the early, pre-Socratic philosophers were interested in is what Aristotle later called an *arche*, a Greek word meaning "beginning," "origin," or "source," and which is familiar to us through Jung's use of the term "archetype." As one historian of philosophy put it, these axial-age Greeks were looking for "the original and controlling stuff and first principle of the universe, the nature of which provides an explanation of the existing universe, and its origin, as a whole."[6] To use an anachronistic phrase that would not apply until the modern age, the pre-Socratics wanted to know what made the universe tick. In this sense we can see these early questioners and thinkers as the first scientists.

We can also see them as the first "absentminded professors." A tale about Thales of Miletus (c. 624–546 B.C.), in Asia Minor, now Turkey, that Plato tells illustrates this. In the *Theaetetus*, Plato tells how Thales was once so engrossed in looking at the stars that he didn't notice a well and fell right into it. This prompted a Thracian maidservant to remark that Thales was so concerned with what was happening in the sky that he was

oblivious to what was right in front of him. (Thales was an early astronomer and accurately predicted a solar eclipse in 585 B.C., so his stargazing
was at least fruitful.) The story later became one of Aesop's fables. Such
observations as the maidservant's soon became commonplace—"Anyone
who gives his life to philosophy is open to such mockery," Plato remarks—
and the kind of obsessiveness that prompted them could be dangerous.
Archimedes of Syracuse, famous for his cry of "Eureka," is said to have
been killed in 212 B.C. by a soldier who ordered him to meet the Roman
general Marcus, then busy conquering the city. Archimedes' fame was
so great that the general wanted to meet him, but Archimedes was so
engrossed in contemplating a mathematical diagram that he ignored the
soldier who, in a fit of anger, killed him. Nietzsche said that philosophers
"lived dangerously," and at least in this instance he was right. But the
moral of the story is clear: philosophers live dangerously because their
obsession with concepts and ideas—a left-brain concern—can alienate
them from "life."

Thales, who was one of the Seven Sages of ancient Greece, believed
that everything is made of water, or, more accurately, that water is the
essence or *arche* of everything. "All is water," he said, "and the world is full
of gods." Here we see an overlap between the mythic view of the world
and the rising "scientific" one, a blending of the old and new consciousness that would last for some time. Water, Thales noted, sustained life
while in its absence things died; he also maintained the view that the
Earth floated on a kind of cosmic sea, a carryover from the mythic notions
of Oceanus, the great World Ocean that was believed to encircle the universe. The philosophers who followed Thales proposed *arche*s of their
own. Thales' student, Anaximander, proposed that the *arche* was not a
substance or stuff like water, but a kind of *principle* that, somewhat con-
fusingly, also had stufflike qualities. Anaximander's *apeiron*, the name of
his *arche*, means the "infinite" or "indefinite." *Apeiron* is limitless and
indefinable; since it explains everything, it must be beyond everything,
and because it is the source of all characteristics, it must be characterless
itself. As it is through the *apeiron* that heat gets its hotness, water its wet-
ness, air its dryness, and earth its solidity, the *apeiron* itself cannot be
hot, wet, dry, or solid. Anaximenes, a student of Anaximander, proposed

a less abstract *arche* and believed that the fundamental stuff of things was air. Heraclitus, the "dark philosopher," said it was fire. They seemed to be following a pattern, and it took the philosophers Leucippus and Democritus sometime later to complete the set of the ancient elements. They proposed that earth, or at least solid matter, in the form of atoms, was the basic stuff out of which everything else was made, an idea that gained remarkable currency in the modern age.

ORDER IN THE FLUX

We may not be impressed with Thales' ontological analysis, nor with that of the philosophers who followed him, although later philosophers like Martin Heidegger believed that we had taken a wrong turn at Plato and needed to get back to the pre-Socratics.[7] But our sophistication can blind us to the significance of their attempts to answer the childish question "What is the world made of?" This is a query that, with an enormous amount of technology and expense, we still ask today: witness the recent excitement over the Higgs boson. What is important about Thales, Anaximenes, Heraclitus, and the others is that, as Richard Tarnas puts it, they "made the remarkable assumption that an underlying rational unity and order existed within the flux and variety of the world" and they made determined attempts to grasp it. The emphasis here is on "rational unity." As Tarnas says, these early philosophers made it their task to discover a fundamental principle at work in the world, and to provide "impersonal and conceptual explanations" of it "based on their observations of natural phenomena."[8] Whatever the world is made of, these early philosophers inaugurated a new departure for humanity. They began to think about things, rather than just accept them. Neanderthal and Schwaller de Lubicz's ancient Egyptians may have enjoyed an intuitive unity with the cosmos that we experience only rarely, if ever. But I am not sure if they wondered about things in the way that we, if we are lucky, still do.

A HARMONIOUS MAN

Talking about Thales, Anaximenes, and the other early Greek thinkers, I have repeatedly used the word "philosopher." This is something of an anachronism, as it was not until the advent of another pre-Socratic thinker that the word even existed. This was Pythagoras of Samos (c. 571–c. 497 B.C.), and if we exclude mythical and semimythical characters like Hermes Trismegistus, Orpheus, and Zoroaster, we can think of him as our first secret teacher.[9] Along with several other things, Pythagoras is traditionally held to be the first person to use the term "philosopher," meaning "lover of wisdom." He also introduced the word "cosmos" into our vocabulary. It comes from a Greek word, *kosmos*, meaning "an orderly or harmonious system," and it is opposed to another Greek word, *khaos*, or "chaos," which for the Greeks meant a formless void, the inchoate state of things before creation.

In *The Caretakers of the Cosmos*, I point out that although scientists often use the words interchangeably, "universe" and "cosmos" do not mean the same thing. Essential to the idea of a cosmos is the necessity of beauty, hence our word "cosmetic," which for the Greeks meant "that which beautifies," but for us means "makeup," something essentially false or "just for show." So for Pythagoras and the philosophers who followed him, we can have stars, planets, galaxies, and so on, but unless these are related to each other in a beautiful, harmonious order, we do not have a cosmos. Another term still in use that has its source in Pythagoras is "theory," from the Greek *theoria*, which means to "contemplate" or to "see" with the mind's eye, or "*nous*." "Theory" for us means an idea or concept, but we can see its roots in the notion of "speculation," which links both to "spectacle" and to "theater," both of which involve a kind of seeing.

One of the difficulties in writing about the pre-Socratics is that little of what they wrote has survived. All we have are enigmatic fragments, and in the case of Pythagoras, who, like Socrates and Christ, taught orally, we don't even have that. (Pythagoras may have left some poetry written under the name Orpheus, but that is uncertain; why he may have chosen Orpheus as a pen name will become clear shortly.) What have come down to us are accounts of Pythagoras's life and teaching by later philosophers. The Neoplatonists Porphyry and Iamblichus wrote accounts of his life, but in these how much is truth, how much myth, and how much hearsay attributed to Pythagoras by the devotees of his school is, at this point, impossible to sort out. Most of the stories about Pythagoras should be taken with several grains of salt as the sort of thing that accumulates around an exceptional individual. I leave it up to the reader to decide whether or not Pythagoras had a golden thigh, or could be seen in two places at once, or if he was indeed the Hyperborean Apollo (or at least his son)—Hyperborea being a mythical land to the north—or that he could converse with a certain river and also with demons, that he descended to the underworld, or, as is perhaps most known, could truly hear the "music of the spheres."[10]

This celestial music, said to be the euphonious hum of the planets as they gently turned around the Earth in their crystalline spheres, is a development of one of the two discoveries that, if they know anything about Pythagoras, most people credit him with. One is the famous Pythagorean theorem which, as we've seen, Schwaller de Lubicz believed the Egyptians knew well before him. If the stories of Pythagoras's travels are true, he may indeed have learned it from them. Pythagoras is also said to have discovered the musical octave. One day, passing a blacksmith, he noticed that the iron rods the smithy was hammering let out different tones depending on their size. It was through this that Pythagoras discovered that different musical notes are related to each other harmoniously because there is a simple ratio between the notes and the length of the string producing them. This story itself may be a folk tale, but Pythagoras did experiment with the monochord, an ancient single-stringed musical instrument with a movable bridge, and it was most likely through his observation of this that he recognized the relation between the length of string and its tone.[11] Having said this, Pythagoras may have learned about the octave during a stint in Babylon, where some scholars have argued its secrets had been known for some time.[12] However Pythagoras hit upon the octave, it is the source of his central insight: that there is a harmonious order at work in the universe, and that this order is most fundamentally expressed through numbers, something Schwaller de Lubicz believed the ancient Egyptians knew as well. Pythagoras was supposed to be so attuned—an instructive metaphor—to this cosmic order that, just as he could hear the octave emerge from the smithy's hammer blows, he could also hear the gentler, more heavenly tones of the planets above.

A SHORT LIFE OF PYTHAGORAS

Pythagoras was the son of Mnesarchus, a gem engraver and merchant from Tyre, and his wife, Pythias, and was born on the Greek island of Samos in the Aegean Sea. He is believed to have studied with Anaximander, from whom he adopted the idea of the *apeiron,* as well as with Thales. He is also thought to have studied with Pherekydes of Syros, an enigmatic figure who is said to be the first Greek philosopher to teach the notion of the transmigration of souls, an idea that Pythagoras and his followers would also adopt.[13] It was said that Pythagoras could remember his past lives and that he could also see the past lives of his students. Sometimes considered one of the Seven Sages of Greece, Pherekydes is seen as a transitional figure, bridging the mental gap between the older mythological thought and the rising pre-Socratic philosophy.

Iamblichus, writing nearly a millennium after Pythagoras's death, claimed that Pythagoras had spent twenty-two years in Egypt, and that he also studied among the Chaldeans and possibly with the Zoroastrians in Persia.[14] He was said to have been initiated into the religious mysteries of certain "barbarians"—which simply meant non-Greeks—and that, according to Porphyry, it was "from his stay among these foreigners that Pythagoras acquired the greater part of his wisdom."[15] He studied, it is said, in all the schools that were available at the time, even reaching the country that for many was the real Hyperborea, the "land beyond the North Wind," ancient Briton, where he may have made contact with the Druids, who, along with Pherekydes, also believed in the transmigration of souls.[16]

Although Pythagoras traveled in search of knowledge, his journeys may also have been in the service of Polycrates, the enlightened tyrant of Samos, a lover of learning and art. It is believed that Pythagoras was engaged in several diplomatic missions for Polycrates.[17] Such political assignments are not uncommon among some secret teachers, and figures such as Swedenborg, Madame Blavatsky, Gurdjieff, and Aleister Crowley have been suspected of espionage and other political intrigues.

After his travels, Pythagoras returned to Samos and it is said that for a time he lived in a cave, which he fitted out as a place to study philosophy. He is thought to have started his first school then, which was called the Semicircle, but this was short-lived. There appears to have been some disagreement with Polycrates. Pythagoras seemed to think, as Plato would after him, that either philosophers should be kings or that kings should be philosophers, and he may be responsible for inaugurating the tradition of trying to inject philosophical idealism into the practicalities of political life. Evidently this didn't go over well with Polycrates, and at around 530 B.C., Pythagoras left Samos and moved to Crotona, one of the largest Greek cities in southern Italy. It was here that his real teaching began. His reputation preceded him; almost immediately on his arrival, he was asked to address the people on the right conduct of life. He must have been a persuasive orator. His audience asked him to get involved in the local government, and for a time his philosophical-political ideas seemed to have found a home. It is said that after his speech, hundreds of locals joined his newly formed Pythagorean Brotherhood, the first philosophical school in Europe, and the first esoteric one too; at least it is the first for which we have any historical records.

Pythagoras's influence in the public life of Crotona and what was known as Magna Grecia or "Greater Greece" was widespread. But again it was short-lived. It is unclear what prompted it, but at some point the populace of Crotona rose up against Pythagoras and his disciples. The rebellion may have been sparked by the disciplined, often ascetic life that Pythagoras maintained was essential to the pursuit of wisdom, or it may have been a result of the suspicion that the average person often has toward the activity of a secret "elite." It may have been that the Pythagorean attitude toward women—which gave them the same status as men—and the overall communal character of the school attracted the animus of powerful members of the community. It is also suggested that Cylon, a corrupt nobleman of Crotona, sought admission to Pythagoras's brotherhood but was denied, and so led the rebellion against him. Whatever the cause, Pythagoras and his brotherhood were attacked. Their meeting-houses were burnt down and many of the disciples were driven into exile or slain. Pythagoras himself fled the massacre and headed to Metapontion, another Greek Italian colony, where he spent his remaining days and started another school. It is said that he died after fasting for forty days.[18] Empedocles said that in his life, Pythagoras experienced "all things that are contained in ten, even twenty generations of men," and even this brief outline suggests that it is difficult to disagree with him.

IT'S ALL IN THE NUMBERS

Pythagoras's central insight was that number was at the heart of the cosmos. This may not sound too remarkable. For us, living in the scientific age, number is indeed everything. From our bank balance and body mass index to our PIN codes and Facebook friends, number is central to our lives. But between Pythagoras's idea of number and our own there is a world of difference. We see number as essentially a unit of measurement, of quantity, and we apply it to practically everything, so much so that the Traditionalist philosopher René Guénon argued that we live under "the reign of quantity."[19] That physical reality can be measured accurately and that predictions based on these measurements will also prove accurate is at the core of modern science and technology. We obviously have much to thank for this, but Pythagoras saw numbers very differently. For him they were essentially *qualitative*. That is, where we see 1, 2, 3, and so on as merely integers expressing the amount of something, for Pythagoras numbers had characters, much in the way that, say, people do. For him, 1, 2, 3, and so on expressed certain fundamental, archetypal characteristics that gave pattern and shape to reality. So where we use numbers to denote the quantity of something—the distance between London and Paris or the price we have to pay for some item—Pythagoras and his followers were interested in understanding the *meaning* of a number, to discover its essence in itself. For them, number was a universal principle, as fundamental, if not more so, as light or sound. Indeed, for Pythagoras, light and sound, as well as everything else, were in essence expressions of the metaphysical character of number. As David Fideler writes, for Pythagoras, number is "the principle, the source, and the root of all things."[20]

For Pythagoras, One is technically not a number. The Monad or Unity is the *principle* behind numbers, which are the "manifestation of diversity in a unified continuum."[21] The One is the fundamental source out of which everything else emerges. It is with Two that all existence begins. Two, or the Dyad, introduces multiplicity and strife, the tension between opposites, but also the possibility of understanding, of relating the opposites to each other. (Again, Schwaller de Lubicz speaks like a Pythagorean when, in his early work *A Study of Numbers*, he speaks of the primal, inexplicable "scission" of the absolute nonmanifest One into multiplicity, a mystery that in the form of the Big Bang still tantalizes science.)

The opposition of subject and object is overcome by Three, or the Triad, which is precisely the relation between these two, between knower and known, which is knowledge. Here, at the very beginning of western thought, we have the recognition that oppositions are unified through the introduction of a third element, the notion of a "transcendent function," mentioned in the Introduction. This third element *harmonizes* the other two; it "fits" them together to create order, which is what "harmony" means. Things are in harmony when they fit together well, when they are ordered, when the balance and proportion between them is correct, and this can apply to everything, from a musical composition or an architectural design, to our diet, which we are told should be "balanced."

This basic pattern of existence, what Gurdjieff centuries later would call "the law of three," was expressed by Pythagoras in a figure he called the *tetraktys*, which is a pyramid of ten points, with one point at the top and four at the bottom, with a row of two and then three in between. For Pythagoras and his followers, all of creation is symbolized in the *tetraktys*. Here we have the undifferentiated unity of the One, which becomes the polarity of opposites in Two, then their harmony and reunification in the higher synthesis of Three, resulting in the manifestation of the world in Four. For Pythagoras, the *tetraktys* was so important that he called it the *kosmos*, or *Pan*, which means "the All."

The *tetraktys* is an example of what the Pythagoreans called "number-shapes," the way that numbers form certain kinds of figures, which tell us about the world. The Pythagoreans wrote numbers as a series of dots. Odd numbers were seen to form squares while even ones formed oblongs, and this is something one can discover for oneself.[22] We may have abandoned this kind of thinking, yet we still think of numbers as "figures," and when we want to find the answer to something, we say we will "figure it out," a Pythagorean inheritance we all share. The kind of mathematical relationship Pythagoras saw between the lengths of iron rods and the tones they emitted seemed to exist throughout the rest of creation too. It was the work of the philosopher, the lover of wisdom, to seek out this hidden order and to harmonize himself with it. He or she must balance his own inner world, his soul, and out of its initial chaos form a cosmos, that is, give it beauty through achieving a spiritual order.

Again, the fundamental process at work in arriving at order, whether in the inner or outer cosmos, was the harmonizing of the tension between two opposites, between the limited and the unlimited, the *peras* and the *apeiron*. Our word "perimeter," or the "period" that ends a sentence or indicates a certain length of time, is an echo of the Greek *peras*. It was in this that Pythagoras differed sharply from his other philosophers. Where Thales, Anaximenes, and the others sought the fundamental "stuff" out of which the cosmos was made, Pythagoras was focused on *form*. Number was not a thing or a kind of material, but that which gave form and limit to matter. All things have form, and all form can be understood in terms of number, and number itself is the result of harmonizing the limited and the unlimited. Without the limited, the unlimited, as Anaximander knew, would be formless, a kind of chaos. It is the limiting power of form that allows for a cosmos to exist.

A PHILOSOPHICAL LIFE

It was also the power of limit, in the sense of a disciplined way of life, that created the inner cosmos, the ordered beauty of the soul. Pythagoras differed from his Ionian contemporaries in maintaining that philosophy was not only a search for rational answers or concepts to account for natural phenomena, but a way of being in the world, a way of bringing oneself into harmony with the order that permeated existence. It was a way of bringing oneself into balance with the cosmos, of fashioning a well-tempered soul. The musical metaphor is peculiarly apt, because music for Pythagoras was well suited to harmonizing the mind and the soul. Its mathematical order excited the mind while the soul enjoyed that order's beauty; indeed, Pythagoras is said to have calmed an excited youth by having a certain mode of music played, a recognition that the harmony and order found in music can have a direct and predictable effect on the psyche, an insight that Gurdjieff shared and said was true of all "objective art."[23] Music was central to Pythagoras's teaching, as it was to the cosmos, and the goal of the philosopher was, like Pythagoras, to be able to hear the harmony of the spheres.

Members of the Pythagorean Brotherhood were vegetarians. This was in part because of dietary reasons; the idea behind the philosophical life was to become pure, and coarse flesh would work against this. But Pythagoras also believed that by eating animal flesh, we may inadvertently eat a human soul that had transmigrated there. Beans were also famously forbidden, as the flatulence they produced would have interfered with the contemplative calm the brothers desired. Some kind of physical exercise aimed, as it is today, at promoting well-being and a balanced lifestyle was also a part of the Pythagorean discipline.

Pythagoras's students were divided into two levels, although he also had secret teachings that he reserved for a select group, a not uncommon procedure in esoteric schools. The *akousmatikoi* or "auditors" went through a three-year probation period and were limited to listening to Pythagoras's lectures, which were said to have been given behind a screen. The *mathematikoi* or "students" proper endured a five-year period of silence, during which they were not allowed to ask any questions, merely to reflect on the teachings they absorbed. All property was held in common, and the brothers' daily routine consisted of studying mathematical diagrams that modeled the harmony in nature and the cosmos. They would also study the heavens and learn the fundamental principles of music. Music seemed to unify the total range of the Pythagorean life, relating the mind, the emotions, and the body. As David Fideler writes, "The divine harmony can be grasped through the mind, yet can also be perceived through the senses."[24]

Apollo was the god of order and beauty, and his lyre produced beautiful harmonies; it is no surprise that Pythagoras was his devoted servant, and there is a tradition that sees in the god's name the essence of the Pythagorean teaching. Apollo is said to mean to "become one, not many" (*hoi polloi* in Greek means "the many").[25] Whatever we may think of the myths and tall tales associated with Pythagoras, it is clear that with his school began the study of mathematics, music, and astronomy that would form much of the western intellectual tradition that followed.

ORPHEUS AND THE MYSTERIES

That music played a large role in Pythagoras's philosophy links his teachings with the Orphic mystery tradition. Orpheus was a musician—his lyre was said to have come from Apollo—whose playing was so beautiful it was said to move not only men's souls, but also stones, trees, and even demons and the gods. He was a human who achieved a semidivine status, and most of us know about his ill-fated attempt to rescue his wife, Eurydice, from the underworld. In the earliest version of the myth, he does succeed, but later versions have him breaking Hades' condition that on his journey back to Earth, he not look back at Eurydice; he does, and she is forced to return to the depths. The Orphic teachings aimed at freeing the soul from this fate, and for centuries Orphism was one of the most important of the Greek Mystery religions. They are called "mysteries" because what exactly was made known during their rites was never revealed and remains a mystery—participants took a vow of secrecy under pain of death—but also because from what we do know of them, it is clear they were concerned with the central mysteries of life and death.

The little we know about the Mysteries comes from brief remarks made by some of their initiates. The Greek poet Pindar said that whoever took part in the Mysteries "knows the end of life, and its divinely-bestowed beginning." The Roman statesman Cicero said that not only did he find "reason to abide in joy" at the Mysteries, but also "to die with greater hope."[26] *The Golden Ass,* by the Roman writer Apuleius, depicts in fictional form an initiation into the Mysteries of Isis, and among the

Greek greats said to have been initiated were the dramatist Sophocles and the fount of western philosophy, Plato.

The most famous of these initiations, the Eleusinian Mysteries, were performed in Eleusis in Greece from around 1500 B.C. to their end in 392 A.D., when the Roman Emperor Theodosius I closed the sanctuaries and ordered the destruction of many other pagan religious sites.[27] A few years later, in 396 A.D., the coup de grâce was delivered when Alaric, king of the Visigoths, invaded, accompanied by many Christians, and wiped out whatever was left. The Eleusinian Mysteries were founded, so the story goes, by the goddess Demeter in honor of the god Dionysus, in thanks for the release of her daughter Persephone from her captor, Hades, who had brought her to the underworld. Persephone was allowed to return to Demeter for half a year, and the myth is supposed to represent the return of spring after the barren winter. If nothing else, it does represent a rebirth and in this sense is related to similar themes and rites of other death and rebirth religions, like that of Isis and Osiris in Egypt, and that of Demeter's fellow Greek, Dionysus, as well as Christianity.

The rites involved a celebration and procession from Athens to Eleusis and were open to every Greek speaker, man, woman, or slave, the only exception being murderers. These rites were a more participatory kind of worship, as opposed to the stale respect shown to the distant gods of Olympus. There were two levels of Mysteries, the Lesser and the Greater. In the Lesser Mysteries, participants were given knowledge of the higher worlds, of what lay beyond the earthly plane and the release from it through death. But in the Greater Mysteries, the participants were given an experience of this. As Joscelyn Godwin points out, the Lesser Mysteries were a collective experience, while the Greater Mysteries were experienced individually, and apparently not everyone was worthy of them.[28] The experience of the Lesser Mysteries culminated in the participants being shown an ear of corn; this and the other vegetal symbolism associated with the rites—wheat, pomegranates, poppies—suggest the ever-recurring forces of life, stirring within nature and ourselves, and revealed to the initiate that he too will return after a brief departure.

In the Greater Mysteries, a potion known as the *kykeon*, a mixture of barley, mint, and water, was consumed, and the secrets of the afterlife were revealed to the participants. Those who received the *kykeon* were known as *epoptai*, the name for those who had beheld (*epopteia*) the sacred secrets—a link, perhaps, to the *theoria* or contemplation of the Pythagoreans. What exactly they beheld and what exactly was in the *kykeon* remains unclear, although some scholars have suggested that the *kykeon* contained some hallucinogenic (or "entheogenic," "god-engendering") substance; LSD from ergot, a fungus found on corn and other grasses, and "magic mushrooms," have been suggested.[29] That drugs may have been in wide use in ancient and classical times is the thesis of a fascinating book, *The Chemical Muse: Drug Use and the Roots of Western Civilization* by D. C. A. Hillman. He argues that Pythagoras, as well as other early philosophers, were very familiar with them.[30] As Albert Hofmann, the discoverer of LSD, remarked, "Greece was the cradle of that experience of reality in which the ego felt separated from the exterior world," and the Mysteries must have "addressed some profound spiritual necessity, some yearning of the soul."[31]

PURIFYING THE SOUL

Initiates into the Mysteries were also given knowledge to help them on their journey after death from the underworld to the heavenly spheres, much as the *Egyptian Book of the Dead* and the *Tibetan Book of the Dead* give advice on how to avoid the traps and snares facing the souls of the newly departed. Initiates were given the password to the paradise of Demeter and were told that on their journey through the underworld they should avoid drinking from the spring of Lethe "near the white cypress," which contains the "waters of forgetfulness," but to make sure they drink from the spring flowing from the "Lake of Mnemosyne," or memory. To remember your spiritual self was essential to avoid either remaining in Hades, a dim realm of shades and shadows, or to being born again.

The aim of the Orphic Mysteries was to avoid having the soul fall again into the body after death. Through the observance of certain rites and an ascetic way of life—the Orphics, too, were vegetarian and if not celibate, were sexually abstemious—those who follow the path of Orpheus would become pure, would experience a *katharsis*, the Greek root of our "catharsis." They would be "cleansed," and through this would avoid being reborn, which, as in the case of eastern ideas of reincarnation, was seen as a punishment for our sins. Orpheus began as a reformer of the Dionysian Mysteries, the wild, orgiastic rites of the god of drunkenness and madness. Nietzsche pitted the gods of madness and of order—Dionysus and Apollo—against each other, and recognized that in the tension between them lay the roots of Greek art.

The mythologist Carl Kerényi saw Dionysus as an "archetypal image of indestructible life," the *élan vital* or "life force" beyond reason, which cannot be understood but only experienced. Dionysus is a "death and resurrection" deity. In one version of the Dionysian myth, he is the son of Zeus and Persephone. The Titans—earlier, godlike powers that Zeus has tamed—jealous of Zeus, eat the child, except for his heart, which Athena rescues and gives to Semele, a Theban princess with whom Zeus had relations. In revenge for the murder of Dionysus, Zeus destroys the Titans, and out of their ashes makes mankind. Semele later gives birth to Dionysus again, but is herself destroyed by Hera, Zeus's jealous wife. As in many myths about the creation of mankind, a residue of the god—our spiritual spark—remains within us, and the rites of the Dionysian Mysteries were aimed at releasing this, through orgies, drunkenness, and other, more "transgressive" acts, inspired by "divine madness." In later years, the Dionysian Mysteries, as well as the others, were enormously popular in Rome; their transgressive character proved too much, even for decadent Romans, and they were outlawed. But Dionysus did not disappear. Of all the gods of ancient Greece, Dionysus is the one who still remains with us, as the divine madness of sex, drugs, rock and roll, and raves is still a popular means of "getting out of it," out, that is, of the limits of the rational mind.

Dionysus, like Orpheus, was linked to music, but Orpheus sought a less mad way of releasing the soul from the bondage of the body. In one version of Orpheus's death, after rejecting the sexual advances of the Maenads, the female followers of Dionysus who engaged in orgiastic and cannibalistic rites, he is torn to pieces by them, but his head lives on and floats down the River Hebrus to the isle of Lesbos, where it continues to sing. Orpheus started his own, tamer version of the Dionysian Mysteries, a kind of ascetic, more speculative rite, which had the same goal of release from our earthly bonds, but which pursued this more consciously, in a more controlled and meditative way. As Christopher Bamford puts it, "the Orphic way of life" provided the "possibility of any individual attaining by his own efforts . . . a transcendent purity synonymous with divinity."[32] In this sense, we can see Orphism as a kind of precursor to Pythagoras and his school.

Yet there is a difference between what the initiates of the Mysteries experienced and the kind of life led by the Pythagorean Brotherhood. While the *epoptai* of the Eleusinian Mysteries spent an evening enraptured with visions of the beyond, induced by the possibly hallucinogenic *kykeon*, they afterward returned to their everyday lives, which were not necessarily devoted to the pursuit of wisdom. In a sense, the Mysteries were the ancient Greek equivalent of modern festivals like Burning Man. They were spectacular and revelatory, but afterward you went home. For all its significance, the experience was passive. It was something that happened to you.

The philosophical life is different. The Pythagoreans wanted to understand the revelations of the Mysteries, and not wait for death to release them from the burdens of the body. Although informed by the religious spirit of Orphism, they wanted to cultivate their intellects as well as their souls. The ritual observances of Orphism were not enough. This is why the Pythagorean Brotherhood was a school and not only a religious community. Its members spent years contemplating the universal harmony, through mathematics, astronomy, and music, and they pursued this wisdom because they loved it. Not everyone who participated in the Mysteries would have the same perseverance. The catharsis that the Dionysiacs achieved through their mad revels, and which the Orphics reached through their rites and practices, was made available to the Pythagoreans through their desire to grasp the rational order of reality. Purifying the soul of its earthly dross was essential, but equally necessary was disciplining the mind.

THE PERMANENT NEEDS Of HUMAN NATURE

The balance achieved by the Pythagoreans between the intellectual spirit and the religious soul seems like a temporary truce between the older, mythological way of being and the newer, critical form of consciousness. The type of consciousness that appeared during the axial age was indeed new and differed from its mythological predecessor, yet as the classicist Francis Cornford remarked, "the philosophic Muse is not a motherless Athena."[33] What Cornford means is that philosophy's appearance was not unprecedented, as Athena, the goddess of wisdom, was said to have emerged fully formed from Zeus's brow after it had been split open by Prometheus's ax—an image that both Julian Jaynes and Jean Gebser use to describe the painful wrenching of a new form of consciousness out of an older one and which again suggests the *aggressive* character of linear, left-brain thinking.

Cornford's book *From Religion to Philosophy*, first published in 1912, argued that, unlike the accepted view that the pre-Socratics represented a complete break with the mythological past, and the first step in what we would call a modern, "scientific" type of thought, the "fresh spirit of rational enquiry" they represented had its roots in earlier Greek religion and mythology. The rationalistic assumptions of Cornford's contemporaries saw mythology and religion as little more than superstition, and the pre-Socratics for them were the first signs of an awareness unburdened with these constraints. In recent times, Peter Kingsley has followed Cornford and proposed that not only was the new philosophy a child of its mythological predecessor, some of its most influential practitioners, such as Parmenides and Empedocles, had roots in ancient shamanistic practices and that these dark origins have been obscured by later philosophical tradition.[34]

Cornford argued that while what would in time become the scientific mode of thought did have its beginnings with the Ionian pre-Socratics, such as Anaximander, who did not believe in the gods, there was another school, and that these "two traditions" were "moved by distinguishable impulses along lines diverging, more and more widely, towards opposite conclusions." These impulses, Cornford writes, "are still operative in our own speculation, for the simple reason that they correspond to *two permanent needs of human nature,* and characterize two familiar types of human temperament" (my italics). This seems to be another expression of the fundamental duality of human consciousness.[35] The other school of early philosophy was represented by Pythagoras, and there is reason to believe that, aware that the older form of consciousness was on its way out—although he did not think in terms of "forms of consciousness"—Pythagoras tried to salvage what he could of it, and embodied this in his teaching.[36]

PLATO

Probably the most important figure in western philosophy who was initiated into the Mysteries is Plato, who speaks of them in the *Phaedo,* his dialogue on the immortality of the soul. Plato's importance to the western intellectual tradition was summed up by the philosopher Alfred North Whitehead, who said that all subsequent philosophy was only a footnote to him.[37] Plato inherited much from Pythagoras, and in him the "two traditions" and "permanent needs" of human nature and thought achieved a remarkable if temporary synthesis. If there is a single most important secret teacher, we would not be far wrong in bestowing that title on Plato. As the historian of esotericism Wouter J. Hanegraaff argues, practically all of western esotericism has its roots in Platonism.[38]

We do not know much about Plato's life. He was born to an aristocratic Athenian family in 427 B.C. and he died, at the age of eighty or eighty-one, in 347 B.C. It is said that he was called Plato because of his broad physique, although, like much else said about him, this might be just a legend. Plato's family had political connections in high places and it is thought he saw military service in his youth. Like most young men of his class, he was widely read and tutored in music and mathematics, and he was also educated in the philosophy of Pythagoras and Parmenides, and most likely the Sophists, lecturers in rhetoric and argument, who sold their knowledge for a price. The most important experience of Plato's life was his meeting with the philosopher Socrates, who appears as a central figure in the early Platonic dialogues; Socrates took up philosophical arms against the Sophists, whom he perceived as intellectual opportunists, lacking integrity.

We know little of Socrates' life aside from his depiction in Plato's dialogues; other sources, such as Plato's student Xenophon and the playwright Aristophanes, are secondhand and fragmentary. Like Christ, Socrates taught orally, and also like Christ, we are dependent on the reports of his followers for what we know of him. As some have pointed out, there is scant factual evidence for Christ's historical existence and only a little more for Socrates'.[39] Socrates' intelligence, intellectual honesty, disdain for honors or riches, and resolute pursuit of the good, true, and beautiful, impressed Plato, as did his concern with ethical and moral questions, as opposed to the more naturalistic ones of the pre-Socratics. For Plato, Socrates embodied the philosophical life, and it was his execution at the hands of the Athenian state on the charge of corrupting Athenian youth that turned Plato away from politics.

After Socrates' death in 399 B.C., Plato left Athens and for many years traveled around the Mediterranean studying mathematics, astronomy, philosophy, and religion with Pythagoreans in Italy and with the priests of Egypt. It was around this time that he began writing. Although known as a philosopher, Plato also wrote poetry, and his dialogues themselves, written in a vivid dramatic style, have a literary genius uncommon among philosophers. In 385 B.C. Plato opened his Academy, where budding lovers of wisdom studied mathematics, astronomy, natural science, and philosophy. The Academy was set in a grove sacred to the goddess Athena, and tradition says that over the entrance were the words "Let no one ignorant of geometry enter," an admonition that may have given quite a few later philosophers pause; Nietzsche, for example, was famously bad at math. Plato's aim in founding the Academy was to stop the disintegration of Greek culture and to prepare Greek citizens to take positions in politics and government, a step toward actualizing his belief, voiced in the *Republic*, that philosophers should be kings, or kings, philosophers.

As in the Pythagorean school, Plato's students participated in communal activities and dedicated themselves to living the philosophical life. As Owen Barfield told C. S. Lewis, philosophy was not an academic subject for Plato, it was a "way."[40] Plato's Academy remained open in different forms until the Byzantine Emperor Justinian I shut it down in 529 A.D. Justinian feared that the pagan philosophy it taught was a threat to Christianity, and his closure of the Academy is generally seen as the end of Antiquity.

Plato's ideas about philosopher kings hit a wall when he tried to put them in practice. In 367 B.C. Plato was invited to become the personal tutor of Dionysius II, the ruler of Syracuse in Sicily. Dionysius II, however, did not make the grade and, being paranoid—as most rulers are—he suspected Plato of plotting against him and placed him under arrest. Eventually Plato was released and he returned to Athens and the Academy, where he found a new student, Aristotle, who would have his own turn at creating a philosopher king when he became tutor to Alexander the Great. Plato spent his last years writing, crystallizing the insights of a lifetime devoted to philosophical inquiry. It is said that he died peacefully in his sleep, although other accounts say he passed away while attending a wedding.

THE IMMORTAL SOUL

In the *Phaedo*, a record of Socrates' last words, Plato examines different ideas about the afterlife and the immortality of the soul. In the end Socrates suggests that the soul is immortal because it can have knowledge of and a share in the Good, the True, and the Beautiful, which are eternal. Because we can participate in these timeless values, there must be some part of us that is timeless too. Only like can know like, Socrates tells Phaedo, his student. Socrates has spent his life pursuing an understanding of the essence of these things, the indispensable quality that makes them what they are, much to the dismay of the people who have been on the receiving end of his inquiries. Socrates called himself a "gadfly," who "stung" his listeners out of their complacency with his unending questions, rather as Gurdjieff was known as the "arch-disturber of sleep" who remorselessly "stepped on people's corns," that is, their self-love and vanity. In Socrates' case, the corns were ignorance and self-importance.

The *Euthyphro* gives an example of Socrates' often numbing pursuit of his essences—in this case, of piety.[41] He never arrives at an *explicit* definition of these fundamentals and, given what we know of them, as I point out in the Introduction, we can understand why. But he does arrive at an understanding of them: that they are timeless and exist in some way beyond the physical world and that his soul participates in them because he has sought them through his pursuit of knowledge. Convinced of the truth of this and fortified by his experience of the Mysteries, Socrates asks his friends not to mourn his death nor to weep at it, but to recognize that it is only his physical body that will die, not his soul. It is being released from a long bondage; as W. B. Yeats said centuries later, we are "fastened to a dying animal."[42] Socrates' bonds are loosening. His last words are "we ought to offer a cock to Asclepius." Asclepius was the Greek god of medicine, and sacrificing a cock to him was done in thanks for recovering from an illness. Socrates sees life as an illness, and his death is the restoration of health: his return to the timeless realm of the soul.

THE FORMS

Plato too believed that philosophy was a preparation for death in the sense that the true philosopher does as much as possible to separate his mind or soul from his body during life, something we know that Pythagoras and the Orphics were also interested in doing. This does not mean practicing asceticism or embracing a kind of romantic death-worship; but it does mean being moderate in sensual pleasure and indifferent toward riches and honors. It also means making clear distinctions between what we can know in an absolute or "pure" sense and what of our knowledge varies.[43] True knowledge, true wisdom, cannot come from the senses, Plato argues, because the perception of things they provide is unstable and shifting and often deceptive.

This seems to fly in the face of science, but a moment's thought shows this is true. We see the sun come up and go down, but we know it does neither, and that the perception that it does is really a result of the Earth's rotation. We certainly do not see that the Earth is round—at least we did not until the advent of space exploration—but we know it is, and that knowledge was arrived at through reason. If you take a pencil and put it halfway into a glass of water, it appears to bend, something ancient sailors noticed when they put their oars into the water. We know the pencil and the oars do not bend, but they appear to. This does not mean that the kind of knowledge provided by the senses is wrong or illusory in some fundamental way, but that it is relative. Under certain conditions, certain observations can be made, and certain deductions derived from them.

Aristotle, Plato's student, will take argument with his teacher and begin the appreciation of empirical knowledge, knowledge accrued by observation, that is the basis of science. His ideas will dominate the western mind for centuries. We have got into the habit of thinking that science provides us with the most accurate or "true" knowledge because of its phenomenal success in its practical application. But Plato was not interested in observing nature or in the practical application of knowledge but in grasping the kinds of "essences" Socrates was after, and that is a good distinction between science and philosophy. We are back again with the pursuit of George Steiner's "sovereignly useless." Philosophy is not "good" for anything—a reflection most nonphilosophers will agree with—but its pursuit enriches our lives. It has no utilitarian value but is a good in itself.[44]

In the *Phaedo*, Socrates speaks of "absolute beauty" and "absolute goodness." He was not speaking of the "most beautiful thing" but of that which gives beautiful things their beauty, and of that which gives good things their goodness. Socrates' friends agree that such absolutes exist, and he asks them how they know this. Have they ever seen absolute goodness or beauty, and not only good or beautiful things? They agree that they have not, and Socrates suggests that the best approach to grasping these absolutes is not through the senses but through the "unaided intellect," that takes no account of sight, sound, touch, or any other sensory means. It is not the body or senses that know in this way, but the soul, the mind.

Plato took Socrates' essences and absolutes and with them developed his theory of the Forms, or Ideas. It is his most important contribution to western consciousness and it had a profound influence on western esotericism and thought in general. Its truth or value has been debated practically since Plato first presented it; in the *Parmenides*, he himself subjects it to some of the harshest criticism it has received. Like all good philosophers, Plato does not shy from questioning his own ideas. Put simply, Plato believed that the Forms were the fundamental blueprints of reality. Just as a carpenter must have an idea of a chair before he can make an actual chair, or an artist an idea of what he wants to paint before he makes his painting, so too for all of reality. Beautiful things are related to each other because they all participate in the Form or Idea of Beauty, which exists in a nonphysical realm outside the physical world, just as the carpenter's or artist's idea exists in their minds.

To speak of a nonphysical realm being "outside" is, of course, confusing, but we are saddled with a language geared toward dealing with the physical world and must make the best of it. We never see Beauty, but only things that participate it in.[45] A sunset, a flower, a painting, and your girlfriend are all beautiful because they in some way reflect the "essence of the beautiful." We can't observe this essence as we can observe the things that participate in it, but through the mind we can grasp the necessity for it, and insofar as we do, we share in it. So through philosophy, the love and pursuit of wisdom, we can awaken that part of us that exists outside the senses, outside the body, and enter the timeless realm of the Forms.

Plato believed that the physical world, the world of the senses, was a copy or reflection of the "real" world of the Forms, and he believed that as long as we remain limited to what the senses tell us, we are not in true contact with reality. Socrates' dialectic is a rigorously logical method of critical investigation, and hence embodies the new "mental" left-brain structure of consciousness; but when Plato wanted to propose a positive insight, he turned to myth. As Whitehead said, "The father of philosophy, in one of his many moods of thought, laid down the axiom that the deeper truths must be adumbrated by myths."[46] In this way, Plato catered to our "permanent need" for something more than logic.

In a famous myth in *The Republic*, Plato tells us that we are like prisoners in a cave who are forced to sit and look at a wall. We are not allowed to turn around, so we do not see that behind us our captors have devised an interesting way to keep us occupied. They have a bright, roaring fire going, and before it they use puppets of different shapes and sizes to create shadows that appear on the wall. As they parade these objects in front of the fire, we see the silhouettes they cast. As they are all we can see, we sit entranced and watch the show, which we take for reality, and some of us even devise theories to account for the sequence in which the shadows appear. It would be the same as if we were somehow locked in place in a movie theater and made to look at what was on the screen, with no knowledge of how the images got there.[47]

Every now and then, however, a prisoner manages to turn around. He sees the fire and the people carrying the puppets and he realizes that what he had been looking at all his life was not reality, but only a shadow of it. Our prisoner manages to escape his bonds and he makes a dash for the exit from the cave. Outside he sees the trees, clouds, sky, and sun and is dazzled by his first glimpse of Reality: he no longer sees shadows, but the real things responsible for them. Delighted with his discovery, and wanting to share it with his fellow prisoners and help them escape, he returns to the cave to tell them. But they are so used to seeing shadows that they don't believe his story. They say he is mad, wrong, or simply telling lies, and angrily turn their heads back to the wall. Saddened by their disbelief and mockery, he leaves them to their chains. Such, Plato says, is the fate of the philosopher.

A PORTABLE TOMB

Plato's cave is the body and the limitations of the senses, but another subterranean metaphor he uses to depict the human condition is perhaps more striking. In the *Cratylus*, a dialogue about the origin of language, Socrates makes a play on words that has a deep philosophical import. The joke isn't apparent in English, but in ancient Greek it works. Socrates says that according to the Orphics, the body, or *soma*, is the tomb, or *sema*, of the soul, which is "buried" in our present life.[48] As the Hermetic writings will later say, the body is our "portable tomb."[49] As in the myth of the cave, the body here is a prison. For most of us, our release from this incarceration will only come with death. But for some there is a way for the soul to escape its prison, or at least to be let out of it every now and then, before that final release. And according to tradition, there is a good chance that Plato may have learned of this way in Egypt.

In *The Quest for Hermes Trismegistus*, I write about the work of Jeremy Naydler. In his short book *Plato, Shamanism and Ancient Egypt*, Naydler argues that there is good reason to believe that Plato did spend time in Egypt, and that while there he was initiated into some of the Egyptian Mysteries. Naydler is not alone in thinking this. Thomas Taylor, the nineteenth-century Platonic scholar who was the first to translate all of Plato into English, and whose work influenced such important figures as William Blake and Ralph Waldo Emerson—and who deserves to be seen as one of our secret teachers—claimed that Plato was initiated into the Greater Mysteries in an underground chamber beneath the Great Pyramid of Giza. Taylor tells us that the Mysteries "enkindled and brought from its dormant state" what was already latent in the "Divine Plato," namely his spiritual knowledge. Plato himself argued that all knowledge is really memory, so Taylor's remarks make good Platonic sense. Taylor relates that "After three days in the Great Hall," Plato was "received by the Hierophant of the Pyramid" and given "the Highest Esoteric Teachings." According to Taylor, Plato remained with the pyramid for three months, during which time he was prepared to go out into the world, "to do the work of the Great Order, as Pythagoras and Orpheus had been before him."[50] One of the esoteric teachings that Plato is thought to have learned during his time in Egypt was a method of separating the soul—or, as we would say, consciousness—from the body, and that this entailed a way of "dying" while in life.

As we've seen, Socrates believed that philosophy was a preparation for death. A literal interpretation of this suggests a kind of world-rejection and pessimism, the kind of anti-life philosophy that Nietzsche suspected in Socrates and Plato. But if that was the case, why shouldn't the philosopher just commit suicide and get it over with? To "practice dying," in the way that Naydler suggests Plato had in mind, means something else.

PLATONIC SHAMANS

Naydler argues that some form of shamanism was involved in ancient Egyptian spiritual practices, and that works like the *Egyptian Book of the Dead* were not only funerary texts but were guides on how to separate what the Egyptians called the "*ba*" from the physical body. The myth of Osiris's dismemberment at the hands of his evil brother, Set, is paralleled, Naydler argues, by dismemberment motifs in shamanic initiation rituals; we have already seen that Peter Kingsley argues that much of early Greek philosophy has shamanic roots.[51] Egyptian ideas about the soul are complex and often confusing, but the *ba* corresponds roughly to what we mean by consciousness.[52] The Egyptians depicted the *ba* as a bird with a human head, hovering over the body of the deceased; to modern eyes, these images seem to suggest accounts of "out-of-the-body-experiences," which suggests that the body in question may not have been dead after all. Most Egyptologists see these images as depictions of the soul leaving the body after death and they believe that this teaching was part of the common Egyptian religion. Naydler argues that in fact these images are depictions of the *ba* leaving the body while it was still in life, and that the knowledge of how to do this was reserved for the priests; it was, he maintains, an *esoteric* knowledge, not divulged to the masses.

The Egyptians believed that the *ba* leaves the body at death, and also in sleep during our dreams, but Naydler argues that the Egyptian hierophants also knew that it can be released from the body in states of deep relaxation or trance. For this to happen, Naydler argues, "the central requirement was that the psycho-physical organism be stilled." "The *ba* only comes into its own," Naydler writes, "when the body is inactive and inert."[53] The kind of physical inactivity Naydler speaks of seems to me to be rather close to the kind of contemplative calm sought after by the Pythagorean or Platonic philosopher.

While the body is active, its noisy demands obscure the *ba*, but when it is quiet, the *ba* can be known and felt. In order to experience the *ba* consciously, while awake and alive, consciousness must be withdrawn from the body and gathered into a unity. The Egyptians believed that consciousness was spread out among the different parts of the body, or rather that the different parts of the body had their own kind of consciousness, an idea that, centuries later, P. D. Ouspensky would explore.[54] To experience the *ba* while awake, the consciousness of the rest of the body had to be stilled, while that of the head, where the *ba* resided, had to be concentrated, as if one were tightening a fist. This unified consciousness could then separate from the body and experience the spiritual states associated with dreams and with the journey of the soul in the afterlife while still awake and alive. In essence, what this means is that our "I" could feel itself to be an independent reality, not dependent on the body or limited by its restrictions. For the ancient Egyptians as well as for the Pythagorean/Platonic philosopher, we "have" a body, but *we* ourselves are something different from it.

Whatever the source of Plato's ideas, with the rise of his student Aristotle, his philosophy lost its dominant position and the long dialectic between myth and logic—the two "permanent needs of human nature"— in the western mind began. We are still involved in this. Plato may have lost top billing for a time—for many years he certainly shared it with his brightest pupil—but his eclipse was by no means permanent. And when he reemerged into the spotlight, it was in a very appropriate place: Egypt.

CHAPTER THREE

THE SECRET GNOSIS

The School of Athens" by the Renaissance painter Raphael, part of the frescoes decorating the Apostolic Palace in the Vatican, depicts a gathering of some of the major figures in classical philosophy. At the center, drawing the viewer's attention and dominating the scene, are Plato and Aristotle. A barefoot Plato, with gray beard and straggly hair, holds a copy of his *Timaeus* in his left hand while with his right he points upward to the heavens. Aristotle, younger and better dressed, holds a copy of one of his important works, the *Nicomachean Ethics,* and with his other hand points downward toward the earth. The gestures are traditionally thought to show the difference in their approach to knowledge and philosophy: Plato concerned with comprehending the transcendent ideas, Aristotle focused on gathering empirical knowledge about nature. Here, in pictorial form, is the contrast between the universal and the particular over which many subsequent philosophers lost much sleep. But what is interesting from our perspective of looking at the history of western consciousness through the lens of our two brains is that Plato stands on the right, while Aristotle is on the left.[1] With Aristotle, the kind of close attention to empirical data that would slowly mature into our own modern science began. With this, the move away from myth and more intuitive modes of knowing gained momentum.

Aristotle's impact and influence on western consciousness is as great as Plato's. Some would say it is even greater. It is no exaggeration to say that Aristotle's approach to knowledge came to define and dominate the western mind, and did so until only fairly recently. But as far as I can tell, he does not figure into the esoteric aspect of our story. Indeed, much of esoteric philosophy finds itself in opposition to Aristotelianism. His emphasis on the evidence of the senses, on logic, on the strictures of rational discourse is often at odds with the inner analogical and metaphorical character of much of esoteric thought, and Aristotle's dictums provided many walls for esoteric thinkers to bang their heads against. Through the long years of the Middle Ages, Aristotle was the Christian philosopher of choice, eventually wedded to the faith through the efforts of St. Thomas Aquinas. During this time his former teacher Plato was held in much lower esteem as a dangerous pagan to be avoided.

Aristotle was born in 384 B.C. in Stagira, in northern Greece, and came from a prestigious Macedonian family; his father was physician to the Macedonian king Amyntus III, the grandfather of Alexander the Great. After his father died, Aristotle went to Athens and, at seventeen, joined Plato's Academy, where he remained for twenty years. With the death of Plato, he left Athens and went to Assus in Anatolia, where a graduate of Plato's Academy was ruler. Here and also on the island of Lesbos—home to the seventh-century B.C. poetess Sappho—he carried out extensive research in zoology and marine biology, practically inventing the disciplines. Where mathematics was central to Plato's philosophy, Aristotle focused on biology, the shifting forms of life in contrast to the eternal verities of geometry. Aristotle was not interested in the "supersensible" Ideas, but in how something becomes what it is, what he called its inherent "entelechy," or "goal"—how each substance actualized its inner potential. Aristotle's approach was systematic and aimed at a workable classification of phenomena; his writings cover an extraordinary range of subjects, everything from botany, chemistry, and ethics, to poetics, politics, and psychology. He is in fact the first systematic thinker and his methods are still at the root of the western educational system. This shows his difference from Plato, who never devised a system and whose dramatic dialogues move from topic to topic. Plato is also a much better writer and we can say that, with Aristotle, the tradition of unreadable philosophers begins.

While he was Plato's student, Aristotle paid lip service to the Forms, but he was really out of sympathy with Plato's ideas and soon abandoned them, arguing that they had failed to account for how the particulars that shared in the transcendent universals appeared in the first place. Rather than focus on what seemed to him vague notions of unearthly forms, Aristotle set his sights firmly on the phenomenal world. Thus began the "bifurcation" in western thought—to use Alfred North Whitehead's term—that has run like a fissure through it ever since.

THE LYCEUM

In 343 B.C. Aristotle was summoned back to Macedonia by Philip II, who wanted him to tutor his thirteen-year-old son, Alexander. Later, while on his campaigns, Alexander sent biological and botanical specimens back to Aristotle, who had returned to Athens to start his own school. At his Lyceum, which he founded in 335 B.C., Aristotle built up a huge "research library" and taught his students his methods of classification, the necessity of systematizing knowledge, and the rigors of formal logic. The students who gathered around Aristotle became known as the "Peripatetics," because he often taught while walking.

There were some differences between Aristotle's Lyceum and Plato's Academy. In the Lyceum, the emphasis was on "scientific research and data collection," which made it very different from a "semireligious philosophical school like Plato's Academy."[2] Another difference is that while Plato's school was rather like a private club, Aristotle's Lyceum was open to everyone—except women. Plato's Academy was open to women, and for his time Plato was very outspoken about the ability of women to learn philosophy. Another difference was that the dialogical method was downplayed. Aristotle lectured, much as university teaching is done today, and did not engage his students in dialogue. His reasoning was that, as they were students, they did not yet know enough to provide intelligent answers. This is very different from Plato's idea that truth emerges through the give-and-take of philosophical exchange, in which opposing or contrasting views can arrive at a conclusion partaking of both, a form of the "transcendent function."

IS IT LOGICAL?

In Plato's early dialogues, Socrates is central, and the emphasis is on critical reasoning; but Plato did not set out a systematic formal logic. Aristotle decided to fill this gap. We have all been exposed to Aristotle's logic in one form or another. It has become so fundamental to our way of thinking that we accept it as given, as "natural," and we find it hard to believe that at one time it was new and unusual. Essentially, it is a means of avoiding contradiction in thinking and of making sure our conclusions follow from our premise—terms that originate with Aristotle. It is an indispensable tool for thought—an "organon," as Aristotle's pupils called it—and it is difficult, if not impossible, to conceive of thinking or engaging in philosophical argument without it. We can think of it as a set of traffic signs and signals directing our reasoning. Readers who have taken Philosophy 101 will be familiar with the form of the "syllogism," which stems from a Greek word meaning "to reason with." The most famous one runs: "Socrates is a man. All men are mortal. Therefore Socrates is mortal." Other similar constructions follow this pattern and readers can refresh their memory by consulting any handbook of logic, if the thought of doing so doesn't fill them with dread.

Fundamental to Aristotle's logic are the notions of identity and noncontradiction. Put in its simplest form, this tells us that A is A, that A is not not-A, and that A is either A or not-A. However we look at it, in Aristotelian terms, something either is or it isn't. There's no middle ground. This is generally called the "law of noncontradiction" and it is related to the "law of the excluded middle." This states that something cannot be both true and false and must be either one or the other.

This is a trait of left-brain thinking, its insistence on an "either/or" approach to knowledge and understanding. This "black-or-white" approach has its virtues and we use it every day; life would soon become chaotic without it. But it is not the only way we can think of things or perceive the world. Earlier we saw that Schwaller de Lubicz believed that the ancient Egyptians had a more "both/and" approach that was more in line with how

Iain McGilchrist argues the right brain interacts with the world. The kind of perception that could appreciate the "simultaneity of opposite states" informs practically all of esoteric thought. The esoteric scholar Antoine Faivre includes it in his "four fundamental elements" of esotericism. Under the heading "Correspondences"—the belief, central to esoteric thought, that there exist relations "among all parts of the universe, both seen and unseen," the "network of connections that links everything with everything else"—Faivre writes "the principles of noncontradiction and excluded middle of linear causality are replaced here by those of the included middle and synchronicity."[3] Synchronicity, Jung's name for the phenomena of "meaningful coincidence," tells us that something which in logical terms should not be meaningful or have any connection to my inner world nevertheless does. And the notion of correspondence tells us that something is more than itself, that it is also a symbol of some higher significance. For Aristotle, as for Gertrude Stein, a rose is a rose and nothing else. For an esotericist, a rose is a rose, but it is also much else.[4] And the "excluded middle" or "*tertium non datur*"—the "third not given"—is precisely the result of the "transcendent function," which produces a "third" alternative, a synthesis of two opposing propositions that "transcends" both of them.

PHILOSOPHY IN DIFFICULT TIMES

We can see Aristotle as the end of the first phase of philosophy, its early creative stage. After him the seeds of doubt begin to grow, and the world that philosophy found itself in changed. After Alexander the Great's death in 323 B.C., squabbles among his generals led to his empire being divided into separate states. Life became more complicated as wars, migrations, the mixing of different peoples and cultural beliefs, and other disruptions introduced a sense of uncertainty and instability into things, much as in our own time. The cosmic order which in earlier times seemed reflected in human affairs was now a distant memory, as everyday life became increasingly complex, confusing, and often dangerous. From an attempt to grasp the fundamental realities of existence, philosophy shifted to more ethical and practical concerns, and became more and more a kind of "self-help" teaching, aimed at survival in difficult times. Its focus was on a disengagement with the world and a detachment from one's own passions and intellectual doubts. More than anything else, peace of mind became its goal.

Cynicism, whose name comes from the idea that its practitioners "lived like dogs" (*kynikos*, the root of "cynic," is Greek for "doglike"), rejected society's conventions and advocated a return to "nature." In practice this meant an ancient Greek version of "letting it all hang out" and "getting off the grid," exemplified by Diogenes of Sinope (404–323 B.C.), who wore rags, barked at passers-by, ate scraps, and urinated in the marketplace. Diogenes believed that only by rejecting society's norms and listening to the needs and demands of "nature" could one lead a true and good life. He has been depicted as living in a barrel, surrounded by dogs, which he preferred to people, and as holding aloft his lantern by daylight as he searches for an honest man. While Diogenes and his followers believed in virtue, for us being cynical means suspecting the worst of everything.

Skepticism arose out of the recognition that there was widespread disagreement among philosophers about practically everything, and that logic and reason could be used to support antithetical arguments, something the Sophists had taught. Skeptics doubted the possibility of knowledge—either through reason or the senses—and advocated "suspending judgment" (*acatalepsia*) about the truth or falsity of all propositions. Either side of an argument could be maintained with equal reason; there was no way to choose between them, so one should, in effect, abandon the attempt. This suspension, they claimed, would result in a state of *ataraxia*, a kind of imperturbable tranquillity or "release from worry," which they maintained was the most desirable state, something that much "mind, body, spirit" literature aims at in our own time.

The Epicureans also sought *ataraxia*. Epicurus (341–270 B.C.) held that the world consisted fundamentally of atoms and "the void," the space in which the atoms moved. His materialist philosophy sought to free men from their worries about the gods and other superstitions, as well as the fear of death. There was no soul and at death nothing happened except that the atoms of one's body returned to the flux. Like the Cynics, he advised a retreat from the public world, but a much more decorous one, and taught that one should "cultivate one's garden." One should, as he said, "live unknown." "Epicurean" for us means refined and delicate tastes, but this is in some ways a misnomer. Although advocating a kind of materialist hedonism, Epicurus really argued for the simple life. Pleasure was the only good, and one should arrange one's life to have as much of it as possible. This did not mean that we should jam as much pleasure into our lives as we can, as if it was an "all you can eat" buffet and we'd be losing out if we didn't stuff ourselves. Such gluttony is simply quantitative. Epicurus preached discrimination aimed at providing the highest quality of pleasure. Self-discipline and self-control were central tenets of Epicureanism.

The Stoics were much more catholic in their tastes. Where the Epicureans taught that one must pick and choose what to attend to in life in order to experience the highest degree of pleasure, the Stoics argued that we must put up with everything life throws at us, whether good or bad. This is because it is all part of the divine reason or *logos*, a cosmic unity that is ultimately good and of which we are inescapably a part. Our own sense of "being stoic" and having a "philosophical attitude" toward life stems from this belief. The founder of Stoicism was Zeno of Citium (335–263 B.C.) not to be confused with Zeno of Elea (495–430 B.C.), famous for his paradoxes. The term "stoic" comes from the *Stoa Poikile* or "painted colonnade" where Zeno taught in Athens, competing with Plato's Academy and Aristotle's Lyceum.

The Stoics were materialists and believed, with Heraclitus, that the fundamental substance of reality was fire; they also believed that the cosmos would be destroyed in some final conflagration but was reborn cyclically. They rejected Plato's Forms but believed there was a world-*logos*, or reason, with which our actions must be in accord. They also believed that as the world was a unity of which we are a part, all men are inherently brothers and therefore equal. If in our own life this equality was not apparent—many slaves adopted Stoicism—this was of no matter. In the end any inequities will be evened out; we should not complain about our lot, as it is a necessary part of the world order and things are irrevocably fated to be as they are. This order is not apparent to the senses but can be recognized through logic. The Stoics believed that as one is a citizen of the world, one has a duty to be engaged in political affairs. Stoicism saw no difference between Greek and non-Greek, a "one world" philosophy radical for its time. Like the Epicureans and the Skeptics, Stoics sought a kind of *ataraxia*, but they saw this more in terms of being free from the passions. They sought to quiet the soul and arrive at *apatheia*, a freedom from emotions; our "apathy," which derives from this, is a negative version of what for the Stoics was a positive state of emotional calm. Stoicism proved remarkably successful; probably its most famous exponent was the Roman emperor Marcus Aurelius (121–180 A.D.), whose *Meditations* offer guidance on how to maintain *apatheia* in the midst of conflict.

RETURN OF THE MYSTERIES

The "self-help" philosophies that sprang up in the Hellenistic Age provided some rational guidance in an increasingly complex and intimidating world. But for many, these reasonable teachings were not enough, and some sought a more intense emotional experience—more right brain, we might say—to give meaning to their lives. By the time of Rome, the ancient Mysteries, accompanied by some newer, exotic ones, became increasingly popular. The established religion—the Roman pantheon, a warmed-over version of the gods of Olympus—no longer commanded devotion and respect, and increasingly Romans found themselves worshiping at strange altars. Rome was remarkably tolerant about religion, and as long as a conquered people paid respect to the Roman gods, they could worship their own gods too. But the tables were often turned, and the gods and goddesses of a defeated people quickly made their way to Rome, where they enjoyed conquests of their own. Rome became a kind of spiritual marketplace—similar to our own time—and deities of many lands and peoples found new and fervent followers in the Eternal City.

One of the most popular of the Mysteries was that of Isis, the Egyptian goddess of love, marriage, and the home, but also of the moon and magic, whose name means "throne." She was the sister-consort of the Egyptian resurrection god, Osiris, and the mother of Horus, a warrior god depicted as a hawk or falcon and seen as the protector of Egypt. In many ways, Isis was similar to the Greek goddess Demeter, and there was a fruitful union of Greek and Egyptian deities during the period of Hellenized Egypt. Isis had been worshiped in Egypt for centuries; the earliest references to her are from the fifth dynasty, c. 2465–2325 B.C., and she is mentioned frequently in the Pyramid Texts, c. 2350–2100 B.C., associated with the *Egyptian Book of the Dead.* With the conquest of Egypt by Alexander and then Rome, her worship spread; as early as the fourth century B.C. she was being worshiped in Piraeus, the port of Athens, which Socrates often frequented. There had always been a strong link between Greece and Egypt. In the *Timaeus,* an Egyptian priest tells Solon, one of the Seven Sages of Greece, that the Greeks were "only children," and goes on to inform him about the lost continent of Atlantis and that Egyptian civilization was eight thousand years old—a dating which puts it in line with Schwaller de Lubicz's estimate.[5] As Arthur Versluis writes, all throughout the classic, Hellenistic and Roman age, "Egyptian tradition was regarded by the Greco-Romans as synonymous with magic and ancient wisdom as well as divinatory power."[6]

Isis was the daughter of the earth god, Geb, and the sky goddess, Nut. Married to her brother, Osiris, she taught the Egyptians the arts of the home, weaving, baking, and brewing (the Egyptians were fond of beer). Osiris's brother, Set, however, grew jealous and murdered Osiris, hiding his body in a leaden coffin which he threw into the Nile. Isis eventually found Osiris but Set was so furious at the discovery that he hacked Osiris's body to pieces, flinging them to the winds—the shamanic dismemberment motif of which Jeremy Naydler speaks. With some effort, Isis gathered Osiris's body parts, all except his penis. With some help from Thoth, the god of magic, and some improvisation, Isis was able to conceive a child, Horus, by Osiris.

Osiris was then obliged to enter the underworld, which, like the Greek Hades, he ruled. Horus eventually grew up and avenged his father. As the broken-hearted widow of Osiris, Isis is often depicted in mourning. Via Delos (Apollo's island), Magna Graecia, Herculaneum, and Pompeii—all of which had temples in her honor—Isis eventually arrived in Rome, where a temple to her and the Greco-Egyptian syncretic god Serapis was erected on the Capitoline Hill during the time of Julius Caesar, and where she was worshiped for centuries.

Isis was the perfect wife and mother: unobtrusive but ready to take charge when needed. She used her magic for healing and is often depicted nursing the baby Horus, an image that later reappeared in Christian iconography as Mary nursing the baby Jesus. As many women pray to Mary for help and guidance, rather than direct their prayers to Jesus or God, so too did many call on Isis "the mighty mother" for strength and comfort. "Of all the gods of the Mystery religions," writes Joscelyn Godwin, "perhaps best loved was Isis—loved for her warm humanity, and for incarnating all the best aspects of women as lover, wife, mother, and widow."[7]

Another mother goddess was somewhat less reassuring. Originating in Phrygia—west central Anatolia—Cybele was like Isis in personifying all that was warm and loving in a mother. But she also had a dark, grasping, devouring side that likened her to Hecate and the Indian Kali, whose worship included violence, pain, and murder.[8] Known as the *Magna Mater* or Great Mother, Cybele was often identified with the Greek Rhea, mother of Zeus, but was more widely worshiped in her Dionysian role as the goddess of dark rites and orgiastic descent into divine madness. Cybele was first symbolized in a black stone—most likely a meteorite—that was set as the face of a silver statue. During the Second Punic War, when the Carthaginian Hannibal was advancing on Rome, her statesmen consulted the Sibylline Books—a collection of oracles from a sibyl, or prophetess, that guided Roman governors throughout the Republic and Empire—and was told that only if the Great Mother was brought to Rome would it triumph. Taking no chances, a messenger was sent to the Delphic Oracle for a second opinion and received the same instruction. In 194 B.C. the black meteorite was fetched from Pessinus in Asia Minor, where King Midas was said to have ruled, and brought to Rome. She was installed in a temple atop the Palatine Hill and was worshiped there until her cult was banned by the emperor Valentinian II in the fourth century A.D.

Cybele's cult was banned because of the "transgressive" character of her worship. Many of her male followers castrated themselves in memory of her tragic young beloved, Attis. There are different versions of the story, but in essence Attis was a beautiful young man with whom Cybele fell in love—in some versions she is his grandmother, indirectly by way of Zeus. But Attis became bethrothed to Midas's daughter. Cybele was enraged at this and, appearing in her full form before Attis, she drove him mad. Attis ran to the mountains and, at the foot of a pine tree, castrated himself, dying in the process. But through the ministrations of Zeus and a satisfied Cybele, he was resurrected; along with Osiris, Dionysus, and Christ, Attis is an archetypal death and resurrection figure.

Many of Cybele's followers took Attis's lead and, as mentioned, castrated themselves as the Great Mother's worshipers danced and writhed through the streets of Rome. Others were less radical, though their self-harming—slashing and cutting themselves into a frenzy—was no less wild. Many dressed in women's clothes, wore makeup, and greased their long hair. As with Dionysus, with whom Cybele is often identified, raucous music, chanting, dancing, drinking, and more lascivious acts made up her worship. As with the Dionysian rites, many found this aspect of Cybele's worship too much. Laws were made to segregate her worshipers, and no Roman citizen was allowed to join in their processions, nor to become priests or priestesses in her cult. No Roman could wear the bright-colored clothes or engage in the revelries that made up the Phrygian forms of worship. Eventually her worship was banned, and those who wished to continue it were forced to form secret societies and to conduct their services in private. In the sixth century, the emperor Justinian had any remaining devotees tortured and executed, often burying them alive.

The ecstatic character of the Great Mother's worship was shared by other cults, most of which participated in what will strike most of us as rather extravagant rites: the taurobolium, or bull-sacrifice, and criobolium, or ram-sacrifice. A priest or priestess stood in a deep trench, covered by wooden planks in which fine holes were cut. The bull was then slaughtered and its blood ran through the holes onto the worshiper who, in some versions, drank it. Initially aimed at ensuring the well-being of the emperor, the empire, or one's community, it later became a ritual of personal renewal—death and resurrection. Its similarity to Jewish and Christian practices involving the Paschal Lamb is striking. In the last days of paganism, the taurobolium was performed in defiance of rising Christianity; the place of the ritual was on a site where St. Peter's now stands.

One Mystery religion in which a bull played a central role was that of the Persian cult of Mithras, which grew out of Zoroastrianism and which was limited to men. It spread mostly through the military, forming a kind of Roman Freemasonry. According to Manly P. Hall, Mithraic initiation rites were often performed in underground temples fashioned to look like caves, which the initiate entered by descending seven steps—representing the ancient planets—and upon whose walls were painted mystic symbols.[9] Here the candidate underwent grievous trials, where he was pursued by the wild beasts and demons of his lower nature. Part of the Mithraic rites involved the tauroctony, or sacrifice of a bull, in which Mithras, the intercessor between man and the gods, stabs the animal with a sword while turning his face toward the sun. Mithras was extremely popular in the Roman world and his cult spread from Syria to Scotland, mostly among soldiers but, like Stoicism, also among slaves. As in modern Freemasonry, there were no social distinctions: rich or poor could be initiated; and also like Freemasonry, initiates were bound by secrecy. As more than one historian of the Mysteries has noted, there are several similarities between the Mithras cult and another that was to become much more successful: that of Jesus Christ. Mithras was a savior god who interceded on man's behalf with the Persian god Ahura Mazda. He was born on the twenty-fifth of December and his birth was witnessed by shepherds. He was considered a manifestation of the Logos—the mind or divine intelligence behind the cosmos. He will return at the end of the world to judge mankind, and after a last battle with, and victory over, evil—Ahura Mazda's archenemy, Ahriman—he will lead the faithful to life eternal.

SOOTHSAYERS AND WONDERWORKERS

This time was also one in which prophecies, predictions, visions, and other means of gaining supernatural knowledge became increasingly popular. If, as the Skeptics believed, reason was no sure road to secure knowledge, other ways were available and the Romans, like other ancient peoples, made use of them. Prophecy by a variety of methods was commonplace. Probably the most popular was by means of reading an animal's entrails. The unfortunate creature—most often a bird—was sliced open and its intestines scrutinized for some indication of the gods' intentions, much as in less brutal times a gypsy fortune-teller or grandmotherly spiritualist would consult your tea leaves. Although this gory method was very popular, as indeed was animal sacrifice in general, less gruesome means were also available. Yet the fact that people resorted to such crude expedients suggests how far consciousness had shifted from its earlier intuitive, participatory mode. What may have come naturally at an earlier time now needed to be extracted through extreme methods. Some part of our earlier consciousness, however, still remained. Sibyls, women prophets who, while in some altered state of consciousness would communicate obscure and often incomprehensible oracles, were respected as divine messengers of the gods and many would make the journey to seek their pronouncements; we have seen how important the Sibylline Books were and how they were responsible for the Great Mother coming to Rome.

In second century A.D. a Roman family known as the Juliani conducted what today would be considered a form of spiritualism or "channeling." It was a kind of father-and-son act. The elder Juliani would practice theurgy, magical rituals aimed at contacting the gods, and through these rites put his son into a trance. While in this state, the boy would answer questions and utter strange sayings whose source was believed to be divine. The Juliani called themselves, or were considered to be, "Chaldeans," an ancient name for the Babylonians, much as today some modern forms of spiritual teaching attach the term "Egyptian" to themselves, in order to profit from the pedigree. Most of what the Juliani communicated is lost, but some of their sayings were recorded; these fragments came to be known as, or at least associated with, the Chaldean Oracles. Modern scholarship suggests that the Oracles are a commentary on an original "mystery poem"—something, perhaps, like the philosophical poems of Parmenides and Empedocles—that is lost but which was considered to be of Chaldean or Babylonian origin. The Chaldean Oracles were later attributed to the Persian sage Zoroaster, and as such, they were influential on the development of western esotericism. When Gemistos Plethon lectured Cosimo de' Medici on the *prisca theologia*, he saw Zoroaster as the initiator of the Golden Chain of Adepts, and the Oracles as the fount of the ancient wisdom.

Whatever the source of the Oracles—and the nineteenth-century

Platonist Thomas Taylor believed that at least some of them did originate with Zoroaster—the visionary teachings they pronounce are in keeping with the philosophy we have so far recognized in the ancient Egyptians, Orpheus, Pythagoras, and Plato: that the human soul and spirit are not irrevocably linked to the body, and through certain practices they can regain their heavenly inheritance.

Magic and sorcery were also very popular, and tales of miracles, magical feats, and dark spells captured the ancient imagination just as they do today. Love potions, poisons, spells to gain power, riches, influence, or to discover hidden treasures, become invisible, heal, cause harm, or become immortal: these and other similar perennial human desires sent many to seek audience with those who knew the ways of fulfilling them. As today, many of the individuals offering their sorcerous services at a price were mostly adept at parting a fool from his money. There were some, however, who seemed to have exhibited genuinely remarkable abilities. One such was the magician, philosopher, and wonderworker, Apollonius of Tyana.

APOLLONIUS Of TYANA

There is little definite factual knowledge of Apollonius. Most recent scholarship places him c. 15–100 A.D. He was born in Cappadocia in Asia Minor (again, modern Turkey) to a prestigious Greek family, and most of what has come down to us about him can be found in the *Life of Apollonius of Tyana*, written by the philosopher Philostratus, most likely between 220 and 230 A.D. Philostratus's biography, commissioned by Julia Domna of Syria, second wife of the Roman emperor Septimus Severus, is supposed to be based on a diary kept by a companion of Apollonius, Damis, but there is debate over whether Damis existed or not. As with Pythagoras, it is difficult to sift fact from fiction, and in general we need several grains of salt when looking into Apollonius's biography.

Apollonius appears to have been a Pythagorean and to have shared in the Pythagorean revival that began around the first century B.C. He was a wandering philosopher-magician and is said to have traveled to India, Egypt, Syria, Greece, and Rome, and to have had run-ins with at least two emperors, Nero and Domitian. He was vegetarian, avoided wine, wore his hair long, did not shave, dressed only in linen, condemned animal sacrifice, and at the age of twenty took a five-year vow of silence. He is said to have written many books, none of which has survived, but fragments of his writing appear in later philosophers, although whether these are actually by Apollonius is still anyone's guess. To Arab alchemists, Apollonius was known as Balinus; in the Middle Ages, a ninth-century Arabic version of the *Emerald Tablet of Hermes Trismegistus*, the most famous alchemical text, found in a work called *The Secret of Creation*, was erroneously attributed to him.

As in the story of Pythagoras, Apollonius traveled in search of knowledge. He studied with the Persian magi, Egyptian hierophants, India fakirs, and Greek philosophers. Like Orpheus, he sought to reform the cults he encountered and he was initiated into the Mysteries of Eleusis. In this Apollonius seems much like other philosophers and sages of the time, but he stands out among them because of the many reports of his miraculous or paranormal powers. He was reported to heal, to have "second sight," to be able to transport himself to faraway places, and to predict the future. On one occasion Apollonius passed some men on their way to execution. He insisted that the confession of one of them had been obtained under torture and he compelled the guards to put him last in the line as he said that a reprieve would come for him. The guards did and a reprieve did come. On another occasion, while in Ephesus, where he taught for some time, Apollonius stopped in his tracks and cried, "Strike the tyrant, strike!" then stood staring at the ground before him. Those around him were astounded and believed he had gone mad, but then Apollonius informed them that at that very moment the emperor Domitian, who held Rome in a reign of terror, had been murdered. Soon after, messengers from Rome arrived and corroborated Apollonius's account.

Some other stories of Apollonius's powers are perhaps less believable, such as accounts of him raising people from the dead, and the tale of "the vampire of Corinth" sounds too good to be true. At a wedding banquet for his friend and student Menippus, Apollonius noticed something strange about the bride-to-be. Watching her closely, Apollonius realized she was really a lamia, a kind of vampire, and he urged his friend to abandon the wedding and leave the banquet. Menippus, however, was too entranced with his betrothed's beauty, and so Apollonius used his magic to defeat her spell. Suddenly all the guests, fine decorations, and marvelous food disappeared, and what remained was the monstrous figure of the would-be bride. (The poet Keats used this tale as the model for his poem "The Lamia.") This and other tales, such as Apollonius's descent into the underworld and that he was the son of Proteus, an ancient Greek sea-god who could change his shape, sound just a bit too pat; the lamia encounter is most likely a cautionary tale about excess of material comfort. But Apollonius was most likely a real Pythagorean philosopher blessed with natural paranormal powers—or cursed, as he suffered throughout his life the calumny to which most magicians are subject. As Colin Wilson writes, Apollonius was most likely "a philosopher, a natural medium, and something of a seer."[10]

JESUS CHRIST, THE SECRET TEACHER

Was Apollonius a secret teacher? The fact that he is no longer well-known whereas he was once one of the most famous sages of antiquity—memorials in his honor dotted Asia Minor—suggests he was. But what about his better-known contemporary? There are many similarities between the life of Apollonius and that of Jesus. Both their births were foretold by a supernatural being and both were miraculous. Both were precocious youths who left home and became itinerant preachers. Both urged people to devote their lives to the spirit, not material things. Both gathered disciples who believed in their divinity. Both performed miracles: healing, raising the dead, casting out spirits. Both aroused strong opposition, were arrested and condemned. (An enemy of Apollonius, Euphrates, accused him of plotting against Domitian and of sacrificing a young boy to scrutinize his entrails for portents of Domitian's downfall; Apollonius presented himself voluntarily at Domitian's court and refuted the charges magisterially.) Both returned to life after death, appeared before their disciples, and were eventually raised up to heaven. And both had later followers who wrote books about them. During the rise of Christian antipaganism in the third century A.D., Apollonius was held up as a kind of pagan Christ, and there is some speculation that Philostratus's biography was written as a kind of propaganda to show that the pagans had their own miracle worker and spiritual teacher and that the Christians had not cornered the market. To counter these claims, in the fourth century the Christian historian and polemicist Eusebius argued that Apollonius was a fraud, or worse, the Anti-Christ, and that any magical powers he had came from the devil.

There are also indications that the life of Jesus was in many ways similar to those of other "death and rebirth" gods. I've already mentioned the similarities between Jesus and Mithras. In *The Jesus Mysteries*, Timothy Freke and Peter Gandy argue that Jesus was not a real individual but a composite figure made up of elements of the "godman" myths prevalent at the time, those of Osiris, Dionysus, Attis, and other "resurrection" gods.[11] Freke and Gandy argue that elements of the Jesus story such as the virgin birth, being a "god made flesh," being born in humble surroundings, offering the opportunity of being "born again," descending into hell, and the idea of a return and judgment on the "last day" can all be found in the myths of Osiris, Dionysus, and other "godmen."[12] Freke and Gandy argue that the Jesus myth was a symbolic Mystery teaching devised by Hellenized Jews and that, like the Greek Mysteries, it originally included an outer and inner initiation. At some point, some Jews stopped at only the outer initiation and took the story of Christ's crucifixion literally, not symbolically, and their teachings became orthodox or historical Christianity. Those who understood that the true Christian message could be received only after the inner initiation became known as Gnostics and were eventually wiped out.

Possibly more books have been written about Jesus Christ than any other individual. As mentioned earlier, most biblical scholars agree that there is little corroborative evidence about his historical reality. What evidence we do have is documentary, based on written accounts, not archaeological, i.e., no physical traces of Jesus's existence have come to light, at least so far. Although most scholars accept that he was a real person, there is little consensus about the facts of his life or his teaching, and attempts to draw an accurate portrait of the "historical Jesus" have proved frustrating. Practically everything we know about him comes from the Gospels, which were written well after his death and most likely not by his apostles, although there are references to a Jew named Jesus in the Jewish historian Josephus and in the Roman historian Tacitus. The significance of these references, however, is also considered debatable. It is a delicate and controversial matter. It has been argued over the years that, among other things, Jesus didn't die on the cross, but escaped to raise a family, and that he was not a human being but a mushroom.[13] In one sense, whether or not Jesus existed is irrelevant. It is clear to most devotees of the western esoteric tradition today that Hermes Trismegistus was not a real individual, but this has not prevented them from taking Hermeticism seriously. That Jesus may not have existed does not mean that we should not love our enemies.

A SECRET CHRISTIANITY?

Seeing Jesus as a secret teacher means that the Christianity that has come down to us and remains a powerful presence in the western world is not the same teaching that esotericists believe Christ himself taught, or that the Jesus myth embodied. This should not really shock us; the philosophy that Plato taught is not the same philosophy that one finds in universities today. This includes Catholicism, Orthodox Christianity, and Protestantism, as well as the other major tributaries of the central Christian stream. There does seem to be textual evidence for this, of the kind that scholars recognize. In 1958, while examining manuscripts at Mar Saba, an Eastern Orthodox monastery near Jerusalem, the historian Morton Smith came upon what appeared to be a remarkable discovery. Paging through an ancient tome, Smith chanced upon a hand-copied letter purporting to be from the early church father Clement of Alexandria (c. 150–215) to one Theodore. Clement was one of the earliest and most respected of the church fathers and no letters of his were thought to have survived, so to come across one was exciting. But what his letter said was even more spectacular. It spoke of a "secret gospel" attributed to Mark, which he wrote in Alexandria, in addition to the canonical Gospel of Mark. This secret gospel, the letter revealed, was "for the use of those being perfected," in order to "lead the hearers into the innermost sanctuary of that truth hidden by the seven [veils]."[14] The letter quotes a story from this secret gospel, telling of a young man who, like Lazarus, was raised from the dead. Wearing "a linen cloth over his naked body," he meets Jesus, who stays up the night with him, teaching him "the mystery of the kingdom of God." Tantalizingly, Smith did not discover exactly what this "mystery" was, as the letter broke off in midparagraph.

Smith spent many years researching the letter and came to the conclusion that it was authentic, although the copy he came upon was made in the eighteenth century. He was especially impressed by the fact that the tale of the young man fit perfectly into the canonical Gospel of Mark, and this led Smith to conclude that the passage was originally a part of Mark's Gospel but was later taken out and reserved for those who had been initiated into Christ's inner teaching. That the young man wore only a linen cloth suggested the passage depicted an initiation, as that was traditionally what was worn while undergoing one. Smith believed that there were also other teachings not included in the "secret gospel," which Jesus imparted to his disciples orally.

As Richard Smoley writes in *Inner Christianity,* "That the Christian faith may originally have been closer to an occult lodge or a secret society than to a religion should not come as a complete surprise."[15] As Smoley points out, secrecy is a common theme in the Gospels. Jesus speaks in parables, which conceal his meaning as much as they convey it, a characteristic of much esoteric communication. When he heals people, he asks that they do not speak of it. Nicodemus's nocturnal visit to Jesus, depicted in the Gospel of John, may, Smoley suggests, be seen as another account of an initiation.

The rise of critical biblical scholarship in the nineteenth century, with its rationalist assumptions, chipped away at the great edifice of Christianity. But the scholarly and scientific blows it inflicted could be absorbed and the faith maintained. Smith's discovery was different. It did not undermine Christianity scientifically, by showing, say, that the Bible could not be read as history, as it had been for centuries. Smith's discovery, if it was one—controversy about its authenticity remains, as about practically all scholarship that challenges the received wisdom about church history—showed that our *ideas* about Christianity, what it is really about, may need revising.

Smith's was not the only discovery that suggested this. Fragments of an apocryphal text written in Greek, known as the Gospel of Thomas, had been known since the late nineteenth century, but in 1945 the full text in a Coptic translation appeared. It was part of a collection of fifty-two ancient writings from the early days of Christianity discovered in Nag Hammadi in Egypt, and which have come to be known as the "Gnostic Gospels." The texts were used by those early Christians that Timothy Freke and Peter Gandy believed underwent the inner initiation mentioned above and achieved *gnosis,* which, they argue, was the true aim of Christ's teaching. The Gospel of Thomas reads much more like a collection of sayings than a narrative, and its simplicity suggests that it may be older and hence closer to Jesus's own time than the canonical Gospels.[16] But even more than its age, what the Gospel of Thomas actually says is remarkable. From the start it identifies itself as a "secret gospel." The Dutch historian and theologian Gilles Quispel studied the text and, as Elaine Pagels writes in *The Gnostic Gospels,* "Quispel was startled, then incredulous to read: 'These are the secret words which the living Jesus spoke, and which the twin, Judas Thomas, wrote down.'"[17]

The mention of Jesus having a twin brother was startling to be sure, but equally so were the "secret words" Jesus spoke. As Pagels writes, while some of the "secret words" appeared in the New Testament, in this setting they seemed strange and full of new meaning, while others were "as cryptic and compelling as Zen *koans.*"[18] For example: "Split the wood and you shall find me," "Lift up a stone and I am there," "Be passers-by," "I have cast fire upon the world, and see, I am watching until it blazes," and "Whosoever finds the meaning of these sayings will not taste death," which sounds remarkably like the aim of the Mysteries as well as that of Pythagoras and Plato. One such enigmatic saying ran, "If you bring forth what is within you, what you bring forth will save you. If you do not bring forth what is within you, what you do not bring forth will destroy you." This sounds very much like good psychotherapeutic advice, and it's no surprise that C. G. Jung, who had been studying Gnosticism since the 1920s, was excited by the discovery; in 1952, one of the scrolls making up the Nag Hammadi Library—as the collection came to be called—was purchased by the Jung Foundation and was named the Jung Codex in honor of the man many saw as a kind of modern Gnostic.

What was also striking about the Gospel of Thomas is that the picture of Jesus it presents is very different from the traditional one. This Jesus does not forgive sins nor does he perform miracles. He does not claim to be the Messiah or preach the end of the world, all things the traditional Jesus does do. The teaching he brings is not about salvation, traditional Christianity's aim, but enlightenment, or *gnosis,* a knowledge that can transform those who receive it. In the Gospel of Philip, this is made clear: "Ignorance is a slave. Knowledge is freedom. If we know the truth, we shall find the fruits of truth within us. If we are joined to it, it will bring fulfilment."[19] Other passages in other Gnostic Gospels also portray a Jesus rather different from the one we are familiar with. The Gospel of Philip has Jesus kissing Mary Magdalene on the mouth and thereby offending the other disciples; both Baigent, Leigh, and Lincoln's *Holy Blood, Holy Grail* and and Dan Brown's *The Da Vinci Code* are based on the idea that Jesus and Mary were husband and wife, or at least lovers, and that Jesus didn't die on the cross but survived and fathered children. Other texts also offer a very different idea of what Christ and the orthodox Bible taught. The *Testimony of Truth* portrays the serpent in the Garden of Eden as a gnostic hero, encouraging Adam and Eve to eat of the Tree of Knowledge, and God as a jealous hoarder, guarding his treasure and kicking the couple out of paradise when they disobey him. The feminine spirit, for the most part minimized in accepted Christian tradition, is here celebrated; in one strange text, *Thunder, Perfect Mind,* it speaks gnomic sayings: "I am the first and the last, the honored one and the scorned one, the whore and the holy one . . . the silence that is incomprehensible, the utterance of my name."[20]

THE GNOSTICS

Who were the Gnostics? Until the discovery of the Nag Hammadi Library, most of our knowledge about them came from prejudiced sources, the church fathers who railed against and condemned them as the first "heretics," a word that derives from the Greek *hairetikos,* which means "able to choose." Heretics are those who choose something other than the received church dogma. What the Gnostics chose was *gnosis* over belief and experience over faith, a choice that is the essence of esotericism. What Pagels's *The Gnostic Gospels* and other recent books about primitive Christianity argue is that there was a struggle in the early years over exactly what Christ taught and how that teaching should be spread. Although there is not one "Gnostic teaching" and much difference between the various Gnostic sects that emerged in the first few centuries after Christ, generally speaking the Gnostics were those early Christians who believed that Christ taught the way to *gnosis,* to an immediate, inner experience of spiritual reality and that, through this, everyone potentially could share equally in the divine, could become a "Christ." The Christians who rejected this idea and who interpreted Christ's teachings and the story of his life literally, who believed that he was the unique "son of God," that only he could experience spiritual reality firsthand, who accepted the story of the crucifixion as historically real and unique and that Jesus died for our sins, laid the foundations for what we know as Christianity. There was a battle between these ideologies in the first centuries of the Christian era, Pagels and others tell us, and needless to say, the Gnostics didn't win.[21] One interesting possibility, mentioned earlier, is that the Gnostics themselves may have *predated* the "official" Christians. That the Gospel of Thomas may be older than the canonical Gospels suggests this, and so it may be the case that the official Christians themselves were the real "heretics."[22]

One of the earliest critics of the Gnostics was Justin Martyr (c. 100–162 A.D.), a philosopher who went through Stoicism, Aristotle, Pythagoreanism, and Plato before converting to Christianity. He became one of its most vocal apologists until he was beheaded in Rome for refusing to sacrifice to the gods. In his Second Apology, he condemns Gnostic teachers such as Simon Magus, Valentinus, and Marcion as "wicked and deceitful."[23] The account of Justin's trial suggests that he took his Christianity very literally; when his accusers told him that if he did not make sacrifice to the gods he would be tortured without mercy, Justin replied that this was what he and all true Christians want, to "be tortured for our lord Jesus Christ and so to be saved."[24] As Jesus was tortured and died a horrible death before ascending to heaven, the literal Christians believed that if they suffered the same fate, so too would they go to heaven.

Although different Gnostic sects had different interpretations of the crucifixion, they generally rejected Justin's somewhat gruesome conviction that the sure way to become one with Christ was to meet a gory end.

Justin Martyr wasn't the only early Christian to speak ill of the Gnostics. For the church father Irenaeus, Bishop of Lyons (c. 130–202 A.D.), Gnostic beliefs were an "abyss of madness" and their gospels "full of blasphemy." He was especially troubled by the Gnostic teacher Basilides of Alexandria (c. 117–138 A.D.), because of his casual attitude toward sin and carnal pleasures.[25] Hippolytus of Rome (170–235 A.D.) wrote an epic *Refutation of All Heresies* in which, along with attacking pagan philosophy, he criticized thirty-three Gnostic sects—evidence, as mentioned, that there was much disagreement among the Gnostics themselves. Tertullian of Carthage (160–225 A.D.), known as the "founder of Western theology," castigated the Gnostics for refusing to believe in the physical reality of Christ's resurrection. Today, acceptance of the literal truth that Christ rose from the dead and that, at the Last Judgment, true Christians will also emerge from their graves seems limited to the more fundamental among believers, readers perhaps of the Left Behind series of apocalyptic fiction. Tertullian made it the linchpin of faith, arguing that precisely because it was absurd, it must be believed, rather like the "leap of faith" of the father of existentialism, Søren Kierkegaard.

This is just a selection of the kind of attacks the "true" Christians launched against the "heretics." Reams have been written by the defenders of the faith, arguing that the Gnostics were everything from lascivious sensualists to agents of the devil. What was it that the Gnostics believed that so enraged their fellow Christians? And why was it so important for them to eradicate the Gnostics who, collectively, we can see as secret teachers?

As mentioned, there were many different Gnostic sects and no one specific "Gnostic teaching" or authority to which all of them adhered. Gnostic groups did not organize themselves hierarchically and were on the whole antiauthoritarian and more loose and liberal in their structure than the orthodox Christians. For one thing, they allowed women much more freedom and power and had no qualms about learning *gnosis* from them. And indeed, so diverse and occasionally contradictory were Gnostic beliefs that some of their enemies claimed that they wrote a "new gospel every day."[26] This led to the church fathers seeing in their sometimes daunting collection of beliefs a confused mess of contradictions, fantasies, and downright lies, a criticism they had no hesitation to profit by.

The church fathers exaggerated this aspect of Gnostic mythology, to be sure, just as they studiously ignored the contradictions in their "official" dogma—or, as Tertullian did, championed them as tests of faith. Yet anyone who has spent some time studying the different myths associated with Gnosticism can be forgiven for turning away with a sense of metaphysical dizziness. The Gnostic cosmos is populated with quite a few spiritual entities and it is often difficult to keep track of them and their significance. Yet having said this, some basic orientations and attitudes were shared by practically all of the early Christians who considered themselves Gnostics, or were considered such by the "official" church.

A fALSE WORLD

One central Gnostic theme is that the world we live in, the physical world of matter and the senses, is evil, or at least seriously flawed. It is a kind of false world, a prison of sorts, created not by the "true God," who is beyond the cosmos—and everything else—but by a "demiurge" or craftsman who subsequently became convinced that he was indeed the true God and fell to lording it over his creation. This demiurge—the term is Greek and is what Plato calls the creator of the world in the *Timaeus*—was for the Gnostics associated with Yahweh, the God of the Old Testament. As I say in the Introduction, the situation here is rather similar to how Iain McGilchrist portrays the relationship between the right and left brain, with the left brain, the "emissary," usurping power from its "master," the right. McGilchrist speaks in terms of psychology and neuroscience; the Gnostics spoke in myth and metaphysics. Yet what each says is very much the same: our true consciousness and relation to the world has been obscured, and a false or at least incomplete and inadequate one has been substituted for it.

The true God exists in what the Gnostics called "the Pleroma," a non-manifest dimension of reality beyond—or before—space and time; as mentioned, it can be seen as something like Jean Gebser's "Origin," and it shares its position with other similar nonmanifest spheres of reality such as the *En-Sof* of Kabbalah, the Sunyata of Buddhism, and the Hermetic and Neoplatonic One. The true God is not alone, though; he shares this nonmanifest existence with a feminine divine principle called "Ennoia," which means "thought" in Greek. Unlike the God of the Old Testament who creates the world out of nothing—*creatio ex nihilo*—the Gnostic God emanates creation out of his (or her) own being, rather as the sun emanates light and heat.[27]

The "emanationist" cosmology of Gnosticism is central to esoteric thought and can be found in other traditions, such as the Kabbalistic Tree of Life, which portrays a hierarchy of being, beginning with the unmanifest *En-Sof* and descending through different levels of decreasing spirituality, the *sephiroth* or "vessels," until it reaches the lowest, the physical world of time, space, and matter. A similar "ladder of being" is central to Neoplatonic and Hermetic cosmology, and it plays a central role in the cosmologies of modern esotericists like Rudolf Steiner and Gurdjieff.

The emanations from the true God are called "aeons," and one of them is Sophia, which we know means wisdom. Sophia is the youngest of the aeons and hence the furthest from the true God. In her desire to know the true God, Sophia emanates a kind of creation of her own, but something goes wrong, and the result is a dark mass, a kind of chaos, the "formless and void" state before creation in Genesis. Sophia decides to create a being that can bring order to this void, and hence gives birth to Ialdaboath, who is the demiurge; he is also known as an "archon," a term that comes from a Greek word meaning "petty official," a kind of cosmic bureaucrat, punctilious and overzealous in his duties. Essentially, Ialdaboath gets the bit between his teeth and in a flush of hubris, out of the chaos he creates other archons who help him in creating the world of space and time and everything in it, including humanity, which they will rule.

Ialdaboath is quite pleased with himself and, ignoring Sophia's warnings, declares (much as does the God of the Old Testament) that "There is no other God but me," rather as the left brain refuses to acknowledge the existence or at least the importance of the right. He is utterly convinced of his supreme importance and just as utterly ignorant of the true God beyond his material cosmos; he dismisses anything Sophia has to say about him. And like any clichéd oriental despot, Ialdaboath—or Yahweh—rules like a petty tyrant. And so we find ourselves here, in a world unimaginably distant from true reality, subject to the rule of the archons, trapped in some cosmic prison. (Sophia, too, becomes trapped in it, and part of the Gnostic narrative is the search for her in order to release her from her bondage.)

We are, as Heidegger put it, "thrown into the world," having no idea where we come from or why we are here, with no sort of Rough Guide to help us find our way around. It is a gloomy situation, and some interpreters of Gnosticism, like the philosopher Hans Jonas, have likened its vision to the kind of world portrayed by the existentialists, devoid of meaning and purpose.[28] Echoes of the Gnostic vision also sound in Gurdjieff's "Fourth Way," which sees humanity as similarly trapped, locked in a kind of cosmic prison.[29] But there is a saving grace in our predicament. Within us, sunken beneath the constricting layers of matter, is a spark of our divine inheritance, some small part of the true God's emanation. Through realizing this, through achieving *gnosis,* the knowledge of our true spiritual nature, we can escape from the rule of the archons and ascend through the spheres of the false world and return to our source.

The Gnostics are those who pursue and achieve this knowledge, and Jesus is the secret teacher who leads them to it. He is one of the "messengers of light" sent by the true God to lead mankind—or at least some of it—out of the snares of the archons. Not all of us are up for the task; unlike orthodox Christianity, which maintains that salvation is available to all who accept Christ as their savior, the Gnostics were more selective. They characterized people as three kinds: "hylics," who are sunk deep in gross matter and the flesh and have no concern for the spirit; "psychics," who are less carnal but given to accepting the dogmas of traditional religion; and "pneumatics," who are spiritually awake and who can achieve and understand *gnosis.*[30] Hylics have no interest in the spirit and psychics are happy to bank on faith and belief, but only pneumatics have a chance of escaping the archons.

In recent times this notion of a false world has become very popular, in a wide cultural sense, as the success of films such as the *Matrix* series show. Other films, such as Peter Weir's *The Truman Show*, Vincenzo Natali's *Cube*, and Alex Proyas's *Dark City* treat of a similar theme. Gnostic ideas started to revive in the twentieth century, mostly through the work of Jung, who was himself influenced by the work of the Gnostic scholar G. R. S. Mead, but can also be found in the novels of Hermann Hesse and Thomas Pynchon, as well as in the science fiction of Philip K. Dick and other writers.

By now the term "gnostic" has become rather broad and seems to have blended with the philosopher Paul Ricoeur's notion of what he calls "the hermeneutics of suspicion," the belief, prominent in our time, that ideas and philosophies cannot be taken at face value, but must be examined for their "true" or "hidden" motivations. So for Marxists, religion is "really" "the opium of the people," and for Freudians spirituality is "really" camouflage for "sex." We may believe that what this amounts to is a "hermeneutics of cynicism." One sign that we live within a "gnostic" milieu is the popularity of a variety of conspiracy theories and the sensibility that goes with them: the disturbing feeling that nothing we learn about on the news or from any other "official" source can be believed and that the true state of things is being kept from us. Those who can unravel the tight skein of falsehoods and red herrings and arrive at the "true" source, whatever that may be, can be seen as modern Gnostics.

GNOSTICS AT WORK

Gnosticism has been accused of promoting a radically pessimistic world-rejection, a Manichean dualism that has nothing but contempt for the physical world, including the human body. The Persian prophet Mani (215–277), the founder of Manicheanism, "the religion of light," drew on Gnostic sources, as well as those of Zoroastrianism, Christianity, and Buddhism in his bid to create a dualistic world religion based on the eternal battle between darkness and light, or good and evil. Later dualist Christian sects, such as the medieval Bogomils and Cathars, seem to share in this Gnostic attitude. But as mentioned, not all Gnostics shared the same beliefs and attitudes, and while some did despise the physical world and their own bodies, others held less radical views. As Stephan Hoeller, a modern Gnostic teacher, writes, from the Gnostic perspective: "Humans are caught in a predicament consisting of physical existence combined with ignorance of their true origins, their essential nature and their ultimate destiny," and their only hope of escape lies in an attitude of "non-attachment and nonconformity to the world."[31] While this is true, how each Gnostic practiced this was different. Some were able to do this from within the rising orthodox church.

Valentinus (c. 100–c. 160 A.D.), whom Hoeller calls "the greatest of Gnostic teachers," was, according to Tertullian, in the running to be pope.[32] Valentinus was born in Alexandria, but in his thirties he moved to Rome, where it is said he studied with a disciple of St. Paul. He lost his bid to be pope to Pius I in 140, but Valentinus continued to teach, although he is said to have been soon denounced as a heretic. Valentinus is said to have developed the most systematic and complex Gnostic doctrine, blending Greek, Christian, and oriental ideas into a kind of "Gnostic orthodoxy"; sadly, most of his writings have not survived, except for the "Gospel of Truth," which is part of the Nag Hammadi texts. Yet for many years, his followers considered themselves true Christians and carried on their worship within the church that ultimately condemned them.

Basilides of Alexandria, whom we've already mentioned and who taught between 117 and 138 A.D., also saw himself as a Christian and a theologian. He was said to have been tutored by a disciple of St. Peter, Glaucias, who he claimed passed on to him a "secret doctrine." Exactly what Basilides taught is unclear, as accounts of his teachings by the church fathers Irenaeus and Hippolytus differ. What is clear is that it was a fantastically complicated system involving 365 "heavens" ruled over by Abraxas, who was associated with the God of the Old Testament. It was the lower angels of these heavens that created our physical world. Basilides taught that Christ did not die on the cross, but was saved from crucifixion by Simon of Cyrene, who took his place. While Simon suffered in Jesus's place, the Gnostic Christ laughed at those who took the body seriously. Basilides didn't take it seriously, but instead of treating it with ascetic rigor, he had an attitude of "do what you like," hence Irenaeus's anger, mentioned earlier, toward what he saw as Basilides's profligacy.

Carpocrates, who flourished in the second century A.D., took things a bit further. He was said to have taught a radically antinomian doctrine, one that made a point of flouting the rules. If this world is false, created by a second-rate god, then there's no need to follow moral strictures and anything goes. Carpocrates' disciples were said to ingest semen and menstrual blood as holy sacraments—a practice revived in the twentieth century by the antinomian magician Aleister Crowley, who taught his followers to "do what thou wilt"—and to have included intercourse during their worship.[33] Much of the accusations of licentiousness and promiscuity aimed at Carpocrates and the Gnostics in general were rooted in orthodox propaganda, so we need to take them with much salt. Yet the antinomian strain in Gnosticism would emerge in different ways throughout the spiritual history of the West.

The first Gnostic "villain"—from the church's point of view—was Simon Magus, who appears in the book of Acts and who was accused of using magic to impress the Samarians with his greatness. He was a contemporary of Jesus and Apollonius, and like them had a reputation as a wonderworker. He has the distinct honor of having a sin named after him. When he saw Peter and John healing through the Holy Spirit, he offered them money if they would tell him how they did it. The practice of trying to buy spiritual things with money was henceforth called "simony." He was accompanied by a woman who he claimed was an embodiment of the true God's "Thought," but who was also a reincarnation of Helen of Troy. He claimed he had found her working as a prostitute in Tyre, an example of the "reversals" common to Gnostic narratives: the serpent, Cain, Judas, and other biblical bad guys are often portrayed as Gnostic heroes. Here the sacred, holy Thought of God supported herself as a whore. It is unclear what Simon taught, and in the official accounts he converts to the true faith, although as Richard Smoley suggests, this is probably more propaganda.[34]

The greatest threat to the early church was the Gnostic teacher Marcion, who is still regarded as one of the most dangerous of heresiarchs. Marcion (c. 85–160 A.D.) was born in Pontus on the Black Sea and was raised in a Christian family; his father was a priest, possibly a bishop, as well as a ship owner. Marcion followed in his father's footsteps and grew up to become a successful businessman as well as a priest. In 140, he went to Rome, where he made substantial donations to the fledgling church. He also tried to make more doctrinal contributions, attempting to win Christians around to his point of view. He was unsuccessful, so, like any good entrepreneur, he started his own church. At this he was successful, dangerously so. Many Christians took to his doctrine, especially in Syria, where until the fifth century there were large Marcionist communities. Marcion taught that there were two gods, the God of the Law, which was the demiurge, and the Good God beyond. He denied that Jesus had a real physical body, a heretical belief that became known as Docetism. The only scriptures he accepted were the Sermon on the Mount, some parts of the Gospel of Luke, as well as the Epistles of St. Paul.

Marcion wanted to purge Christianity of its Jewish elements—hence his rejection of the Old Testament—and we can see his efforts to pare down the faith as the first attempt to establish an "official" church canon, something the church didn't do until the Council of Nicaea in 325. By then, Marcionite churches were thriving. Some writers on Gnosticism wonder if Marcion should be considered a "true" Gnostic, as central Gnostic elements such as *gnosis,* an elaborate mythology, and the divine spark are absent from his teaching. Although tarred with the Gnostic brush, the absence of *gnosis* and the Gnostic cosmology in his teachings may be attributed to his determination to purge Christianity of its Jewish roots.

THE ROOTS OF GNOSTICISM

While clearly growing in Christian soil, the roots of Gnosticism spread into different religions and beliefs. The exact debt it owed to these is unclear and most likely will remain so. Scholars continue to debate over how much Gnosticism received from its predecessors and what the medium of transmission was. For our purposes, it is enough to give a general idea of the different spiritual sources available to it at the time. One such was the Jewish wisdom tradition, contained in the book of Proverbs, in the Wisdom of Solomon, and in the apocryphal Ecclesiasticus, also known as the Wisdom of Sirach, as well as the better known Ecclesiastes. In these,

Wisdom is personified as a woman, much as in the Gnostic tradition, and the general atmosphere of these works is pessimistic: that there is nothing new under the sun would not be out of place among other Gnostic aphorisms. Other Jewish traditions, such as the Merkabah, or "throne mysticism," would also have been known to the early Gnostics. This tradition, which arose around the time of the destruction of the Temple of Jerusalem (70 A.D.), predated Kabbalah and was based on the vision of Ezekiel, who saw a cloud of fire within which was a blazing chariot, surrounded by strange creatures. Through meditating on this vision, aspirants aimed to "ascend" to heaven in the chariot and reach the heavenly throne. This and other forms of "Jewish Gnosticism," as the Kabbalah scholar Gershom Scholem called it, were prevalent at the time of early Christianity and most likely contributed significantly to the makeup of Gnosticism proper.[35]

The Gnostics were part of a strange phenomenon of their time, what we can call "the retreat to the desert." Colin Wilson has called this "the third great evolutionary step taken by the human race," after the creation of cities and the religious and philosophical awakening of the "axial age."[36] Practically overnight, large numbers of people abandoned the cities and made an exodus to the desert, where they established communities dedicated to "contemplation and knowledge of the infinite" in an attempt to satisfy a craving for some meaning beyond the decadent world.[37] One such group was the Essenes, a kind of fundamentalist Jewish religious group, who established themselves near the Dead Sea and who are thought to be responsible for the Dead Sea Scrolls, discovered in Qumran on the West Bank in 1946. As with so much else from this time, there is a great deal of debate about exactly who the Essenes were and what they believed; one highly controversial matter is whether Jesus and John the Baptist may have been members of their sect. What does seem clear is that the Essenes felt that the traditional Jewish faith had broken the covenant with God and that a new one had to be established.

Like other sects we have looked at, the Essenes had two levels, what we might call full-time and part-time members. Full-time Essenes lived at Qumran and adopted a celibate, ascetic life devoted to ritual and prayer; part-timers could live in the city, be married, and carry on a normal routine while dedicating part of their life to worship. Like the Gnostics, the

Essenes had a dualistic worldview, in which good and evil, truth and falsehood, were engaged in an eternal combat, with the human soul as the battlefield. Like later Christianity, the Essenes were not ethnocentric; anyone of pure heart and soul could be saved, although like the Gnostics they recognized that not everyone was up to the task. Also, like the later Christians, the Essenes shared in the expectation of some apocalypse that would bring an end to the sinful world and the establishment of righteousness, a Messianic belief central to the Jewish faith. They spoke of an individual known only as the Great Teacher; who he may have been has never been discovered, which certainly qualifies him as a secret teacher.

Another dualist teaching that informed Gnosticism was Zoroastrianism. It remains unclear exactly when Zoroaster, after whom the religion is named, was born, or if indeed he was one person or several. Current scholarly opinion has Zoroaster's birthplace as Bactria, in what is now Afghanistan, and his doctrines took hold most firmly in Persia. Today, Zoroastrians are known as Parsis and worldwide they number fewer than 150,000, the major Parsi communities being in India. As mentioned earlier, Zoroaster holds an important place in the Hermetic Chain of Adepts, equal to if not more important than that of Hermes Trismegistus, and he is one of the key figures of the "axial age." According to one historian, Zoroaster was the first to teach doctrines such as "individual judgment, heaven and hell, the future resurrection of the body, the general Last Judgment, and life everlasting for the reunited soul and body."[38]

All of these doctrines would play an enormous role in the development of Christianity, Judaism, and Islam. They would also inform Gnosticism, but the most significant Zoroastrian teaching to make its way into Gnostic doctrine was its dualism. Zoroastrianism is a monotheistic religion within which opposites play a central role. There is the one Good God, Ahura Mazda, which means "wise lord," from whom two forces, a beneficent spirit called Spenta Mainyu and a destructive spirit named Angra Mainyu, emerge. Although in Zoroastrianism creation is good, evil is a reality, even though it will eventually be defeated at the end of time. Over the centuries, Ahura Mazda and Spenta Mainyu coalesced into Ohrmazd, and Angra Mainyu became Ahriman, the original Zoroastrian trinity downsizing to a duality. Rather than an emanation of the Good

God, Ahriman took on a reality of his own, and came to be seen as equal in stature. Good and evil, or light and darkness, became coeval powers, present from the beginning, and engaged in a titanic war. It was this development of Zoroastrianism that Mani adopted into his "religion of Light." While recognizing the power of evil, Zoroaster saw the world as essentially good, an assessment that differs from the generally pessimistic notions of the Gnostics.

We have already mentioned that Platonism was an ingredient in the Gnostic mix. It would difficult for it not to be: Greek thought and Greek ways of understanding the world informed practically all forms of belief at this time. The Gnostics did not escape this, although how they used Greek ideas was peculiar to themselves; as one scholar remarked, Gnosticism was "a kind of Platonism run wild."[39] Nevertheless, the Gnostics absorbed much from Plato and Greek philosophy, however they used it: the idea of the demiurge; the soul's descent from the spiritual world into matter; the dualism of mind and matter, or spirit and world; the nature of God and the return to our source. They were not, however, the only denizens of the desert to borrow much from the Greeks, nor were they the only ones in pursuit of *gnosis*. Other spiritual communities at this time sought the kind of direct, incontrovertible spiritual experience that informed Gnosticism. But what they made of this was something different.

CHAPTER FOUR

FROM THE ONE TO THE ONE

In 331 B.C. Alexander the Great had an idea: he would found a city in his own name and it would be in Egypt.[1] The location of this future metropolis—or, to be more exact, cosmopolis, as the denizens of Alexander's city would come from all corners of the known world—was soon decided and Alexander's surveyors and architects had been sent to the site to begin work. But then something happened. Alexander, the student of Aristotle, was a great reader of Homer, and he carried his precious copy of the great poet's work in a golden casket, which, legend has it, was forever at his side. In the *Odyssey*, Homer had spoken of Pharos, an "island in the stormy sea off the Egyptian coast," and this mention of the "only harbor" and "good landing beach" on the whole of the otherwise featureless Egyptian coastline struck Alexander. The Greek historian Plutarch records that one night Alexander had a dream in which a man of ancient and wise appearance stood beside him and recited Homer's verse about the Egyptian island. Alexander saw his dream as a vision and took the hint. The next day he ordered his architects and surveyors to abandon the first location for his city and take their tools to where the poet had advised the master of the known world to put down stakes. Thus, the story goes, Alexandria, fabled city of antiquity, home to the legendary lighthouse and library, was born.

At first, Alexander took a hands-on approach to the job. He rode on his horse Bucephalus across the desert, pointing out to his architects where temples would be and where the palace would rise and what form the harbor would take. There was a decided lack of chalk in Egypt at the time, and so the lines of measurement that Alexander's surveyors indicated were laid with barley flour. As Justin Pollard and Howard Reid note in their book *The Rise and Fall of Alexandria: Birthplace of the Modern World,* flocks of birds attacked the measurements as soon as they were traced, creating what must have been a strange scene.[2] But although the net of lines and angles measuring what we might call the Platonic Form of Alexandria was quickly erased by crowds of hungry birds, the city they gave birth to would remain for centuries and, at its height, would rival Rome itself. Yet Alexander never saw it. Impatient with the foundation work of his eponymous city, and tempted by fresh conquests, he left the site after a few days and headed to the desert shrine of Ammon, one of the great creator gods of Egypt, where the priests there would declare him "master of the universe" and a true son of Ammon, effectively making him a god.

Alexander then pushed on to the "ends of the earth and the Great Outer Sea," getting as far as India and, as mentioned, sending shipments of specimens back to Athens for his old tutor Aristotle to examine. Returning westward after his failed India expedition—his troops had mutinied and demanded he turn back—Alexander stopped off at Babylon, where he died in 323. Some believe he was poisoned and that Aristotle himself was party to the plot, but this has never been corroborated. What we do know is that shortly after a drinking binge—Alexander was fond of wine—he took ill and never recovered. Legend has it that at thirty-three, seeing that he had become master of practically all there was to rule, he cried at having no worlds left to conquer.

The story is apocryphal and most likely a distortion of Plutarch's remark that, at being told that there were infinite worlds, Alexander wept because he had not yet conquered this one. Its meaning, however, is clear. The moral seems to be that had Alexander paid more attention to Aristotle, the lure of battle and command might not have gained such mastery over him, and he might have dedicated his later life to something more durable than the temporal success of conquest.

After Alexander's death, his empire began to crumble. Egypt came under the rule of Alexander's general Ptolemy Soter I. There was much debate as to the location of the last resting place of the great king—it would become a sacred site and draw pilgrimages—but after much discussion, Ptolemy Soter I solved this particular problem by kidnapping Alexander's body. He brought it to Memphis, where it was entombed among the pharaohs. Some years later, Ptolemy II Philadelphius, Ptolemy Soter I's successor, brought the golden sarcophagus containing Alexander's body back to his city. Where it is buried remains a mystery, although in recent years a site outside of Alexandria has attracted much attention.[3] In any case, however great Alexander was, for the purposes of our story he merely helps to set the scene. For it is his city, and not its founder, that would have an enormous influence on the esoteric history of the West, harboring within its walls quite a few secret teachers.

A CITY OF SECTS AND GOSPELS

By the time Caesar Augustus had conquered Egypt in 30 A.D.—which led to the suicide of Mark Antony and his lover, Cleopatra VII, the last of the Ptolemies—the Ptolemaic dynasty had ruled Alexandria for three centuries. During this time a remarkable fusion of Greek and Egyptian religious ideas had taken place. Although the Greeks and later the Romans were the dominant social and political force, Egyptian spirituality still maintained its preeminence. As Herodotus, the "father of history," remarked, the Egyptians "were scrupulous beyond all measure in the matter of religion," and their knowledge of the mysteries of life, death, and the beyond had been renowned through the centuries.[4] The Greek and Roman rulers of Alexandria were in awe of the Egyptian priesthood and were more than happy to acknowledge their wisdom. Although at different times the city would be plagued by persecutions and pogroms—first by the Romans against the Jews and Christians and then by the Christians against the pagans—for the most part an enviable religious tolerance was maintained. And where the Greeks and later Romans saw resemblances between their gods and those of Egypt, a convenient syncretism occurred.

Rather than argue over top billing, a fusion between Greek and Egyptian gods often took place. One such god was Serapis, who was an amalgamation of the Egyptian gods Osiris and Apis (a bull deity), but who was depicted with a Greek appearance and who also enjoyed characteristics attributed to Hades, Demeter, and Dionysus. Serapis was an extremely popular deity, especially during the Roman period. His cult came to a disastrous end in 391 A.D. when a Christian mob, roused by Patriarch Theophilus of Alexandria, destroyed his temple, the Serapeum, during a pagan pogrom, along with many other pagan sites. Any remnants of the cult were put down a few years later when the emperor Theodosius I suppressed all pagan religions.

But before this, Alexandria was home to a dizzying assortment of faiths, beliefs, philosophies, and religions. It was, as the novelist Lawrence Durrell, author of *The Alexandria Quartet*, called it, "a city of sects and gospels." Greeks, Romans, Egyptians, Jews, Babylonians, Persians, Phoenicians, Indians, and other peoples filled its maze of streets and squares and temples. Platonists, Pythagoreans, Zoroastrians, Buddhists, Christians, Stoics, and many other followers of many other beliefs met, argued, and learned from each other. As in our own time, the Alexandrian Age provided a spiritual marketplace, a bevy of competing teachings, some fraudulent, others profound, meeting a variety of intellectual, emotional, and religious needs.

One attraction of this hive of philosophies and faiths was the fabled library of Alexandria, the largest of ancient times. Founded by Ptolemy Soter I, it remained in existence—if in reduced form—until the sack of Alexandria by the Arab leader Amr ibn al'Aas in 639 A.D. Legend has it that when asked what to do with the library, Amr ibn al'Aas replied that "either the books contradict the Koran, in which case they are heresy, or they agree with it, in which case they are unnecessary," and ordered that they be burned to heat his soldiers' baths.

The truth of this remains debatable, but by the time of Amr ibn al'Aas's conquest, the library had already suffered extensive buffetings. It was once burned accidentally by Julius Caesar in 48 B.C., when he tried to prevent Ptolemy III, whom he was battling, from reaching his ships; pillaged by the emperor Aurelian in 273 A.D.; and ransacked by Patriarch Theophilus at the same time that he laid waste to the Serapeum. As Pollard and Reid remark, with the loss of the library, "most of the knowledge of the first thousand years of Western civilization was lost."[5] We know of some of its contents from remarks in various works, but of most of what was lost, we do not know. Had the library survived, our ideas about the ancient world and what it knew may well have been very different.

Exactly how many works were housed within the library is unclear; estimates range from five hundred thousand to more than a million, but as no catalogue of the library's contents has ever been discovered, we will never be sure. According to Alberto Manguel in *The Library at Night*, "the Library of Alexandria revealed a new imagination that outdid all existing libraries in ambition and scope."[6] Earlier libraries were aimed at safekeeping and were mostly the work of collectors. The library of Alexandria was the first true research library, available to scholars from all over the world. Initially begun in order to better follow the teachings of Aristotle, Alexander's tutor, the library grew to encompass all that was written at the time. Ptolemy ordered that any ship docking in Alexandria had to deposit any books it might be carrying at the library, where they would be copied and eventually returned; as Manguel remarks, "like so many solemn kingly promises, this one was not always kept, and often it was the copy that was handed back."[7] Such a collection was bound to attract the best minds of the time. A quick name check of some of the figures associated with Alexandria provides a prestigious list: Euclid, whose geometry is still taught today; Archimedes of "Eureka" fame; Galen, the greatest physician of antiquity; Claudius Ptolemy, whose geocentric universe was in place until the time of Copernicus; and Eratosthenes, who knew the circumference of the Earth and was a chief librarian at Alexandria.

But while the preeminence of Alexandria as an ancient haven of *episteme* is unchallenged, it was also home to the pursuit of *gnosis*. Yet not everyone interested in this particular form of knowledge was a Gnostic.

THE OTHER GNOSTICS

We've seen that in the early days of Christianity, a struggle took place between various Gnostic sects and what would become the official church over what exactly was the true Christian teaching. Most of the early church fathers rejected the various Gnostic beliefs, but while rejecting the Gnostics, some early church fathers had more sympathy with the idea of *gnosis*, or direct spiritual experience, and strove to incorporate it into Christian doctrine. These orthodox Gnostics, as they might be called, laid the foundations for an esoteric Christianity based on a Christian *gnosis*, which would inform a powerful stream within the western esoteric tradition. One such orthodox Gnostic was the church father Clement of Alexandria, whose letter to Theodore speaking of a "secret gospel" we looked at in Chapter Three.

Clement was born in Athens, where he received a classical education, but he seems to have spent most of his life in Alexandria. Our hard knowledge about him is scant, but from allusions in his written works, some scholars have suspected that he may have been an initiate of one of the mystery religions; he does at least seem to be well-informed about them, as about Greek philosophy, which he respected, while rejecting pagan religion. Clement sought out spiritual knowledge from a variety of sources, and he makes a reference to six mysterious "blessed and memorable men" whom he does not name but from whom he says he learned much.[8] One of these men is thought to have been Pantaenus of Alexandria, a Christian scholar who was dean of the first Christian school, known as the Didascalia; among other works, it would produce the first translation of the New Testament from Aramaic and Greek into Coptic, the language of the Egyptian Christians. The idea behind the school was to develop a philosophical argument for Christianity that could hold its own against the Platonists and which would not offend the critical sensibilities of the Greek Egyptians it wanted to attract. Pantaenus is thought to have originally been a Stoic before converting to Christianity; if so, he would have been well versed in the sinewy twists and turns of Greek dialectic. Clement became his star pupil and would eventually succeed Pantaenus as head of the Didascalia. Pantaenus is said to have embarked on an evangelical mission to India and left Clement in charge; he was eventually martyred during one of the Christian pogroms that became a familiar feature of the time.

Clement saw the need to develop a *philosophy* of Christianity if he was to succeed in attracting educated Greeks to the new religion, and he taught a very eclectic curriculum, drawing on Plato, Aristotle, the Stoics, and the Epicureans, integrating different aspects of Greek philosophy into his Christian catechism. He wrote many works, of which his *Stromata* ("miscellany") is perhaps the most important. This is a collection of aphorisms and reflections aimed at portraying the good Christian life and at leading the reader to an understanding of its mysteries. It was not a systematic work, and Clement drew on whatever was appropriate to make his points. It was in this eclectic and practical spirit that Clement saw the value of some Gnostic notions, if he nonetheless rejected the central Gnostic teachings. "The life of the Gnostic," he says in his *Stromata*, "is, in my view, no other than works and words which correspond to the tradition of the Lord." With this in mind, Clement was able to wed some Gnostic notions to his orthodox beliefs.

THE NEED FOR SYMBOLS

One such notion was the need to conceal the true meaning of Christianity in symbols and allegories, that is, to read scripture analogically, not literally, which, as we've seen, was a hermeneutical approach of the Gnostics. This is necessary, Clement believed, because not everyone can read the Gospels in the same way, and this is because there are spiritual differences between people. (Clement seems to be speaking of this in his remarks about Mark's "secret gospel" in his letter to Theodore.) Clement saw these differences in much the same way as the Gnostics did. He speaks of three levels or tiers of human understanding, what he calls the "heathen," the "believer," and the "gnostic," which correspond quite clearly to the Gnostic grades of hylic, psychic, and pneumatic. But although Clement believed in a "true Gnosis," he could not accept the central Gnostic doctrine of a false god, and his Gnosticism remained strictly within the bounds of the church.

A similar idea to Clement's notion of reading the Gospels symbolically was developed by the Jewish philosopher Philo of Alexandria (20 B.C.– 40/50 A.D.). Alexandria had a large Jewish population and it was there that the Septuagint, the Greek translation of the Hebrew Bible, emerged. Philo came from a wealthy Alexandrian family and he strove to develop a philosophical justification for Judaism that would satisfy the dialectical appetite of the Greeks. He believed that Greek philosophy was actually rooted in the wisdom of Moses; as in the case of Hermes Trismegistus and Zoroaster, Moses too was believed to have received a divine revelation, a knowledge of the perennial philosophy or *prisca theologia,* which was handed down through the ages. Philo saw Moses's teaching as the "summit of philosophy," and believed that it was his wisdom that informed Plato's ideas. Philo introduced the notion of the "Great Chain of Being," the hierarchical structure of reality, into the biblical account of creation, seeing God as the absolute One, from whom the *logos* or Forms (Sophia in the Jewish tradition) emanated, through whom the created world was brought into being. But he also saw that the Bible needed to be read allegorically, not literally, and had to be understood on different levels. Genesis, he said, should be read as a "metaphor for the history of the soul," and not as a literal account of creation. With his Hellenic approach to the Bible, Philo had, according to one account, "created the philosophical space in which the early church fathers would grow Christianity," his influence reaching to St. Paul, the Gospel of John, and the Epistle to the Hebrews.[9]

ORIGEN

Another church father who saw much good in *gnosis* was Origen (185–252 A.D.), who enjoys the dubious honor of being declared heretical centuries after his death; he was officially condemned in 553 A.D. by the Second Ecumenical Council of Constantinople. The Byzantine emperor Justinian I felt Origen's works were so dangerous that he ordered them destroyed. Although some Christian thinkers have tried to return him to the fold, he remains the black sheep among the early church fathers.

Origen was born to a Christian family and was raised in Alexandria. His father, Leonides, taught Greek, and his mother was Jewish. He had an excellent education in Christian scriptures and Greek philosophy, and attended the Didascalia under Clement's tutelage. Origen also attended the "secret lectures" of the mysterious secret teacher Ammonius Saccas, who had for another student Origen's younger contemporary, the Neoplatonic philosopher Plotinus, whom we will meet further on. Origen's brilliance was obvious from the start, and was reflected on his family: his father was often referred to as "Leonides, father of Origen." Leonides, however, came to a bad end, being beheaded in 202 during a pogrom instigated by the emperor Septimus Severus.

With his father's death, Origen's family was left destitute and Origen supported them by teaching and by copying manuscripts, but he was also helped by a wealthy Christian woman who paid for his education. It was during the Severian pogrom that Clement left Alexandria (he would die c. 215, but exactly where is unknown), and the next year the Bishop Demetrius made the eighteen-year-old Origen head of the Didascalia. As a young man, Origen was of a passionate, somewhat impulsive nature, and a reading of Matthew on the question of eunuchs led him to castrate himself, much like the devotees of the Great Mother Cybele, "for the kingdom of heaven's sake." The fact that many of his students were women may have had something to do with his rash act, and Origen later admitted that his extreme devotion was unnecessary and beyond the call of Christian duty.[10]

Like Clement, Origen taught an eclectic curriculum, bringing Christian doctrine and Greek philosophy together, and his students enjoyed a remarkable degree of freedom, following whatever scholarly paths attracted them, while living a simple life punctuated by prayer and fasting. Origen himself was said to spend all day teaching and all night studying scripture, setting an ascetic example for his students. He spent ten years as a teacher, leaving Alexandria for brief sojourns in Rome and Arabia. He later became friends with Ambrose of Alexandria, a wealthy man Origen had converted to Christianity. Ambrose became his patron and for the rest of his life he promoted Origen's work. Origen was a prolific writer and estimates of his output range in the thousands. And it was in his writings that the Gnostic strain in his ideas appeared.

As Philo did with Judaism, Origen sought to introduce Platonic notions into Christian doctrine. His savvy with Greek dialectics served the Christian cause in good stead when Origen was called upon to refute the criticisms of Christianity produced by the Platonic philosopher Celsus, who saw Christianity as a kind of "revolt of the masses" against the true philosophy of the Greeks, with its appeal to the rabble and uneducated, to blind faith rather than reason. Christians appreciated Origen's riposte, *Against Celsus,* but when it came to finding a place in their religion for the very Platonic notions Celsus tried to woo them back to, they balked. Origen's Platonizing of Christianity can be seen in his treatment of the Trinity, which he saw hierarchically, in the sense of the "Great Chain of Being," or ladder of reality, reaching from God to the mineral kingdom, with the angels, man, animals, and the vegetable world in between. Where Christian doctrine presents the Trinity as a "mystery" to be accepted on faith, however aberrant to reason, as Tertullian said the resurrection of the body must be, Origen tried to have it make good Platonic sense. As Philo did, Origen saw God the Father as the absolute One, a God that was "wholly other," beyond our human conceptions, and as such he could not be responsible for something like creation. And as Philo did with Sophia, Origen saw Jesus the Son as an emanation of God, as the *logos*, the Word, equivalent to the Platonic Forms, which were at work fashioning the world. The Holy Spirit, the third member of the incomprehensible Trinity, Origen saw as embodied in the church and its saints.

While this arrangement does not strike us as threatening or shocking, it eventually led to Origen's posthumous condemnation because it seemed to agree with the Arian heresy, promulgated by the fourth-century Alexandrian theologian Arius. In a nutshell, this argued that Jesus was not of equal stature as God, that, in effect, he occupied a slightly lower link in the Great Chain of Being. It was Arianism that occupied the minds of the attendants at the Council of Nicaea—along with Docetism—in 325 and which led to the dogma that Jesus was "begotten, not made," i.e., was of the *same* being as God, and not an emanation from him, nor "created" by God in any way. Origen had lived before Arius, but his attempt at a "subordination of the divine Persons"—as his hierarchical scheme was called— was a pre-echo of Arius's heresy. As Origen wrote in *On First Principles,* "The God and Father, who holds the universe together, is superior to every being that exists . . . the Son, being less than the Father, is superior to rational creatures alone (for he is second to the Father). The Holy Spirit is still less and dwells within the saints alone. So that in this way the power of the Father is greater than that of the Son and of the Holy Spirit, and in turn that of the Holy Spirit exceeds that of every other holy being." Origen also believed that between human beings and the upper levels of his hierarchy, there were intermediary spirits, some good, some bad, his version of the Gnostic archons, which was later codified into the Christian angels and demons. It was ideas such as these that also led to Origen's condemnation.

Origen had other Gnostic ideas. Like Philo and Clement, he believed that we need to read scripture symbolically, and like them he detected three levels of meaning, that of "body, soul, and spirit," which lines up well with the Gnostic hylic, psychic, and pneumatic and Clement's heathen, believer, and gnostic. For Origen, "just as man consists of a body, soul, and spirit, so in the same way does the scripture."[11] He spoke out sharply against the absurdity of reading the Bible as literal truth, asking "who is so silly as to believe that God, after the manner of a farmer, 'planted a paradise eastward in Eden,'" and that one could have a first, second, and third day "without the sun and moon and stars?"[12] Origen's tripartite hermeneutics was considered standard Christian doctrine until a ruling at the Eighth Ecumenical Council of Constantinople in 869 made it Christian dogma that man consists of only body and soul, relegating spirit to a doctrinal limbo. Origen also believed in the preexistence of souls before their earthly life and he taught reincarnation, an idea that some Gnostic sects embraced and which was not uncommon in early Christianity.

One idea that most likely made him anathema to more hardline literalist Christians was his acceptance of universal salvation, the belief, known as *apocatastasis*, that at the end of time, even the devil will be redeemed and the original paradise will be restored. In essence, Origen believed that God was fundamentally not interested in punishment and had better things to do than torture errant souls for eternity. Those with a taste for fire and brimstone more than likely felt this was too liberal a stance and saw Origen as a dangerous revisionist, although everything he taught was in no way antithetical to Christ's glad tidings.

Origen would eventually be branded a heretic by the church, but in his own life he suffered for it deeply. When the emperor Caracalla unleashed fury on Alexandria, slaughtering thousands of its citizens indiscriminately because of what he perceived as their lack of respect, Origen and Ambrose fled to Caesarea in Palestine. A later falling out with Demetrius, the bishop of Alexandria, led Origen to move there permanently. He was increasingly under attack by other churchmen for his provocative views, but he never left the church and would come to its aid when it called. During his last years, he founded a school. When the emperor Decius started new persecutions, believing that Christian magic was somehow behind a return of the plague, Origen was arrested, imprisoned, and tortured. He was eventually released, but died not long after from his injuries.

THRICE GREATEST HERMES

Along with the early church fathers, another group in Alexandria who shared with the Gnostics a hunger for *gnosis* were the Hermetists. Who they were, we do not know; no names have come down to us and they signed their works with pseudonyms. So there is no equivalent among the Hermetists to Valentinus, Basilides, Marcion, or other Gnostics who were their contemporaries. Given this, they were perhaps the most secret teachers of all. We do know whom they worshiped and what they believed, as far as we can tell from their writings. They were disciples of Hermes Trismegistus, the "thrice greatest one," master of magic, philosophy, and all learning, and they believed that mankind had a divine mission: to journey back through the planets to their invisible divine source and awaken their consciousness to an awareness and grasp of the cosmos. The means of doing this was through *gnosis*, which we can see as a form of "cosmic consciousness."[13]

Earlier, I mentioned that a remarkable syncretism characterized the religious atmosphere of Alexandria and pointed to the god Serapis as evidence of this. Another example is the creative fusion that took place between the Egyptian god Thoth and the Greek god Hermes. Both gods had much in common, and when the Greeks of Alexandria recognized this, a union of the two deities seemed natural. Thoth is the god of speech, writing, language, and magic; he is a moon god and is responsible for creating hieroglyphics, and along with Ma'at, the goddess of Justice, he stands with Ra on his solar barque. Thoth is depicted as an ibis-headed man holding a pen and tablet. The ibis was sacred to Thoth, and thousands of the birds were sacrificed in his honor yearly, so many that the species was practically wiped out in Egypt. It is he who records the outcome of the weighing of the soul when the dead are judged in the Duat, the Egyptian underworld. Thoth is a guide to the underworld; he is associated with Osiris and is believed to have composed parts of the *Book of the Dead.* We remember that it was through Thoth's help that Isis was able to revive the dismembered Osiris and to conceive the child savior, Horus, through him.

Hermes too was a "psychopomp," a guide leading souls to Hades. He is a messenger god, a god of writing, of speech and eloquence. He is also an interpreter, hence the discipline of hermeneutics, the science and art of understanding how we understand things, grows out of his activity. While Thoth's worship can be traced back to 3000 B.C.—Hermopolis, one of the oldest cities on earth, was the center of his cult—Hermes' origins are both somewhat later and more humble. He begins as a cairn or pile of stones, known as a *herm,* that Greek travelers left at crossroads; hence Hermes is a god of travelers and crossroads, both earthly and spiritual. These *herm*s, which date from around 600 B.C., later became stylized pillars, with a bearded Hermes displaying an erect phallus. Hermes is a trickster god— Thoth could be one too at times—and he is also a god of thieves, merchants, and bankers; one still finds his visage overlooking banks today.

When these two gods began to be conflated, what emerged was not a syncretic god like Serapis, but a new character altogether. Exactly when the figure of Hermes Trismegistus first appeared is unknown; several instances have been suggested, but there is still no scholarly consensus on them.[14] In the fifth century B.C. the Greek historian Herodotus identified Thoth and Hermes with each other in his *Histories,* and the phrase "three times great" may date back earlier than this, to the Egyptian Late Period.[15] But it is clear that by the second century A.D. the incomparable sage Hermes Trismegistus, incorporating characteristics of Thoth and Hermes, had become a well-known figure in Alexandria, embodying the pursuit of sacred wisdom and secret spiritual teachings, and the attainment of esoteric knowledge.

As mentioned in the Introduction, until the early seventeenth century, Hermes Trismegistus was considered a real person, although an unusually accomplished one. Church fathers like Clement, Lactantius (240–320), and St. Augustine (354–430) acknowledged his eminence. For Lactantius, he presaged the incarnation of Christ, and St. Augustine believed he was a contemporary of Moses. For both, he lived well before Plato. In addition to inventing writing and magic, Hermes Trismegistus was the creator of civilization, of medicine, chemistry, laws, art, astrology, alchemy, music, mathematics, and much more. According to the Egyptian historian Manetho, Hermes Trismegistus was the author of some thirty-six thousand books. The Neoplatonist Iamblichus credited him with a somewhat smaller number, a mere twenty thousand. Clement speaks of forty-two books written by him, while the Alexandrian alchemist Zosimus called Hermes "a thousand times great."

Since the early eighteenth century, occultists have called the Tarot the *Book of Thoth*, giving it an Egyptian provenance most modern scholars reject.[16] Yet Eliphas Levi claimed that the true *Book of Thoth* was Egypt itself, or what was left of it, its pyramids, obelisks, temples, and Sphinx, which can be read and interpreted like a secret text, an idea he shared with Schwaller de Lubicz.[17] Throughout the Middle Ages and the Renaissance, Hermes Trismegistus was known as "the Egyptian," as it was he who embodied the sacred knowledge of those holy people. And it was in his writings and those by his disciples, known to us as the *Hermetica* or *Corpus Hermeticum*, that Hermes Trismegistus communicated the divine revelation he had received at the dawn of time. This was the *prisca theologia* and "perennial philosophy" that was later handed down from adept to adept throughout the ages, and which we've already encountered in one form or another.

As we now know, Hermes Trismegistus was not a real person and his writings, the *Corpus Hermeticum*, were not written "before the Flood," or even before Plato, who was supposed to have been profoundly influenced by them. But if this is so, who was Hermes Trismegistus, and who did write the *Corpus Hermeticum*?

We do not know where or when or by whom the name "Hermes Trismegistus" was first uttered, but by the time of the composition of the works attributed to him, in the second and third centuries of the Christian era, we can assume legends and tales of his remarkable accomplishments and wisdom were widespread.[18] Early scholars believed that the ideas expressed in the *Corpus Hermeticum* were Greek through and through, and that the Egyptian elements that run throughout them—most clearly in the *Asclepius,* the most well-known Hermetic writing until the rediscovery of the *Corpus Hermeticum* in the fifteenth century—were really an exotic window dressing, lending the works a mysterious, mystical lure. Although the influence of Platonic ideas in the *Corpus Hermeticum* is clear, many scholars today believe that the tone and atmosphere of the writings is nonetheless Egyptian, and that the teachings they present are a late codification and Hellenization of ancient Egyptian wisdom.[19]

Although the *Corpus Hermeticum* and Hermes Trismegistus themselves could not have influenced Plato—as the Renaissance Hermeticists believed—that Plato very likely "went to school in Egypt" suggests that the Platonic ideas informing the authors of the Hermetic writings were themselves rooted in Egyptian thought.[20] What seems to be the case is that in Alexandria in the second and third centuries of the Christian era, several different authors over many years wrote a variety of philosophical, cosmological, mystical, spiritual, and magical texts communicating the ancient Egyptian wisdom in a Hellenized form, and that these unknown authors—or secret teachers—attributed these texts to the remarkable sage Hermes Trismegistus and his disciples. They did this not out of good marketing strategy, but as a sign of the worship and respect they had for the wisdom they were communicating.

One possible reason they acted in this way is that they foresaw an imminent disaster approaching Egypt. In the *Asclepius,* Hermes tells his disciple Asclepius that "A time will come when it appears that the Egyptians have worshiped God with pure mind and sincere devotion in vain. All their holy worship will turn out to be without effect and will bear no fruit. For the gods will withdraw from earth to heaven and Egypt will be deserted." Dark days will reach the land of the Nile, Hermes warns, and the river will run with blood. Religion will be forsaken, crime will be the norm, and evil will rule the land. But Hermes also tells Asclepius that there will be a resurrection of the spirit; the ancient ways will be restored and Egypt, once "the temple of the whole cosmos," will again become "an image of heaven."[21] At the time of writing, with Egypt overrun by foreign invaders—first Greeks then Romans—and infiltrated by foreign religions—Greek, Roman, Christian, Gnostic, Jewish—it may be that Egyptian esotericists thought it best to collect the ancient wisdom in a series of writings so that it may survive the deluge ahead.

THE CREATION ACCORDING TO HERMES

What was the ancient wisdom the unknown Hermetists wanted to save? In the *Poimandres* or *The Divine Pymander*, the most famous text from the *Corpus Hermeticum*, Hermes Trismegistus recounts a mystical experience in which the true relations between God, man, and the cosmos were revealed to him. It was an experience of *gnosis*, an immediate, direct revelation of spiritual insight. Like the Gnostics who were their contemporaries— some Hermetic texts were among the Gnostic scrolls found in Nag Hammadi—the Hermetists sought a knowledge that would cut through the knotted bundle of doubts and perplexities that Greek dialectic had become. Earlier we saw that soon after Plato, philosophy had become an arena of competing "discourses," to use a popular academic term, with the result that many felt that philosophy itself, the "love of wisdom," had become something to avoid, and that reason could not lead one to any certainty. Frances Yates points out that by the time of the Hermetic writings, dialectic had reached a standstill and nothing new could be expected to come from it. *Gnosis* was something different. As the Gnostic and Hermetic scholar G. R. S. Mead remarked, with *gnosis* comes "certitude, full and inexhaustible, no matter how the doubting mind . . . may weave its magic."[22] The doubting mind for Mead was Greek; what it knew was "discursive knowledge," "the noise of words," and "the appearance of things."

For "Greek" here we can read "the left brain," with its meticulous attention to particulars and its tendency—some might say obsession— with prying discreet, individual objects—parts—out of the whole. The whole, the province of the right brain, was what the Hermetists were after, and in his mystical experience of *gnosis*, this is what Hermes Trismegistus got.

While in a relaxed state, in which his body was calm—a state much like that described by Plato as "practicing dying," and in which Jeremy

Naydler suggests the ancient Egyptian priests could release their *ba* from the body—Hermes Trismegistus is visited by *Nous,* or the Divine or Universal Mind. *Nous* tells Hermes about the creation of the world. Much of the story will be familiar to us. Wanting to create the world, *Nous* first creates a craftsman, a demiurge, who does the job, much as in the Platonic and Gnostic creation myths, although in the Hermetic account, the craftsman does not go rogue and usurp power from his master. The craftsman creates seven helpers to aid him in his task; these will turn out to be the seven ancient planets, whose crystalline spheres will encircle the Earth. With the job done, *Nous* decides that he would like to share his creation with another, so he creates Man. (Needless to say, Man here is used in the classical sense of human, meaning men and women.)

Man is quite taken with creation, and wanting a closer look at Earth, he peers through the seven spheres and is immediately smitten with Nature. Nature, too, is smitten with him, and their attraction to each other causes man to fall to Earth, where the two embrace (Nature here, as in all classical accounts, is a woman). Plummeting through the seven spheres, man's originally wholly spiritual being becomes weighted down with elements of the planets, and he finds himself sunken into brute matter, his inherent spiritual state now obscured by the dense resistance of the physical world. Like the Gnostics, Hermetic Man finds himself trapped, "fallen" into a world that constrains his freedom and denies his spiritual roots. At the very least he has become, as the Hermetic writings have it, a creature of "two worlds," an earthly being subject to "fate" yet with a memory of and yearning for his spiritual source, however distant and diminished its influence has now become.

THE JOURNEY THROUGH THE PLANETS

The Hermetists shared with the Gnostics the idea that they had fallen from an original spiritual state into a world of brute and oblivious matter, but their response to this situation was different. For one thing, the Hermetists did not see the world as evil, nor did they believe it was a product of a usurper god. Another difference is that while the Gnostics worked within the Judeo-Christian tradition, the Hermetists' milieu was Egyptian, although some interpreters have seen their teachings as a kind of "pre-Christian Christianity." Both, however, saw *gnosis* as the answer. But while the Gnostics sought *gnosis* as a way of escaping from a false world, the Hermetists saw *gnosis* as a way of recovering their spiritual state within the world. And for them, this ultimately meant a way of transforming the world, of redeeming it and themselves from their fallen state. At the risk of overgeneralizing, we can say that if for the Gnostics the world was a prison they wished to escape, for the Hermetists it was one they wished to transform into a cathedral.

Just as the Gnostics believed that the way back to their source, the true God beyond the cosmos, led through the gauntlet of the archons, the Hermetists believed that the way to regain their true spiritual state led via a "journey through the planets," a return trip back to *Nous*. During this voyage they would either divest themselves of the dense, planetary characteristics they had acquired on their descent, or transform them into positive values. This "ascent through the spheres" was not accomplished via a rocket ship but through an inner voyage, the kind of "journey into the interior" that would become a mainstay of the esoteric tradition. Fundamentally, this was a meditative and contemplative practice aimed at transforming consciousness, much as the "practice of dying while still alive" and the initiation into the Mysteries were. The Hermetists knew that their origin and goal lay "beyond the cosmos," but they knew this "beyond" was not some far-off destination in the depths of space, but a "beyond" outside of space, that metaphorically "interior" realm we call "the mind." The "progress through the Hebdomad," as Stephan Hoeller calls the journey through the seven planets, took place inwardly, and its stages were marked by an increase in consciousness. As Hoeller writes, "as the initiate's interior powers increase, the stranglehold of the cosmos and the planets decreases."[23]

As one side of our nature is subject to planetary, stellar, and cosmic forces, the aim of the "progress through the Hebdomad" was to master these and to actualize oneself as a "microcosm," as a small cosmos in oneself. From being a part of the whole, and subject to its constraints ("fate"), one became a reflection of the whole itself. The aim was to come to a vision of what they called "the One, the All," or, as the modern Christian

Hermeticist Valentin Tomberg calls it, "the totality of things."[24] The Hermetist undertook a guided ecstatic inner ascent during which he would confront the planetary forces working on him and master or transform them from limitations into useful powers, at each stage approaching closer to *Nous*. A similar "ladder of ascent" can be found in other traditions: in Kabbalah, as the path upward through the Sephiroth; in Tantra, as the awakening of the Kundalini power through its ascent of the chakras; and in more modern esoteric teachings, such as Gurdjieff's "Ray of Creation," Rudolf Steiner's "evolution of consciousness" through the planetary spheres, and in C. G. Jung's "individuation," in which the role played by the planets is now couched in psychological terms, as the "archetypes."

COSMIC CONSCIOUSNESS

The ultimate aim of the journey through the planets was *gnosis*, or, as mentioned earlier, "cosmic consciousness." Although this term did not come into widespread use until the publication of R. M. Bucke's *Cosmic Consciousness* (1901)—a remarkable book arguing that mankind is evolving into a new, wider mode of consciousness, and which influenced important figures in the "secret history of consciousness" such as William James and P. D. Ouspensky—as I suggest in *The Quest for Hermes Trismegistus*, descriptions of *gnosis* given in the *Corpus Hermeticum* and other Hermetic writings are strikingly similar to those given by Bucke and the inner explorers who followed him.[25] As the term suggests, this was a consciousness of the cosmos, of the "network of connections linking everything to everything else" mentioned earlier, and which I have linked to a right-brain mode of perception. In Book XI of the *Corpus Hermeticum, Nous* explains to Hermes that "within God everything lies in the imagination," and goes on to give a description of what he can expect from *gnosis*.

> Command your soul to go anywhere and it will be there quicker than your command. Bid it to go to the ocean and again it is there at once . . . Order it to fly up to heaven and it will need no wings . . . If you do not make yourself equal to God you cannot understand him. Like is

understood by like. Grow to immeasurable size. Be free from every body, transcend all time. Become eternity and thus will you understand God . . . Consider yourself immortal and able to understand everything: all arts, sciences, and the nature of every living creature . . . Sense as one within yourself the entire creation . . . Conceive yourself to be in all places at the same time . . . Conceive all things at once: times, places, actions, qualities and quantities: then you can understand God.[26]

Much of this passage reminds us of the remark by the philosopher C. D. Broad, quoted in Chapter One, that "Each person is at each moment capable of remembering all that has ever happened to him and of perceiving everything that is happening everywhere in the universe." And as I suggest in that chapter, the reason we usually aren't aware of "everything happening everywhere in the universe" is that, as Henri Bergson suggested, our brain serves an *eliminative* function, allowing only enough of "reality" into our awareness to help us survive. The reader may remember that I associated this eliminative function with the left brain's tendency to fix on the part while ignoring the whole. The passage from the *Corpus Hermeticum* above suggests that what the Hermetists were aiming at was a shift from a left- to a right-brain mode of consciousness, from our everyday form of consciousness that attends to our daily necessities, to one that is aware of "the network of connections linking everything to everything else."

In *The Eighth Reveals the Ninth*, one of the Hermetic texts found among the Nag Hammadi scrolls, we find a long string of what seem nonsense words: "Zoxathazo a oo'ee Zozazoth," and so on. What exactly the Hermetists did with these is unclear, but one suggestion is that they chanted them in order to induce an altered state of consciousness, or that they were a sign that such a state had been achieved. As Stephan Hoeller writes, "this heavenly mystery [*gnosis*] is not profitably approached in rational terms," and "the utterance ensuing from such extraordinary states of consciousness also must be of an other than ordinary kind."[27] The idea would be that on reaching *gnosis,* the rational mind—or left brain—responsible for ordered speech would be "short-circuited," as it were, which, as we saw earlier, would make a logical account of the experience difficult, if not impossible. Many of the Hermetic texts speak of such states, which were expressed in hymns of praise (another important difference from the Gnostics) or in a profound "sacred silence." At the end of the *Poimandres*, Hermes says, "You whom we address in silence, the unspeakable, the unsayable, accept pure speech offerings from a heart and soul that reach up to you." We have already pointed out that the implicit meanings and insights provided by the right brain more times than not elude clear, explicit statement.

Another aspect of the Hermetic *gnosis* that we have already touched on is its peculiar ability to enter into things, to see and to experience their "insides." Earlier I spoke of this in regard to Schwaller de Lubicz's "intelligence of the heart" which allows us to "tumble with the rock which falls from the mountain" and "rejoice with the rosebud about to open," and Owen Barfield's ideas about "original" and "final participation." In Book XIII of the *Corpus Hermeticum*, Tat, a disciple of Hermes Trismegistus, tells his master that

> I have been made steadfast through God; I now see not with the eyes
> but by the operation of spiritual energy in the powers. I am in heaven,
> in earth, in water, in air; I am in living creatures and plants; I am in the
> womb, before the womb, after the womb. I am present everywhere.[28]

This passage reminds us of Jesus's remark in the Gnostic Gospel of Thomas: "Split a piece of wood and I am there." As mentioned, Iain McGilchrist argues that the right-brain mode of perception is more "participatory" than the left, it allows us to "get inside" things more, in the way that Bergson's "intuition" also does. Given that the wisdom associated with the *Corpus Hermeticum* is considered ancient, and that Barfield and Schwaller de Lubicz and others suggest that our early ancestors had a more participatory form of consciousness, and that McGilchrist argues that our right-brain consciousness is older than our left, this again suggests to me that what the Hermetists were about was linked in some important sense to a shift from left- to right-brain consciousness. Again, this is not to reduce Hermeticism to an expression of brain function, but to show that the whole Hermetic tradition, its pursuit of *gnosis* and cosmic consciousness, is not some weak-minded wild goose chase, but a recognition of the value and irreducibleness of our other mode of consciousness.

DRAWING DOWN THE GODS

The parts of the Hermetic writings touched on above have a mystical, philosophical, and ecstatic character, yet as we know, Hermes Trismegistus was the master of magic. The most magical of the Hermetic texts is the *Asclepius,* which was famous throughout the Middle Ages and which was censured by St. Augustine because of its instructions in the art of theurgy. This is the calling down to earth or making present the gods and their powers—or, conversely, the raising up of the theurgist to them. In the *Asclepius,* Hermes tells his disciples how one can draw the divine energies from the stars and infuse them into representations of the gods—how, that is, one could "animate" statues and symbols of the gods by permeating them with a spiritual "life force" borrowed from the *Anima mundi,* or "soul" of the world, which the theurgist funnels through his imagination. This kind of "star magic" would later inform the Renaissance Hermeticism of Marsilio Ficino, who developed a kind of prophylactic and therapeutic astrology with it. This would attract good stellar forces and repel baleful ones, using music, art, poetry, and scents, as well as magical sigils and symbols, as spiritual "magnets," capturing these energies. It was the potentially "demonic" character of this magic that would turn Augustine and later churchmen against Hermeticism, which for a time, like Platonism, was seen as a Christian fellow traveler.

Theurgy would form an important part of the last phase of pagan philosophy, in a kind of Platonism that had as much to do with magic as it did with the love of wisdom, and which perhaps could have appeared nowhere else but in Alexandria. The last exponents of what came to be called Neoplatonism claimed to possess magical and clairvoyant powers, and they saw philosophy as being as much concerned with making vital contact with living spiritual beings as with the subtleties of dialectic—even more so, perhaps. It was a visionary philosophy, and although the Neoplatonists make no mention of the Hermetists (they were, however, critical of the Gnostics), they shared with them a desire to return to the source, and they too sought to climb up the "ladder of being" through the intermediary spheres to the One. The theurgic element in Hermeticism that repelled

Renaissance churchmen was for these late pagans the essence of their teaching: the belief that through meditation, ritual, and solemn rites, one could manifest divine powers and participate in them. Here the Platonic Forms, once abstract and impersonal, have become living entities that the theurgist can communicate with, not merely contemplate. Although the church would ban such practices, its own belief in the "real presence" of Jesus in the Eucharist, brought about through transubstantiation, the alchemical transformation of the communion host and wine into the body and blood of Christ, is an echo of the "god-making" powers conferred upon the theurgist.

PLOTINUS AND THE MAN HE WAS LOOKING FOR

The thinker most associated with Neoplatonism, however, was a visionary and a mystic, not a magician, although his approach to Plato would pave the way for the more magical Platonism to come. Plotinus (204–270) is thought to have been born around 204 in Lycopolis, Egypt, but there is really no consensus on his ancestry or his early life, and he never made public the date of his birth. Hard biographical information about most of our ancient secret teachers is scant, but in Plotinus's case this is doubly so: he took a dim view of his personal life, believing that all that mattered was the spiritual and philosophical life, which for him meant the pursuit of the One, the transcendent source of being. Plotinus was exceedingly chary about revealing any details about his background, the only titbit of personal gossip forthcoming from him was the fact that he continued to nurse at his governess's breast until his eighth year—exactly why he spoke of this is unclear.[29] So contemptuous of the body was Plotinus that the biography of him written by his disciple Porphyry (234–305) begins, "Plotinus, the philosopher of our time, seemed ashamed of being in a body." We know that in the Platonic tradition, the body is seen as an impediment to pure thought—"to rise up to very truth is altogether to depart from bodies," Plotinus wrote in his *Enneads*—but he seems to have taken the notion of philosophy as an escape from embodiment to an extreme. His shame about his "detestable vessel" led to Plotinus's proscription against any portrait being painted of him.[30] Yet the motive behind all this secrecy was not a desire to create a veil of mystery—to, in effect, draw attention to himself through his ostentatious attempts to avoid it—but that his ideas, his philosophy, should attract and bond his students to him, not his personality. If any man lived completely for philosophy, it was Plotinus.

Plotinus began his philosophical life in his late twenties. At the age of twenty-seven, he came to Alexandria seeking a teacher. His search for one in the public lecture halls was disappointing and he almost despaired of his quest until someone told him of a remarkable teacher who spoke not in the lecture halls, but at the city's docks. No doubt piqued by so odd a choice of venue, Plotinus took his friend's suggestion and went to hear this unusual savant. When he did, he knew his quest was over. "This," he said, "was the man I was looking for."

The man Plotinus discovered was Ammonius Saccas (175–242), mentioned earlier, about whom little is known, and who qualifies as a secret teacher. There is some debate over whether or not he was a Christian. Porphyry says that he was brought up Christian but abandoned the faith for philosophy, while Christian writers claim that he remained Christian throughout his life. Some scholars have suggested that a way out of this confusion is to assume there were two Ammoniuses in Alexandria at the time, one a philosopher, the other a Christian. My own feeling is that if Ammonius was as central an influence on Plotinus as is believed, it is difficult to accept that he was a Christian while tutoring Plotinus in philosophy. Although Neoplatonism would influence Christianity, there is little to suggest that Christianity influenced Plotinus's thought, and in the last centuries of paganism, Neoplatonism and Christianity were bitter rivals.

What we know of Ammonius Saccas is that he came from a humble background and that he worked as a porter on the Alexandrian docks, hence his nickname "Saccas," which means "sack bearer." In 193, he founded a school, but he left no writings and taught orally; the little we know of his philosophical ideas comes from accounts in Porphyry and later Neoplatonists (Plotinus himself also taught orally and only wrote down his ideas after his student Porphyry compelled him to late in life). Ammonius attended lectures in philosophy for many years but he also learned much from contact with the people he met at the harbor: sailors, traders, and fishermen, some of whom may have stimulated his interest in foreign teachings, those of Persia and India, a curiosity he passed on to Plotinus. There was a revival of interest in Pythagorean thought at the time, and like Pythagoras, Ammonius demanded a vow of secrecy from his students, whom he separated into three classes—novices, initiates, and masters—rather like the three levels of understanding we have seen in the Gnostics, Clement of Alexandria, and Origen. As he was Origen's teacher, we may wonder if Origen's three-tiered notions of scripture and the human being may have its roots in Ammonius's lectures.

Like Philo, Clement, and Origen, Ammonius taught that we should interpret myths and legends symbolically, not accept them as literal truth, seeking their correspondences with our interior world, that is, the life of the soul. The practice of reading the Greek myths analogically that became part of Neoplatonist practice most likely had its roots in Ammonius's hermeneutical approach. He took few students, and he seems to have had an exoteric teaching that he voiced in public lectures and an esoteric one he reserved for his close disciples. He was an eclectic teacher and drew on many sources for his ideas, even on dreams; it is said that he thought so much about philosophy during the day, that his thinking continued during sleep, and that many of his insights came to him in dreams. He was known as a *theodidactos*, or "God-taught," and it is believed that he was the first to use the term *theosophia*, or "divine wisdom." Centuries later Madame Blavatsky, one of the founders of the Theosophical Society, would celebrate Ammonius Saccas as an enlightened forebearer, and she spoke of the Alexandrian Philalethians, or "lovers of truth," a name that Ammonius embraced as well. Along with his eclecticism, which blended Plato with Egyptian and even Indian ideas, what Blavatsky shared with Ammonius was the belief, which we encountered in Chapter One, that there is a universal teaching, a perennial revelation, at the basis of all myths, religions, and philosophies, and that, at bottom, there is no conflict between them. It is said of Ammonius that he aimed to show that there is a fundamental agreement between Plato, Aristotle, and even Christianity, as they were all expressions of this timeless wisdom, a philosophical project that would occupy Renaissance Hermeticists like Pico della Mirandola and which forms the essence of the Traditionalist school of esoteric thought.

Ammonius believed in an absolute transcendent deity, utterly beyond human comprehension, an idea that we have seen in Philo and also in Origen, and he also believed that the human soul was a kind of immortal "radiation" from the immortal universal soul that emanated from this One. As the human soul was a radiation of the universal divine soul, through meditation, contemplation, virtue, and the love of wisdom, the human soul can raise itself to union with its source. It is this belief in *henosis,* a Greek word meaning the union of the individual soul with its divine source, that is at the foundation of Neoplatonism.

THE LAST DAYS OF PLOTINUS

Plotinus stayed with Ammonius for eleven years. After the death of his master, and intrigued by his remarks about the mystic teachings of the Persians, Chaldeans, and Indians, Plotinus decided that he would go on a journey to the East. His mode of transportation may seem odd, but without independent means, travel in the ancient world was not easy. To get to the Orient, Plotinus decided to join the army of the emperor Gordian III, which was embarking on an invasion of Persia. Gordian III was assassinated en route; his campaign collapsed and Plotinus found himself lost in the wasteland. It took him two years to reach the ancient city of Antioch. From there he boarded a ship to Rome, where he remained for most of the rest of his life, retiring in his last days to an estate in southern Italy, bequeathed to him by a friend.

In Rome, Plotinus became something of a celebrity. The emperor Gallienus and his wife became followers, and with them came a host of other prominent citizens, including many members of the senate, as well as many influential women. Plotinus became tutor to many of their children and was well rewarded in exchange; he was often called on to arbitrate in disputes. One of his students, Malchus of Tyros, was nicknamed "Porphyry" ("clad in purple") because of Phoenician descent—purple dye came from Tyre—but perhaps also because Malchus means "king" and purple was the color of royalty. Porphyry stayed with Plotinus for six years, but left Rome for Sicily on Plotinus's advice, to recuperate after a severe mental strain led to thoughts of suicide. During Porphyry's absence, Plotinus died, finally jettisoning the detestable vessel he had spent his life trying to ignore. After leading an abstemious life dedicated to work, contemplation, and the pursuit of the good, Plotinus contracted what may have been leprosy. An ungenerous reflection would be that his body took a last revenge against his abuse. There is some debate over the actual nature of his disease, but becoming a leper would be one compelling reason to leave Rome and retire to a secluded estate. His last words are said to have been "Strive to give back the Divine in yourself to the Divine in all." Readers familiar with the work of Rudolf Steiner may hear in this a pre-echo of Steiner's own late definition of his esoteric teaching, Anthroposophy, which he characterized as "a path of knowledge to guide the spiritual in the human being to the spiritual in the universe."[31]

FROM THE ONE TO THE ONE

Giving back "the divine in oneself to the divine in all" can be seen as the essence of Plotinus's work, as well as the core concern of Neoplatonism. Plotinus himself, we should reflect, did not see his work as a new approach to Plato, merely the refining of certain aspects of his philosophy left in a rough form at the master's death. Or, as some commentators remark, Plotinus thought out of his own concerns, and looked to Plato for confirmation of his insights. We can see his work as "Plato +". If in Plato the philosopher finds wisdom through contemplating the Forms, and the best wisdom in contemplating the Form of Forms, i.e., the Good, with Plotinus the philosopher goes a step further and from contemplation reaches union, or *henosis*, when he becomes one with the object of contemplation or, with the later "magical" Neoplatonists, is made "godlike" himself.

It is surprising that Plotinus makes no mention of the Hermetists, who were his contemporaries. He did write critically of the Gnostics: in *Against the Gnostics,* he chides them for their world rejection, their antinomianism, their abandonment of moral responsibility and the pursuit of virtue, in favor of their elite "secret knowledge."[32] One suspects he had the Carpocratian variety of Gnosticism in mind. The Hermetists did devote themselves to virtue and purification—a central Plotinian ideal—and they did not see the material world as evil, but even more so, as we've seen, they devoted themselves to union with the One, with the *henosis* that transforms the natural, carnal self into something more godlike, to which Plotinus also aspired. It may be that Plotinus associated the Hermetists with the Gnostics, as both pursued *gnosis*. Plotinus did not believe there was a "magic formula" for union with the divine, a special dispensation that only members of an elite sect could enjoy—the "one thing needful," to borrow from the Gnostics' Christian rivals.[33] Although Plotinus himself experienced *gnosis*—that is, direct spiritual knowledge—he was a true philosopher and he got there by effort. He knew that work, thought, discipline, and virtue were the sine qua non of achieving union with the divine.

But Plotinus did see things differently from the Hermetists, at least as far as his account of creation goes. Unlike the Platonic, Judeo-Christian, and Hermetic creation stories, Plotinus does not posit a creator or demiurge or any deliberate plan for creation. For Plotinus, the One did not decide to create the cosmos; it is an irrepressible outcome of the overflow of its divine being, just as the sun's light and warmth is essential to its being a sun. The sun does not choose to shine; it must, or it would not be a sun. In a sense, for Plotinus there is no act or moment of creation per se, and he treats Plato's account in the *Timaeus* as an allegory. All is part of the One, which is eternal. Creation is ongoing, not a temporal or historical event. We can say Plotinus had a "steady-state" view of creation rather than a "Big Bang" one, which means that he did not see an end to creation; it is everlasting.

In his creation story, Plotinus posits another version of the Great Chain of Being, which we've seen in Philo, Ammonius, and Origen. There is the One: absolute, transcendent, beyond all attributes, beyond anything we can say about it. It is not Mind, nor God, nor the Good—although we will use these terms to refer to it—but somehow beyond these. It is beyond everything because it is the source of everything, and hence cannot be a "thing" itself. It is the One and the All. All things come from it and to it all things wish to return. It is the Good toward which all other goods are drawn.

From this indescribable, incomprehensible source, two spheres of being emanate, the Intellect, or *Nous,* and the World Soul, or *Anima mundi.* The three together are called the "three hypostases," or ultimate principles. They are the fundamental, transcendental—nonsensible— realities out of which all things come into being. From the One comes *Nous,* from *Nous* comes the World Soul, and from the World Soul comes Nature and the material world. As with Jean Gebser's structures of consciousness, with each new structure being further removed from "Origin," in Plotinus's system, the further an emanation is from the One—in terms of ontology, not spatial distance—the less spiritual and more dense it becomes, yet each emanation retains elements of the other emanations. And so the One is present in the All, as Gebser's structures remain active although superseded by later structures.

Like Gebser's Origin, the One is not lessened by its emanations; it is an eternal spring, an inexhaustible source that loses nothing by creating. Plotinus speaks of the process of creation as "the unfolding of a seed," which moves "from simple origin to . . . the world of sense . . . from a store of indescribable power . . . that must not halt within the higher range . . . but continue to expand until the universe of things reaches the limit of its possibility, lavishing its vast resources on all its creatures, intolerant than any one should have no share in it." In this portrayal of a kind of ontological geyser, continuously gushing creative energy out of itself and into its creations, Plotinus's vision is like that of Henri Bergson's *élan vital,* the surging life force at work in the world. It is no surprise that for many years Bergson lectured on Plotinus in university, and it is also no surprise that Plotinus's ideas informed Goethe and other Romantic philosophers and poets.

The One is self-sufficient and self-content, but the Intellect and World Soul look back to their source; they contemplate it, and through their contemplation, an overflow of creative energy arises that permeates all of creation. This contemplation is shared, to differing degrees, by the All. All is in touch with All, or, as Plotinus would say, All is linked to All through "the sympathy of all things," the "network of connections linking everything to everything else." "A sympathy pervades this single universe, like a single living creature," Plotinus writes, "and the distant is near." This "sympathy of all things" will inform later esoteric readings of the world, whether through Hermetic, alchemical, and Kabbalistic "correspondences"—"as above, so below"—or in Jung's notion of synchronicity, the "meaningful coincidences" that tell us that our relationship to the world is a much more participatory one than our scientific minds would have us believe, or through the analogical hermeneutics of symbolism, which sees poetic and metaphoric reflections of the whole in each of its parts, through the kind of perception that we have associated with a more right-brain mode of consciousness.

At the very bottom of the Plotinian ladder is matter, which is a formless chaos until it receives the imprint of the Forms of the Intellect through the mediation of the Soul. While necessary for the sensible cosmos to exist—which existence itself is a necessity—matter is a kind of afterthought, an unavoidable canvas on which the Intellect and Soul create the beauty of the world, a sensuous mirror reflecting the supersensible. (We must remember that for Plotinus, as for all our secret teachers, *consciousness*, not matter, is primary; true being resides in states of consciousness, in a ladder of spiritual activity.) The Intellect, or *Nous*, is the realm of the Intelligible Forms, the Platonic blueprints for everything in existence. A perfect harmony exists in *Nous*, with every part related to every other part seamlessly; the Forms are ordered, not a mosaic or jumble. Because it is spiritual, not material, *Nous* is ever present, outside of space and time; as William Blake, a reader of Plotinus through his friend Thomas Taylor, said, "one thought fills immensity." Unlike many neuroscientists and modern philosophers of mind, who tell us that the mind is something in us individually, in our brains as an epiphenomenon of neural firing—a kind of steam given off by our neurons—for Plotinus (and the entire esoteric tradition) we are in Mind, in "Mind at Large," as Aldous Huxley called it, and because of this are connected to each other.

We see evidence of *Nous* everywhere, in the patterns of nature from sunflowers to spiral galaxies. Like Pythagoras, Plato, and the Hermetists, although regretful of his embodiment, Plotinus saw the created world as a work of beauty and wonder. But the world is not only harmonious; it is alive, a single, sentient organism, carrying within itself the imprint of its source. While *Nous* provides the forms that the created world will exhibit, it is the *Anima mundi* that gives life to everything. It is the life force running through the cosmos. The World Soul brings the cosmos of space and time into being, and it is through it that it is animated, or "ensouled." Again, unlike modern science, which sees life as an accidental product of a meaningless universe, the result of a chance combination of physical forces, for Plotinus the entire cosmos is alive, intelligent, and responsive to human entreaty—this is the basis of the later theurgic philosophy of Iamblichus (245–325) and Proclus (412–485), the last of the Neoplatonists. It is through the *Anima mundi* that the Forms of the Intellect become something more than abstract ideas, just as it is through his soul that the philosopher is a "lover of wisdom," and not a dry logician. And it is through his soul, which is linked to and is a part of the World Soul, that the philosopher is immortal. The Plotinian ladder of being is recapitulated in man, who contains within himself his source in the *Anima mundi, Nous,* and the One. In Plotinus's philosophy, the aim of the philosopher is to climb this interior ladder, and to regain a place with his source in the One. The similarity to the Hermetic "journey through the planets" should be clear.

In the *Enneads,* the collection of his writings edited and organized by Porphyry, Plotinus uncharacteristically speaks of himself when trying to give a description of the kind of mystical union he sought:

Often I have woken to myself out of the body, become detached from all else and entered into myself; and I have seen beauty of surpassing greatness, and have felt assured that then especially I belonged to the higher reality, engaged in the noblest life and identified with the Divine; and there established, I have attained to that supreme actuality, setting myself above all else in the realm of Intellect. And after this repose in the Divine, descending from Intellect to reasoning, I am perplexed as to how my descent comes about, and how my soul has become embodied—a soul, though in the body, of such manifest excellence.

As in the Hermetic account, for Plotinus man is of two natures: he is an amphibian, living in two worlds simultaneously. One part of him is in direct contact with the higher worlds, another part is immersed in the lower ones. Man can choose which part of his being he values, and to which part he directs his energies and attention. To focus on the body and its desires—linked to what Plotinus called the "lower soul"—or to the temptations of the world is to cut oneself off from the divine. To turn one's attention first to reason, then to the higher intellect, is to renew the link to our origin in the One. To contemplate this One is the true happiness toward which man can aim; all else is a distraction.

This did not mean that Plotinus counsels us to retire to a cave and live the life of an ascetic. Contemplation of the source begins with contemplation of its fruits, with the beauty and order of the world, and this is aided by the pursuit of virtue. This leads to a good that is independent of the travails of life. Journeying within, one frees oneself of the body's tyranny and comes to recognize one's unity with the World Soul. In the intelligible Forms, we see the radiance of the Good. Finally, rather than perceive the Forms from without, we attain union with them. The philosopher no longer reflects on the good and true, using his intellect to understand them; he has become one with them. The reality he had contemplated is no longer outside him. He and it are one.

This *henosis*, however, cannot be commanded or willed, although the philosopher works daily preparing the ground for it. He must be patient and allow it to happen. It is not exactly a kind of grace, as Plotinus does not believe that the One *does* anything; it does not bestow this union. But it is always present, always available, just as the stars are always present; it is only the proximity of the sun that obscures them. The philosopher must make himself a worthy vessel for the presence of the One by emptying himself of coarse matters. Or, to change the metaphor, he must quiet the racket within himself so that the sacred silence can be heard. It is solitary work, with no aim other than itself. Unlike Plato, Plotinus did not dream of philosopher kings, but of teachers who, like the One itself, radiate their knowledge and wisdom so that those who are drawn to the philosophical life and are capable of it may be guided in their quest. Ultimately, through purifying himself, pursuing the virtues, and through contemplating the good, the true, and the beautiful, the philosopher comes to see and to participate in the ever-present, self-evident, and eternal One, "the solitary returned to the Solitary."

AfTER pLOTINUS

After the austere and sublime heights of Plotinus's teaching, there would seem to be little left for Neoplatonism to do. In effect, what takes place after Plotinus is a kind of retreat from these timeless philosophical peaks and a return to the roots of Greek spirituality in pagan mythology and the Mysteries. With Porphyry, Iamblichus, and Proclus, we can see what we might call the "last stand of paganism" before its passing. With Christianity on the rise, these thinkers may have felt that they had to make the old religion more acceptable to those who had developed their critical thinking through philosophy. The result is an early attempt at a philosophy of religion, a way of understanding the ancient ways through the lens of Platonic thought.

We have Porphyry to thank for forcing Plotinus to write; otherwise the *Enneads* might never have been produced. (We also have him to thank for editing Plotinus's writings which, from all reports, were often chaotic.) Porphyry himself was a highly cultured and learned thinker who wrote a great deal, but only little of this has survived. He wrote a spirited criticism of Christianity, *Against the Christians,* arguing like Celsus against what he saw as their lack of reason and dependence on emotional persuasion, not philosophical argument. He also wrote on the virtues of vegetarianism and other forms of abstinence and made an attempt to harmonize Plotinus's thought with Aristotle, an early essay in the kind of synthesizing and integration of previous Greek philosophy that would occupy later Neoplatonists. We can say that with Plotinus, the great current of philosophy that started with Thales reaches an end; those who came after him are less creative and original; they are more scholarly and aim to find ways of reaching agreement between ostensibly opposed viewpoints in order to develop an all-inclusive philosophical system. Such system building is generally associated with the completion of a movement of thought. As the philosopher Hegel, one of the great system builders, remarked, "the owl of Minerva flies at dusk."

Porphyry was more interested in religion than Plotinus. Although he showed religion due respect, it is clear that Plotinus believed that his philosophical, contemplative approach was sufficient and that the rituals of religious observance were unnecessary. When invited to make a pious visit to his local temples, Plotinus declined, remarking that "they should come to me, not I to them."[34] This did not mean that Plotinus did not believe in the gods, only that his own approach to venerating the divine was preferable. He had a similar feeling toward magic or theurgy. He believed magic worked, but only within boundaries of the natural world. It was a way of using the "sympathy of all things" arising from the World Soul. But the higher realms were unaffected by it, and it was these with which he was ultimately concerned. We can see the later development of Neoplatonism as a contradiction of Plotinus's ideas about theurgy and the gods.

Porphyry begins this change with his belief that traditional religious observance was still important. Plotinus's approach was, he knew, limited to only a handful of determined individuals and could never appeal to the masses. But the myths informing pagan religion, he also saw, needed to be read symbolically, with a philosophical eye, an idea we've already encountered with Ammonius Saccas. Porphyry argued for an esoteric reading of Greek mythology, seeing in it coded knowledge about the soul and its need for, as well as its way of, salvation. His esoteric reading of Homer is most clearly presented in his work *The Cave of the Nymphs*. Porphyry was also a great reader of the Chaldean Oracles, whose devotees, we've seen, were practitioners of magic and divination. Yet while he was most likely the teacher of Iamblichus, Porphyry was also a critic of theurgy, and in his *Letter to Anebo*—supposedly an Egyptian priest—Porphyry spells out a series of questions about theurgy's efficacy and his preference for a more philosophical approach.

Iamblichus had no doubts about the efficacy and importance of theurgy, and we can see his "magical Platonism" as a retreat from Plotinus's solitary mystical heights to a kind Neoplatonic religious service. Iamblichus was born in Chalcis in Syria, into a wealthy family that descended from Syrian priest-kings. We know little about his life. He most likely studied with Porphyry, but ultimately rejected his philosophy in favor of a kind of baroque system that introduced a multiplicity of superhuman beings into Plotinus's relatively simple ontology. Iamblichus elaborated on Plotinus's three hypostases, adding further differentiations between them, increasing the number of intermediary spheres between man and the One, as well as the beings who inhabit them. He was also a devotee of Pythagoras and saw him as the supreme arbiter, introducing Pythagorean "number mysticism" into Plotinus's ideas. For one thing, he added a second One, thus introducing Pythagoras's "dyad."

Iamblichus disagreed with his teacher Porphyry about theurgy. His rebuttal to Porphyry's criticisms, *On the Mysteries of Egypt*, argues that we cannot achieve union with the One through our mind alone—Plotinus's way—but require the aid and assistance of the gods. Hence the need for theurgy. What was essential was not *thinking* our way to the One, Iamblichus argued, but the "performance of mysterious acts which surpass all understanding, duly executed in honor of the gods, and the power of unutterable symbols, intelligible to the gods alone."[35] In other words, it is the power of ritual, symbols, and magic words that "effects the theurgic union."[36] Here we are back to the Gnostics and the Hermetists, who employed rituals and prayer to achieve *gnosis*, although Iamblichus's remarks about the importance of divination and "divine possession" sound very much like modern accounts of mediums and "channeling."[37] But here we also have an early appearance of a split in the western esoteric tradition, to which we will return further on, between what will come to be known as the *via negativa* and the *via positiva*, the way of pure contemplation, which divests itself of imagery and works, and the way of ritual, symbolism, and practice, which embraces them.

We can also say that Iamblichus's insistence on "mysterious acts which surpass all understanding" and "the power of unutterable symbols" puts him in closer proximity to a more right-brain approach than Plotinus's more cerebral method. For Iamblichus, symbols and rituals are *objectively* effective; they contain real power. They do not compel the gods, but the gods recognize them and respond to their affinity with them, because the symbols and rituals are themselves godlike. As mentioned earlier, this understanding of the significance of ritual would inform the theology behind the Christian sacraments. Although modern critics see his ideas as a "charter for irrationalism," Iamblichus's standing in antiquity was impressive.[38] He was regularly called "the divine Iamblichus," and the emperor Julian the Apostate (331–363), who tried to revive the pagan religions, said that he preferred Iamblichus over Plato.

Proclus was born in Constantinople but went to Athens, where he studied at the Platonic Academy. He was so good a student that he was eventually made its head. Although the Academy would continue on until its closure by Justinian in 529, we can see Proclus's time there as its last blaze of glory. Proclus is most known for his long and detailed commentaries on previous philosophers, and in general we can see his work as an attempt to systemize the ideas of Iamblichus. Like Iamblichus, he was a great believer in theurgy, and he made daily orisons to the sun and other deities while living an abstemious life. Like Porphyry, he was a devotee of the Chaldean Oracles, so much so that he rated them higher than Plato. Like Iamblichus, he argued that we have need of the help of the gods in order to attain salvation, and he was especially devoted to the importance of ritual objects, which for him were portals to the divine realms; through theurgy, even the most mundane items could be raised to divine status.

Where Plotinus focused on the intellect as the royal road to *henosis,* Proclus saw the need to integrate our emotional and religious aspects into this pursuit; hence the need for ritual, prayer, and religious observance. Plotinus's thought seems to hover over history, but Proclus was much more a man of his time, attuned to the proliferation of sects and cults that characterized late antiquity. His loyalty to the fading gods of Greek mythology caused him some trouble in an increasingly intolerant Christian milieu; at one point he was exiled because of his worship of the pagan deities. His *Platonic Theology* is a monumental attempt to integrate Greek mythology, Pythagoreanism, Orphism, and the Chaldean Oracles into a systematic philosophy of pagan religion, to present a coherent pagan theory of the gods rooted in Platonic thought, and to see in the Olympian pantheon allegories of abstract ideas. It is a massive work, containing within itself a universe of divine beings and multiple levels of reality which in its baroque complexity reminds us of the Ptolemaic geocentric universe, with its epicycles on epicycles, needed to "save the appearances." The pagan world in which both emerged was on its way out, but both, in different ways, would inform the new world that would take its place.

CHAPTER FIVE

GREAT PAN IS DEAD

In 415, during the reign of Honorius—generally considered one of the worst Roman emperors—Cyril, the Christian patriarch of Alexandria, incensed with antipagan zeal, encouraged a mob of Christian fanatics in an act that in sheer brutality serves as symbol for the end of paganism. At the very least it was a grim example of what was in store for any who refused to reject pagan ways and convert to the new faith.

Cyril's predecessor, Theophilus, had already ordered the destruction of all pagan temples in Alexandria. But to make the message crystal clear, an even more violent reminder seemed necessary. Cyril was suspicious of the influence of Alexandria's last Neoplatonic philosopher, the brilliant Hypatia (370–415), one of the most remarkable women in western history. A mathematician, dialectician, philosopher, and astronomer—she is credited with developing the astrolabe—Hypatia's well-reasoned arguments easily outpaced the emotional rhetoric of the Christians, and her persuasive oratory was a threat to the increasingly militant faith. More specifically, her influence over Orestes, prefect of Alexandria, and other city officials troubled Cyril, who had already banished the Jews from Alexandria—after confiscating their goods—and he believed that Hypatia advised the prefect in ways contrary to Christianity. Cyril was on close terms with a group of desert monks, as well as with the *parabalani,* "the reckless ones," Christian fanatics who were feared for their exuberant faith and penchant for violence. Historians debate the extent of his responsibility, but it is generally agreed that Cyril's detestation of Hypatia communicated itself to these extremists, who decided to rid Christianity of this despicable evil.

Enraged with pious indignation, and led by a particularly zealous cleric named Peter, the mob attacked Hypatia as she returned home from the academy. Pulling her from her chariot, they dragged her into the Caesarean Church where they stripped her, beat her to death, and then scraped the flesh from her bones with oyster shells (some accounts say roof tiles). They then took her remains to a place called Cindron and burned them. Thus Hypatia became "the greatest of the pagan martyrs," as well as one of our secret teachers.[1] Cyril went on to have a long and illustrious career in the church, and according to one Christian Web site, is considered "the most brilliant theologian of the Alexandrian tradition."[2]

Although Proclus was three years old when Hypatia was murdered, and the Platonic Academy in Athens would remain active until 529, this gruesome assassination seems to mark a turning point. For the Neoplatonists who remained in Alexandria, it was a sign that they should leave the city, which was no longer a safe haven for philosophy. And so began what we might call an "esoteric exodus." Increasingly, the stream of ideas and teachings emanating from Greek thought—and rooted, perhaps, in the Egyptian Mysteries—would have to act secretly, would, that is, have to go "underground," a survival tactic not uncommon in the history of the western esoteric tradition. For roughly the next millennium, the ideas we have looked at in previous chapters, stemming from Pythagoras, Plato, and Plotinus—and also from the Gnostics and Hermetists—would lead a covert life, subtly informing more mainstream developments, adding a secret leaven to the now triumphant Christianity and the soon to rise Islam. Like a subterranean current, esoteric ideas moved below the surface, occasionally bubbling up to ground level, but more times than not remaining like a hidden spring at which a few daring souls took refreshment.

DIONYSIUS THE AREOPAGITE

One last emanation from the Neoplatonist school would inform perhaps the most mystical and esoteric expression of western Christianity, and there is some poetic justice in the fact that the source of this final efflorescence was a Christian student of Damascius (458–538), last teacher of the

Platonic Academy. This unknown philosopher—truly a secret teacher—was well versed in the complex Neoplatonic theology of Proclus, and with this he performed an act of spiritual fusion. Taking the Neoplatonic hierarchy of intermediary realms (and their inhabitants, all the gods and daimons) as a model, he developed what would become the Christian "celestial hierarchy." This is the ladder of spiritual beings comprising the Seraphim, Cherubim, Thrones, Dominions, Virtues, Powers, Principalities, Archangels, and Angels, that reaches up from our fallen state back to God.[3] We do not know who this mystic and visionary was. He is known as Dionysius the Areopagite, but that is not his real name. He is called this because he was confused with the Athenian converted by the apostle Paul and mentioned in Acts 17:34; he was also confused with St. Dionysius, the patron saint of France. Because of this he is often called "Pseudo-Dionysius." He was most likely active around 500 and probably had been born in Syria, but there is little we actually know about him. His works, *The Divine Names, Mystical Theology, Celestial Hierarchy, Ecclesiastical Hierarchy,* and a collection of ten epistles had a huge influence on Christian theology and mysticism throughout the Middle Ages, and if we can credit one figure with the rise of the Gothic cathedrals, it's Dionysius.

To be sure, the elements of the Gothic style came from many sources; the pointed arch, for example, came from Islam, most likely through Muslim craftsmen taken prisoner during the Crusades.[4] But the inspiration for it came from Dionysius's Neoplatonic–Christian theology. As William Anderson writes in *The Rise of the Gothic,* what compelled Abbot Suger in the twelfth century to rebuild the cathedral of St. Denis according to Dionysius's mystical vision, thus inaugurating the age of the Gothic, was "the desire to create in stone and glass an interior expressing the Neoplatonic idea that our visible and corporeal light derives from a higher incorporeal light."[5] So when we look today with delight at stained-glass windows in our churches, we have Dionysius the Areopagite to thank for them.

According to Arthur Versluis, "Dionysius the Areopagite stands as a central figure in the history of western esotericism," an assessment shared by Joscelyn Godwin, who calls him "the father of Christian esotericism."[6] Dionysius deserves this high standing for several reasons. One is that he laid the foundation for a Christian *gnosis* by providing a Christian equivalent to the intermediary spheres of being in the Neoplatonist ladder of reality, in other words, the whole realm of the angels. Through this synthesis, an invaluable part of the Neoplatonic cosmology was saved from oblivion as the pagan worldview shrank in the face of rising Christianity. If one no longer "journeyed through the planets" back to *Nous,* one could still contemplate the angelic hierarchies.

Another reason Dionysius is important is that he introduced a dichotomy that continues to run, not only through western esotericism, but through the West's spiritual heart. As with Plotinus (and Philo, Origen, and Ammonius Saccas), for Dionysius, the one God, the source of all being, is transcendent, utterly beyond human conception. Yet he is also in some inexplicable way available to us. The way of reaching God through the recognition of his transcendence is known as the *via negativa,* mentioned in the previous chapter. This is the way of "negative theology," the "emptying out" of all ideas, images, or preconceptions about God (or the One) in order to allow his "dark brilliance" to shine within oneself. On this path—which informed the great movement of Christian mysticism in the Middle Ages, specifically Meister Eckhart and the anonymous author of *The Cloud of Unknowing*—one aims to remove anything coming between oneself and the divine. One means of doing this is by way of negation, through expressing what God is *not.* (Hinduism has a similar approach to grasping the incomprehensible Brahma in its doctrine of "neti-neti," "not this, nor that."[7])

In a sense, this leads to a kind of spiritual "black hole," an emptiness which is really a fullness (Dionysius often uses paradox to try to convey his meaning). God in this sense is everything but also nothing, as he is beyond everything: he is literally "no thing." Like Zen koans, such paradoxical statements inhibit the logical mind, allowing for a sudden illumination. As Dionysius writes, "Through the inactivity of all his reasoning powers the mystic is united by his highest faculty to That which is wholly unknowable; thus by knowing nothing he knows That which is beyond knowledge."[8] This would not be out of place coming from one of Plotinus's *Enneads.*

Yet, paradoxically, Dionysius also articulated the opposite path, the *via positiva,* which proceeds through imagery, symbols, through positive statements about God's goodness, love, omniscience, and so on.[9] In this way, the formless, transcendent God is revealed to us. Poetic symbolism, which, to be sure, is not the same as "idolatry," does not define the divine; it alludes to it, points in its direction. It is not explicit, but seeks to embody the divine's implicit transcendent reality. A symbol is not the thing; *that* is idolatry. But it provides a *way* to the thing. It does not say, it shows. Images and symbols provide a means through which we can ascend the spiritual hierarchies, just as the Hermetists used images and symbols to make their "journey through the planets." This is because symbols and images can activate our latent powers of intuition, of the right-brain mode of consciousness, and it is precisely a change in consciousness that esotericism is after.

In a very real sense, the distinction between the *via negativa* and the *via positiva* is that between mysticism and esotericism. Where the mystic seeks direct union with the divine, eschewing any intermediary realms, the esotericist wants to know and explore these realms, and his means of doing so is through imagery and symbols—through, that is, imagination. Where the mystic desires union, the esotericist seeks knowledge—in other words, *gnosis*—and he reaches it through the imagination. Achieving *gnosis* through the use of disciplined spiritual imagination will become one of the fruits of the esoteric exodus out of Alexandria.

DARK AGES

Although composed in the last days of paganism, it was not until the ninth century, some three hundred years after he flourished, that Dionysius's writings would become available in the West. Before then, a tremendous upheaval took place. The great power of Rome, the greatest empire the world had yet seen, tottered and fell. It was the breakdown of a civilization, and it did not take place overnight. If Rome was not built in a day, it also took longer than that for it to fall. It was in decline for at least a century. Some historians, like Edward Gibbon, saw Christianity as greatly responsible for Rome's collapse. "I have described the triumph of barbarism and religion," Gibbon says at the end of *The Decline and Fall of the Roman Empire*. Other historians point out that there were many factors, and that no single one can be held solely accountable.

The empire had grown too large: by 285, it had already split into a western and eastern part, with Byzantium its eastern capital. It had become too corrupt: it depended too much on hired foreign armies, and had a history of mad, sadistic emperors. But one reason why Rome disintegrated must be because it was one of the most materialistic civilizations in history, fostering a culture of power, wealth, indulgence, and little else. It is clear that once the Christians came to power, they persecuted their rivals just as much as the Romans had persecuted them. But it is also clear that Christianity offered a view of life that in essence, if not always in practice, was more spiritual, more meaningful to the average person than what was available in the empire. It was a vision of a world transformed, and there was good reason why many embraced it. The world rejection that Christianity taught was arguably a valid response to the world in which it appeared, in which life was cheap and the individual dispensable, and charity and love in short supply. There was a felt sense that something had to change, that life was about something more serious than what most people saw around them—a not uncommon feeling in our own time—and for many, Christianity met that need. It is one of the tragedies of history that what began as an alternative to fire and the sword too soon descended into the very thing it came to overcome.

Whoever or whatever was responsible, by 476, when Romulus Augustulus, the last emperor of the western Roman empire, was deposed by Odoacer, the first king of Italy, ancient Rome was no more. In recent times historians have questioned the accuracy of the term "dark ages," yet the fall of Rome nevertheless ushered in an age of what we can call "endarkenment." Different barbarian hordes—Goths, Huns, Vandals—filled the power vacuum and hacked away at the corpse of the empire. It was a time when "violence, ignorance, and anarchy swept over Europe like a tide."[10] The learning that had characterized Athens and Alexandria was scattered on the winds. It was not a time when esoteric knowledge, or any other kind, could flourish, yet here and there, in small, inconspicuous ways, some of what remained was gathered and preserved. In 529, the same year that saw the end of the Platonic Academy, Benedict of Nursia, the "father of Christian monasticism in the West," founded the first Benedictine monastery in Monte Cassino, Italy.[11] So began "the most important religious order in western Christianity."[12]

There had been monastic Christian communities in the deserts of Egypt, and by this time, the Celtic church, independent of Rome, had also set up monastic communities in the British Isles.[13] Benedict imported the idea to a West ravaged by war, famine, and social collapse, and strove to create small, self-sufficient enclaves where the work of civilization could carry on. The dictum *ora et labora*, "pray and work," became the guiding spirit behind the Benedictine order, in which the disciplines of spirit and fruitful action were combined. Benedictine monks were devoted to God, but they also tilled the land. In a way, we can see the early monasteries as attempts to live "off the grid," to detach themselves from the turbulent macrocosm around them and achieve a harmony in a microcosmic way. As Rodney Collin writes in *The Theory of Celestial Influence*, in the monastery "all that was of value of the past was kept—Greek and Roman manuscripts copied, Byzantine symbology transferred to painted miniatures, secrets of music and medicine preserved, the '*opus dei*' or work of regeneration attempted."[14]

Whether or not "esoteric schools," as Collin suggests, were behind the movement, which quickly spread, the effect was the same. The monasteries acted as a kind of time capsule, in which the elements of a new flowering could be preserved amid the chaos and dangers of the outer world. Here the seeds of a new beginning could be kept safe and nurtured until the time was right for them to sprout. It is difficult for us to grasp exactly what it meant to live in this time.[15] In our age of almost instantaneous retrieval of the past, the idea that the past is not always available seems strange. Yet it was certainly true in the Dark Ages, and they were dark for precisely this reason. The "Great Memory," in William Anderson's term, on which new generations draw for inspiration, is not always available, and at this time it would be some centuries before what was left of the western mind could call on it again.[16]

Yet what was preserved was shared. Another important service the monasteries performed was the communication of ideas. Pilgrimages from monastery to monastery—a kind of spiritual tourism—helped spread knowledge from one center to another, and kept lines of communication open at a time when travel remained unsafe. The age this fractured fledgling Europe found itself in may not have been as dark as earlier accounts suggest, but it was certainly dim, and the light would not return to it for some time. And when it did, it came, as all dawns do, from the East.

FACING EAST

As different peoples in the West picked over what remained of the Roman Empire, another world civilization was coming to power: Islam. Readers familiar with Hermetic history may wonder why in writing of Alexandria, I made only a brief mention of alchemy. Although its roots lie in Egypt—indeed the word "alchemy" is thought by some to stem from the Arabic *al-kemi*, "out of Egypt"—alchemy as a practice and subject of study does not really appear in the West until the thirteen century, with figures like Albertus Magnus (Albert the Great, 1200–1280) and Thomas Aquinas (1225–1274).[17] Its heyday as a more spiritual, as opposed to a predominately practical, discipline concerned with the transmutation of metals is even later, following the Renaissance. (Other forms of alchemy also arose in China and India, roughly around the same time as it did in Egypt.[18]) Although in the popular mind, alchemy is still seen as at best a precursor to chemistry and at worst the fanciful pursuit of turning lead into gold, students of esoteric history know that at its heart it was—is—a spiritual discipline, aimed at the transformation of the self, a goal it shares with other esoteric practices. Alchemy was active in Alexandria and although the *Corpus Hermeticum* does not speak of it, in figures like Zosimus of Panopolis (fl. ca. 300 A.D.), called "the father of alchemy," we can see a blend of alchemical and Hermetic ideas and teachings, especially in his famous *Visions*.

Space does not allow me to go into detail about Zosimos and his Hermetic and Gnostic connections; readers can find more about this in *The Quest for Hermes Trismegistus*.[19] One thing I will mention is that the *Emerald Tablet of Hermes Trismegistus*, the most famous alchemical text of all, is not part of the *Corpus Hermeticum*. The alchemists themselves did not make much use of these Hermetic writings, although they did see Hermes Trismegistus as the patron saint of their work.[20] The earliest known version of the *Emerald Tablet* is found in the work of the great Arabic alchemist Jabir ibn Hayyan (721–815), known to the West as Geber, and dates from the ninth century. It is believed to be a translation from Syriac. As yet, no Greek original of the *Emerald Tablet*—the language in which the *Corpus Hermeticum* was written—has been found.

Alchemy spread from a fading Alexandria to a rising Arabic East when Amr ibn al'Aas, mentioned earlier, conquered the city in 639. Amr ibn al'Aas may not have appreciated the wealth of literature he had acquired by plundering the city—as his alleged burning of the library's collection suggests—but those around him did, and Arab scholars and philosophers soon demanded translations of the Greek and Latin texts that had fallen into their hands. Works on mathematics, medicine, philosophy, and other disciplines were speedily turned into Arabic, as were many alchemical texts. The first known Arab alchemist was Khalid ibn Yazid (660–704) of Damascus. He is said to have studied under a Byzantine monk named Morienus, who had himself studied under Stephanos (fl. 610–640), one of the last alchemists of Alexandria, who left the city in the end and headed to Byzantium. Khalid was an Umayyad prince, and Morienus agreed to tutor him in hopes of converting him to Christianity. Morienus apparently succeeded in transmuting some lead into gold, but his hopes of transmuting Khalid into a Christian soon faded when the prince, angry that his court alchemists could not match Morienus's skill, had them executed. Understandably, Morienus fled. Khalid's less reprehensible contribution to alchemy was to have many Greek alchemical texts translated into Arabic.

The most important Arab alchemist was, as mentioned, Jabir ibn Hayyan, who was born in Tus, Khorasan, in Iran. It is said that our word "gibberish" is rooted in Jabir's incomprehensible writings, but there is debate about this. He began his alchemical studies in Kufa (in present-day Iraq), where he is said to have studied with Ja'far al-Sadiq (700–765), a learned man who was known as the sixth Imam, a spiritual leader in succession from the Prophet Mohammed. Ja'far al-Sadiq was also a Sufi, a follower of the esoteric path in Islam. Jabir came to be known also as

"Al-Sufi," and like the Sufis, as well as like the ancient Egyptians, he believed that the true seat of human intelligence was not the brain, but the heart, an idea we have spoken of in connection with Schwaller de Lubicz. Like the Arab world in general, Sufism profited by the esoteric exodus from Alexandria, and it embraced the Neoplatonism and Hermetism that had made their way east. Like Neoplatonism and Hermetism, Sufism sought union with the divine, what it calls *tawhid*, or "unity of being," and it employed meditation, prayer, ritual, and most famously dance, to achieve this end. The order of the Mevlevi dervishes, founded in the thirteenth century by the Sufi mystical poet Rumi (1207–1273), with their hypnotic whirling, is the most recognizable image of the Sufis in the West.

The beginning of Sufism dates from the first two centuries following the founding of Islam in 622, rather as Gnosticism dates from the first two centuries following the founding of Christianity. It is said to get its name from the rough wool or *suf* garments its practitioners wore, to distinguish themselves from the fine apparel worn by the Islamic court. The Sufis were ascetic ecstatics devoted to the love of Allah, and they traced their lineage back to Ali, the Prophet's son-in-law, hence they are part of Shia Islam.

In Baghdad, Jabir came under the protection of the court of Harun al-Rashid (763–809), the famous caliph of *The Thousand and One Nights*. Here he practiced alchemy, but also pursued Aristotelian science; more than Plato, Aristotle became the Arabic philosopher of choice; outside of the esoteric community, Jabir is known today much more for his work in chemistry than for his alchemical contributions. Harun al-Rashid was a lover of learning and culture, and among many other cultural and scholarly projects, in 750 he established the "House of Wisdom" in Baghdad, a seat of learning that rivaled Alexandria and made Baghdad a center of knowledge, culture, and trade. This was the "Golden Age of Islam," a time when the Arabic world was the unchallenged hub of science and civilization. While Europe slumbered in its Dark Ages, the Arabic world was alight with enlightenment. Yet much of the light it enjoyed had its source in the esoteric teachings it had inherited from the West.

PAGANS AND THE PROPHET

As the source of his alchemical knowledge, Jabir cited the Greek and Egyptian gods, as well as Pythagoras, Hermes Trismegistus, and Agathodaimon, a figure who appears in the *Corpus Hermeticum* as one of Hermes' disciples.[21] While a triumphant Christianity sought to eliminate all trace of its pagan rivals, the Arabic world in which Neoplatonism, Gnosticism, and Hermetism found themselves seemed to welcome them with open arms, at least for a time. As the Greeks found important similarities between their god Hermes and the Egyptian Thoth, so the Arabs found that Hermes Trismegistus had much in common with their prophet Idris (whom they also associated with the biblical Enoch). When Alexandria became unsafe for pagan philosophy, many of its Neoplatonists and Hermetists left and made their way to the ancient city of Harran in northern Mesopotamia (now Anatolia in Turkey).

Harran is no more. It was founded in 2000 B.C. but in 1271 A.D. it was destroyed by Mongol invaders, and all that remains of it are ruins. But in its day it was an important trading hub—its name means "crossroads"—and it appears in the Bible as the place Abraham visited after leaving the city of Ur.[22] Harran is also the site of an ancient copper industry, but it was its ancient university that attracted many Alexandrian pagans fleeing Christian intolerance. With them they brought the eclectic wisdom that characterized Alexandria, teachings from the Magi, the Chaldeans, the Jews, the Greeks, even the Christians. Yet it was Hermes Trismegistus that made the strongest impact on the Harranians, who came to worship him as a great teacher and sage. Parts of the *Corpus Hermeticum* became a sacred text in Harran, and the ancient city became one of the last outposts of pagan thought. When Christians tried to convert the populace, most refused, which led to Harran being known as the "city of pagans." For Christians this became a mark against the Harranians, but their loyalty to Hermes Trismegistus served them well when dealing with their later Arab conquerors.

By the mid-seventh century, Syria and Mesopotamia came under Arab rule, and in 744 the Umayyad Caliph Marwan II moved his capital to

Harran. The capital was soon moved back to Baghdad, and in 830, while on campaign against the Byzantines, the Abbasid Caliph al-Ma'mūn passed through Harran. When he asked the people what their religion was, they answered, "We are Harranians." Not satisfied with this, he pressed them to be more specific. Were they Muslims, Christians, Jews, or Magians—all people protected by the Koran? The Harranians replied no. When al-Ma'mūn asked about their holy books and prophets, they were even less forthcoming. Al-Ma'mūn accused them of idolatry and informed them that if they had not converted to Islam or to some other belief sanctioned by the Koran by the time he returned, he would be forced to execute them.

Understandably some Harranians converted to Islam and some to Christianity. But the majority refused and remained pagans, yet they sought some way out of their dilemma. They consulted a Muslim jurist, who suggested that they call themselves Sabians, one of the religions sanctioned by the Koran, and who were known to worship the angels in the form of the seven ancient planets—a strong link to the Hermetists. For a sacred text they chose the *Corpus Hermeticum* and for their prophets they chose Hermes Trismegistus, whom, as mentioned, the Arabs associated with their prophet Idris, and Agathodaimon, whom the Arabs equated with Seth, a son of Adam. This protective coloring proved successful and the pagans of Harran were allowed to live. Thus Harran's Hermetists—now known as Sabians—were allowed to work and study undisturbed and Harran remained a haven for philosophy for some time.[23]

Perhaps the most famous of Harran's pagans was the Arabic scholar Thabit ibn Qurra (835–901). Thabit attended Harran's university, where he quickly established his brilliance. But following a schism among Harran's Hermetists, Thabit left Harran for Baghdad. Here Thabit became close to the caliph. He earned favor in the court and was invited to study at the House of Wisdom. Some of Thabit's fellow Harranians followed him, and together they formed an independent Hermetic school in Baghdad. They too took the name of Sabians, and hearing of this, many of Harran's Hermetists left Harran to join Thabit's pagan community. Here they formed a Neoplatonic academy, with the Hermetic books as their central texts.

Thabit wrote on a wide range of subjects: mathematics, logic, astronomy, medicine, astrology, magic, the "occult sciences"; it is unclear if he had an interest in alchemy, as no alchemical texts by him have come down to us. Thabit also made many translations from Greek to Arabic, and as a whole the Harranian Hermetists were known as excellent translators, a talent that was also observed in the mysterious Brethren of Purity, a community of Hermetic scholars in tenth-century Basra, that produced an encyclopedia of esoteric science, the *Rasā' il,* which proved important for Sufism. The Brethren of Purity were mysterious, in the sense that we know little about them; their dates are uncertain, as is their membership and their links to Sufism, Shiism, Ismailism, or to the Sabians of Harran. Their aim, however, was to integrate the teachings of the ancient philosophers with the Koran, and like many we have looked at, they recognized a primordial revelation of sacred knowledge from which Hermes Trismegistus, Pythagoras, Plato, as well as Abraham, Jesus, and Mohammed, drew.[24]

Thabit's core love was philosophy. Thabit and his followers saw themselves as "the heirs and propagators of Paganism," the philosophy of Plato and the Neoplatonists. For Thabit, it was pagans who "civilized the world and built cities," who "taught the hidden wisdom," and to whom "the Deity revealed itself." It was pagans who "discovered the art of healing the soul . . . and the body" and who "filled the earth with wisdom, which is the highest good." According to Thabit, "without paganism the world would be empty and miserable."[25]

Thabit wrote this celebration of pagan philosophy while living in Baghdad; this suggests that for a time at least, the Muslim world was tolerant of, and even open to, the influx of Hermetic and Neoplatonist ideas. To say that the deity—Allah—revealed itself to "philosophers"—a term of abuse for fundamentalist Muslims—was tantamount to heresy. But Thabit was able to say it without censure. This liberality of thought would continue for some time, and after Thabit's death, the work of his followers would carry on, contributing to Islam's Golden Age of learning. Yet by the middle of the eleventh century, the tide had turned and a new orthodoxy was establishing itself. Thabit had said that "happy is he who, for the sake of paganism, bears the burden of persecution with firm hope."[26] It would not be long before one of the Prophet's pagans would have an all too concrete opportunity to test the truth of this noble sentiment.

SUHRAWARDI, MARTYR AND ILLUMINIST

By the mid-eleventh century, the liberalism that allowed pagans like Thabit ibn Qurra to express their love of pagan philosophy without censure had faded and a new intolerant fundamentalism had settled into the Arab world. An orthodoxy once open to the influx of esoteric ideas and insights coming from a declining West had now closed ranks. Much as would happen with the Renaissance Hermeticists' attempts to leaven the *logos* of Christianity with Hermetic ideas, Arab religious thinkers decided that since with the Prophet and the Koran they had all that was necessary for salvation, there was no need to adulterate their pure teachings with Greek philosophy. The eclectic, syncretic, and synthesizing character of esotericism was anathema to those who believed they had the Truth at hand. And so paganism and the philosophies associated with it became heretical. No one felt the force of this conservatism more than the Persian theosopher, Neoplatonist, and Gnostic Suhrawardi (1155–1191), who was executed in Aleppo (present day Syria) on charges of heresy.

Our knowledge of Suhrawardi's life is minimal. He was born in Suhraward, a village located near the present-day towns of Zanjan and Bijar Garrus in northwest Iran. He studied Aristotle and the great Persian polymath Avicenna (980–1030) in nearby Maragheh with Majd al-Din Jaili, who was the teacher of the theologian and philosopher Fakhr ad-Din ar-Razi. He then went to Isfahan, where he studied logic with Zahir al-Farisi. After this, Suhrawardi seems to have spent some years on an "initiatory quest" or "journey for knowledge," an itinerary common to many of our secret teachers. He traveled through Anatolia, during which time he came into contact with many Sufi masters, among them Fakhr al-Din al-Mardini. Fakhr al-Din al-Mardini was an unusual Sufi, professing Aristotelian leanings along with more mystical ones, and this uncommon combination would have a lasting effect on Suhrawardi. Suhrawardi's early biographer, Shams al-Din Shahrazuri, relates that Suhrawardi became a Sufi, yet some accounts suggest that while he studied with and learned much from them, he never fully joined the Sufis. That he is rarely mentioned in histories of Sufism suggests he was more of a fellow traveler than true convert.[27] Yet the point seems merely academic. Sufi or not, Suhrawardi lived the Sufi life: he was an ascetic; had no interest in wealth, power, or rank; prayed incessantly; and loved *sama*, the Sufi music and dance. He was prone to solitary meditation, often kept a vow of silence, and frequently wore the *suf* garments that gave the Sufis their name. Yet he also seemed to move among the finely dressed courtiers of Anatolia, and one of his early works is dedicated to one of the minor rulers in this area.

One reason why Suhrawardi may have declined to take the final step to becoming a full Sufi is that he saw as his task the fruitful and necessary dialogue between philosophy and ecstatic surrender, between thought and mystical vision, a rare blend he first encountered in Fakhr al-Din al-Mardini. He recognized the importance of Aristotle—Avicenna had taught him that—yet he saw that the Greek sage's philosophy needed to be surpassed. Yet he also saw that the ecstatic love of the divine that Sufism pursued was itself not enough. His work was "addressed precisely to those who aspire at once to both mystical experience and philosophical knowledge," and he made clear that it should be transmitted only "to him who is worthy, chosen from among those who have given evidence of a solid knowledge of the peripaticians' philosophy, while their hearts are nevertheless captured by love for the divine Light."[28] Suhrawardi saw that what was needed was both the heart and the mind, the essence of esoteric work, or, as we might say, both sides of our cerebral hemispheres, whose creative union brings a true vision of reality. Thought or feeling alone did not suffice. What was needed was to root thought in the self-evident soil of inner spiritual experience.

Suhrawardi arrived in Aleppo in 1183; according to Shahrazuri, at his entry into the city he was dressed as a dervish. Salah ad-Din Yusuf ibn Ayyub (1138–1193), known to the West as Saladin, had conquered Aleppo that year, and he had made his son, al-Malik al-Zahir, temporary governor. Suhrawardi soon became close with the young governor and eventually became his tutor, but he also very quickly gained the enmity of the local jurists and *ulama,* or scholars of the Koran, for his skill in debate and dialectics. Although like them a Sunni Muslim—here, perhaps, is another reason for his reluctance to fully convert to Shia Sufism—Suhrawardi did not hesitate to point out where dogma had got the better of their thought. Had Suhrawardi lived a century or so earlier, this might not have caused him much grief. But in the climate of orthodoxy that reigned at the time, such forthrightness was costly. As mentioned earlier, the term "philosopher" is one of abuse for orthodox Muslims, suggesting a penchant for the "noise of words" the Gnostics had deplored, and it was becoming very clear that Suhrawardi belonged to their ilk.

It was during this time that Suhrawardi completed his major work, *Hikmat al-Ishraq* (*The Philosophy of Illumination*, 1186), also known as *Oriental Theosophy*, in which he attempted to revive the philosophy of ancient, pre-Islamic Persia, an esoteric metaphysics of Light that had much in common with the wisdom traditions of Alexandria, especially Neoplatonism.[29] As Suhrawardi wrote, "There was among the ancient Persians a community of people guided by God who thus walked the true way, worthy Sage-Philosophers . . . It is their precious philosophy of Light, the same as that to which the mystical experience of Plato and his predecessors bears witness, that we have revived in our book."[30] It was this same philosophy of light, transmitted by Dionysius the Areopagite, that would inspire the soaring, illuminated interiors of the Gothic cathedrals.

As Gemistos Plethon would some centuries later, Suhrawardi spoke of an initiatic chain, a school of ancient adepts, comprising Hermes Trismegistus, Zoroaster, Pythagoras, Plato, and Plotinus, as well as a series of Iranian-Islamic teachers. This mystical lineage, he argued, articulated the one true revelation, the *prisca theologia* and perennially illuminating philosophy, that it was his goal to resurrect. His aim was to revive "the ancient wisdom which has never ceased to be taken as a pivot by the Imams [Guides] of India, Persia, Chaldea, Egypt, as well as those of ancient Greece up to Plato, and from which they drew their own theosophy; this wisdom is the Eternal Leaven."[31]

Such objectives and beliefs, while essential to the esoteric history of western consciousness, did not go down well with Aleppo's orthodoxy. The jurists and *ulama* complained that Suhrawardi defended the "philosophers" too well, that his ideas were heretical, and that they would influence the young governor and mislead the people. They also accused Suhrawardi of claiming to be a prophet and of performing magic—both highly heretical acts. Suhrawardi denied these charges, but the accusations stuck and his protestations were ignored. As Socrates had centuries earlier, Suhrawardi found himself accused of corrupting the young. And just as Socrates' accusers did, those who saw Suhrawardi as a threat demanded he be put to death.

Letters from Aleppo's magistrate reached Saladin in Damascus, his capital, and they did not speak well of the "philosopher." Suhrawardi, the magistrate declared, was a threat to the public good and a heretic. These charges were brought against Suhrawardi by those he had bested in debate, and were fueled by envy of his influence, but by this time this barely mattered. Saladin saw the magistrate's point—he had no love for "philosophers" and most likely felt that one dead one was better that many angry mullahs—and ordered his son to execute his tutor. (Saladin, a conservative Sunni, may have felt that Suhrawardi's teachings were much too Shia; and Suhrawardi's belief in the fundamental unity of all religions— the essence of the perennial philosophy—might not have been too popular during the Crusades.)

Al-Malik al-Zahir at first declined to order the execution, but when pressured, he capitulated. Exactly how Suhrawardi was murdered is unclear. Some accounts say he was starved to death, denied food or drink. Some say he was strangled, others beheaded, and still others suggest a crucifixion.[32] However it was done, Suhrawardi was henceforth known as the Shaikh al-Maqtul, "the murdered Master," as well as the Shaikh al-Ishraq, "the Master of Illumination." Like Hypatia, Suhrawardi died for his philosophy.

THE IMAGINAL WORLD

In recent times, Suhrawardi's philosophy has gained a new following through the work of the French philosopher and historian of religion Henry Corbin (1903–1978), one of the great esoteric scholars of the twentieth century and a central figure in what we can call a modern "esoteric academy," the Eranos Conferences held in Switzerland from the 1930s on. Through Corbin's works—*The Man of Light in Iranian Sufism, Cyclical Time and Ismaili Gnosis*, and *The Voyage and the Messenger* among others—the modern reader is introduced to an idea that runs throughout esoteric thought but is articulated in Corbin's "spiritual hermeneutics" in perhaps its clearest and most eloquent expression. This is the notion of the *'âlam al-mithâl*, or, as Corbin calls it, the *Mundus Imaginalis,* or Imaginal World. This, Corbin writes, is a "very precise order of reality, which corresponds to a precise mode of perception," which, for Suhrawardi, is based on a "visionary spiritual experience" that the Shaikh al-Ishraq considered "as fully relevant as the observations of Hipparchus or Ptolemy are considered to be relevant for astronomy."[33]

What this means is that the world of visions that informs Suhrawardi's philosophy is perceived through the organs, not of the senses, but of the *imagination*—we can call them "organs of inner vision"—and what they perceive in this realm is as real as what astronomers see when they observe the stars. That is, the Imaginal World, though located (metaphorically) within our own our psyches (and where are *they* located, precisely?) and hence to that extent "subjective," is in reality as "objective" as the outer world known to our senses. Earlier I spoke of Dionysius the Areopagite's notion of the *via positiva,* the approach to the spiritual by way of images and symbols, that is, through the imagination. It is through Suhrawardi's *'âlam al-mithâl,* Corbin's Imaginal World, that one passes when taking that route.

Corbin coined the term "Imaginal" for this realm of being which occupies the same place in Suhrawardi's ontology as the intermediary realm of the Neoplatonist's *Anima mundi,* the Hermetic "journey through the planets," and Dionysius's angelic hierarchy. This was necessary in order to differentiate it from our term "imaginary." Brought up on "realist," utilitarian notions of reality (that is, left-brain notions), we think of the imagination as either a poor substitute for actuality—as when we "imagine" what we did last summer—or flights of fancy ("that's just your imagination"). We may accept a more valued appreciation of it when we realize that it is imagination that fuels great works of art and informs all breakthroughs in science. Yet the idea that the imagination constitutes an *entire world of its own,* just as objective as our sensory world, with its own laws, geography, history, and, most difficult to accept, inhabitants, is, for most of us, too much to swallow. Yet this is precisely what Suhrawardi and all the other secret teachers tell us.

The "Imaginal" is the world that lies between the purely intelligible—that is, conceptual—world of Plato's Forms (the Intellect in Plotinus's philosophy) and the purely material world of the senses.[34] It is, as Corbin writes, "ontologically as real as the world of the senses and that of the intellect."[35] It partakes of and informs both in the sense that in it, the pure abstract Ideas are clothed in *symbols,* and the brute objects of the physical world can become imbued with symbolic significance. We enter it every night when we dream, and some intrepid explorers have entered it while fully conscious. To jump ahead somewhat: C. G. Jung's "descent into the unconscious," Swedenborg's journeys to heaven and hell, Rudolf Steiner's "readings" of the "Akashic record," to name perhaps the most well-known modern journeys into the interior, all took place within the *Mundus Imaginalis.* While there, each of these "mental travelers"—in the secret teacher William Blake's phrase—discovered, as Aldous Huxley did following his own voyages into these inner realms, that the mind "still has its darkest Africas, its unmapped Borneos and Amazonian basins" and that "the creatures inhabiting these remoter regions of the mind are exceedingly improbable." As all our secret teachers did, Huxley recognized that at "the antipodes of everyday consciousness" (we could say, left-brain consciousness), we find "the world of Visionary Experience."[36] It was that world that Suhrawardi sought to explore.

THE INNER VOYAGE

Suhrawardi wanted to anchor his philosophy in his immediate experience, his *gnosis.* And so like the Hermetists and Gnostics, he undertook the inner voyage.[37] His destination was *Nâ-Kojâ-Abâd,* "the country of no-where."[38] This did not mean a place that did not exist. It meant an *interior* place, an inner location that could not be found in any external "where" or on any map—that is, any physical terrain. In Suhrawardi's "hierarchy of light," our physical world occupies the same position as it does in the Hermetic ladder of planets and the Neoplatonist chain of descending emanations. We experience it as an "outside," "external" world because we are far removed from its source, which, paradoxically, is within ourselves. For Suhrawardi, creation is an overflow, a radiance, from an original Supreme Light of Lights. This is a pure, immaterial light, as is the spiritual light of Neoplatonism. Radiations emerge from this Supreme Light in a descending scale, giving rise to what Suhrawardi calls "horizontal light," which serves the same function as the Platonic Forms. In a sense we can say that, according to Suhrawardi, our physical world is made of "hardened" or "dense" light, something that used to be science fiction but which seems to becoming science fact.[39]

Borrowing from Zoroastrianism, Suhrawardi sees this "ladder of light" as an angelic hierarchy, in which each angel *is* the different level of reality or state of consciousness (the two are the same). And as with the Gnostics and the Hermetists, it is the theosopher's desire to ascend this angelic ladder and return to his source. As we have seen with other inner voyagers, the first step in this journey is to detach oneself from the body, from worldly matters and concerns. By doing this, one is ready for the voyage within, remembering, in a slight paraphrase of Corbin, that the metamorphosis of the knowing subject is the real voyage for the gnostic philosopher.[40]

Rather than present his accounts of inner voyaging in abstract, conceptual terms as Plotinus did, Suhrawardi gives us a series of visionary tales, spiritual stories in which the narrative, characters, and setting symbolize the spiritual realities the inner voyager encounters, much as we know dreams do. As Suhrawardi wants to present an Imaginal World, one of images, he can't do otherwise. Yet in our dreams we are still subject to the influences of the sleeping body; what Suhrawardi has in mind can be seen as a kind of "conscious dreaming," dreaming while wide awake, perhaps more awake than in our normal waking state. Although the stories differ in detail, in essence they share the same structure. Freeing his consciousness from the concerns of the body and entering a meditation, the voyager finds himself in the presence of a supernatural being, much as Hermes Trismegistus does at the beginning of the *Poimandres*. The being asks the voyager, who is generally known as "the stranger," who he is and where he comes from. The stranger replies that he is a traveler who aspires to return home, to his true homeland beyond the world of the senses. This journey will take him beyond Mount Qâf, the "cosmic mountain," which is made up of the celestial spheres he must surmount, much as the Hermetists did. There, beyond Mount Qâf, the stranger will find his true, higher self, and he will approach the "spiritual city," Hūrqalyā, which starts at the "convex surface" of the "Ninth Sphere, or Sphere of Spheres" which encompasses the whole cosmos.

When he steps beyond this sphere, something remarkable and, for most modern minds, incomprehensible happens. The entire outer world is seen to be contained *within* the inner one. Paradoxically, by going inward, we find ourselves *outside* the "outer world." As Corbin puts it, "once the journey is completed, the reality which has hitherto been an inner and hidden one turns out to envelop, surround or contain that which at first was outer and visible."[41]

In *The Caretakers of the Cosmos*, I speak of our "inside out" condition, expressed in the aphorism of the "unknown philosopher" Louis Claude de Saint-Martin that "It is necessary to explain things by man and not man by things," meaning that we are wrong to try to explain man by the world, when the world should be explained in terms of man.[42] The same can be said for our consciousness. We generally think of ourselves as "contained" within the world—the cosmos—and of our consciousness as contained within our head, or brain. But beyond Mount Qâf, beyond, that is, the top of the ladder of light, the opposite appears to be true: the cosmos is contained within our consciousness, which is itself not limited to some metaphorical space within my skull, but is the space in which all "spaces" can exist. We see that the hitherto outer world has become a symbol of the inner one, and that a correspondence exists between all the different levels or worlds and the states of consciousness associated with them.

TRUE IMAGINATION

Our first reaction to this may be "That's fine, but how do you know this isn't just your imagination, in our usual sense of the word? How do you know it isn't a fantasy?" The inner voyager has to ask himself this too, and learn the difference between the *imaginatio vera*, the "true imagination," and sheer subjective fancy. True imagination has a cognitive, noetic value;

it is an organ of *knowledge*. We learn from it and can come away from our inner voyaging with some practical, effective understanding, and not merely the pleasure of having been on a "trip." As the poet and Blake scholar Kathleen Raine says, there is a "learning of the imagination," and like anything worth knowing, its lessons demand hard work and concentration. True imagination is not sheer whimsy or arbitrary novelty; it works within a canon of symbols, images, and metaphors, a tradition that is manifest in its expressions. While our modern positive notion of imagination looks to it for the "new" and "original"—which often amounts to the subjective and "shocking"—the Imaginal tradition finds the original in what is close to the origin, to the primal, the archetypal, and which appears in different but resonant symbols in the different esoteric teachings.

These symbols have a definite relation to each other, much as the grammar and syntax of any language do, and the traveler in the Imaginal must learn to read them as he must read any language. This requires not "free association" or "blue sky thinking," but a "new discipline of the imagination," an "active imagination," a controlled inner seeing, not a parade of random thoughts.[43] In this sense, the imagination is an instrument one must learn to use properly, just as a scientist must learn to use his microscope. In effect the inner voyager must learn how to discriminate between the objective landscapes and figures he encounters and his or her own subjective imagery, just as we learn how to discriminate between good art and bad. If we recognize the difference between a focused imagination, intent on its object, and the diffuse wanderings of daydreams and gratification fantasies, we are halfway there.

TREES OF LIFE

The need for a disciplined imagination is a central part of another visionary tradition, whose codified form began to emerge first in France and then in Spain in the twelfth and thirteenth centuries. In Chapter Three, I spoke of the Jewish mystical tradition of Merkabah, the "throne mysticism" based on Ezekiel's vision of a flaming chariot. The practice of visualizing Ezekiel's chariot in order to ascend with it to the divine—much as the Hermetists ascended through the planets to *Nous*—was part of the Jewish Heichalot, or "divine palace" mystical tradition of the first centuries A.D. This continued as an active tradition, embracing fasting, prayer, meditation, and incantation, until the emergence of Kabbalah in its modern form.

Kabbalah, which means "receiving," had in some form or another always been part of the mystical side of Judaism. It signifies a vast, complex, and sometimes confusing amalgam of esoteric, meditative, and magical lore. It is not one specific teaching—there is no central "book of Kabbalah"—but a general "umbrella term" covering a wide-ranging tradition, including theosophy—the wisdom of God—ecstatic meditative states, and magical and esoteric practices focused on the hidden power of words. Letters and words have a significance and status in Kabbalah quite unlike that in other esoteric traditions—understandably, given Judaism's proscriptions on imagery. It is said that to speak the name of God correctly—known by the Greek term "Tetragrammaton," which, oddly enough, means "four-letter word"—is to destroy the universe. Hence the true pronunciation of YHVH remains secret, while it is the word "EMETH," or "Truth," written on the Golem's forehead, which brings it to life in the old legends; rubbing out the "E," which leaves "METH," or "death," destroys it. While the ecstatic and magical aspects of Kabbalah are important and remain popular today, it is its theosophical or esoteric character, in the sense of *gnosis* or knowledge, that is its real heart. Much as Stephen Hawking does in our time, Kabbalists want to know the mind of God.

Depending on your source, Kabbalah has its origins in Adam, Abraham, or Moses, each of whom, legend has it, received a divine revelation. But one likely and more historical beginning for Kabbalah as we know it may be in the interpretation of the Talmud developed in the Jewish academies that flourished from the sixth to tenth centuries A.D. Like the other primal revelations we've discussed, Kabbalah shares in the perennial philosophy and *prisca theologia*, and in essence it is the esoteric reading of the Torah, a way of understanding God's plan in creation and our place in it. For most of its history, it was an oral tradition, passed down through the generations, and protected and kept hidden from unworthy hands. But by late antiquity it had begun to take on the written form in which it is popularly known today. Although mainstream Judaism considers it nonsense, Kabbalah's ecstatic side has a vital life in the Hassidic tradition, which began in the eighteenth century, and since the 1970s, Kabbalah has been one of the staples of New Age and "mind, body, spirit" literature. One of the earliest texts in Kabbalah is the *Sefer Yetzirah*, or *Book of Creation*, which was most likely composed sometime before the sixth century A.D. Legend ascribes it to the first-century Rabbi Akiva, who was martyred by the Romans, but it was most likely written later than this.

In the *Sefer Yetzirah*, creation is understood as the result of ten emanations or *sephiroth* (translated as "numbers" or "vessels"), containers of the creative energies emerging from the unmanifest and incomprehensible Godhead, which is known as the *En-Sof*, or "limitless light."[44] As with many of our secret teachings, this invisible source is beyond anything we can comprehend. Yet we are not completely cut off from it, and Kabbalah has its own rationale for bridging the gap between the *via negativa* and *via positiva*. Although as in Islam, Judaism forbids any representations of the divine in order to avoid idolatry, in the Kabbalistic tradition, the *via positiva* is condoned as long as the practitioner knows that the imagery and symbols he employs are a means to the divine, and not ends in themselves. So while it is understood that God is ultimately beyond any of our conceptions, the Kabbalist nevertheless meditates on God's countenance, visualizing the "hairs of his head," his "cranium," the "nostrils of the ancient," his "ears, hands, feet," and other parts of the metaphorical anatomy of the divine. The *Shi'ur Qomah*, for example, a Midrashic text of the Heichalot tradition, provides the precise measurements of God's macrocosmic body. As one commentator remarks, "for the Kabbalist, it was acceptable to portray God's attributes in physical terms, on the understanding that it was an appropriate understanding of something that was beyond all corporeal expression."[45] As in other esoteric traditions, one aim of Kabbalah is to discipline the *nephesch*, or "animal soul," so that it can make way for the *neschamah*, or "higher soul."

Between the unmanifest source of creation and our own world there stands what is known as the *Otz Chiim*, or Tree of Life, a diagram of the heavenly *sephiroth* whose elegant simplicity belies the complex reality it symbolizes. The Tree of Life is another version of the ontological ladder we have seen with the Neoplatonists, the Hermetists, and the Gnostics, and while it shares with them the archetypal theme of a kind of "stairway to heaven," which the Kabbalist climbs in order to know God, the breadth of its application can be stunning. As one esoteric scholar remarks, "the Tree of Emanation is an almost infinitely complex constellation of symbols . . . a glyph for the whole of existence that bears within it countless interrelated glyphs."[46] If for the Hermetist "that which is above is like that which is below," the Kabbalist takes this same formula of "correspondence" and applies it tenfold.

The ten *sephiroth* run from *Kether*, which is called "the Crown," the first emanation from the Godhead, to *Malkuth*, "the Kingdom," which is the physical world. In between are *Chokmah*, "Wisdom"; *Binah*, "Understanding"; *Chesed*, "Mercy"; *Geburah*, "Severity"; *Tiphereth*, "Beauty"; *Netsach*, "Victory"; *Hod*, "Glory"; and *Yesod*, "Foundation."[47] Connecting the ten *sephiroth* are twenty-two "paths" that correspond to the twenty-two letters of the Hebrew alphabet, which, for Kabbalists, has esoteric significance. Much as Pythagoras believed that numbers lay at the foundation of things, the Kabbalists believed that the Hebrew alphabet did.

From its beginning in the Godhead to its end in our physical universe, creation passes through four levels, or "worlds," which correspond to the four levels of scriptural interpretation, from the literal to the anagogic. Kabbalists intent on understanding the secret meaning of creation meditate on the different "paths" between the *sephiroth*, while visualizing different combinations and permutations of letters, numbers, and geometric forms. Entering the Imaginal World, they find the landscapes and beings appropriate to their understanding, their encounters corroborated by the symbolic necessities of the journey. Each of the creative energies contained in the *sephiroth* permeates the universe and enters into combinations with each other. And just as the Neoplatonic theurgists employed symbols and performed "mysterious acts" to attract the divine powers, the Kabbalist knows what symbols, names, or numbers "correspond" to the heavenly energies he wishes to understand. If an esoteric understanding of the world is based on analogy—on the right-brain perception of the "network of connections linking everything with everything else"—then the Tree of Life is the most complex and systematic representation we have of this.

The *Sefer ha-Zohar*, or *Book of Splendor*, another central Kabbalist text, is a voluminous, complex, and often meandering mystical interpretation of the Torah. It appeared in Guadalajara, Spain, in 1286 and was said by its "discoverer," Moses de León (1250–1305), to be an ancient work passed down through the ages, written by the second-century wonderworking Rabbi Shimon bar Yohai, a student of Rabbi Akiva. Most modern scholars believe it was written by León himself. Its five volumes comprise many different aspects of the tradition, including magical spells, and like Suhrawardi, it includes stories and tales, most featuring Rabbi Yohai and his ten companions.

Another important work, the *Bahir* or *Book of Illumination*, appeared in France in the eleventh century. It is a fragmentary work, attributed to the first-century Jewish sage Nehunya Ben HaKanah, but its true authorship is unknown; its jumbled character suggests that more than one hand was involved in its conception. Its gnomic paragraphs speak of the mystical significance of the shape of Hebrew letters, as well as the sacred names in magic, and describe, in a Neoplatonic fashion, the emergence of the subsequent *sephiroth* out of the first emanation of the divine, *Kether*, "the Crown." Some scholars of Kabbalah, such as Gershom Scholem, suggest a pronounced Gnostic influence on the *Bahir*.

Although for most of its existence Kabbalah remained strictly within a Jewish milieu, in the Renaissance it was linked with the Hermetic and Platonic traditions. With these, it formed what became known as "Christian Kabbalah," the most fiery proponent of which was Pico della Mirandola, whom we will meet further on. One of the heretical nine hundred theses that Pico was called on to defend before a panel of learned theologians in Rome was "There is no science which gives us more assurance of Christ's divinity than magic and the Kabbalah." It is understandable that the panel disagreed and that this, along with most of Pico's other theses, were condemned. Pico's Christian-Platonic-Hermetic variant on the ancient Jewish tradition informed the Kabbalistic magic associated with nineteenth-century occult figures like Eliphas Levi and groups like the Hermetic Order of the Golden Dawn, and continues to inform popular occultism today, although scholars of the Jewish mystical tradition like Gershom Scholem have worked to purge Kabbalah of its popular occult character and return it to its roots.[48]

THE MIDDLE PILLAR

In looking at the western esoteric tradition through the lens of the integration of our two modes of consciousness, one is unavoidably drawn to the tripartite arrangement of the Tree of Life, its three "pillars." In between the pillar of Mercy—made of *Chokmah, Chesed,* and *Netzach*—and the pillar of Severity—*Binah, Geburah, Hod*—stands the "middle pillar" of "harmony" or "balance," *Kether, Tiphereth, Yesod,* and *Malkuth.* We can say that in Kabbalah, the middle pillar symbolizes the transcendent function, the dynamic integration of the opposites, a kind of mystical "Goldilocks" state, in which the balance between the two extremes is achieved and an esoteric condition of being "just right" is reached. *Tiphereth,* "Beauty," is located at the center of the Tree of Life, and is the *sephira* with the most links to the other *sephiroth.* It is also the midpoint between *Kether* and *Malkuth,* between, that is, the first emanation from the unmanifest *En-Sof* and ourselves.

In Kabbalah, the first three *sephiroth* are known as "the Supernals." Although not quite so unmanifest as the *En-Sof,* the Supernals are still far beyond human comprehension, and they exist in a realm that lies on the other side of what is known as "the Abyss."[49] Although the Godhead is always in their sights—metaphorically, at least—we can say that for most Kabbalists, *Tiphereth* is the bull's-eye. This suggests that this central *sephiroth* and its middle pillar symbolize the union of our two modes of consciousness with which this book is concerned, the pillar of Severity encompassing "hard," left-brain thinking, and the pillar of Mercy housing the "softer" mode of the right.

THE RETURN OF NATURE AND
THE RISE OF THE GOTHIC

In 824, Emperor Louis the Pious, son of Charlemagne, asked the Byzantine emperor Michael the Stammerer for the loan of a book. It was the Greek text of Dionysius the Areopagite's *The Celestial Hierarchy.* As Louis could not read Greek, he sent the manuscript to the monastery of St. Denis, located north of Paris. Here, in 636, the relics of St. Denis, the patron saint of France, were interred in the basilica, and from the tenth to the eighteenth century, it was in St. Denis that most of the kings of France found their final resting place. The monks at St. Denis, one of whom was Louis's cousin, tried to translate the manuscript into Latin, but as their Greek was not much better than Louis's, the result was less than satisfactory.

Some years later, in 845, John Scotus Eriugena (815–877), an Irish monk and theologian, accepted an invitation to come to France, to teach in the Palace School founded by Charlemagne. While there, he agreed to translate the manuscript; as he was one of the few at that time who could read Greek properly—his training as an Irish monk saw to that—this was fortunate. He finished the translation by 862, and thus, as we've seen, introduced to the endarkened West the light of Neoplatonism, seen through the acceptable gauze of Dionysius's Christian ontology. Not since St. Augustine had Platonic ideas made such inroads into Christianity.

Eriugena—the name means "born in Ireland"—translated more of Dionysius's work and he also wrote books of his own, the most famous being *Periphyseon* (later titled *De divisione Naturae, On the Divisions of Nature*). His philosophy combined his own interpretation of Dionysius with the beliefs of Gregory of Nyssa (335–395) and Maximus the Confessor (580–662), theologians of the eastern Orthodox church who were influenced by Neoplatonism. Eriugena's central vision is the Neoplatonic one of a transcendent God from whom all things flow hierarchically and to whom all things return. For Eriugena, the divine emerges "from itself" and returns "into itself," and like Origen, another Platonic Christian, Eriugena was a believer in *apocatastasis,* the doctrine that ultimately all beings will be saved and will share in the return of the original paradise. As with Origen, this belief led to trouble with the church.

Like Dionysius, Eriugena emphasizes the "wholly other" character of God, and his work is in the school of "negative theology." Yet Eriugena's vision included the natural world, which had been ignored—demonized even—by the church as the province of paganism and the devil. Eriugena thought otherwise. He spoke of nature's "manifest theophanies"—how

God appeared through it—and saw its beauty as evidence that the God-head manifested both in negation, the *via negativa,* and in the celebration of the whole cosmos, the *via positiva.* For Eriugena, the divine flows from formlessness into infinite forms, a Neoplatonic version of the Hermetic formula of "the One, the All." If for most of the Middle Ages "the medieval mind perceived the physical world as symbolic to its core," with Eriugena it began to appreciate the natural world for its own sake.[50]

This renewed concern with nature also manifested in the twelfth-century School of Chartres, a center for Platonism in northern France, and at the time the most important institution of learning in western Europe. Its members read Eriugena, Dionysius, the Neoplatonists, and whatever Plato they could find. In his *Cosmographia,* Bernardus Silvestris (1085?–1178?), one of the philosophers of Chartres, outlined a Neoplatonic cosmology delineating the hierarchical structure of the cosmos. In his scheme, the highest spirits dwell near the Godhead in the "Eighth Sphere"; the angels are associated with the planets; and the divine hierarchy reaches down to the "sublunary discarnate beings," before beginning its ascent.[51] Although the church had tried to expunge Plato from its worldview, the Greek sage seemed to be making a comeback; in 1147, Pope Eugene III even commended Silvestris's *Cosmographia,* a sign that the injunction against pagan philosophy was weakening.[52]

Eriugena's reading of Dionysius emphasized the Neoplatonic centrality of light; in the School of Chartres, the focus was on what we can call "sacred geometry." Of the few works of Plato available to the Chartres philosophers, one was a partial Latin translation of the *Timaeus,* in which Plato provides a myth of the creation. Timaeus himself, who does most of the talking, was a Pythagorean, and not surprisingly he voices the belief that number and geometry are at the root of existence. The philosophers at Chartres were impressed with this; it seemed to lead to a rational understanding of Genesis, and they began to think of God as a mathematician. In the natural forms around them they could see sacred geometry at work—we saw some examples of this in Chapter One where I speak of the Golden Section—and in their manuscripts they began to picture the Creator with a compass. The idea that number, harmony, and proportion—

all fundamental Pythagorean concerns—were at the heart of all creation took hold. When these met Dionysius's celebration of light, the ingredients for the Gothic were in place.

THE AESTHETIC ABBOT

The man responsible for putting them together was Abbot Suger (1081–1151). Little is known of his early life. He was born into a humble family and at the age of ten began his education at the Abbey of St. Denis. During this time he met the future king Louis VI of France, with whom he became friends; he would also later befriend Louis VII. By 1109, Suger had become secretary to the abbot of St. Denis. Suger was a responsible, capable man who earned the respect of those around him. Louis VI used Suger as an envoy on many missions, some to Rome, and on his return from a mission to Pope Gelasius II, who reigned for a year in Montpellier, in 1122 Suger was made abbot of St. Denis.

Suger had long wanted to remodel the abbey church. He was an aesthete and a patron of the arts, a man who, like Eriugena, saw the "manifest theophanies" of nature, and also those in the works of man. He loved precious stones, gold, and stained glass, and collected many pieces of fine craftsmanship. He was also a reader of Dionysius. In 1137, Suger decided to get to work.

One of his aims in reconstructing the church was to have it be filled with light, which, following Eriugena and Dionysius, Suger believed was the closest thing on earth to the divine. God may dwell in an impenetrable holy darkness, but when he manifests, he first appears as radiant light. One result of Suger's light philosophy was the huge rose window above the west portal at St. Denis, the first of its kind. The rose window would soon become a signature of the Gothic and serve as a kind of Christian mandala, harmonizing the twelve apostles around the figure of Jesus or his mother, while allowing the divine effulgence to illuminate the cathedral's interior. Another result was the high stained-glass windows that we associate with the Gothic. In order to accommodate these, which demanded thinner walls than those of Romanesque churches, many new architectural features were required: the pointed arch, the ribbed vault, and the flying buttress, as well as techniques in producing stained glass which modern methods have been unable to duplicate. Suger wanted to create a semblance of heaven on earth, and the effect these cavernous illuminated interiors had on people used to the sturdy and stolid Romanesque churches must have been astonishing. With the later additions of the soaring spires, Gothic masterpieces like Chartres seemed to embody in stone and colored glass the hierarchical cosmos of the Neoplatonists. They acted as a kind of spiritual rocket ship, sending its congregation shooting to the heavens, as well as a mystical lightning conductor, drawing down to Earth the divine energies, much as the Neoplatonic theurgists drew down the power of the gods.

The interiors, designed according to sacred geometry, formed a space unlike that of the everyday, and must have produced a sense that by stepping *inside*, one was entering a much larger world.[53] And when some of the earliest harmonized music, in the transition from plainsong to polyphony, was performed in places like Notre Dame de Paris, the otherworldly effect must have been transformative.[54] The harmonies of sound and space must have given the congregation a sense of Pythagoras's music of the spheres.

THE MYSTERY OF THE CATHEDRALS

The rise of the Gothic took place between 1150 and 1220, a brief period which saw a transformation of western consciousness, only some aspects of which I can touch on here. It occurred during what has been dubbed the "twelfth-century Renaissance." It was a remarkable burst of creativity and imagination the aim of which was, according to some commentators, to embody a new image of mankind, to harmonize disparate elements in the medieval consciousness, and to present a "symbolic realization of universal humanity."[55] One reflection of this was the more human, personal character of the figures represented within the cathedrals' walls, compared to those of Romanesque churches, which, for all their power, were rough-hewn and abstract. Just as the aim of Christianity was to perfect man, so too the Gothic images of Christ would present his humanity more perfectly. This required greater artistry, and more than one Gothic craftsman could echo the goldsmith and lay brother Hughes de Dorgnies's remark, "Let others sing Christ with their mouths; Hughes sings with his goldsmith's work," a pre-echo of Blake's belief that we worship God best through works of the imagination. This is an example of what William Anderson calls "Gothic joy," a renewed appreciation of beauty.[56]

We do not know the names of the masons who built these marvels, which deserve our awe and wonder as much as the Sphinx and pyramids do. Even on a sheer technical scale this is true: according to Jean Gimpel in *The Medieval Machine,* in France from the eleventh to the late thirteenth centuries, more stone was quarried than in the whole history of ancient Egypt.[57] Those responsible for building the Gothic cathedrals were truly secret teachers, and what they had to teach us still remains a mystery. Much has been written about the symbols, images, and designs that decorate the Gothic cathedrals. Some, like the mysterious alchemist Fulcanelli—his real identity has never been disclosed—declare that they speak of alchemical and esoteric knowledge in a secret language, what Fulcanelli called *argotique,* a kind of esoteric slang.[58] In *Le Mystère des Cathédrales,* Fulcanelli claims that the term "gothic" originates not with the Goths, but with the French word *argot,* which Fulcanelli defines as "a language peculiar to all individuals who wish to communicate their thoughts without being understood by outsiders."[59] Fulcanelli calls this a "spoken cabala," the "green language" in which he claims "all the Initiates expressed themselves."

If nothing else, this does seem to fit the esoteric character of revealing by concealing, of keeping sacred secrets safe from profane hands. Others, like P. D. Ouspensky, believed the Gothic cathedrals were the work of hidden esoteric schools that used the church as "an instrument for the preservation and propagation of the ideas of *true Christianity,*" of "true religion or true knowledge" during the "superstitious, bigoted and scholastic Middle Ages."[60] Ouspensky and Fulcanelli may be right, and anyone who has visited Chartres, Notre Dame, or any other of the great Gothic cathedrals can be excused for believing that some deep, interior, and not wholly conscious work is taking place as one gazes at their strangely moving symbols and images. More than one student of the Gothic has noted that along with the Christian and Platonic iconography—a figure of Pythagoras, for example, sits over the west portal at Chartres—symbols and decorations linked to an earlier pagan past also appear.

As William Anderson has pointed out, chevrons, spirals, and lozenges—all patterns associated with the Great Goddess of the Neolithic period—form decorations on many Romanesque churches, which also incorporate the image of the Sheila-na-gig, a female figure revealing exaggerated genitals. Debate continues over the meaning of these figures, but there is a strong argument that they represent some continuation of a pre-Christian fertility religion. Many Christian churches dedicated to the Virgin were built over ancient pagan sites dedicated to goddesses such as Venus, Diana, Cybele, and Isis. A common feature of many of these churches is that they possess statues of the Black Virgin, which are believed to have miraculous powers. Chartres had one, until it was destroyed by anti-Christian sansculottes during the French Revolution. And in the center of the rose window of Chartres's north transept, Mary, Jesus's mother, surrounded by radiating lozenges, has a black face.

Why these Virgins should be black remains a mystery.[61] As we saw in Chapter Three, the original cult statue of the goddess Cybele had a black meteorite in place of its face. The earliest known images of a mother holding a child on her lap, as representations of Mary and the baby Jesus are often presented, are of Isis suckling her infant son, Horus, and an ancient name for Egypt was, as we've seen, "*khem*," which is supposed to refer to the black alluvial soil of the Nile. Does the Black Virgin look back to early forms of the sacred feminine?

One characteristic of early Christianity—if not throughout its whole history—is the emphasis on the masculine side of the divinity at the expense of the feminine. (If Leonard Shlain is right, the feminine has had a hard time of it during the entire reign of the left brain.) It is no secret that practically all of the Gothic cathedrals were dedicated to Our Lady, Notre Dame. We know that the Gnostics had more appreciation of the feminine than did the Christians who became the official church, and that part of their mythology concerned the search for the goddess Sophia (Wisdom) and her release from bondage. We also know that Sophia was a central character of the Solomonic books of the Old Testament. The

Royal Portal of Chartres, the three doors that open into the cathedral in the west front, are surrounded by carvings depicting the works of knowledge, science, and art (it is there that we find Pythagoras). Surmounting these is a statue of the Virgin, seated on the throne of wisdom, from which she gives her blessing and guidance.

Given that the School of Chartres was for a time "the most important civilizing force in Europe," as well as "the greatest shrine of the Virgin in western Europe," one can't help but ask why the two are associated.[62] Was this an attempt to bring the feminine—which, all concerns about the simplistic character of the idea noted, we can associate with a right-brain mode of being—back into a masculine, left-brain dominated worldview? The official attitude of the church toward the feminine can be gleaned from these remarks by Bernard of Cluny, a twelfth-century Benedictine monk. "Woman," according to Bernard, was "sordid, perfidious, fallen." She "besmirches purity, meditates impiety, corrupts life . . . woman is a wild beast, her crimes are like the sand . . . woman is a guilty thing, a hopelessly fleshy thing, nothing but flesh . . . all guile she is, fickle and impious, a vessel of filth, an unprofitable vessel."[63] With such an assessment of the feminine coming from the author of *De Contemptu Mundi* (*On Contempt of the World*), woman's long association with nature could not have helped her case. It is also clear that such a negatively biased view would call out to be compensated by a more positive assessment.

There were other signs of a heightened appreciation of the feminine at this time. Toward the end of the eleventh century, Europe saw the mysterious appearance of the troubadours, Provençal poets who sang of their idealized love for an unobtainable woman. Much of their poetry was influenced by the Arthurian legends, which captured the medieval imagination, and spoke of the knight who dedicates his valorous deeds to his lady love, Lancelot and Guinevere being the archetypal pair. Both the Arthurian legends and the troubadours elevated women to something like a spiritual savior; William of Poitiers (1071–1126), the first of the troubadours, declared "By her alone shall I be saved," although apparently this did not prevent William from also being "one of the greatest deceivers of ladies."[64] From the Mediterranean this popular movement of Platonic love—in the sense of its being unconsummated, although not always—spread to northern France, where the singers were called *trouvères* and then to Germany where the *Minnesingers* were known as the "terror of the husbands."[65]

The church did not think well of this development, and there is some suggestion that the cult of the Virgin was created as a response to this growing erotic spirituality, in which "a vision of woman entirely at variance with traditional manners" was celebrated.[66] For the troubadour, "woman was set above man," a kind of Gnostic reversal of the church's official view, and was seen to embody an ideal love, far beyond "any attainable in this life."[67]

Although a satisfactory account of the origin of the troubadours remains unwritten, links have been made between them and Sufi and Arabic poetry, which speak of the mystic's love for the divine in highly erotic terms, and with the kind of Neoplatonic spirituality we have seen in Suhrawardi.[68] That the Arab movement reached far into Spain and southern France suggests at least that this is a strong possibility. An argument has also been made that the troubadours were influenced by the Cathar heresy, a resurgence of Gnostic spirituality in the twelfth and thirteen centuries that for a time presented a viable threat to the dominance of Rome. In *Crusade Against the Grail,* the German esotericist and SS officer Otto Rahn argued that "all troubadours were Cathars," and that the rhetoric of courtly love was a code—or "green language"—for heretical beliefs, an argument put forward in the early twentieth century by the French Rosicrucian Joséphin Péladan in *Le secret des troubadours* (*The Secret of the Troubadours*).

What was it about the Cathars that so troubled the church and what role, if any, did they play in the esoteric history of the West?

CHAPTER SIX

SPIRITUAL LOVE IN
THE WESTERN WORLD

In 1244, in the Languedoc region of southern France near the foothills of the Pyrenees, a massacre took place that we would not be far wrong in calling "the last stand of medieval Gnosticism." At the end of a long and devastating spiritual war, conducted with the kind of "meticulous brutality that might arouse envy even among modern practitioners of genocide"—or so believes Richard Smoley in *Forbidden Faith: The Gnostic Legacy from the Gospels to the Da Vinci Code*—225 high priests of what the church called "the Great Heresy" preferred to burn to death rather than recant their beliefs.[1] The siege of their stronghold, the near impregnable castle of Montségur, lasted for months, and the heretics had strong support from local nobles. But as the days wore on and the heretics' protectors reached terms with the papal forces, it became clear that the end was in sight. It's doubtful the true believers would have been spared had they chosen to reject their religion and return to the "true faith," and they seem to have accepted their destiny with equanimity, even joy. Accounts say they went to the flames singing. Legends also say that just before the end, a small group of the Elect managed to escape their stronghold and carry away with them a treasure. What exactly that treasure was and what happened to it remains a mystery.

The "war against the Cathars," or the Albigensian Crusade, began in 1209, when Pope Innocent III decided to wipe out a religious movement within western Christianity that in essence revived the doctrines of the Gnostics of old. It was called the Albigensian Crusade because the first bishopric of this heretical sect was established in the French town of Albi. But the sect's other name, the Cathars, tells us more about their spiritual character. It comes from the Greek word *katharos*, meaning "purified." We have encountered this before, in speaking of the cathartic, purifying effect of the Dionysian and Orphic mysteries. The Cathars sought a similar purity. As some radical Gnostics sects did, they embraced an austere metaphysical dualism, seeing the physical world of matter as the work of an evil God, and as good only that which emanates from spirit. The hard historical evidence linking the Cathars to the Gnostics and the Manicheans is, according to scholars, meager and highly controversial; yet a familiarity with the beliefs of these groups suggests the kind of "ahistorical continuity" between them that Arthur Versluis speaks of. There are enough similarities between the Cathars, the Manicheans, and the Gnostics to suggest that all three, as well as other, less-known sects associated with them, shared the sort of spiritual dualism that the church wanted to expunge, once and for all.

WHO WERE THE CATHARS?

The Cathar movement came to public awareness in 1143 in Cologne. During a theological dispute, it became clear that some of the participants, among them the local archbishop, held doctrines antithetical to the church. He spoke of a "baptism by fire," rather than water, that was performed by a laying on of hands and not with the baptismal fount. Followers of the strange faith were vegetarians and teetotalers, and they allowed marriage only between virgins, considering sex, even if for procreation as the church affirmed it, something sinful. The archbishop declared that their religion had many followers throughout the world, and he claimed that the origins of his belief came from the East, Byzantium, where the doctrines of the true Christianity had been preserved since the days of the martyrs. Threatened with execution, many of the archbishop's flock recanted their heresy and returned to the fold. The archbishop didn't, and he and a few fellow staunch believers were accordingly burnt.

One heresy that preceded the Cathars and came from the East was that of the Bogomils, a dualistic religious sect that appeared in Bulgaria in the tenth century. Very little is known about them.[2] Their name, said to derive from the sect's founder, means "beloved of God," or "chosen of God," or "worthy of God's mercy." Where and how the Bogomils originated is a matter of debate. Some accounts trace them back to the Massalians, the fourth-century anticlerical "praying people" who embraced a radical dualism and who believed that after a "baptism by fire," they were free from evil and could do as they pleased, an antinomian attitude embraced by some Gnostics. The Bogomils are also said to be linked to the Paulicians, another dualistic sect who had a peculiar regard for the apostle Paul. Some accounts trace them back to ancient Dionysian and Orphic cults still thriving in Eastern Europe in the seventh century.

Wherever the Bogomils descended from, they embraced certain practices that clearly resonate with those of the Cathars. They rejected the Old Testament, likening its God to the Gnostic demiurge, and dismissed the sacraments of the church. They saw the cross as the instrument of Christ's torture and not to be revered, yet paradoxically they embraced Docetism, the belief, shared by many Gnostics, that Christ's body was only a "phantom," and that he did not suffer crucifixion. Like the Cathars, the Bogomil priests were ascetic, abstaining from meat and wine. They saw the established church as an instrument of the devil, whom they considered the creator of the physical world which, needless to say, they believed was evil. They lived simply, as the first apostles did, and looked with scorn, as the Cathars would, on the church's increasing temporal power and wealth. As the Gnostics did, they had their own way of interpreting scripture, and tended to make heroes of biblical villains. And as in some of the Gnostic sects, their followers were divided into two camps, the Perfects and the Believers. Perfects were completely committed to the faith and its austere requirements; Believers were allowed a less strenuous worship. The way from Believer to Perfect was demanding and arduous, requiring much study, ascetic practice, and the performance of a rite that would find a central place in the sacraments of the Cathars. This was known as the *consolamentum*, "the consoling," which completed their rejection of this evil earth and hastened their return to the higher spheres from which they had fallen.[3]

There is a sense that the Bogomils, like the Cathars, were already well established at the time of their discovery, as if they had planted "sleepers" in different parishes and conducted their worship alongside conventional churchgoers. As with the Gnostics, it could be said that the Cathars were the true Christians, and that the established church had become dogmatic and corrupted, its initial spiritual force spent. In a strange paradox, at the same time as the Gothic movement looked toward the eternal heavens, the established church sought greater and greater temporal power; popes were not satisfied with celestial authority and sought more and more secular control. The Cathars abhorred this and, with some justification, saw the church as an obstacle to the true faith. The Cathars themselves seemed an embodiment of this. Their life of the spirit was so devout, their acts of mercy and charity so genuine that their preachers earned the name *les bonshommes*, "the good men."

These good men, however, soon also earned the enmity of the church. In 1145, Bernard of Clairvaux, founder of the Cistercian Order, was sent to the Languedoc to battle the heresy. He had little luck, and in 1163, another outbreak occurred in Cologne. The Languedoc seemed fertile soil for the sect. It was a region associated with a flowering of culture unheard of in the Middle Ages, so individual that some sources speak of a "Languedoc civilization," with its own arts, literature, and language, Occitan. ("Languedoc" means the "language of the *oc*," *oc* meaning "yes" in Occitan, which was spoken in an area of Europe that included parts of Italy, France, and Spain.) This coincided with a religious tolerance and openness to different faiths; many Jews lived in the Languedoc, and it was in Provence that the Kabbalistic *Sefer ha-Bahir* emerged in the twelfth century.

According to Denis de Rougemont in *Love in the Western World*, the Languedoc was the scene of "one of the most extraordinary spiritual confluences in history," bringing together "a strong Manichean religious current," and "a highly refined rhetoric," stemming from the Sufis and Platonism.[4] The Crusades had opened up traffic with the eastern Mediterranean, which allowed for an influx of new ideas, the conduit for which may have been the military-religious order of the Knights Templar. It is not surprising that with an increasingly corrupt church, a return to a more genuine spirituality would take place here and that it would spread quickly. By the end of the twelfth century, the Cathar faith was well established, even making inroads into the courts of the nobility.

The church tried to stem the spread of the Great Heresy, and between 1204 and 1206 it held a series of public debates in the Languedoc. These had little effect. With more of the region's nobility siding with the Cathars, the church recognized that words were not enough and stricter measures were called for. In 1209, the crusade against the Cathars began with what is known as the "sack of Béziers." A crusader army reinforced by mercenaries fell upon the French town, which was a Cathar stronghold. When asked how the army were to differentiate between Cathars and those who remained faithful to the church, Abbot Amalric, the papal legate, spiritual leader of the crusade, is reported to have said, "Kill them all; God will know his own." God had his work cut out for him; accounts give the number of dead at twenty thousand. This suggests the level of violence condoned by the church and mandated by the crusade's zealous leader, Simon de Montfort, who devastated whole towns and put entire populations to the sword in the name of Christ.

The Cathars and the nobility that protected them had little chance of surviving such slaughter and a truce was reached in 1229 with an agreement known as the Peace of Paris that officially put an end to the heresy. Yet many Cathars continued to worship in secret, secluded in their castles in the Pyrenees. In order to root them out, Pope Gregory IX established the Inquisition, a highly effective spiritual secret police staffed by Franciscan and Dominican monks, which would be overseen by the papacy itself. After the fall of Montségur, small enclaves of Cathars continued to exist for some time in northern Italy, but with the efficiency of the Inquisition, these were eventually rooted out, and by the thirteenth century, Catharism was effectively eliminated.

A CATHAR *GNOSIS*?

Some writers on the Cathars wonder if they should be considered Gnostics at all.[5] This is not only because of a lack of hard historical evidence linking them to the early Christian sects. While embracing the radical dualism popularly associated with the Gnostics, the Cathars did not, it seems, pursue *gnosis*. It could be said that with the esoteric exodus from

Alexandria, the two main elements of "classic Gnosticism" parted company and went separate ways.[6] The *gnosis* element in Gnosticism and Hermetism went to Persia, where it was developed in the work of Suhrawardi. The dualistic element was carried on by Mani and his followers and thrived in Babylonia. We've seen that there is enough circumstantial evidence to suggest a connection between Manicheanism and the Bogomils, and between the Bogomils and the Cathars. But is it true that the Cathars embraced a world-rejecting religion without any element of *gnosis*?

Earlier I mentioned the Cathar practice of the *consolamentum*, which was another name for the "baptism of fire." What was the *consolamentum*? It seems it may have been a version of the "secret teaching" and "inner initiation" of primitive Christianity mentioned earlier. There I remarked on Timothy Freke and Peter Gandy's idea that there was a "inner initiation" involved in early Christianity that was rejected by the Christians who would go on to build the established church. In John 3:5, Christ tells Nicodemus that "Except a man be born of water and spirit, he cannot enter into the kingdom of God." Baptism by water is the conventional sacrament initiating someone into the church, but the second baptism, that of "spirit," is something else, and seems to have been more along the lines of the ancient Mysteries or a kind of *gnosis* experience. Water for the Cathars was a symbol of matter, of the physical world into which we are born, and hence for them was a reminder of our fallen state. Baptism by spirit—or fire, a symbol of spirit—initiated one into the higher life beyond the physical world, into the kingdom of God.

As Richard Smoley suggests, the *consolamentum* may have been something along these lines, a second baptism that marked one's second birth into the life of the spirit. It was not administered lightly. A candidate first had to go through a two-year probationary period in which he or she was taught much along the same lines as the church did. After this, if the candidate was serious enough about the faith to receive the *consolamentum*, he first had to fast for forty days, emulating Christ's sojourn in the desert. Then a period of silence was enforced and other ascetic practices carried out. After this, the candidate was brought to a room lined with torches, where there was an altar upon which was a copy of the New Testament. The candidate stood in the middle of a circle formed by the worshipers, where the Lord's Prayer was recited and appropriate passages from the New Testament were read. All this was in preparation for the *consolamentum* proper. Placing the New Testament on the candidate's head, the other members placed their right hands on him while the elder recited, "Holy Father, accept this thy servant into thy justice and bestow the grace and Holy Spirit upon him." With this the ritual concluded with a "kiss," not on the lips but by placing the New Testament on the participant's shoulder.[7]

What took place *inside* the candidate during this initiation? Clearly there is scant "hard" historical evidence to tell us, and inner experience is always difficult to interpret, even our own. One scholar of Catharism suggests that the result of the ritual was that the soul of the candidate "rediscovered the spirit from which it had been separated."[8] This certainly sounds as if the *consolamentum* was a true initiation, in the sense that it was the kind of transformative experience associated with the Mysteries or with the awakening of *gnosis*. Smoley suggests that what occurred during the *consolamentum* may have been like similar experiences in other religions in which some kind of "spiritual energy" is transmitted from the guru to the disciple. According to J. G. Bennett, a student of Gurdjieff who experienced such a transmission at first hand, in the Sufi tradition there is the idea of *Baraka*, or "effectual grace," which can be transmitted by someone of "a high degree of attainment."[9] Similar practices can be found in other traditions, and we are all familiar with eager *chelas* mobbing a charismatic guru hoping to absorb some of his radiant grace—followers of the Bhagwan Shree Rajneesh, for example, come to mind. Something similar is also the case with fans of movie stars, rock stars, and other celebrities.

Whatever happened during the *consolamentum*, the church did not look kindly on it, because it controverted its own teaching that the sacraments of the church were both necessary and sufficient for salvation. This meant that *extra Ecclesiam nulla salus*, "there is no salvation outside the church." Nothing else was needed, no "inner initiation" or "secret gospel." Such ideas, the church believed, were dangerous and could only lead the faithful away from the true path.

The Cathars saw things quite differently. The church itself had taken a detour and was no longer heading toward paradise, but deeper into the world of matter, into power, wealth, and secular influence. Innocent III himself claimed supremacy over all the kings of Europe and did his best to show he meant it. Whatever true spirit the church had at its start seemed to have congealed into its opposite, and for those of a living faith, this was a travesty of Christ's glad tidings. It seems we are really talking about two very different kinds of religion: one based on an *inner experience*, which, because of its nature is available to only a few, because they accept the difficulties that come with having it, and the other centered on dogma and the official rules of the exoteric church.[10] Christ had little time for the scribes and Pharisees who knew the letter of the law but not its spirit, and who tried to prevent those who did know the spirit from experiencing it. Tragically this made little impression on the devout who condoned the slaughter of thousands in his name. What the Cathars may have aimed at was the return of a true *gnosis*, a true experience of the spirit, to a church that had lost touch with it, or, as is likely, began its career by denying it fiercely in favor of a literal reading of the law.[11]

SOUL LOVE

Earlier, I mentioned a possible link between the Cathars and the troubadours. At first sight this seems unlikely. The troubadours sang of love, mostly but not exclusively unconsummated, while the Cathars—at least their *parfait* or Perfect, those who had taken the *consolamentum*—scorned sexuality as a trap luring souls deeper into the folds of matter. While it is true that some troubadours and their idealized women might succumb to the temptations of the flesh, they had self-discipline enough for us to characterize their pursuit of Eros as spiritual. We can even see them as embracing a kind of medieval tantra, the eastern form of spiritual practice that includes sex in its worship. While tantra has become widely popular among New Age devotees, it is often for the wrong reasons. It is not, as many believe, aimed at better and more powerful orgasms, but at transmuting sexual energies into something finer, into states of consciousness receptive to spiritual insights. Although the troubadours may not have spoken of it in these terms, there is reason to believe that they may have had something similar in mind.

The idea that sexual love can be a means of achieving spiritual insight has a long history in the West. In Plato's *Symposium* we learn that the love of physical beauty is the first step toward the love of beauty in itself, which leads to the love of the good, the Form of Forms, and so to the divine. Socrates voices this idea during the drinking party and it is no coincidence that the person he has learned this from is a woman, Diotima, a philosopher and seer. More than two millennia later, Goethe ends the second part of *Faust* with the words *"Das Ewig-Weibliche / Zieht uns hinan,"* "the Eternal-Feminine / Draws us upward."[12]

A more modern and little-known rendition of the same theme is *Amorous Initiation,* a novel by the Lithuanian poet, philosopher, and esotericist O. V. de Lubicz Milosz, in which "the realization of the unity of the sensual and the spiritual . . . leads the narrator to a higher state of consciousness and to contemplation of the Divine discernible in Creation."[13] So while the delights of sexual love may only mire us deeper in the depths of the fallen world, they can also help us rise up out of it into the clear light of the spirit. The church did not think well of the troubadours, but it could hardly have been their slips into carnality that troubled it. Men and women had fornicated well before the troubadours arrived, so it must have been something else. That something else may have been the knowledge that through a spiritualized sexuality, men and women were able to transcend their earthly limits and enter the sphere of the soul without the need or guidance of the church, which looked upon such pursuits as highly dubious. Sex for the church was a regrettable but necessary means of procreating the race; it saw it in strictly utilitarian terms. The idea that it could be an end in itself and could initiate one into the deeper dimensions of life must have been threatening.[14]

In *The Mystery of the Grail,* the controversial Italian esotericist Julius Evola suggests that "the troubadour literature"—which Evola associates with the Grail legends and which themselves center around the notion of a pure love—"had, to a certain extent, an esoteric dimension and secret tendencies" linked to a "superior knowledge and a spirituality purer than the Catholic one."[15] "The literature of love," Evola argues, "had a secret content," which was associated with the kind of doctrine of purification the Cathars sought and which led to them becoming "Perfect Ones." This "secret content" and "doctrine" was incompatible "with the more exoteric Catholic teachings," as were the Cathars' beliefs.[16] For Evola, the church had usurped the role of Wisdom-Sophia—or denied it outright—and had exiled the "true doctrine," while its increasingly secular objectives distanced it from a "vivifying knowledge," the kind sought, perhaps, by the Cathars and troubadours.[17] This knowledge was of the soul, and for the troubadours it was personified in the "unobtainable woman," who symbolized a love that transcended the earthly.

Individual troubadours ostensibly sang of different women, but they were all, according to Evola, really singing of the "same woman": the symbols of Sapientia, Lady Intelligence, Sophia, the feminine embodiment of a higher knowledge and experience.[18] As mentioned, the cult of Mary may have been created in order to keep the spiritualizing power of the feminine within the bounds of the true faith. If so, the plan worked to some extent, but as the popularity of the troubadours suggests, it was not a total success.

DANTE AND BEATRICE

Perhaps the most famous and influential expression of the "spiritualized feminine" in western literature is the figure of Beatrice, the Florentine woman who inspired Dante Alighieri's *La Vita Nuova* (*The New Life*), and who appears as his psychopomp, or "soul guide," leading him out of purgatory and into paradise in *The Divine Comedy*. Needless to say, *The Divine Comedy* is one of the great works of world literature and Dante ranks with Homer, Shakespeare, and Goethe as one of the titans of European letters. What is perhaps less well-known is that his account of an inner journey from hell to heaven may be informed by the pursuit of the kind of knowledge associated with the western esoteric tradition. It may be the case that Dante is one of our secret teachers.

Dante was born in Florence in 1265 and died in exile in Ravenna in 1321. His family was of the impoverished nobility, and Dante was proud of an ancestry that he could trace back to Roman soldiers who settled along the banks of the Arno. He speaks little of his father, and sonnets he wrote satirizing him suggest a lack of filial respect. His mother died when

Dante was fourteen—some accounts say ten—and he had a half sister and half brother from his father's second marriage. But there is little mention of Dante's family or of his wife, who bore him three children, in his writings. What is clear is that Dante was devoted to his native city and it was his involvement with its politics and ongoing struggle between the Guelph and Ghibelline parties—supporting the papacy and the Holy Roman Emperor, respectively—that, in 1301, threw him into exile. It was during this banishment that Dante wrote *The Divine Comedy*, a work inspired by his encounter with the beautiful Beatrice and in which he hoped to write "that which has never been written of any woman."

In *La Vita Nuova*, Dante tells of his first seeing Beatrice when she and he were nine. "The moment I saw her I say in all truth that the vital spirit, which dwells in the inmost depths of the heart, began to tremble so violently that I felt the vibration alarmingly in all my pulses, even the weakest of them. As it trembled, it uttered these words: 'Behold, a god more powerful than I, who comes to rule over me.'" Unlike in a Hollywood romance, Dante remained the distant admirer, satisfied with the merest glimpse of his beloved. He receives no more than these, but when he does, they are transformative. "Whenever and wherever she appeared," Dante writes, "I felt I had not an enemy in the world . . . I glowed with a flame of charity which moved me to forgive all who had ever injured me; and if at that moment someone had asked me a question, about anything, my only reply would have been 'Love.'"[19]

Such remarks may strike our cynical ears as so much sentimental gushing. For Dante, they were the meaning of his life. He meets Beatrice only once again nearly a decade after his first encounter, but his path and hers were not to coincide, and she eventually marries a banker. At one point she ignores him and he is crushed at the idea that she is making fun of him. He rises above his heartache and is determined to sing only her praises, filled with trepidation over what he believes are portents of her impending death. Her father dies and so does her friend, and Dante himself dreams of her dying. He breaks off writing *La Vita Nuova* when he learns she is dead, and for a time finds solace in a young woman who briefly takes Beatrice's place. Beatrice is finally transfigured into an angelic being, a spiritual *inspiratrice*, who will lead Dante to the "beatific vision," his direct experience of God.

Scholarship has still not decided if Dante's Beatrice was a real person or an allegorical or symbolic figure. Many critics agree that the most likely candidate was Beatrice Portinari, who was born in the same year as Dante and died in 1290 at the age of twenty-four. Beautiful women who die young and who serve as muses are not infrequent among romantic poets. Edgar Allan Poe made the early death of a beautiful woman the theme of many of his stories, and his own child-bride, Virginia Clemm—she married Poe at thirteen—died at the age of twenty-five. Novalis, the German Romantic poet and esoteric philosopher, became infatuated with the twelve-year-old Sophie von Kühn; they married and Sophie died of tuberculosis at sixteen.[20] The names of these poets' tragic muses are instructive. Other sightings of Sophia are more fleeting. In 1872, the Russian spiritual philosopher Vladimir Soloviev watched as the young girl sitting across from him in a second-class carriage of the Moscow-Kharkov express become the living embodiment of the Divine Woman. Soloviev was to have two more such visions, one while studying Gnostic texts at the British Museum in London, the other while visiting Bedouins in Egypt. Many women today reject the role of the muse, wanting to be appreciated for who they are personally, not for how well they can accommodate the idealized vision projected onto them. Yet for Dante and a group of poets associated with him, the ability of some women to reflect the higher light of the spiritual formed the essence of a powerful devotion.

THE FEDELI D'AMORE

Dante began to write poetry at eighteen and he soon did what all aspiring writers do: send his work to established poets in order to get some feedback on it. In this case it was a group of poets who were working to regenerate the cultural and spiritual standards of Florence. They were known as the "Fedeli d'Amore," "the Faithful of Love." Their leader was Guido Cavalcanti (1250–1300), a poet who developed the *dolce stil nuovo*, the "sweet new style," which became Dante's own and which transformed the poetic expression of the time.

Cavalcanti was one of the wittiest and wealthiest of Florence's poets, and he was also a reader of the alchemist and theologian Albertus Magnus and the Peripatetic Arab philosopher Averroes. Along with innovations in style and language, the *dolce stil nuovo* developed the themes of the troubadours and of "courtly love" into an exploration of the philosophical, psychological, and spiritual experience of Eros. The poem Dante sent the Fedeli d'Amore described a dream in which "Love"—the spiritualized aspect of Eros—appeared to him with Beatrice. The poetry of the Fedeli d'Amore focused on the members' own spiritual and mystical experiences, and they paid great attention to dreams and other visions, something Dante himself did throughout his life. Cavalcanti read Dante's poem and recognized his talent; he replied with a poem of his own and invited Dante to join the group. The two became close friends, although some years later, the convoluted twists of Florentine politics led Dante to agree to Cavalcanti's exile in 1300, a year before Dante fell victim to the same political machinations. After a few months as an outcast, Cavalcanti decided to return to Florence, but came down with fever—possibly malaria—and died along the way.

There is much speculation about the possible esoteric influences at work in the Fedeli d'Amore and Dante. Much of this has a political cast dealing with opposition to the church. In 1840, the Italian political radical and Dante scholar Gabriele Rossetti—father of the Pre-Raphaelite painter and poet Dante Gabriel Rossetti—published a book, *Il mistero dell' amor platonico nel Medioevo* (*The Mystery of Platonic Love in the Middle Ages*). He argued that the Fedeli d'Amore were adepts of a secret doctrine that they referred to using different women's names, but by which they meant the same "woman," Sophia, an idea referred to by Julius Evola. *Dante, hérétique, révolutionnaire, et socialiste* (*Dante, Heretic, Revolutionary, Socialist*) by Eugène Aroux argued that Dante's rhetoric concealed subversive political doctrines. Luigi Valli's *Il linguaggio segreto di Dante* (*The Secret Language of Dante*) suggested that Dante and the other poets of the Fedeli d'Amore spoke in their own "green language" in order to avoid the Inquisition. These suspicions were brought together by the Traditionalist René Guénon in

The Esoterism of Dante, and for an overview of the question, the interested reader should begin there.

The Fedeli d'Amore seem to have practiced a kind of erotic spirituality which involved the development of what they called the *cor gentile,* "noble heart," a kind of aristocracy of the soul—not one inherited by blood or wealth—and which aimed at achieving *l'intelleto d'amore,* "the intellect of love." We cannot but notice the similarity to Schwaller de Lubicz's "intelligence of the heart." They were, according to some accounts, a "secret group devoted to Sapientia"—that is, Wisdom—and "custodians of a secret doctrine," incompatible with the exoteric teachings of the church.[21] Even more than this, they were "a conscious elite" who were "devoted to achieving a harmony between the sexual and emotional sides of their natures and their intellectual and mystical aspirations," and who saw themselves as having "a conscious civilizing mission," of the kind usually associated with "esoteric schools."[22] Their aim was to introduce their ideas into society at large in order to transform it. The fact that much of their poetry was based on their practical experience with dreams and visions and that it aimed to express a body of knowledge anchored in Neoplatonism and other "wisdom" traditions suggests a link to the kind of pursuits we have seen in individuals like Suhrawardi.

THE TEMPLAR CONNECTION

The source of the Fedeli d'Amore's inspiration remains debatable; two of the most often suggested candidates are the Knights Templar and the Sufis. The Order of the Knights Templar was established in 1118 to protect Christians traveling in the Holy Land during the Crusades. Eight knights in service to Hugh de Payens, a French nobleman, received permission from King Baldwin II of Jerusalem to use the Temple Mount, a site sacred to Christians, Jews, and Muslims, as their headquarters. The ruins of the Temple of Solomon are said to lie beneath the Mount; and the Dome of the Rock, the Muslim shrine that houses the stone from which Mohammed ascended to heaven, is also there. At the time Hugh de Payens and his knights arrived, it was the sight of the Al Aqsa Mosque, which they were given to use. The knights renamed this the "Templum Domini," the Temple of the Lord, hence their name Knights Templar.

Their popularity soon spread, and Christians wanting to defend the Holy Land against the heathens were expected to support the Templars. Although the Knights took a vow of poverty, they received many donations of money, land, matériel, and volunteers; any nobleman wishing to join them had to donate his land and wealth to the order. Many did, and the Templars' resources increased. Although they lived communally, the Templars soon became fabulously wealthy, and in a short time they became the most powerful bankers in Europe; much of modern banking has its roots in Templar wealth. In 1129, at the Council of Troyes, the Templars were officially sanctioned by the church. At this time they also received the important blessing of Bernard of Clairvaux, founder of the influential Cistercian Order (as we saw earlier, in 1145, Bernard would be sent to Provence to nip the Cathar heresy in the bud). In 1139, a papal bull issued by Pope Innocent II granted the Templars free passage and exemption from taxes. They were also given the medieval Christian equivalent of a "license to kill," and were made answerable only to the pope. Usury—lending money at a profit—and killing were both forbidden by the church, but the Templars got around these restrictions. With their military prowess and success, they quickly became one of the most powerful forces in Christendom.

In 1291, Acre, the last Christian outpost in the Holy Lands, fell and the Crusades were over. The Templars wished to return to France and to acquire lands in the Languedoc, home to the Cathar heresy. But the tide was turning against them. They were immensely wealthy and powerful, and answered to no one but the pope, a status that caused some trepidation in France, especially with King Philip IV (inaptly named the Fair), who was already in debt to the Templars. He had recently asked for another loan in order to continue a war against England, and the Knights had refused, so Philip had reason to hold a grudge against them.

Exactly what led to the Templars' downfall is still debated. The likely scenario is that Philip, angry at the Templars' refusal of a loan and envious of their wealth, persuaded Pope Clement V, his childhood friend, that there was something not quite right about them and that they should be investigated. The Cathar schism was still fresh in people's minds—why did the Templars wish to acquire land in Cathar country?—and the charges of heresy and blasphemy brought against them found willing believers. They were said to deny Christ's divinity, to have spit and urinated on the cross, to practice sodomy, to consort with demons, and to worship a god called Baphomet. Eventually, on Friday, October 13, 1307, Templars were rounded up across France and arrested (giving rise, it is said, to the bad reputation of Friday the thirteenth). The Inquisition stepped in and obtained confessions by its usual method of torture. Many were killed, and in 1314, Jacques de Molay, the last Templar Grandmaster, was burned at the stake in Paris. Legend has it that before he died, de Molay put a curse on Philip and Clement, saying that they would both be judged by God within a year. If true, de Molay was right: both Philip and Clement died less than a year after his execution.

The fate of the Templars has given rise to much speculation. One suggestion is that not all of the Templars were arrested and that some escaped to Scotland, where they were eventually involved in the rise of Freemasonry. Templar themes abound in Masonic history, and with the unknown masons responsible for the Gothic cathedrals, the Templars are seen as esoteric ancestors from whom modern Freemasonry is descended.[23] Their very name suggests "sacred geometry," and the building of Solomon's Temple is a central part of Masonic practice, the "temple" being man's spiritual constitution. Like the Cathars, the Templars are said to have saved a treasure from the destruction of their ranks. Much mystery surrounds this Templar treasure, if indeed it ever existed. It is said to have been a collection of ancient scrolls, much like the Gnostic Gospels of Nag Hammadi, revealing the true history and nature of the church: that it is the opposite of Christ's real teachings. Others suggest that the treasure has something to do with the Ark of the Covenant.

In our context of Dante and the Fedeli d'Amore, another suggestion seems more apt: that the Templar treasure was not an object or thing but a teaching, a belief or set of ideas. Something similar can be said of other such "secret treasures," such as the philosopher's stone of the alchemists or the Holy Grail. Such symbolic interpretations of "lost mysteries" may seem dull compared to the search for and discovery of some actual tangible thing, some miraculous substance that can turn lead to gold or the fabled goblet from which Christ drank at the Last Supper. But if there is some link between Dante and the Templars, this approach strikes me as the most promising.

As the Templars' wealth was well-known, their "secret treasure" could not have been gold or jewels. That the Templars were thought to have obtained this treasure in the Holy Land is suggestive. We have seen that with the esoteric exodus from Alexandria, the teachings of the Neoplatonists, the Gnostics, and the Hermetists moved east and found a home in thinkers like the pagans of Harran and Suhrawardi. These teachings in some way centered around Sophia, around wisdom and the love of it. Solomon is associated with Wisdom and with Sophia, and the Song of Solomon—also known as the Song of Songs—is an overtly sexual work that can be read as an expression of the erotic spirituality associated with the Fedeli d'Amore. The yearning of the lovers to unite is also the yearning of the self to be united with the soul, or the philosopher with Sophia, much as may have been the aim of the Cathar *consolamentum*. Given that the Templars were accused of sexual perversions and blasphemy, it seems not too farfetched to wonder if they may have practiced some form of the erotic mysticism associated with the Sufis, and that they sought the kind of direct spiritual experience and embraced the kind of perennial philosophy—with its idea of the essential unity of all religions—we have been looking at in this book.

THE SUFI CONNECTION

There are clear links between the Templars and Dante. Dante uses the seal of the Templar Grandmaster, an eagle and a cross, as a symbol in *The Divine Comedy*. He also has especially vile places in hell set aside for Philip the Fair and Pope Clement V. The elect in heaven wear white robes similar to those worn by the Templars. Some, like René Guénon, have argued that Dante was a member of an auxiliary branch of the Templars, La Fede Santa ("The Sacred Faith"), an idea first presented by Gabriele Rossetti. Others have suggested that Brunetto Latini (1210–1294), Dante's teacher, was a Templar, or at least a member of La Fede Santa, and that he initiated Dante. The descriptions of hell in *The Divine Comedy* are supposed to be literal accounts of Dante's initiation experience in an underground cave.[24] Perhaps most suggestive is the fact that Dante's last guide in *Paradiso*, who leads him to his mystical vision, is Bernard of Clairvaux, who gave the Templars his blessing and who wrote their rules. Dante is also said to have taken a mysterious journey to Paris while the immolation of Jacques de Molay took place.[25]

It may be true that, as William Anderson writes, many of Dante's "most obscure allegorical passages receive their most coherent explanation when related to the crisis of the Templar order."[26] Yet while the Templars certainly have a high status in the esoteric history of the West—Guénon believed the Kali Yuga, our present spiritual "dark age," began with their destruction, while one writer declares that "the Knights Templar remain . . . the single greatest force for turning the spiritual mind of the west"—there are some problems with seeing them as practitioners of sexual mysticism and exponents of the *prisca theologia*.[27]

The Templars were fundamentally a military order, and while a few of them may have made contact with mystical orders or individuals in the East, the majority of them most likely had little time or interest in esoteric knowledge. Their rules included a strict vow of celibacy, which would make them "a most unlikely channel for themes devoted to the praise of beautiful ladies."[28] And while Bernard of Clairvaux blessed the Templars, he had, we've seen, a less positive attitude toward the Cathars, with whom the Templars are linked in this chain of associations. Yet there does seem a strong connection between the kinds of themes that concerned the Fedeli d'Amore and Dante, and the kind of erotic mysticism that the Templars may have encountered in the East.

As Henry Corbin has shown, the Arab Andalusian Sufi master and saint Ibn 'Arabi (1165–1240) had his own "Beatrice experience" in Mecca in 1201, decades before Dante. While staying with a noble Iranian family, 'Arabi met Nizam, the *shaikh*'s daughter, who "combined extraordinary physical beauty with great spiritual wisdom."[29] "She was," Corbin writes, "for Ibn 'Arabi what Beatrice was to be for Dante." Corbin makes the point that both the allegorists and the literalists are wrong when they argue over whether or not Beatrice or Nizam were "real" people or "only" symbols. Both were "real girls," but at the same time each was "a theophanic figure, the figure of *Sophia aeterna* (whom certain of Dante's companions invoked as *Madonna Intelligenza*)."[30] By "theophanic," Corbin means that it is through Beatrice and Nizam's beauty that the divine appears; they, and other of the troubadours' "beautiful ladies," are simultaneously flesh and blood individuals, but also archetypes, something along the lines of walking, talking Platonic Forms of beauty.[31] That is to say, when seeing Beatrice and Nizam, Dante and Ibn 'Arabi engaged in a form of what Schwaller de Lubicz called *symbolique,* the ability to see mutually exclusive ideas simultaneously. This is a function of Schwaller de Lubicz's "intelligence of the heart," whose similarity to the Fedeli d'Amore's *intelleto d'amore* we have noted. This is an ability, it seems, that has its source in the right brain and is accomplished through the use of the imagination, allowing us to grasp realities that elude our usual left-brain view of the world, which can only see things in terms of "either/or."

"If we fail to grasp this twofold dimension simultaneously," Corbin writes, "we lose the reality both of the person and the symbol," something those who argue that Beatrice or Nizam must be either "real" or allegorical, are prone to do.[32] That such "double vision" is part of both the Sufi and troubadour tradition Corbin makes clear by linking Ibn 'Arabi with the great Persian Sufi poet Rumi, mentioned in Chapter Six, whom he calls "the Iranian troubadour of that religion of love whose flame feeds on the theophanic feeling for sensuous beauty."[33] Corbin goes on to say that "Fedeli d'Amore [is] the best means of translating into a Western language the names by which our mystics called themselves in Arabic or Persian."[34]

"The Faithful of Love" can be understood to mean something more than a particular group of poets working in a particular historical moment at a particular place, as literal historians would limit them to. They can represent a wider, larger association of sympathies and vision across time and space, the kind of "ahistorical continuity" we have spoken of before. Sensibilities common to the Fedeli d'Amore and to the erotic mysticism of the Arab poets were shared by the Sicilian poets who gathered in the court of the Holy Roman Emperor Frederick II, who preceded Dante by a generation and who shared Neoplatonist themes with the troubadours.

For them, as for Dante and the Sufis, "the soul could be ennobled and purified through love and through the appreciation of poetry and music," a belief we saw sprouting in the fertile soil of "Gothic joy."[35] "Beauty will save the world," Dostoyevsky's Prince Myshkin says in *The Idiot,* and the "faithful followers of love," both those of Dante's local group and others, agree with him.

DANTE'S INNER VOYAGE

Like all great masterworks, *The Divine Comedy* can be read on several levels, and Dante, in his adoption of four levels of reading—his "polysemous interpretation"—tells us that there are different ways to understand his account of his inner journey. In a letter to his benefactor, Can Grande ("Big Dog"), to whom he dedicated *The Divine Comedy,* Dante spelled out what he meant. There were, he said, two basic ways of reading, the literal and the symbolic, a distinction we have come across before. But symbolic reading itself has gradations, what Dante called the allegorical, the moral, and the anagogic.

The literal reading of Dante's journey is simply the state of the soul after death. His narrative can be read as a Christian vision of what happens to the soul when we die. "Allegorical" in Dante's time had a particular meaning; it meant showing how events in the Old Testament prefigured those in the New Testament, how the Old Testament is a kind of "pre-echo" of Christ's coming, and how he is its fulfilment. The moral sense is a kind of psychological reading; it tells us of the state of the soul. The literal sense of Dante's opening line "Midway along the journey of our life/I woke to find myself in a dark wood" tells us that, at around thirty-five, Dante found himself in a dense forest. The moral reading means that Dante found himself in a state of alienation, of uncertainty about himself and his life, what we call a "midlife crisis."

The level of interpretation that concerns us most is the anagogic, the spiritual, which in modern terms we can say relates to changes in Dante's consciousness. "The inner journey of the poet" that Dante undertakes is, as Kathleen Raine puts it, "an exploration of the psyche, of the inner worlds and states of the poet himself."[36] As Swedenborg would say some centuries later, the hells Dante enters are not literal places of torment, but "states" of the soul, constricting circles of selfishness and egocentricity which the poet must confront before he can be free of them. Here the literal, left-brain approach must be abandoned and a more metaphorical tack taken, something Dante told Can Grande in his letter.[37] And while *The Divine Comedy* is full of Dante's personal animosities and political views, as well as some fairly orthodox Christian teaching, it is also an attempt to synthesize all the knowledge that was available at the time, of both the spiritual and the secular worlds, into a universal vision. It is an attempt, that is, at unifying our two disparate cognitive halves into a coherent whole.

It is not too difficult to find signs that Dante's inner journey shares in many of the esoteric themes encountered in this book. The three main settings for his inner voyage—hell, purgatory, and paradise—can be seen as the basic blueprint for spiritual awakening. Hell is the material world we find ourselves in, with its allurements and traps and restrictions. It is a kind of false half-life, and like many of us, when Dante awakens to the fact that it is leading nowhere, that its temptations are hollow—when, that is, he finds himself in the dark wood—he is disturbed and seeks a way out of it.

Purgatory represents the initiatory trials, the purifications and spiritual struggles necessary to free the soul from the weight of matter and prepare it for its spiritual awakening. This happens in paradise, when the soul, hitherto lost in darkness, has risen in the light of the divine and, having been freed from false desires and vision, shares in the brilliance of the true light and beholds the unity of all creation. That it is the Virgin who grants Dante the supreme vision, and that this consists of an "exalted light," tells us that his mystical experience is in the Sophianic and Neoplatonic tradition. Dante even tells us that when Dionysius the Areopagite thought of the "angelic orders," he named them "true and best."[38] That Dante's journey takes place from Good Friday to Easter links it to similar "rebirth" narratives we have looked at, and that he sees God as three concentric circles symbolizing the Father, Son, and Holy Spirit reminds us of one of Plotinus's few concessions to imagery, when he depicts the One, the Intellect, and the World Soul in the same way.

Dante's inner geography is also in line with the different but similar ontological ladders we have encountered so far. The journey from the circles of hell, up through Mount Purgatory and paradise, leads to the same celestial trajectory as the Hermetic "journey through the planets." Having passed from the earth, Dante must travel through the "seven heavens" (the planets) that will lead him to the "eighth" and "ninth heaven," rather as the Hermetist traveled to the "eighth" and "ninth sphere," or as the Kabbalist worked his way through the *sephiroth*. Here, the seven deadly sins of hell, after being transformed through Dante's struggles in purgatory, become the cardinal virtues in service to the divine order, just as the Hermetist transmuted the heavy weight of the planets into spiritual energies transforming the soul.

At the top of this mystical spiral, Dante has a vision of the transcendent God, of the Neoplatonic One, the "tenth heaven" that is beyond time, space, and matter. Here Dante is beyond words; he has reached the union with the divine sought by those who walk the *via negativa*. Yet Dante asks the "Light supreme" to relent a little, so that he is not entirely overcome and so that, in his words, he "may burn/One single spark of all Thy glory's light/For future generations to discern."[39] Like all writers, Dante wants to communicate his experience, to capture it so that it will not disappear, "as the sun melts the imprint on the snow."[40] The ultimate experience of the divine may be beyond expression, but Dante the poet, a traveler on the *via positiva*, knows that man needs beauty, images, and symbols in order to truly love. We should be thankful that the divine granted Dante his wish, and dimmed its glory, so that we can share in some small part of it.

This plea for the need for images and symbols links Dante to the Imaginal World, to Suhrawardi's intermediary realm, through which the reader of *The Divine Comedy* has just journeyed. Like "the stranger" in Suhrawardi's initiatory tales, Dante meets an inner figure who will serve as his guide, something C. G. Jung would also do some centuries later when he embarked on his own descent into the underworld. In the first two parts of Dante's voyage, through hell and purgatory, his guide is Virgil (70 B.C.–19 B.C.), the Roman poet who, like Homer before him, and like Orpheus before Homer, made the journey into the underworld. But

Virgil, who represents the best of the classical world, can only take Dante so far. When he reaches the limits of the earthly realm he must hand over his charge to Beatrice, who will take Dante further. We can say that philosophy and reason (the left brain) must allow insight and intuition (the right brain) to take charge now. In order to reach Beatrice, Dante has had to climb through Mount Purgatory, much as the stranger in Suhrawardi's initiatory tales must make his way up the difficult slopes of Mount Qâf, the cosmic mountain, in order to find his true self and reach the spiritual city, Hūrqalyā.

The outskirts of Hūrqalyā, we've seen, start at the "convex surface" of the "Ninth Sphere, or Sphere of Spheres" which encompasses the whole cosmos, much as the *Primum Mobile* or "Ninth Heaven" of Dante's geocentric system is the last layer of materiality before the transcendent realms of the unmanifest source. In pointing out these similarities between Dante's journey and Suhrawardi's account of his own inner voyages, I am not suggesting that Dante somehow knew of Suhrawardi's work, although we have seen that there is reason to believe that the Arabic and Sufi versions of central Neoplatonic themes most likely informed the Sophianic tradition within which Dante worked. More important, and initiatory in its own right, is the recognition that Dante and Suhrawardi's accounts are similar because they both *journeyed to the same place,* to the "inner worlds and states of the poet himself." That is, into the human mind or, as we have already called it, the *Mundus Imaginalis,* the Imaginal World that resides within and without all of us.

Although Dante's and Suhrawardi's inner worlds are decorated, so to say, with the symbols and iconography of their own particular place and time—Catholic and Islamic, as the case may be—the basic terrain, the fundamental geography is the same. We can say that both share a kind of similar topography of the imagination. This is a tradition, not in Guénon's sense of a specific doctrine handed down through the ages, but in Kathleen Raine's sense of a "learning of the imagination." It is a tradition that has its source, not in a "secret teaching," revealed to mystic sages at the dawn of time, but in the human mind itself.

DANTE'S COSMIC CONSCIOUSNESS

In his book *Cosmic Consciousness,* R. M. Bucke includes Dante in the list of historical figures in whom he argues that the "cosmic sense," the next stage of human consciousness, has appeared. Dante is in good company: Jesus, the Buddha, Plotinus, and Jacob Boehme, among others, are with him in the top ranks. Although a Christian may be satisfied with knowing that at the end of his journey Dante "saw God," Bucke relates Dante's vision to other traditions, and says that Dante's "expression . . . of the Cosmic vision . . . is a parallel statement with the Qur'an, the Upanishads, Suttas, the Pauline Epistles," but also with works of literature like Honoré de Balzac's *La Comédie humaine* (a twist on Dante's "divine" comedy), Walt Whitman's *Leaves of Grass,* and Shakespeare.[41]

As William Anderson notes, Bucke was the first to locate Dante's mysticism in the context of the perennial philosophy, and not solely in the Christian tradition.[42] This is important, but I would go further and say that Bucke places Dante's vision not only in the context of the perennial philosophy, but also in that of the evolution of consciousness. This suggests that, although it is decorated in Christian iconography, Dante's vision was not rooted solely in the Christian faith. Or we can say that, while the setting and cast of characters of Dante's journey are Christian, the *mechanism* of Dante's vision, what *happens to his consciousness* while it is taking place, transcends the Christian narrative. But this is merely to state the premise of the perennial philosophy: that the fundamental vision transcends any specific expression of it, "transcends" in this sense, meaning not limited to it. If, as the title of a book by Frithjof Schuon, one of the Traditionalists, has it, there is a "transcendental unity of religions," then the "transcendental" vision related to this cannot be limited to any one religion, just as, say, the "poetic experience" can't be limited to any one poet or subject matter of poetry.

P. D. Ouspensky, no stranger to mystical states of consciousness, addressed this issue more than a century ago. Considering the difficulties involved in trying to express the insights of mystical experience, Ouspensky saw that invariably a man who has had mystical experiences uses, for expressing and transmitting them, those forms of images, words and speech which are best known to him, which he is accustomed to use most often and which are the most typical and characteristic for him. In this way it can easily happen that different people describe and convey *an entirely identical experience quite differently* [my italics]. A religious man will make use of the usual clichés of his religion. He will speak of the Crucified Jesus, of the Virgin Mary, of the Holy Trinity, and so on. A philosopher will try to render his experience in the language of the metaphysics to which he is accustomed . . . A theosophist will speak of the "astral" world, of "thought forms" and of "Teachers." A spiritualist will speak of the spirits of the dead.[43]

Ouspensky himself carried out a series of experiments inducing altered states of consciousness, and he said of his own mystical experiences that they were nothing like anything he had read in other accounts of similar experiences.

Ouspensky's remarks take us a good way toward understanding the need for a *language* of mysticism, a language of "higher states of consciousness" that transcends that of the different religious or philosophical contexts in which they occur. It also helps us to make sense of the perennial thorny question, invariably raised by skeptics, of why different accounts of mystical experience *are* so different, why they do not share in the same commonality that accounts of our normal, everyday world do. If I go to my local supermarket, my experience of it will not be exactly the same as someone else's, but neither will it differ radically or in any fundamental sense. Because we are different people, our perspectives on it will naturally differ, but not enough to suggest that we really visited two very different places. But when Suhrawardi, Dante, Swedenborg, Steiner, Jung, and other inner voyagers tell of their journeys, they do seem to be speaking about very different experiences. Swedenborg goes to heaven and hell, Steiner reads the "Akashic record," Jung enters the "collective unconscious," although Corbin's notion of the Imaginal World and Kathleen Raine's ideas about the "learning of the imagination" can help us here.

It strikes me that this idea of a kind of "meta-language," which can help us decipher different mystical experiences, would be of most help if it concentrated on what was happening to the person having them, rather than on their content. "Comparative symbology," of the kind that Henry Corbin, Kathleen Raine, Jung, and others have worked out, is important and essential. It is through this that we can begin to map out these strange inner but oddly *objective* worlds, by showing the similar themes, images, and symbols that these "different but the same" interior terrains—in the sense that the Fedeli d'Amore's "beautiful women" were all different but also all the same Woman—possess. But it is just as important to look at the seer as at what is seen. In this context I am less interested in whether or not Dante saw God in some strict sense, as a devout Christian might be, as in what was happening to Dante when he saw him. What was going on in Dante's consciousness when the "cosmic sense," as Bucke puts it, came to him?

My own guess is that Dante somehow brought together the usually opposed cerebral hemispheres. Or, if we want to avoid localizing what took place too strictly in Dante's brain, we can say that he brought together our two usually opposed modes of consciousness, our two ways of knowing, and reached that rare harmony that I call the "Goldilocks state." Dante was one of those infrequent geniuses who can unify the opposing sides of human nature as well as the cognitive expressions specific to each. Dante was able to pursue both *episteme* and *gnosis*. He was aware of and conversant with all of the rational (Aristotelian) knowledge of the day. He studied politics and was an active politician. He studied jurisprudence and wrote on government. He knew philosophy and theology well and was well versed in the Scholasticism of Thomas Aquinas—who is among the many famous characters he encounters in the underworld. He knew his Bible. He studied history and knew the Ptolemaic astronomy of the time. Dante was also an extremely contemporary man, "up-to-date," and what sets *The Divine Comedy* apart from earlier epics is his clear grasp of current events and the introduction of "real life" characters into his spiritual narrative. Dante was a hard-nosed, no-nonsense, clear thinker who, if he believed it was the right thing to do, could send his friend into exile. But he was also a poet, one attuned to beauty and the charms of the erotic, and an intensely religious man who felt the concrete reality of the spirit. And he was also a mystic in pursuit of Sophia. Dante held the entire world of his time in himself and felt its contradictions. *The Divine Comedy* was a way of bringing the disparate elements of his world together to form a picture of the whole. He was, as John Ruskin called him, "the central man of all the world," holding in perfect balance "the imaginative, moral and intellectual faculties at their highest." That unity of being is certainly one of the central aims of the esoteric tradition.

A similar unity, I suggest, happened in Dante's consciousness. I am not the first to suggest that Dante's vision was the result of a fruitful cooperation between the two sides of his brain. William Anderson, to whom I have referred often in this chapter, suggests as much in his remarkable book, *Dante the Maker*, to which I am gratefully indebted. For all I know, others have said so too. Anderson makes the suggestion in several places, but one passage in particular struck me as especially insightful, given what Iain McGilchrist says about the "inhibitory" relationship between the two cerebral hemispheres, how each one works to achieve a cooperative balance by "inhibiting" the excesses of the other. Anderson refers to the "two kinds of knowledge" posited by Thomas Aquinas, the "active searching" for knowledge and the "intuitive possession" of it, which we can, as Anderson does, relate to the left and right brain. As Anderson writes,

> if we remember what Aquinas says of the two kinds of knowledge—
> that the lower, reason, is the active searching for knowledge, and the
> higher, intellect, is the intuitive possession of it—then we get a glimpse
> of what that higher knowledge, symbolized by Beatrice as the light
> between truth and the intellect, might be when gained through the
> proper balance between the two hemispheres . . . What Dante experi-
> ences in the purification of his will as he ascends Mount Purgatory, and
> in the enlightenment of his intellect as he soars into the heavens is *a
> constant interchange between the hemispheres, each correcting and balancing
> the other* [my italics].[44]

This expresses one of the central concerns of this book: the fruitful interplay of the opposites. In terms of the erotic spirituality we have been looking at, we can say that when the Lover and the Beloved—the philosopher and Sophia, or reason and intuition—combine in their mystic marriage, their *hieros gamos,* they produce interesting offspring. I have used Jung's idea of a "transcendent function" as an overall term to refer to this result. One form in which the transcendent function manifests, Jung tells us, is the mandala, the magic circle of Tibetan Buddhism that Jung, following his own inner voyage, came to see as a symbol of the Self, of the totality of the psyche, the union of the conscious and unconscious minds.[45] Mandalas appear in different ways, one of which is the great rose windows of the Gothic cathedrals. Just before his vision of God, Dante has a vision of an enormous rose, the petals of which are the souls of the faithful, and which symbolizes divine love.[46] Everyone he has met in heaven, including Beatrice, has a place in it.

Is it too much to suggest that, just as it would in Jung, the transcendent function produced in Dante a kind of mandala, that is, a symbol of the unification of the opposites, of the All and the One, that represented the unity in diversity of the outer world, as well as the unified consciousness necessary to produce it? It is instructive that Dante gave up politics and became convinced that it was only through art, through the *via positiva,* the effective combination of intellect and intuition—the critical (left) and creative (right) powers—that he could pass on some of the knowledge he had gained. He even went beyond the aims of the Fedeli d'Amore by writing a work that would transcend the cultural milieu of fourteenth-century Florence and act as a kind of "time-release capsule," making available the timeless ideas and symbols of the unitive experience for generations after him. In this way he helped make the inner journey of the poet possible for ourselves.

MEISTER ECKHART AND THE *VIA NEGATIVA*

While Dante was creating perhaps the greatest initiatory work of the medieval *via positiva,* a German contemporary of his was laying the groundwork for perhaps the greatest medieval expression of the opposite path, the *via negativa.* As mentioned earlier, the esoteric and the mystic paths, though related, are not identical. The esotericist seeks the experience and knowledge of the intermediary planes that lie between the material world and the One; he is interested in the Imaginal World, and in the different levels of reality and consciousness it encompasses. The mystic has little interest in anything but union with the divine. Both ways are rooted in the Neoplatonic ladder of being, but while one is interested in mapping out each step of the way, the other wants to reach the top by the shortest route possible.

While Dante projected an entire cosmos in order to contain his beatific vision, the theologian and philosopher Meister Eckhart (1260?–1327?) worked to empty his consciousness of everything but the immediate presence of God. Eckhart's focus on the direct and unimpeded experience of the divine exemplified the great wave of lay mysticism and spirituality that swept through the Rhineland in the fourteenth century and troubled an unstable church already challenged by the Cathars and Knights Templar. As the Mysteries of antiquity provided a more powerful emotional experience than the routine worship of the gods, so too the grassroots spirituality fed by Eckhart's vision offered a more transformative form of devotion than the increasingly legalistic strictures of the church.

This independent spirituality attracted many followers and took different forms, such as the contemplative Friends of God, led by Eckhart's followers, John Tauler (1300–1361) and Henry Suso (1295–1365), and the more antinomian Brethren of the Free Spirit. The church has never taken kindly to amateur spirituality, believing that such matters should be left in the hands of professionals, and it took steps to dampen what it called "enthusiasm" whenever it appeared. In 1311, the Brethren of the Free Spirit were declared heretical by Pope Clement V—who ordered the arrest of the Templars—and accordingly persecuted. The less rambunctious Friends of God were not persecuted; they in fact remained within the church and were a kind of response to the Dionysian revels of the Brethren of the Free Spirit, although the fact that they died out after only two generations may have saved them from the Brethren's fate. Along with the Black Death and the Hundred Years' War (1337–1453), the inability of the church to accommodate a more living spirituality was a factor adding to the turbulence and chaos of the late Middle Ages. The time was rife with a sense of imminent disaster and apocalypse. The end of the world, many believed, was coming. A century earlier, the Calabrian monk and mystic Joachim of Fiore

(1135–1202) had prophesized that a new age of the Holy Spirit was on its way, following the ages of the Father and the Son. Mankind, Joachim said, would then achieve direct contact with God, and no longer have need for the church, a prediction the Brethren of the Free Spirit, who were followers of Joachim, had tried to make true. Rome was not happy with this, but Dante put Joachim in Paradise, and the fact that the beginning of the age of the Holy Spirit coincided with the purported year of Meister Eckhart's birth, 1260, may not have been entirely the work of chance.

Dante and Eckhart shared much in common; for one thing, the combination of mystical insight and intense intellectual hunger, although in each the expression of this union took different forms. Both also had trouble with the authorities. Dante, we know, was exiled. In his later life, Meister Eckhart was accused of heresy, tried, and was found guilty, although he died before receiving the verdict. He was accused of pantheistic tendencies; like Eriugena, he spoke of nature's "manifest theophanies" and preached that there was no need to hear sermons, "for every creature is full of God and is a book" and that "God is present in a stone or a log; only they do not know it."[47] For such beliefs, he was posthumously found guilty of being "deceived by the father of lies," and, like Socrates and Suhrawardi, of "sowing thorns and thistles among the faithful and even the simple folk" by the men who tried him.[48] Yet Eckhart's remarks are not strange or threatening to anyone with a sense of Schwaller de Lubicz's "intelligence of the heart" or Bergson's intuition or the "participatory" mode of consciousness associated with the right brain. Yet these subtle insights are invariably lost on those who view life literally.

In some sense we can say that the parallel positive and negative ways, rooted in Dionysius the Areopagite and embodied in Dante and Eckhart, reached a kind of culmination at this point, just as Europe was about to undergo the transformation that would eventually lead to the modern world. As Evelyn Underhill said in her classic work *Mysticism*, "These two giants stand side by side at the opening of the [fourteenth] century; perfect representations of the Teutonic and Latin instinct for transcendental reality."[49] For Teutonic and Latin, we can read *via negativa* and *via positiva*, a differentiation that would inform the Protestant Reformation in the sixteenth century and which would change the face of Europe.

Although supressed after his death and forgotten for centuries, Meister Eckhart's work was rediscovered in the nineteenth century, mostly through the work of the German Romantic philosopher and Christian theosopher Franz von Baader (1765–1841), and he has since become a central figure in modern western mysticism. Some recent scholars suggest that Eckhart's true lineage is within the German philosophical tradition, and wish to save him from the dubious world of New Age mysticism. Yet the German philosophical tradition itself contains many who were fellow travelers with mystics, so the differentiation is perhaps more academic than useful. In recent times, Eckhart has been enormously influential, and figures as disparate as the philosopher Martin Heidegger, the Zen scholar D. T. Suzuki, the contemporary spiritual teacher Eckhart Tolle, and the Christian priest and theologian Matthew Fox find common ground in their inheritance from Meister Eckhart.

A fAITHfUL HERETIC

Eckhart von Hochheim was born around 1260 in Tambach, a Thuringian village in northeast Germany near the town of Erfurt. Little is known of his childhood and family life; some accounts say he was the son of a knight, yet others dismiss this. It is possible he may have studied in Paris as a youth under the Aristotelian philosopher Siger of Brabant.[50] What we do know is that at around sixteen, Eckhart entered the Dominican novitiate at Erfurt. In 1280, he was sent to the famous Dominican House of Studies, the *Studium Generale,* at Cologne, which was founded by Albertus Magnus. Eckhart was there for only a short time before Albertus Magnus died, but accounts say he met the great philosopher and theologian and was taught by some of his students, one of whom was Thomas Aquinas. Albertus Magnus brought the ideas of Plato, Aristotle, and Plotinus and the theology of Christianity, Islam, and Judaism into a creative synthesis, a version of the perennial philosophy; he was also, as mentioned, one of the first in the West to study alchemy. Eckhart absorbed this heady curriculum, which also included the work of Porphyry, Proclus, Augustine, Origen, Dionysius, and Eriugena. Although Albertus

Magnus's Neoplatonism was soon eclipsed by the scholasticism of his pupil Aquinas, the mystic spirituality he fostered had a powerful influence on the Christians of the Rhineland.

Eckhart proved a brilliant student and able administrator, and following his ordination as a priest in 1293, he went on to have a remarkable career in the church. In Paris, he worked as a lecturer and studied for his degree as master of theology. Between 1293 and 1302, when he was granted the degree, which was the highest academic honor at the time—and from which his title of "meister" comes—he was made prior of Erfurt and also vicar of Thuringia. Other titles came, including being made regent master at the St. Jacques Dominican House of Study, the First Provincial of Saxony, the vicar of Bohemia, as well as professor of theology. Eckhart is generally considered a mystic; if he was one, he was in the tradition of Emanuel Swedenborg and Rudolf Steiner, two other men deemed mystics who were also highly efficient organizers.

Eckhart was put in charge of reforming several of the Dominican Houses and he was also made responsible for the spiritual guidance of Dominican nuns and several women's lay spiritual groups, such as the Beguines. These popular women's groups reflect both the turn toward the feminine and the interest in independent spirituality common to the time; as one commentator remarked, they contributed to "one of the most spectacular upsurges of mystical spirituality in the history of Europe."[51] Not surprisingly, Clement V, who had suppressed the Templars and declared the Brethren of the Free Spirit heretical, suppressed the Beguines, and in 1310, the mystic Marguerite of Porete was burned at the stake for heresy in Paris. Among other things, she was accused of promoting the "heresy of the free spirit," a charge laid against Eckhart as well. Marguerite, along with other women mystics, such as Hildegard of Bingen (1098–1179) and Mechthild of Magdeburg (1207–1294), a Beguine, was an influence on Meister Eckhart's beliefs. Eckhart believed in an equality of the sexes and promoted a casual friendship between men and women, in contrast to the more sharply segregated policy of the church. He was also, as Albertus Magnus was, open to insights from other faiths, and was conversant with Jewish thinkers like Moses Maimonides and the Sufi saint Ibn 'Arabi, among others. Much of what we know of Eckhart's teachings comes to us from the many nuns and Beguines who memorized his sermons and wrote them down, although in their efforts to erase Eckhart's work, the Inquisitors seized many of these accounts and destroyed them. Were it not for the efforts of these spiritual women, the little we have of Eckhart's writings might have been even less.

What troubled the church was that Eckhart preached the same sort of union with God that the Sufi mystics sang of under the cover of a mysticism of the erotic. "God and I are one," Eckhart told his congregation. "Through knowledge I take God into myself, through love I enter into God."[52] Other sayings make the same point. "The eye through which I see God is the same eye through which God sees me; my eye and God's eye are one eye, one seeing, one knowing, one love." "Our Lord says to every living soul 'I became man for you. If you do not become God for me, you do me wrong.'"[53] Probably the most well-known, as well as the most threatening from the church's perspective, is "God needs me as much as I need him," an insight that achieves the dual heresy of diminishing God's omnipotence while emphasizing man's importance.[54] This sort of union with the divine has always been frowned upon by the church—understandably, as it subverts its authority, although Eckhart made a spirited defense of his faithfulness and orthodoxy and, as in the case of other heretics, much of what he says can be found in scripture.[55] Yet as we've seen throughout this book, "dynamic" religion, meaning personal and experiential, does not get along well with the "static" variety, and it is usually the dynamic individuals who suffer from this dissonance.

According to Eckhart, the fundamental ground of all being is God—or, in Neoplatonic terms, the One—and through a process of letting go, of emptying ourselves of everything that stands in the way of recognizing and experiencing this—the *via negativa*—we can come to know God and to be One with Him. Or to be more precise, not to *know* God, which we cannot, as he is beyond knowledge, but to love him and to feel his love. This process of inner emptying is at the heart of the anonymous fourteenth-century mystical work *The Cloud of Unknowing*, whose title encapsulates the essence of the *via negativa*, and whose aptly unknown author was, like Eckhart, influenced by Dionysius the Areopagite. The aim of this work was to instruct a novice on the essentials of the contemplative life. Physical withdrawal, in the clichéd sense of retiring to a cave, is not essential. This work can and should be done in the midst of life. Eckhart himself said that if it was a choice between mystical rapture and giving a sick person soup, one should forget the rapture and get the soup. What was important, both for Eckhart and the unknown author of *The Cloud of Unknowing*, was "psychological withdrawal," a letting go of attachments, possessions, relationships, and personal concerns. As the old Sufi saying has it, one should be in the world, but not of it. As the psychologist Ira Progoff remarked, "the aim of the work is to lead beyond all theological conceptions and doctrines, and beyond all attachments to religious objects and observances."[56] We should, the anonymous author tells us, learn to love God without his characteristics; love him not because he is good, loving, or merciful, but simply because he *is* (the similarity to the Neoplatonic conception seems fairly clear here). "It is good to think about the kindness of God, and to love Him and to praise Him for it, [but] it is far better to think about his naked being and to praise Him and love Him for Himself."[57]

As with Eckhart, this "ground" of "naked being" is the same as our own, and by losing one's self in order to find it, one finds one's "true self," as it *is*. This is best achieved by getting rid of everything that can take our minds away from this. As Progoff writes, "Attachment to the symbolic forms and sacred figures of man's religions can easily become an impediment in the ultimate quest of the spirit."[58] The philosopher Alfred North Whitehead said, "Religion is what the individual does with his solitariness," an insight with which Eckhart and those that followed him would agree.[59]

Eckhart had different names for this process of getting rid of whatever comes between oneself and God, but probably the most well-known is *Gelassenheit*, a German word that does not have an exact English equivalent but can be understood as "detachment," "releasement," or simply "letting go." It plays a central role in the philosophy of Martin Heidegger, whose concern with our "forgetfulness of being" is close to Eckhart's own vision, with his attention to *Istigkeit*, or the sheer "is-ness" of things, and it is also used by Iain McGilchrist to characterize the right brain's mode of letting things be as they are, as opposed to the left brain's tendency to manipulate them into how it thinks they should be. The "dispassionate equanimity" related to the Greek notion of *ataraxia* (Chapter Three) comes close, but is too negative. We can see it as a positive letting-go in order to let things be as they are. "When a man's heart grieves for nothing, then a man has the essence and the nature and the substance and the wisdom and the joy and all that God has," Eckhart tells us. "Then the very being of the son of God is ours and in us we attain to the very essence of God," he says of this kind of detachment.[60] One cannot help but think of the Buddhist quieting of desire and of countless "dropouts" who quit the rat race in order to find a better life. "I have no money, no resources, no hopes; I am the happiest man alive," Henry Miller declared at the start of his most famous work, *Tropic of Cancer*, an account of *la vie bohème* in the Paris of the 1930s.[61] Eckhart might not have appreciated the book, but he would have agreed with Miller's joy.

Yet while Eckhart and those who followed him continued on their solitary path toward the "dark brilliance" and "empty fullness" of the divine, the western mind was gearing up for a trip down the *via positiva* unlike any it had seen for some time.

CHAPTER SEVEN

AN ESOTERIC RENAISSANCE

In the spring of 1336, just before the start of the Hundred Years' War, the Italian poet Petrarch (1304–1374) did something that marked a shift in western consciousness: he climbed a mountain to see the view. Petrarch is second only to Dante in the ranks of Italian literature, and is considered Italy's greatest lyrical poet. With Dante he shared the inspiration of an unrequited love, in his case the mysterious and elusive Laura.[1] Petrarch's passion for the literature of antiquity is seen as the spark initiating the Renaissance.[2] Yet for some, it was his strange desire to scale an inhospitable height, for no reason other than a scenic one, that marks him as one of the first "modern" men.

The mountain in question, Mount Ventoux, in the Provence region of France, is today easily accessible and is famous for being on the route of the Tour de France. In Petrarch's time it was a formidable peak and the idea of climbing it, or any other mountain, simply to see the view, was unheard of. Yet that is what Petrarch did. In a letter to Dionigi di Borgo San Sepolero, an Augustinian professor of theology and Petrarch's former confessor, Petrarch says, "Today I climbed the highest mountain in this region, which is not improperly called Ventosum (Windy)." "The only motive for my ascent," he explains, "was the wish to see what so great a height had to offer."[3] Petrarch had lived beneath the mountain's shadow since his childhood—his family had moved to Avignon, then seat of the papacy, when he was eight—and one wonders if there is any connection between Petrarch's climb and the fact that the area had been home to the Cathars and troubadours.

That Petrarch's desire to climb Mount Ventoux was unusual for the time is clear in the response of an old shepherd he and his brother, who accompanied him, encountered on the way. When Petrarch told the old man of his plan, he reacted with alarm and tried to dissuade the two from what was clearly a mad idea. The shepherd himself, some fifty years earlier, had the same notion, but he did not succeed, and all he got from scrambling on the rocks was torn clothes and a bruised body. Since then, no one else had thought to do it, until now, and he warned Petrarch that nothing good would come of it.

As Owen Barfield has argued, it was not until the Romantics of the late eighteenth century that the idea of contemplating nature as something beautiful *in itself*—and not as one of God's "manifest theophanies" or for utilitarian purposes—became popular. In *A Journey to the Western Islands of Scotland* (1775), the English man of letters Dr. Johnson often complains of the many lakes and mountains he and his companion James Boswell had to go around; they made the trip long and tedious, Johnson grumbled. And in 1777, Goethe made his own mountainous ascent when he scaled the Brocken, the highest peak of the Harz Mountains, a climb that, even four centuries after Petrarch's, was still considered crazy.[4] Yet after the publication of William Wordsworth's and Samuel Taylor Coleridge's *Lyrical Ballads* in 1798, "nature" suddenly became something that people went out of their way to experience "in the wild." Before then, untamed nature was not sought out, and the idea of a beautiful garden was of a well-sculpted topiary.[5]

The fact that Petrarch was moved by some obscure desire to see what the top of Mount Ventoux "had to offer" makes him for many the first sign of a significant change in western man's attitude toward the world. That Petrarch himself is troubled by his curiosity comes through in his account. We have seen that a shift in the western perception of nature had begun with Eriugena and the rise of the Gothic. Until then the natural world had been seen as the province of pagans and the devil, unworthy of man's consideration and a temptation to avoid. But with the return of the "sacred feminine," nature too was seen in a new light. Petrarch participates in this, yet his conscience as a good Christian makes his dazed appreciation of "the wide expanse of view" spread out before him uneasy, and he chides himself for admiring "the things of the world," when his thoughts should be focused on his soul.[6] He takes comfort in a passage from St. Augustine, yet his guilt in enjoying the view surrounding him seems forced.[7] Petrarch is torn between two worlds, the Christian one that makes him scorn the "worldly object before me," and the new vistas that startle him.[8] Yet it seems clear that for all his guilt about his "weakness," this strange new world has captivated him.

This sense of Petrarch straddling two ages and two worlds has struck several commentators. For the cultural historian Jacob Burckhardt, Petrarch's "indefinable longing for a distant panorama" makes him "one of the first truly modern men."[9] For the philosopher Ernst Cassirer, Petrarch's "desire to immediately contemplate nature" is "testimony to the decisive change in the concept of nature that began in the thirteenth century."[10] For Hans Blumenberg, Petrarch is both "deeply Medieval" and "early modern."[11] And for the archetypal psychologist James Hillman, Petrarch's ascent emphasizes "the complexity and mystery of the man-psyche relationship," making him a "discoverer" of nature, but also of the inner worlds too.[12] That Burckhardt speaks of an "indefinable longing for a distant panorama" reminds us of the notion of *Sehnsucht,* a German word central to German Romanticism that has no strict English equivalent, but which can be approximated by "unfulfillable longing." In *Faust,* Goethe writes of an "unbelievably sweet yearning" that drove his hero to roam "through wood and lea."[13] This is the essence of *Sehnsucht* and Romanticism; if Petrarch was afflicted with this nearly half a millennium before Goethe, he was clearly ahead of his time. Poets had of course written about nature before, but the sense of some "indefinable longing" associated with it is new. The "distant panorama" that Petrarch sought in the outer world was mirrored in the new *inner* panoramas that western man was beginning to seek out in himself.

A CHANGE IN PERSPECTIVE

Another philosopher who saw profound significance in Petrarch's ascent was Jean Gebser. For Gebser, Petrarch's ascent marks "the discovery of landscape" and ushers in a new epoch, what Gebser calls the "perspectival world." For Gebser this was "the first dawning of an awareness of space that resulted in a fundamental alteration of European man's attitude in and toward the world."[14] For Gebser, Petrarch was the "first to emerge from a space dormant in time and soul and into 'real' space." If we compare the sense of space that we find in medieval tapestry with that of perspective painting, which was just beginning to appear around the time of Petrarch's ascent of Mount Ventoux, we can get some idea of what Gebser means.

In medieval tapestry, figures and their landscapes are flat, two-dimensional; differences in size are determined not by spatial location, but by importance, so, for example, a church or other religious subject in the background will appear larger because of its spiritual significance.[15] There is a sense that people of the Middle Ages did not feel space in the same way we do, as an empty expanse through which we move, or as a box in which we are contained. In *Saving the Appearances* (1957), Owen Barfield suggested that medieval man did not feel he was within space as if it were a container. Rather, for Barfield, medieval man *wore* the world like a garment. Medieval man, Barfield suggests, saw the world quite differently than we do. For him the air was "filled with light proceeding from a living sun, rather as our own flesh is filled with blood from a living heart." The night sky was not a "homogenous vault pricked with separate points of light, but a regional qualitative sky . . . from which . . . the great zodiacal belt . . . the planets and the moon . . . are raying down their complex influences on the earth."[16] Barfield says that although he may not have heard it, medieval man believed in the music of the spheres and he took for granted the correspondences between things on Earth and those above: the moon's correspondence with growth, the sun's with gold, Venus's with copper, that of Mars with iron, and Saturn with lead. For Barfield, this meant that our medieval ancestors lived in a much more "participatory" relationship to the world than we do. They were "in" the world in a way that we are not, much more like figures in a painting than objects in a box. There was, we can say, a felt continuity between themselves and the world around them.

All this changed, Gebser argues, with the rise of the "perspectival age." If people of the Middle Ages were like figures in a painting, we are much more like visitors to a gallery. Prior to this change, western man was "unperspectival." He did not see the world in terms of his physical location within it, but in terms of its hierarchical significance and symbolic meaning. With the rise of perspective, this sense of hierarchical significance and participatory continuity faded. Although the separation of consciousness from the world began, Gebser believed, around 1225 B.C. with the rise of the mental-rational structure of consciousness, it did not reach its peak until the emergence of the "perspectival age." It was at this point that the separation of consciousness from the world—and, according to Gebser, from its unmanifest source, "Origin"—became complete. Petrarch's trepidation in gazing on the "wide expanse" that left him "dazed" was, we've seen, informed by his conscience as a good Christian. But it was also informed by his awareness that with his ascent of Mount Ventoux, he had cut loose his moorings and was now adrift. It was as if some figure in a medieval tapestry suddenly found that he could step out of the fabric of his world and move about at will. Or as if we found ourselves able to move about freely in a film, a thrill that "virtual reality" entrepreneurs hope to cash in on. As many sensitive minds do, Petrarch experienced in advance what would soon become commonplace; as Ezra Pound said, artists are the "antennae of the race." With Petrarch's ascent of Mount Ventoux, human consciousness, at least in the West, became aware of distance, depth, and all that we take for granted as "empty space." We had detached ourselves from our ground and were now floating freely. In a very different sense, we were "in" the world, but not "of" it.

ROOM TO MOVE

The new vistas of space that dazed Petrarch also presaged a change in how western man saw himself. As one scholar argued, "the man of the Middle Ages was humble, conscious almost always of his fallen and sinful nature," and felt himself to be "a miserable foul creature watched by an angry God"—as his religious authorities persuaded him he was.[17] Now there was a shift to a rather opposite view. Man began to appreciate that he was something more than a sinful wretch who had to endure this "vale of tears" in order to find salvation in the next world. Petrarch's rediscovery of the genius and greatness of the past made it clear that he had revealed a "new foundation for the appreciation of man."[18] Petrarch had tapped the "Great Memory" and found that there was reason to celebrate man in his own right, and not see him as only a miserable sinner. The great poets and thinkers of the classical age could provide profound insights and offer models of moral and spiritual development that did not depend on diminishing the human. The "humanities" became a guide to the good, the true, and the beautiful within the human soul. Man could stand on his own two feet and embrace the world around him, knowing that it was not sinful to do so, but an expression of his own humanity.

This new freedom was exhilarating but with it came a danger. It was at this point, Gebser argues, that the mental-rational structure of consciousness entered its "deficient mode." What had been an advantage was now becoming a handicap. We can say that, with its deficient mode, the mental-rational structure had become overripe and was beginning to rot. The separation of consciousness from Origin that marked the beginning of the mental-rational structure and made possible the rise of philosophy, logic, science, and all the rational forms of thought that we rightly value, now began to work to our disadvantage. By entering this mode, consciousness's separation from Origin had become total and man no longer felt a connection to the world. Just as Petrarch felt dazed and confused by the vistas he saw before him, western consciousness began to experience the uncertainty of its place in the cosmos.

In a certain sense we can say that Petrarch's arduous climb marked childhood's end for western man. To have the apron strings cut and to move about freely is without doubt necessary and exciting, but it can also be frightening. The celebration of the purely human values that characterized the Renaissance and led to our modern, scientific outlook—for which, needless to say, we have much to be grateful—also led to our loss of meaning and alienation, to our sense of being, in the novelist Walker Percy's phrase, "lost in the cosmos." From here on in, it became more and more clear that we were on our own.

Yet any freedom worth having is dangerous, and the same "perspectival shift" that opened the way to our uncertain modern universe also sparked the last great revival of Hermetic thought. Some of those who benefited by Petrarch's mad adventure were the readers of a rediscovered Hermes Trismegistus.

A BYZANTINE PLATO

George Gemistos Plethon's (1355–1452/54?) attendance at the Council of Ferrara-Florence (1438–1445) is one of the secret turning points in the history of western consciousness. It was during this visit that Gemistos adopted the name Plethon, a variant of Plato's own. Gemistos's knowledge and advocacy of Plato's philosophy so impressed the Florentine humanists he met during his visit, that all who heard him would have agreed with Marsilio Ficino that Gemistos had "spoken of the Platonic mysteries like a second Plato."[19] Like many we have encountered in this book, Gemistos Plethon is one of our secret teachers.

Plethon (although he didn't adopt the name until late in life I will refer to him by it) was born in Constantinople and raised in a well-off and educated Christian family. As a young man, he studied in Constantinople and also in Adrianople, which at the time was the capital of the Ottoman Empire; like Cairo and Baghdad before it, Adrianople had become a center of learning and we can assume Plethon made the most of it. Not much is known of Plethon's early life. It is said that at the age of fifteen, he "visited Western Europe in the train of Emperor John Palaeologus," and it seems he was educated with the aim of becoming a teacher of philosophy.[20] Plethon was lucky in his choice of career. Much more of Greek philosophy survived in the eastern empire than in the western, and the Byzantine church had also absorbed more of Neoplatonism than its western counterpart. Around 1407, when he was past fifty, Plethon left Adrianople and traveled through Cyprus and Palestine before returning to Constantinople. A few years later, he moved to Mistra, a town in the southern Peloponnese near the ancient site of Sparta that was known for its tolerance, and where the ancient Hellenistic traditions that Plethon loved still survived.

Plethon's love of Plato and the Neoplatonists was not without danger.

One of Plethon's students in Mistra, George Scholarius, who would later become patriarch of Constantinople, took argument with Plethon's appreciation of Plato, who was still considered a dangerous influence in the Aristotelian-dominated church. The Byzantine church was more open to Platonic ideas than Rome, but any criticism of Aristotle was still fraught with peril. Scholarius convinced the Byzantine Emperor Manuel II Palaeologus that Plethon's ideas bordered on heresy. The emperor knew and respected Plethon, but to placate Scholarius he had Plethon confined to Mistra. Plethon had little interest in religious disputes, and the more relaxed atmosphere of Mistra suited him; his confinement in fact was wholly beneficial. In Mistra, Plethon taught philosophy, astronomy, and history, and edited various collections of classical writers. He also wrote several works arguing how the fragmenting Byzantine Empire could be reorganized along the lines of Plato's *Republic*. Like Meister Eckhart, Plethon was an able administrator and held many important positions. He was also a judge and a member of Constantinople's senate, and was frequently consulted on a number of issues by the emperor and other officials.

In 1428, the emperor John VIII Palaeologus consulted Plethon on the possibility of unifying the eastern and western churches. One motivation for this was the fact that the Ottomans were edging closer to Constantinople, and the Byzantine church needed help in keeping the Turk at bay. Plethon himself had no love for the Latin church, and his advice was solely motivated by realpolitik. In 1438, the emperor invited Plethon to join the advocates of the Greek church attending the Council of Ferrara, which was to discuss the unification (it was soon moved to Florence for several reasons, one of which was plague).

Plethon was a secular thinker, but his knowledge and wisdom were assets. Along with several other advisers—one of whom was his ex-student now enemy, Scholarius—Plethon made the journey west. It was unusual for a man of his age to take such a trip—Plethon was in his eighties—but odd as it sounds, it was the turning point in his career. His voyage to Italy must have been interesting. On board ship with him was the German philosopher, theologian, and later cardinal (1449), Nicolas of Cusa (1401–1464). Nicolas had been in Constantinople to help with arranging the council. His philosophy of "learned ignorance" (*de docta ignorantia*), founded in the "negative theology" of Dionysius the Areopagite, and of the reconciliation of opposites—including different faiths—helped create the pro-Neoplatonic intellectual atmosphere that made possible the "esoteric Renaissance."[21]

PLATO, ARISTOTLE, AND THE *PRISCA THEOLOGIA*

Plethon was bored by doctrinal disputes, and to keep busy while the churchmen split hairs, he agreed to speak to the Florentine humanists about Plato and, more specifically, about the *prisca theologia* of which Plato was a central exponent. Plethon benefited in having had access to many more philosophical texts in the original Greek than his Latin counterparts; much of what they knew of Aristotle and others had come to them second hand through Arabic sources, which Plethon corrected. It is no exaggeration to say that Plethon, the "second Plato," reintroduced the first to western Europe. His command of dialectic was exemplary and the churchmen whose familiarity with Aristotle he improved were at once in awe and in fear of this Greek whose lectures were fragrant with heresy. Plethon's main argument was that Plato's thought was much more in harmony with Christianity than Aristotle's—for all of Aquinas's scholasticism—and that where Aristotle differed from Plato, he simply misunderstood him.

One of Plethon's lectures was about Aristotle's and Plato's ideas of God. Plethon showed that Plato's idea of God was much more grand and in line with the church's than Aristotle's, and he is generally credited with sparking the Plato versus Aristotle debate that raged throughout the Renaissance.[22]

Yet while Plato was important to Plethon, he shared his place of honor with another. Plethon was a keen reader of the Chaldean Oracles, which he believed originated with Zoroaster, the great Persian sage and religious prophet. As mentioned earlier, we know the Chaldean Oracles really emerged in second-century Rome with the theurgic family known as the Juliani. Plethon didn't know this; for him, the Chaldean Oracles were a fount of the "primal theology" he impressed his audience with in Florence, and Zoroaster was their source. Plethon had come to the Chaldean

Oracles through a collection edited by the eleventh-century Byzantine monk and philosopher Michael Psellus (1017–1078/96?). Psellus, like Plethon, was a scholar and lover of Greek and he also had a hand in another work that, even more than the Chaldean Oracles, would have an enormous influence on the "esoteric Renaissance."

Plethon believed the "Chaldeans" had corrupted some of the oracles, and he deleted the suspect ones from Michael Psellus's collection. He wrote a commentary on the rest, calling it *Magical Sayings of the Magi, Disciples of Zoroaster.* The result has been described as "the most extraordinary kind of Oriental mysticism and magic."[23] It may be that Plethon came to see Zoroaster as the source of the "primal theology" through a Jewish scholar named Elissaeus, with whom Plethon studied during his time in Adrianople.[24] Elissaeus may have been a follower of the Ishraqi school of illumination, stemming from Suhrawardi, who we know anchored his "science of lights" in the pre-Islamic Persian theosophy of Zoroaster. As with Suhrawardi and the Imaginal World, through meditation and prayer, the devotee of the Chaldean Oracles achieves a visionary state, a kind of "inner theurgy."[25] Suhrawardi we know had his own version of the chain of adepts, an idea that Plethon discoursed upon to his Florentine audience. Plethon's great initiates included Zoroaster, Eumolpus (founder of the Eleusinian Mysteries), King Minos of Crete, the oracle of Dodona, Chiron, and the Seven Sages, as well as more familiar figures like Pythagoras, Plato, Plotinus, Porphyry, and Iamblichus.[26] If indeed Plethon received his inspiration for his ancient lawgivers and sages from Elissaeus the Jew, who instructed him in the illuminist philosophy of Suhrawardi, then it seems we can trace at least one spark of the esoteric Renaissance back to Alexandria, as Suhrawardi himself received inspiration from the esoteric exodus from that city.[27] This would not be the only influence coming from that city of sects and gospels.

Plethon left Florence in 1441 and returned to Mistra, where he started his own polytheistic "mystery school." Here he and his students studied philosophy and said prayers to statues of the pagan gods. The Council had not been a success and the proposed unification of East and West did not take place. There is a sense that Plethon had some intuition of a coming crisis and tried to preserve what he could of the Hellenistic world he loved. As with his ideas about reforming the Byzantine Empire along

Platonic lines, Plethon seems to have thought beyond the need to reform the church—as many of the Florentine humanists did—and more toward a revival of the pagan religions, something along the lines of Suhrawardi's Zoroastrian "science of lights." The philosopher and scholar George of Trebizond, who attended the Council of Ferrara-Florence, was scandalized by Plethon's prediction that a new universal religion, based on a revival of paganism, would take the place of Christianity and Islam. Trebizond was a staunch Aristotelian and he countered Plethon's pro-Platonic philosophy with a work of his own.[28]

Plethon's last and most heretical work, *Nomoi* (*Book of Laws*), brought together a medley of beliefs, combining Zoroastrianism with astrology, Neoplatonism, and the Brahmins of India, as well as elements of Sufism and mystical Christianity, all linked together through his pagan polytheism which he hoped would provide the basis for a new society. It was never published, and after Plethon's death, the book fell into the hands of his ex-pupil Scholarius, who burned it but saved just enough to justify his actions to the authorities.

THE RETURN OF HERMES TRISMEGISTUS

Plethon's Florentine lectures met with great success, and with no one more than Cosimo de' Medici (1389–1464), the city's great power broker.[29] Cosimo had heard Plethon, and his words had fired him. The idea of a "primal theology" at the root of all religions impressed him deeply, and Plethon's championing of Plato led Cosimo to an inspired idea: he would start his own Platonic Academy, right there in Florence. It would, of course, require someone knowledgeable in Greek and well versed in philosophy to head it. Luckily such a person was immediately at hand.

It is unclear exactly who put the word in Cosimo's ear, but the name Marsilio Ficino (1433–1499), a young scholar of Greek and philosophy, was spoken of highly. In 1459, the twenty-six-year-old Ficino was interviewed by Cosimo and made a good impression. By 1462, Ficino was installed in a villa in Careggi, in the hills above Florence, and a revived Platonic Academy was open for business. It would do well. Soon Ficino's

Platonic Academy attracted numerous artists, poets, and philosophers eager to learn about the ancient philosophy, which Ficino expounded with style and insight. Important figures from his time and beyond felt his influence, so much so that it is no exaggeration to say that Ficino "wrought a deep and lasting change in European society" and that "the whole intellectual life of Florence . . . was under his influence."[30] We may agree with James Hillman that making Ficino solely responsible for the quattrocento is an overstatement, but it is one that comes fairly close to the truth.[31]

Around the same time, Cosimo, an obsessive collector of books and manuscripts, had acquired a collection of Plato's texts that required translation into Latin. Plethon's intuition of a coming crisis had come true. The Latin church did not come to the aid of its Greek cousin, and in 1453, a year after Plethon's death, Constantinople fell to the Ottomans. As the Turk drew near, many Christian scholars fled, bringing with them whatever of their libraries they could carry, selling what they could to fuel their flight. It was through this frantic escape that Plato had arrived at Cosimo's door.

Cosimo was an old man but he had a noble ambition: he wanted to read all of Plato before he died. To this end he gave Ficino the task of translating his new collection. But just as he was about to begin, Cosimo ordered him to stop. Another collection of texts had arrived, and these, Cosimo believed, were even more important. One of Cosimo's book scouts had come across something in Macedonia that he knew his employer would like. It was a near complete collection of the *Corpus Hermeticum*, the sacred works of the ancient sage and teacher Hermes Trismegistus. It had been lost for a millennium. Scraps of it had appeared over the centuries, and the collection that came to Cosimo's and then Ficino's hands was most likely the version of the Hermetic writings put together by Michael Psellus, who had edited the Chaldean Oracles that so impressed Plethon.[32] Plato was of course important. But Hermes Trismegistus shared top billing with Zoroaster as a source of the *prisca theologia*.[33] It was from this source that the divine Plato had drunk and so, Cosimo thought, Hermes had precedent. Ficino agreed and got to work. It was a great sacrifice for Cosimo. He got to read the *Corpus Hermeticum*, but died before Ficino could get back to Plato.

That Plato took a backseat to Hermes has not been lost on commentators. Frances Yates, whose groundbreaking work opened the door to the "esoteric Renaissance," calls the situation "extraordinary."[34] Some of the Hermetic writings were known in the Middle Ages. The Greek original of the *Asclepius* had been lost, but a Latin translation—incorrectly ascribed to Apuleius, author of *The Golden Ass*—was well-known. It had been through this work that Ficino and the other Florentine humanists had come to understand the importance of Hermes Trismegistus. It was the *Asclepius* that drew the ire of St. Augustine, who condemned its advocacy of theurgy, and which led him to condemn all magic as the work of demons. It is also in the *Asclepius* that Hermes makes his gloomy prophecy about Egypt's coming "dark days." But while the *Asclepius* is a work of magic and prophecy, the works of the *Corpus Hermeticum* have a different character. Most of the Florentine humanists were also good Christians and they could be expected to hesitate when dipping into a work of magic that an important figure like Augustine considered dangerous. But these texts were different, and the belief that with them they had gained access to a source of the "primal theology" excited Ficino and his friends.

A MELANCHOLY PLATONIST

Ficino was the son of a doctor and one suspects that he would have followed in his father's footsteps had it not been for the influence of his mother. She appears to have been of a dark, brooding, melancholy nature and also to have possessed certain psychic gifts. Accounts say she predicted her mother's death and her husband's riding accident accurately, and that with her frail physique and emotional sensitivity, she was considered somewhat odd.[35] Ficino seems to have inherited his mother's characteristics. He had a melancholy nature which his physical frailty and deformity—he was hunchbacked and dwarfish in appearance—could not have helped. The picture one gets of him is of a sensitive, retiring, physically shy but mentally active individual, who enjoyed company, conversation—although he had a stammer—music, and the arts.

Yet in a sense Ficino did inherit his father's role as a healer. Ficino's particular attraction to Hermetic ideas led to his developing them into a kind of Renaissance psychotherapy.[36] His father had attended men's bodies, but he would heal their souls. It was as a "Doctor of Souls," a name he had given to Plato, that Ficino would be known to his contemporaries, and it was in the same capacity that a kind of Ficino revival took place in the 1980s and '90s. This was mostly through the work of James Hillman, whose influential book *Re-Visioning Psychology*, published in 1975, cast the "loveless, humpbacked, melancholy" Ficino as a precursor to Hillman's own doctrine of the "centrality of soul," crucial to his "archetypal psychology."[37]

Ficino first came across Plato through his Latin teacher, who also introduced him to his second love, music; as part of his later esoteric practice, Ficino would compose music and sing the Orphic Hymns, something Gemistos Plethon did as well. His interest in Plato was further piqued by lectures he attended at the University of Florence, where his instructor encouraged him to continue with Greek. Ficino had a knack for it, and the little Plato he encountered provided much more felicitous examples of the language than Aristotle. Yet Aristotle's influence was inescapable, and Ficino's obvious preference for the hated Plato soon got him into trouble. He was accused of heresy by the archbishop of Florence, forbidden to study Greek, and advised to reread his Thomas Aquinas. Ever the accommodating soul, Ficino did as he was told—but continued with Greek. He took classes in medicine at the University of Bologna and it seemed he was on his way to a medical career after all when Cosimo's desire to reinstate the proscribed Plato led him to headhunt for the right man for the job. Ficino may have been born under a bad sign—he was a Libra, and Saturn was in the ascendant at the time of his birth, apropos, it seems, for his future career. But here at least the stars were in his favor.

It is as a translator and explicator of Plato's philosophy that Ficino is best known, and it is clear that he took his role seriously. He reenacted the *Symposium* every November 7, the date of Plato's original philosophical drinking party, although in most ways his dedication to the philosophical life was much more ascetic. He rose early, worked steadily, was vegetarian and sparing in that. In many ways Ficino's daily life is reminiscent of the Pythagorean ideal. His sexuality remains ambiguous. He may have been homosexual. He did speak of a "unique friend," Giovanni Cavalcanti, a poet and member of Ficino's Platonic Academy, who lived with Ficino for many years in Careggi. Not surprisingly, Ficino characterized their relationship as "Platonic love"—a term he introduced to the West—and their friendship, and Ficino's others, is thought to have been chaste. As his appreciation of the *Symposium* suggests, Ficino was more likely interested in an eroticism of the soul, not the body.

The soul, in fact, was everything for Ficino. His major work, *Platonic Theology*, a massive tome consisting of eighteen books which Ficino labored on for five years, has the immortality of the soul as its central concern. It was an attempt to bring together Platonic philosophy and Christianity, a union that would occupy many Renaissance minds yet which his Byzantine benefactor Plethon opposed.[38] The notion of an immortal soul had already been part of Christian doctrine, but it was not made Christian dogma until the Lateran Council of 1512–1517, a decision almost certainly influenced by Ficino's work.

HERMETIC THERAPY

Ficino also explored the secrets of Hermes Trismegistus. Magic throughout the Middle Ages was considered demonic. We have seen the bad reputation the *Asclepius* had. Another work that Ficino knew, not ascribed to Hermes Trismegistus but linked to him, was the *Picatrix*, an Arab manual of spirit evocation and astrology based on a variety of sources: Hermetic, alchemical, Sufi, and others. One source is thought to have been Jabir ibn Hayyan, who, as we've seen, was known to the West as Geber. It was most likely written in the eleventh century and translated into Latin in the thirteenth century. It is a kind of guide to talismanic magic, talismans being certain symbols thought to attract celestial energies. In a Neoplatonic sense, the *Picatrix* is a text on theurgy.

Ficino's reading of the Neoplatonists convinced him that their theurgic practices were not, as St. Augustine had argued, demonic, but were based on the use of natural forces, on, in fact, the *Anima mundi*. To draw down beneficial stellar influences and to repel baleful ones became for him a kind of practical astrology, a way of using the vital energies of the

Anima mundi to compensate for the celestial cards one was dealt at birth. In Ficino's case, the fact that at his birth Saturn was in the ascendant accounted for his melancholy character; the fact that he had also inherited his mother's disposition, and that he had chosen philosophy as a career, only made things worse. Astrologically, Saturn is the planet of time, limits, restrictions, and responsibilities; it is also known as the "Great Teacher." All philosophers have what we might call an excess of Saturn, hence their serious, pensive character. We can say in Ficino's case, he had it doubly so. To compensate for this, the philosopher needs to balance things with more jovial (Jupiter) and venereal (Venus) influences. Ficino developed a theurgic means of doing this.

Medieval man felt the influence of the stars as a fate he was unable to avoid, yet Ficino shared in the new sense of man's own inherent powers by using the stars' own energies to guide his destiny. Through the power of the Hermetic talismans, Ficino could draw down the venereal and jovial energies needed to counterbalance his saturnine disposition. They acted, in a way, as "astral magnets." The talismans were able to do this because, as symbols, they were closer, in an ontological sense, to the *Anima mundi*. And as they were Hermetic symbols, and stemmed from the *prisca theologia*—that is, the ancient source—they were even more powerful. Through the power of correspondence, they were able to attract the desired celestial energies or repel unwanted ones. Ficino in fact believed that through knowledge of the correspondences between symbols and the *Anima mundi*, the Hermetist could "repair" parts of the world that had "fallen from grace," a belief that caused him some trouble with the church.[39]

Talismans and the symbols they employed occupied a position closer to the Platonic Forms out of which, as a good Neoplatonist, Ficino believed God had created the world. In this sense they occupied a similar place to Suhrawardi's Hūrqalyā, the intermediary Imaginal World that exists in between the realm of pure intellect (the Forms) and the physical world. Through using the power of the talismans Ficino was, in a sense, drawing on God's own powers. In this way he had shown that man could now become a cocreator with God.

Along with the talismans, Ficino also devised a way of using the natural correspondences between earthly things and the *Anima mundi*. The participatory mode of consciousness associated with the right brain is aware of the "network of connections that links everything with everything else," and earlier we saw an example of this in Owen Barfield's description of how medieval man saw the world around him. For the Hermetist, certain colors, scents, music, natural forms, minerals, times of day, numbers, and other items were associated with different celestial and planetary energies. In some way, these are able to absorb beneficial forces from the stars. Ficino's "Hermetic therapy" worked by using the knowledge of these correspondences to create an environment that would attract the stellar influences one desired; hence Frances Yates's remark that someone following Ficino's Hermetic prescriptions was rather like the client of an expensive psychiatrist, who could afford to buy beautiful objects and spend time meditating on paintings or listening to music. Strumming a lyre, singing an Orphic Hymn, burning incense, drinking wine, and meditating on a talisman while at ease in your private chamber were the means by which Ficino's therapy worked. Through their knowledge of the Hermetic correspondences, Ficino's "patients" could create a kind of celestial "strange attractor," funneling the stellar influences into their own home. Ficino brought together many of his ideas about "Hermetic therapy" in his Renaissance "self-help" books, *On Making Your Life Agree with the Heavens* and *The Book of Life*, giving his readers a knowledge that allowed them a kind of control over their lives denied to their medieval ancestors.

THE MAGIC OF ART

It is clear that Ficino's "therapy" employed the *via positiva* and it is through his impact on the artists of the Renaissance that he had his greatest influence on the western soul. While the Neoplatonic theurgists wanted to imbue statues of the gods with life, the Renaissance artists who came under Ficino's spell did something perhaps even more miraculous. As Frances Yates writes, "it is chiefly in this imaginative and artistic sense that we should understand the influence of the Renaissance magic . . . inaugurated by Ficino . . . The operative Magi of the Renaissance were the artists and it was a Donatello or a Michelangelo who knew how to infuse the divine life into statues."[40] This ability of the Renaissance artist to imbue inanimate objects with a strange, powerful life—which remains as vital today as when it first appeared—is a clear example of the new confidence in man's own godlike powers, symbolized by Petrarch's ascent of Mount Ventoux. One example of Ficino's influence on a Renaissance masterpiece is Botticelli's *Primavera* (1482), which, aptly enough, is an allegory of the return of life in the spring. The painting, Yates tells us, was directed by Ficino and represents "a practical application of [Ficino's] magic, as a complex talisman, an 'image of the world,' arranged so as to transmit only healthful, rejuvenating, anti-Saturnian influences to the beholder."[41] Ficino believed that the purpose of art was to remind the soul of its origin in the divine world, to create a kind of "homesickness" for the higher realms. It gave, in a way, a direction for the yearning for "distant panoramas" which, we've seen, began with Petrarch.

RETURN Of THE MAGI

Another Renaissance magician who in his own way sought out distant panoramas was the philosopher Giovanni Pico della Mirandola (1463–1494), who came into Ficino's orbit in 1484. Pico was born in Mirandola, near Modena, and was raised in a brilliant and wealthy family. Even as a child he displayed an astonishing memory, and early on his mother decided he would have a career in the church. As a teenager, he studied law in Bologna. For the next several years, he went to various Italian and French universities where he mastered Greek, Latin, Hebrew, Arabic, and Chaldee. Pico's temperament was the polar opposite of Ficino's tact and circumspection, his fiery character earning him recognition as the "most romantic of the Humanists."[42] When his mother died in 1480, Pico turned his attention to philosophy. At around the same time, he began a friendship with a young Dominican monk, Girolamo Savonarola (1452–1498), who later became infamous through the "Bonfire of the Vanities," a public burning of books, artworks, musical instruments, practically anything that could possibly give rise to an "occasion of sin" or to celebrate man at the expense of God. (Today a similar cultural vandalism is regularly performed by the

Taliban and more recently ISIS.) Savonarola's rabid antihumanism—Ovid and Dante were among those whose works he destroyed—can be seen as a desperate attempt to push back the clock, to, in a sense, reject the shift in western consciousness triggered by Petrarch's ascent of Mount Ventoux.

Pico had read the Chaldean Oracles and had discovered the Kabbalah. He was familiar with the works of the *Hermetica,* and the idea of the *prisca theologia* led him to the notion of synthesizing the Christian, pagan, and Hebrew traditions into one doctrine. This was the basis for the nine hundred theological theses he planned to defend in a public debate in Rome. In 1486, while waiting to start the debate, he published the theses. Pope Innocent VIII had a look at them, got wind of Pico's plan, and put a stop to it. Thirteen of Pico's theses were condemned outright, and the rest did not fare much better. The general criticism was that they "reproduced the errors of pagan philosophers" and that they seemed to endorse magic.

Pico's magic was not the harmless natural kind that Ficino had convinced the authorities was behind his talismans and "Hermetic therapy." Pico had somewhat grander designs, and an idea of why the church found his theses dangerous can be seen in the one we have already quoted: "There is no science which gives us more assurance of Christ's divinity than magic and the Kabbalah." Pico's bold statement was meant to assert Christ's supremacy, but for the learned theologians who questioned him, he seemed to be saying that Christ was merely one magician among others, an idea with which the church could not agree. Faced with certain arrest, Pico fled Italy but was stopped in France, where he was imprisoned.

Pico was eventually allowed to return to Florence a few years later but something had changed in him, and the follower of Plato, Hermes, and the other sages of the *prisca theologia* had now become a disciple of the dour Savonarola, agreeing with him that "the least little child of the Christians is better than Socrates and Plato." He gave away his fortune and burned his poetry. He had decided to become a wandering evangelist but was prevented from starting this new career by his untimely death at thirty-one. The cause of his death remains a mystery and there is some suspicion that he may have been poisoned, a not uncommon occurrence in Renaissance Florence.

Before his flight and arrest, Pico was able to deliver his famous

Oration on the Dignity of Man, which contains the essence of his theses. Its celebration of the new belief in man's own powers contrasts sharply with his later chastened humility. Pico's aim was to show that humanity could get to the roots of being itself, to the *logos* behind creation. Where Ficino limited himself to drawing on the beneficial energies of the *Anima mundi*, Pico went further and argued that man had access to godlike powers, to the Forms themselves. The *Oration* has been called "the manifesto of humanism" but Pico's aim was for something much more like "superhumanism."[43] In a sense we can see him as the godfather of the "human potential movement" that began in the 1960s.

The *Oration* begins with a remark by Abdala the Saracen—thought to be a cousin of Mohammed—who, when asked what in the world was most worthy of wonder, had answered "man." Pico remarks that in the *Asclepius*—perhaps not the best work to use in his defense—Hermes says much the same: "What a great miracle is man." (So would Shakespeare in *Hamlet:* "What a piece of work is a man!") Pico's central argument is, as Colin Wilson put it, that man is a god who "has forgotten his heritage and come to accept that he is a beggar."[44] His aim was to remind man of his roots, something the entire Hermetic tradition wished to do.

Pico points out man's peculiar position in the cosmos. Unlike all other created beings, man has no fixed nature nor fixed place; as the *Asclepius* and *Poimandres* tell us, man is dual-natured, with equal parts of the earth and the spirit. He is also a microcosm, a little cosmos, containing the whole of creation in his own being. "The Supreme Maker decrees," Pico writes, that man "should have a share in the particular endowment of every other creature . . . We have given you, O Adam, no visage proper to yourself."[45] "We have made you a creature neither of heaven nor of earth, neither mortal or immortal, in order that you may, as the free and proud shaper of your own being, fashion yourself in the form you may prefer."[46]

As Petrarch had discovered, man was not chained to the earth nor was he only a lowly worm, wretched and sinful. Man, Pico tells us, can make of himself what he will. He can "descend to the lower, brutish forms of life" or "rise again to the superior orders whose life is divine."[47] (In Pico's posthumously published *Treatise Against Astrology*, he embraces Ficino's belief that man can alter his fate and free himself from the dominance of the stars.) It is man's choice how he will live, which parts of himself he will develop and which reject: "Whichever of these [the brutish or the superior forms of life] a man should cultivate, the same will bear fruit in him."[48]

Critics as far apart as the Traditionalist René Guénon and the feminist thinker Charlene Spretnak have seen Pico's call to arms as little more than an expression of a dangerous hubris. For them, Pico's philosophy is an attempt to "bring everything down to purely human elements" and results in the complete "humanization" of the world, at the expense of both nature and the sacred.[49] There is much to consider in these criticisms and we should remember that Pico himself abandoned his own philosophy in favor of Savonarola's antihumanism. Yet such caveats should not obscure the importance of Pico's ideas. I think we must agree with Frances Yates that "the profound significance of Pico della Mirandola in the history of humanity can hardly be overestimated."[50] After him, western man was confident again in his own powers and in his ability to act upon the world and control his destiny.

Someone who agreed with Pico was Giordano Bruno (1548–1600), who was burned at the stake at the Campo de' Fiori in Rome in 1600. His execution marks an unmistakable shift in the church's attitude toward Hermes and magic. Bruno was born in Nola, then part of the Kingdom of Naples, in the foothills of Mount Vesuvius, an appropriate birthplace for someone of his explosive character. His life was one long, wearying, and eventually disastrous conflict with the ecclesiastical authorities.

Bruno's execution is generally seen to be the result of his championing of the Copernican heliocentric solar system against the longstanding Ptolemaic geocentric one. Copernicus's groundbreaking ("universe shattering," actually) book *On the Revolutions of the Heavenly Spheres* was published in 1543, just before he died. Like Ficino, Copernicus was a wary sort and it was only with great difficulty that his friends finally persuaded him to let his work see print. As Lynn Picknett and Clive Prince make clear in *The Forbidden Universe,* Copernicus was well steeped in the Hermetic philosophy, and they make a strong argument that the central idea of Copernicus's theory—that the Sun, and not the Earth, is the center of our patch of the universe—was itself a Hermetic insight.[51] Their book is key to understanding how much of the science that would soon denounce the Hermetic, occult, and esoteric view of the world as superstitious nonsense, itself emerged from the very worldview it sought to annul.

Yet while Bruno accepted Copernicus's "discovery"—Aristarchus of Samos (310–230 B.C.) had presented his own heliocentric theory ages earlier, and Copernicus himself gives credit to two members of the *Aurea Catena*, Pythagoras and his disciple Philolaus (a teacher of Plato), for helping him—the real reason for his auto-da-fé was his belief in an infinite universe filled with innumerable worlds, a vision that is much more like our own, and which he shared with Nicolas of Cusa, Gemistos Plethon's shipmate. For Bruno (and Nicolas), the Earth was not the center of the universe but one star among countless others in a space that was endless. The fact that Bruno also wanted to see a return of the ancient Egyptian religion—much as Gemistos Plethon wanted to see a revival of pagan beliefs—with himself at its head could not have helped. Bruno believed the church had brought about the decline of man and was responsible for the kind of spiritual "dark days" prophesied in the *Asclepius*. Like Pico, Bruno made it his mission to reawaken men to their true position in the cosmos, and in perhaps his most controversial work, *The Expulsion of the Triumphant Beast*, he celebrates the return of the Egyptian gods and portrays himself as their avatar.

TRIALS OF THE MAGICIAN

Like many at the time, Bruno began his career in the church. At seventeen, he entered a Dominican order. It was when he was preparing to be ordained, at the age of twenty-four, that Bruno's remarkable powers of memory seem to have become apparent. Pico, too, displayed an impressive memory, but Bruno seems to have surpassed even his. In *The Art of Memory* (1966), Frances Yates argues that Bruno revived "magical memory," an ancient mnemonic discipline that would become an indispensable part of the magician's armory. In order to remember their long orations, Roman rhetoricians would memorize a series of places in an imaginary building and they would decorate these "inner rooms" with various images related to the subject of their speech. As they inwardly walked through their "memory palaces," the different images reminded them of the appropriate part of their speech, some of which were hours long. Today, with concerns about memory loss and ADHD due to overindulgence in computers and video games, the kind of memory the ancients seemed to enjoy and which Bruno revived strikes us as nothing short of magical. As we will see, it was precisely for magical purposes that Bruno developed it.

Bruno's intransigence began when he threw away images of the saints, keeping only a crucifix, something the participants in the Protestant Reformation (1517–1648) were busily doing themselves. At the same time, he seems to have recommended several "dangerous" books to a fellow monk; one of these may have been the works of the humanist Erasmus, whom the church had banned. More offenses followed, the most serious being his defense of the Arian heresy. Bruno was forced to flee Naples and the Inquisition, and he did not stop running until his arrest in 1592. For thirteen years, Bruno traced a dizzying route through much of Europe, crisscrossing the Continent in a fruitless search for a stable resting place. Many of Bruno's troubles were of his own making. His querulous, often paranoid character lost him his friends and earned many enemies.

Yet Bruno did more than argue, and during his *Wanderjahre,* he earned a degree in theology, lectured in philosophy, was in and out of the church, put on and took off his monk's habit, gave demonstrations of his "magical memory," and performed other feats that seemed to many much more like "black magic." From Italy he entered France, then Switzerland, then England, where he tried to get a teaching position at Oxford, and where he lectured on the return of the Egyptian gods as well as the Copernican system. He then went to Germany and Bohemia (today the Czech Republic). In Prague, Bruno spent six months at the court of the Holy Roman Emperor Rudolph II, known for his alchemical and all-round eccentric interests; other of Rudolph II's guests included the magician John Dee and his "scryer" Edward Kelly, the astronomers Tycho Brahe and Johannes Kepler, and the alchemists Michael Maier and Michael Sendivogius.[52] Bruno informed Rudolph II that he, the emperor, was the "new Hermes Trismegistus." Bruno's flattery did not secure him a home in Prague— most likely Bruno really reserved the notion of being a new "thrice great one" for himself—and he was forced to move on.

More travels and controversy followed. The end was in sight in 1591, when Bruno attended the Frankfurt Book Fair. Bruno had written about his "magical memory" and a reader of his work invited him to Venice to tutor him in this art. It was a dangerous risk to return to Italy, but Bruno needed the work and he bet on the Inquisition having a worse memory than his. Yet his argumentative personality once again cost him, and his patron, weary of Bruno's demands and concerned about his claims to godhood—and his own possible complicity in them—mentioned his name to the Inquisition. Bruno was soon arrested on charges of blasphemy, heresy, magic, and preaching the belief in many worlds. For his encounter with his inquisitors, Bruno had armed himself with a selection of magical talismans, more powerful than the kind Ficino used, and it seems he carried himself off well. But then the pope stepped in, and in 1593 Bruno was on his way to Rome.

He remained in jail for the next seven years, the length of his trial. Heliocentrism was not made heretical until 1616, so technically it did not figure in the charges against Bruno. (The church held its anti-Copernican position until the mid-eighteenth century; today it maintains an observatory.[53]) Along with preaching the belief in innumerable worlds, the worse charges against Bruno were those of practicing magic. It was Bruno's bad luck that he was up against a character as martial as himself, Cardinal Bellarmine, who would confront Galileo, another willful personality, some years later. Bruno recanted on many points where it was clear he had contradicted church dogma, but on the issue of innumerable worlds he refused. He might have taken a feather from Galileo's cap—if we can excuse the anachronism—and recanted this as well, muttering under his breath "There are still many."[54] But Bruno found compromise difficult, and like others the church found too dangerous to ignore, he was sent to the flames.

MAGICAL MEMORIES

Bruno is remembered today as a martyr to free thought and a victim of the church's tyranny. But his real importance is as a magician and visionary, and it is in his ideas about "magical memory" that this is most clear.

Bruno took seriously the Hermetic injunction that in order to understand God, one must make oneself equal to him. His means of doing this was through his "magical memory." Bruno devised a method of impressing on his consciousness divine images of the celestial archetypes, what he called "the seals of the stars," much in the way that Ficino had used talismans to attract beneficial astral energies. For Bruno, these images were "shadows" or reflections of the Platonic Forms—the title of his book *The Shadow of Ideas* says as much. Taking the images from the Hermetic books, Bruno made talismans and then fixed these symbols in his memory, furnishing his mind in the same way that the ancient rhetoricians furnished their "memory palaces."

As with Ficino, these Hermetic images had great power, and it was through them that Bruno believed he performed magic and impressed his will upon the world. Ficino would never be so bold as to say it, but Bruno had no hesitation in declaring that in this way he became a cocreator with God. His images, ranging through the Great Chain of Being from minerals to man, constituted an inner universe, at the center of which was the magician, just as the sun was at the center of the new Copernican cosmos. In this way Bruno stood outside space and time and achieved the "cosmic consciousness" that was the goal of the ancient Hermetists. From humbly using the "natural" energies of the *Anima mundi,* the Renaissance magician had now become something much more like God himself.

THE END OF MAGIC

By the time of Bruno's death, the church had turned away from anything to do with magic or Hermes Trismegistus. It had seemed for a time that there was a good chance that at least some Hermetic ideas would find a place within the church's compass. Ficino's attempt to bring Plato and Christ together had made an impression, and not a few within the church thought that if not a union of the two, at least a broadening of the church's view to include worthy fellow travelers like Hermes was possible. Evidence for Hermes' brief high standing can be seen in the mosaic pavement at the entrance to the Cathedral of Siena, put in place by Giovanni di

Stefano in 1488. Here Hermes is flanked by two sibyls, ancient oracles who, like Hermes himself, were considered prophets of Christ. An inscription relates that Hermes was a contemporary of Moses, whose representation seems to be bowing before the Egyptian. Another figure may be Asclepius, and Hermes' hand rests on a tablet containing a passage from the *Asclepius*.

Even more striking are the Hermetic frescoes in the Appartamento Borgia in the Vatican. Painted by Bernardino di Betto—better known as Pinturicchio—for the "Borgia pope" Alexander VI, a devotee of magic, the frescoes display the career of Hermes in his many forms, one of which is as the teacher of Moses. Other figures include Isis and the Apis bull, which was identified with Osiris, and formed one half of the syncretic god Serapis whose Serapeum in Alexandria was destroyed by Patriarch Theophilus in 391. The bull was a symbol of the Borgia family, and in the frescoes, the Borgia bull is identified with Apis. The connection with Osiris suggests that in some way Alexander VI saw himself as linked to the ancient Egyptian gods, and he may have had an interest in their revival that predated Bruno's.[55]

There were other hopeful signs. In 1540, the humanist, biblical scholar, and Catholic apologist Agostino Steuco coined the term *philosophia perennis* ("perennial philosophy") to account for the harmony he saw between the pagan philosophies and the church. In 1579, the alchemist and bishop of Aire, François Foix de Candale, argued that the Hermetic books should be made canonical, an outlook that informed the Venetian philosopher and scientist Francesco Patrizi when, toward the end of the century, he petitioned Pope Clement VIII to have Hermetic ideas taught in Christian schools. Patrizi shared with Plethon a criticism of Aristotle and held the belief that Plato and other pagan thinkers heralded Christ.[56]

Many respected minds defended Plato and Hermes, but it was not the best time to ask the church to embrace magic. Works like Cornelius Agrippa's (1486–1535) *Three Books of Occult Philosophy* (1531), a mammoth compendium of the dark arts and "one of the most important works in the western magical tradition," seemed to return to the kind of thing associated with the *Picatrix*.[57] A pious Christian, Agrippa argued for the need to know the true God and the importance of a strong faith, but with its focus on planetary spirits, elementals (spirits of fire, water, air, and earth), the evil power of menstrual blood, folk remedies, numerology, and other suspect practices, to many his work smacked more of sorcery than philosophy.[58] Agrippa himself had been taught by the cryptologist and abbot Johannes Trithemius (1462–1516), who had also taught Paracelsus. Trithemius was accused of conjuring demons, and his association with the unlucky Doctor Johann Faustus (1480–1539), whom he called "the most accomplished alchemist that ever lived," could not have helped his reputation; stories of Faust's pact with the devil began to appear in 1587.[59]

John Dee (1527–1609), Queen Elizabeth I's astrologer and a guest of Rudolph II, contacted angels through the services of his medium, Edward Kelly, by all accounts a dubious character. The angels spoke to Dee in a curious language he called "Enochian," named after the biblical figure whom the Muslims associated with Hermes Trismegistus.[60] Dee was as much a mathematician and early scientist as a magician, and in the early days before science's triumph, its association with magic—through their shared use of mathematics—did not serve it well.[61] The rising antimagic sensibility conflated anything to do with mathematics or numbers with evil "conjurations," and books of mathematics were considered just as pernicious as those containing spells.[62] Dee—who according to his biographer, anticipated in some ways Newton and Galileo—was eventually accused of black magic; his library was vandalized and he died in poverty and obscurity.[63]

What turned the consciousness of the time so vehemently against magic? In one sense we can see it as a turn away from the *via positiva* embodied in the Renaissance and a movement toward the *via negativa*. It was precisely accusations of a concern with worldly beauty and magic made against Catholicism that prompted Martin Luther to nail his famous theses to the door of the Wittenberg church in 1517, thus inaugurating the Protestant Reformation. Among other things, Luther was disgusted with the practice of "indulgences." These were assurances given to the faithful that for a price, a priest would intercede on their behalf or that of a loved one, arranging things so that their salvation would go smoothly. It was a way to secure a good seat in heaven, more or less. The money went to help rebuild the basilica of St. Peter in Rome, which may have been a worthy cause; like the Gothic cathedrals, we can see it as an expression of the *via positiva*. Yet Luther and the Protestant Reformation he triggered were very much informed by the *via negativa*, and saw such designs as so much frippery. Like Meister Eckhart, they were interested in a direct route to God and had no time for intermediaries.

More to the point, they saw little difference between a priest arranging things in the afterlife and a magician consulting the *Picatrix* to command a demon. In fact, as D. P. Walker argues in *Spiritual and Demonic Magic: From Ficino to Campanella*, the Catholic Mass can be seen as a kind of Ficinian magical ritual.[64] All the elements are there: music, magical words, incense, lights, wine, and a form of theurgy or, more precisely, theophagy, the ingestion of the god in the form of the Communion wafer. It was this sort of practice, coupled with a polytheistic pantheon of saints and the images associated with them, that sent Protestant iconoclasts raging in cities like Zurich, Copenhagen, and Geneva, destroying statues and paintings in a way that made Savonarola's bonfire seem like a picnic.

The Reformation had no interest in magic, and the church already had its own. Neither needed or wanted Hermes or anyone else. The kind of fundamentalism the Protestants endorsed was much like the kind that sent Suhrawardi to his death and had the Arab leader Amr ibn al'Aas burn the books of the library of Alexandria. The Protestants burned books too. In England in 1550, during the reign of the teenage king Edward VI, the first raised as a Protestant, huge bonfires blazed in Oxford, and entire libraries were thrown into them. Among the volumes burned were works of mathematics and science. Much like Abbot Amalric, who during the "sack of Béziers" made no distinction between Cathar and faithful, and ordered his army to "kill them all," leaving it to God to "know his own," the Protestant Puritans ignored the difference between magic and anything else they couldn't understand.

HUMAN OR SUPERHUMAN?

The church had other reasons for closing ranks and shutting the door on the *prisca theologia*. For a time during this period, there was a jockeying for position among the different competitors for what we might call the dominant view of man's place in the cosmos.[65] Brief alliances were made, but in the end, of the four competing views—that of the church, rising science, humanism, and the Hermetic philosophy—it was Hermeticism and the esoteric or "occult sciences" that fared the worst.

Ironically, it was not the church nor nascent science that dealt the Hermetic tradition a serious if not fatal blow, but the very humanism that emerged from Petrarch's interest in the past and penchant for mountain climbing, and which informed the Hermetic revival itself. In 1610, the French Huguenot Isaac Casaubon, considered the most learned man in Europe, was asked by James I of England to write a criticism of Cardinal Caesar Baronius's *Annales Ecclesiastici,* a vast Counter-Reformation history of the church. James I was trying to find a "middle way" between the extremes of Catholicism and Protestantism, and he thought Casaubon was the man for the job. The undermining of Hermes Trismegistus's reputation was really only some collateral damage incurred during Casaubon's research.[66]

Baronius had repeated the church father Lactantius's remarks about how Hermes Trismegistus had prophesized the coming of Christ. Casaubon knew that as a sage of the *prisca theologia,* Hermes Trismegistus was supposed to be a source for Plato's philosophy. But Casaubon also knew that there was no mention of Hermes in Plato, or in any of the other pagan philosophers who were supposed to have received Hermes' wisdom. Casaubon's scholarly instincts were piqued. Consulting the *Corpus Hermeticum* closely, Casaubon came to the conclusion that the Greek it was written in was a form of Greek that came *after* Plato. It was not the Greek of the time before Plato; it was a later Greek, not an earlier one. It was, in fact, the Greek of Roman Alexandria. Casaubon's conclusion was that whoever wrote the *Corpus Hermeticum,* it was not written at the "dawn of time," nor during the time of Moses, or at any time earlier than the first centuries after the birth of Christ. These texts were not as old as they were believed to be.

In the end, Casaubon decided that the writings attributed to Hermes Trismegistus were really written by Alexandrian Christians who concocted these forgeries in order to bring pagans to the true faith, by showing that one of the great pagan sages of the past had anticipated the incarnation of Christ. Plato did not learn from Hermes; the authors of these works incorporated Platonic ideas into them. And they did not speak of "Egyptian wisdom"; the Christian parallels were too clear for that and accounted for the mistaken idea that the thrice-great one had somehow got advance knowledge of Christ. It was a pious fraud, but a fraud nonetheless. This was more or less the understanding of the *Corpus Hermeticum* for centuries, but more recent scholarship questions much of it.[67]

Casaubon was only following his scholarly instincts and did not intend to cast doubt on the authenticity of the *Hermetica*. Yet what was at work here were really two different notions of humanism. I've suggested that the humanism associated with Pico was really a kind of "superhumanism." It wanted to expand the idea of the human so that it would embrace the godlike. William Blake captured its essence in "The Everlasting Gospel" when he wrote "Thou art a Man: God is no more/Thy own Humanity learn to adore." Blake wasn't celebrating atheism; the god he rejects is "Old Nobodaddy," the demiurge of the Gnostics, whom he associates with Urizen, his mythological embodiment of an unrestricted rationality.[68] Blake wanted man to celebrate his powers, specifically his imagination. We can see the struggle between Urizen ("Your reason") and Los, Blake's symbol of the imagination, as that between the left and right brain.

A similar opposition developed in the early days of humanism. One side looked to Greek philosophy, to Neoplatonism and Hermetism, and was passionate about metaphysics and science. It saw the world from a "cosmic" perspective and was interested in the big questions: life, death, destiny, God. It was speculative, inspired, and used intuition as much as intellect. The other side took Rome, not Greece, as its model. Its concerns were good form and rhetoric; the Latin orators were its guides. Rome had no philosophy or religion of its own and borrowed what it had from the Greeks, but it excelled at practical pursuits, like making roads and building empires. This form of humanism was urbane, sophisticated, and skeptical. It focused on getting things "right," and was less prone to excess than Pico or Bruno. It counseled curbing enthusiasm in favor of cool appraisal. Its version of humanism is the one we are more familiar with today. We can see it as a kind of "only humanism."

It does not take too much to suggest that "superhumanism" is more slanted toward a right-brain perception, while "only humanism" veers more to the left, with its exactitude and eye for detail. If this is so, we can see Casaubon's critical nit-picking as left-brain humanism bringing down the right.[69] What Pico, Bruno, and others saw as a message of man's inherent godhood, Casaubon and earlier humanists like Eramus saw as exaggerated gushing; as Frances Yates said, "an atmosphere of unadulterated humanism is not one which is congenial to the Magus."[70] The "only humanist" is always bringing the "superhumanist" down to earth and chiding him for his bad grammar and excesses. Casaubon himself has gone down in history as the archetype of the dry-as-dust grammarian. A character of this description is named after him in George Eliot's novel *Middlemarch*, and the pedantic scholar in Umberto Eco's anti-esoteric novel *Foucault's Pendulum* shares his name as well. Oddly, the right-brain-oriented humanism, with its interest in mathematics and philosophy—which its left-oriented brother disliked—would soon grow into modern science, occupying the now empty space left by the retreat of Hermes. And the church, now free of its cosmic rival, would for a time have unchallenged dominance in man's spiritual concerns.

Casaubon's almost offhand undermining of the authenticity of the *Corpus Hermeticum*—and, by association, that of the *prisca theologia*—happened in 1614. In the years that followed, the Hermetic view slowly but surely lost ground. Marin Mersenne's attack on the esoteric tradition as a whole—spelled out in the Introduction—took place in 1623. Any vision of the world that saw it as a living intelligent whole, infused with spirit, interconnected by subtle correspondences and invisible forces with which the mind of man could participate, and linked to a higher nonmanifest reality, was henceforth seen as not only incorrect, or heretical, but increasingly as *pathological,* as, indeed, insane. At best it was the product of an ignorant, superstitious sensibility, a debilitating atavism that should be swiftly eradicated.

Three centuries after Petrarch's mind-shifting ascent of Mount Ventoux, Gebser's deficient mode of the mental-rational structure of consciousness was in full swing. The brief détente between the two sides of our brain that Iain McGilchrist argues took place during the Renaissance was over. After this there was a decided shift to the virtues of our left cerebral hemisphere: to analysis, measurement, and precision; to parts rather than the whole; to formulae rather than mythologies; to explicit facts rather than implicit meanings; to an "either/or" rather than a "both/and"; to clarity, detail, and an increasing desire to apply the knowledge thereby gained to achieving mastery over the world rather than participating with it. It was the beginning of the kind of world we know today, and in the face of it, the esoteric tradition was forced to go underground.

CHAPTER EIGHT

ESOTERIC UNDERWORLD

In 1614, the same year that Isaac Casaubon revealed the truth about Hermes Trismegistus, a pamphlet appeared in Cassell, Germany, announcing the existence of a strange secret society. The anonymous authors of this mysterious document would not have known about Casaubon's bombshell. It took some time for the fallout from Casaubon's revelation to take effect, and many who were Hermetically inclined carried on in spite of it.[1] So the appearance of the *Fama Fraternitatis* ("The Fame of the Fraternity"), the title of this strange pamphlet, can't be seen as a response to Casaubon's erudition. Yet the timing is so apt that one is almost forced to suspect a connection. My own suspicion is that something like Jung's synchronicity was involved, in this case on a historical scale.

The pamphlet spoke of the Brotherhood of the Rosy Cross, or, as they are also called, the Rosicrucians, and it called on all who read it to join the society in its work. This was nothing less than a total reconstruction of Europe, a complete reformation of the science, politics, religion, and social systems of the time. The pamphlet was couched in an obscure Hermetic, alchemical, and astrological language, with clear anti-Catholic and anti-Habsburg sentiments—the Habsburgs being the then-reigning royal house of Europe. Two more similar documents appeared in the following years, and soon practically all of Europe was witness to a "Rosicrucian furore," with wild speculation about the mysterious society dominating the Continent. Yet who or what the Rosicrucians were remained unknown. Many sought them out, as the pamphlets had advised, but all attempts to make contact failed. Try as they may, no one could find them.

The Rosicrucians were so hidden, so secret it seems, that soon they were nicknamed "the Invisibles." Even René Descartes was piqued by the Rosicrucian mystery and tried to reach them, but to no avail. After a while, the fact that all attempts to contact the Rosicrucians proved futile turned interest into contempt and the Rosicrucian furore dwindled into the Rosicrucian hoax. The mysterious society became the butt of jokes and vilification, with accusations of witchcraft and other evils made against it. Finally the Lutheran pastor and literary man Johann Valentin Andreae (1586–1654), one of the authors of these strange documents, admitted that at least one of them, a weird alchemical text called *The Chemical Wedding of Christian Rosenkreutz*—a kind of surrealist novel depicting in symbolic form the Great Work of spiritual transformation—was what Andreae called a *ludibrium*, which means a "serious joke." For most, this put an end to the Rosicrucian mystery. It had been, after all, a hoax all the time. Or had it?

If the people caught up in the Rosicrucian furore were unclear exactly what the excitement was all about, the Rosicrucians themselves, at least according to their documents, were less confused. The *Fama Fraternitatis* tells the story of the society's founder, Christian Rosenkreutz, and his search for wisdom in the East. Like many before him, Christian had journeyed in search of secret knowledge and his initiatory quest has become a kind of archetype for the western seeker of wisdom. Whether he ever existed or not is another story. He is supposed to have been born in 1378 and to have died in 1484, which would have made him 106 at his death. He came from a noble family and, as a child, was given to monks who taught him Latin and Greek. As a young man, Christian accompanied a monk who wished to visit the Holy Lands. En route the monk died, but Christian carried on. He became ill in the mysterious city of Damcar (most likely Damascus) and remained there, where he learned much wisdom from the Arabs. He had further travels in Egypt and North Africa, where he perfected his esoteric knowledge, as well as that of science and mathematics. The sages he met along the way all seemed to be in accord with each other and were happy to share what they knew, a sign perhaps that what Christian was taught was the *prisca theologia*. That he learned it in the East may suggest that it had something to do with the mysterious treasure of the Knights Templar.

After more travels and learning, Christian returned to Europe wishing to share his knowledge, which he hoped could help in a reformation of Christendom. Alas, he met only derision and petty envy. After fruitless attempts to disseminate what he had learned, he decided to build a temple to house his knowledge and to gather like-minded fellows to whom he could pass it on. Five years later, Christian and his companions set out again to spread the word. Later they separated, each going to a different land. Before this, each had taken a vow. They agreed to heal the sick without payment, to wear the dress of the land they found themselves in, to meet each year at the temple, the Sancti Spiritus, or "House of the Holy Spirit," to find someone to take their place when needed, and to keep silent about the brotherhood for one hundred years.

Soon after this, Christian died and he and his followers—the original Rosicrucians—slowly passed into myth, but their descendants secretly kept the work of the society going. When the hundred years had passed, it was agreed that the society should reveal itself. In 1604, a year marked by heavenly events such as the discovery of "new stars" (Johannes Kepler sighted a supernova—an exploding star—that year, and it is named after him), which portended great changes in the land, Christian's tomb was rediscovered in a secret room in the Sancti Spiritus. His uncorrupted body lay within a seven-sided vault, which was lit by a kind of miniature sun. Geometrical figures decorated the walls and among other mysterious objects were copies of works by Paracelsus, as well as a strange book containing Christian's secret knowledge. The members who found Christian's tomb took it as sign to reveal themselves to the world and announce that a great change was on its way and to spread the word among the populace. Hence the mysterious documents eventually turning up in Cassell.

What was the "Rosicrucian furore" about and what was the "general reformation" that the members of this mysterious secret society called for? Many have asked these questions and many have provided answers, some more profitable than others. Manly P. Hall's queries suggest the general tone of inquiry. Were the Rosicrucians, Hall asks, "an organization of profound thinkers rebelling against the inquisitional religious and philosophical limitations of their time" or just a group of visionaries "united only by the similarity of their viewpoints and deductions"? Were they a religious or philosophical brotherhood, or were their designs less innocuous? Did they seek "the political control of Europe," or were they merely esoteric dilettantes, playing some sort of practical joke?[2] Was it all a silly game enjoyed by a group of Protestant students, or something much more serious, as Andreae himself suggested?[3]

Questions about who or what the Rosicrucians were remain to this day, which has not stopped their name being adopted by more than one occult organization claiming them as their ancestors.[4] Like "gnostic," "Rosicrucian" has been taken up by many enthusiasts as a catch-all term indicating a general interest in the occult or the esoteric. For our purposes, it has a more specific connotation. In *The Rosicrucian Enlightenment*, Frances Yates argues persuasively that the Rosicrucian phenomenon was part of an attempt involving Frederick V, the Elector Palatine of the Rhine, to free Europe from Habsburg and Catholic dominance. In Frederick V, a Protestant, many placed their hopes for a Christendom healed of religious strife and open to a more tolerant and pluralistic view. The Rosicrucian manifestoes were, in Yates's view, designed to promote interest and support in this campaign, and to spell out the vision of a new, progressive Europe. For Yates, they convey "an apocalyptic message of universal reformation leading to a millennium."[5]

Such sentiments were not unusual at the time. We've seen that Joachim of Fiore's vision of a coming age of the Holy Spirit influenced many dissatisfied with the church, and there is reason to believe that the authors of the Rosicrucian documents were themselves informed with Joachim's vision.[6] According to Christopher McIntosh, this was a time when "religious and social upheavals had gone hand in hand." Germany especially was a hotbed "of messianic and millennialist ideas."[7] In this instance, however, the dream of a new Europe sadly did not come true. In 1620, at the Battle of White Mountain near Prague, Frederick V's forces were defeated by the armies of Ferdinand II, the newly crowned emperor of the Holy Roman Empire. Ferdinand II was a fanatically intolerant Habsburg Catholic and had inherited the throne from Matthias, who had succeeded to it himself after the death of his brother, Rudolf II. This was one of the first battles of the Thirty Years' War (1618–1648), which devastated the Continent and left whole regions destroyed. Many believe that if Frederick V had been victorious, the war would have been avoided, and rather than bloodshed and ruin, a more progressive Europe may have risen instead.[8]

SECRET SOCIETIES

The events leading up to the Battle of White Mountain are detailed and complex, and trace the century-long struggle between Catholics and Protestants following Luther's theses turning up at the Wittenberg church. That an esoteric brotherhood professing Hermetic, alchemical, and astrological beliefs should be involved in the strife is curious enough, but for our purposes, what is most interesting is that after making much hue and cry about the coming millennium and asking the populace to join in its work, the Brotherhood of the Rosy Cross ducked out of view—or, to be precise, wasn't in it to begin with.

Such secrecy may have been prompted by sheer prudence. The Rosicrucian manifestoes made no bones about their views. In the *Confessio Fraternitatis* ("The Confession of the Brotherhood"), the second pamphlet to appear, the authors "do now altogether freely and securely, without hurt, call the Pope of Rome Antichrist," and Mohammed, too, comes in for a drubbing.[9] Their vision of a mankind free from material cares and miseries—"hunger, poverty, sickness and age"—would prompt any monarch to fear for his throne.[10] Yet such views were not new, and as we've seen, the church had already dealt with several reformists and revolutionists. Bruno wished to revive the ancient Egyptian pantheon, and the philosopher Tommaso Campanella (1568–1639) envisioned a church remodeled after the Hermetic utopian city of Adocentyn, described in the *Picatrix*, in which Ficinian star magic would be the order of the day. Campanella was imprisoned and tortured for his efforts, although after his release, he did perform some Hermetic therapy with Pope Urban VIII who, like Alexander VI, had a taste for magic.[11]

The union of politics and the occult these projects embodied suggest that the Hermetic utopia envisioned by the Rosicrucians was not new. What was new was that the proponents of this dream worked covertly. They were an "occult underground" and they laid the foundations for what would become a kind of esoteric counterculture. Whatever the motivation of the individuals behind the Rosicrucian phenomenon, that they operated in secret at a time when the Hermetic sciences had lost their respectability is at the very least a remarkable coincidence. Before this, magicians and seers spoke openly. Plethon, Ficino, Pico, and Bruno addressed the powers that be and compelled them to listen, if not always to agree. John Dee, whom Yates sees as a major influence on the Rosicrucian phenomenon, engaged in a kind of occult politics that led him to the court of Rudolf II. His "mystic imperialism" was sanctioned by Queen Elizabeth I, whose astrologer he was, and he even coined the term "the British empire," much to the queen's delight. But now such visionaries had to work behind the scenes.

There had always been "elite" or "select" spiritual groups in the past. We have seen some of them with Pythagoras, and other teachers like Ammonius Saccas were said to have reserved certain teachings for special students. Even Jesus, it seems, may have had a secret gospel. There has always been a sense that esoteric knowledge was strictly for the few. Trithemius, who taught Cornelius Agrippa, counseled that "To the vulgar, speak only of vulgar things, keep for your friends every secret of a higher order."[12] Such sentiments seem elitist to us but they make perfect sense and merely stem from the recognition that not everyone is interested in esoteric ideas and not everyone can understand them. But with the "invisible Rosicrucians," something new seems to have started. In the centuries that followed, the idea that there were mystic sages and masters *in hiding* became more and more prevalent. These "secret teachers," as it were, became a central theme in esoteric lore. Following Hermes Trismegistus's fall from grace, not only was the knowledge that he and great sages like him taught "occult," meaning hidden. Now its teachers were too.

PANSOPHIA

The "universal reformation" envisioned by the Rosicrucians was informed by a school of thought known as "Pansophy," which means "all wisdom" or "universal wisdom." It aimed at a synthesis of Hermetic and occult philosophy, nondogmatic Christianity, and the rising new natural sciences.

As with the attempts to wed Plato and Hermes with Christianity, Panso-phy wanted to have the best of both worlds. It was an expression of the same sentiment that lay behind the notion of the *prisca theologia* or *philoso-phia perennis*. We can see it as an early attempt to unite the two approaches to knowledge, the epistemic and the gnostic, that with the deficient mode of the mental-rational structure—and the rise of left-brain dominance— were quickly moving apart. (To coin an ugly word, we can say that Panso-phists sought "epignosis.") For the Rosicrucians and those who followed them, there was no categorical divide or opposition between the sciences of the invisible and the visible worlds. Each complemented the other, and both were needed to have a true, full vision of reality. The same was true in the religious sphere: the dogmatic insistence on the truth of only one belief led to a narrow and limited view.

The proponents of Pansophy, however, had their work cut out for them, for it was precisely such narrow, limited views that increasingly dominated both the church and the nascent science that would soon oppose it. Ferdi-nand II's vehement opposition to any compromise with the Protestant upstarts was paralleled by Marin Mersenne's equally fanatical detestation of everything to do with the Hermetic view of the world. Each had their truths secure in hand and would brook no opposition. The idea of the com-bined pursuit of natural and supernatural knowledge bringing about a progressive, tolerant, and pluralist new world left both cold.

Others were more enthusiastic. John Dee was a Pansophist, and com-bined the study of mathematics with that of the angels. Another was Rudolf II, during whose reign there was a considerable degree of religious tolerance, patronage of science, and the pursuit of occult knowledge, par-ticularly alchemy. Another Pansophist was the Bohemian philosopher, educator, and scientist John Amos Comenius (1592–1670), known today as the "father of modern education."

Comenius is not as well known in the English-speaking world as he should be. In central Europe he is a national hero and his birthday is a holiday. A teacher's college and an adult education program in Hungary are named after him, and Rembrandt painted his portrait. He was asked to be the first president of Harvard, but declined because he was then leader of the Bohemian Brethren, a mystical strain of Protestantism that began with Jan Hus, who was burned at the stake by the Inquisition in 1415. Comenius led the Brethren across a war-torn Europe, and he himself lost his wife, child, and home in the conflict. UNESCO confers a Comenius medal for outstanding achievements in education.

Comenius embodied the utopian, educative strain of the Rosicrucians and he pursued the ideal of knowledge being open and shared by all who desired it, one pursued earlier by Michael Psellus, who offered free university education to any who wanted it.[13] In many ways we can see Comenius's efforts as developing a kind of late Renaissance "information highway," a network of philosophers, teachers, and scientists willing to pool their insights in the service of the common good. The collapse of the Rosicrucian dream with the defeat of Frederick V and the eruption of the Thirty Years' War threw Comenius into despair and precipitated a kind of Rosicrucian "diaspora," with followers of the Brotherhood hounded and forced to go into exile. This spiritual heartbreak is conveyed in Comenius's moving work *Labyrinth of the World,* which depicts a society in which "everything is wrong" and which may present the first dystopia in modern literature.[14]

In the years following the Rosicrucian phenomenon, one outstanding Pansophist was the physician, polymath, and Hermeticist Robert Fludd (1574–1637), against whom Michel Mersenne seems to have taken particular umbrage, if his diatribes against Fludd's work are anything to go by. Fludd's vast knowledge and vast ambition led to his writing vast works with vast titles. His early defense of the now discredited Rosicrucians was called *Apologia Compendiaria Fraternitatem de Rosea Cruce suspicionis et infamiae maculis aspersam, veritas quasi Fluctibus albuens et abstergens* (*A Compendious Apology for the Fraternity of the Rose Cross, pelted with the mire of suspicion and infamy, but now cleansed with the Waters of truth*).

Within that considerable mouthful Fludd managed to conceal a joke, as *fluctibus* means "flood" or "waters" in Latin; so the filth unwarrantedly cast on the Rosicrucians will be cleansed by Fludd himself. This is one of the few light moments in Fludd's work, which in essence aims at proving, at length, that the magic of the Rosicrucians, which he links to the *prisca theologia,* is both holy and scientific, something Mersenne went to equal lengths to deny. Another vast work, *Utriusque Cosmi Historia*—I will not burden the reader with its full title—is a history of the two worlds, the macrocosm and the microcosm. In it, Fludd brought together a wealth of knowledge about medicine, mathematics, music, divination, astrology, "magical memory," and the rising science of mechanics in an enormous attempt to "encompass the whole of learning" and to "summarize the knowledge of both the universe and man."[15] Fludd's Hermetic approach had some hard results. Seeing the heart as the sun and the blood as the planets—the Copernican view based on the Hermetic vision—Fludd's accurate recognition of the cardiovascular system anticipated his contemporary William Harvey, who is generally credited with discovering it.

ALCHEMY

A Pansophist who was at the heart of the Rosicrucian ideal was Paracelsus, like Fludd a physician who combined Hermetic science with a close reading of the "book of Nature." Paracelsus was an alchemist and a healer—he is credited with laying the groundwork for what we today call "natural" or "alternative" healing as well as modern pharmacology—and some background in alchemy is necessary in order to understand his importance.

We've seen that alchemy began in Egypt and that, with the fall of Alexandria, it made its way to the Arab world. In the twelfth century, Arabic alchemical texts began to be translated into Latin, mostly through Spain, where, as we've seen, the beginnings of codified Kabbalah began to take root. In 1142, Peter the Venerable, abbot of Cluny, asked Robert of Chester to translate the Koran into Latin. Chester did, and in 1144, he went on to translate Morienus's *The Book of the Composition of Alchemy* as well, producing the first work of alchemy to appear in Latin.

Alchemy's entrée into western consciousness was by way of scholars and men of learning and had little to do with its later clichéd image of boastful charlatans engaged in the futile pursuit of turning lead into gold. Chester's translations sparked an "Arabic craze," and a flood of new translations followed, which fueled part of the "twelfth-century Renaissance." We've already looked at Albertus Magnus, who was also known as "Doctor

Universalis," which suggests that although he did not use the term, Magnus would not be averse to being call a Pansophist. Two who followed Magnus's example were Roger Bacon (c. 1214–c. 1292) and Magnus's pupil, Thomas Aquinas. Both were practitioners of the Hermetic art.

Bacon was another polymath and seems to have practiced Pansophy before its time. Like later Hermetic scholars, he was accused of sorcery and he spent some time in prison. After his death, his books were nailed in place and left to rot, so convinced were his accusers that he had been in league with the devil. Like Petrarch he seems to straddle two ages, that of the medieval and the beginning of modern consciousness. He was accused of wizardry—he was called "Doctor Mirabilis" because of his supposed magic powers—but he was also an early champion of what became known as the "scientific method."

In *Opus Maius* (*The Greater Work*), Bacon developed what he called a "new method" based on "experience" rather than "argument," which seems a pre-echo of Paracelsus's later attack on dusty dogmatic thinking as opposed to the immediate study of nature. Bacon's "experience" is seen as a precursor to his namesake Francis Bacon's "experimental method," and Francis Bacon himself had Rosicrucian leanings, as can be seen in the utopian themes of his *Advancement of Learning* and *New Atlantis,* with their call for a "fraternity in learning and illumination." Yet as Peter Marshall writes in *The Philosopher's Stone: A Quest for the Secrets of Alchemy,* Roger Bacon had met Sufis while in Spain and his "experience" may have more to do with "Sufi gnosis, involving divine inspiration," than with the kind of detached observation we associate with modern science, a suspicion with which Henry Corbin agrees.[16] Yet Bacon was also often accused of black magic. That he was reported to have a "talking head" made of brass, rather like the animated statutes of the *Asclepius,* could not have helped his reputation, but then Pope Sylvester II (c. 940–1003), a student of Hermeticism and supporter of all learning, had one as well, so Bacon was in good company.

Like the participants in the Renaissance pagan revival, Bacon had a talent for invention and he had plans and designs for "mechanical marvels" such as a flying machine, a submarine, and a kind of early CCTV system involving mirrors.[17] He was introduced to alchemy by his teacher, Robert Grosseteste, who was the chancellor of Oxford and the bishop of

Lincoln. Bacon defined alchemy as "the science of a certain Medicine or Elixir" and separated it into two approaches, what he called "speculative" and "practical" alchemy. Speculative alchemy is concerned with understanding the "generation of things from the elements," and applies a more theoretical approach, while practical alchemy confirms alchemical theory and can bring many material benefits, especially in medicine. It accomplished this by "speeding up" natural processes and by "making things better or more abundantly by art than they are made in nature."[18] One practical benefit was the ability to prolong life. This was the main concern of Chinese alchemy, and it would gain more importance in western alchemy in later years. Fulcanelli, whom we met in Chapter Five, is said to have discovered this secret and, like Christian Rosenkreutz, he is believed to have lived an inordinately long life.

SUMMA ALCHEMICA

Thomas Aquinas is most known for his *Summa Theologica*, the first attempt at systemizing Christian theology, and which wedded Aristotelian logic to Christian faith. But he also believed in the alchemical transmutation of metals. One of the oddest works of alchemy, the *Aurora Consurgens* (*Rising Dawn*) is attributed to him and it has received much attention in Jungian circles. Marie-Louise von Franz, Jung's interpreter and an important thinker in her own right, singles it out for special study.[19]

Von Franz started with the belief that the attribution to Aquinas must be apocryphal—as with Albertus Magnus, many later alchemical texts were attributed to Aquinas but it is clear they were not from his hand. But this one seemed different. Von Franz learned that shortly before his death, Aquinas underwent a strange experience in which his personality was transformed. While working on his *Summa*, he suddenly pushed it away and left it unfinished. When pressed by his colleagues to continue, Aquinas said he could not and that he now felt that everything he had written seemed to him only so much worthless straw. For weeks before this, Aquinas seemed afflicted with a strange absentmindedness. He seemed to have had a kind of mystical experience while saying mass. At the altar he entered a trance and remained silent and still for some time until someone shook him and he came to.

Similar trance states occurred. A friend took him to visit a cousin who was a countess and with whom Aquinas had spoken openly many times. The friend thought that the countess might be able to communicate with Aquinas to find out what was afflicting him. But during their visit, Aquinas again sat perfectly still and silent the entire time. It was after weeks of this that he abandoned working on the *Summa* and rejected all of his accomplishments. A similar experience would happen to Swedenborg some centuries later, what the historian of psychology Henri Ellenberger called a "creative illness," a sudden psychological crisis precipitating a complete change of orientation.[20] In Swedenborg's case, it led to his abandoning his early scientific work, much as Aquinas abandoned his theology.

Aquinas eventually regained a degree of normality and he returned to his church duties. He was asked to attend a congress in southern France. En route, he hit his head on a tree branch and fell from his donkey. He stayed in a nearby monastery and his illness returned, with it a conviction that he would soon die. The monks, delighted at having an important guest, implored Aquinas to teach them something. Gathering his strength, he is said to have begun a seminar on the Song of Songs (or Song of Solomon). It was while lecturing on this that he collapsed and died.

SOPHIA AND THE PHILOSOPHER'S STONE

Von Franz believed that the *Aurora Consurgens* is based on notes taken during Aquinas's fatal seminar. The text seems to recount some sort of "life-shattering experience," which could well have been Aquinas's "creative illness."[21] It describes a vision of Sophia, the Wisdom of God, the feminine spiritual element, which at that time was making a reappearance through the Gothic cathedrals. The philosopher's stone, the great goal of the alchemical quest, is identified with Sophia; and the text, in von Franz's interpretation, describes the process through which the author achieves a new psychic alignment, in which ignored elements of the psyche are reintegrated and a new wholeness is achieved.

The stages of the alchemical process are understood as the necessary transformation of the psyche, from the *nigredo* or darkness of depression, through the purging whiteness of *albedo,* to the final redness of *rubedo,* in which the male and female principles are joined in the *hieros gamos,* or "sacred marriage." In Aquinas's case, the idea seems to be that with his intense focus on sharp Aristotelian logic, he had ignored the need for a more intuitive openness—had, we could say, overemphasized his left-brain virtues at the expense of the right—with the result that he experienced what Jung called an *enantiodromia,* a sudden shift from one point of view or perspective to its opposite. (That Aquinas knew of the "intuitive grasp" of knowledge as opposed to the "active search for it" we have seen in William Anderson's remarks about Dante's similar awareness in Chapter Six.) The "sacred marriage" of the successful alchemical work, which brings the opposites together, achieves this necessary compensation harmoniously and not through the drastic means of a nervous breakdown. Aquinas's rejection of his theological efforts (his left-brain work) is paralleled by other accounts of *gnosis,* in which the sudden vision is so overwhelming that it leaves the plodding process of deductive reasoning far behind.

The kind of spiritualized alchemy found in the *Aurora Consurgens* was not typical of the time. And indeed many esotericists have taken argument with what they see as Jung's "psychologizing" of alchemy; Schwaller de Lubicz and Julius Evola, for example, both reject Jung's approach. Titus Burckhardt, a writer in the Traditionalist school, sums up this response. For Burckhardt, the "secret depths" of the soul that the alchemist wished to reach should not be confused with "the chaos of the so-called collective unconscious," and the alchemist's "'fountain of youth' in no wise springs from an obscure psychic substratum; it flows from the same source as the spirit."[22] Jung believed that the alchemists were engaged in what he called "active imagination," a way of entering into a dialogue with the unconscious, but that they did not know this was what they were doing, and erroneously believed in the reality of physical transmutation.[23] Burckhardt rejects the idea that the alchemists pursued their goal "like sleepwalkers [making] passive 'projections' of the unconscious contents of their souls."[24] But while Burckhardt argues that the alchemists "were never ensnared in any wish-fulfilling dreams of making gold," others, like Schwaller de Lubicz, argued that an actual transformation of matter did take place in their work.[25] For better or for worse, the idea that alchemy is about turning lead into gold—or effecting transmutations in matter—is one that simply won't go away.

PUFFERS AND MASTERS

More representative of early western alchemy was the work of those known as "puffers," because of the bellows they used to keep the alchemical furnace burning. Puffers had no interest in the spiritual side of alchemy and were intent on making gold, or on convincing others, usually kings, that they could. Some may have genuinely believed in their practice, but others were out-and-out frauds, keen on receiving ill-gotten gains through pandering to human greed and gullibility. In the Rosicrucian manifestoes, the authors are eager to differentiate themselves from these charlatans, emphasizing that true alchemy is concerned with the regeneration of man himself. Yet not all who sought the philosopher's stone or universal solvent or the elixir of life were confidence men, and some accounts suggest that on some occasions at least something more than greed and gullibility were at work.

One of the most fascinating accounts of a genuine alchemical transmutation concerns the Frenchman Nicolas Flamel. Flamel was a scrivener by trade—that is, a kind of clerk—and he was known for his generosity and good works. He donated much money to charities and churches, far more than a scrivener could afford, and even paid for hospitals to be built. But he was also suspected of being an alchemist, and rumor had it that he had actually succeeded in discovering the secret of the philosopher's stone. When Flamel died in 1417, his house was invaded by a mob seeking to discover his secrets. In 1612, one of his alchemical works was published and it revealed how Flamel and his wife, Pernelle, had cracked the alchemical code. Flamel had a dream in which an angel came to him and showed him a beautiful old book filled with wonderful illustrations. Years later, Flamel bought a book and remembered his dream: the book he had bought and the one the angel had shown him were the same. It was written by an Abraham Eleazar and it described the art of transmuting metals. Flamel told Pernelle that he could understand only a small part of the book, yet he knew it contained a real treasure.

For twenty years, Flamel and Pernelle—the archetypal *frater mysterium* and *soror mystica*, that is, male and female principles—struggled over the book, but to little avail. Eventually, Flamel made the pilgrimage to Santiago de Compostela in Spain, hoping to meet someone who could enlighten him. He was in luck. Canches, a Jewish merchant, recognized the book as a work of Kabbalah and he explained its mysteries to the alchemist. Flamel invited Canches to return to Paris with him; he did, but he died along the way.

Three years later, at noon on Friday, January 17, 1382, Flamel and Pernelle succeeded in the Great Work: they had made the "red stone" and changed mercury into gold. They repeated their success that spring, and from then on, the Flamels' riches grew, and they generously shared them. One odd part of the story is that after Flamel's death, finding nothing in his house, the mob broke into his and Pernelle's tombs and found that they were empty. Rumors spread that the alchemical couple had escaped to India; one later report places them at the Paris Opera in 1761.

Flamel's story sounds unbelievable, but he did exist, he did practice alchemy, and he did possess great wealth which he shared with needy causes. The French think so well of him that there is a street in Paris named after him—in the Fourth Arrondissement—and in 1900, his house was restored as a national treasure. Others seemed to have replicated Flamel's success. In 1618, the scientist Jean Baptiste van Helmont (1579–1644), one of the founders of chemistry (he discovered gases and even coined the name), was given some "transmutation powder" by a stranger. With it, van Helmont was able to transmute four ounces of mercury into gold. Helvetius—the pseudonym of the Dutch scientist Johann Frederick Schweitzer—left a detailed account of how in January 1667, he changed half an ounce of lead into gold, using a tiny portion of an unknown substance given to him by a strange visitor. When Helvetius complained that such an amount—about the size of a turnip seed he said—would be insufficient, the stranger took it and broke it in two, telling Helvetius that even this small crumb would be enough for the job. It was. Helvetius's success convinced even the philosopher Spinoza, an adherent in his own way of the perennial philosophy.

In 1601, the Scotsman Alexander Seton, a contemporary of Helvetius, came to the rescue of a Dutch sailor who had shipwrecked off the coast near Edinburgh. Seton later visited the sailor in Holland and performed a successful transmutation for him. He then toured Europe, giving more demonstrations before learned doctors, who made detailed accounts. In 1603, the Elector of Saxony, Christian II, imprisoned and tortured Seton, trying to discover his secret. An apprentice alchemist, Michael Sendivogius, helped Seton escape. Seton soon died from his injuries, but not before he gave Sendivogius some of his "powder of projection." Sendivogius became famous as a master alchemist but could not himself manufacture the powder.

One late and tragic tale of transmutation concerned a young scientist named James Price, who in 1782 invited a group of fellow scientists to witness his discovery. Under their watchful eyes, Price succeeded in turning mercury, nitre, and borax first into silver, then into gold, using a white and red powder respectively. Price's paper on the experiment drew much attention, but it failed to explain exactly how the transmutation took place. Seton also said that the experiment took a toll on his health and he feared he could not repeat it. When members of the Royal Society demanded another demonstration, Price reluctantly agreed. But when the scientists arrived at his laboratory, Price killed himself by drinking prussic acid.[26] As late as the 1890s, the Swedish playwright August Strindberg, a passionate student of alchemy, believed he had succeeded in extracting gold from iron, an alchemic opus he recounts in his remarkable work, *Inferno*.

That budding chemists were fascinated with alchemy should be no surprise; alchemy is generally seen as a mistaken but helpful precursor to chemistry. And indeed, the Hermetic Art has been responsible for some important chemical discoveries. We've seen that one of the fathers of chemistry, van Helmont, was a devotee. Johann Friedrich Böttger, the German chemist who in 1708 discovered the secret of making porcelain, was too.[27] Robert Boyle, another founder of chemistry, was a practicing alchemist with links to the Rosicrucians.

THE HERMES OF THE NORTH

One of the most important alchemists to make essential contributions to science was the cantankerous "Hermes of the North," Paracelsus. His real name was Philippus Aureolus Theophrastus Bombastus von Hohenheim, but he thought so highly of himself that he adopted his new name, which means "higher" or "better" than Celsus, the first-century Roman physician (25 B.C.–50 A.D.), not the second-century Platonist who wrote critically of Christianity (see Chapter Four). Paracelsus's high self-regard is arguably warranted. According to the historian of esotericism Nicholas Goodrick-Clarke, Paracelsus is celebrated today as "the first modern medical theorist, the founder of iatrochemistry [pharmacology], homeopathy, antisepsis, and modern wound surgery."[28] We can add to this that he wrote the first treatise on an occupational illness—a work on miner's disease, or silicosis—that he was the founder of balneology (the study of the medicinal effects of baths), and paved the way for an effective treatment of syphilis. Yet Paracelsus's self-praise earned him a bad reputation, and for a time it was said that the word "bombast," meaning highfalutin but insincere rhetoric, originated with him. It doesn't, but it may as well have.[29] Like Giordano Bruno, Paracelsus was a brilliant, volatile, and impatient character who did not suffer fools gladly and did not hesitate to tell them so. Like Bruno, he made many enemies and, like Bruno, Paracelsus's life was a long, wearying, and ultimately unsuccessful search for a stable and secure home.

Paracelsus was born on December 17 in Einsiedeln, Switzerland; he remains a Swiss national hero, and in Switzerland there is a chain of pharmacies named after him, an odd legacy for a secret teacher. In 1943, Joseph Goebbels, Hitler's spin doctor, applauded G. W. Pabst's biopic of Paracelsus, in a bid to appropriate the Swiss savant as a Nazi folk hero. What Paracelsus may have thought of this is, of course, unknown. I saw the film ages ago and I remember it being not bad.

Paracelsus's father, who worked as a doctor, was the illegitimate son of a Swabian nobleman; his mother, who died when Paracelsus was young, was a bondswoman of the Benedictine order. Paracelsus was frail and weak as a child, and because of the Swabian wars, Paracelsus and his father soon moved to Villach in Carinthia. Here Paracelsus's father taught him the basics of medicine. Paracelsus attended monastery schools and also the mining school of the Fuggers, an important banking family. He visited many mines in the area and was later apprenticed to a mine in the Tyrol. Alchemy held that metals "grew" in the earth, and there is a long German tradition about the secrets and magic of caves. Paracelsus's early exposure to medicine and "earth magic" set the foundation for the alchemist to come.

After studying with Trithemius, who exposed him to Pansophy, Kabbalistic, and alchemical ideas, between 1509 and 1512 Paracelsus worked for his bachelor's degree in Vienna. He then went to Ferrara in 1513, and in 1516, received his doctorate in medicine. After this, rather than settle into a comfortable university appointment, like Christian Rosenkreutz, Paracelsus took to the high road in search of knowledge. For seven years he journeyed across Europe, following a dizzying itinerary that had him in Italy, France, Spain (where he studied Kabbalah), Portugal, England (where he visited tin mines), Germany, Scandinavia, Poland, Russia (where he met shamans), Hungary, Turkey, and Egypt (where he studied alchemy). On much of his journey he worked as an army surgeon. He also fought, and his sword was named "Azoth," an alchemical term meaning "philosophical mercury," considered the "first principle of metals." As he traveled, he absorbed local traditional knowledge of remedies and cures, learning from anyone he could. This folk knowledge combined with his firsthand work as a surgeon informed Paracelsus's revolutionary approach to healing.

At the time, surgeons were considered little more than barbers or butchers; aside from a basic instruction in medicine and anatomy, their qualification for the work was that they possessed the tools of the trade. True doctors were scholars, learned university men well read in Galen—an influential Greek physician of second-century Rome—and Aristotle, and looked down on the messy business of stitching wounds or amputating limbs. Paracelsus was more down-to-earth and wanted to promote a medicine that would combine empirical knowledge with practical skill. He thought little of medical men who based their prestige on books rather than experience. He was also scornful of apothecaries who made a good living by selling doubtful herbal remedies that dated from the ancients;

they were more miss than hit, but the prestige of the past ensured their popularity. For a man of the Renaissance, Paracelsus had little love for the old. His impatience with the medical status quo also informed his social and religious ideas. He was sympathetic to the Brethren of the Free Spirit and other forms of grassroots spirituality popular at the time, and in 1525, he was arrested for supporting a peasant rebellion in Salzburg and just missed being executed.

In early 1527, in Strasbourg, Paracelsus fell in with a group of influential Protestant reformers. He treated one of them successfully, and Wolfgang Capito, his patient's friend, an acquaintance of Ulrich Zwingli, the Swiss Reformation leader and correspondent of Luther, introduced Paracelsus to the humanist circles of Basel. In Basel, Paracelsus cured the publisher Johann Froben of a septic leg and became friends with Erasmus, whom he treated for gout and kidney problems. Paracelsus was Catholic, but he was sympathetic to the Reformation, although with typical penetration he called Luther and Pope Clement VII "two whores debating chastity." His skill at curing Froben led the Protestant theologian Johannes Oecolampadius to secure Paracelsus the position of town physician. This should have been the start of a stable career, but things did not work out that way.

Paracelsus's position included the right to lecture at the university, and he was eager to use this to promote his new ideas about medicine. The university authorities were not so eager. They had not been consulted about Paracelsus's appointment and they made their displeasure known. Paracelsus could have quieted things by submitting to the formal act of reception necessary to an external graduate. It would have been a simple show of respect, but Paracelsus's impatience got the better of him and he refused. He then issued a proclamation in which he insisted that he would lecture daily on his own ideas, not Galen's or Aristotle's, and in German, not Latin. This in itself was revolutionary and in line with Luther's similar treatment of the Bible, which he had recently translated into his mother tongue to make it available to the common folk.

To make things even worse, during the student festivities on St. John's Day (June 24), Paracelsus burned copies of Galen and Avicenna, declaring that they and other old dogmatists were worth less than the hairs of his beard; even esotericists, it seems, burn books sometimes. Paracelsus had a talent for invective and had a way of making a point. Lecturing on the benefits of putrefaction—"Decay is the midwife of great things," he once said—he illustrated his thesis by presenting a group of learned dons with some of his shit.[30] It is no wonder he made few friends and many enemies. "I am different: let this not upset you," Paracelsus once said. Sadly it did.

The university faculty responded to Paracelsus's book burning by disputing his right to lecture or to sponsor doctoral candidates. Paracelsus protested and the town council took his side, a rare occasion in his life. At the same time, Paracelsus complained about the apothecaries' business practices. This only made him more enemies. The tables turned when Paracelsus's friend and protector Froben died. Satirical pamphlets about him appeared calling him "Cacophrastus" (*kakos* means "bad" in Greek) and singing Galen's praises. When he complained again to the council, they ignored him. Injury was soon added to insult. A wealthy churchman had promised to pay Paracelsus a tidy sum if he cured him. Paracelsus did, but the churchman only gave him a pittance. Paracelsus took his grievance to the law, but he was awarded only a modest fee, and his ferocious outburst at the injustice put him in contempt of court. Fearing arrest, he took to the road, and remained on it the rest of his short life.

The rest of Paracelsus's story is a tragic tale of a brilliant but explosive personality banging his head against several walls, while at the same time achieving deep insights into the links between man, nature, and the spiritual worlds. Paracelsus wrote many books on medicine, philosophy, theology, and prophecy during his wandering, most of them couched in a difficult prose. As the Rosicrucians did, he envisioned great changes ahead and saw signs in the sky that confirmed this. His insights, however, were lost on most who encountered him. In 1529, he reached Nuremberg but the local physicians got wind of his coming and banded against him. He challenged them to a kind of duel and cured nine out of fifteen lepers (how well the locals did is unclear). He developed a new treatment for syphilis—"the French disease"—and argued that the current cure, based on mercury and American guaiac (pockwood) was ineffective. The Fuggers, who had cornered the lucrative guaiac market, were not pleased with this and banished him from town; his book about syphilis was banned. In *Paragranum,* which he wrote in Beratzhausen, he argued that medicine must be built on "four pillars": nature, astrology, alchemy, and virtue. In 1531, he completed his *Opus Paramirum* (*Work Beyond Wonders*), which contained his theory of the three substances, sulfur, salt, and mercury, that made substantial changes to alchemical theory. It also spoke at length of his new chemical-based medicine—as opposed to the traditional "four humors" approach—as well as sex, digestion, nutrition, and also "illnesses of the imagination," a remarkable anticipation of neurosis and psychosomatic disturbances.

It would be tedious to recount all of Paracelsus's travels and travails—the interested reader is directed to Philip Ball's excellent biography *The Devil's Doctor*. For some time he wandered among Swiss peasants in the Alps, eventually reaching Innsbruck dressed in rags. He fought the plague in Sterzing but received little thanks. By the late 1530s, some recognition of his work began to appear. In September 1537, in Pressburg, he was feted at a ceremonial dinner in his honor. His reputation and finances recovered, and in Vienna he was granted two audiences with King Ferdinand. He visited his home town of Villach again, but then began another bout of wandering. His own health was poor, and in late 1540, he accepted an invitation to settle again in Salzburg. His years in the wilderness were finally over but luck was not with him. On September 21, 1541, he had a stroke and a few days later he died. He was forty-eight. There is some suspicion he was poisoned and some legends say he was pushed from a cliff, or fell from it in a drunken stupor. Most likely he was simply worn out by a lifetime of struggle.

ALCHEMICAL CHANGES

Paracelsus shared with Ficino, Pico, and the Renaissance magicians the new vision of man sparked by Petrarch's ascent of Mount Ventoux, and it is no surprise he inspired the Rosicrucians. God had given man powers and abilities and it was his duty to use them. It was a sin and insult to God if one didn't. It was not enough to know what the ancients, however worthy, had said. Man must use his own senses and intuition to reach the truth. This was not given, once and for all, in ages past, but must be gained again and again by man through his own efforts. Paracelsus's alchemy was based on the idea, voiced by Roger Bacon, that man can improve on nature, can speed up or intensify her processes.

We should note that with alchemy, the character of the esoteric quest changes. If in the Platonic and Gnostic traditions the emphasis is on a knowledge, a remembering or awakening (*gnosis*), that aids the seeker in the return to the source—the journey through the planets or the ascent of the Chain of Being—in alchemy the emphasis is on *transformation*.

This in itself should alert us to a difference. The Neoplatonic One is unchanging, eternal, and immutable. It is the essence of *being*. Alchemy is about *becoming*, about growth, change, development, about something lowly turning into something "higher." (*"Aurum nostrum non est aurum vulgi,"* "Our gold is not the vulgar gold," the alchemist Gerhard Dorn said.) The two are not mutually exclusive, and indeed, there are what we can call different "styles" or themes or motifs of esoteric work that overlap and run parallel with each other. There is the "quest" motif, as seen in the search for the Holy Grail. In this we "find" something, a hidden magical treasure like the Golden Fleece. There is the "mystic marriage," the union of *yin* and *yang*, male and female, microcosm and macrocosm, that forms part of alchemy as well as Hermeticism—and is also one of the central themes of this book. Here we are "reunited" with a lost or forgotten other half—in our case, our other brain. We can say that alchemy is about "making" something.

Paracelsus believed that God created things in what he called their "prime," not their "ultimate" form, a nod, perhaps, to Aristotle's notion of "entelechy." His vision was of a world in constant transformation, a living, growing, dynamic unity. Alchemy's focus on transmuting lead into gold, or the ignoble into the noble, seems to fit in with the evolutionary ideas that would come to dominate the modern mind. It also seems to depend to a greater degree on man's own efforts, which is in line with the alchemical insight that what is really the subject of transformation is oneself. To that extent, the alchemist was a kind of "self-made man," a very modern notion indeed. He is not given anything except his natural powers and abilities, and it is up to him to make the most of them. It is through his use of these that he can become something *more*.

The Belgian Gerhard Dorn (1530–1584), a follower and translator of

Paracelsus, makes this point. He developed the "inner" aspect of Paracelsus's work and paid less attention to furnaces and alembics, focusing instead on the powers of the mind—no mystery then that Jung made much of Dorn's writings. Dorn is the author of one of the most oft-quoted alchemical maxims: "Transform yourselves from dead stones into living philosophical stones!" A similar formula of his makes much the same point: "Never look outside for what you need, until you have made use of the whole of yourself," an aphorism that would not be out of place among the Gnostic sayings found in Nag Hammadi. "As faith works miracles in man," Dorn said, "so this power, the *veritas efficaciae* [true efficacy], brings them about in matter. This truth is the highest power and impregnable fortress wherein the stone of the philosophers lies hid." As Peter Marshall remarks, for Dorn, the philosopher's stone is man, or at least can be discovered within him.[31]

IMAGINAL MEDICINE

Paracelsus says much the same. His medicine is based on the macrocosmic/microcosmic principle, which says that man is a small universe, that all the powers of the cosmos, both visible and invisible, also reside in him. Paracelsus sought to activate the correspondences that exist between the greater and lesser cosmoses. Our health depends on these being well aligned. According to Nicholas Goodrick-Clarke, Paracelsus was the first to systematically apply this Hermetic approach to nature.[32] As Goodrick-Clarke expresses it, Paracelsus believed that man can have a "direct knowledge of Nature on account of a sympathy between the inner representative of a particular object in his own constitution and its external counterpart."[33] This sympathy between the inner world and the outer—the essence of the macro/microcosmic polarity—is our primary means of "acquiring intimate and total knowledge."[34] Paracelsus's task as a physician was to grasp the correspondence between man's inner world and that of nature, an idea we have come across in Owen Barfield. It was through this knowledge and way of knowing that Paracelsus effected his cures and laid the groundwork for much of both modern mainstream and alternative medicine.

Paracelsus's "direct knowledge" sounds very much like the kind of "direct perceiving" Stan Gooch suggests our Neanderthal ancestors enjoyed and which allowed them "a real knowledge of aspects of human life and human biology, of some of the functions of the planet's geology and perhaps some knowledge even of atomic and molecular structure." It is also reminiscent of Schwaller de Lubicz's "intelligence of the heart," Bergson's "intuition," and the other variants of these we have come across in this book. This way of knowing involves something more than the brain, or at least something more than only one half of it. The whole person must be involved.

Something similar seems to have been at work in an account of the effects of the powerful psychoactive drug ayahuasca, reported by the anthropologist Jeremy Narby in his book *The Cosmic Serpent*. Narby wanted to know how the indigenous Amazonian people who use ayahuasca in their religious ceremonies learned of its properties, and also those of the thousands of other plants they used. Such knowledge, Narby thought, could not have come through trial and error. The natives told Narby that they learned all of this from the plants themselves: they told them all about it, while they were under the influence of the drug.

Narby tried ayahuasca himself and had a remarkable experience in which two giant boa constrictors spoke to him and passed on ancient wisdom.[35] His experience led Narby to research snake symbolism in world culture, and he was surprised to discover how often the combination of snakes and secret knowledge turned up, something Leonard Shlain also remarked upon in *The Alphabet Versus the Goddess*.[36] We have seen that psychedelic and other mind-altering drugs, like ayahuasca, work by inhibiting the brain's—possibly the left hemisphere's—"filtering mechanism," allowing more of "reality" than we usually perceive to enter consciousness. This "more" entails the "network of connections linking everything to everything else," and which would include, one assumes, the correspondences between our inner world and nature's. We should also note that we have seen that this more "open" consciousness is *older* than our own, and that the wisdom Narby's boa constrictors imparted was ancient. What Narby's natives learned in the ayahuasca trance, Paracelsus seems to have perceived naturally—although the fact that Paracelsus regularly prescribed opium and used it liberally himself may suggest that he too relied on some help.[37]

THE INNER FIRMAMENT

Central to Paracelsus's ideas was the imagination. He called it the "inner firmament," the microcosmic parallel to the starry sky above. As Petrarch knew when gazing from the summit of Mount Ventoux, vast distances stretch *within* us as well as without us. It is through understanding and grasping these that man can align his own being with that of the cosmos.

"The first step in the operation of these sciences," Paracelsus said, "is this: to beget the spirit from the inner firmament by means of the imagination."[38] As were Giordano Bruno and Suhrawardi, Paracelsus was acutely aware of the power of the imagination. We have seen that with his ideas about the "illnesses of the imagination," Paracelsus knew that the mind has a direct influence on the body, something Cornelius Agrippa understood as well. Agrippa had written that "imagination does, of its own accord . . . change the physical body with a sensible transmutation, by changing the accidents in the body, and by moving the spirit upward or downward, inward or outward."[39] Agrippa is saying that our moods have a direct impact on our physical health, something modern medicine recognizes as well.[40]

Paracelsus concurs and goes even further. "Resolute imagination is the beginning of all magical operations," he says. "It is possible that my spirit . . . through an ardent will alone, and without a sword, can stab and wound others."[41] Such power, it would seem, would be behind the otherwise unaccountable efficacy of "black magic" and the "evil eye," convincing accounts of which crowd dozens of books about the paranormal and the history of magic. The novelist John Cowper Powys, whose *A Glastonbury Romance* is one of the great mystical novels of all time, was so disturbed by his own ability to "exercise some kind of 'evil eye' on people" that he developed a kind of neurosis about it and engaged in obsessive rituals in order to protect those around him. "The feeling that comes over me at such times," Powys wrote, "is one of most formidable power." As his readers know,

Powys had a gargantuan imagination and it is not surprising that he felt at times that he "really *was* endowed with some sort of supernatural power."[42]

As became clear in the Renaissance, the artist and the magician are very close cousins, and the tie linking them is the imagination. "Thoughts are things," Annie Besant and C. W. Leadbeater said in their classic Theosophical work *Thought Forms*; and according to Agrippa, Powys, and Paracelsus, they can be very powerful things indeed. It was with this in mind that Owen Barfield gave a warning in *Saving the Appearances* about what he called the *responsibility* of the imagination. "Imagination is not," Barfield wrote, "simply synonymous with good. It may be either good or evil."[43] As with many things, it depends on the use to which it is put. As the poet and magician W. B. Yeats warned the members of the Hermetic Order of the Golden Dawn, "whatever we build in the imagination will accomplish itself in the circumstances of our lives."[44]

As we saw in Chapter Five, imagination is not the same thing as fantasy. That, for Paracelsus, was the "madman's cornerstone," an "exercise of thought without foundation in nature."[45] We know what Paracelsus means. Obsessive thoughts, ruminating over some mistake, pointless brooding over ills and problems can lead to serious mental disturbances. But even less excessive states like daydreaming can be wasteful. We can think of fantasy as the mind idling; the engine is running, but the car isn't going anywhere. Insights can come to us in this state, but in order to grasp their significance, we have to put the motor in gear, as it were, and drive—that is, focus our mind on them.

This is imagination: the directed focus of the mind, throwing a spotlight on reality. As mentioned earlier, this has a distinct *noetic* character; it shows the imagination as an "organ of knowledge."[46] It is through this that we can "surpass given reality" and "surmount the solitude of the self," which, as Paracelsus, Swedenborg, and other inner voyagers knew, "can become an obsession bordering on madness."[47] Imagination takes us *out* of ourselves by taking us *into* ourselves, into that greater self that Paracelsus and our other secret teachers had knowledge of and wanted to share. Paracelsus's "true imagination" is not an escape from reality but a means of grasping *more* of it. As Colin Wilson writes, "Imagination is the explosive flare that lights up inner spaces, revealing meaning."[48] Paracelsus knew this, but like Christian Rosenkreutz, those he tried to teach this to—most of them at least—lacked the imagination to grasp it. But then, Paracelsus's own pedagogic methods were not always inviting.

IMAGINATION AND THE PHILOSOPHER'S STONE

One alchemist who seems to have picked up the Paracelsian torch is Mary Anne South (1817–1910). Her story takes place in the mid-nineteenth century, but if the reader does not mind the anachronism, this seems the place to tell it. Her work, as obscure as it is—in typical alchemical style, much of it is willfully baffling—seems to be saying that the secret ingredient in the alchemical opus is the mind itself.

Mary's father, Thomas South, with whom she lived in Hampshire, England, had a deep interest in mesmerism and hypnosis, both of which derived from the work of the Bavarian physician Franz Anton Mesmer. Mesmer believed that the universe was permeated by currents of vital energy, which he called "animal magnetism." For a time in the eighteenth and nineteenth centuries, Mesmer's ideas were immensely popular although, as in the case of Paracelsus, the medical establishment was dead against them. It was only by accident that a student of Mesmer's discovered hypnosis. Making "magnetic passes" over a patient—in order to get his "animal magnetism" flowing—it was found that he had entered a trance. Thomas South was also profoundly interested in spiritualism, the belief that the living could make contact with the dead through people called "mediums," who entered a trance in order to speak with them. Thomas belonged to a circle who studied such things and who performed séances. Mary shared his interest, as well as Thomas's love of the ancient world. He taught her ancient Greek and Latin, and from being his pupil she became his secretary and then colleague. Lyndsay Clarke based his novel *The Chymical Wedding* on the sometimes strange relationship between Mary and her father.

Thomas attached great importance to the ancient Greek Mysteries. He rejected the idea accepted by most nineteenth-century classicists—and made widely popular some years later by Sir James George Frazer in *The Golden Bough* (1890)—that the Eleusinian Mysteries were merely a way in which people ignorant of science could "explain" the seasons, why, that is, leaves fall in autumn and flowers bloom in the spring. (We remember this is because Persephone is allowed to leave Hades once a year but must return.) Thomas believed something more profound was at work and Mary agreed. They believed that the ancient sages of Egypt, Greece, and Rome knew something that modern science had forgotten but which was just beginning to be rediscovered by the mesmerists, spiritualists, and other "psychic researchers"—although the name was not yet coined—of their time. Both believed, much as Porphyry did in the third century, that the Mysteries and myths of the ancients spoke symbolically and that if one could crack their code, the ancient wisdom could be revived.

Among the ancient works that Mary and her father studied was the *Hermetica,* and they paid special attention to the fabled *Emerald Tablet of Hermes Trismegistus.* Mary decided to translate the *Emerald Tablet,* and it was while doing so that she and her father felt they discovered something profound. Alchemy was seen then—as it is for the most part today—as a precursor of chemistry. But the more they looked into Hermes' wisdom, the less this seemed to make sense. They came to the conclusion that what alchemy was about had more to do with the ancient Mysteries than with chemicals and their combinations. The Hermetic Art, they realized, was a code for the Mysteries of the ancients. And what the Mysteries taught had to do with what the mesmerists and spiritualists of their time were rediscovering: the mysteries of the mind itself.

In 1846, Mary published a short book, *Early Magnetism,* which related the work of Mesmer and the hypnotists to the ancient Mysteries, as well as to mysticism and spiritual revelations, and Mary herself seems to have experienced some sort of mystical experience around this time. Her father thought the book came close to expressing the insights they had uncovered between the ancient Mysteries and mesmerism. But it seems he felt that they deserved a more substantial effort. He decided to provide this in an epic philosophical poem, not surprising for a student of the ancient Greek philosophers. Mary took a different route and produced a very strange and unwieldy work entitled *A Suggestive Inquiry into the Hermetic Mystery with a Dissertation on the More Celebrated of the Alchemical Philosophers,* published in 1850 at the Souths' own expense.

Thomas was intent on his poem and gave little attention to Mary's book. But when he finally read it, he was shocked—panic-struck would not be an exaggeration. Something in the book so disturbed Thomas that he recalled all the copies that had been sent out to libraries or for review. He also gathered any copies they had left, and on the lawn of their home in Hampshire he burned them. Only a few copies survived and the book wasn't reprinted until 1918, some years after Mary had died at the age of ninety-two. Thomas seems to have destroyed his poem as well.[49] Mary was devastated, but she seems to have agreed with the destruction of her work, although it did end her literary ambitions. Years later she gave one of the few surviving copies to Anna Kingsford, a leading English Theosophist, and the book had a kind of "cult" life in theosophical circles.

Why did Thomas South burn his daughter's book? Some have suggested sheer jealousy motivated him: Mary had done a better job of communicating their insights than he had and he couldn't accept this. While there may be some truth in this—Thomas South's poem was, at best, inspired doggerel—the fact that Mary seems to have agreed with her father's extreme act, and that he also seems to have destroyed his own work, suggests that something else may also have been involved. Her father died shortly after destroying the book, but Mary made no effort to republish it nor to write another. In 1859, she married a clergyman named Atwood with whom she spent the rest of her life (she is often listed as Mary Atwood in histories of alchemy) and no further revelations came from her.

The Mason W. L. Wilmhurst, who wrote about the Souths, suggests that the "responsibility of publicly displaying a subject of extraordinary and sacred moment" proved too much for them; he also suggests that Thomas had somehow "got religion" and wanted to recant his pagan beliefs.[50] As Colin Wilson argues, neither of these reasons seems adequate. The occultist A. E. Waite, writing on alchemy, gave Mary short shrift and argued that her basic idea was that alchemy was a spiritual discipline, having nothing to do with transmuting matter. This, however, was not news, and a sort of Christian spiritual alchemy, which saw Christ as the philosopher's stone, had been around for some time. It was certainly not something that warranted burning her book. But a look at *A Suggestive Inquiry* in fact confirms the opposite of Waite's suggestion.[51] Mary does believe that an actual transmutation does take place, and the first part of her book offers evidence for this—although given that she is at pains to conceal as much as she reveals, her writing requires some unraveling. The examples of transmutation that she offers are much like those I mentioned earlier: Flamel, Helvetius, van Helmont, and so on. Yet in the second part of the book, "On the True Subject of the Hermetic Art and Its Concealed Root," she tells us that "No modern art or chemistry . . . has anything in common with Alchemy."[52] So while she seems to be saying that an actual transmutation does take place, it is not brought about by chemical means.

The essential ingredient, she tells us, is what the alchemists called the *prima materia*, the "first matter" or the Universal Matter, the fundamental stuff out of which everything is made, something like the *arche* sought by Thales and Anaximander during the axial age. Those she calls "pseudo-Alchemists" believed that transmutation could take place from one metal to another *as they were,* in their present form. Her remarks about these "puffers" can easily be read to mean that she rejected transmutation per se. "Since species are indestructible," she writes, "therefore, the transmutation of metals has been regarded as a sophistical proposition and not a true art." Yet, she continues, "it is not species that they [the true alchemists] profess to transmute; nor do they ever teach in theory that lead as lead or mercury as mercury . . . can be changed into gold, any more than a dog into a horse or a tulip into a daisy . . . but it is the subject matter, the radical moisture of which they are uniformly composed that . . . may be withdrawn by art and transported from inferior forms, being set free by the force of a superior ferment or attraction."[53] This "subject matter" and "radical moisture" is the *prima materia*. The alchemist must first arrive at this, and then the transmutation can be achieved.

What is this *prima materia*? Mary knows, but she does not want to let the cat out of the bag too easily. She speaks not so much in a "green language" but in a very convoluted one, which leads the reader to suspect she is writing gobbledygook. But this is part of alchemical and esoteric practice. What she has to say is important and she does not want it to fall into unworthy hands. Her book was the first overall survey of alchemy, an attempt to convey its essence to an interested reader. It would be read not only by alchemists but also by the simply curious. Gurdjieff's jaw-breaking masterpiece, *Beelzebub's Tales to His Grandson,* is replete with esoteric insights and knowledge, but it is written in so rebarbative a style that only the most dedicated reader gets to these. Many are put off, and this was Gurdjieff's intention; he did not want casual readers but true seekers. *A Suggestive Inquiry* is similarly dense and circuitous, but a determined reader can find clues to Mary's meaning.

She speaks of "concentrating the vitality" and a "concentrative energy."[54] She quotes Plotinus's account of his mystical experience in Thomas Taylor's translation—the Souths were members of a secret society founded by Taylor: "Often when by an intellectual energy I am roused from body and converted to myself . . . and become the *same* with a nature truly divine . . . I arrive at that energy by which I am elevated beyond every other intelligible" (italics in the original).[55] She also makes liberal reference to the theurgic powers of the Neoplatonists, which, we remember, could bring life to inanimate objects. "Nothing vitally alterative is achieved," she tells us, "unless the vital force be present and in action."[56] One comes away from these and similar remarks feeling that she is talking about the mind, consciousness, and the imagination. Her ideas about the philosopher's stone and *prima materia* seem to echo Gerhard Dorn's counsel that the alchemist should "Never look outside for what you need, until you have made use of the whole of yourself." What the alchemist needs to perform the transmutation is within himself, and it is his mind. Somehow, by some act of concentration brought about through the mesmeric trance, the mind, the imagination itself reaches into matter and changes it. This was the Great Arcanum and it was this that Thomas and Mary South agreed should not be revealed. As was Owen Barfield, they were aware of the responsibility of the imagination.

This idea should not trouble those who take a more Jungian view of alchemy, nor those who reject Jung and believe some real transmutation, and not only a psychological realignment, takes place. Jung himself, with his ideas about synchronicity, suggests that in some strange way the mind, or at least its unconscious part, can "arrange" reality and produce those strange experiences of "meaningful coincidence," when a correspondence between what is happening in my mind and what is happening in the world takes place. And while Mary Anne South's theory of transmutation does involve an "inner alchemy," it does result in a real "outer" transformation. But then, such "participation" between inner and outer is a central theme of this book, and it is something that we have reason to believe the ancients that Mary and her father studied knew more about than we do.

THE MYSTIC COBBLER

Mary Anne South did not have a monopoly on writing difficult books. Another master of inner alchemy whose prose provides its own peculiar challenges is the "Teutonic philosopher" Jacob Boehme. Unlike Mary, Boehme was not a student of the ancient mysteries but an untutored, pious Bohemia shoemaker. But perhaps Boehme did not need to study. In 1600, he had a mystical experience in which he "saw and knew more in one quarter of an hour than if I had spent many years at a university."[57] Boehme seems to have had an experience of the kind of "knowing" we looked at in Chapter One. The result of Boehme's vision was a geyser of alchemical, gnostic, and mystical insight, expressed in a style that is at once exasperatingly vague and strikingly vivid. Yet Boehme's often incomprehensible writings were enormously influential, informing the work of William Blake, Jung, Martin Buber, Coleridge, Novalis, and the philosophers Hegel, Schelling, and Heidegger, among others. The Romanian physicist Basarab Nicolescu has even argued for strong parallels between Boehme's mystical vision and the findings of postquantum physics.[58] Other of Boehme's readers included, not surprisingly, Mary Anne South and her father, and Frances Yates has pointed out the similarities between Boehme's ideas and those of his contemporaries, the Rosicrucians.[59] While Yates recognizes there is no direct historical connection between them, the "ahistorical continuity" we have mentioned seems to have been at work here.

Jacob Boehme was born in 1575 in Alt-Seidenberg, near the town of Görlitz in Silesia (modern-day Poland). He was the fourth of five children to be born to his parents, Jacob and Ursula. Jacob's father was a well-off Lutheran peasant, and after it appeared that his son was too poorly to herd cattle—and that he often went off on his own, forgetting about them—he apprenticed him at the age of fourteen to a shoemaker. Jacob was a dreamy child, with a slight build and self-effacing character. His early biographer and disciple, Abraham von Franckenberg, relates that at some point in his youth, Boehme met a stranger who foretold that he had important work to do and that he was destined for greatness. Most modern researchers consider this story apocryphal and indeed there are several legends about the young Jacob that need to be taken with some salt.

Boehme had only an elementary education, although he read the Bible and was later fond of Paracelsus and other mystical writers. His apprenticeship lasted three years, after which he traveled, exactly where is unclear. One story is that he was forced to leave the apprenticeship because his workmates and master didn't care to have a prophet in the house; Boehme himself, with his taste for reading, most likely found them coarse and vulgar.[60] He returned to Görlitz in 1600, set himself up as a shoemaker, and married Katherine Kuntzschmann, who bore him four children. Not long after this, the destiny foretold by the mysterious stranger began to unfold.

One day Boehme found himself staring at a burnished pewter dish. The sun's reflection on it seems to have sent him into a mystical trance. As Franckenberg tells it, it was as if he suddenly saw into the heart of nature and could understand the world and everything in it. He was "introduced into the innermost ground or center of the recondite or hidden nature," and saw what he later called "the signature of things."[61] The experience unsettled Boehme and he walked out into some nearby fields to clear his head. But the feeling of actually *seeing* into the trees, leaves, and grass around him remained. Paracelsus had said that it was possible to see into the essence of things: "we may look into Nature in the same way that the sun shines through a glass."[62] Boehme seems to have experienced this. He seems to have had a profound experience of Bergson's "intuition" and Stan Gooch's "direct perceiving," and it remained with him the rest of his life. R. M. Bucke includes him with those in whom the "cosmic sense" has appeared, but admitted that his writings were "well-nigh unintelligible to the merely self-conscious mind."[63]

Boehme kept his vision to himself. It was not until another similar experience happened that he decided he must write it down. He spoke of his initial vision—not mentioning the pewter dish—and it was here that he spoke of "learning more in one quarter of an hour" than if he had been for years at university. He saw and recognized, he said, "the Being of All Beings, the foundation and that which is beyond foundation and is fathomless." He saw "the birth of the Holy Threeness of God, the origin and primordial condition of this world and all creatures through divine wisdom."[64] There were, Boehme saw, three worlds. Two of these, the divine world, which is "angelic and paradisiacal," and a dark world of fire and "wrath," are beyond the senses. The third world, our own, Boehme says, is the product of an everlasting struggle between these two invisible worlds.

Boehme came to write down his vision only after a period of intense depression and resistance. But after a number of "violent storms," his spirit broke through and he experienced the Godhead "as a bridegroom embraces his beloved bride." The result was his first book, *Aurora*, also known as *Morgenröte* (*Morning Redness in the Rising Sun*). It soon gathered a small group of readers; one of these, the nobleman Karl von Endern, made several copies and distributed them. One fell into the hands of Gregorius Richter, the pastor of Görlitz, who was not pleased with what he read. He fumed that a humble, uneducated cobbler like Boehme should have the temerity to write of such things. Aside from this, it smacked of heresy.

It's doubtful Richter grasped much of Boehme's vision, but he no doubt noted the several sharp criticisms of the deadness that the Lutheran church had fallen into that Boehme had included. Richter decided to teach this uppity shoemaker a lesson, and one Sunday in church Boehme was astonished to find himself under attack. In a sermon on false prophets, Richter singled Boehme out and loudly criticized his work. Boehme had none of Paracelsus's aggressiveness, and after the service he approached Richter apologetically to ask what he had done wrong. Richter shouted, "Get thee behind me, Satan!" and told him to leave town. He remained Boehme's enemy for the rest of his life. The next day Richter convinced the town council to banish Boehme. The dismayed prophet spent an uncomfortable evening outside the town gates. The council saw better the day after and allowed Boehme to return on the condition that he wrote no more.

Boehme was an obedient sort and he agreed. For several years he didn't write a word. But word of *Aurora* had spread and Boehme found that he had a following. Alchemists, doctors, philosophers, even clergymen visited the shoemaker—eventually he went into the linen trade—and spoke with him about his vision and pressed him to break his oath and write again. Boehme impressed them by being able to tell a plant's properties simply by looking at it; he was also able to understand the meaning of a foreign word simply by its sound. Language and words were important to Boehme, and he sought to understand the original, Adamic language of Eden. "There was," George Steiner wrote, "no deeper dreamer on language, no sensibility more haunted by the alchemy of speech, than Jacob Boehme."[65]

It was the prompting of his friends and followers, and his belief that what he had experienced was God's will—"When the sun goes up in my spirit, then I am certain"—that, in 1618, led him to return to writing. In the last years of his life—he died in 1624—Boehme produced a torrent of words, not all of them understandable, doing his best to convey to his readers what he meant by "the signature of things." Yet once again, his nemesis Richter made things difficult for him. A friend gathered some of Boehme's writings and had them printed under the title *The Way to Christ*. Unfortunately, a copy again reached Richter and he reacted explosively. He attacked Boehme again from the pulpit and published a hysterical polemic against him, saying his work stank of shoe polish and the devil, incensed that this ignorant upstart should claim to understand God. Boehme was again told to leave town, but by this time he had made many influential friends, and through one of them, he was invited to the Prince Elector's court in Dresden. Here he spoke with many Lutheran theologians; they agreed that much of what he said escaped them but that there was nothing heretical in it. Boehme had found a new home and he moved his family there. Sadly, he died of gastric fever shortly after. The story is that at the moment of his death he said, "And now I go to Paradise." His archenemy Richter had preceded him but the pastor who took his place refused to preach a funeral sermon for him, and the one who finally did admitted to being bullied into it.

THE SIGNATURE Of THINGS

After his death, Boehme's fame spread over Europe, and in Görlitz today there is a statue to him. He is considered the founder of modern Christian theosophy, which is not the same as Madame Blavatsky's brand. The

Christian mystic seeks union with God. The theosopher seeks this as well, but he also wants the knowledge and understanding of him. According to the Christian existentialist philosopher Nikolai Berdyaev, Boehme is "the greatest of Christian gnostics," and Berdyaev's own profound philosophy draws much from Boehme's notion of the *Ungrund*, "the groundless," the fundamental absolute "nothingness" at the source of reality, what Berdyaev called "meontic freedom."[66] Like Meister Eckhart, Christian theosophy draws much from the *via negativa*. "If you can swing yourself up for a moment into that in which no creature dwells, then you will hear what God speaks," Boehme tells us.[67] In England, Boehme's theosophy was carried on by John Pordage and Jane Leade, who started the Philadelphian Society in 1670, a pious organization dedicated to Boehme's work. Boehme's wilder flights of insight were the inspiration for the Dutch Christian Kabbalist Johann Gichtel, "the hermit of Amsterdam," who edited the first major collection of Boehme's writings. Like Boehme, Gichtel was hounded by church authorities and was saved from suicide by a mystical vision.[68] Later Christian theosophists inspired by Boehme include the Kabbalist Friedrich Oetinger; "the unknown philosopher" Louis Claude de Saint-Martin; and Karl von Eckartshausen, whose mystical work *The Cloud Upon the Sanctuary* sent Aleister Crowley on his dubious road to illumination.[69]

Boehme's vision is fundamentally Christian but he expresses it in a difficult alchemical language, much of which he borrowed from Paracelsus. What sets him apart from other Christian mystics is the sense of a titanic struggle going on at the heart of reality, the tension between what Boehme called Love and Wrath. Wrath is a force of "dryness, harshness, and contraction," much like the "granulation" that Schwaller de Lubicz says is a result of "cerebral consciousness." Love unifies. This antagonism is not rooted in Lucifer's mutiny, as in the standard Christian account of the origin of evil. For Boehme it emerges from God's own nature. God himself is self-divided. Boehme sees God as a dynamic process of self-creation, rather than an eternal order and hierarchy: "Nowhere in nature is there calmness, eternal order—everywhere there is the conflict of opposing principles."[70] The opposing principles are Being and Nothingness. In one sense we can say God is fighting for his life.

A great spiritual Yes and No are at odds with each other and the result is the universe. This battle goes on in ourselves, and Boehme uses the alchemical symbols of the seven planets and metals and Paracelsus's three forces (sulfur, salt, mercury) to try to convey his vision of what is happening in our inner world. We spend most of our time enveloped in Wrath, in the pursuit of our own aims and desires. It is by letting go of these—Boehme, like Meister Eckhart, speaks of *Gelassenheit*—that we can feel God within us and take part consciously in his struggle. Adam fell victim to his own will and rejected Sophia, who was supposed to be his consort. By doing this, he lost his original wholeness, but he—and we—can regain this through a process of spiritual regeneration, in which we fuse together the disparate parts of our being into a new, higher unity. Without putting too fine a point on it, I think we can see Boehme's struggle between self-will and *Gelassenheit* in terms of the tension between the two sides of our brain.

This fusion takes place through understanding what Boehme calls the "seven characteristics," which for him serve the same purpose that the seven planets did for the Hermetists. They mediate between the original unity and the multiple worlds we inhabit. They exist here in a confused mixture, but by meditating on them we can understand their essence and, as we can with the two opposing forces, bring them into unity.

No doubt this highly selective account of Boehme's difficult philosophy does little justice to the depth and intensity of his work. What strikes me most about Boehme is that, as with the alchemy in which his ideas are rooted, he presents a much more modern view of existence than what went before. We no longer think of an eternal order in the universe, but of Big Bangs, exploding stars, and colliding galaxies. God did not make us as final, fixed creatures; we have evolved to who we are through a long and strenuous struggle. We live, in J. G. Bennett's phrase, in a much more "dramatic universe" than the ancients did, and Boehme's vision seems in line with this.[71] He died just as Marin Mersenne's attack on the Hermetic world was gaining steam. The world that came after this was something different.

CHAPTER NINE

THIS IS THE MODERN WORLD

As the seventeenth century progressed, the Hermetic, Pansophic vision lost ground. Yet this was also a time when works on alchemy flourished. Many illustrated alchemical texts were printed in this period, and much of what is popularly known about alchemy comes from them. Texts like the *De Lapide Philosophico* and the *Theatrum Chemicum Britannicum*, as well as earlier ones from the late sixteenth century, like the *Splendor Solis* and the *Rosarium Philosophorum*, were much sought after and today provide modern readers with the familiar but still unsettling imagery we associated with alchemy.

Red dragons, green lions, hermaphrodites, kings and queens lying naked in a bath, smiling suns and moons, the homunculi or "little man," the alchemical egg, an old king being executed, the ouroboros (a snake eating its own tail), and other images equally strange and evocative inhabit the alchemical landscape. Like the "green language," these images were meant to reveal secret knowledge to those who could grasp it, and conceal it from those who could not. A later offspring of "alchemical art" are the works of "hyperphysical cartography" that appeared throughout the seventeenth and eighteenth centuries, examples of which are the Rosicrucian enthusiast John Heydon's *The Wise Man's Crown* (1655) and the anonymous *Secret Figures of the Rosicrucians* (1785–1788).[1]

These were complex and sophisticated attempts to "map" universal knowledge, to illustrate the varied correspondences between the macrocosm and the microcosm. At a time when much of the physical globe was being mapped, such "metaphysical maps" brought together alchemical,

Kabbalistic, Hermetic, and scientific knowledge to form complex diagrams made of concentric circles, triangles, text, and illustrations in order to create a representation of the "unseen." Editions of Jacob Boehme's writing, like *Theosophische Werke,* published in Amsterdam in 1682, are full of haunting illustrations that often offered more ready access to Boehme's profound ideas than the difficult terrain of his prose.[2]

The alchemical side of the Rosicrucian experiment was carried on by people like the German Michael Maier, who for a time was the personal physician of Rudolf II, the alchemical Holy Roman Emperor. Like Paracelsus, Maier combined alchemy with medicine, and following the great Swiss savant, he was the most important "alternative health" figure of the time.

Like Robert Fludd, whom he very likely met during his years in England, Maier defended the Rosicrucians when they came under attack. He is even thought to have tried to drum up support for Frederick V with King James I of England, father of Elizabeth, Frederick's bride. A Christmas greeting Maier sent the king contained an illustration of a rose with eight petals, in the center of which Maier had written in Latin: "Greetings to James, for a long time King of Great Britain. By your true protection may the rose be joyful." It was in fact James I's decision not to help Frederick V in his battle against Ferdinand II that many believe turned the tide against the Rosicrucian dream and led to Frederick V's defeat.

James I, however, was not the best king to ask to support an esoteric enterprise. He had a hysterical fear of magic and witchcraft and wrote a book, *Demonologie,* condemning it. This is not surprising; in 1590, a coven of witches had apparently confessed to trying to drown James I and his queen, Anne of Denmark, as they returned to England after their wedding. James I—who was James VI of Scotland at the time—then began a pogrom on witches. Later he refused an audience with John Dee when Queen Elizabeth's astrologer badly needed support. In effect this condemned Dee to the poverty and neglect of his final years.

Maier is responsible for some of the most remarkable works of alchemical art, most representative of which is his *Atalanta Fugiens* (*Atalanta Fleeing*), which appeared in 1618, a kind of seventeenth-century example of multimedia. Through poetry, images, and music, Maier uses the myth of Atalanta's ravishment by Hippomenes, as told by Ovid, to illustrate the *coniunctio oppositorum,* or union of the opposites at the heart of alchemy. Maier was not the first to link alchemy and music. Indeed, some of the earliest operas dealt with similar themes, such as Jacapo Peri's *Euridice,* which dates from 1600. Claudio Monteverdi, opera's first "star," was a practicing alchemist.

Like the late Neoplatonists, Maier believed that ancient myths needed to be interpreted symbolically, and in his *Arcana Arcanissima* (*The Secret of Secrets*) of 1614, he gives an alchemical reading of Greek and Egyptian mythology. Here the hero of his tale journeys in search of the phoenix, the fabled bird that returns to life out of its ashes. At the Nile delta he meets Hermes, who shows him the divine creature's dwelling place. Maier's *Themis Aurea,* of 1618, is in large part a defense of the Rosicrucians. Here he depicts the brotherhood as inheritors of an ancient esoteric tradition, and argues that they are dedicated scientists and healers committed to using their knowledge and wisdom in the service of a better world. Maier himself, sadly, was a victim of the Rosicrucian pogrom and Thirty Years' War. By all accounts he was killed in 1622, during a siege of Magdeburg by forces loyal to the Habsburgs. Yet the Rosicrucian dream of using knowledge to create a better world had not died. Some still believed that like the phoenix, it too would rise again from the flames.

AN INVISIBLE CHURCH

One of the most ironic outcomes of the Rosicrucian diaspora is that many of the ideas at the heart of the Rosicrucian experiment, and the Hermetic philosophy that informed it, would serve as the basis for a worldview rather different than the one the Rosy Brotherhood had in mind.

Following the Rosicrucian debacle, Johann Valentin Andreae turned his attention away from Hermetic science and focused his energies on establishing a kind of Christian utopia, exemplified in his visionary work *Christianopolis,* "the City of Christ." Readers of this pious work familiar with the Rosicrucian philosophy will find ample evidence of it within its pages. Andreae's aim in presenting the "serious joke" of the Rosicrucian manifestoes was, it seems, to inspire their readers not so much to *join* the Rosicrucians, as to *become* them. The literal idea of some secret society clandestinely planning to subvert the status quo was the joke. No such group existed—at least not yet. This is where the "serious" part of the hoax came in. The aim of the manifestoes was to express the ideals of the mythical fraternity and inspire those moved by them to go out and work to make them real. In this way they would indeed join the fraternity, which was an "invisible" brotherhood of people of like mind, working, each in their own way, to bring about much needed change.

Those who understood Andreae's meaning and answered this call included Robert Fludd, Michael Maier, and John Comenius. Jacob Boehme had come under the influence of someone with a similar idea, Caspar Schwenckfeld, a German Pietist, theologian, and preacher who wrote of an "invisible church," not one of stone, and the idea of a "hidden" "interior" church is at the heart of Karl von Eckartshausen's *The Cloud Upon the Sanctuary,* an eighteenth-century mystical classic.[3] One of the problems facing organized religion is that it too easily hardens into a "static" state. By Andreae's and Boehme's time, this was happening to the Protestant church. It sought a "confessional conformity" when what was needed was a spiritual transformation, an ongoing one, as the danger of inspiration crystallizing into dogma is ever present. The vilification of the Rosicrucians that followed the defeat of Frederick V led Andreae to abandon his esoteric approach. Instead, he repackaged the Rosicrucian ideals in a highly Christianized form, and organized various "Christian societies" in order to disseminate them.

THE INTELLIGENCER

Like much else, most of Andreae's societies were eradicated during the Thirty Years' War, but at least one member of one of them managed to escape the carnage and attempt to revive the Rosicrucian dream. Samuel Hartlib belonged to one of Andreae's societies, but when life under the Habsburgs' wrath proved too perilous, he left his native Poland and headed to England. Hartlib was in contact with Comenius and shared his

ideas about universal education and Pansophy. He was also in contact
with Elizabeth, the exiled queen of Bohemia, who held court in The
Hague. After the death of Frederick V in 1623, those who still believed in
the Rosicrucian ideals gathered around his queen, who still had hopes of
somehow challenging the Habsburgs' rule.

Hartlib was so inspired by the Rosicrucians that he became one. He
was a passionate astrologer, Hermeticist, and follower of Paracelsus, and he
tried to establish a "Pansophic college," the Collegium Lucis, or "College
of Light" in Chichester. Its aim was to produce "teachers of mankind."[4]
Hartlib's Rosicrucian college never quite got off the ground, but Hartlib's
most vital role was as a kind of seventeenth-century networker. He was
what was called an "intelligencer": he pursued a Pansophic goal by keeping
up-to-date on a dizzying number of topics and shared his knowledge with
his numerous contacts. One of his ideas was what he called an "Office of
Addresses," a kind of "citizen's information bureau," which made available
a wide range of material on a number of subjects, what we might call an
early form of Wikipedia. One of Hartlib's contacts was John Worthington,
an academic associated with the Cambridge Platonists, a group of Pansophic philosophers led by Ralph Cudworth, who kept the Hermetic torch
burning in spite of Isaac Casaubon's debunking. Others in Hartlib's address
book included the diarist Samuel Pepys and the poet John Milton.

The England Hartlib arrived in was much like Bohemia before the
Thirty Years' War. On the brink of its own civil war—which pitted the
Roundheads against the Cavaliers and saw the public beheading of Charles I
in 1649—England's intellectual and political climate was strangely liberal
and promising. In 1640, Hartlib addressed Parliament, expounding his
philosophy of Pansophy and universal education, and proposing practical
ideas that Parliament could act on. He must have felt his speech was a success, as he urged Comenius and John Drury, a Scots preacher who had met
Hartlib in Poland and who shared his belief in educational and religious
reform, to come to London. It seemed that finally, there was a good chance
that the Rosicrucian dream might come to fruition.

Sadly, it was not to be. Comenius and Drury were well received by
Hartlib's circle, but in 1642 civil war broke out and all plans for a universal reformation were shelved. Drury left for The Hague and Comenius

headed to Sweden. In *The Way of Light,* written during his time in England, Comenius called for the spread of knowledge and for a "college" to be founded in order to accomplish this. At the end of *Labyrinth of the World,* Comenius's pilgrim escapes from the maze of worldly events and finds himself in "the Paradise of the Heart," where angelic teachers impart to him "secret knowledge of diverse things." Similar angelic teachers peopled Andreae's *Christianopolis.* Comenius called these angelic teachers an "invisible college"—much like the "invisible church" of Caspar Schwenckfeld. His hope that such an institution could be founded on earth had not diminished, although the necessary conditions seemed as elusive as ever.

THE INVISIBLE COLLEGE

In 1645, while civil war raged, several scientific enthusiasts—or "natural philosophers," as they were then called —gathered in London in informal meetings to share their passion and discuss ideas. Two of the people involved had close ties to the Rosicrucian dream through their contact with Charles Louis, Frederick V's son. One was Theodore Haak, an exile from Bohemia, member of Hartlib's circle and a follower of Comenius. Another was John Wilkins, the future bishop of Chester and author of a popular work *Mathematical Magick,* which refers to the Rosicrucian manifestoes and is based on some of the ideas of John Dee and Robert Fludd; the title, Wilkins said, came from Cornelius Agrippa.[5] Around the same time, Robert Boyle, an alchemist and the founder of chemistry, referred to an "invisible college" in some letters. In a letter of 1646, written to his former tutor, Boyle asked for some books that would make him "extremely welcome to our Invisible College." Boyle wrote that the members of this "invisible college" endeavored to "put narrow-mindedness out of countenance" and strove to "take the whole body of mankind to their care," rather Rosicrucian-sounding ideals. In a letter of 1647 to Hartlib, Boyle called him "the midwife and nurse" of this college and said that the "whole society is concerned in all the accidents of your life."[6]

It seems clear that Boyle's "invisible college" was the circle around Hartlib, and it was out of this that Hartlib had hoped to create an educational establishment along Pansophic and Rosicrucian lines. What did emerge from Hartlib's vision was something different. There is, it seems, a clear link between Hartlib's "invisible college" and the founding of the Royal Society, the oldest and most prestigious scientific society in the world.

The events leading up to the founding of the Royal Society in 1660 are complex, but in essence it involved natural philosophers from two independent groups coming together. One group, led by John Wilkins and inspired by Hartlib, held Pansophic and Rosicrucian ideals. The other was motivated more by the ideas of Francis Bacon. Bacon, we've seen, followed some Rosicrucian ideals, but his ambition and pragmatism led him to move more toward the kind of mechanical view of the world promoted by Marin Mersenne. Bacon famously said that nature "must be put on the rack and tortured for her secrets," but before becoming a symbol of the archetypal experimental scientist, he embraced a Hermetic view of the world and, according to the Italian historian Paolo Rossi, was a firm believer in the *Anima mundi*.[7] Given this, it is surprising that Bacon joined Mersenne in attacking the work of Dee, Fludd, and Paracelsus. But like Dee and Michael Maier, Bacon sought the favor of James I and he knew the paranoid king held no truck with magic. While it seems he saw the virtue and value of the Hermetic view, Bacon also knew that it was best to play his esoteric cards close to his chest. With the prevailing wind moving in a mechanical direction, Bacon decided it was favorable for his career to bend with it. The fact that Bacon enjoyed several court appointments and that his upward mobility led to being made lord chancellor in 1618 seems to argue that he played his cards right.

Among Hartlib's correspondents was Baron Skytte, a Swedish nobleman who shared Hartlib's ideas and who was among the group of natural philosophers partial to the Pansophic view. In 1660, the proto-Royal Society sought the king's endorsement—indeed, they could not be a royal society without it. Propositions concerning the society's aims and ideals were put before Charles II, the first king of England following the Restoration, by Baron Skytte. Many of the Baconian group were Royalists who were in exile during Oliver Cromwell's Commonwealth, but had now returned. Hartlib, whose ideals informed the Pansophic group, had found favor during the Commonwealth, and he was now looked on with suspicion. The proposals Baron Skytte had put before the king were of a Pansophic character, but Hartlib's dreams were sadly dashed again. At a meeting, Skytte's view of the society was soundly voted out; even Boyle's support failed to move the Baconians. They pursued the royal charter on their own and received in it 1662. Skytte returned to Sweden and Hartlib died the next year. One factor involved in the rejection of the Pansophic vision must have been that in 1659, an edition of Dee's *Spiritual Diary* was published, giving his account of his communication with angels. It contained a preface by Meric Casaubon—Isaac's son—that accused Dee of consorting with devils.

In the midst of religious and political tensions, the Baconians prudently distanced themselves from ideas about "universal wisdom" and narrowed their prospects down to pursuing "real" science, the Marin Mersenne brand. They were also acting in response to the anti-Baconian sentiment that dominated during the dour years of the puritan Cromwell's Protectorate. The "official" history of the society's founding, published in 1667, underplayed its early Pansophic connection, and failed to mention anything about an "invisible college." John Wilkins, who shared Hartlib's views, remained as the society's secretary, but his active role was diminished. Pansophy, it seems, was dead. Or had it, like the esoteric current as a whole, only moved underground?

"LET NEWTON BE!"

The most famous member of the Royal Society was Isaac Newton (1642–1727), generally considered the greatest scientific genius of all time. It is not too much of an exaggeration to say that Newton created the modern world practically single-handedly. His major work, *Mathematical Principles of Natural Philosophy*, published in 1687, usually referred to as the *Principia*, is considered the most important book ever written, even more than the Bible. We live in a Newtonian universe, or at least we did until the arrival of Einstein.

It would be tedious and unnecessary to point out all of Newton's contributions. From the law of gravity to the infinitesimal calculus, history can be divided into pre- and post-Newton periods. As Alexander Pope wrote in honor of his passing, "Nature, and Nature's Laws lay hid in night: God said 'Let Newton be!' and all was light."

Yet in what has to be the greatest irony in the history of western esotericism, the man responsible for the clockwork cosmos that William Blake railed against—accusing him of "single vision and Newton's sleep"—and contemporary New Agers hold responsible for practically all our ills, was himself a passionate, obsessive devotee of the Hermetic sciences. Newton not only wrote reams about alchemy—some one million words to be exact—he was committed to discovering the philosopher's stone and was particularly fascinated by the story of Nicolas Flamel. In recent years, the fact that Newton's discoveries, which led to our modern world, were secondary to his main pursuits has become more or less common knowledge. But for a long time any whiff of the alchemical retort associated with Newton was quickly blown away. It was only in the 1940s that the fact that Newton, father of the modern world, was secretly a secret teacher came, appropriately, to light.

In 1936, the economist John Maynard Keynes bought a collection of Newton's papers, which had been languishing in neglect; some had even been kept hidden. When Keynes began to read them, he was astonished. Keynes discovered that Newton was "different from the conventional picture of him." In 1946, in an address to the Royal Society, part of a tercentenary celebration of Newton's birth, Keynes spelled out exactly how different.[8] Newton was, Keynes wrote, "more extraordinary than the nineteenth century cared to make out of him"—the century par excellence of the mechanical view of the world and the deficient mode of Gebser's mental-rational consciousness structure. Newton was not, Keynes came to see, "a rationalist . . . who taught us to think along the lines of cold and untinctured reason." He was not "the first of the age of reason," Keynes said, but "the last of the magicians . . . the last wonderchild to whom the Magi could do sincere and appropriate homage." Newton was a magician because "he looked on the universe and all that is in it as a riddle." It was a "secret" strewn with "mystic clues" that turned it into a "philosopher's treasure hunt" fit for an "esoteric brotherhood."

That Newton belonged to such a brotherhood, in spirit if not in literal fact, is for the most part ignored today. If it is acknowledged, it is a source of embarrassment or, at best, a grudging admission that to some small degree, Newton's interest in alchemy did play a part in his discoveries. Even *Time* magazine had to admit that Newton's "laws" owed "something to alchemy."[9] More robust appraisals deny that Newton's alchemical interests have any importance at all. Christopher Hitchens—with Richard Dawkins, one of the most vocal modern advocates of atheism—responded to Keynes's revelations by calling Newton "a spiritualist and alchemist of a particularly laughable kind."[10]

This, however, was not the opinion of those who knew Newton. For his contemporaries, Newton was a serious student of Hermetic science who pursued it with a dedication that left most of his fellows looking like amateurs. He was, as the cliché goes, looking for the mind of God. One suspects that with his Pansophic interests, Newton may have had a better chance of finding it than his counterparts do today.

GENIUS AT WORK

Newton was born in Woolsthorpe, near Grantham, on Christmas Day in 1642. His father, a farmer, had died three months earlier. Newton's mother remarried, and when he was three, she abandoned Newton to be brought up by his grandmother. Newton was a sickly, solitary child who hated his mother and stepfather so much that he planned to set fire to their house with them in it. In a confession he wrote at the age of twenty, this murderous fantasy rated very highly.[11] He did not form close emotional relationships, and his early abandonment led to a basic mistrust of life. A colleague at Cambridge said of Newton that he was "of the most fearful, cautious, and suspicious temper that I ever knew."[12] Newton spent most of his adult life as a recluse; he was, as the psychologist Anthony Storr writes, "preoccupied with his work to the exclusion of almost everything else, with little social contact with other human beings, and no close relations with either sex."[13]

Newton seemed to have a pathological reluctance to publish his work, fearing that his ideas would be stolen or subject to criticism that he could not endure. Probably the most famous example of his paranoia is the feud with the philosopher Gottfried Wilhelm Leibniz over who had invented calculus first; Leibniz, like Descartes, had also tried to make contact with the Rosicrucians. Newton had similar feuds with John Flamsteed, the first Astronomer Royal of England and founder of the Greenwich Observatory, and Robert Hooke, a fellow member of the Royal Society, with whom Newton quarreled about priority in gravity and other touchy subjects. These proprietary squabbles seem much like the "petty envy" Christian Rosenkreutz encountered when he wished to share the knowledge he had gained in the East. For all his Hermetic obsessions, Newton seems not to have embraced the Rosicrucian ideal of sharing knowledge, as his costive attitude to publication suggests. According to one biographer, "Newton hardly ever published a discovery without being urged to by others; even when he had arrived at the solution of the greatest problem that astronomy has ever faced he said nothing about it to anybody."[14]

Newton showed a facility with mechanics from an early age, but his life's work began when as a boy he bought a prism at a county fair. Thus started the fascination with light that resulted in his treatise *Opticks*, which was published in 1704. Newton might have become a farmer like his father, but in 1661, he won a scholarship to Cambridge. He was what was called a "sizar," a student who earns his keep doing menial tasks. At first Newton seems to have been an average student, giving no sign of what was in store. In 1665, Newton graduated and, because of the threat of plague, he left Cambridge and returned to Woolsthorpe, where he remained for two years. There he experimented with his prism, made his first forays into inventing calculus, and, most famously, had an apple fall on his head.

Whether an apple really did hit Newton's head or not, an idea certainly did. What came to Newton was the hunch that whatever it was that made the apple fall also kept the moon from falling into the Earth, or the Earth falling into the sun. What that something eventually turned out to be was a mysterious force which no one had seen and which acted on things at a distance, that is, with no medium carrying its influence from source to target. In other words, gravity. Pretty much everything Newton is known for came out of those two years in Woolsthorpe. After this time, he made no new major discoveries.

Newton returned to Cambridge in 1667 and was made a Fellow. Two years later, at the age of twenty-seven, he was made professor of mathematics, occupying the Lucasian Chair in Mathematics, which Stephen Hawking, who would also like to know the mind of God, until recently did as well. In 1668, Newton's fascination with optics led to his inventing the first practical reflecting telescope. This brought him to the attention of his peers; four years later, he was made a member of the Royal Society. By the early 1680s, he had turned his mind to gravity again, his interest pricked by Robert Hooke's remarks about having devised a proof that whatever force acted between the planets, it was inversely proportional to the square of the distance between them. This had occurred to Newton too, some twenty years earlier, but his reluctance to publish meant that no one knew it.

Newton's caution led to his feud with Hooke, much to Hooke's regret; Newton was a bad enemy and he went out of his way to erase Hooke's reputation, very successfully in fact.[15] The architect Christopher Wren—responsible for rebuilding much of London after the Great Fire of 1666—offered a prize to whoever could devise the kind of proof Hooke mentioned. (Most historians consider Hooke's claim wishful thinking, as he never delivered the proof he claimed to have.) The astronomer Edmund Halley—after whom the comet is named—mentioned this contest to Newton and asked what he thought. Newton remarked that yes, the inverse square law was correct, and that he had already calculated it. Halley asked to see the proof but Newton had shelved it and promised to send it to Halley later. Halley told the Royal Society of Newton's claim and suggested that when Newton delivered on his promise, the society should publish it. Three years later, Newton came through, and the *Principia* was born. In a very real sense it marked the end of Newton's life as a scientist.

ALCHEMICAL NEWTON

But not as an alchemist. One project Newton turned to after the *Principia* was biblical chronology. This had been a topic of great interest since 1654, when Bishop James Ussher had argued that, according to his close reading of the Bible, the world had begun in 4004 B.C., on Sunday, October 23, to be exact. Newton's own starting point was 4000 B.C. There were other similar chronologies—Johannes Kepler, one of the giants on whose shoulders Newton famously stood, had devised one—but Newton's is unusual for the fact that he projected it into the future and, in a vision of what he called "alchemical history," predicted that the end of the world would come around the middle of the twenty-first century.[16] The fact that Newton also predicted that Christ would return in 1948 may suggest that we can take his future history with some grains of salt.[17]

Another biblical mystery that gripped Newton was the secret of Solomon's Temple. Like the Hermeticists and Neoplatonists, Newton believed that Egypt was the source of all wisdom. He believed that the ancients had held the key to all knowledge, and the secret to discovering this was hidden in the symbols of the Hermetic tradition. Newton also believed that Solomon was the greatest philosopher of all time, and he devoted much time and thought to "reconstructing" Solomon's Temple, which he saw as a kind of "frame" through which he could understand the pattern of history.[18] Like the Traditionalist school of René Guénon, Newton believed that "the first religion was the most rational of all others till the nations corrupted it." Like Gemistos Plethon, Newton believed that at the "dawn of time," man did know the mind of God. He had forgotten it since, but Newton was determined to remember.

Newton's interest in alchemy may have begun in his early days at Grantham School, when he lodged with a chemist. His lifelong hypochondria may have started then too. Like Paracelsus, Newton took laudanum—a mixture of opium and alcohol—and he also concocted unusual remedies for mostly imaginary ills, the "illnesses of the imagination" Paracelsus had warned about. He read much at this time: Aristotle, Plato, and Francis Bacon, whose own Rosicrucian views settled into Newton's mind. One powerful Hermetic influence came from his tutor, Henry More, one of the Cambridge Platonists who, like John Worthington— one of Hartlib's networkers—dismissed Isaac Casaubon's erudite nit-picking. More believed that behind the natural world was a universal spirit, something along the lines of the Neoplatonist's *Anima mundi,* and he passed this on to Newton.

By 1663, Newton began a "philosophical" notebook in which he jotted down reflections on a number of topics, one of which was "Of Gravity and Levity." Another was optics and the mystery of color. As Peter Marshall argues, Newton's intuitions about gravity and color emerged from his interest in alchemy, which spoke of "hidden forces at work in nature and stressed the possibility of transformation."[19] Changes in color during the alchemical process were taken as a sign of transformation; this was known as the "peacock's tail." According to Marshall, Newton had an inordinate fondness for red, decorating his room at Cambridge in it. Red symbolizes the last stage of the alchemical opus, and another name for the philosopher's stone is the "red elixir."

Newton read widely in alchemical literature and built up an extensive library on the subject, one of the largest of the time. Ramon Lull, Basil Valentine, Michael Maier, Michael Sendivogius, the Rosicrucian manifestoes, Jacob Boehme, and other important alchemical authors found space on Newton's crowded shelves.[20] Newton annotated Maier's works, and he wrote at length on the Rosicrucians. Newton also made transcripts of many alchemical works, translated others, made detailed cross-references between different texts, and compiled an alchemical glossary of over seven thousand items. Much of his notes was written in code, partially out of Newton's paranoia but also out of the belief that such knowledge should be kept from unworthy hands. He himself tried to live piously and believed that "They who search after the Philosopher's Stone [are] . . . obliged to live a strict religious life."

Newton also knew, as did Mary Anne South, that "alchemy does not trade with metals as ignorant vulgars think," and that its work "is not of that kind which tends to vanity & deceit but rather to . . . the knowledge of God." This is in order "to glorify God in his wonderful works" and "to teach a man how to live well." The knowledge of how this can be done can be found in nature, but it was also found in what Newton called the "sacred signatures," works of spiritual truth such as Genesis, the book of Job, and other biblical texts.[21] Other important "signatures" were the *Corpus Hermeticum* and the *Emerald Tablet*, which Newton translated and about which he wrote a long and detailed commentary. [22]

Newton's perseverance in his alchemical studies became legendary.

More than one acquaintance observed that he could go for long periods without food or rest and that he was never so happy as when he had gained a new insight in his work. He had a genius for absentmindedness. William Stukeley, an early Freemason and the antiquarian responsible for the modern interest in ancient sites like Stonehenge, knew Newton and was one of his first biographers. Visiting Newton, Stukeley was kept waiting. After some time, Stukeley grew hungry and decided to eat the lunch that Newton had ignored. When Newton finally appeared, he lifted the lid on his lunch plate and remarked, "Dear me, I thought I had not dined," and put it back.[23]

As Lynn Picknett and Clive Prince make clear, recognition that Newton's alchemical pursuits informed his scientific work appeared as early as the 1960s, but such insights were out of step with the accepted picture of the father of "the age of reason" and made little impact.[24] Yet more than one scholar saw that the work for which Newton is justly recognized today came about not in spite of his alchemical interests, but because of them. As Picknett and Prince write: "If Newton had never become privy to the Hermetic philosophy, he would never have achieved his work and the world would be—literally—much the poorer for it. It is universally acknowledged that if the *Principia* had never been written, our modern technological world would not exist. But without the *Hermetica*, Newton would not have written the *Principia*. Emphatically Newton did not make his great scientific discoveries *despite* his esoteric belief, but *because* of them."[25]

NEWTON'S BREAKDOWN

The strain of writing the *Principia*, as well as conducting his alchemical research, took its toll on Newton, and by the early 1690s, it was beginning to show. In 1693, he began a strange work, *Praxis*, in which it seems that he claims to have achieved "multiplication," another name for "transmutation," the central aim of alchemy. Peter Marshall ponders this possibility and asks whether, if it was true, would Newton have had to rethink the mechanical philosophy that he presented in the *Principia*?[26] According to the historians of science J. Edward McGuire and Piyo M. Rattansi, Newton did leave a draft of sections of the *Principia* that he intended to rewrite for a new edition, which would include more of his ideas about the Hermetic sciences.[27]

That edition did not appear, but the idea remains a tantalizing suggestion. Marin Mersenne died in 1648. He would undoubtedly have applauded the *Principia,* but we do not know what he would have thought about its author's alchemical pursuits or quest for the mind of God. We can only speculate on what impact a Hermetically widened *Principia* would have had on western consciousness. In mid-1693, Newton suffered a nervous breakdown. He abandoned *Praxis* after only a few short chapters and it remained unfinished. His paranoia increased and he believed that his friends Samuel Pepys—Samuel Hartlib's neighbor—and the philosopher John Locke were conspiring against him. Newton was always subject to depression, often violent outbursts, and strong feelings of guilt. After a sleepless week, Newton's mind cracked and he was overwhelmed with delusions. The overwork and solitude were a strain, but there is also the suggestion that he was poisoned by the fumes of some alchemical experiment.

By the end of the year, Newton had recovered, but he seems to have experienced the kind of *enantiodromia* that turned Thomas Aquinas against his *Summa*. He abandoned science and alchemy and, in 1696, left Cambridge for London. There he turned his attention to theological questions. He became president of the Royal Society in 1703, and remained so until the end of his life. He was appointed warden of the Mint, and later master of the Bank of England, an ironic position in that alchemy was illegal and subject to the death penalty. This was not out of religious reasons but because of the odd chance that alchemists *could* make gold. If so, it would ruin the economy. Having Newton in charge of the treasury was rather like leaving a fox in charge of the chicken coop. But Newton brought the same dedication to this task that he had to his alchemical and scientific ones. He had no qualms about sending counterfeiters to the gallows and did so whenever necessary. He died in 1727, having brought into existence a world quite unlike the one he believed we actually live in.

THE MASON'S WORD

One of the books in Newton's alchemical library was the *Theatrum Chemicum Britannicum,* a compilation of English alchemical literature compiled by Elias Ashmole, published in 1652. It was one of Newton's most consulted works and there is small wonder why. Ashmole had gathered many texts that were available only in manuscript form and were sequestered in private libraries. The number of alchemists represented is impressive: Thomas Norton, George Ripley, and Edward Kelley are among them, and Ashmole also includes Geoffrey Chaucer's satiric poem, "The Canon Yeoman's Tale," which lampoons "puffers" and tells the story of a fraudulent alchemical priest. Ashmole was a solicitor, alchemist, antiquarian, and astrologer, and he had a particular fascination with the Rosicrucians. He copied out by hand English translations of the Rosicrucian manifestoes and wrote a letter in Latin asking to join the fraternity. He never sent the letter—not because he had changed his mind, but because like so many others he didn't have their address.

Ashmole was one of the founders of the Royal Society; he was part of the group who favored Francis Bacon's experimental approach to natural philosophy. He supported the Royalists during the civil war, and when the monarchy was restored, he received many benefits. Like Newton, Ashmole acquired a huge library, and like the Hermetic Holy Roman Emperor Rudolf II, he was an obsessive collector of curiosities, unusual natural or man-made objects, a hobby that many at the time with the funds and leisure enjoyed. In 1677, Ashmole donated his library and collection to the University of Oxford; it formed the basis of the Ashmolean Museum, the first university museum in the world. Another of Ashmole's curious accomplishments is that he is one the first men in England to be initiated into Freemasonry.

Ashmole's initiation took place under less than propitious circumstances. It happened in 1646, when he was a prisoner of war. He had been captured by the Roundheads (supporters of Parliament against the king) in Lancashire, and Ashmole's initiation was one of many that took place under the auspices of battle.[28] Ashmole's involvement with Freemasonry continued throughout his life. In 1682, he noted in his diary that he had attended a lodge meeting at Mason's Hall in London as the senior member, and that they later dined at the Half Moone Tavern in Cheapside. Ashmole died in 1692.

Ashmole was not the only person involved in the Royal Society who had links to Freemasonry and the Rosicrucians. Sir Robert Moray, a Scot, was a soldier of fortune and a spy and, like Ashmole, he fought on the side of the king during the civil war. Also like Ashmole, his initiation took place in wartime; in Moray's case, it happened in Newcastle. In 1641, just before the outbreak of the civil war, Scotland was involved in a revolt against England. Successful, the Scots headed south and captured Newcastle, and there, in March 1641, Moray was made a Freemason. Scotland later sided with Parliament against the king, but Moray was one of the few Scots who fought on the side of the Royalists. During the Commonwealth, Moray lived in France, but with the Restoration, he returned to England and was instrumental in the Royal Society gaining Charles II's patronage. Moray was friends with the "inner alchemist" Thomas Vaughan, who published the first English translation of the Rosicrucian manifestoes; Thomas's twin brother, Henry Vaughan, the metaphysical poet, used alchemical motifs in his work.[29] Other members of the Royal Society, like Christopher Wren, were Masons. Oddly Newton was not, given his interest in Solomon's Temple, a central theme in Masonic philosophy.

That Freemasonry was in some way connected to the Rosicrucians is not an unusual idea. In 1638, the Scot Henry Adamson published a poem, "The Muses Threnodie," that contained the lines: "For what we presage is not in grosse,/For we be brethren of the Rosie Crosse;/We have the *Mason Word* and second sight/Things for to come we can foretell aright."[30] This suggests that Freemasonry and the Rosicrucians were linked, and that both were privy to paranormal abilities. In 1676, a Masonic pamphlet featured a humorous reference to what must have been an interesting dinner party. It read: "To give notice, that the Modern Green-Ribboned Cabal, together with the Ancient Brotherhood of the Rosy Cross, the Hermetick Adepti and the company of Accepted Masons intend all to dine together on the 31 of November next."[31] The association of Masons, Rosicrucians, and Hermeticists is clear, and the notice also advised those attending to bring their spectacles, otherwise some of the guests might prove "invisible." Such links suggested to one Masonic researcher that Freemasonry was a direct descendant of the Rosicrucians. In his "Historico-Critical Inquiry into the Origins of the Rosicrucians and the Freemasons," Thomas De Quincey, the "English opium eater," argued that the Freemasons "arose out of the Rosicrucian mania." De Quincey seems to have recognized that Andreae's "hoax" had a serious intent and speaks of its "elevated purpose." He concludes that "Freemasonry is neither more nor less than Rosicrucianism as modified by those who transplanted it to England."[32] Those who transplanted it were Hartlib, Comenius, and Fludd.

It would be gratifying to accept De Quincey's conclusion, but there are problems with it. There are clear resemblances between the Rosicrucians and Freemasonry, but the dates argue against a direct lineage. There is evidence for Freemasonry that is earlier than the Rosicrucian diaspora. In 1583, James VI of Scotland—soon to be James I of England—made William Schaw his master of works. Schaw oversaw all building under James VI's rule and he was responsible for organizing the different lodges of builders. Along with all the other necessary requirements in order to secure work, Schaw made a curious addition to what each stonemason would have to provide. He made it a rule that each new applicant would be tested in "the art of memory and the science thereof."[33] Mention of an "art of memory" reminds us of Giordano Bruno and the Renaissance adepts. Is it this memory Schaw referred to? He could be thinking of ordinary memory, a useful tool in any practice. But why refer to it as an "art" and "science"? If Schaw was speaking of "magical memory," then this seems evidence that some Hermetic ideas were involved in stonemasonry well before the Rosicrucian experiment.

THE ROOTS OF FREEMASONRY

As with so many of our secret teachers and teachings, the origins of Freemasonry are shrouded in the mists of time. They also suffer from a surfeit of suggestions. We have already seen one Masonic origin story link it to the Knights Templar. The Templars, in fact, serve as a connecting thread running through a fascinating and fatiguing assortment of possible sources for the roots of Freemasonry. In recent years, a shelfload of books have appeared anchoring Freemasonry in a number of speculative foundation stories, ranging from the shroud of Turin and John the Baptist to the Essenes and the Ark of the Covenant.[34] Manly P. Hall suggests that Freemasonry reaches back to lost Atlantis, and that it and the Rosicrucians were responsible for the founding of America.[35] Hall's suggestions echo in the work of David Ovason and Robert Hieronimus, whose books argue that the United States was intended to be a kind of Rosicrucian utopia and that Washington, D.C., was designed according to the sacred geometry associated with Freemasonry.[36]

An offshoot from Masonic mythology are the Illuminati, a breakaway group that for a time in the late eighteenth century briefly troubled the government of Bavaria. Currently they are enjoying a comeback in popular culture. From Dan Brown to Jay-Z—and with much in between—the Illuminati are either planning to destroy the Vatican, or are a super-exclusive elitist club, open to rich rap stars and politicians intent on establishing a New World Order.

Although more conservative ideas about Freemasonry's origins exist—according to the historian Jasper Ridley, they have little if nothing to do with the Templars—Masonic history itself can be extravagant.[37] The most common story accepted by Masons is that Freemasonry goes back to the murder of Hiram Abiff, architect of Solomon's Temple. Hiram Abiff knew the secret of the temple—the Mason's "Word"—and when three "ruffians" accosted him and demanded it, he refused. They murdered him, and in the ritual that raises a Freemason to the third degree and makes him a Master Mason, Hiram Abiff's murder is reenacted.

In a Masonic text known as the "Old Charges" that dates to 1400, part of what is known as the Cooke and Regius manuscript, it is said that Masonry goes back to antediluvian times. After the Flood, its secrets were recovered, and they are the basis for the knowledge of Hermes Trismegistus and the wisdom of Pythagoras. In other accounts, God himself is a Mason; evidence of this is the fact that he built the universe in six days. Adam was a Mason too, and it was Masons who built the Tower of Babel.[38] For some, Freemasonry reaches back to the ancient Mystery schools.[39] For others, mostly since the French Revolution, the Masons are secretly dedicated to world dominion. In 1924, the conspiracy theorist Nesta Webster published *Secret Societies and Subversive Movements,* in which she claimed that Freemasons, communists, and Jews were planning to take over the world. Webster's work was in many ways a rehash of the notorious *Protocols of the Elders of Zion,* a scurrilous forgery published in Russia in 1905, which claimed that the Masons, in league with a cabal of international Jewry, were busy undermining western civilization. Some of the *Protocols'* appreciative readers were Adolf Hitler and the Traditionalist Julius Evola.

The *Protocols* were proven to be a forgery—in 1921, a series of articles in *The New York Times* did that—and Nesta Webster's hysterics did not reach far beyond the lunatic fringe (although Winston Churchill took them seriously), yet an aura of danger still surrounds the Masons. Today the occult or mystical aspect of Freemasonry has given way to its character as an Old Boys' Club, membership of which is helpful in one's career advancement. Yet for all its protestations, Freemasonry has never quite shaken off the suspicion that it is up to no good.

THE CATHEDRAL BUILDERS

In the most likely account of the origins of Freemasonry, it emerges from the medieval stonebuilders' guilds. As Jasper Ridley remarks, during the Middle Ages there was a common feeling that the masons were somehow "different" from other people.[40] For one thing, while most people then rarely left the town they were born in, masons moved around; they, as it were, followed the money. Very few buildings then were made of stone, and masons had to travel to reach the castles, churches, cathedrals, and abbeys they worked on. Their work too was different; often it involved the sacred. The masons who did the fine-tuning, working on the cathedral carvings, formed a kind of elite.

Much of this work involved sacred symbols, alchemical glyphs, and the secret "green language." Whether every mason who worked with these understood them is unknown, but we must assume some did. In France, such elite masons were known as the *Compagnonnages*. In Germany they were called the *Steinmetzen*. These master carvers worked with what was called "freestone," a softer material that allowed for precision work. The rank-and-file masons, who laid the building's foundations, worked with "rough stone," a harder, unwieldy material. Over time "freestone mason" was shortened to "freemason."[41] These "freestone masons" needed to recognize fellow masons in foreign towns, and so they developed secret signs, handshakes, and passwords, and guarded these fiercely. This helped to ensure that only true masons would be allowed to do their work, which, as it was involved with cathedrals and other sacred sites, was connected to the great religious monuments of the past, such as Solomon's Temple.

Masons were also required to lead a moral and religious life. They had a duty to God and to the church. They must obey the king and show fealty to their master. One "charge" given to masons was not to sleep with their master's wife or daughter. Another forbade card-playing, fornicating, or frequenting pubs.[42] A mason was also never to reveal his master's secrets, his tricks of the trade, as it were—a possible source of the story of Hiram Abiff.

These ethical and moral strictures—or something much like them—became part of later Freemasonry and epithets like "upright," "four square," and "on the level," which indicate soundness, integrity, and fairness—why should a "square" deal be better than a "round" one?—have entered common language. But while Freemasonry's origins remain a mystery, another mystery is what is known as the shift from "operative masonry" to "speculative masonry," which happened sometime between 1550 and 1700.

OPERATORS AND SPECULATORS

At some point, emphasis shifted from actual masons working with stone—"operative"—to an interest and concern with the *meaning* and *symbolism* of architecture, with "speculating" about it. We can see this as a reverse of the shift that turned alchemy into chemistry. "Inner alchemy" began with an interior transformation, but the chemistry that appeared in the seventeenth and eighteenth centuries concentrated on "real" changes in the chemical combinations of matter. "Freestone masonry" began as a "hands-on" experience with actual stone, and transformed into a "spiritual masonry," aimed at building an "inner" temple.

Exactly why and how this happened is unknown, but we can assume that "speculative masonry" shared in the wide hunger for a more immediate and liberal religious experience that characterized the Rosicrucian experiment and the heretical movements that preceded it. What is clear is that by the early eighteenth century, the masons were no longer a "trade union" submitting to the strictures of the Catholic Church, but had become a society of "intellectual gentlemen who favored religious tolerance and friendship between men of different religions, and thought that a simple belief in God should replace controversial theological doctrines."[43]

In a development that has never been satisfactorily explained, aristocratic men of cultured leisure suddenly took a profound interest in the activities of stonecutters and laborers. Or more precisely, not in their activities, but in the meaning behind them. One source for this interest must have been the King James and other vernacular versions of the Bible. These took control of religious thinking away from the church, and their account of the building of Solomon's Temple aroused curiosity about the masons' work. The result was that ideas of religious tolerance, promoted by the Rosicrucians, became part of the masons' legend, which was associated with sacred architecture. These ideas had their roots in the Pythagorean and Platonic vision we have looked at in this book. Masonic symbolism is Hermetic in origin. The Masonic Great Architect, who creates the universe and shapes the rough stone of humanity, making it a fit temple, finds his ancestor in the Platonic and Hermetic cosmic craftsman. Part of the Masonic initiation ritual includes a kind of Hermetic ascent through the planets, and in Mozart's Masonic opera, *The Magic Flute* (1791), which depicts the archetypal struggle between darkness and light, Egyptian and Hermetic symbols abound. In *The Lost Keys of Freemasonry*, Manly P. Hall even sees a connection between the legend of Hiram Abiff and the kind of Egyptian initiation rituals aimed at separating the soul from the body, and which Plato spoke of as "practicing dying."

DEISM AND THE DIVINE ARCHITECT

The Masonic origin story recounted in James Anderson's *Book of Constitutions,* published in 1723, depicts God as the Divine Architect. This concept fit in well with the Deism of the Enlightenment, a religious position that grew out of Newton's mechanical cosmos. This saw God as the Creator of the Universe, but a creator who, once his handiwork was done, no longer interfered with his creation. Once set in motion, the clockwork universe would carry on with no need of supernatural intervention. The meaning of the Creator's work could be understood through reason and observation, not revelation.[44] The slow accumulation of scientific fact would reveal the truth about God, a religious position known as "naturalism," a philosophy with which William Blake found much fault because it allowed no place for free will or the imagination, and reduced man and the universe to little more than very complicated machines.[45] In this way, we can see Deism as a very left-brain religion, relying solely on reason and the senses and leaving out of account anything that reason cannot explain.

While not all Freemasons were Deists, their desire to avoid sectarian squabbles led to their anchoring spirituality in what we might call a religious common sense, which emphasized reasonableness over everything else. While for a time Deism made possible a truce between religion and the swiftly rising scientific outlook, the need for a Creator soon fell away. When Napoleon remarked to the French astronomer Laplace that he had left God out of his account of the universe, Laplace replied that he had no need of that hypothesis, a sentiment echoed recently in Stephen Hawking's *The Grand Design,* which argues that there was no need for God, given that the universe arose from "spontaneous creation."

Deism allowed men of the Enlightenment to compartmentalize their spiritual and scientific beliefs and so avoid for a time the religious bickering that had characterized the last few centuries. This sense of harmony and reasonableness informed English Freemasonry, which soon found a place within mainstream society. The Grand Lodge of England was established in 1717. With its emphasis on moral and ethical responsibility, it quickly became associated with the values of sobriety and propriety, egalitarianism and civic-mindedness. Within the Masonic lodges, men from different social backgrounds and standing could meet each other as equals, just as those of different religious beliefs could. It was this belief in the equality of men that drew the founding fathers of the American Revolution to Freemasonry, which spread throughout the colonies via military "field lodges," the kind through which Elias Ashmole and Robert Moray were initiated, rather as Mithraism spread among Roman soldiers.

While much has been written about the "Masonic roots of America," we should be cautious in ascribing the kind of detailed "secret" planning that Manly P. Hall and other writers see in the beginnings of the United States to the fact that Masonic emblems and motifs make up much of American symbolism, from the Great Seal to the Washington Monument. It is true that many signatories of the Declaration of Independence were Masons, but as Michael Baigent and Richard Leigh argue in *The Temple and the Lodge,* there is no evidence that a Masonic conspiracy was at work in the founding of America, although they do admit that some Rosicrucian ideas may have reached the New World as early as the Jamestown settlement.[46] The truth is that there were Masons on both sides during the American Revolution, and British generals and those of the rebels were equally brothers in the craft. Yet while we shouldn't see in the origins of America a Masonic–Rosicrucian plot to create the New World, we should recognize that the progressive and Masonic notions of liberty, equality, tolerance, brotherhood, and the "rights of man" that made up the American vision were "in the air," and that they permeated the Zeitgeist through the spread of Freemasonry. Many people who would never read the intellectual sources of these ideas—David Hume, John Locke, or Voltaire (who was a Mason)—nevertheless discovered them within the progressive atmosphere of their Masonic lodge.

CONTINENTAL FREEMASONRY
AND HIDDEN SUPERIORS

While English Freemasonry found a home within the established order of society, its continental counterpart soon became a Masonic black sheep.

This was because of its association with the Jacobite cause, which wanted to return the Stuarts to the English and Scottish thrones. In 1688, James II, a Catholic, had unexpectedly sired a male heir. This horrified the English nobility because they saw the threat of a possible Catholic dynasty. They convinced James II's daughter Mary, a Protestant, and her husband, William of Orange (Holland), to force James II to abdicate.

When William's troops reached England's shores, James II escaped to France, where he remained in exile. For the next sixty years—until 1745, and its collapse at the Battle of Culloden—the Stuart cause found support in France, Sweden, Spain, and other countries that had a stake in returning a Stuart to the throne. The Jacobite cause ("Jacobus" is the Latin equivalent of James) bled into Scottish Freemasonry, and secret Masonic fraternities devoted to the Stuarts flourished and gave the craft a subversive, threatening character. In order to make clear its fealty to the Hanoverian regime, English Freemasonry had to publicly renounce its Jacobite elements, some of which had acquired a bad reputation through their involvement with the Hell Fire Club, a society devoted to paganism and general carousing.[47] In effect, English Freemasonry went through the same purging that the Royal Society had: it rejected its politically incorrect elements and produced a document, James Anderson's *Constitutions*, that asserted its unthreatening, compliant character.

English Freemasonry was limited to three main degrees: Entered Apprentice, Fellow Craft, and Master Mason. There were "optional" and "higher," more mystical degrees, but these were now available only on the Continent. The subversive taint associated with continental Freemasonry infected these higher degrees, and soon continental Freemasonry was seen as dark, mysterious, and altogether sinister. One element of continental Freemasonry that became a central part of modern esotericism was the idea of "hidden superiors." This was introduced in the 1740s by the German Baron Karl Gotthelf von Hund, who founded a form of Freemasonry known as "Strict Observance," which traced its origins back to the Knights Templar. It was called "Strict Observance" because it demanded unquestioning obedience to certain leaders Hund referred to as "unknown superiors," hidden chiefs whose identity was secret.

Hund was a typical eighteenth-century Masonic "noble traveler," who made his way across Europe, acquiring initiations as he went. He was first initiated into Freemasonry in 1741, in Frankfurt. Hund later claimed that in Paris in 1743, he was initiated into this new Templar Freemasonry by someone he knew only as "the Knight of the Red Feather." Who this was has never been confirmed, but Hund hinted that his initiator was Charles Edward Stuart, "Bonnie Prince Charlie," the Young Pretender, who, he claimed, was the Grandmaster of all Masons. Hund initiated others, and his Templar-based Freemasonry would have a long history. In 1908, during a séance, René Guénon received a message from Jacques de Molay—the last Templar Grandmaster—telling him to "revive the Temple," that is, to start a new Templar-oriented Masonic lodge. Guénon did, but it did not last, and in 1911 he received another message telling him to close the lodge. Guénon did, and his association with Freemasonry ended in 1917.

Hund continued to promote his Strict Observance Rite, but in the early 1750s, he was faced with an embarrassing situation. When new converts asked for more information about his "hidden superiors" and their work, Hund had to admit that he could tell them nothing. He had not heard from his masked leaders for some time and feared he never would. They said they would contact him again with new instructions, but Hund heard nothing more. Like the "invisible Rosicrucians," Hund's "hidden superiors" were nowhere to be found.

Baigent and Leigh suggest that Hund's "hidden superiors" were important Jacobite Masons and that with the collapse of the cause in 1745, they had simply disappeared. They were arrested, possibly dead, or had drifted back into life. Hund may also have been the dupe of Masonic con men: he was wealthy, earnest, idealistic, passionate about chivalry and its codes, hence his perpetuation of the Templar–Freemasonry myth. Or he may have made it up, with good intentions. Strict Observance was designed to bring rigor back to what in many ways had become something of a gentleman's club, and it continued on, even with the end of the Jacobite cause. Another possibility is that Hund's "hidden superiors" were something else entirely . . .

Whatever the truth behind Hund's "hidden superiors," along with the "invisible" Rosicrucians, they came to have a very concrete influence on esoteric history, transforming in the centuries to come into Madame

Blavatsky's "hidden masters," the "secret chiefs" of the Hermetic Order of the Golden Dawn, and Gurdjieff's "inner circle of humanity," to name just a few of their incarnations: elusive, mysterious individuals who guide a faltering humanity on its path to enlightenment.

A SCANDINAVIAN DA VINCI

One important esoteric figure who may have found his way to continental Freemasonry was the scientist, religious philosopher, and "inner voyager" Emanuel Swedenborg. According to the research of Marsha Keith Schuchard, Swedenborg was initiated into a Jacobite lodge in London in 1710, during his first visit to the city, and he is thought to have renewed his contacts with this group and to have made contact with other similar societies during the 1740s, when he came to London again.[48]

Swedenborg was born in Stockholm in 1688. His father, Jesper Swedberg—the name was changed to Swedenborg in 1719 when the family was ennobled—was a regimental chaplain, pastor, and theologian who later became a bishop. Swedenborg was a deeply religious man, but his spirituality took a form radically different from his father's. By the end of his life in 1772, Swedenborg was known throughout Europe as the man who had visited heaven and hell and returned to tell about them. He did, in lengthy, unwieldy volumes which recounted in dry, precise detail the facts about the spiritual worlds. Today, in secular Sweden, he is hardly mentioned without some note of embarrassment, but Swedenborg's readers included some of the most creative and influential people of the last two centuries. A short roll call would include William Blake, W. B. Yeats, Helen Keller, Jorge Luis Borges, Arnold Schoenberg, C. G. Jung, August Strindberg, and Ralph Waldo Emerson.

Although a Christian, Swedenborg's vision transcends his religion; D. T. Suzuki, who introduced Zen Buddhism to the West, called him "the Buddha of the North." Most people who know of Swedenborg associate him with the New Church, which is based on his teaching. This rose up more than a decade after Swedenborg's death and he had nothing to do with it. Swedenborg did speak of a "new church," but he saw it more along the lines of Johann Valentin Andreae's "invisible brotherhood," Caspar Schwenckfeld's "invisible church," or the "interior church" of Karl von Eckartshausen, an "open community where regenerated men and women would find rules for life through divine grace and love," not a sect.[49] Having said this, I should mention that one New Church missionary was John Chapman, otherwise known as "Johnny Appleseed," an early conservationist who spread Swedenborgian ideas as well as apple trees across much of the eastern United States. Swedenborg's vision of "regenerated man" had its roots in a symbolic reading of the Bible as well as in Hermetic, Neoplatonic, and Kabbalistic thought, and along with Newton he was one of the great Pansophic thinkers of his time.

As a child, Swedenborg had visions; he often spoke of "unseen" playmates who told him things that astounded his parents, and by his early teens he had developed a curious habit. While at prayer, he discovered how to control his breath so that it seemed he was hardly breathing. Doing so, he said, allowed him to focus more intently on God. Breath control has long been recognized as a means of altering consciousness; the young Swedenborg seems to have discovered this for himself. This habit stayed with him, and it informed his reflections on the link between breath and the brain, one of Swedenborg's many insights into neurophysiology which were later confirmed by modern science. Another curious phenomenon the young Swedenborg experienced was something he called "the sign." This was a kind of inner light, an interior "flame" that Swedenborg saw whenever his meditations led him in the right direction. This "confirmatory brightness," as he called it, assured him that he was close to some breakthrough.

The teenage Swedenborg was introduced to Hermetic ideas by his brother-in-law Erik Benzelius, a brilliant scientist and theologian. Benzelius was a Hebraist. He had edited Philo of Alexandria and he knew F. M. van Helmont, who had annotated Knorr von Rosenroth's translation of the *Kabbalah Denudata* (*The Kabbalah Unveiled*). F. M. van Helmont was the son of the alchemist and chemist Jean Baptiste van Helmont, and the "M" stood for Mercurius. Benzelius, an important Swedish Enlightenment figure, was a Pansophist with a deep interest in the Kabbalah; he was also a friend of the philosopher Leibniz.

Swedenborg was also exposed to the Hermetic tradition in his university studies. The professor who presided over his dissertation lectured on Pythagoras, Plato, and Plotinus, and the emanationist doctrine of Neoplatonism found a place in Swedenborg's later scientific and spiritual writings. Swedenborg also read Pansophic thinkers like Comenius.

Swedenborg showed a real flair for science, but his father's religious beliefs had no place for this. After graduating from university, Swedenborg took Benzelius's advice and traveled. Swedenborg sought out knowledge and he met others, like himself, with an intense passion for learning. In London, Paris, Amsterdam, Rome, Milan, Hamburg, and other cities, Swedenborg met and conversed with many of the leading scientists of the day. Many shared a Rosicrucian, Pansophic ideal. He absorbed mathematics, mechanics, astronomy, anatomy, and other disciplines with an embarrassingly voracious intellectual appetite. Swedenborg also learned many "hands-on" skills, picking up watchmaking, cabinetry, brass working, marble inlay, and other trades from the many craftsmen he lodged with. While in London during his first visit, he invested in scientific instruments. His letters to Benzelius were read by the Collegium Curiosorum, "the Guild of the Curious," Sweden's equivalent of England's Royal Society. Swedenborg's reports led to him becoming the editor of Sweden's first scientific journal, *Daedalus Hyperboreus* (*Northern Inventor*), and the guild asked him to meet with John Flamsteed, England's Astronomer Royal. Swedenborg also met with Edmund Halley and he tried, unsuccessfully, to meet Newton. Swedenborg entered the competition sponsored by Greenwich Observatory for devising a method of establishing longitude at sea; he just missed winning, but was beaten by John Harrison, inventor of the chronometer.

On his return from his five-year grand tour, Swedenborg worked with Christopher Polhem, Sweden's most famous inventor. Swedenborg had already devised plans for a number of inventions, ranging from a submarine, an aqueduct, and a machine gun, to an airplane, automobile, and eighteenth-century home entertainment system.[50] While with Polhem, he put his engineering flair to great use. Among Swedenborg's efforts were a dry dock at the port of Karlskrona; Sweden's first salt works; the Tröllhättan Canal—which links Sweden with the North Sea—and perhaps his most remarkable feat of engineering: moving the king's navy fifteen miles across land in order to fight the Norwegians in the Battle of Fredrikshald in 1718. Yet Swedenborg's engineering ability, remarkable as it was, was not his real passion and his sights were set on bigger game.

SOUL SEARCHING

In 1719, when his family was ennobled, Swedenborg fulfilled his responsibilities as a member of the Swedish Diet. He had already been appointed a special assessor of mines. But Swedenborg's "ruling love"—as he would later call it—compelled him to pursue the Big Questions, such as the structure of the cosmos, and the relationship between the soul and the body. For the next few decades, along with all of his practical obligations, Swedenborg studied the works of the great scientists and traveled to meet them, intent on cracking the cosmic riddle.

Many of Swedenborg's insights into astronomy and neuroscience were ahead of their time and were subsequently confirmed by later scientists. He wrote reams on the structure of the cosmos, human anatomy, and the workings of the brain, along with technical treatises on mineralogy and mining. He was up-to-date on the latest developments in the new science of Descartes and Newton—like Samuel Hartlib, Swedenborg was a dedicated "intelligencer"—but Swedenborg also recognized the limits of this burgeoning worldview. Newtonian science limited itself to laws based on sensory evidence, but Swedenborg wanted to get behind phenomena to their causes. "The sign that we are willing to be wise," he wrote, "is the desire to know the causes of things, and to investigate the secret and unknown operations of nature," a dictum suitable for an alchemist's laboratory.[51]

In his first major work, *The Principles of Natural Things*, Swedenborg speculated on the nature of the universe.[52] He wanted to know how the finite physical world emerged from an infinite, unmanifest source, a question that occupied many previous minds. Swedenborg's speculations led him to ideas that in many ways anticipated our notions of holograms and fractals, as well as the "implicate order" and "unbroken wholeness" of the physicist David Bohm.[53] The French astronomer Laplace, mentioned earlier, shares credit with Immanuel Kant for developing the nebula theory of solar and planetary formation, but Swedenborg may have anticipated them, and inspired Kant, who inspired Laplace.[54] Swedenborg's contributions to astronomy, ignored for years, were confirmed by his countryman, the Nobel Prize–winning physicist and chemist Svante Arrhenius, in his book *Emanuel Swedenborg as a Cosmologist*, published in 1908. Arrhenius was one of the first scientists to investigate the "greenhouse effect," and he was an early advocate of "panspermia," the notion that life came to Earth from outer space, an idea once again in the news.[55] Swedenborg himself believed in a very strong form of the "anthropic cosmological principle," arguing not only that our universe is one in which intelligent life forms like ourselves must come into being; he believed that the universe existed *in order for* beings like ourselves to exist.[56]

Swedenborg made equally important discoveries about the brain, such as the existence and importance of neurons, and the significance of the frontal lobes for higher mental functions. He also recognized important differences between the cerebral hemispheres and, as mentioned in Chapter One, he paid special attention to the cerebellum, which, along with Stan Gooch, he believed played a crucial role in spiritual experiences.[57]

Swedenborg's anatomical studies convinced him that the purely material and mechanical explanations for life were inadequate. Any serious attempt to understand its nature required understanding the soul. It was clear that life had its roots not in chemical reactions, but in the same unmanifest source that, he argued, lay behind the universe. As the Neoplatonists did, he saw the answer in a gradual descent from a purely spiritual origin to our own physical world. But where and how did the two meet? Where was "the seat of the soul"? This was not an unusual question. Descartes himself believed that it lay in the pineal gland, a mysterious organ within the brain whose function is still not completely understood, although its importance in the production of the amino acid melatonin, necessary for the production of the neurotransmitter serotonin, is clear. For the ancient Hindus, the pineal gland was the location of the "third eye," the "opening" of which led to visionary states. Swedenborg himself was interested in such states, and in the 1740s, during another stay in London, he made efforts to achieve them.

COUNT ZINZENDORf,
THE MORAVIANS, AND RABBI fALK

In 1744, Swedenborg returned to London. As Marsha Keith Schuchard suggests, Swedenborg's trip may have involved an intelligence mission for the Jacobite cause, but what emerged was something else. Along with meeting scientists, Swedenborg became involved in the Fetter Lane congregation of the Moravians, the name Comenius's Bohemian Brethren adopted after they came under the protection of Count Nicholas Ludwig von Zinzendorf. While a student, Zinzendorf started a religious society, the Order of the Grain of Mustard Seed, dedicated to spreading the message of the Gospels; some of its later members included the archbishops of Canterbury and Paris and Christian VI, King of Denmark.[58] During a visit to Dusseldorf, Zinzendorf had a mystical experience looking at a painting of Christ.[59] It depicted Jesus with his crown of thorns and it moved Zinzendorf powerfully. He had a sudden, vivid experience of the "fully human" Christ, the opposite of the Gnostic Docetist view that saw Christ's body as a phantom. Zinzendorf's Christ was human, through and through, and for Zinzendorf this included his sexuality. It became clear to the count that only by experiencing Christ's full humanity could one be saved. This was the inspiration for Zinzendorf's form of sexual spirituality, centered around the crucified Christ.

Deep meditation on Christ's sexual organs, as well as his wounds, would, Zinzendorf believed, lead to spiritual experience. This meditation, however, was not limited to the inner world. In a form of Christian tantra, Zinzendorf preached that the true Christian experience required the practice of ritualized sex. Zinzendorf believed that for the truly faithful, "all the senses must be mobilized, the whole body must participate."[60] Zinzendorf believed in the Kabbalistic idea—also found in alchemy— that in sexual union, male and female "repair" the rifts in the fallen world and achieve a unified, androgynous state.

Zinzendorf believed that through the Kabbalah, Jews and Christians, Protestants and Catholics could all come together, a vision of religious unity that occupied many at the time. Sexual climax echoed the original emanation of the *sephiroth* out of the Godhead. For Kabbalists, God himself makes love to his *Shekhinah,* his female emanation. Zinzendorf Christianized this erotic mysticism and saw the Holy Spirit as feminine; the product of her union with God was Christ. Along with Kabbalah, Zinzendorf was also influenced by the teachings of Sabbatai Zevi, the "false messiah," who saved himself from decapitation by Sultan Mehmet IV in 1666 by renouncing his messianic claims and converting to Islam. Many of Zevi's followers abandoned his teaching after this ignominious retreat, yet others saw it as similar to Christ's crucifixion, and embraced debasement and humiliation as ways to holiness. This "reversal" shared in the metaphysics of antinomianism and led to a form of "holy sinning," different expressions of which we have come across in this book. "Holy sinning" means in effect that "anything goes," and for Zinzendorf that "anything" meant sacred sex. Along with visualizing Christ's genitals and seeing his wounds as a vagina—hence making him a cosmic androgyne, like the Kabbalistic Adam Kadmon—the Fetter Lane congregation often enjoyed "love feasts" that resulted in communal unification of the opposites.

Swedenborg himself was deeply interested in the spiritual aspects of sex, a study that he pursued well into his later years. In one of his last books, *Conjugial Love,* written in his eighties, Swedenborg says that in heaven angels engage in mutually satisfactory and perpetual sex. Throughout his life Swedenborg kept mistresses—he remained a bachelor—and he advocated sex outside marriage. This was not a cover for licentiousness, but a recognition of the profound link between sexuality, altered states of consciousness, and spirituality, something we have come across in the Fedeli d'Amore. Swedenborg himself practiced a form of erotic meditation that allowed him to maintain an erection and hover in the erotic trance for long periods.

Along with worshipping with the Moravians in Fetter Lane, it seems likely that Swedenborg met a fascinating, enigmatic figure during this visit to London. Rabbi Samuel Jacob Hayyim Falk was born into a Sabbatian community in Galicia (Poland) where he became known as a *Ba'al Shem,* a "Master of the Divine Name," a title given to practicing Kabbalists. He was almost burned as a heretic, and after traveling through Europe, he arrived in London in 1742. He set up an alchemical laboratory on London Bridge, and ran an esoteric school from his house in the East End. Falk seems to have been the magical magnet attracting a diverse group of esotericists: Rosicrucians, Freemasons, alchemists, Kabbalists, and Moravians.

One of his students was Cagliostro, the colorful magician and healer who stormed across Europe, spreading his own brand of Egyptian Freemasonry which, it is said, was taught to him by the mysterious Comte de Saint-Germain. Reminiscing about his years in the Hermetic Order of the Golden Dawn, W. B. Yeats spoke of "hidden superiors" from whom the order's legitimacy derived, and some have suspected that Falk may have been whom Yeats had in mind.[61] Swedenborg seems to have been among this circle, and he was most likely introduced to Falk through one of the Moravians. Swedenborg learned different Kabbalistic eroto-spiritual meditations from Falk, and from all accounts these contributed to the crisis that changed Swedenborg's life.

ON THE WAY TO HEAVEN

By the time Swedenborg met Falk, he had been practicing his breathing exercises for years. It seems he had also tried automatic writing and wanted, as had John Dee, to communicate with angels. Something else Swedenborg practiced throughout his life was a curious ability to hover in that strange state between sleeping and waking. This condition, known as "hypnagogia," allows for a conscious experience of the unconscious; Swedenborg shared this facility with other secret teachers, such as Rudolf Steiner and C. G. Jung.[62] His breathing exercises, extended experiences of hypnagogia, and Falk's eroto-spiritual Kabbalistic meditations contributed to Swedenborg's breakthrough into the spiritual worlds.

In July 1744, Swedenborg seems to have had his "creative illness." One day he entered a trance and became uncommunicative; the two "good Israelites" in the room with him may have been Falk and an associate. The next day Swedenborg seems to have had a mental breakdown. Like Sabbatai Zevi, he believed he was the Messiah and that he would be crucified. The following day, Swedenborg disrobed, rolled in the mud, and handed out money. He had already experienced a visitation by Christ. After hearing a thunderous boom and a great rush of wind, Swedenborg seems to have had an out-of-body experience, at the end of which he found himself face-to-face with Jesus. Soon after, Swedenborg abandoned his scientific "search for the soul" and devoted himself to the symbolic exegesis of scripture—the "spiritual hermeneutics" of Henry Corbin— and his voyages to the spiritual worlds, heaven and hell.[63] His multivolume work *Arcana Coelistia* contains Swedenborg's "internal" interpretation of Genesis and Exodus.

Swedenborg's accounts of his journeys to heaven, hell, and the intermediary realm he called the "spirit world" are the most readable of his writings and are collected in his book *Heaven and Hell,* a kind of Rough Guide to the afterlife. Here Swedenborg speaks of his own voyages in the *Mundus Imaginalis,* the Imaginal World that Suhrawardi entered several centuries before him. As we've seen, mystical or visionary experiences take on the symbols and expressions of the culture of the person having them. In Swedenborg's case, these were Christian. But Swedenborg's Christianity is esoteric and his interpretations of the angelic and devilish realms do not depend on faith or belief. Swedenborg himself abhorred the Catholic Church and felt the Atonement was an insult to the dignity of man. Like Blake, Swedenborg's Christianity is "man-centered." His ultimate vision is of the Grand Man, the macrocosmic human, what he called the "human face of God."

Swedenborg's heaven is not unlike life on earth, except that time, space, and other physical constraints no longer apply; they are, Swedenborg tells us, "states" rather than physical realities, and what appears to us as sequential and separate in heaven is simultaneous and unified—a distinction not unlike that between left- and right-brain consciousness. His heaven is not filled with cherubs and harps, but with effort and work, what he calls "the active life."[64] Swedenborg's hell seems as harrowing as Dante's. Insatiable desires, incessant bickering, and interminable darkness torment its inhabitants. After death, one reaches either destination, Swedenborg tells us, by passing through the "spirit world," a kind of bardo realm or purgatory, where the truth about oneself unavoidably comes to light. What strikes most modern readers about Swedenborg's heaven and hell is that they are psychological and spiritual states, and not places we go to. They exist here and now; we enter them through our choices and decisions. Those interested in growing beyond themselves and in the work of the divine naturally enter heaven. Those who cling to the self and its desires are already in hell.

Not all are taken with Swedenborg's spiritual travelogue. Ralph Waldo Emerson, one of his readers, whose Transcendentalism is rich in Hermetic, Neoplatonic, and eastern ideas, said of Swedenborg's hell that "a vampire sits in the seat of the prophet and turns with gloomy appetite to images of pain."[65] William Blake rejected Swedenborg's neat distinction between the angelic and devilish, and sought a "marriage of heaven and hell." One idea emerging from Swedenborg's work has had an undeniable impact on modern esotericism and culture at large. This is his doctrine of "correspondences." Its essence is the recognition that there are direct links between the heavenly and earthly worlds and that the phenomena of the physical world are a kind of symbol or "alphabet" of the higher ones. "The whole natural world corresponds to the spiritual world," Swedenborg wrote, "not only the natural world in general, but also in every particular."[66]

As the Nobel Prize–winning writer Czeslaw Milosz—nephew of the mystical Swedenborgian poet O. V. de Lubicz Milosz, friend of Schwaller de Lubicz—put it, "Swedenborg's world is all language."[67] For Swedenborg, one "reads" the world as one reads a book, and the language of things points to their spiritual source. Through reading the book of the world and the scriptures symbolically, Swedenborg, like Joachim of Fiore, the Rosicrucians, and others, came to see that humanity was on the brink of a new age, one sign of which was the "new church," made up of spiritually akin minds—not mortar and bricks—that Swedenborg believed would come after him.

Swedenborg's "correspondences" grew beyond his use. One reader of Swedenborg was the nineteenth-century French poet Charles Baudelaire. While many readers—perhaps most—probably won't avail themselves of *Arcana Coelistia*, they may be aware of how Baudelaire used Swedenborg's idea. In his poem "Correspondences," Baudelaire takes Swedenborg's idea and applies it to the haunting, elusive resonances that link colors, scents, shapes, and sounds. "Nature is a temple," Baudelaire tells us, through which we pass "symbolically." Baudelaire's poem creates an atmosphere of shifting forms and landscapes in which "perfumes and colors are mixed in strange profusions." The effect is a sense of "the strange expansion of things infinite," the suggestion that things are *something more* than they seem, that some mystery envelops them, an aura of possibility, the analogical way of seeing the world that we have seen is linked to a right-brain mode of consciousness. Swedenborg believed that in an earlier time the truth of correspondences was common knowledge, but that we have lost it because of our self-obsession, which suggests something like the loss of our more right-brain mode of consciousness.

Baudelaire's poem triggered a fascination with synesthesia, the strange condition in which sensory modes blend, in which one hears colors and sees sounds, and which suggests a *unity* behind phenomena. Perhaps the best-known example of this is Arthur Rimbaud's poem "Vowels," which ascribes different colors to the letters: A, black; E, white; I, red; O, blue; and U, green.[68] Such associations harken back to the Kabbalistic notion of an Adamic language (Boehme), a primal speech in which the unity between speaker and world is undefiled. The art movement that emerged from this, Symbolism, was responsible for some of the most important works of the late nineteenth century, from the operas of Richard Wagner to the paintings of Gustave Moreau and Odilon Redon—both of whom were occult enthusiasts—and the intensely Hermetic poetry of Stéphane Mallarmé. Along with the Modernism that followed, Symbolism was saturated in occult, Hermetic, and esoteric ideas. It showed that the world was not the mechanical clockwork of the materialist scientist, but a forest of question marks, each suggesting some possible answer to the riddle of life. And Swedenborg was responsible for this.[69]

CHAPTER TEN

THE ROMANTIC CENTURY

The years leading up to the French Revolution saw one of the most esoterically charged periods in modern western history. As the Baroness d'Oberkirch, an observer of high society at the time, remarked, "Never, certainly, were Rosicrucians, alchemists, prophets and everything related to them so numerous and so influential."[1] We may think we have a monopoly on such interests, as our insatiable curiosity about conspiracy theories, aliens, religious sects, gurus, and other exotic items suggests. But the period leading up to the rise of the guillotine also saw the birth of "popular occultism." Not only was the popular press filled with stories that would suit our own tabloids, the literary genre of "occultism" finds its roots here too.[2]

Probably the most influential work of this kind was the multivolumed *Le Monde primitif* (*The Primal World*) by the eccentric Court de Gébelin, which appeared in 1773 and was an immediate best seller. Court de Gébelin was a Protestant theologian with a passion for ancient languages, which he believed held the key to what he called a lost, "primitive"—in the sense of original—science, which had become corrupted and debased over time. This form of the *prisca theologia* could, he believed, be retrieved through a deep study of the earliest forms of human speech. The encyclopedist and mathematician Jean le Rond d'Alembert was one of Court de Gébelin's readers, as was Louis XVI, and the popularity of *Le Monde primitif* proved so great that Court de Gébelin eventually built his own museum, where he lectured to packed audiences. His most popular ideas were those about the Tarot, and it is here that this enigmatic pack of playing cards makes its "occult" appearance.

The Tarot deck had been in circulation since the Renaissance and its origins are most likely found in the Neoplatonic and Hermetic influences of the time, which were expressed in images based on the ancient practice of "triumphs" or parades.[3] But it was not until Court de Gébelin that an Egyptian origin of the cards was proposed. Court de Gébelin argued that the Tarot came "out of Egypt," and that it contained the lost knowledge of these mysterious people. Following Court de Gébelin was a curious character known as Alliette, who wrote under the pseudonym "Etteilla," his named spelled backward. Etteilla added that the Tarot, initially conceived by Hermes Trismegistus, was created after the Flood, by a council of magi who spent many years on its design. Etteilla called it "the Book of Thoth," a misnomer that remains associated with the Tarot to this day. Etteilla seems to have been a very astute occult businessman; he sold talismans, held classes in practical magic, and, not surprisingly, gave Tarot readings.

Another who promoted "popular occultism" was Antoine Fabre d'Olivet, whose mission was to synthesize every known fact, an expression, it seems, of Enlightenment Pansophism. Like Court de Gébelin, Fabre d'Olivet studied ancient languages—Latin and Greek, as well as Arabic, Chaldee, Syrian, Samaritan, and Chinese—and also plunged into the young discipline of Egyptology. Fabre d'Olivet believed that the ancient wisdom of Egypt was embedded in the Old Testament, specifically Genesis. This had suffered in translation and he sought to restore the ancient Hebrew to its pristine origin. Like many we have come across in this book, Fabre d'Olivet believed that in its true state, the Bible needed to be understood on different levels and that in its most important sense it needed to be read symbolically.

LIBERTY, EQUALITY, AND MESMERISM

Esoteric ideas also fed the growing social tensions that would, in a few years, give way to revolution. One such influence was the work of the

THE SECRET TEACHERS OF THE WESTERN WORLD

German scientist and healer Franz Anton Mesmer. Mesmer belongs to
that select group of people who have added to our vocabulary. The word
"mesmerize" comes from him, but in this Mesmer has suffered an historical irony. For us "mesmerize" is a synonym for "hypnotize," yet in reality
the hypnosis that arose from Mesmer's work had nothing to do with it. It
emerged from the recognition that Mesmer's fundamental idea was wrong.
When treating one of his patients, the Marquis de Puységur, a student of
Mesmer, noticed something strange. The young man had fallen asleep but
when de Puységur tried to wake him, he couldn't. He had entered a trance.
When, exasperated, de Puységur shouted, "Stand up," to his amazement
his patient did, but he remained asleep. De Puységur spoke to him and
asked questions, all of which he answered while remaining unconscious.
He seemed to be in a state similar to somnambulism, "sleep-walking."
When he finally did awake, he had no memory of what had occurred. The
marquis had accidentally discovered hypnosis, but the phenomena would
not be named until 1843, when the Scottish physician James Braid coined
the term.

The exact mechanism of hypnosis remains obscure but the effect seems
to be to narrow consciousness down to a single point. Given that the person hypnotized usually does not remember what has happened while he
was in the trance, we can assume that what is narrowed down is our usual
left-brain ego awareness. In *Frankenstein's Castle,* Colin Wilson suggests
that the remarkable abilities people often display while under hypnosis
may be rooted in the powers of the right brain. If this is the case, then we
can see hypnosis as a means of putting our left brain to sleep while the
right remains awake and open to the suggestions of the hypnotist.[4]

Mesmer is often called the discoverer of hypnosis, but what he actually
believed was that the universe was filled with an invisible vital energy
which he called "animal magnetism," "animal" in this sense meaning animated, living, or, in older parlance, ensouled.[5] This energy permeates the
cosmos and connects everything with everything else. This unseen vital
fluid is responsible for our health; illnesses are caused by blockages of our
animal magnetism, and the "mesmeric passes" that caused the Marquis de
Puységur's patient to fall into a trance were aimed at increasing the circulation of animal magnetism within his body.

It is not too difficult to see the similarities linking Mesmer's animal magnetism, the Neoplatonic "sympathy of all things," and Marsilio Ficino's ideas about helpful and baleful stellar influences. We can also see that Mesmer's ideas about a "universal fluid" will inform Eliphas Levi's thoughts on "astral light," what he calls the "universal agent," which he links to the imagination and which Madame Blavatsky will borrow from when speaking of the "Akashic record." There are also clear resonances between Mesmer's animal magnetism and the "orgone energy" of Wilhelm Reich and the *chi* of traditional Chinese medicine. Mesmer's animal magnetism also bears a family resemblance to the "Odic force" of Baron von Reichenbach—which would reappear in the twentieth century as "Kirlian photography"—and the "soul force" of Joseph Rodes Buchanan, associated with psychometry, the ability to psychically "read" the history of objects. Mesmer's own links to the Hermetic and Paracelsian tradition are evident in his doctoral dissertation, "The Influence of the Planets on the Human Body" which he submitted in Vienna in 1768, a sign that the discredited esoteric view of man and the cosmos was still active. Mesmer was not an occultist—at least he considered himself a man of science—but in *The Discovery of the Unconscious*, Henri Ellenberger suggests that during his university days, Mesmer was supported by secret societies.

Early on in his practice, Mesmer used actual magnets, which seemed to encourage the sluggish animal magnetism of his patients. He had a high success rate. But he soon came to see that he himself was a magnet; it was his own vital animal magnetism that enlivened his patients. He married a wealthy Viennese widow and soon became a popular patron of the arts, as well as a sought-after physician. He was friends with the composers Gluck and Haydn—both Masons—and knew the Mozart family well.

In 1778, Mesmer moved to Paris, encouraged by his success in Vienna, but also by one important failure, Maria Theresia Paradies, a young blind pianist whom Mesmer claimed he could cure. Her parents allowed her to live with Mesmer, and Maria believed that his magnetic treatment worked. But many didn't and they wondered why so many of Mesmer's patients were young women and why certain parts of their bodies—such as their thighs and bosom—needed so many magnetic passes. An examination showed that, sadly, Maria's sight had not improved, although she herself believed it had. She was removed from Mesmer's home, and when the Viennese police intervened, Mesmer decided to leave Vienna.

Paris was a strangely tense city. Mesmer's haughty manner and powerful personality served him well, and soon he began to repeat his early successes. Mesmer set up "magnetic baths" and devised a group treatment called *banquets* that allowed for several patients to be "mesmerized" simultaneously. There was also a great deal of what we might call "group therapy," with patients stimulating each other's magnetism. The cure began with the "magnetic crisis," a kind of "mesmeric convulsion," after which the clots in one's magnetism were unblocked and one's natural, "primitive" health was restored. It was the frequent dishabille of Mesmer's female patients, and the orgasm-like fit of the "magnetic crisis" that soon had tongues wagging.

As with Paracelsus, the medical establishment was not keen on Mesmer. They thought his cures were fakes, his treatment quackery. And like Paracelsus, Mesmer was vain and arrogant. His downfall began when he was forced to submit to an investigation by the Academy of Sciences, the French equivalent of England's Royal Society; one of the committee's members was Benjamin Franklin. They ignored Mesmer's successes— these were chalked up to hysterical patients and the power of suggestion— and focused on Mesmer's central claim: to have discovered an all-pervasive vital fluid. Not surprisingly, they found no evidence for this and branded Mesmer a fraud. Mesmer became the target of abuse. His aristocratic clientele and superior manner were out of step with the Revolution, and he left France. He continued to find patients and was able to retire comfortably but embittered near Lake Constance. He died in 1815.

RADICAL SPIRITS

Mesmer had started "Societies of Harmony" around France, designed to spread his message of "natural health." Like Jean-Jacques Rousseau, whose ideas about the "social contract" and "noble savage" helped fuel the Revolution, Mesmer believed that health was man's natural state, and it was only a corrupt society that sickened him. Although he was not political and in fact courted royalty and the aristocracy, Mesmer's ideas were absorbed by radicals wanting to bring the leisured class down. As today, they believed that vested interests prevented "the people" from gaining access to "miracle cures." They argued that just as an individual's natural health and regeneration were triggered by the magnetic crisis, so too society must go through a similar crisis before its own health could be regained. A radical "getting back to nature" was envisioned, a return to a pristine state of pure harmony.

Some agents of harmony combined mesmerism with Swedenborg's beliefs about the regeneration of man. Esoteric Freemasonry was often the linchpin uniting the two.[6] One group, the Order of Elect Cohens ("priest" in Hebrew) was led by the Swedenborgian, Rosicrucian, and Freemason Martinez de Pasqually, who is believed to have been initiated by Baron Hund's "unknown superiors." They used theurgic means of prophecy, a method also used by the group around the Benedictine Antoine-Joseph Pernety, who made contact with a supernatural entity he called "*la chose*," "the thing."

Another group was led by Jean-Baptiste Willermoz, a Strict Observance Mason from Lyons, who had been initiated into the Elect Cohens. Willermoz was also a member of one of Mesmer's Societies of Harmony. When Pasqually died in 1774, Willermoz took his master's theurgy and combined it with Mesmer's ideas. He gathered a group of women he called the *crisiacs*, who were peculiarly susceptible to Willermoz's magnetic passes. In their "magnetic trance," these modern-day sibyls communicated gnomic messages from Swedenborg's "spirit world." Most pronouncements concerned the coming new age and the return of the ancient wisdom— much like today's "channelers"—but at times the communications were more obscure. Willermoz would then call in one of the most important figures of the time for help in deciphering the secret code.

THE UNKNOWN PHILOSOPHER

Like Willermoz, Louis Claude de Saint-Martin was a member of Pasqually's Elect Cohens. At first attracted to theurgy, he eventually abandoned it for a more meditative, theosophical approach, influenced by Jacob Boehme, whom he translated into French. Saint-Martin had been initiated into Pasqually's lodge while stationed in Bordeaux in 1767. From early childhood, the frail Saint-Martin was drawn to the mystic path and interior world, and he pursued this in an unusual way. With Europe at peace, he recognized that an army commission would provide the time and independence needed for his studies, and he remained a military magician with the rank of lieutenant until 1771.

With Pasqually's death, Saint-Martin began the series of writings for which he is known today. I say "known," but for much of his career, Saint-Martin's authorship was obscure. He signed his mystical, philosophical works as "the Unknown Philosopher," partly because of the uncertain climate of the time, but also because of Saint-Martin's association with several secret societies. In Lyons, he became friends with Willermoz and frequented the city's many esoteric circles. He was also friends with Mesmer's disciple de Puységur. Saint-Martin joined a Society of Harmony, but in the end he left, concerned that Mesmer's focus on a physical fluid was too materialistic and would attract the curiosity of dubious astral spirits.

One astral spirit that troubled Saint-Martin had been called up by Willermoz's *crisiac*s. This entity, which Willermoz called "the Unknown Agent," had commanded him to establish an esoteric group within his Rectified Scottish rite, an outgrowth from Strict Observance which abandoned Baron Hund's Templar roots in exchange for Pasqually's theurgic slant. This new group would receive messages from the Unknown Agent directly. Willermoz asked Saint-Martin for advice on decoding these communications, yet something about these directives from beyond disturbed Saint-Martin and he soon abandoned the attempt to decipher them.

Saint-Martin's vision, which he expressed in poetic, metaphysical works like *Of Errors and Truth*, *The Man of Desire*, *The New Man*, and *The Spirit of Things*, can be summed up in his notion of "repair," a metaphysical responsibility incumbent upon man that shares much with the practice of *tikkun* associated with the Kabbalah of Isaac Luria.[7] Saint-Martin rejected the rising mechanical view and its increasing diminution of man.

He shared Pico della Mirandola's view that man was endowed with god-like potential and Marsilio Ficino's belief that through these powers man could "repair" the fallen world. This indeed was our responsibility and task. "The function of man differs from that of other physical beings," Saint-Martin wrote, "for it is the reparation of the disorders in the universe."[8] Saint-Martin believed that behind our humble recognition that the Earth was no longer the center of the universe lay diffidence and laziness. He believed that "the present-day avoidance of the belief that we are the highest in the universe is the reason that we have not the courage to work in order to justify that title." Such duties are too laborious and we would rather, he said, "abdicate our position and our rights than realize them in all their consequences."[9]

Saint-Martin recognized that man was a sleeping god, a spiritual giant afflicted with amnesia, and his job was to sound as clear and persuasive a wake-up call as possible. In this he was a herald of Romanticism, the sudden awakening of man's imaginative powers that characterized the new century. For some yet unknown reason, the late eighteenth and early nineteenth century saw what we can only call an explosion of imaginative energy, a widespread recognition of the vast inner spaces that Petrarch had briefly glimpsed from the vantage point of Mount Ventoux. Across Europe, artists, poets, musicians, and philosophers were suddenly ablaze with a godlike and often demonic energy, an expression of the "superhumanism" we saw in Pico della Mirandola. Often this was triggered by an interest in the occult and esoteric, a development I chart in my book *A Dark Muse*.

Saint-Martin's work was an attempt to halt the spread of the "only humanism" that, by our own time, has become the unquestioned assessment of ourselves. Saint-Martin's books provide sudden flashes of insight into what by the 1960s would be called "human potential," the recognition that lying dormant deep within us are "vestiges of the faculties resident in the Agent" which produced us—in other words, the divine. With Paracelsus, Saint-Martin knew that the key to awakening these latent abilities was the imagination. He knew that although the soul leaves the body at death, yet "during life, the faculties may extend beyond it, and communicate with their exterior correspondents without ceasing to be united to their center."[10] Like Plato, Plotinus, and others, Saint-Martin knew that we are something more than our physical shells. This was a vision that would set Europe afire in what we can see as the Romantic century.

BLAKE AND COLERIDGE

Much of Saint-Martin's vision was shared by his younger contemporary William Blake. It is even possible that they met. In 1783, the Reverend Jacob Duché, ex-chaplain to the Continental Congress, founded the London Theosophical Society, a radical Swedenborgian group that also studied the works of Jacob Boehme. Along with other esoterically inclined individuals—such as the painter Philip de Loutherbourg and the Swedish alchemist Augustus Nordenskjold—one of its members was Blake. In 1787, Saint-Martin visited the group, along with Cagliostro, who was a friend of de Loutherbourg and who often stayed at his home in Hammersmith. For all his bad reputation—most of it unearned—Cagliostro was a sincere student of Hermeticism and a devoted Mason and he would have had sympathy with Saint-Martin's doctrine of "repair." It is unknown if Blake was there during their visit; if so, it would have been an interesting evening.

Blake is usually seen as a naïve natural mystic, responsible for childlike works like the *Songs of Innocence,* and for visionary insights about seeing a "world in a grain of sand and a heaven in a wildflower," which have by now sadly become clichés. Or he is seen as a raving madman, producing wild, ecstatic paintings and incomprehensible epic poems centered around his unwieldy personal mythology. Both of these pictures of Blake are false.

Although Blake did have visions early on—his father once beat him for talking about angels in a tree—he was not unschooled and his later visionary works are not, as some Jungians have suggested, spontaneous expressions of the archetypes. As the poet and Blake scholar Kathleen Raine has argued, Blake was a student of the esoteric tradition, and his immense body of work is best understood as his own synthesis and expression of the "perennial philosophy": one of his poems is entitled "The Everlasting Gospel." We have seen that Blake, like Boehme, whom he studied, had a deep intuition about the ongoing creative tension between our opposing modes of consciousness, and an uncanny insight into our "fallen state" of left-brain dominance, which he depicted as the tyranny of Urizen, the symbol of reason and the limiting of energy, and opponent of his contrary, the imagination.[11] Imagination was all for Blake. "This world of Imagination is the World of Eternity; it is the Divine bosom into which we shall all go after the death of the Vegetated body." "There exist in that Eternal World the Permanent Realities of Every Thing which we see reflected in the Vegetable Glass of Nature."[12] Blake saw as his task the "mental fight" that would free man from the chains of the encroaching materialist view. He labored to cleanse the "doors of perception" and "open the immortal eyes of man Inwards, into the worlds of thought, into Eternity, Ever expanding in the Bosom of God, The Human Imagination" (*Jerusalem*).

Although Blake wrote of wildflowers and grains of sand, he was not a "nature poet," as was William Wordsworth, with whom he took argument. With Saint-Martin, the Gnostics, and many others, Blake believed man had fallen from his original spiritual state into this dense, difficult world of matter, what he called "the land of Ulro," and the "dark Satanic mills" (Milton), which are usually seen as symbols of the Industrial Revolution, were for Blake the "starry wheels" of the Newtonian clockwork universe. For Blake, the land of Ulro congealed around men's minds when they lost touch with their true being, which was the imagination, which Blake saw as the essence of Jesus's teaching. He called Jesus "the Imagination" and said that he "was all virtue and acted from impulse not from rules," a sensibility shared by many who sought a more immediate spiritual life, and not one bordered by dogma.

Blake saw the imagination as the primary force behind creation, an insight shared by his younger contemporary, Samuel Taylor Coleridge, one of the Romantic poets who carried on Blake's "mental fight." In his *Biographia Literaria,* Coleridge distinguishes between imagination and fancy in a way that later "spiritual hermeneuts" like Henry Corbin would applaud. "Primary" imagination Coleridge held to be "the living power and prime agent of all human perception." It was a "repetition in the finite mind of the eternal act of creation in the infinite I AM." Fancy, Coleridge saw, as a rearranging of things already created. It is "no other than a mode of memory" which receives "all its material ready-made from the law of association." In between these, Coleridge placed what he called "secondary imagination," the creative imagination of the artist, poet, and thinker, which echoes the primary imagination of the "infinite I AM." Secondary imagination creates just as the primary imagination does, but on a lower level; fancy does not create, but only "plays" with what is already created.[13] Unicorns or flying pigs are fanciful, but Blake's apocalyptic paintings are works of creative imagination. We see here the difference between daydreams and creative insight, as well as that between what Paracelsus called "true imagination" and whimsy.

Coleridge was also, like Blake, profoundly aware that "the essential duality of Nature arises out of its productive unity." This is a more abstract way of expressing Blake's dictum that "Without Contraries there is no Progression." Like Blake—and Boehme, whom he read—Coleridge saw that this duality, or in his term, "polarity," was organic. The mechanistic philosophy, which by the mid-nineteenth century could more or less claim victory, Coleridge saw as an atomistic mosaic, "the relations of unproductive particles to each other." Like Blake, for Coleridge this was a "philosophy of Death" and held good only for "dead nature." All life, however, he knew consists in the "strife of opposites," in their uniting and separating to form new unities and divisions, what he called their "polar tension."[14] Coleridge appreciated Blake's insights and developed his own; both drew on the reservoir of symbols and intuitions that make up what Kathleen Raine called the "learning of the imagination," the universal tradition housed in our minds.

THOMAS TAYLOR

One secret teacher who tutored Blake and Coleridge and many poets after them was the "English Platonist" Thomas Taylor. Taylor produced the first English translations of the complete works of Plato and Aristotle, as well as many translations of Plotinus, Proclus, and "the divine Iamblichus." Taylor also wrote important essays on the Orphic tradition and the use of Orphic mythology by the Neoplatonists. During his lifetime, Taylor's work was criticized or ignored by the literary and philosophical main-stream but it was read avidly by many of the most important figures in English literature: along with Blake and Coleridge, these included Shelley, Keats, Yeats, as well as Yeats's friend the mystic poet "AE" (George Russell). Taylor's worked crossed the Atlantic and informed Ralph Waldo Emerson and his fellow Transcendentalists; in his book *Representative Men*, Emerson ranked Taylor among "the Immortals" and appropriately placed him next to Marsilio Ficino and Pico della Mirandola. In reading Taylor's work, Emerson said, one encounters "the majestic remains of literature," as if one was "walking in the noblest of temples." He was "a better man of imagination, a better poet, than any English writer between Milton and Wordsworth." Other important figures in esoteric history who spoke highly of Taylor were H. P. Blavatsky; her secretary, the Gnostic and Hermetic scholar G. R. S. Mead; and the esoteric encyclopaedist Manly P. Hall. Another of Taylor's readers was Mary Ann South.[15]

According to John Livingston Lowes in his classic study *The Road to Xanadu*, Taylor was one of Coleridge's "darling studies," and his translations fired the poet's imagination and inspired signature Romantic works like "The Rime of the Ancient Mariner" and "Kubla Khan." "Thomas Taylor, the Platonist" Lowes wrote, "fired with the ardour of a devotee, was doing for England what Marsilio Ficino, three centuries before, had done for Italy."[16] A one-man Platonic Academy, Taylor made available the perennial philosophy which, for him, was "coeval with the universe itself; and however its continuity may be broken by opposing systems, it will make its appearance at different periods of time, as long as the sun himself shall continue to illumine the world."[17] Taylor was also an early advocate of animal rights. Following Thomas Paine's *The Rights of Man* and Mary Wollstonecraft's *A Vindication of the Rights of Women,* in 1792, Taylor published under a pseudonym *A Vindication of the Rights of Brutes,* which argued that animals deserved the same treatment as humans, well in advance of today's "biocentricism."[18]

One appearance the perennial philosophy made, as Kathleen Raine has shown, was as an inspiration for the Romantic movement in England. It is no exaggeration to say that for Raine, English Romanticism *is* Neo-platonism, in symbol, imagery, and aim, and that Taylor was the source. I am not sure if it is still taught today—it is a sad sign of the times if it is not—but one of the earliest poems I learned in school was Coleridge's "Kubla Khan," with its haunting images of a "stately pleasure dome," "Alph, the sacred river," and the "damsel with a dulcimer." I did not know at the time, nor do many realize today, that these images and the rest of Coleridge's strange dream landscape were born from his reading of Taylor's translations. In a "wish list" Coleridge wrote to a friend shortly before writing the poem, he asked for copies of Taylor's translations of Iamblichus, Proclus, and Porphyry (he also asks for a work by Ficino).[19] The "caverns measureless to man," "sunless seas," and "caves of ice" that evoke a strange nostalgia for *somewhere we have never been* and stimulate a thirst for the beyond are, according to Raine, memories of our past existence in the spiritual realms, symbols of that "learning of the imagination" that, in different ways, informed the work of Dante, Suhrawardi, Plato, and other inner voyagers.

Taylor was born in London in 1758, the son of a Dissenting minister. He would have become a minister himself, except for an unacceptable marriage, which made him the black sheep of his family and forced him out on his own. He abandoned his religious studies—he would soon display his lack of sympathy with the church—and had to fend for himself. Most of Taylor's life was lived in poverty. He early on showed a great love of mathematics, but his interest in it was Pythagorean, and although for much of his adult life he worked as a banker, his attraction to numbers was more mystical than calculative. He suffered poor health, was quiet, earnest, and somewhat dreamy. At one point he invented what he called a "perpetual light" that used phosphorus. Taylor may have dreamed that this eternal flame would lead to riches and fame; unfortunately, while demonstrating his invention at Freemason's Hall, it exploded and nearly caused a fire.

He had a talent for languages and a powerful memory. It is said that he and his wife conversed only in ancient Greek and it was in his early twenties that he first encountered Plato. He was soon enthralled and it was while reading Proclus that Taylor had a mystical experience. It affected him so much that he named his son after the philosopher. Like the Hermetists he was translating, Taylor believed that one can only know the divine by becoming it, and at least once in his life he did. He spoke little about his experience but did record a "perpetual serenity, unceasing delight, and occasional rapture." One effect of his illumination was that his soul would "spontaneously utter musical sounds"—much as lyrical poets like Keats, whom he influenced, did—which indicated an "inner harmony," "echoes of the perpetual felicity she enjoys."[20]

Taylor was saved from the dreary life of a bank clerk by being invited to give a series of lectures on Plato at the house of the successful artist and friend of Blake, John Flaxman. Many of the intelligentsia of the time attended, and Flaxman and his friends were able to secure Taylor a position with the Society for the Encouragement of the Arts (later the Royal Society of the Arts). It was at these lectures that Taylor met Blake. The two became friends and Blake soon sat, at least for a time, at Taylor's feet. Taylor told Blake that the ancients wrote obscurely, in myths and arcane symbols, and that they needed to be read and deciphered in order to reach their true meaning. Blake listened to Taylor, absorbing the Neoplatonic philosophy that, along with the Gnostics, Boehme, Swedenborg, Paracelsus, and alchemy—and of course the Bible and his own visions—Blake would transform into his own unique mythology. In England today, Blake's poetry, set to music by Sir Hubert Parry, forms the patriotic hymn "Jerusalem"; few who appreciate it realize they are responding to Blake's esoteric vision.

Taylor spoke of Orpheus, Hermes, Zoroaster, and the *prisca sapientia*, the "primal wisdom" of the ancients, much as Marsilio Ficino had to Renaissance artists, and it is interesting to note that in his paintings, Blake tended toward Michelangelesque figures. Blake, however, had a more prophetic than philosophical temperament and his spiritual homeland was more Jerusalem than Athens or Alexandria. At one point, he submitted to learning mathematics from Taylor but soon gave it up, deciding that God was not so much a geometer as an artist. Blake's antipathy to measure and what he called "ratio" and its stifling circumference of the free imagination was embodied in his painting of Newton, which shows him at the bottom of the sea—water is a Neoplatonic symbol of "matter," formless without the animating soul—armed with a compass, capturing the vital continuity of life in neat geometric patterns.

GOETHE

The Romantics did not know, as we do, that Newton was as much an esotericist as Blake. Another who took argument with Newton's mechanizing of reality was Blake's older contemporary, Johann Wolfgang von Goethe, Germany's greatest poet and one of the chief architects of the Romantic movement. It is said that his early work, *The Sorrows of Young Werther*, written when he was twenty-five, taught Europe how to cry. It also made Goethe an overnight success, something Blake, who labored in obscurity, never had.

Goethe was not a visionary and his work is not prophetic. He is much more urbane and classical, and his most famous work, the archetypal magical cautionary tale, *Faust*, is filled with an often caustic wit. Where Blake thundered against "single vision and Newton's sleep"—induced by the landscape of Ulro—and developed a complex gnostic mythology to replace it, Goethe had a more measured response to the limitations of Newtonian science.[21] He also had the supreme self-confidence that comes with the knowledge of one's genius. Goethe decided to beat Newton at his own game, and his *Farbenlehre*, or *Theory of Colors*, is his riposte to Newton's *Opticks*.

Goethe has been called the "last universal man," a tribute to the breadth and depth of his interest and accomplishments. He was a Pansophist, "the last man who grasped everything thought to be significant in the realm of knowledge: the several arts and their histories, medicine, law, literature, classical culture, the sciences, philosophy."[22] Goethe believed Newton had reached his conclusions about color through "torturing" nature and rejected them. For Goethe color was really a product of the "polarity" between light and dark.[23]

Goethe also was an early evolutionist. For the popular mind, Charles Darwin "discovered" evolution in the mid-nineteenth century, but there were many evolutionary thinkers before him, and Goethe was one of them. Goethe's greatest evolutionary triumph came in 1784, with his discovery of the intermaxillary bone in humans, which linked us to other mammals, a revolutionary idea at the time. Some see "Goethean science" as "analogy run wild," but it has increasingly proved more than a poet's fancy and has informed recent developments such as chaos theory and complexity.[24]

Goethe's evolutionary ideas came from what he saw as nature's "transformative" character, its constant growth and metamorphosis, which Goethe believed was the work of an animating spirit, much like the *Anima mundi*, and not the result of random mutations or "survival of the fittest." Goethe's beliefs, and indeed all of his scientific pursuits, were influenced by his interest in alchemy and Hermeticism.[25] As a young man, he was introduced to alchemical ideas by his spiritual mentor, the Pietist Fräulein von Klettenberg, a follower of Count Zinzendorf, who gave him Paracelsus, Basil Valentine, J. B. van Helmont, and George Starkey to read.

Goethe also profited by some alchemical medicine. At one point, he had a nervous breakdown and was treated for it by a mysterious Dr. Metz. Metz spoke of a "universal medicine" and the Kabbalistic and Hermetic texts that showed how to prepare it. Whatever Dr. Metz's miracle cure was, it worked. "The salt was scarcely taken," Goethe wrote, "than my situation appeared relieved; and from that moment the disease took a turn which, by degrees, led to my recovery."[26] Goethe later set up an alchemical laboratory in his parents' house. Here he tried to make "liquor silicum," melting quartz flint with a mixture of alkali. This should have produced a transparent glass, which Goethe intended to use as his *prima materia*, but after many attempts he admitted he had failed.

Goethe devoured Boehme, Swedenborg, Thomas Vaughan, and the *Corpus Hermeticum*, and he became particularly fascinated with the Rosicrucian manifestoes. As it was for the "invisibles," the rose and the cross was a powerful symbol for Goethe, an emblem of the unification of the opposites, and he began a poem, *"Die Geheimnisse"* ("The Mysteries"), about the brotherhood but left it unfinished. A reading of Andreae's *Chymical Wedding of Christian Rosenkreutz* inspired Goethe's own enigmatic alchemical fable, *The Fairy Tale of the Green Snake and the Beautiful Lily*, which would have a profound effect on Rudolf Steiner.

ACTIVE SEEING

Another aspect of Goethe's work which had a great impact on Steiner, and which puts him in the tradition of Imaginal thinkers such as Suhrawardi, Paracelsus, and Henry Corbin, are his studies in plant "morphology"—a term, incidentally, that he coined. These are contained in his book *The Metamorphosis of Plants,* published in 1790. Goethe was at the height of his fame, but his ideas were so strange that his usual publisher wouldn't accept the work.[27] Goethe argued that all existing plants had their roots in a common ancestor, what he called the *Urpflanze* or "primal plant," a kind of botanical Platonic Form, and that all the organs of plants were modifications of one structure, the leaf. Goethe believed that he could actually *see* his *Urpflanze* with his imagination, which, like Suhrawardi and other Imaginal thinkers, Goethe believed was an organ of knowing. Goethe came to this discovery during an early morning visit to Palermo's botanical gardens, recounted in his *Italian Journey.*[28] He found his thoughts returning to an "old fancy," and looking at the variety of plants, Goethe asked, "Among this multitude might I not discover the Primal Plant? There certainly must be one. Otherwise, how could I recognize that this or that form *was* a plant if all were not built upon the same basic model?" From this meditation, Goethe's ideas blossomed into a full-grown theory of knowledge based on what he called "active seeing," a way of observing phenomena by imaginatively *participating* with them, a form of "direct perception."

Goethe's "active seeing" was a means of putting himself *inside* what he was observing, as Schwaller de Lubicz's "intelligence of the heart" put him inside a rock or a bird. It was, we can say, a form of right-brain consciousness, or rather a combination of right and left. Well in advance of Werner Heisenberg, Goethe had hit on the fundamental insight that "The phenomenon is not detached from the observer, but intertwined and involved with him."[29] We do not observe the world from behind a plate-glass window. We are "in" it, and the kind of attention we direct at it determines the kind of world we see. Goethe observed this phenomenon, not with the cold detachment of the mechanical scientist, but with the warmth and involvement of the artist. He was "involved" in what he observed, and that involvement was key. Truth for Goethe was not reached by treating nature as a machine. It was "a revelation emerging at the point where the inner world of man meets external reality . . . It is a synthesis of world and mind," something Paracelsus and others knew and which today, after a century of quantum physics, we may be just beginning to understand.[30]

This is an essential insight and bears repeating. Truth for the modern scientist is, as in *The X-Files,* "out there" in the "objective" world, and our consciousness merely reflects it as a mirror would. In more recent times, developments like postmodernism and deconstructionism deny any "objective" truth—some go so far as to deny any "objective" world—and consider all pronouncements about it "subjective" and relative, although how they account for the supposed truth of their own statements escapes me. Goethe is saying that truth, reality, knowledge—all are aspects of the same thing—are not simply "out there," nor are they only "in here," but they arise from the meeting of the inner and the outer, from the polarity of both. "There resides in the objective world," Goethe wrote, "an unknown law which corresponds to the unknown law within subjective experience."[31]

"Meaning," then, is not only subjective, "inside our heads." There is real, "objective" meaning in the world, but we only "access" it by our active engagement with it, not by passively reflecting it. If we think of a book, this may become clearer. The "meaning" of a book is in its words, sentences, paragraphs, and chapters. It is "really" there, in black and white. But unless I *read* it, that meaning remains mute. Reading is more than my simply looking at the pages and reflecting them, as a mirror would. I have to make the mental effort of absorbing the words, connecting them, and assimilating them to my experience. The meaning isn't something I make up arbitrarily. It isn't "subjective" in that sense, but in order for it to emerge, I have to meet it halfway. I have to direct a certain energy and focus to it, what the philosopher Edmund Husserl called "intentionality." Without this, I can read a page several times without grasping what it says. We all have had the experience of looking at our watch to see the time and forgetting it immediately after. We saw the watch, we "reflected" it, but we did not "actively see" it; not enough of ourselves was in the act of seeing to grasp the time. Goethe is saying the same about the world.

There is meaning in phenomena, but unless we direct the same kind of attention to them as we do to reading a book, we won't see it. The kind of science that sees the world as a machine is like someone looking at a book and saying it is made of paper and squiggles of ink. It is, but that is not all it is. Goethe's "active seeing" is a way of reading the world, of getting past its squiggles and ink—the matter of which it is made—to its meaning.

NOVALIS

Goethe's approach to understanding the world as a living spirit was shared by his younger contemporary Friedrich von Hardenberg, whose works, most of which appeared after his death, were published under the pen name Novalis. Novalis was the archetypal Romantic. He died from tuberculosis—"consumption"—in 1801 at the age of twenty-eight, and if there is one Romantic symbol that captures the essence of *Sehnsucht*, it is the elusive "blue flower" of Novalis's unfinished novel, *Heinrich von Ofterdingen*.

Like his remark that "all philosophy is homesickness," Novalis's blue flower symbolizes the feeling that the earth is not our true home, and that we have arrived here from "somewhere else." But like Goethe, Novalis was more than a poet, and for all his homesickness, he had a deep love of the earth. In his short life, Novalis attempted, like Goethe, to encompass the whole world, and addressed himself to mathematics—something Goethe and Blake hated—chemistry, mineralogy, geology, physics, politics as well as Plato, Pythagoras, and the Neoplatonists. In this he embodied the Hermetic, Pansophic ideal of a truly global knowledge, a pursuit captured in his aphorism "The genuine poet is all-knowing—he is an actual world in miniature."[32] This vision of a macrocosmic/microcosmic unity informs all of Novalis's work and is voiced again and again throughout it. We can see it in other aphorisms, such as "We will come to understand the world when we understand ourselves," and "Man is a sun and his senses are planets."[33]

Like Goethe and Meister Eckhart, Novalis was no retiring mystic, but an able administrator. Like Swedenborg, he was appointed an assessor of mines, and this position allowed him to combine his interest in mineralogy with alchemical reflections on the forces of growth within the earth. By his early twenties, he became well-known and gathered around himself some of the most influential thinkers and writers of the time: the philosophers Friedrich Schlegel, Johann Gottlieb Fichte, and Friedrich Schelling; his fellow poet Ludwig Tieck; and, on occasion, even the Olympian Goethe. These kindred spirits Novalis called the "Friends in the Night," the band of fellow seekers with whom he shared the quest for universal knowledge.

Like Blake, Goethe, and Coleridge, Novalis saw the world as a unity of polar forces and the creative tension between them, and he recognized that the human mind had a unique role in bringing them into life. "The brains," he wrote, "the thinking organs—are the world producers—nature's genitals."[34] He planned a vast encyclopedia that would embrace his wide, Pansophic view. It was never completed and remains, as much of Novalis's work does, in fragments. But each fragment is a spur to further thinking and meditation, and Novalis looked at his aphorisms as "pollen," seeds sent out to impregnate other minds.

As the Neoplatonists did, Novalis sees the world as a gradation of consciousness, as increasing or decreasing levels of spirit. Man's task was to unite the levels, to join nature and spirit and thereby become God, as the ancient Hermetists believed. This is the alchemical work of spiritual transformation which will regenerate the earth just as it does man. As a fragment of his *Encyclopedia* has it, "Paradise is strewn over the earth— and therein has become unknown. Its scattered lineaments are bound to coalesce—its skeleton is bound to become enfleshed. Regeneration of paradise."[35] Here Novalis shares with Saint-Martin and Blake a sense of man's—our—great responsibility, our task of awakening ourselves so that the world too may be awakened.

NATURPHILOSOPHIE

A similar sensibility informed what was known as *Naturphilosophie*, an early nineteenth-century philosophical and scientific movement practically forgotten today, that shared much with Romanticism and took its cue from

Goethe's ideas about a "living" nature. Where the increasingly dominant mechanical view saw the world as a collection of atomistic bits, pushed and pulled by physical forces and subject to strict causality, *Naturphilosophie* saw the world as an expression of spirit, as, in Goethe's words, "God's living raiment." In different ways the different thinkers associated with this school—G. H. Schubert, Friedrich Schelling, Carl Gustav Carus, Alexander von Humboldt, Franz von Baader—all sought to express the essential unity of nature and spirit, of the inner and outer worlds. Unlike the mechanistic view, which sees the two as absolutely separate, with a material, causal world as primary, and our consciousness of it an accidental development, *Naturphilosophie* saw the world and our consciousness of it as a unity, as two sides of one ever-growing, ever-differentiating "life," ranging from inanimate matter to our thoughts.

Rather than being driven by causal forces, this "living nature" had its own teleology. It was *purposive* and was moving *toward* something, rather than being blindly pushed from behind. For the *Naturphilosophen*, nature "was steadily transformed from a simpler, less organized, earlier state to a higher, more developed, later state," which sounds rather like the fundamental aim of alchemy.[36] Nature's aim was total expression, and the diversity of nature was the product of the polarity between nature's urge to manifest and the "restraints" to which it subjects itself. The physical forces of electricity and magnetism, studied by many Romantics—Percy Bysshe Shelley was a keen student, and *Frankenstein*, written by his wife Mary Shelley, is based on the idea of electricity as the source of life—were an expression of the polarity through which nature differentiates itself. As in Boehme, whose ideas informed much of *Naturphilosophie*, this results in a much more "dramatic universe," filled with tension and growth, rather than a mechanical one, filled with law and repetition.

It also results in a much more symbolic nature, one that is more like a work of art than a machine, or like a person with whom we have a relationship. As did Pansophy, *Naturphilosophie* did not see itself as an alternative to mechanical science, but as its complement. It provided a way of "reading" nature, of deciphering its text and metaphors, its correspondences with our inner world.

As Antoine Faivre writes, for *Naturphilosophie* the world is full of "symbolic implications" and "invisible processes" that correspond to human feelings. So for Faivre, as for Novalis, "knowledge of Nature and knowledge of oneself go hand in hand."[37] Man, for *Naturphilosophie*, was not one accidental creature among others, but nature's most recent and successful attempt to produce a being that could understand itself; that is, man is nature's attempt to become *self-conscious*. And just as nature resides in us, we, the human, reside in nature. We share with it certain basic patterns, certain archetypes, that can be found in different but similar manifestations throughout its variety.

It was the recognition of these patterns that led Goethe to believe that with his *Urpflanze* he had reached the source of all possible plants. In a letter to the philosopher and poet Johann Gottfried Herder, Goethe said that with the aid of his "primal plant," "one can then invent further plants *ad infinitum*, which, however, must be consistent." They would be plants that *could* exist, not "shadows or glosses of the poet's or painter's fancy," but ones that "possess an inherent rightness and necessity."[38] Here again is the difference between Coleridge's "primary imagination" and mere fancy. Nature is not some infinitely plastic stuff that, subjected to external laws and the mechanical forces of causality, can be made to take any shape we choose, that can be, as Bacon advised, "tortured" into delivering the desired results. She manifests according to her own inner necessities, which the poet, scientist, artist, and philosopher can grasp through understanding the same necessity within themselves, the "unknown law" in the subjective world aligning with the same law in the objective one.

THE NIGHT SIDE Of NATURE

Another aspect of nature that occupied *Naturphilosophie* was what came to be called its "night side," and what we would call the "paranormal," the darker, mysterious operations of the human mind. G. H. Schubert was a physician and naturalist with an interest in "animal magnetism" and other unusual phenomena, such as clairvoyance and prophetic dreams. His book *Symbolism of Dreams*, published in 1814, was a huge success and was later read by Freud and Jung. Like his fellow *Naturphilosophen*, Schubert saw God in both nature and the human soul, and he was fascinated by the strange powers of what would soon be called "the unconscious." His book *Views from the Nightside of Natural Science* (1808) was a powerful influence on the Romantics, especially E. T. A. Hoffmann, the writer and music critic—an early champion of Beethoven—whose short stories deal with visions, trance states, dreams, and other strange mental phenomena.

Hoffmann is most known today in English-speaking countries for Offenbach's light opera *Tales of Hoffmann* and Tchaikovsky's ballet *The Nutcracker,* but he is a more psychologically disturbing writer than these works suggest; his stories and novels, full of esoteric references and "altered states of consciousness," read like a meeting between Edgar Allan Poe and Hans Christian Andersen. Other *Naturphilosophen* like Joseph Ennemoser, a mesmerist whose work would influence Madame Blavatsky and Adam Karl von Eschenmayer, another "animal magnetism" enthusiast, shared Schubert's interest in nature's night side.

The most popular book on the subject was *The Seeress of Prevorst,* by the poet, physician, and friend of Goethe, Justinus Kerner, which became a success in 1829. It tells the story of a remarkable psychic. Kerner was consulted by relatives of a woman named Friederike Hauffe, from the town of Prevorst, who was suffering from a wasting disease (one suspects tuberculosis). She was also subject to frequent trance states in which she saw spirits of the dead. Kerner's investigation revealed that Friederike was capable of much more. She was able to predict the future and could see into the human body and accurately diagnose diseases, a talent the twentieth-century psychic and prophet Edgar Cayce later displayed. Friederike could also read through her stomach; when Kerner blindfolded her and placed manuscripts on her midriff, she could read them perfectly. She told Kerner that her spirit could leave her body. She also told him that if he put her in a "magnetic trance," the spirits would tell her what treatment he should give her. While in her trance, she displayed clairvoyance and related information given to her by the spirits that proved accurate. Friederike also produced the knocks, raps, and other sounds associated with "poltergeists"—a German term meaning "noisy spirits"—and was able to levitate objects. She produced a complete and complex "spiritual teaching" and spoke of an ancient "universal language" that was spoken in the "inner world." These phenomena drained Friederike's energies, and three years after meeting Kerner, she died.[39]

In 1845, *The Seeress of Prevorst* was translated into English by Catherine Crowe, a British author of children's stories and popular novels, and became a huge success. In her day, Crowe was a well-known figure and counted among her acquaintances Charles Dickens and Charlotte Brontë. She was also interested in "altered states of consciousness"; in his memoirs, Hans Christian Andersen tells of seeing her inhaling ether at a party in Edinburgh.[40] Crowe had an interest in psychic phenomena, and many of her stories deal with supernatural themes. She was a reader of *Naturphilosophie* and the German Romantics. Although Coleridge had a taste for the supernatural, as did his friend Thomas De Quincey, Germany was seen as the land of ghosts, visions, and strange phenomena. In 1849, Crowe produced her own book on the subject, *The Night-Side of Nature*; another success, this became her most popular work, staying in print for more than a century. It was also the first real attempt to treat the paranormal scientifically, predating the Society for Psychical Research by more than thirty years.

Although by today's standards Crowe's work would not be considered "scientific"—her accounts are anecdotal for the most part—their sheer number are enough to convince an open-minded reader of the reality of her subject. She ranges over dreams, precognition, doppelgängers, apparitions, spirits, ghosts, poltergeists, mesmerism, and much more with a patient, insightful, and critical mind; her still readable book remains one of the few sources in English for insight into "abnormal psychology" in the days before Freud. Throughout her book she refers to theurgy and the Neoplatonists, and her central idea is what she calls "the dweller in the temple"— the soul—which, when released from the constraints of the body, enjoys what she calls "spiritual seeing, or intuitive knowing." She speaks of "one universal sense, which does not need the aid of the bodily organs; but, on the contrary, is most efficient when most freed from them," an insight we have come across before.[41] "It has been the opinion of many philosophers," she writes, "that in the original state of man . . . that knowledge which is now acquired by pains and labor was intuitive. . . . Degraded in its nature . . . man has lost the faculty of spiritual seeing; but in sleep, when the body is in a state of passivity . . . the spirit, to a certain degree freed from its impediments, may enjoy somewhat of its original privilege."[42]

HERE COME THE SPIRITS

By the 1830s, mesmerism was a popular topic in America, but it had really been there from the start. Benjamin Franklin had been among the group that denounced Mesmer as a fraud, but another hero of the Revolution, the Marquis de Lafayette, told George Washington that he was considered one of Mesmer's most enthusiastic students and that he was as devoted to Mesmer's ideas as he was to American independence.[43] But it was not until some decades later that ideas about "animal magnetism" and the "magnetic trance" became widely known. Their audience was primed for them to some degree by the work of the Transcendentalists. We've seen that Emerson was a reader of Swedenborg and Thomas Taylor, and references to Hermes, Pythagoras, Zoroaster, the Neoplatonists, and other esoteric sources abound in his writings and journals.

In 1851, Bronson Alcott, another Transcendentalist, introduced Hermes to the Boston literary crowd in her salons, and more than one commentator has remarked that in many ways the Transcendentalists paved the way not only for Madame Blavatsky and the Theosophical Society, but also for our own modern New Age.[44]

Emerson was not the only American writer interested in these pursuits. Edgar Allan Poe was introduced to mesmerism through a book, *Facts in Mesmerism*, published in 1840 by the English cleric Chauncy Hare Townshend, a friend of the novelist, esotericist, and early psychic investigator Lord Edward Bulwer-Lytton. Lytton was a friend of the French magician Eliphas Levi and his supernatural stories, like the classic "The Haunted and the Haunters," approach ghosts scientifically. His mammoth Rosicrucian novel, *Zanoni*, is one of the most important esoteric works of the nineteenth century, packing into its dense pages an encyclopedic amount of Hermetic lore; and his early science fiction novel, *The Coming Race*, anticipates Nietzsche's ideas about the "superman" by more than a decade.[45]

Poe used Mesmer's ideas in some of his stories, such as "The Facts in the Case of M. Valdemar," "A Tale of the Ragged Mountains," and most directly in "Mesmeric Revelation." This last was read by a Swedenborgian group who believed the account of the spirit world Poe gave was accurate and wrote to Poe to tell him so. Typically tactless, Poe wrote back that he had made it up.

Yet Poe was interested enough in mesmeric visions to attend magnetic séances held by "the Poughkeepsie Seer," Andrew Jackson Davis, whose voluminous spiritualist tract, *The Principles of Nature,* became an instant best seller when it appeared in 1847.[46] Poe's own attempt at a cosmological work, *Eureka,* was a flop, yet it communicated much that he had already said in "Mesmeric Revelation," and its many intuitive bull's-eyes concerning black holes, the expanding universe, curved space, galactic clusters, and other astronomical insights that have since been verified suggest that in some way he too had experienced some "direct perception."[47] Poe's *Marginalia* shows that he was interested in dreams, trance states, and that strange intermediary state between sleep and waking known as "hypnagogia," of which Swedenborg made much use.

Mesmerists, Swedenborgians, spirit healers, and clairvoyants formed a kind of traveling sideshow in America, bringing their messages from beyond to backwoods families as well as to cultured societies. But it was not until a particular encounter in an unassuming farmhouse that a full-blown spiritualist craze would begin. In March 1848, in Hydesville, New York, in an area of the country known as the "Burned-Over District" because of the many religious revival movements it had seen, something strange happened. On a farm where the Fox family lived, two sisters began to hear strange "knocks" and "raps" that seemed to come from nowhere. A search of the farmhouse could not locate their source, and the girls began to speak of a "Mr. Splitfoot," who they pretended was behind the sounds.

Hearing the noises again one evening, as a joke, Kate Fox said, "Mr. Splitfoot, do as I do!" and snapped her fingers. Immediately another "snap" was heard. Her sister Margaret joined in and did the same and when the "snaps" continued, their mother did too. Mrs. Fox seems something of an amateur psychic investigator, as she then proceeded to ask Mr.

Splitfoot questions, which "he" answered correctly. She then asked the obvious question, "Are you a spirit?" suggesting "he" knock twice if so. Two thunderous bangs replied. Eventually it turned out that Mr. Splitfoot was the spirit of a man who had been murdered in the house before the Foxes lived there. "The invasion of the spirit people," as one writer called it, had begun. After this, spirits started turning up all over the country and in other countries too.

Soon table-turning, ghostly hands, musical spirits—floating tambourines turned up frequently—and the mediums who contacted them appeared in abundance on both sides of the Atlantic. Spiritualism even entered American politics. In 1872, Victoria Woodhull, a medium, mesmerist, early communist, and advocate of "free love," became the first woman to run for the U.S. presidency; needless to say she didn't win.[48]

Speaking with spirits and contacting the dead were not, technically, new. Homer, Virgil, and Dante had written about such communications, and the oracles of ancient Greece and Rome were as commonplace as e-mail is today. Theurgists contacted astral entities, and magicians like John Dee spoke to angels. But now it wasn't poets, sibyls, or high priests who made contact, but ordinary people. Andrew Jackson Davis had little education—more than he claimed, most likely, but by no means could he have been called an intellectual or philosopher. The Fox sisters were adolescents. It seems the spirits were moving with the spirit of the time and had decided to become democratic.

There were, of course, spiritual celebrities. The most famous was the Scot Daniel Dunglas Home, whose performances were extraordinary and to this day have never been explained by any rational—that is, reductive— means.[49] Home could not only contact the dead, predict the future, and generate "raps." He could hold live coals, levitate an oak table or piano, and, most famously, float out one third-story window and in through another. He could also elongate his body and materialize figures from the past. After Home attended a lecture on Cagliostro, the Grand Copht turned up in Home's bedroom and chatted with him, sitting on his bed.[50]

Exactly why the spirits chose the middle of the nineteenth century to make a mass appearance remains unclear—if we accept that something more than sheer chicanery was involved. Setting aside any possible social, economic, political, or other "reasonable" answer, we can consider an idea proposed by an obscure English esotericist, C. G. Harrison, and later developed by Rudolf Steiner.[51] This suggests that in the nineteenth century, certain occultists, concerned with the rise of materialism, conferred on how best to deal with the situation. The conservatives maintained that the esoteric knowledge of the reality of the spirit must remain secret, otherwise it could become trivialized and watered down. The radicals wanted to disseminate the knowledge as widely as possible, to ensure the greatest effect. The radicals won out and "the invasion of the spirit people" was planned to counter the dominance of materialist science.

THE FRENCH CONNECTION

France, too, saw its own master spiritualist. The educationalist Hippolyte Léon Denizard Rivail was one of France's most well-known intellectuals; he was a kind of Comenius of his time, a proponent of "universal education," ready and able to dispense it. He was also a follower of Mesmer. Two daughters of a close friend had taken up the spiritualist craze, and Rivail took the opportunity to study them. The sisters were especially interested in "automatic writing," letting the spirits guide their hand. Rivail wrote a series of questions for them to put to their contacts. Their answers amazed Rivail.

The spirits had communicated a complex and profound spiritual philosophy, which included Mesmer's ideas about "animal magnetism." But there was more. The universe, it seemed, was pervaded by spirits and we, our bodies, are only temporary homes for these invisible souls. Each life allows the spirit to advance somewhat in its evolution, but it must return to another body to take the next step. In essence, Rivail's experiment led to a fusion between spiritualism and reincarnation, and after a séance in which the spirits obligingly danced tables and chairs around the room, Rivail abandoned his work as an educationalist to spread the word.

He adopted a new name, Allan Kardec—the spirits had suggested it, based on names he had in past lives—and wrote a book under it. *The Spirits' Book* appeared in 1856 and was an overnight sensation. Kardec's "spiritism," the name he chose to differentiate his teaching from mainstream spiritualism—which, like Swedenborg, did not accept reincarnation—was, until his death in 1869, extremely popular in France. Today it is one of the major religions of Brazil.

THE PROFESSOR OF TRANSCENDENTAL MAGIC

Around the same time as Rivail was hearing from the spirits, another Frenchman was making other esoteric waves. Alphonse Louis Constant was an ex-priest turned radical socialist writer and artist, but when his young wife left him for the editor of a political journal, he made the transformation that would change his life, becoming, in due course, "the Professor of Transcendental Magic." Constant came under the influence of an eccentric Polish mathematician and astronomer named Józef Maria Hoene-Wronski, who had developed a visionary system of messianic philosophy. Hoene-Wronski had studied at the Marseille observatory for several years, but when he published his findings he was forced to leave. Hoene-Wronski's theories about the origin and structure of the universe were decidedly Pythagorean, and he combined a mathematical mysticism with a messianic belief in a coming new age. Hoene-Wronski's commitment to an absolute and universal visionary knowledge was combined with his attempts to "square the circle," to develop a perpetual motion machine, and to invent a "prognometre," a device that would accurately predict the future.

Hoene-Wronski called his system *Messianisme,* and it sparked in the cuckolded socialist a profound if uncritical study of the Kabbalah, Hermeticism, and other esoteric traditions. Abandoned by his wife, Constant plunged into these deep waters, and when he emerged he was reborn. He took a new name, Eliphas Levi, the Hebrew equivalent of his old one, and began a career as an occultist. The first fruit of this transformation was *Dogme de la haute magie* (*Dogma of High Magic*) which appeared in 1854. Its follow-up, *Rituel de la haute magie,* appeared in 1856. (As mentioned, in 1896, both were translated as one volume, *Transcendental Magic,* by the occult scholar A. E. Waite.) With these and some later works—like *Les clefs de grand mystères,* published in 1861 and translated into English by Aleister Crowley as *The Keys of the Great Mysteries*—Levi triggered what has been seen as the first "occult revival" of the modern world.

There had been a kind of dud English occult revival earlier in the century, when Francis Barrett published *The Magus* in 1801. But although Barrett held classes in occult studies, his work is really a collection of earlier magical texts and is a dull read, lacking the romance and mystery of Levi's work. Most modern students of magic and the Kabbalah recognize that Levi is an often unreliable source. His work is full of dark musings about the Talmud and *Zohar,* but his command of Hebrew was practically nonexistent and, as A. E. Waite pedantically points out, much of what Levi writes about Kabbalah and other traditions is nonsense. Yet in an important sense this misses the point. What Levi captured in his dramatic and sonorous prose is the *adventure* and excitement that linked a renewed interest in the occult with the Romantic spirit of the age. Levi may be wrong on most things, but he is never dull, and he appeals directly to the imagination and to the belief, embodied in Romanticism, that we are much more powerful beings than we assume.

Magic, for Levi, was not about conjuring spirits or performing miracles, although he delved into both; it was about restoring fallen man to his true stature of a god. Levi's magic was "a science which confers on man powers apparently superhuman."[52] With Paracelsus, Goethe, and Blake, Levi emphasized the importance of the imagination. When combined with the will—which had received great attention through its association with the "power" of the mesmerist, something the novelist Honoré de Balzac, a devotee of Swedenborg, had written about—this can master the "astral light," what Levi called a "universal agent." This astral light was not only, like Mesmer's "animal magnetism," a subtle medium for the magician's will; it was also a kind of cosmic film on which everything that has ever happened has left its trace, an idea of which Madame Blavatsky would make much use. It was the magician's task to master the astral light—that is, his imagination—and this was accomplished through the power of his will.

Like Samuel Hartlib, Levi was a kind of "intelligencer," and made contact with others who shared his Hermetic interests. One such was

Edward Bulwer-Lytton, who witnessed Levi perform a magical ritual on the roof of the Pantheon, a large bazaar on Oxford Street in London.[53] Levi had performed an earlier ritual in London, after a mysterious woman in black approached him and requested him to perform a ceremonial invocation. He did and succeeded in conjuring the spirit of Apollonius of Tyana. Levi also received occult visitors, students eager to learn from the Professor of Transcendental Magic, as he came to be called. Many flocked to his small Parisian apartment, such as the English Rosicrucian Kenneth Mackenzie, and Levi's Italian disciple Baron Nicolas-Joseph Spedalieri.

One central occult idea that Levi contributed—and which has since been recognized as inaccurate—was uniting the Tarot with Kabbalah. Levi linked the twenty-two "paths" on the Kabbalistic Tree of Life, symbolized by the twenty-two letters of the Hebrew alphabet, with the twenty-two Tarot "trumps," known as the "major arcana"; he also linked the four minor suits (wands, cups, swords, discs) with the four letters of the Tetragrammaton, the unpronounceable name of God.[54] (YHVH had already been linked to the four ancient elements—fire, water, air, and earth—the fixed signs of the zodiac, and the four Evangelists.)

Levi also popularized the idea that the Tarot was the mysterious *Book of Thoth*, a nonexistent work the "search" for which still titillates modern seekers.[55] The Tarot became a kind of esoteric archetype for Levi. He found evidence of its influence practically everywhere, and he believed it originated in a kind of "universal Kabbalah." Levi's Kabbalistic study was mostly of the Christian Kabbalah that emerged from Pico della Mirandola, and did not reach to its Jewish sources; it is not surprising that Kabbalah scholars like Gershom Scholem would find his ideas absurd.

Nevertheless, bringing Kabbalah and the Tarot together was a brilliant stroke and was accepted by practically all subsequent occultists. If later research suggests that Levi's linkage of the Tarot with Egypt and a "universal Kabbalah" is based more on his stirring imagination than historical facts, this does not mean that it is entirely rubbish. The fundamental "method" of esotericism is analogy, and Levi's' mistake has been a very fruitful one. His work reached not only other occultists like the Hermetic Order of the Golden Dawn and began a tradition of French occultism that included René Guénon and Schwaller de Lubicz, it also influenced some of the major figures in French culture. The poets Baudelaire and Arthur Rimbaud; the novelist J. K. Huysmans; the founder of Surrealism, André Breton; the composers Claude Debussy and Erik Satie; and the painter Odilon Redon were all touched by Levi's ideas. On a less high-brow note, the image of Baphomet—supposed idol of the Templars—that adorns many heavy-metal album covers as well as clothing was originally designed by Levi.[56] He is seldom credited.

THE INCOMPARABLE HPB

Levi died in 1875, shaken by illness and the hardships of the Franco-Prussian War. That year was something of an esoteric milestone. Along with Levi's death, it saw the birth in England of the dark magician Aleister Crowley, a central if controversial figure. It also saw the founding of the most influential esoteric organization of modern times. On September 13, 1875, on New York City's east side, the Theosophical Society was born. Three figures played essential roles in its birth: William Quan Judge, a twenty-four-year-old Irish immigrant who had just passed his New York bar examination; Colonel Henry Steel Olcott, a middle-age agricultural-ist, journalist, ex-Civil War officer, and a member of the commission that investigated Abraham Lincoln's assassination; and a remarkable Russian immigrant, the journalist, traveler, psychic, revolutionary, spiritualist, and all-around curmudgeon, Helena Petrovna Blavatsky, known to her acquain-tances as HPB. Although she remains to many outside the esoteric milieu a very secret teacher, to those who recognize her importance, she is as much a creator of the modern world as Marx, Nietzsche, and Freud.[57] In many ways, were it not for Blavatsky's impact, the rest of this book could not have been written, as many of its remaining figures emerged, one way or another, from the esoteric treasure chest she very energetically opened.

Madame Blavatsky led a life, as the cliché goes, shrouded in mystery, and it is not until her appearance in New York in 1873 at the age of forty-two that any verifiable accounts of her activities begin.[58] We know that she was born Helena von Hahn in 1831 in Ekaterinoslav, then in Russia, now Dnipropetrovsk in the Ukraine. Her mother was a popular novelist and daughter of a princess; her father a military man descended from German nobility. From an early age Helena displayed psychic abilities—or so her sister said—and was headstrong. Her mother died when Helena was eleven and she then lived with her maternal grandparents. The discovery of her great-grandfather Prince Pavel Dolgorukov's occult library—he was a Strict Observance Rosicrucian Freemason—was a revelation, as was learning about Prince Pavel's involvement with a plan to "change the map of Europe" along esoteric lines. Ideas about "hidden superiors," "invisible" esoteric masters, and "universal reformations" took hold at an early age.

Two other events set Helena on her road of discovery. One was meeting Prince Alexander Golitsyn, a Freemason who traveled through Europe and the East in search of fellow seekers of knowledge. Alexander's grandfather and namesake had been a Freemason, a student of Louis Claude de Saint-Martin and Karl von Eckartshausen and an acquaintance of Franz von Baader. An intimate of Tsar Alexander I, the elder Golitsyn had encouraged the tsar to read Saint-Martin, Eckartshausen, Boehme, and Swedenborg. Young Prince Golitsyn talked to the teenage Helena about his travels and about the men and women he had met, who, like him, were, as Gurdjieff would later call himself, "seekers of truth." He encouraged her to travel "in search of the unknown," and at the first opportunity she did.

That chance occurred after the second event that set her on the path to destiny: her marriage at seventeen to Nikifor Blavatsky, the forty-something vice governor of the province of Erivan in southern Russia. Why she made this questionable and unconsummated alliance—HPB remained a lifelong celibate—is unclear, but soon into it she wanted out, and after three months she galloped off alone in the direction of Tiflis. After a failed attempt to ship her to her father in Odessa (she escaped to Constantinople), from late 1849 to her passing through immigration in Battery Park in July 1873, what actually happened in her life remains highly debatable.

If Paracelsus's, Giordano Bruno's, and Apollonius of Tyana's itineraries were packed, young Helena's sounds dizzying. From leaving her crestfallen husband to turning up in lower Manhattan—with occasional pit stops back home—her boot heels wandered to Turkey, Egypt, France, North

America, South America, England, Germany, Greece, India, and other parts, in search of inner wisdom and ancient knowledge. Along the way she fought on the barricades with the Italian nationalist Mazzini, crossed the United States in a covered wagon, survived the wreck of the *Eumonia*— a sea disaster as famous in its day as the *Titanic*—held séances in Cairo, taught music in Russia, ran an artificial flower factory, and much more.

Although it is difficult if not impossible to verify much that either she or others said she did, the remarkable thing is that there seems enough circumstantial evidence to suggest that at least some of her adventures were true. The most controversial part of her travelogue is her journey to Tibet at a time when white European males found it impregnable. She allegedly arrived there in the late 1860s, on her third attempt, at the command of two Hindu teachers. One of these teachers, the Master Morya, she claimed in later life to have had visions of since her childhood, and to have met in London in 1851 at the Great Exhibition. He told her she had a special mission and that it would require devoting three years of her life to receiving occult training in Tibet. Blavatsky claimed that in a secret location in the Himalayas, Master Morya and his colleague Koot Hoomi taught her the occult knowledge and esoteric teachings that she brought to the increasingly materialistic West in order to save it from complete self-destruction.

When Blavatsky arrived penniless in New York in 1873—traveling steerage from France in order to help a stranded family—she was a woman with a mission, and she did her best to let everyone know. One person she went out of her way to inform was Colonel Olcott. Olcott had an interest in spiritualism and was reporting on a "haunting" in a farmhouse in Chittenden, Vermont, for *The Daily Graphic*. Blavatsky read his articles and went to Chittenden purposely to meet him. The gentlemanly Olcott was bowled over by Blavatsky's forthright and blowsy manner. She smoked like a chimney, wore extravagant clothes, and had a "colorful" vocabulary. But what impressed Olcott most were her psychic powers. Upon her arrival, the farmhouse was visited by Russian, Georgian, and Kurdish spirits, dancing to Blavatsky's tune. HPB showed Olcott that she was something more than a passive medium; she was a *magician*. The control over "phenomena" that she displayed in Chittenden convinced Olcott that

Blavatsky was a woman of *power*. Then and there Olcott became her press agent, Platonic soul mate, and "chum"—or, depending on your point of view, partner in a folie à deux.

Blavatsky told Olcott about her mission and her masters (Olcott would soon meet one himself) and the colonel informed his readers of her amazing powers. She was not just another spiritualist and she soon drew fire because of her claim that the spirits mediums communicated with were more likely astral hobos and ectoplasmic deadbeats, bored lowlifes of the "other side," and not dear Aunt Betty or Uncle Tim. Mediumship, spiritualism were not the true spiritual path, she argued. They were passive, retrograde practices. The true path of spiritual evolution demanded the kind of control and discipline she had mastered in Tibet and which she was ready to teach to the right students. After a few misalliances and a failed "Miracle Club," the way ahead became clear. With Olcott, Judge, and several other seekers, the Theosophical Society was born.

ANCIENT WISDOM, MODERN WORLD

There were occult or esoteric societies prior to the Theosophical Society. One was the Orphic Circle, a mesmerist group associated with Emma Hardinge Britten, a prominent spiritualist and the author of *Art Magic* and possibly another influential work, *Ghost Land*, both of which appeared in 1876. Britten was an early member of the Theosophical Society before she had a falling-out with Madame Blavatsky. Another group was the elusive Hermetic Brotherhood of Luxor, led by the mysterious Max Théon, which incorporated some ideas of the eccentric mixed-race occultist Paschal Beverly Randolph, whose interest in drugs and sex-magic predates Aleister Crowley's and whose turbulent life ended when he blew his brains out in 1875 at the age of forty-nine. Joscelyn Godwin suggests that both groups may have had a hand in triggering the "spiritualist craze."[59]

But the Theosophical Society was something different, and much of its early success came from Blavatsky's powerful personality and media savvy. She was an excellent self-promoter, getting her name in the papers regularly, and she and Olcott made an impressive team. The Theosophical

Society was also concerned with more than spirits and mesmerism, which, by the late nineteenth century, were beginning to lose their appeal. As we saw in Chapter One, part of its focus was on recovering the lost knowledge and wisdom of the ancients, of philosophers and mystics like Plotinus, Iamblichus, and Porphyry, which had been forgotten in the modern age. It also aimed to study the phenomena of spiritualism and mesmerism scientifically—again in advance of the Society for Psychical Research—and to develop ways of actualizing the psychic powers latent in man. But it was Blavatsky's mission to "form a nucleus of a universal brotherhood of humanity, without distinction of race, creed, sex, caste or color" that perhaps set the Theosophical Society apart from earlier groups and linked it to the kind of "universal reformation" we saw with the Rosicrucians and Freemasons and with which she believed her great-grandfather had been involved. This egalitarianism, combined with an emphasis on personal spiritual experience and effort, made it an agent of the kind of "superhumanism" associated with Pico della Mirandola and Romanticism, and fit well with the democratic temper of the time. It appealed to people seeking a more rewarding spiritual life than that offered by the church but also to those of a scientific bent who nonetheless were dissatisfied with the increasingly reductive approach of modern science.

Blavatsky found herself battling on three fronts—against religion, science, and spiritualism—and she did surprisingly well. The Theosophical Society's motto, "There is no religion higher than truth," had wide appeal. Many early theosophical recruits came not from society's outcasts, as one might suspect, but from its best and brightest. Two prominent early members were the Civil War hero and purported inventor of baseball, Abner Doubleday, and "the Wizard of Menlo Park," Thomas Edison, who had by this time invented the phonograph and was on his way to the lightbulb.

UNVEILING ISIS

Blavatsky's first major work of occult philosophy, the massive *Isis Unveiled*, appeared in 1877 and was an immediate success, its first edition of one thousand copies selling out in a week. Many more printings followed and the book has never gone out of print. A review in *The New York World* gives us a clue as to what Blavatsky aimed to accomplish. It called the book "an extremely readable and exhaustive essay upon the paramount importance of re-establishing the Hermetic Philosophy." Strange stories gathered about how it was written; Blavatsky apparently was able to "see" passages in books she didn't possess and had no access to, through the medium of the "Akashic record," Levi's "astral light."

Some spiritualist critics, happy to nip at Blavatsky's heels, argued the book was full of plagiarisms—Blavatsky quotes a legion of authors—but a reader today isn't bothered by such pedantry. What he or she discovers is a torrent of esoteric inspiration, synthesizing practically all previous occult philosophy with the then latest developments in science, history, and other disciplines. Blavatsky had read and assimilated an enormous amount of material—akashically or otherwise—and presented it to the modern reader in a forceful, driven, at times exasperated—she does not shy from table-thumping—but readable style. With its championing of truths and realities that narrow scientific reductionism ignored—everything from mesmerism, precognition, and reincarnation, to "elementals," planetary evolution, and magic, with much else in between—*Isis Unveiled* reintroduced ideas that had been obscured by limited "left-brain thinking" to an audience eager for clues as to what lay *beyond,* and kick-started an occult revival.

Along with ideas about the Akashic record, Blavatsky argued that, contrary to Darwin and his followers, the entire universe, from the smallest clod to the greatest galaxy, is involved in a long, continuous process of cosmic and spiritual evolution, the essential element of which is consciousness. As the cultural historian Theodore Roszak pointed out, Blavatsky presents the first philosophical—not religious—critique of Darwinism, anticipating Samuel Butler's *Life and Habit* (1878), which is generally credited with this, by a year. Blavatsky also argued the central theme of the "perennial philosophy": that all religions have emerged from a common, primal source, once again voicing the recurrent Hermetic insight, and wish, that the different faiths should abandon their fruitless squabbles and focus on the real work of getting mankind up a step on the evolutionary ladder. It was an exciting and moving vision, and it came at the right time. Western consciousness, fed on reductive science, had by then entered a metaphysical black hole, one expression of which was the idea of the unavoidable "heat death" of the universe brought about through the irrevocable process of entropy, "the second law of thermo-dynamics." This argued that all of the energy in the universe would eventually flatten out into a lukewarm, lifeless, cosmic puddle and would remain that way throughout eternity. In contrast, Blavatsky offered a vision of a growing, expanding, conscious universe, in which the smallest part—Blake's grain of sand—was able to contain the whole, and with it, move toward achieving Godhead.

INDIA AND DOWNFALL

By the end of 1878, Blavatsky made a decision that would eventually lead to her downfall: she chose to leave New York and relocate to India. Exactly why she did remains unclear but by February 1879, she and Colonel Olcott had reached the subcontinent. It was from here that the Theosophical Society would achieve its greatest victories, but it is also here that Blavatsky's reputation suffered a blow from which it never really recovered. After five years of unqualified success in which the society attracted thousands of recruits, including many among the higher classes and British expatriates, and Blavatsky and Olcott received many honors and much good press—both had converted to Buddhism—a dark cloud appeared in the form of an old friend.[60] Emma Coulombe, whom Blavatsky had known from her séance days in Cairo, wrote to HPB from Ceylon (now Sri Lanka), telling of hard times. Blavatsky invited her to join the society and keep house for her in Bombay (now Mumbai). It was an offer she would later regret.

Soon after this, in 1884, HPB and Colonel Olcott went to England and France. In London, the recently founded Society for Psychical Research (SPR) suggested they investigate the claims made about Blavatsky's psychic powers. She had already recruited Alfred Percy Sinnett, an influential newspaper editor, whose books *The Occult World* and *Esoteric Buddhism* were very popular and introduced Blavatsky's ideas to many readers, among them Rudolf Steiner and W. B. Yeats. Sinnett spoke of her miraculous ability to "materialize" objects, the most uncanny of which were letters from her mystic Masters, who, by now, were called "Mahatma," which means "great soul." These letters appeared, literally, out of nowhere, usually falling from the empty air above their recipient's head. Sinnett himself carried on an extensive correspondence with the Masters in this way, more than thirteen hundred pages of elaborate esoteric communication, in red and blue ink, which are available for study in the British Library. HPB called the magic that provided the letters "precipitation," and it was something she had learned in Tibet. Newspapers around the world carried accounts of Blavatsky's "materializations," and the SPR was keen to investigate them. HPB and Olcott agreed.

By this time, Emma Coulombe, angered by some perceived slight, had told a Christian missionary magazine that HPB's powers were a fake and that she had been recruited to help her old friend pull the wool over many eyes. The "precipitated" letters were simply slipped through cracks in the floorboards, and the Masters were phoneys too. Most damaging, Emma said she had letters from Blavatsky to prove it. Blavatsky had few good words about the Christian missionaries—she was a fervent critic of Christianity and chided the missionaries for taking the natives away from their own infinitely preferable religion—and she also was less than complimentary about the British Raj. The magazine was only too happy to hear Emma's revelations, and soon the rest of the world heard about them too, including the SPR. The upshot was that when Richard Hodgson arrived to investigate HPB's "precipitations," he swallowed Emma Coulombe's story whole and reported to the SPR that Blavatsky was one of the greatest impostors in history. She was also most likely a Russian spy, working against the British in the "Great Game," the tussle for influence in Tibet and northern India between the tsar and Queen Victoria.

Blavatsky denied Emma's claims, said her alleged letters were forgeries, and came back to India to defend herself. She was also incensed by Hodgson's accusation that she was a spy. But Olcott and others in the society thought it would be a mistake to launch a legal battle in which Blavatsky would be obliged to reveal the true identity of her Masters, something she had sworn never to do. In any case, any action would lead to a show trial against Theosophy, and everyone wanted to avoid that. Blavatsky was a volatile character and liable to explode in the process of rebutting the allegations against her. In the end, HPB took the calumny upon herself, and in 1885, left India—a country she loved and would never see again—and for some years became something of a wanderer, crisscrossing Europe as had the mages of old. She may have found some recompense in the fact that in 1986, the SPR retracted Hodgson's report as highly flawed and stated that Madame Blavatsky had been "unjustly condemned." A century after she took the blame, Blavatsky, if not completely cleared, at least had something of a day in court.[61]

SECRET DOCTRINES

Blavatsky eventually settled in England in 1887, where she spent her last days. Many of them were occupied in producing her second enormous work of occult philosophy, *The Secret Doctrine*, which was published in 1888 and is even longer that *Isis Unveiled*. Blavatsky claimed it was a commentary on stanzas from *The Book of Dzyan*, an unknown ancient work written in the equally unknown ancient language of "Senzar," which HPB said she learned during her time in Tibet.

The Book of Dzyan, Blavatsky tells us, is the source of all eastern and western "wisdom traditions," and the two volumes of *The Secret Doctrine* amount to a cosmic history of man and the universe. They speak of the Earth going through different stages of evolution—what she calls "rounds"—and of the different "root" and "sub" races that have lived on it prior to us, such as the Atlanteans and the Lemurians. Much has been made of Blavatsky's attention to race, mostly by a few racist esotericists and by critics of esotericism who believe it is racist by definition. Yet anyone who reads much of Blavatsky's huge oeuvre soon sees that race actually plays a very small part in it, and that what there is must be seen in light of her overarching mission to inaugurate a new, modern, universal "brotherhood of man." There is much evidence in Blavatsky's life to show that she was not racist.

As with *Isis Unveiled*, it is difficult to give a précis of *The Secret Doctrine*, but its central aims can be summed up in three propositions. One is that it seeks to establish the existence of one absolute Reality, which precedes all manifestation and transcends our ability to speak of it, something we've heard in regard to the Hermetic One, the Neoplatonic *Nous*, the Kabbalah's *En-Sof*, the *Sunyata* (or void) of Mahayana Buddhism, Jacob Boehme's *Ungrund*, and the negative theology of Meister Eckhart. Blavatsky also wants to establish the eternity of the universe as a "boundless plane," in which the ebb and flow of creation, its "periodicity," is played out. For Blavatsky, the universe is ever creating itself out of itself, its apparent "destruction" merely the prelude to a new "creation" (so no final "heat death"). And, perhaps most important, she argues for the identity of every individual soul with the Oversoul, a universal consciousness through which each soul undergoes the process of a cosmic evolution, a transformative journey through all states of existence, from stone to God. With these objectives, Blavatsky takes the reader on a thrilling, challenging, and not infrequently bewildering voyage through the occult history of the world. Whether she is successful depends on the reader, but those who persevere will find that the sudden stunning views and insights are worth the effort.

Writing *The Secret Doctrine* took its toll on Blavatsky, who was never in good health and whose enormous size and scandalous diet did not help; in her last days she weighed more than two hundred pounds and had to be pushed around in a perambulator. In London, she started an Esoteric Section of the Theosophical Society—an offshoot of her earlier Blavatsky Lodge—in which she instructed selected students in the finer details of her ideas. She later formed an Inner Group from some of its members, some of whom went on to play important roles in esoteric history. The fiery suffragette and socialist Annie Besant came in to the Theosophical fold in 1889, after reviewing *The Secret Doctrine* for *The Pall Mall Gazette*. After meeting Blavatsky, she was converted, a life change for the atheist Besant that churned up much gossip. She would take over running the Theosophical Society from Colonel Olcott in the new century. G. R. S. Mead went on to become a respected scholar of Gnosticism and Hermeticism and to start his own Quest Society, and William Wynn Westcott was one of the founders of the Hermetic Order of the Golden Dawn.

Blavatsky received many visitors. W. B. Yeats was charmed by her and said she had an "air of humour and audacious power." She told Yeats that "nothing mattered but what happened in the mind. If we cannot master the mind, our actions are of little importance." Probably the most influential and surprising of Blavatsky's visitors was Mohandas Gandhi, who later described Theosophy as "Hinduism at its best."

Gandhi was taken to meet Blavatsky in 1889, when he was a young law student trying his best to be English. He had met two young Theosophists and was embarrassed to admit that he had never read the *Bhagavad Gita*, a classic of Indian spirituality. Such works had been frowned upon by his Christian missionary teachers. After he met Blavatsky, it became the most important book in Gandhi's life; his doctrine of *Ahimsā*, nonviolence, he said, emerged from his reading of it. Gandhi joined a Theosophical lodge and remained deeply interested in Theosophy for the rest of his life. On January 30, 1948, the day he was assassinated, Gandhi had written about Theosophy in his journal *Harijan*, saying that "Theosophy is Hinduism in theory, and Hinduism is Theosophy in practice." Such accounts are regularly left out of most writing about Blavatsky's influence in the world.

Blavatsky died on May 8, 1891, at the age of sixty. She had a medley of ailments and, unlike today's spiritual people, treated her body with contempt; the idea of being concerned with her "health and well-being" would have prompted an unprintable remark and a drag on her ubiquitous cigarette. She may not have known it, but the years after her passing saw something like an esoteric Big Bang, the consequences of which we are still trying to understand.

CHAPTER ELEVEN

TOWARD THE NEW AGE

The decades following Madame Blavatsky's death saw a remarkable blossoming of esoteric ideas, an occult revival that continued until the outbreak of World War I, and which rivaled the Renaissance and Romantic movement for inspiration, insight, and influence. The fin-de-siècle, as this period is known, is generally considered a time of decadence—epitomized in J. K. Huysmans's eccentric novel *Against the Grain* (1884) and Oscar Wilde's *The Picture of Dorian Gray* (1891)—but it was also a time of intense creativity and experiment. Elements of the ancient wisdom often joined forces with modern and progressive ideas to create an atmosphere in which old familiar ways of life were challenged and practically anything seemed possible. While concerns about the decline of the West and its spiritual exhaustion were rife—witness the success of Max Nordau's study *Degeneration* (1892), which argued that practically all of modern art and literature was inspired by disease—the years between 1890 and 1914 were also filled with an exuberance and optimism that to our more cynical eyes seems incredible. The century about to dawn offered, it seemed, a blank slate on which western man could write his destiny, and for many the future looked infinitely promising.

R. M. Bucke's *Cosmic Consciousness,* for example, a riposte to Nordau published in 1901, saw mankind moving into a higher stage of consciousness and liberated from material concerns through a kind of world socialism. Nietzsche's prophecy of a coming superman informed speculations on human evolution, and the belief in progress and mankind's perfectibility combined with ideas of karma and reincarnation to produce an effervescent, highly charged milieu. New developments in science and technology suggested a power over the physical world unlike any before, while investigations into the "night side" of nature revealed the hidden abilities of the human mind.

It was a paradoxical time, when the stridently modern met ancient "lost" knowledge and produced a curious sensibility, in which much that was "up-to-date" had its roots in the mysterious past. Some writers have suggested that the occult revival of this time was a reaction to the rise of modernity and an attempt to avoid it, what the historian of the occult James Webb called "the flight from reason."[1] But as in the Renaissance, in many cases the "modern" itself had its source in what had been long forgotten. As in our own time, with science and mysticism often neighbors— witness Fritjof Capra's *The Tao of Physics*—Einstein's relativity theory and notions of non-Euclidean space informed accounts of astral travel and the fourth dimension. At the same time, a widespread dissatisfaction with western materialist science and its disenchanted universe—as well as with an increasingly moribund Christianity—led many to take a journey to the East, and to embrace a variety of oriental philosophies that are still with us today.

In fact, it seems clear that much, if not all, of what we consider our own New Age can be traced back to this forgotten "positive *fin-de-siècle*."[2] Many of the interests informing the new, progressive ways of life have a very familiar ring. Yoga, natural medicine, getting back to nature, higher consciousness, experimentation with drugs, free love, feminism, gay rights, meditation, vegetarianism, animal rights, multiculturalism, homeopathy, interest in indigenous people and traditional beliefs, spiritualism (channeling), mythology, communal living, anticapitalism, a fascination with ancient civilizations, occultism and the supernatural, a rejection of cold reason in favor of feeling and intuition, a turning away from modernity and progress while at the same time a fervent millennarian belief in a coming "new age": these and many other alternative ideas informed the western Zeitgeist at the beginning of the twentieth century.

THE SPAWN OF HPB

Many of the prime movers of this early modern occult revival got their start through Theosophy, which by the end of the nineteenth century had become a worldwide movement, informing many areas of life. The Russian painter Wassily Kandinsky and his Dutch colleague Piet Mondrian, for example—two giants of modern art—were Theosophists. Theosophical ideas are at the core of their work, and a good argument can be made that abstract art grew in theosophical soil.[3] Along with the lectures and writings of Rudolf Steiner, himself a major Theosophist, one of the main influences on Kandinsky, generally recognized as the first abstract painter, was the book *Thought Forms,* written by Annie Besant and C. W. Leadbeater, another leading Theosophist, and published in 1905.[4] As mentioned earlier, the basic idea of *Thought Forms* is that "thoughts are things." The illustrations accompanying Besant and Leadbeater's text, portraying different thoughts, feelings, emotions, and ideas in colorful abstract forms, informed Kandinsky's attempt to capture the spiritual world on canvas, an objective he spells out in his influential book *Concerning the Spiritual in Art* (1912).[5]

Other arts were also theosophically informed. Nicholas Roerich, the artist and mystic who designed the sets and provided the inspiration for Igor Stravinsky's scandalous 1913 ballet *Le Sacré du Printemps*—which riotously inaugurated the age of modern music—would later claim to be guided in his expeditions to the Himalayas by one of Blavatsky's Masters. The Russian composer Alexander Scriabin, famous for works like *The Poem of Ecstasy* (1908), was a Theosophist; his last work, left unfinished at his death, was to be a gigantic Mystery drama on Theosophical themes, combining music, art, dance, theater, poetry, and ritual. The American writer Jack London was a Theosophist, and reincarnation is the central theme of his novel *The Star Rover* (1915). And L. Frank Baum, the author of *The Wizard of Oz* (1900), became a Theosophist in 1892.

Theosophy also reached into scholarship, and many who first introduced eastern ideas and philosophies to western minds were influenced by theosophical beliefs. W. Y. Evans-Wentz, who brought *The Tibetan Book of the Dead* to western readers, was a Theosophist, as were the influential Buddhist scholars Christmas Humphreys and Edward Conze. D. T. Suzuki, who introduced Zen Buddhism to the West, was also a Theosophist. Politics, too, had its share. We have already mentioned Gandhi, but Jawaharlal Nehru, who would become the first prime minister of India, was initiated into the society as a teenager in 1902. And our own multifaith aspirations have a pre-echo in the first World Parliament of Religions, which took place in 1893 during the World's Columbian Exposition in Chicago. Here the Theosophists Annie Besant and William Quan Judge, and the Sinhalese religious reformer Anagarika Dharmapala (a student of Blavatsky who had been inspired by Colonel Olcott's Buddhist missionary work) shared a stage with Christians, Jews, Muslims, Hindus—Swami Vivekananda opened the proceedings—atheists and agnostics, a tangible expression of Theosophy's advocacy of the "perennial philosophy."

MOUNTAINS Of TRUTH

Theosophy also had a hand in starting what would later be called the "counterculture." In 1889, Alfred Pioda, a member of the Swiss parliament and a committed Theosophist, planned a "Theosophical cloister" in the sleepy village of Ascona on the shores of Lago Maggiore in Ticino, the Italian-speaking canton of Switzerland. Ascona already had a "radical" reputation: in 1873, one of its residents was the Russian anarchist Mikhail Bakunin. The cloister was to be built on a hill named Monescia overlooking the lake, and Pioda's collaborators included Countess Constance Wachtmeister, Madame Blavatsky's Swedish traveling companion; the German Theosophist and occultist Franz Hartmann; and the Dutch novelist, psychiatrist, and spiritualist Frederik van Eeden, who in 1913 coined the term "lucid dream."

Pioda's plan didn't pan out, but in 1900, Ida Hoffman, a Montenegran piano teacher, and Henri Oedenkoven, son of a wealthy Belgian industrialist, rechristened the hill Monte Verità, the "Mountain of Truth," and founded a "co-operative vegetarian colony" there, devoted to "getting back to nature" and "experimental living," which in many cases meant nudism, sun-worship, and free love. Soon scores of esoteric and cultural notables headed to Ascona, eager to escape the stress of city life and "get off the grid" in the beautiful near-Mediterranean microclimate. Well in advance of the 1960s "love generation," anarchists, vegetarians, nature worshipers, free-love advocates, poets, painters, occultists, and musicians who rejected mainstream society "dropped out" in the curiously spiritual atmosphere of Monte Verità. Among those who climbed the "Mountain of Truth" were the novelist Hermann Hesse, the dancer Isadora Duncan, the choreographer Rudolf Laban, the radical Freudian and sex and drugs guru Otto Gross (a colleague and patient of Jung), the occultist and spy Theodor Reuss, Rudolf Steiner, the sociologist Max Weber, the novelist D. H. Lawrence, and the anarchist Erich Mühsam, who was later assassinated by the Nazis.

The most characteristic figure of Monte Verità was the *Naturmensch* Gustav Gräser, known simply as "Gusto," a poet and painter determined to be free of "civilization." Gusto made his own clothes, plucked food from the trees, made his own furniture, and lived in a cave with his wife and children. In Monte Verità on a rest cure, Herman Hesse submitted to Gusto's natural health regime, which meant exposing his naked body to the elements; in Hesse's case, this resulted in sunburn and torn flesh.[6]

In 1920, the original Monte Verità experiment ended when Hoffman and Oedenkoven moved to South America, but it received a new lease on esoteric life a decade later when the Dutch socialite Olga Fröbe-Kapteyn opened her nearby Casa Gabriella to the famous Eranos Conferences. These prestigious gatherings were presided over by C. G. Jung and included some of the major names of post–World War II spiritual and esoteric scholarship, such as Henry Corbin, Joseph Campbell, Gershom Scholem, Mircea Eliade, and James Hillman. For the Jungian Erich Neumann, the Eranos Conferences constituted a modern "link in the Golden Chain" of adepts; Eliade himself likened them to what took place during the Renaissance and the Romantic movement.[7] Curiously, Fröbe-Kapteyn had originally planned for the auditorium she had built to be used by the Theosophist Alice Bailey, but after holding a few "spiritual summer schools" there, Bailey abandoned the idea, saying that the area was associated with black magic and witchcraft.

PSYCHIC SOCIETIES

Experiments in new ways of living were not limited to Mountains of Truth, and in many European cities the new progressive sensibilities mixed with a revived interest in the occult. Paris, St. Petersburg, London, Munich, Prague, Rome, and other cosmopolitan centers had a thriving occult underground. One expression of this was a determined attempt to understand the spiritual world scientifically, to refine the work started a generation earlier by the *Naturphilosophen*, Catherine Crowe and Bulwer-Lytton.

The Society for Psychical Research was founded in England in 1882 by the classicist F. W. H. Myers, the philosopher Henry Sidgwick, and the psychologist Edmund Gurney. Their motive was the belief that the "objective and intelligent investigation" into spiritualism and related phenomena "could provide answers to the troubling metaphysical questions of the time."[8] As mainstream religion withdrew in the face of an encroaching materialist science, the big questions of life and death and good and evil were seen as either meaningless or unanswerable, and the debate between reason and faith was increasingly polarized. With an inadequate religion and a dismissive science, Myers and his colleagues wondered if the evidence for ghosts, spirits, precognition, telepathy (Myers coined the term), clairvoyance, and other "psychic phenomena" might help throw light on the "actual truth as to the destiny of man."[9] The central question regarding the "destiny of man" was, for the members of the SPR, the possibility of life after death. Myers gathered an enormous amount of evidence for this in his posthumously published masterpiece *Human Personality and Its Survival of Bodily Death* (1903), a massive two-volume work in which Myers developed his own theory of the unconscious—or, as he called it, the "subliminal mind"—in advance of Freud.

Myers's ideas influenced fellow psychologists such as Pierre Janet, Théodore Flournoy, and C. G. Jung. Unlike today, when most scientists shy from public admission of any "spiritual" views, in the positive fin-de-siècle such timidity was rare, and soon after its inception the SPR drew to its cause many of the most famous minds of the time, including

Alfred Russel Wallace, "co-discoverer" with Darwin of the theory of evolution; the physicists William Barrett and Lord Rayleigh; the chemist and Theosophist William Crookes; the philosopher and British Prime Minister Arthur Balfour; the physiologist Charles Richet; and Arthur Conan Doyle, creator of Sherlock Holmes (unlike his creation, Doyle was a fervent spiritualist). Freud and Jung were members, and the SPR also attracted the philosopher Henri Bergson, whom we have met throughout this book, and his friend and fellow philosopher William James.

James straddled the related concerns of psychical research and investigation into mysticism and altered states of consciousness, one result of which is his classic work *The Varieties of Religious Experience*, published in 1902. James agreed with Myers that any account of human life must include evidence coming from "abnormal" psychological states, such as mediumship and mystical experience, and he argued that personal experience was a more valid proof of God or spirituality than any theology, dogma, or system, an idea we have come across before. James himself was not a stranger to such states, and during an experiment with nitrous oxide—well in advance of the psychedelic generation—he experienced "depth beyond depth of truth" and recognized that "our normal waking consciousness, rational consciousness, as we call it, is but one special type of consciousness, whilst all about it, parted by the filmiest of screens, there lie potential forms of consciousness, entirely different." "No account of the universe in its totality can be final," James saw, "which leaves these other forms of consciousness quite disregarded."[10] Needless to say, the materialist account of the universe did leave these other forms of consciousness quite disregarded, and in many instances prided itself on doing so.

James's breadth of inquiry was impressive and, along with Bergson, he also took a deep interest in the rise of what he called the "Mind-cure movement," the gospel of "positive thinking" that formed part of the optimistic character of the fin-de-siècle. In *The Varieties of Religious Experience*, James sings the praises of the "healthy-minded attitudes" of "courage, hope and trust" which have resulted in, by James's account, nothing short of miracle cures, with the blind restored to sight, the lame walking, and invalids free of their ailments. As with much of our own contemporary New Age literature, James recognized that many "mind-cure" tracts are

so "moonstruck with optimism and so vaguely expressed" that many educated people find them difficult to swallow. Yet he argues that this
shouldn't prevent us from recognizing the practical results from what he
calls America's "only decidedly original contribution to the systematic
philosophy of life," an application, in its way, of Paracelsus's recognition of
the power of imagination over our health.[11]

GOLDEN DAWNS

W. B. Yeats, who also experimented with drugs, mostly hashish and peyote, in order to explore other forms of consciousness, left the Theosophical Society because of his interest in ceremonial magic, an occult pursuit
that Blavatsky abhorred. He soon found congenial company in the Hermetic Order of the Golden Dawn, arguably the most famous occult group
of modern times. The Golden Dawn fused Hermetic, Egyptian, Rosicrucian, Kabbalistic, and theurgic teachings into a unique blend that informed most of the popular magic of the last half century. All of its work
was aimed at achieving the "knowledge and conversation" of one's "Holy
Guardian Angel," the order's version of the "higher self," derived from a
medieval Kabbalistic tract known as *The Book of the Sacred Magic of Abra-
melin the Mage*. As with the Theosophical Society, many of the most
influential occultists of the twentieth century emerged from the Golden
Dawn or one of its offshoots: a short list would include Israel Regardie;
Dion Fortune; A. E. Waite; the writer on mysticism Evelyn Underhill;
and the horror fiction writers Arthur Machen and Algernon Blackwood.

The most well-known story of the Golden Dawn's origin—which is
most likely apocryphal—concerns a cipher manuscript found in a secondhand bookstore in London's Farringdon Road. Wynn Westcott—later a
member of Madame Blavatsky's Inner Group—could not decipher it
and he asked a friend, Samuel Liddell MacGregor Mathers, for help.
Mathers was an eccentric character. He combined a natural predilection
for magic with a passion for military history and an inveterate taste for
fantasy and self-dramatizing; oddly enough, he was also married to Henri
Bergson's sister, Moina, herself a medium. Mathers and Westcott cracked

the cipher—it was one devised by Paracelsus's teacher, Johannes Trithemius— and recognized that it contained magical rituals and material on the Tarot, as well as a letter from a Fräulein Anna Sprengel in Nuremberg. The letter gave her address and also said that if more information about the cipher was needed, to contact her. Westcott wrote Fräulein Sprengel, who told him that she was the head of a magical order, *Die Goldene Dämmerung* (The Golden Dawn). She also gave him a charter to start a branch in London, which Westcott, Mathers, and a colleague, William Woodman, did in 1887.

When Westcott wrote to Fräulein Sprengel again, he received a reply saying that she had died, and that no further help would come from Germany. If he and his colleagues wanted more information, they would have to contact the Secret Chiefs, the true heads of the order, themselves. Yeats, we've seen, thought that these Secret Chiefs (or "Hidden Superiors") went back to Rabbi Falk, but for Mathers, they had a more supernatural status. By 1891, about the time Yeats met him, Mathers was in command of the Golden Dawn, and he likened his contacts with the Secret Chiefs to the effect of a lightning flash coupled with the shortness of breath that accompanies inhaling ether. Mathers claimed that he was in sole contact with these powerful beings, who were rather like Blavatsky's Masters, and this, combined with his dictatorial style and the fact that he was leading the London group while living in Paris, led to fractures that would soon break the order apart.

One factor certainly hastening the order's collapse was the initiation in 1898 of Aleister Crowley, the most famous—or infamous—magician of the twentieth century. A poet, mountaineer, chess master and, like Blavatsky, world traveler, Crowley combined a brilliant mind with an unfortunate adolescent need to shock, born of his upbringing in a prosperous Christian fundamentalist family. He also had a hefty inheritance and a taste for unconventional sex, and a variety of drugs that would, within a few years, make him a darling of the tabloids. Yeats and most of the other members found Crowley unbearable, but Mathers considered him an ally. When he initiated Crowley into a higher grade that Yeats had earlier refused, the subsequent squabble led to the order's sundering into opposed camps and eventual fracture.

Crowley soon founded his own magical society, the A∴A∴ (the pyramid of dots is a Masonic device indicating that the society was secret), which is most commonly understood to mean *Argentium Astrum*, or Silver Star, and which more or less carried on in the Golden Dawn tradition. Crowley would also later join and revamp another society, the Ordo Templi Orientis, or O.T.O., a quasi-Masonic group dedicated to tantric "sex magic," claiming descent from the Knights Templar and which still survives today. Crowley's A∴A∴ combined magical workings of an Egyptian-Kabbalistic blend, with experiments in altered states of consciousness, mostly using drugs—what Crowley called "Scientific Illuminism"—as well as rituals aimed at discovering one's "true will." These were based on Crowley's inspired work, *The Book of the Law*, which was dictated to Crowley by a supernatural being in Cairo in 1904. *The Book of the Law* prophesised a coming new age, that of "the crowned and conquering child," and the rise of the religion of *thelema*, Greek for "will." The essence of *thelema* was summed up in Crowley's antinomian formula "Do what thou wilt shall be the whole of the law," which was later taken up as a catchphrase during the 1960s and has carried on to today.[12]

THE OLD NEW AGE

Crowley was part of the general occult boom of the fin-de-siècle, and he knew one of the period's major movers and shakers.[13] The literary critic and editor A. R. Orage was a brilliant "desperado of genius"—according to the playwright George Bernard Shaw—whose journal *The New Age* was the premier sounding board for a remarkable array of progressive ideas. In many ways it was a kind of Monte Verità in print, opening its pages to the occult, Theosophy, socialism, dress reform, psychical research, feminism, and other radical notions. Orage himself was a walking embodiment of the time, being simultaneously a Fabian socialist, Theosophist, psychical researcher (he was a secretary of the SPR), occultist, and Nietzschean; his *Friedrich Nietzsche, the Dionysian Spirit of the Age* (1906) was the first systematic introduction to Nietzsche in English.

Orage and a friend bought the moribund *New Age* in 1907 with money donated by Shaw and a "Theosophically minded banker," and quickly turned it into a vital organ of progressive thought.[14] Along with more obscure writers, it published Shaw, H. G. Wells, and G. K. Chesterton, and its sole editorial policy was that what it printed had to excite argument and debate. Before moving to London and acquiring *The New Age*, Orage had been a teacher in Leeds, where his interest in Plato and the boredom of the classroom led him to Theosophy. He was also a keen student of eastern religion; like Gandhi, the *Bhagavad Gita* was an important work for him, and as an editor, he took the *Mahabharata* as the benchmark of literary style and excellence.

In 1904, Orage gave a lecture to the Leeds and Manchester branch of the Theosophical Society on "Consciousness: Animal, Human, and Superman." Like R. M. Bucke, Orage believed that mankind was on the brink of a new stage in its evolution, what he called "superman consciousness," compared to which our everyday human consciousness is "inferior . . . just as an embryo in an egg is inferior to the bird flying in the air."[15] For Orage, "superman consciousness" is an intensification of our normal self-consciousness, in which the self that we take for granted would become an object of study and analysis by something *higher*. Orage believed that "the activity of the inner senses is beginning to slowly predominate over the outer senses," the basic mechanism of esoteric consciousness. And Orage makes clear that this process proceeds through imagination. For him, "evolution is altogether an imaginative process. You become what you have been led to imagine yourself to be."[16] This amounts to joining the Rosicrucians by becoming one.

Orage's Nietzschean sensibilities soon distanced him from most rank-and-file Theosophists, just as his Platonic dialectic made him an opponent of much murky mysticism. In an article for the *Theosophical Review*, Orage contrasted what he called the "occult arts" with the "occult faculties." While the former can obsess and devour people, often turning them into "cranks"—some people cannot make a decision without consulting the Tarot—"occult faculties" free the mind and enable it to soar. The faculties in question—intuition, insight, and imagination—Orage called "winged thought," "winged judgment," and "winged sympathy." The difference between the two is that while arts can be lost or forgotten, faculties, once acquired, remain.[17]

ANNIE BESANT

Another Fabian socialist who also found herself in the Theosophical fold was, as we have seen, Annie Besant. But while Orage's politics were for the most part theoretical and Platonic, Besant's had a more practical slant. Secularism, woman's rights, workers' rights, and education were only some of the causes she advanced. Born in London in 1847, she gained notoriety in 1877 when she was arrested with the secularist Charles Bradlaugh for publishing a book on birth control by the American family-planner Charles Knowlton. Her championing of equal rights between the sexes cost her her marriage and the custody of her children. A natural public speaker, she came to national attention in 1887 for demonstrating against unemployment in the famous "Bloody Sunday" riots in Trafalgar Square. In 1888, she led a successful fight to improve the working conditions for London's "match girls," then, while on the London school board, improved the lives of thousands of schoolchildren. She also helped dockworkers. Her private life was also eventful, having affairs with, among others, Bernard Shaw.

After reviewing *The Secret Doctrine* for *The Pall Mall Gazette*—whose editor, W. T. Stead, was a spiritualist and later one of the fatalities of the *Titanic*—Besant visited Madame Blavatsky. At the end of their meeting, Blavatsky asked Besant to "come among us." She did. It was a decision that changed her life. She became a regular visitor, and not long after, in August 1890, Blavatsky moved into Besant's home in London's affluent St. John's Wood. A seasoned campaigner, Besant quickly moved up the Theosophical ranks, an ascension not without its costs. Besant was obliged to publicly renounce her earlier views on birth control, and in 1891, she gave a farewell speech to the National Secularist Society. There were, however, compensations. In 1890, she became co-editor of Blavatsky's Theosophical journal, *Lucifer* (which later became the *Theosophical Review*), and in the same year was made president of the Blavatsky

Lodge, a development that left her rival, A. P. Sinnett, with leadership of the less prestigious London Lodge. With Blavatsky's death, Besant became head of the Esoteric Section as well. Not everyone was happy with her success. There would later be a "back to Blavatsky" protest, and schisms would soon lead to the society separating into Indian, American, and English entities, distinct from each other yet united by a sometimes friendly but often bitter rivalry.

Key were the Masters, and after HPB's death, a race ensued to see who could make contact with them. Olcott remained head of the society until his death in 1907, when Besant took over, but he was always a more administrative than esoteric figure, and his contacts with the Masters had always come through HPB. Sinnett's communication with them had dwindled, and he resorted to a series of psychics in order to renew it, but with no luck. William Quan Judge, who had stayed in America, claimed to have made contact and hence was HPB's rightful heir, but Olcott dismissed this. Other, "renegade" Theosophists like Katherine Tingley and Alice Bailey made their own contact, but their influence was limited, and they, like Judge, started their own societies. If Besant was to capture the throne, she needed a secure hotline to the Mahatmas.

C. W. LEADBEATER AND KRISHNAMURTI'S AURA

This came in the form of one of Theosophy's most controversial characters, Bishop Charles W. Leadbeater, who joined the society in 1883. He too wanted to communicate with the Masters, and while in Adyar, India, with HPB, he did—much to Blavatsky's annoyance. Leadbeater claimed he was clairvoyant, and along with being able to communicate with the Masters, he was also able to journey on the "Akashic planes," and to see auras, a kind of energy field around the human body, a development from Mesmer's "animal magnetism" and Levi's "astral light." It was through this strange ability that Leadbeater made a momentous discovery. Leadbeater is best known as the man who discovered the teenage Jiddu Krishnamurti on a riverbank near the Theosophical compound in Adyar in 1909. His aura, Leadbeater said, was remarkable, and Leadbeater announced that

Krishnamurti was destined to become a "world teacher." Besant was thrilled with the idea and agreed, creating special orders within the society to promote her "World Teacher Project."

Krishnamurti played the part of a Theosophical saint for many years, but his avatarship was not accepted by all Theosophists. One in particular, Rudolf Steiner, rejected it vehemently and left Theosophy to start his own movement. Eventually Krishnamurti himself was not happy with his role, and in 1929, at the age of thirty-four, at a large Theosophical gathering, he renounced both his "god-manship" and Theosophy. "Truth," he said, "was a pathless land," one best entered by clearing the mind and allowing the inner silence to be heard, a doctrine similar to the *via negativa* of Meister Eckhart and *The Cloud of Unknowing*. Krishnamurti went on to become an influential itinerant nonteacher of a nondoctrine, traveling around the world, put up by affluent hosts, and inspiring important figures such as Aldous Huxley, Igor Stravinsky, and the physicist David Bohm.[18] He died in 1986.

Leadbeater's "discovery" seemed dubious to many because of his known predilection for young boys, and prior to Krishnamurti, he had already "discovered" two other candidates for the role of "world teacher"; what became of them is unclear. He had also got into Theosophical hot water in 1906 when it came out that he had taught some adolescent Theosophists the basics in masturbation, an ironic echo of Besant's own earlier advocacy of sex education. Yet it was his clairvoyant abilities that enabled Besant to outpace her rivals.

They met in 1890, and after Blavatsky's passing, Leadbeater became Besant's "channel" to the Masters. They had by now become something more than remarkable men, possessed of incredible powers but still flesh and blood, as they had always been for HPB. With Besant and Leadbeater, they were transformed into something more supernatural, and it is with them that the road to the "ascended Masters," by now traveled by many, begins. Besant had little clairvoyant ability—Leadbeater tutored her in it—but the two began a kind of "open door" policy on the astral plane, making it very difficult to verify or disprove anyone's claim to have spoken with a Master or traveled to Atlantis the night before.

Their efforts did garner some results, some of which we have already seen. In another joint work, *Occult Chemistry* (1908), Besant and Leadbeater clairvoyantly investigated the structure of atoms. While this may seem doubtful, there is some possibility that through Stan Gooch's "direct perception," they did achieve some knowledge "even of atomic and molecular structure." In a book called *Extra-sensory Perception of Quarks*, Stephen Phillips, a professor of particle physics, suggests that in describing the structure of a hydrogen atom clairvoyantly, Besant and Leadbeater had hit on the existence of "quarks," strange subatomic particles that were first proposed by the physicist Murray Gell-Mann in 1961. Phillips maintains that the picture of the hydrogen atom given in *Occult Chemistry* would have looked ridiculous to any scientist in 1908, well before the existence of quarks was even suspected, but that today it is not so strange and bears an eerie resemblance to Gell-Mann's model.[19]

HOME RULE

Besant and Leadbeater's clairvoyant claims may be questioned, but what is not in doubt is the success Besant had with more verifiable achievements. Not surprisingly, these came in the realm of politics. In 1893, Besant went to India, where she was met by Olcott, and her journeys around the subcontinent were like a royal procession, with huge crowds turning out to see her. Blavatsky was critical of the British Raj and had always spoken out for Indian independence; along with A. P. Sinnett, who promoted Theosophy during his editorship of the Allahabad *Pioneer,* one of her important Indian converts was A. O. Hume, a British Hinduphile who in 1885 had organized the first meeting of the Indian National Congress. Now a reforming firebrand Theosophist who had fought for the weak and oppressed had landed on India's shores.

For many, promoting Indian spirituality was tantamount to supporting Indian independence, and the thousands who heard Besant's speeches made this known. Like HPB before her, Besant "went native," learning Sanskrit, wearing local dress, and starting a Central Hindu College; her aim was much like Plato's with his Academy millennia earlier: to secure new leadership for India's future. She joined the Indian National Congress and designed its banner, and it would be through the Congress that Gandhi would eventually achieve an independent India. (In his book on Home Rule, Gandhi said that in the early days, all the top members of the Congress were Theosophists.)

It was Besant who initiated Jawaharlal Nehru into the society. Besant campaigned for Indian independence for the rest of her life, a cause that landed her in much trouble. At the outbreak of World War I, she risked charges of treason by borrowing a phrase from her Irish Home Rule campaign: "England's need is India's opportunity"; and as editor of *New India*, she fiercely criticized British rule. In 1916, she started the All India Home Rule League and led it in massive demonstrations. Ordered to leave India in 1917, she refused and was arrested; in the garden of her compound, she flew a red and green flag, India's colors. Nationwide protests demanded her release, and Gandhi wrote letters to the government calling for her freedom. The British were forced to back down, and amid assurances that an independent India was its ultimate aim, released Besant. Her freedom triggered a national celebration and she was made president of the National Congress. Besant died in 1933 (Leadbeater followed the next year), and in 1947, her cause prevailed when India became an independent nation.

OUSPENSKY'S FOURTH DIMENSION

The Russian philosopher and writer P. D. Ouspensky came to Theosophy in 1907, in his late twenties, and remained in the society until the outbreak of World War I. Although early on he recognized Theosophy's faults—that its initial creative surge had hardened into dogma—Theosophical ideas remained with him throughout his life. He was always proud of the fact that during his "search for the miraculous" he was treated as an esoteric V.I.P. when he visited the society's headquarters at Adyar. The compound's three floors indicated a visitor's importance. The ground floor was open to hangers-on, and the second to important financial donors. But the top floor was reserved solely for visitors of the highest Theosophical rank. Ouspensky was admitted to this group immediately on his arrival. According to his contemporary, the Christian existentialist philosopher Nikolai Berdyaev, a critic of Blavatsky and Steiner, Ouspensky was "the most independent and talented Theosophical writer we have." Like Orage, Ouspensky brought a disciplined, critical mind to his esoteric studies, and his brilliance shines through in his writings.

Ouspensky was interested in the "miraculous" from a young age, and one question that obsessed him throughout his life was the mystery of time. Like the writer J. B. Priestley, who was influenced by his ideas, Ouspensky was a "time-haunted man." One expression of this was his fascination with Nietzsche's idea of the "eternal recurrence," the belief that our lives are repeated over and over without change throughout eternity. For Nietzsche, such cosmic reruns were a test of one's ability to affirm life—only the superman, Nietzsche believed, was strong enough to do so—but Ouspensky thought more of how one could escape the wheel of repetition. His novel *Strange Life of Ivan Osokin* (1915), an inspiration for Harold Ramis's film *Groundhog Day*, explored this theme, and in his last days Ouspensky tried to fix the memories of his life in his consciousness so that next time he "recurred," he would *remember*.

Ouspensky was also fascinated with the idea of the "fourth dimension," a late nineteenth-century philosophical puzzle that captured the attention of figures like Albert Einstein and H. G. Wells, whose debut work, *The Time Machine*, popularized it. As chaos theory and fractals enjoyed wide attention in the 1990s, the fourth dimension became a kind of craze during the fin-de-siècle. The writer Charles Hinton wrote several popular books on the subject—he coined the term "tesseract," meaning a "four-dimensional cube"—and developed what he called the "Hinton cube," something like a multicolored Rubik's cube made of smaller movable cubes, that would enable one to see things "four dimensionally."

Many settled for seeing the "fourth dimension" as time, but Ouspensky expanded on the idea, as well as the number of dimensions, and in his still exciting and widely influential metaphysical, work, *Tertium Organum*, (*The Third Organ of Thought*, 1912), superseding Aristotle's and Francis Bacon's—he brought together Hermetic, Theosophical, Neoplatonic, and philosophical ideas to argue his basic vision: the need to go beyond the positivistic logic that dominated the philosophy of the time and reduced the world to the kind of dead mechanism associated with an extreme left-brain perspective.

Ouspensky's inspiration for *Tertium Organum* came from many sources—Nietzsche, Kant, mathematics, Blavatsky, Plotinus, Kabbalah, Hermeticism, nature, sex, art, poetry, and literature—and with *Isis Unveiled,* the book is an attempt to achieve a new Pansophic vision, uniting mysticism and science. One source of Ouspensky's inspiration was the series of experiments with altered states of consciousness he conducted using nitrous oxide and hashish in his small apartment in St. Petersburg sometime around 1911, and which we touched on in Chapter Six. Ouspensky was familiar with William James's account of his own nitrous oxide experiment and with Bucke's *Cosmic Consciousness,* and he discusses both at length.

He was also familiar with the work of his older contemporary, the now forgotten poet and social reformer Edward Carpenter, an intimate of Walt Whitman, whom Bucke considered a modern example of cosmic consciousness. Carpenter's book *Civilization: Its Cause and Cure* (1889), an early argument for "dropping out," can be seen as an inspiration for social experiments like Monte Verità, and like Orage he embodied a medley of the forms of the "new life" cropping up at the time. An early gay activist among other things, Carpenter was also a Fabian socialist, a vegetarian, and a leader of "dress reform"; we have him to thank for the fashion of wearing sandals in the summer. More important, in his book *From Adam's Peak to Elephanta,* published in 1892, about his journey through Ceylon and India, Carpenter describes his mystical experiences of "consciousness without thought." It was these and his Whitmanesque poem *Toward Democracy* (1883) that Bucke saw as evidence of cosmic consciousness.

Ouspensky's own account of his consciousness experiments should be read by anyone interested in understanding the fundamental realities underpinning the esoteric view. His initial access to these inner worlds revealed to him that he had entered a dimension of total unity in which there was "nothing separate, that is, nothing that can be named or described separately." Ouspensky had experienced "the network of connections linking everything with everything else," the fundamental *relationality* of consciousness. Among paranormal and magical experiences—too many to describe here—Ouspensky was also struck by his strange ability to "enter into" things, to feel himself part of them, as Bergson said was true of intuition and Schwaller de Lubicz said of the "intelligence of the heart."

Ouspensky belonged to the generation of "God Seekers" that characterized Russia's esoteric fin-de-siècle—Berdyaev and Vladimir Soloviev were among them—and his work influenced the Russian avant-garde. As Besant and Leadbeater's *Thought Forms* influenced Kandinsky, Ouspensky's *Tertium Organum* inspired many artists seeking new directions for their work. One of these was the painter Kazimir Malevich, with Kandinsky and Mondrian one of the creators of abstract art, who attended some of Ouspensky's lectures. In his translation of the first major book about Cubism, *Du Cubisme* (1912) by Albert Gleizes and Jean Metzinger, the artist Mikhail Matiushin includes passages from *Tertium Organum,* linking Ouspensky's ideas to the new "aperspectival" art—in Jean Gebser's term—emerging with Picasso and Braque in Paris.

Ouspensky understood the visionary function of art, and the ability of the imagination to open other worlds. "In art it is necessary to study 'occultism,'" he wrote. "The artist must be clairvoyant; he must see that which others do not see; he must be a magician."[20] Ouspensky himself was a regular at the Stray Dog Café, a St. Petersburg bohemian watering hole, where he hoisted glasses with the avant-garde elite such as the poets Vladimir Mayakovsky and Anna Akhmatova. Other regulars were the novelists Andrei Bely, whose *Petersburg* (1916) is a hallucinatory modernist novel filled with occult ideas—mostly taken from Rudolf Steiner; and Valery Bryusov, whose *The Fiery Angel* (1908) is a classic account of witchcraft, in which Cornelius Agrippa is a character.[21] At one point Ouspensky even explained the fourth dimension to Leo Tolstoy, mapping out its contours on a tablecloth, while Tolstoy spoke of how his experiences with Freemasonry informed *War and Peace.*

DR. STEINER, I PRESUME?

Another thinker to emerge from the Theosophical milieu who combined an interest in esotericism with an acute philosophical mind was Rudolf Steiner. As mentioned, Steiner broke with Theosophy over Besant's and Leadbeater's promotion of Krishnamurti as the new world teacher. But even before this, he had his own ideas about how esotericism should be pursued. Where Blavatsky and Besant looked toward the East, Steiner was adamantly western, and the Anthroposophy he developed after 1912 was a unique amalgam of Theosophy, German philosophy, and esoteric Christianity.

Steiner was born in 1861 in Kraljevec, a small rural town in what was then Hungary but is now part of Croatia. From an early age he showed signs of clairvoyance. His father worked on the railway, and one day sitting in the station, Steiner saw a strange woman whom he didn't know but who bore a strong resemblance to members of his family. She said, "Try to help me as much as you can—now as well as in later life," then vanished. Steiner kept this to himself but when he saw his father, he noticed he was sad and then learned that a female relative had committed suicide at the same time as the mysterious woman had appeared to him. Like Swedenborg and William Blake, Steiner was a born visionary, and while other boys were busy playing games he was preoccupied with the spirit world.

Something else that preoccupied the young Steiner was geometry. It had the same effect on him as on Pythagoras and Plato, that of introducing him to another world, that of ideas and logical relations, which, although intangible, was as real, if not more so, as the physical world. Steiner was deeply introverted and it was relief for him when he discovered that "one can work out forms which are seen purely inwardly, independent of the outer world." This came as a consolation to the young boy, who felt isolated because no one he knew could answer the many questions that filled his mind. "To be able to grasp something purely spiritual brought me an inner joy," Steiner wrote in his *Autobiography*. "Through geometry," Steiner said, "I first experienced happiness."

This combination of psychic ability and scientific precision characterized Steiner's approach to esoteric knowledge. For him, geometry and his psychic visions occupied the same "spiritual space," an interior universe that was the "setting for spiritual beings and events." Thoughts for the young Steiner were not "mere pictures we form of things"; they were instead "revelations of a spiritual world seen on the stage of the soul." As many secret teachers did, Steiner recognized that our inner world is just as objective as the outer one. As he would later tell his students, the triangles that you or I visualize in our minds are not separate, different triangles, but the same one, just as the ideas of truth, beauty, or goodness we reflect on are not separate ideas, "personal" to ourselves, but objective realities that we encounter, just as we encounter objective realities in the physical world.

Steiner's geometrical insights were soon informed by his wide reading in science and German Idealist philosophy, thinkers like Kant, Schelling, and Hegel, and his psychic experiences found some guidance through meeting a curious individual. At eighteen, while on the train to Vienna, where he studied at the Institute of Technology, Steiner met Felix Koguzki, a middle-age herb gatherer and "simple man of the people." Felix too saw spirits, not only of the dead, but of "living nature," the sort of perception that Paracelsus and Boehme had of the "signature of things." Steiner was relieved to find someone he could talk to about his psychic experiences, and Koguzki shared his insights and understanding of the spirit world with the young visionary.

Steiner believed their encounter was not by chance, and soon after meeting Koguzki, Steiner had another meeting. This was with someone he called "the Master." Who this was is unknown; all we know about him is that he told Steiner that he would find much significance in some passages of the philosopher Fichte, a follower of Kant and friend of Novalis. Fichte wanted to understand the *active* nature of the mind, an insight that would inform the philosopher Husserl's reflections on the "intentionality" of consciousness, touched on in Chapter Ten. The Master also told Steiner that in order to overcome the materialism of the modern world—a mission that, like Madame Blavatsky, Steiner embraced—he would have to begin by understanding it. Steiner did, complementing his psychic experiences and study of idealist philosophy with a solid grounding in nineteenth-century science.

FROM ACTIVE SEEING TO
SUPERSENSIBLE PERCEPTION

The most powerful influence on Steiner, however, was, as mentioned, Goethe, and Steiner first came to public attention as the editor of Goethe's scientific writing. Steiner saw a link between Goethe's "active seeing" and his own recognition of the objective reality of ideas, thoughts, and spirits. It was through a combination of these that he developed his notion of "supersensible perception," the ability to perceive realities of the spirit through a process of thought, a cognition that went beyond the senses. Unlike trance states and mediumship, Steiner's "supersensible perception" was a wholly conscious activity, one that could be pursued through a series of conscious mental exercises, much as Plotinus believed that realization of the One could be achieved through conscious reflection alone. In his book *Knowledge of the Higher Worlds and Its Attainment* (1905), Steiner outlined a process through which one could learn how to achieve "supersensible perception" by developing the powers of intuition, inspiration, and imagination. Steiner was a remarkably versatile individual, and the results of his "supersensible perception" would enjoy a wide application, informing architecture, farming, dance, art, theater, education, and medicine.

Steiner spelled out his ideas about the irreducible reality of the "I," the active nature of thinking, and the fundamental fact of spiritual freedom in his major philosophical work, *The Philosophy of Freedom*, published in 1894. The scientific thinking he was at pains to understand denied the reality of the "I," and reduced its apparent free will to an illusion, as much of contemporary philosophy of mind still does. But Steiner insisted that it is only as a "spiritually free being" that we can engage in thinking at all. Steiner had rediscovered the essential insight, first voiced by the French philosopher Maine de Biran in the early nineteenth century, that when I make an *effort*, I have a direct, unmediated experience of my free will. By definition, no effort can be mechanical. No machine can pull itself together, grit its teeth, and "try harder." Only a being with free will can do that. Yet it was not as a philosopher that Steiner made his mark. Steiner sent a copy of his book to Eduard von Hartmann, author of the once immensely popular *The Philosophy of the Unconscious* (1869), eager to hear his response. Hartmann had a thoroughly pessimistic view of human consciousness—it was, he believed, merely a light illuminating a meaningless world—and thought Steiner had simply muddled the question.

STEINER AND THEOSOPHY

After unsuccessful attempts to launch himself in the literary worlds of Vienna and Berlin, Steiner became a kind of freelance intellectual, lecturing to whoever would have him. Like the Pansophists of old, Steiner was a polymath, and he spoke on a variety of topics, from Marxism to mathematics. In 1900, Steiner was asked to speak to the Berlin branch of the Theosophical Society on the philosophy of Nietzsche. Soon after, he was asked to return to lecture on Goethe's *Fairy Tale of the Green Snake and the Beautiful Lily*. Steiner was a success, and for the first time, he felt he could speak about his spiritual insights in public. More lectures followed. It was clear that Steiner spoke from experience, and also that his vision was focused more on the western spiritual tradition than that of the East. Steiner spoke of Christ's incarnation as the culmination of the ancient Mystery tradition that included Plato, Pythagoras, and the pre-Socratics. Later, Steiner's "supersensible" reading of the Akashic record would reveal mankind's participation in a vast cosmic evolutionary process, stretching back to our pre-physical origins in the spiritual planes.

Steiner's different spiritual "epochs" parallel the Gnostic, Hermetic, and Neoplatonic emanationist "ladder of being" mentioned throughout this book. In books like *An Outline of Occult Science* (1910) and *Cosmic Memory* (1937)—a collection of essays originally published in Steiner's magazine *Lucifer-Gnosis*—Steiner shared his vision of the "evolution of consciousness," which is simultaneously an evolution of the cosmos. This began in an unmanifest source Steiner called "Old Saturn," and gradually solidified through stages he calls "Old Sun" and "Old Moon" into our present physical cosmos, subject to the senses. This incarnation, however, was necessary for the development of our independent egos, and it triggers the ascent back to the spirit realms, through our coming "Jupiter" stage, then through "Venus" and "Vulcan." The similarity with the Hermetic journey through the planets seems clear. The midpoint of this process for Steiner was Christ's incarnation and crucifixion—"the Mystery of Golgotha"—which he considered the single most important event in human history.[22]

In 1902, Steiner was asked to become the head of the Theosophical Society's German branch. Within a few years his importance in the society rivaled Annie Besant's, and the two would have more than one difference of opinion. Steiner crisscrossed Europe, lecturing almost nonstop—he gave some six thousand talks in his lifetime—informing his audiences about reincarnation, the etheric body, the Akashic record, Atlantis, Lemuria, as well as health, diet, art, and much more. His central idea, which we can appreciate whether or not we accept Theosophy or Anthroposophy, is a form of the participatory consciousness we have explored in this book. In his early work, *Goethe's Conception of the World*, published in 1897, Steiner wrote, "Man is not there [in existence] in order to form for himself a picture of the finished world; nay, he himself cooperates in bringing the world into existence." It is through our consciousness, our *ideas*, that the world, for Steiner, becomes "complete." Without our imaginative contribution, all that remains are empty, physical forms.

As had Blavatsky, Steiner believed that mankind was involved in a tremendous struggle against the forces of materialism, which Steiner embodied in the form of the spiritual being Ahriman, the destructive spirit of Zoroastrianism. Along with his counterpart, Lucifer (the fallen angel and spirit of hubris who tempts man with the illusion of pride), Ahriman seeks to deflect humanity from its true evolution by inculcating the belief in a dead, mechanical world, subject to the requirements of technology. As mentioned in the Introduction, it was the creative mediation between these two forces, which left on their own are highly destructive, that Steiner saw as the task of mankind.

THE END OF OLD EUROPE

On June 28, 1914, Archduke Franz Ferdinand of Austria and his wife, the Duchess of Hohenberg, were shot dead in Sarajevo, Bosnia. Their assassin was Gavrilo Princip, a Bosnian Serb, Yugoslavian nationalist, and member of the Black Hand secret society. A month later, Europe erupted into World War I. Although the twentieth century was midway into its second decade, the hostilities that had the armies of Great Britain, France, and Russia on one side, and of Germany and Austria-Hungary on the other killing each other—and which soon drew in Italy, Japan, Turkey, Bulgaria, Romania, the United States, and other countries—can be seen as the true end of the nineteenth century.

The peace and prosperity of La Belle Époque were over, and chaos and barbarity had descended on the world. The positive thrust of the fin-de-siècle was cut short and the optimism that had energized the age had vanished. After an initial spurt of mobilization and hopes for an early decisive victory, the German advance on Paris stalled, and the deadly tedium of trench warfare began. A great gouge known as the Western Front sliced through Belgium, France, and Germany from the North Sea to Switzerland, on opposite sides of which the Allies and the Central Powers maintained a murderous stalemate, with many lives lost for no appreciable gain. In the end, four years later, after a costly Allied victory, some sixteen million people, combatants and civilians combined, had died and much of the Continent was devastated. "Old western culture," as C. S. Lewis called it, was no more. A sense of the impact of the "Great War"—which, until its outbreak seemed unthinkable—can be seen in the title of the Viennese satirist Karl Kraus's play about it, *The Last Days of Mankind*.

Along with its own carnage, the war brought famine, disease, economic collapse, revolution, and the end of empire. When the smoke from the "guns of August" cleared, the Ottoman and Austro-Hungarian empires had ceased to exist. Russia had exploded in a violent Marxist revolution and subsequent civil war; with Germany, where there was fighting in the streets, apparently about to do the same. It was supposed to be the "war to end all wars," a phrase associated with the American president Woodrow Wilson, but which originated with H. G. Wells.[23]

Sadly, Wells, an otherwise very accurate prophet, missed the mark on this one, and twenty years after the armistice on November 11, 1918, Europe and the rest of the world was poised to do it again. A new age had indeed emerged, but with a few possible exceptions—Aleister Crowley had, it is true, envisaged a coming era of "force and fire"—it was not one most visionaries had expected. A few years into the brooding decades *entre-deux-guerres*, the poet T. S. Eliot—himself no mean student of esoteric philosophy—captured the defeated spirit of the time in his poem

The Waste Land, which appeared in 1922 and marked the fractured, broken, alienated mood that would dominate henceforth. With its references to the Tarot, Madame Blavatsky, Hermann Hesse, the Grail legends, *The Golden Bough*, and the Upanishads, Eliot's modernist manifesto remains an example of how esoteric ideas continued to inform the western mind, even as the shadow of meaninglessness crept over its consciousness.

The war would bring different challenges to the new era's secret teachers and it would introduce some new names to their roster. It would also usher in what seems a kind of "golden age" of modern western esotericism, a period when some of the most important and influential figures were working at the same time and in relatively the same place. This "golden age" would eventually lead to our own time, when the teachers were no longer so secret and what they taught became more readily available.

But before this, one rather secretive secret teacher made a somewhat startling debut.

MEETING A REMARKABLE MAN

The beginning of the war found P. D. Ouspensky returning to Russia after his "search for the miraculous" had left him empty-handed. He had gone to Egypt, India, Ceylon, and other places in order to discover "the unknown" and to find "schools" and "teachers" who could show him the way to it. His search had been unsuccessful and the war now seemed to throw his efforts into chaos. He saw it stoically as "one of those generally catastrophic conditions of life in the midst of which we have to live and work and seek answers to our questions and doubts."[24] Ouspensky did not find what he was seeking amid the pyramids of Egypt or the ashrams of India, but in early 1915, in a small, rather seedy backstreet café in Moscow, the miraculous, it seemed, found him.

It appeared in the form of a "Caucasian Greek," a "certain G," whose followers had entreated Ouspensky, a well-known journalist and writer, to meet, and who had been charged with the task of "ensnaring" Ouspensky into such a meeting.[25] Just as Madame Blavatsky had gone out of her way to meet and seduce Colonel Olcott—their relationship was Platonic, but this is the correct word—the disciples of this "certain G" had been given the task of reading Ouspensky's works and ensuring that he would agree to meet their master who, it appears, had plans for him. After a fruitless, months'-long search for "teachers" and "schools," Ouspensky was not in the market for a guru, but after meeting this "certain G," he had indisputably found one. The result can be found in Ouspensky's posthumously published masterpiece *In Search of the Miraculous* (1949), an account of his years as this "certain G's" student, and still the best introduction to his ideas.

Ouspensky's "G" was Georges Ivanovitch Gurdjieff, an enigmatic Greek-Armenian-Russian esoteric teacher whose name has turned up several times throughout this book. Like Madame Blavatsky's, Gurdjieff's early years are wrapped in mystery, an ambiguity that, also like Madame Blavatsky, Gurdjieff went out of his way to perpetuate. Even the year of his birth is uncertain, given variously as 1866, 1872, 1874, and 1877, depending on which biography you read. More certain is his place of birth, which, depending on the year was either under Turkish rule and called Gümrü or under Russian rule and called Alexandropol. At any rate, it and the town Gurdjieff's family moved to when he was a boy, Kars, are now part of Armenia. Gurdjieff grew up in a racial, national, linguistic, and cultural melting pot, a turbulent, unsettled, and shifting world that demanded one think on one's feet, a talent Gurdjieff labored hard to pass on to his students.

From the moment he met Gurdjieff, Ouspensky was impressed. He was, it seemed, a man who *knew*. Gurdjieff knew of Ouspensky's travels and he spoke to him of places he knew well and of which Ouspensky had only heard. They spoke of yoga, India, esotericism, "schools," and the use of drugs to induce unusual states of consciousness. But what struck Ouspensky most was Gurdjieff's insistence on what at first seemed to him an absurd idea but which soon became a central tenet of his own philosophy.

Human beings, Gurdjieff told Ouspensky, are asleep. They are machines who believe they are awake and possess free will. But they are really only machines whose every action, every thought, is mechanical. "All the people you see, all the people you know," Gurdjieff told Ouspensky, "all the people *you may get to know*, are machines, actual machines working solely under the power of external influences."[26] Ouspensky was at first put off by this sweeping indictment of humanity's unconsciousness. It was, in essence, identical to ideas about human psychology promoted by the reductionist science Ouspensky had opposed in *Tertium Organum*. But with a world exploding into war, with each side blaming the other, he had ample evidence to judge its accuracy.

REMEMBER YOUR SELf

Ouspensky was struck by Gurdjieff's knowledge, which combined a psychological acuity equal to Freud's or Nietzsche's with a cosmology that, at first sight, seems frankly outlandish. Many of Gurdjieff's insights into human weakness Ouspensky had come to on his own, but one psychological oddity Gurdjieff spoke of seemed a revelation. This was the notion of "self-remembering," the observation that human beings do not "remember" themselves.

Absorbed in the demands of life, we forget our own existence; we take it for granted, and suffer, as Gurdjieff's younger contemporary, Martin Heidegger put it, a "forgetfulness of being."[27] For most of our life, "we" do not exist—that is, we do not possess a vivid, vital awareness of our own being. It is only in moments of crisis, or when we find ourselves in some strange, new environment—say, finding ourselves alone in a city we have never visited—that an awareness of our own existence comes over us and we have the slightly uncanny feeling of "What? Me, here?" With this often comes a vivid recognition that much of our life is lived in a dream. Ouspensky's own deep ponderings on time, eternal recurrence, and the disorienting feeling of déjà vu, the sense that he had been here *before*, made the importance of "remembering himself" that much more urgent.

I would suggest that the "forgetfulness of being" that Gurdjieff and Heidegger recognized in human consciousness stems from our overly dominant left brain, which reduces the richness of experience to easily managed "symbols," dehydrated surfaces of life through which we can easily maneuver. This allows us to cope with an increasingly complex and demanding environment, but at the expense of living a kind of "half-life," which is doubly dangerous because we mistakenly accept it as the "real thing." It is only in moments of crisis or deep relaxation that, in Yeats's phrase, we complete our "partial mind"—allow in right-brain vividness—and, to paraphrase the poet, for an instant stand at ease, laugh aloud, our hearts at peace—feel, that is, fully alive and are amazed at it, something that occurs to anyone who has ever shaken off their "forgetfulness of being."[28]

FOOD FOR THE MOON

But these moments of self-remembering, at least according to Gurdjieff, are few and far between. Everything around us, Gurdjieff told Ouspensky, encourages our "self-forgetting," this "forgetfulness of being," and it is only through determined and continued efforts at "wakefulness" that we can escape it. This "work," as Gurdjieff's teaching came to be called, is, as the ancient alchemists knew of their work, "against nature." For nature's purposes, it is well that we "sleep," as, contrary to our high opinion of ourselves, we play a rather humble role in the great scheme of things. If we knew the true "terror of the situation," it would, Gurdjieff believed, drive us mad.

The truth about our place in the cosmos is that we are what Gurdjieff called "food for the moon." This requires some explanation.

Gurdjieff's system—often known as the "Fourth Way," to distinguish it from the "way" of the fakir (body), monk (emotions), or yogi (mind)—speaks of what he calls "the Ray of Creation," a variant of the Neoplatonic "Great Chain of Being." For Gurdjieff, this begins with the "Absolute" then passes through "All Worlds"—all the galaxies in the universe—then to "All Suns"—the stars in our galaxy—then our sun, the planets in our solar system, and the Earth, to end in the moon, which for Gurdjieff was the lowest step on his ladder of being.[29]

Unlike the Great Chain of Being, which has a static, timeless character, Gurdjieff's "Ray" is active, is still growing, and the moon is its point of growth. The entire universe, Gurdjieff believed, is alive, an idea he shared with Henri Bergson and Alfred North Whitehead, as well as with the late *Naturphilosopher* Gustav Fechner, who first suggested that our Earth was a single organism, much in advance of James Lovelock's "Gaia" hypothesis, proposed in 1974.[30] The moon is growing into a planet, Gurd-jieff suggested, and Jupiter, the biggest planet in our solar system, is growing into a sun. Whatever we may think of this, the upshot is that the moon "grows" by feeding on organic life on Earth. "Everything living on the earth, people, animals, plants, is food for the moon."[31] The moon is fed by the life energy that organisms give off at death. In the case of humans, this is the soul.

It is not a good thing to find yourself feeding the moon. The moon, for Gurdjieff, is subject to many "laws"—ninety-six, to be exact—and the souls trapped there live a kind of mineral existence and cannot escape. But we can avoid this fate by making "efforts," by "working on ourselves," by trying to wake up, by defeating our mechanicalness—the left brain, remember, works best with machines—by struggling to achieve a state of "self-remembering." By doing this, we not only avoid feeding the moon, we free ourselves of the "laws" we are subject to here on Earth. We can then move up the Ray of Creation, against the stream, as it were, and journey back to the Absolute, which is the source of consciousness, will, and freedom. The similarity to the Hermetic journey through the planets seems apparent, as does the Gnostic theme of "escape." The Earth, Gurdjieff told Ouspensky, was in a very bad place in the universe, and he likened our position to that of inmates in a prison, or sheep awaiting slaughter.

Gurdjieff told Ouspensky of other cosmic "laws," such as the "law of octaves," also known as the "law of seven," and the "law of three." Gurdjieff's octave—again an echo of Pythagoras and the seven ancient planets—explains how something that begins one way invariably turns into its opposite, a theory of *enantiodromia* that accounts for how Christianity began as a religion of love and turned into intolerance and persecution, or how the *liberté, égalité,* and *fraternité* of the French Revolution became the guillotine.[32] The "law of three," "a fundamental law" responsible for all phenomena in the universe, declares that everything is "the result of the combination or the meeting of three different opposing forces."[33] As mentioned, Gurdjieff's "law of three" has Pythagorean roots—as does his belief that the universe consists of vibrations—and is in the company of Hinduism's "three *gunas*"; alchemy's sulfur, mercury, and salt; Boehme's worlds of love and wrath; and Jung's "transcendent function."

SEEKERS Of TRUTH

Where did Gurdjieff learn these laws? Gurdjieff told Ouspensky that in his early days, he belonged to a group of like-minded individuals, "specialists" that, in *Meetings with Remarkable Men* (1963), an account of his early years, he called the "Seekers of Truth." Like many of our secret teachers, as a young man Gurdjieff was fascinated by the mysterious side of life and had a passionate curiosity about the occult, the mystical, and the supernatural. In his adolescence and teens, he encountered precognition, faith healing, spiritualism, even vampirism. A powerful sense of the living reality of the past, of tradition, came to him when he recognized that the poem his father, a bard, recited came from the epic *Gilgamesh*, fragments of which had only recently been discovered. His search led through religion, philosophy, science, but neither priests nor doctors nor scientists could answer his questions. His need to know and to understand his experience led him to join with others with a similar passion—as had Madame Blavatsky—and they banded together to explore ancient sites, to study ancient texts, and to find those then alive who *knew*.

This search, Gurdjieff tells us, led him through Egypt, the Holy Lands, and Central Asia; and on one adventure he found his way to a hidden monastery of an ancient secret society known as the "Sarmoung Brotherhood." The brotherhood flourished in ancient times—2500 B.C., to be exact—but remnants of it still existed. In *Meetings with Remarkable Men*, Gurdjieff speaks of being blindfolded and taken to a secret location somewhere in Turkestan, where he learned, among other things, the "laws" of three and seven. These were taught in the form of "sacred dances" and through the use of a strange apparatus, a kind of tripod with seven arms, each of which was subdivided into seven segments. These could be arranged in different ways and read as a kind of "cosmic alphabet."

Some, like J. G. Bennett, believed in the reality of the Sarmoung Brotherhood and linked it to a Sufi brotherhood known as the Naq'shbandis.[34] Others, however, will consider Gurdjieff's brotherhood something more along the lines of Madame Blavatsky's secret monastery in Tibet. As strict autobiography, *Meetings with Remarkable Men* should be read with several helpings of salt; Gurdjieff's penchant for leg-pulling is well known, another trait he shared with Madame Blavatsky. Yet whatever the reality of Gurdjieff's ancient brotherhood, the insights he says he gained among them are less questionable and have practical applications that soon convince of their value.

A MIRACULOUS ESCAPE

Gurdjieff came to wide notice in 1921, when Ouspensky escaped a White Russian refugee camp in Constantinople and was miraculously transported to London, courtesy of a wealthy reader of *Tertium Organum*.[35] It had become a huge success a year earlier, after the American writer and architect Claude Bragdon, like Ouspensky a devotee of "higher dimensions," published it in an English translation. While Ouspensky taught English to fellow Russian refugees in order to feed his family, *Tertium Organum* was being hailed on both sides of the Atlantic, with important writers like Hart Crane singing its praises. It was with much difficulty and through the efforts of Orage, who had met Ouspensky and had published him in *The New Age*, that Ouspensky learned of this, received much-needed royalties, and obtained his ticket to freedom. Ouspensky had found himself washed to Europe's edges by the Russian Revolution, which had exploded while he and several others were under Gurdjieff's tutelage. The account of their journeys across a country collapsing into chaos makes *In Search of the Miraculous* not only a central work of modern esotericism, but a thrilling and inspiring spiritual adventure story.

On his arrival in England, Ouspensky's savior, Lady Rothermere, wife of a powerful newspaper baron, arranged for him to lecture to the cream of London's intelligentsia. Some of the names in Ouspensky's audience included T. S. Eliot, Aldous Huxley, Gerald Heard, Algernon Blackwood, and Orage.[36] Ouspensky would also lecture to G. R. S. Mead's Quest Society, which Mead had started in reaction to Annie Besant's "neo-theosophy."

All of these writers and thinkers would be influenced by Ouspensky's ideas—Eliot's *Four Quartets*, for example, are filled with Ouspenskian reflections on time—but what startled many that evening was Ouspensky's rejection of *Tertium Organum* and his advocacy of Gurdjieff's grim doctrine. And when Gurdjieff arrived a year later and opened his Institute for the Harmonious Development of Man in the forest of Fontainebleau, just outside of Paris, many who had heard Ouspensky's stark teaching journeyed across the English Channel to learn from the master himself.

One of these was Orage, who went on to become one of Gurdjieff's most important disciples. Another was Maurice Nicoll, a successful psychologist who, with Orage and a few like-minded individuals, had started a "Psychosynthesis Group" to compensate for the fragmenting effect they felt that Freud's psychoanalysis was having. When Nicoll heard Ouspensky, he felt the teacher he had prayed for had arrived. When he headed to Fontainebleau, he knew that if anyone could synthesize his psyche, it was Gurdjieff.

Nicoll was quite a catch. He had been handpicked by Freud's crown prince and later rival to represent his own variant of psychoanalysis, "analytical psychology," in Great Britain. The mentor Nicoll had thrown over to join Gurdjieff's work was C. G. Jung.

THE MADNESS OF C. G. JUNG

Just before the outset of World War I, the Swiss psychologist Carl Gustav Jung feared for his sanity. A falling-out with his friend and mentor, Sigmund Freud, the Viennese founder of psychoanalysis who looked to Jung as his successor, had precipitated a nervous breakdown which Jung's keen professional expertise recognized was developing into a full-blown psychosis. At any rate, it was certainly a textbook example of what Henri Ellenberger called a "creative illness."

In October 1913, a short time after the publication of his first book, *Symbols of Transformation*, announced his rejection of Freud's sexual theory of neurosis—and made his first tentative approach toward the "collective unconscious"—Jung found himself on a train. The journey from Zurich to Schaffhausen was not long, but it took Jung to another world. In a vision, he saw a great flood washing over Europe. Debris and bodies floated on the waves, which soon turned to blood. The vision lasted some time and was like a dream that had *invaded* Jung's consciousness. Other dreams did too, all with the same apocalyptic message. Having treated many patients with similar complaints during his years at Zurich's Burghölzli Mental Clinic, Jung had cause to be concerned. It is ironic, then, that in July 1914, Jung greeted the announcement of war with some relief. He was not, it appeared, going mad. He had simply seen the future.

Such an experience would have frightened Freud, who while privately accepting the paranormal, publicly rejected it. Yet while Jung's visions had been disturbing, the fact that they were evidence of psychic activity rather than madness comforted him. Throughout most of his career, Jung kept his deep, personal interest in the occult, the supernatural, and the "night side of nature" relatively discreet, but the truth was that these pursuits were in his DNA. His grandfather, mother, and other relatives were psychic, and Jung grew up in an atmosphere of spirits, séances, poltergeists, and premonitions.

His desire to maintain a respectable scientific reputation led Jung to mute his interest in occult phenomena until a near-death experience in 1944 convinced him it was time to come out of the paranormal closet.[37] Jung did, and although he still prevaricated, prefacing his revelations with "scientific" disclaimers, he got the message across. In the last years of his life—he died in 1961—Jung became the most widely known and publicly respected figure to take the occult, esoteric, Hermetic, and magical tradition seriously. He was never accepted by the mainstream intelligentsia, but at a grassroots level, Jung's ideas spread, and he is certainly one of the forefathers of our own New Age movement. In many ways, as Madame Blavatsky had opened the door to the Hermetic currents in the late nineteenth century, Jung did the same for the twentieth.

DESCENT INTO THE UNCONSCIOUS

Jung later declared that all the essentials of his psychology emerged during the turbulent years of his "creative illness." After months of fending off madness—and alarming his family in the process—Jung decided to try another tactic. Sitting at his desk, Jung decided to stop holding back the sense of oppression and *let go*. He allowed the fantasies pressing on his consciousness to take over. Almost immediately he found himself in the interior terrain Henry Corbin later called the Imaginal. Jung felt himself drop, and after landing in utter darkness on a soft mass, he discerned the entrance to a cave. He saw a dwarf, and after wading through icy water, came upon a huge, glowing red crystal. Beneath this was the corpse of a blond youth. Floating past, Jung saw a gigantic black scarab, then a brilliant sun.

In his later terminology, Jung had entered the world of the archetypes, the primal psychic blueprints that he argued constituted what he came to call the "collective unconscious," a kind of reservoir of images that our individual minds are connected to and that we share with one another. The collective unconscious is a part of our psyche that is more fundamental than our personal unconscious, the collection of memories and dreams concerning our own individual lives. It is a kind of universal psychic substratum of forms—different from but likened unto Plato's—that rests below our individual awareness, which, as it were, floats upon it like ships on the sea. Jung himself linked the collective unconscious to the Neoplatonic *Anima mundi* and to accounts of creation in the *Corpus Hermeticum*. It was, he believed, the source of myths and religions, and its presence could be discerned in our dreams.

The most startling discovery, however, was that this interior world was inhabited. During another inner descent, Jung found himself in a lunarlike landscape, where he encountered two individuals whom he took to be Elijah and Salome from the Bible. Jung also saw a huge black snake. Later, other figures appeared, the most important of whom Jung called "Philemon," who became a kind of "inner guru" for Jung. Philemon told Jung some extraordinary things. He informed him that he was mistaken to believe that everything in his mind belonged to him. On the contrary, the inner world he had entered was just as objective as the outer one, with its own flora and fauna. What he discovered here no more belonged to him than did the clouds and the birds outside his window. Through Philemon, Jung recognized that "there are things in the psyche which I do not produce, but which produced themselves and have their own life."[38] In other words, there were things in Jung's mind—and our own—that had nothing to do with him personally. Jung was just another inhabitant of this interior world, which he later called the "objective psyche." Like other inner voyagers we have met—Suhrawardi, Swedenborg, Blake—Jung had found his way to a new world, one, as Aldous Huxley had remarked, with its own "unmapped Borneos and Amazonian basins."

Jung did not speak openly of his experience until his last years. His record of his "creative illness," his remarkable *Red Book*, was kept secret during his lifetime, and was published only in 2009, half a century after his death. Jung's reticence is perhaps understandable. After Freud's death in 1939—and Alfred Adler's in 1937—Jung became the most famous living psychologist, and he would remain so until the end of his life. To speak of the visitations of the dead, poltergeists, ghosts, and other "spooky" phenomena that accompanied Jung's "creative illness"—and continued after it—would jeopardize his hard-won professional reputation. (In my book on Jung, I recount his many psychic experiences and his equivocalness about them.)

But throughout his career, Jung was a rather circumspect secret teacher, and those who were allowed into his inner circle—like the initiates of old—were aware of his entrée into the "other world." Like Swedenborg and Steiner, Jung developed a method of inducing these excursions into the interior. Like them, Jung had a knack for hypnagogia, a natural capacity for "dreaming while awake" that proved very useful. But Jung played his cards close to his chest and he only dropped hints of his method here and there; he never came out and spoke about it clearly and openly, at least not in any of his major works.

This method Jung called "active imagination," which I have mentioned earlier. It is a way of entering into a dialogue with the unconscious, of bringing the conscious and unconscious minds—or left and right brains—into creative collaboration. This triggers the transcendent function, a reorientation of the limited ego toward the larger and more inclusive Self, the wider personality that encompasses both cerebral hemispheres. Active imagination is in all essentials identical in aim to the methods of inner journeying we have come across in this book. But where Suhrawardi spoke openly about Hūrqalyā, Swedenborg of heaven and hell, and Steiner of the "Akashic record," Jung demurred—again, perhaps understandably—and spoke only of his empirical findings about the character of the psyche. This scientific caution informed most of Jung's dealings with the occult.

JUNG THE GNOSTIC

For Stephan Hoeller, a contemporary Gnostic thinker, Jung embodies "one of the most important branches of what has sometimes been called the Pansophic Tradition, or the wisdom heritage which descended from Gnostic, Hermetic, and Neo-Platonic sources."[39] Hoeller's book, *The Gnostic Jung and the Seven Sermons to the Dead*, from which I have quoted, is an analysis of Jung's curious Gnostic text, *The Seven Sermons to the Dead*, which he produced in 1916 during his "descent into the unconscious." Like Crowley's *Book of the Law* and Yeats's less well-known but no less fascinating *A Vision* (1925), *The Seven Sermons to the Dead* is a work of "spiritual dictation." It came to Jung after a peculiarly tense period of psychic disturbance, involving himself and his family; had Catherine Crowe known of it, it would have found a place in *The Night-Side of Nature*. The *Seven Sermons* were related to Jung by strange, disembodied voices that claimed to have come from Jerusalem. At the end of their dictation, Jung ascribed the work to "Basilides in Alexandria, the City where the East toucheth the West." Basilides was the Gnostic teacher who especially offended the Christian Justin Martyr (Chapter Four); Abraxas, a Gnostic deity Basilides wrote about, turns up in Jung's *Seven Sermons* too.

The Seven Sermons is a curious work, and Jung himself was of two minds about it. He mostly kept it to himself, but gave copies to selected readers, who were asked to keep it secret. It sometimes reaches poetic power, but more often its bombastic, quasi-biblical style reads like a pastiche of Nietzsche's *Thus Spake Zarathustra*, something that is true of the *Red Book* too. Jung excused the excesses of the work, saying its highfalutin language was that of the archetypes. Crowley's *Book of the Law* exhibits the same excess, so perhaps Jung is right, although the fact that both Crowley and Jung—they were exact contemporaries, born in the same year—came from very religious families may have had something to do with it.

The *Seven Sermons*'s central message is the need to differentiate from the mass, to achieve one's individuality, to emerge as a separate being from the undifferentiated Pleroma. "The natural striving of the creature goeth towards distinctiveness, fighteth against primal, perilous sameness." "Ye all become equal and thus is your nature maimed."[40] It is a doctrine to be found in Nietzsche and William Blake, and would be shared by Yeats, Schwaller de Lubicz, and others concerned about the "leveling" aspect of modern mass egalitarianism. Abraxas plays an important role, as the mediator and reconciler of opposites. He would do the same in Hermann Hesse's Gnostic novel *Demian*, which appeared in 1919, after Hesse himself underwent Jungian analysis. Hesse may have been inspired by Jung's *Seven Sermons*; he was one of its few recipients.

Jung achieved his own "individuation"—or at least discovered a means of achieving it—in the last days of the war. While serving as commandant at an English prisoner of war camp—although neutral, Switzerland interned any combatants that crossed its borders—each day Jung sketched a mandala, the Tibetan "magic circle." He came to see the mandala as both an image or symbol of the Self—the completed partial mind—and also as a means of stimulating the unification of the opposites out of which the Self emerges.

Jung was an effective artist—the watercolors filling the *Red Book* show that—and his mandalas were elaborate. His first, which he called "The System of All Worlds," is like a work of "hyperphysical cartography," mentioned in Chapter Nine. It is also like the Hermetic representations of the universe Jung would soon study during his investigations into alchemy.

Jung studied the Gnostics seriously throughout the 1920s, although his interest in them began in 1912; he even wrote to Freud saying that he believed the wisdom of the Gnostic Sophia may return through the efforts of psychoanalysis. Jung learned much about the Gnostics from G. R. S. Mead, whom he knew and once visited in London; Mead's *Fragments of a Faith Forgotten* (1900) is a classic of Gnostic scholarship. Yet in a search for a historical antecedent to his idea of individuation, Jung abandoned the Gnostics in favor of the alchemists who, as we've seen, he believed practiced active imagination without knowing it.

Jung was aware of a connection between psychology and alchemy. He had read his colleague Herbert Silberer's little-known but fascinating book, *Hidden Symbolisms of Alchemy and the Occult Arts* (1917), which predated Jung's own work by decades. Silberer, like Jung, was a good hypnagogist, and Jung's active imagination and transcendent function may have been informed by Silberer's writings on hypnagogia.[41]

SCHOOLS OF WISDOM

Jung's inspiration for his alchemical studies came from his friend, the sinologist Richard Wilhelm, whose translation of the *I Ching* (the Chinese *Book of Changes*), a work of divination and Taoist wisdom, Jung introduced to western readers in the 1950s. It would become a Bible of the sixties' occult revival. Jung's interest in the *I Ching* stemmed from his fascination with "meaningful coincidences," what he termed synchronicity. He had been interested in this for decades, but like most of Jung's occult interests, he did not speak about it openly until the last decades of his life. It was Jung's interest in synchronicty that convinced him to study alchemy. Wilhelm had sent him a copy of a Taoist alchemical text, *The Secret of the Golden Flower,* and asked him to write a commentary on it. Jung had just painted a mandala featuring a golden castle that struck him as Chinese, something he hadn't intended. The coincidence confirmed Jung's ideas about mandalas and the Self. His commentary to *The Secret of the Golden Flower*—which, like western Mystery teachings, is about creating an "inner body" able to survive physical death—contains some of his most direct remarks about active imagination and the transcendent function.

Jung had met Wilhelm in 1922 at the School of Wisdom established by Count Hermann Keyserling in Darmstadt, Germany, in 1920. A friend of Keyserling's had attended one of Jung's seminars and suggested that Jung lecture at Keyserling's school. Jung did and he became a familiar figure there. Keyserling came from an aristocratic Baltic Russian family, but had lost his fortune in the Bolshevik Revolution. Before this he had traveled around the globe, and his book about his adventures, *The Travel Diary of a Philosopher* published in 1919, was a huge success.

Keyserling used the royalties from his book to establish his School of Wisdom. Keyserling promoted an eclectic philosophy, gathered from spiritual traditions from around the world; he had a "planetary" outlook well in advance of our own "global" sentiments. Although forgotten today, Keyserling was considered an important enough thinker that after his death in 1946, his brain was put on display in a museum in Berne, Switzerland; Einstein's was later added to the collection.[42]

Keyserling's School of Wisdom aimed to synthesize the vision of the East and the West, and along with Jung and Wilhelm, other important speakers there included Hermann Hesse and the Indian Nobel Prize–winning poet Rabindranath Tagore. It was at the School of Wisdom that Jung met Olga Fröbe-Kapteyn, mentioned earlier, and suggested to her that she use her auditorium at Casa Gabriella for a similar purpose. It was out of this that the Eranos Conferences began.

Count Keyerseling's was not the only school of wisdom operating at this time. Understandably, the chaos of World War I turned many people's minds toward the question of renewal and of ways to prevent another such catastrophe from happening. The massive fatalities also prompted a renewed interest in spiritualism and questions about the meaning and purpose of life. Rudolf Steiner had spent the war in Dornach, Switzerland, building a remarkable work of "Anthroposophical architecture," the Goetheanum, an impressive structure of flowing, organic forms erected by Anthroposophists from all the warring nations. Sadly, this fantastic work of Expressionist architecture—one of its gigantic wooden domes was bigger than that of St. Peter's in Rome—burned to the ground on New Year's Eve, 1922.[43] Arson by proto-Nazis was suspected, and Steiner immediately began work on its successor, an equally fantastic temple—now of concrete—built on its predecessor's ruins, and which stands today.

Steiner had come to international prominence with his book *The Threefold Commonwealth* (1919), which proposed a spiritual reconstruction of Europe based on a "threefold" vision of the body politic similar to Plato's *Republic*. The book was a huge success, and for a time Steiner's political ideas made their way onto the ballots. His lectures on the subject were jammed, and on one occasion in Berlin, the lines reaching out of the auditorium were large enough to stop traffic; a lecture in Vienna was attended by some two thousand people. By this time, however, a wide anti-Steiner sentiment had risen and he came under attack by Catholics, Communists, proto-Nazis, and other occultists. An assassination attempt on him in Munich—Hitler's city—by proto-Nazis was foiled when Steiner's followers formed a ring around him and escorted him to safety.

One element of Steiner's "threefold" system that materialized was the Waldorf Schools, which began in 1919 and which have since become a very successful worldwide source of alternative education; the name "Waldorf" comes from the Waldorf-Astoria cigarette company in Stuttgart, whose owner, an Anthroposophist, financed the project. In the last years of Steiner's life, his epistemological concerns—stemming from Goethe—took a backseat to more practical developments, and along with Waldorf education, his "bio-dynamic" farming, Anthroposophical medicine—its roots in Paracelsian remedies—and architectural ideas have become familiar parts of the alternative landscape.

Steiner's own remarkable vitality began to flag in the early 1920s, and after years of lecturing and private teaching—Steiner never refused helping others and this infinite solicitousness took its toll—his health declined. He died in 1925, aged sixty-four, of a still undisclosed illness. At the end, he was concerned about the rise of technology, which he saw as Ahrimanic, and his last remarks called on his followers to create within themselves "the inner strength *not to go under.*"

Aleister Crowley, who would become one of the icons of the sixties' occult revival, spent the war years somewhat ignominiously, writing pro-German propaganda while sitting out the hostilities in New York. Readers can decide for themselves the credibility of Crowley's claims that by doing so he was really supporting the British war effort. When he returned to England at the end of 1919, Crowley's health—bronchitis and asthma—led to a prescription for heroin, then legal, and his subsequent addiction led to him founding his own school of wisdom, the Abbey of Thelema, based on *The Book of the Law*, in Cefalù, Sicily, in 1920. Over the years, Crowley had developed a variety of techniques—mostly involving sex and drugs—for "discovering" one's "true will," and as his reputation in England was abysmal—he was, as Lady Caroline Lamb said of the poet Lord Byron, "mad, bad and dangerous to know"—he sought to put down stakes elsewhere.

Crowley believed that drugs like heroin and cocaine could be taken freely, without fear of addiction, provided the user knew his or her true will. Crowley's still-readable novel *The Diary of a Drug Fiend* (1922)—written under the influence of heroin and cocaine—is a romanticized and idealized portrait of his abbey and of Crowley himself.[44] One reason for heading to Sicily is that Crowley wanted to find a warm climate in which to kick his habit.

Crowley had a vague intuition that we are cut off from our source of inner power—which we can see as the right brain—and for all their dubiousness, his Dionysian tactics for reconnecting with it at times worked. Some visitors to his abbey did find their "true will." Most, however, found the squalor, lack of sanitation, frequent sexual rituals involving sodomy and bestiality, and habitual drug use less to their tastes and left. After the controversial death of his disciple Raoul Loveday and a series of tabloid exposés, Crowley was deported from Italy by its new ruler, Benito Mussolini, in 1923. In the same year, Yeats, his magical and poetical rival, won the Nobel Prize for literature.

Crowley spent the rest of his life addicted to drugs, perpetually insolvent, exiled from more than one country, and burning as many bridges and ruining as many lives as his true will required. He also wrote some of the most important works on "magick"—as he spelled it—in the twentieth century, such as *Magick in Theory and Practice* (1929) and *The Book of Thoth* (1944), one of the most influential books on the Tarot ever written. Crowley spent his last years in an eccentric boarding house in Hastings, near the English Channel, and died in 1947 at seventy-two. In a remarkable *enantiodromia*, the "Wickedest Man in the World" and the "Man We'd Like to Hang"—as the tabloids called Crowley—now has his portrait hanging in London's National Portrait Gallery, a place dedicated to Britain's "best and brightest."[45]

While Crowley was trying to kick his heroin habit and remember his true will, Gurdjieff was establishing himself in Fontainebleau, France. There is a persistent if questionable story that Crowley once went to Gurdjieff's *Prieuré* in order to free himself of heroin; Gurdjieff at times made a living using hypnosis to cure addicts of their addiction. Gurdjieff, too, occasionally hit the tabloids, and the death of the New Zealand writer Katherine Mansfield, one of Orage's discoveries, at Gurdjieff's *Prieuré* in 1923 from tuberculosis cast a shadow over the Institute for the

Harmonious Development of Man. Gossip that Gurdjieff slept with many of his students also fueled the scandal sheets.

In 1924, mounting debts led Gurdjieff to bring a troupe of his students to America—New York and Chicago—to give performances of his "sacred dances." These are the basis of what are known as the Gurdjieff "movements," difficult, complicated positions and steps Gurdjieff developed in order to push his students past their mechanicalness. These performances were a success and Gurdjieff's reputation profited by it. It was at this time that Orage became Gurdjieff's American lieutenant, remaining in New York and carrying on as Gurdjieff's spokesman until breaking with him a decade later over Orage's marriage to Jessie Dwight. Orage returned to London and died in 1934 after giving a talk on Social Credit—a return to the *New Age* days—for the BBC. He was sixty-one.

In July 1924, Gurdjieff, an appalling driver, crashed his Citroën into a tree somewhere between Paris and Fontainebleau. He was found covered in blood, unconscious—he would remain so for five days—his head resting on a cushion, not far from the crash. How he came to be in this position remains a mystery, as do the circumstances surrounding the accident: there is reason to believe Gurdjieff arranged it on purpose. The immediate result was his decision to liquidate his institute, and turn his attention to waking up his fellow men through writing. From 1925 to 1935, Gurdjieff labored at getting his ideas onto paper. One result was *Beelzebub's Tales to His Grandson* (1950), a work whose difficulties make Jacob Boehme seem a model of clarity and concision. A more congenial work, *Meetings With Remarkable Men*, also emerged from this time, as did the aborted *Life Is Real Only Then, When "I Am"* which appeared in fragmentary form in 1974. An earlier work, *The Herald of the Coming Good* (1933), was considered so strange, megalomaniacal, and bombastic that some readers—Ouspensky included—believed it was a work of someone approaching madness. It was soon recalled.

Ouspensky had by this time been long separated from his erstwhile teacher. During the 1920s, he laid low in London, giving talks, acquiring students—most notably Maurice Nicoll, J. G. Bennett, and the physician and writer Kenneth Walker—and working on the account of his time with

Gurdjieff that would become *In Search of the Miraculous*.[46] He also worked on *A New Model of the Universe*, a remarkable collection of ideas he had explored before meeting Gurdjieff—such as eternal recurrence and cosmic consciousness—reworked to include what he had learned from his former master.

When *A New Model* appeared in 1931, it sold well, reestablishing Ouspensky's reputation as a philosopher of the esoteric and introducing him to new readers. One of these, as mentioned, was the novelist and playwright J. B. Priestley, who used Ouspensky's ideas about eternal recurrence in his hit West End play *I Have Been Here Before* (1937). By this time, Ouspensky had established his own school, first in London, then in a huge estate in Lyne Place, his version of Gurdjieff's *Prieuré*. Visitors to Ouspensky's school included Aldous Huxley and Gerald Heard. Important students from this time included Robert S. De Ropp, whose books *Drugs and the Mind* (1957) and *The Master Game* (1968) became countercultural favorites in the 1960s; and Rodney Collin, who later went on to form groups in Mexico and whose major work, *The Theory of Celestial Influence* (1954) I mentioned in Chapter Five.

In 1940, during the Blitz, Ouspensky followed Huxley and Heard by leaving England for the United States. He set up another school, this time in Mendham, New Jersey. But the uprooting, and the loss first of Russia, then Europe—Ouspensky loved Paris, now occupied by the Nazis—his lack of contact with the "inner circle of humanity," and, most painfully, his broken relationship with Gurdjieff—who had, Ouspensky believed, "gone off the rails"—led, sadly, to depression and heavy drinking.

In January 1947, a very ill Ouspensky returned to a bombed-out and heavily rationed London and gave his old English students a wake-up call like no other. From February to June, in a series of startling lectures, Ouspensky rejected the "system" he had spent more than twenty-five years teaching and told his students that they had to start from the beginning and think for themselves.[47] Not long after this, Ouspensky made strange journeys around England, during which he tried to "fix" in his mind his memories so that, as mentioned, during his next recurrence he would "remember." He died on October 2, 1947. He was sixty-nine.

From the 1930s on, Gurdjieff taught in Paris and New York. Like Madame Blavatsky—and also Crowley—he put on weight, and the huge lunches and dinners he would prepare—part of his teaching technique—and fondness for Armagnac, vodka, café noir, and cigarettes, did not help his health. (Again it should be noted that practically all of the "big names" in modern western esotericism—Blavatsky, Crowley, Gurdjieff, Ouspensky, with the exception of Steiner—weren't concerned with health and well-being.)

In Paris, Gurdjieff waited out the Occupation in his small flat on the Rue des Colonels Renard, near the Arc de Triomphe. Here he jammed as many of his students into his rooms as possible and took them on madcap automobile adventures, driving into the Paris countryside until his Citröen ran out of gas, forcing them to make "super efforts." Exactly how he survived during the Occupation is unclear, but then Gurdjieff was nothing if not a survivor.[48] Among his students at this time was the surrealist poet René Daumal, author of the spiritual adventure novel *Mount Analogue* (1952).

Ouspensky had warned his students to stay away from Gurdjieff—his accident, he believed, was a sign something had gone wrong—but after Ouspensky's death, many of them went to Paris to become part of Gurdjieff's groups. Most notable among these was J. G. Bennett, who carried on Gurdjieff's and Ouspensky's work, as well as his own, in England until his death in 1974.

Gurdjieff died in 1949. His age at death is anyone's guess. One account has it that his physician remarked that the state of his internal organs suggested he should have been dead years earlier. It seems he kept himself going through sheer will. His passing was mourned by many. Gurdjieff usually had harsh words about his ex-student Ouspensky, but when shown the manuscript of *In Search of the Miraculous*, he agreed it was an excellent account of his ideas and said he loved Ouspensky for it. He did want *Beelzebub's Tales* to be published first, but Ouspensky, who asked for his masterpiece to remain unpublished, finally trumped his master.

Not long after this, in 1954, an at best dubious account of Gurdjieff's ideas appeared, *Monsieur Gurdjieff*, by a French journalist, Louis Pauwels. It was full of inaccuracies and unsubstantiated claims, but it piqued the public's interest in the occult, and a book Pauwels and a colleague would produce a few years later sparked a full-scale occult revival that is still with us today.

Postwar Europe had fallen under a dark night of rationing and painful reconstruction. But there were positive signs that a new morning was about to dawn.

CHAPTER TWELVE

THE NEXT STEP BEYOND

On June 24, 1947, the American businessman Kenneth Arnold was flying his two-seater monoplane in the vicinity of Mount Rainier, Washington, when out of his window he saw something strange. Nine shining "unusual objects" flying at high speeds moved in erratic patterns across the sky. Arnold, an experienced pilot, had never seen anything like them, and he described their appearance as like a "pie pan," a disc, or a "saucer." Arnold's account caught the public's imagination and the press soon dubbed Arnold's "unusual objects" "flying saucers." As with the spiritualist craze of the nineteenth century, other sightings were soon reported—Arnold himself contributed more—and within a short time the public was aware of the possibility that the Earth was being visited from outer space. Newspapers, magazines, radio, and the new medium of television spread the word. The age of modern UFOs had arrived.

Exactly why the UFO craze caught on—and has never let go—remains unclear. Yet by the 1950s, the idea that visitors from other planets were among us was widely discussed and, among many people, generally accepted. Hollywood soon got the hint and presented us with spacemen of superior intellect and moral purpose, as in *The Day the Earth Stood Still* (1951), or interplanetary invaders intent on world domination, as in *Earth vs. the Flying Saucers* (1956). Good or bad, it seemed the collective imagination was hungry for something new, alien, and *other*.

After the dark days of Hitler, World War II, and the shadow of the mushroom cloud, the mid-twentieth-century mind seemed to be reaching out for the otherworldly and unearthly. This, of course, could have been nothing more than escapism, a desire to obscure a dreary and dangerous reality with dreams and fantasies, and no doubt many, perhaps most, of the UFO sightings were along these lines. But there seems to have been something in the postwar appetite for the unusual that suggests something more.

Immanuel Velikovsky's *Worlds in Collision*, published in 1950, argued that around 1500 B.C. a comet sprung from Jupiter—Velikovsky says it became the planet Venus—nearly hit the Earth, causing global havoc and "proving" some of the miracles in the Bible, like the parting of the Red Sea. It was an immediate hit and topped *The New York Times* best-seller list for eleven weeks. In 1956, *The Third Eye*, an account of life in Tibet by T. Lobsang Rampa, sold millions of copies. The fact that Rampa was the pen name of Cyril Henry Hoskins, an Englishman from Devon who had never seen the Himalayas, was a mere detail. The book was based, Hoskins said, on his previous incarnation as a lama and he went on to write many more, all of which sold well. World War II had put a damper on much esoteric work, and most of the secret teachers of earlier years were dead. But the taste for *something else* remained.

A reader might ask, "Yes, this is true, but what do flying saucers have to do with the occult or esoteric? Aren't they more in line with science and the future?" A fair question, even if bookshops generally put material on UFOs in the Occult section. Yet one secret teacher who would have an enormous impact on the twentieth century took them very seriously.

In *Flying Saucers: A Modern Myth of Things Seen in the Sky* (1958), C. G. Jung argued that the many UFO sightings from around the world were a kind of global "active imagination." He was equivocal about their physical reality, but of their psychic reality he had no doubt. "Flying saucers," Jung believed, were "projections" of the collective unconscious, images of inner unity born of modern man's need for meaning, a mass yearning for "wholeness." They were, in other words, mandalas from outer space, their round shape serving the same purpose as that of the Tibetan "magic circle": an expression of the unified Self. The Cold War was about to thaw in a nuclear confrontation, and the tension between the U.S. and U.S.S.R. produced a planetary schizophrenia. The flying discs were a sign that a profound psychic tension was at work, but they were also a way of circumventing disaster. We know that Jung believed that meditating on the mandala could help trigger the transcendent function, the psyche's ability to grow beyond a seemingly insoluble problem. If the western world was approaching a nervous breakdown, it seemed its unconscious was taking steps to mitigate the collapse.

Jung also believed that just as the mandala signals a new development in the individual, it also did so for the collective. The idea that some great change was on its way had been with Jung for some time, but he only spoke openly about this in the last decade of his life. Jung had been a student of astrology for years, and even used it in his therapeutic work. As early as 1940, Jung had mentioned the "age of Aquarius" in a letter to his translator H. G. Baynes, speaking of "the premonitory earthquake of the New Age."[1]

Others had spoken of a coming new astrological age, a result of the "precession of the equinoxes" mentioned in Chapter One; Edward Carpenter, whom we met in the previous chapter, wrote about it, as did others before him.[2] But Jung was certainly the most high-profile name to do so. He believed he had to keep his speculations secret, but in 1951 he presented them in his strange work *Aion*, whose title is the name of a Gnostic deity. In *Aion*, Jung presented the idea that the archetypes evolve, and that we were currently caught in the shift from one "psychic dominant" to another—rather as Jean Gebser believed that we are moving from one "consciousness structure" to another. The new age, for Jung, would be one that would "constellate the problem of the union of opposites" and this would come about through the "individual human being, via his experience of the living spirit."[3]

Jung presented the same message in his book on flying saucers, but with a bit more gravitas. "My conscience as a psychiatrist," he wrote, "bids me fulfil my duty and prepare those few who will hear me for coming events which are in accord with the end of an era." He goes on: "As we know from ancient Egyptian history, they are the symptoms of psychic changes that always appear at the end of one Platonic month and at the beginning of another. They are . . . changes in the constellation of the psychic dominants, of the archetypes or 'Gods' as they used to be called . . . This transformation started . . . in the transition of the Age of Taurus to that of Aries, and then from Aries to Pisces, whose beginnings coincide with the rise of Christianity. We are now entering that great change . . . when the spring-point enters Aquarius."[4]

By the mid-1960s, Jung's ideas about the coming age of Aquarius would filter down to the burgeoning "counterculture" and would be popularized through Gavin Arthur's astrology column in the underground newspaper the *San Franciscan Oracle*. As a young man, Arthur—in his sixties during the "summer of love"— had known Edward Carpenter and may have heard about the idea from him.[5] By 1969, millions of people knew all about the dawning age through the hit song "Aquarius," by the Fifth Dimension—a pointedly occult name—from the hippie musical *Hair*.

MAGICAL MORNINGS AND MUSHROOMS

Jung's pronouncements seemed accurate, as least insofar as they related to the shift in popular consciousness toward the strange and mysterious that gathered momentum at the end of the 1950s. If there are any doubts about this, a book that appeared at the start of the new decade should clinch it. In 1960, an unusual title turned up in Parisian bookshops. It was *Le Matin des Magiciens* (*The Morning of the Magicians*). Its authors were Louis Pauwels—whose highly inaccurate *Monsieur Gurdjieff* I mentioned at the end of the last chapter—and Jacques Bergier, a physicist and practicing alchemist who, among other claims, said that he had met Fulcanelli (Chapter Five) in 1937.

Pauwels and Bergier shared a dissatisfaction with the narrowness of modern science, but they also believed that much of contemporary science had parallels with ancient beliefs, such as alchemy. But this was only one theme of the book, which rambled on at a brisk pace through a dizzying assortment of occult and esoteric ideas, everything from Gurdjieff, Madame Blavatsky, and the Golden Dawn, to "occult Nazis"—they more or less invented the genre—the philosopher's stone, ancient spacemen, Atlantis, mutants, higher consciousness, ESP, and much more. Much of what Pauwels and Bergier had to say was inaccurate, but in one sense this hardly matters. Their central aim was to show that the universe was a much more mysterious place than we take it to be, and if nothing else, they were successful at that.

Le Matin des Magiciens caused a sensation. In the black-and-white capital of existentialism, nihilism, and *La Nausée*, it was as if a UFO had landed on Boulevard Saint-Michel and sprayed the Paris of Jean-Paul Sartre and Albert Camus with technicolor. Nothing like it had appeared since the prewar occult revival, and people were ready for it. The book was a best seller and did equally well in its English and American editions. The occult revival of the 1960s had begun, and by the middle of the decade it would inform practically all aspects of popular culture, influencing literature, film, television, comic books, and, above all, music.

One factor helping the occult's rise to dominance in popular culture was the growing "psychedelic movement." Experimenting with peyote and other mind-altering drugs had been part of the "new age" fin-de-siècle. Crowley, Yeats, and the pre-Freud sexologist Havelock Ellis had done so, as had Thomas De Quincey and Baudelaire with opium before them. But it was Aldous Huxley's experiment with peyote's derivative, mescaline, that made its mind-altering effects widely known.

In 1943, the Swiss chemist Albert Hofmann discovered the powerful hallucinogenic drug lysergic acid diethylamide, or LSD-25; his account of accidentally dosing himself with it remains a classic of drug literature, and as we've seen, Hofmann believed the ancient Eleusinian Mysteries used some form of psychedelic.[6] But it was Huxley's account of his mescaline experience in *The Doors of Perception* (1954) that popularized what would soon be called "altered states of consciousness."[7] In 1957, R. Gordon Wasson, a vice president of the J. P. Morgan Bank and amateur ethnomycologist, published an article in *Life* magazine, "Seeking the Magic Mushroom," about his experiences with mind-altering psilocybin mushrooms during religious rituals with the *curandera*, or shaman, Maria Sabina in Mexico. In 1958, Huxley published an article, "Drugs That Shape Men's Minds" in the *Saturday Evening Post*. By this time, LSD had become a popular therapeutic/recreational drug among the Hollywood set, and celebrities like the actor Cary Grant sang its praises.

The most well-known advocate of LSD was Timothy Leary, the ex-Harvard psychiatrist turned drug guru who hoped to "turn on" the world and head the counterculture in a "psychedelic revolution." While Hofmann and Huxley in different ways called for the judicious use of LSD as an aid in self-exploration—in effect, echoing the ancient system of initiation—Leary had bigger ideas and advocated widespread use of the powerful substance. His aim was to create a twentieth-century Mystery religion.

Leary first experienced "magic mushrooms" in Mexico in 1960, and soon after, at Harvard, he ran a number of psilocybin sessions with some of the "Beat Generation": Allen Ginsberg, Jack Kerouac, and William S. Burroughs. The Beats were writers and poets who rejected the buttoned-down, conservative character of 1950s America and, like the early participants in the occult revival, sought new experiences and ways of living. This included unconventional sex and drug use, but also an interest in eastern forms of spirituality, like Zen Buddhism. The man most responsible for importing this to the Beat scene was Alan Watts, a student of the Theosophist and Buddhist scholar Christmas Humphreys.

Psilocybin was powerful, but it was a candle compared to LSD's solar flare. Leary was introduced to Hofmann's discovery by a British confidence trickster named Michael Hollingshead; he had obtained an introduction to Leary by tricking Aldous Huxley into providing it.[8] Leary tried the stuff and it went, literally, to his head. He soon became a vociferous tub-thumper for the psychedelic revelation, and his evangelizing cost him his position at Harvard. It also led, in 1966, to making LSD illegal, a development that put research into the therapeutic use of the drug back by decades. Leary started his own secret society—the International Federation of Internal Freedom—and began publishing the *Psychedelic Review*. It featured classics like William James and R. M. Bucke, whose *Cosmic Consciousness* became a psychedelic "must read," and provided hippies with the catch word "cosmic." Leary published Plato too, and he also included work by Gurdjieff, Ouspensky, René Daumal, and other esoteric thinkers.

One of the important texts for Leary was the *Tibetan Book of the Dead*, in the English translation edited by the Theosophist W. Y. Evans-Wentz and introduced by Jung. It was here that he discovered a phrase that would become a central tenet of the psychedelic counterculture: "Turn off your mind, relax and float downstream." Leary included this in his influential book, *The Psychedelic Experience,* coauthored with Ralph Metzner and Richard Alpert—who would soon become the guru Ram Dass—and published in 1964. The book uses the *Tibetan Book of the Dead* as a guide to "tripping," and one of its readers was the Beatle John Lennon.

In March 1966, Lennon and Paul McCartney—two of the most famous people in the world—went to the Indica Bookshop in London—named after a species of marijuana, by then widely popular—looking for something to read. Lennon settled into *The Psychedelic Experience.* Lennon had already had two bad trips, but Leary's message was persuasive and he took the guru's advice about turning off his mind very seriously. One result was that for the next three years, Lennon dosed himself on LSD almost daily. Another was the Beatles' first psychedelic tune, "Tomorrow Never Knows," from their album *Revolver* (1966). The song's lyrics start with a reprise of Leary's Tibetan advice: "Turn off your mind, relax and float downstream." The age of pop psychedelicism and pop esotericism had begun.

THE RETURN OF THE BEAST

By 1967, it was clear that the growing youth culture, psychedelic movement, and occult revival were quickly coalescing into a powerful social force. The indubitable sign of this was the inclusion of C. G. Jung, Aldous Huxley, and the India sages Sri Yukteswar Giri, Sri Mahavatar Babaji, and Sri Paramahansa Yogananda on the cover of the Beatles' trendsetting album *Sgt. Pepper's Lonely Hearts Club Band,* part of the soundtrack to that year's "summer of love." Also included on the crowded cover was Aleister Crowley, otherwise known as "the Great Beast."

After his death twenty years earlier, Crowley had faded from consciousness, but in 1951 two books about him appeared. Charles Richard Cammell's *Aleister Crowley: The Man, the Mage, the Poet* turned a friendly eye on the dark magician, but it was John Symonds's critical—and often very funny—*The Great Beast* that really put Crowley back in the spotlight. Books on witchcraft and black magic were mildly successful in the 1950s, works like Gerald Gardner's *Witchcraft Today* (1954) and *The Meaning of*

Witchcraft (1959). Gardner, who knew Crowley, is more or less responsible for popularizing Wicca, a modern version of the ancient craft. And the Hollywood Hills "acid set" was the milieu in which the Crowley-inspired avant-garde filmmaker Kenneth Anger would produce his *thelemic* masterpiece, the lush and magical *Inauguration of the Pleasure Dome* (1954). Its cast included Marjorie Cameron, widow of the rocket scientist and Crowleyite Jack Parsons, and the writer Anaïs Nin, whose claims to have met Crowley in 1930s Paris must be taken with some salt.[9] In 1958, Symonds followed up *The Great Beast* with *The Magic of Aleister Crowley*, and by 1960, the Beast was included in the potpourri of occult disclosures making up *The Morning of the Magicians*.

According to Ringo Starr and Paul McCartney, *Sgt. Pepper's* cover was made up of "people we like" and "all our heroes," and in an interview shortly before his death, Lennon remarked that the "whole Beatle thing was to do what you want . . . do what thou whilst, as long as it doesn't hurt somebody."[10] Lennon misquoted Crowley, and his caution escaped the Beast, but after *Sgt. Pepper's*, Crowley too was a member of the counterculture.

In fact he became a positive exemplar of it. In the *International Times* for October 1967—an underground newspaper edited by the Beatles' friend Barry Miles—a full-page article on Crowley presents him as a proto-hippie, his sex-and-drug-filled life ample evidence for the claim. That year *The Black Arts* by Richard Cavendish appeared, among whose readers was Mick Jagger, lead singer of the Rolling Stones. Cavendish would later edit the influential 1970s magazine series *Man, Myth and Magic*, which included Mircea Eliade on its board.

The Stones became friends with Kenneth Anger and they produced a somewhat darker version of the Beatles' *Sgt. Pepper's*, *Their Satanic Majesties Request*. The Stones' take on the occult revival was more threatening, as their song "Sympathy for the Devil" suggests. With them we can say that a genre of pop music, "rockult and roll," begins and which would include later groups like Led Zeppelin—whose guitarist Jimmy Page was a dedicated Crowleyan—and other purveyors of heavy metal. By this time Timothy Leary had turned his attention away from Tibetan Buddhism and Gurdjieff, and was seeing himself as a reincarnation of Crowley, a timely discovery. In his autobiography *Confessions of a Hope Fiend* (1973)—a title taken from Crowley's *Confessions of Aleister Crowley* and *Diary of a Drug Fiend*—Leary writes about the "eerie synchronicities" between his life and Crowley's, and in a post-sixties interview for the PBS program *Late Night America,* Leary said he was a great admirer of Crowley and that the sixties themselves were a collective attempt to "do what thou wilt."[11]

THE NEW NEW AGE

As we've seen, the idea of a "new age" is very old and recurs repeatedly throughout western history. By the end of the 1960s, expectations of some millennarian shift were high. The Aquarian Age would arrive, Atlantis would rise—predicted for 1969 by the "sleeping prophet" Edgar Cayce and made into the hit song "Atlantis" that year by Donovan—and we would, according to the organizers of the huge music festival Woodstock, "get back to the garden." Many if not all of the interests that informed the "positive fin-de-siècle" and sent early twentieth-century dropouts to Monte Verità and other alternative spots were the height of fashion, and like other antinomian movements—such as the Brethren of the Free Spirit and the Moravians—the participants believed they were "beyond good and evil."

As in the Renaissance and other periods, nothing was as new as the old. It was a strange time, with technology's most glorious achievement—putting a man on the moon—coinciding with a return to primitive, tribal life, as in Woodstock and any number of communes. And as an example of Gurdjieff's "law of seven" and Jung's *enantiodromia,* the expectations that "peace would guide the planets and love would steer the stars" collapsed when the dark side of the age of Aquarius began to emerge.

This first became clear in the revelation that the brutal slaying of the actress Sharon Tate and her friends in the Hollywood Hills in August 1969 had been the work of a sadistic, homicidal hippie guru named Charles Manson. Then came the Rolling Stones' disastrous concert at Altamont, California, in December, when the antinomian Hells Angels killed one person and terrorized hundreds more. The Tate murders and another, of Leno and Rosemary LaBianca, had taken place just a few days before Woodstock. That Manson and his "Family" were responsible wouldn't become clear until the end of the year, but the juxtaposition is nonetheless striking.

By 1970, the mood had changed from expectations of love to something less wholesome, a shift seen in the increase in violence exhibited by a variety of radical political groups eager to bring on "the revolution." During the massive anti-Viet Nam War march on Washington in October 1967, Kenneth Anger and Allen Ginsberg were content to try to exorcize and levitate the Pentagon simultaneously.[12] By 1971, the Weathermen, a radical leftist group who had organized Timothy Leary's prison escape the year before, had bombed the Capitol. In 1972, they would bomb the Pentagon. (They had earlier christened Manson a "revolutionary hero.") In a letter sent to the *Berkeley Barb*, an underground newspaper, after his escape—he had been arrested on drug charges—Leary himself wrote that to "shoot a genocidal robot policeman in defense of life is a sacred act . . . Shoot to live. Blow the mechanical mind with Holy Acid. Dose them."[13]

As happened with the plummeting hopes of Romantics following the French Revolution's descent into the Reign of Terror and the rise of the guillotine, disappointed expectations of social change shifted into inner concerns. Many elements of the occult revival made their way into mainstream society. With ideas of a coming revolution fading, the occult, once threatening, now became domesticated. Practices like the Transcendental Meditation of the Beatles' guru, Maharishi Mahesh Yogi, were seen to have beneficial results and, with yoga and other forms of eastern spirituality, it made its way into the corporate world. EST, or the Erhard Seminars Training of Werner Erhard, also made corporate inroads, as did the other motivational and transformational techniques at the root of today's "self-help" literature—a reprise, in many ways, of the fin-de-siècle's "positive thinking." Yoga centers, health food stores, and oriental medicine shops began to appear on Main Street America. Belief in Tarot, astrology, synchronicity, telepathy, and other occult practices became commonplace. In 1970, the best-selling novelist Kurt Vonnegut wrote an article about the new popular occultism for *McCall's* magazine, in which he called Madame Blavatsky "the Founding Mother of the Occult in America."[14]

An occult publishing boom flooded the market with cheap reprints of esoteric classics, works by Crowley, Mathers, A. E. Waite, Levi, Regardie, and others. New works like Francis King's *Ritual Magic in Modern England* (1970) and Colin Wilson's *The Occult* (1971)—which looked at the magical and esoteric through the lens of existential philosophy—brought the subject up-to-date. Works by Stan Gooch—another British writer—on Neanderthal man and his links to the paranormal appeared.

The View Over Atlantis (1969) by the Platonist and friend of the Rolling Stones John Michell—whose first book, *The Flying Saucer Vision*, appeared in 1967—argued that England and the rest of the world were covered in "ley lines," hidden streams of a mysterious occult force. It ushered in the fascination with "Earth mysteries" that would continue on to today's crop circles and constituted a kind of esoteric environmentalism. In works like *The Roots of Coincidence* (1972), respected writers like Arthur Koestler—famous for attacks on reductionist science in *The Act of Creation* (1964) and *The Ghost in the Machine* (1968)—took telepathy, precognition, and synchronicity seriously, and many universities established departments in parapsychology, following in the footsteps of J. B. Rhine, who, at Duke University in the 1930s, had set up one of the first research units in the paranormal.

THE NEW HUMANISM

This interest in the hidden powers of the mind paralleled what was called the "human potential movement," a late twentieth-century version of Pico della Mirandola's "superhumanism." It emerged from the humanist psychology of people like Carl Rogers and Abraham Maslow. Rogers argued against the reductionist psychologies of Freud as well as the behaviorism of J. B. Watson, whose 1960s representative, B. F. Skinner, denied the reality or desirability of free will in his influential book *Beyond Freedom and Dignity* (1971).

Like Gurdjieff, behaviorism saw human beings as machines, motivated solely by stimulus and response; unlike Gurdjieff, it believed there was nothing we could do about this. Skinner's book argued that in order to create a safe and fair society, we should abandon notions of free will and allow ourselves to be "conditioned" to be good. Against this mechanical view of human psychology, Rogers emphasized the reality of the self, the person, as a real agent of change. His "person-centered" psychology also rejected the Freudian notion that we are helpless slaves to unconscious desires.

Abraham Maslow also rejected Freud and behaviorism and broke new psychological ground by studying healthy people, rather than sick ones. Maslow discovered that human psychology was informed by a "hierarchy of needs," at the top of which was the need to "self-actualize," Maslow's version of Jung's "individuation." Maslow saw that self-actualizers, those who work to fulfil their potential, enter the "farther reaches of human nature," and that our higher spiritual and creative needs are just as much a part of our makeup—our biology—as our lower physical ones. Against the mechanical view of human nature and the nihilism of existentialism—which saw human beings trapped in a meaningless universe (much as the Gnostics did)—Maslow argued that healthy, purposeful people regularly experience what he called "peak experiences," sudden, unexpected moments of joy and happiness, in which the meaningfulness of their life and the world is self-evident—moments, perhaps, when the warring sides of our brains reach a surprise accord.

One place in which the ideas of humanistic psychology were put into practice was the Esalen Institute, an alternative educational establishment founded on California's beautiful Big Sur coastline in 1962 by Michael Murphy and Richard Price. Murphy and Price had been students of Alan Watts, and their aim in opening their institute was to explore what Aldous Huxley had called the "human potentialities." Esalen was a success, and a list of the important figures who taught there reads like a who's who of alternative thinking: Joseph Campbell, Fritjof Capra, Stanislav Grof, Buckminster Fuller, Michael Harner, and R. D. Laing are only some of the names.

Esalen was a sort of West Coast Eranos, but unlike Eranos, it was open to the public, offered workshops and group therapy sessions, and its approach was less scholarly and more "hands on." With the Gestalt encounter groups led by the psychologist Fritz Perls, it was even "touchy feely," an aspect of Esalen about which Maslow, a frequent contributor, had serious reservations.[15] Maslow believed that Esalen's emphasis on "spontaneity" and "experience" could lead to a counterproductive anti-intellectualism, in which the sensual hot tub replaced the cerebral think tank.[16]

A misunderstanding of Maslow's self-actualization—a process requiring both intellect and feeling, and hence both sides of our brain—fed the shallow expression of "human potential" that informed the "Me Generation" of the 1970s. This "culture of narcissism," in the historian Christopher Lasch's phrase, emphasized the "self" component of self-actualization, and its devotees seemed overly fixated on producing bigger and better versions of themselves. This skewed view of human potential was compensated for by the rise of "transpersonal psychology," a view of the human psyche that incorporated elements of the sacred, spiritual, and nonhuman. Maslow's own work was informed by this, and like Jung, he considered spirituality a central part of human nature. Transpersonal psychology took Maslow's lead and developed a complete vision of the human psyche based on it.

TRANSPERSONAL PSYCHOLOGY

Transpersonal psychology has its roots in the work of Roberto Assagioli, a thinker whose important ideas are not well known and deserve more attention. In this sense, Assagioli remains a secret secret teacher. Assagioli was an early Freudian and colleague of Jung; like Jung, he studied under Eugen Bleuler at the Burghölzli clinic in Zurich. He came into Freud's orbit in 1909, but broke away from him earlier than Jung, in 1910, apparently without a "creative illness." Like Jung, he rejected Freud's narrow, reductive view of human psychology and his emphasis on the sexual root of neurosis. Also like Jung, Assagioli was interested in the spiritual aspects of human psychology, those parts of our being that transcend the personal. Hence his psychology was "transpersonal."

Like Jung, Assagioli wanted to counter the fragmenting effect of Freud's psychoanalysis, and against this he developed his system of psychosynthesis. (Jung also spoke of "psychosynthesis" before he hit on "analytical psychology," and he may have got the idea from Assagioli.) Unlike Jung, Assagioli did not hesitate to say that the spiritual was an actual, objective reality. Jung, more circumspect, spoke only of his "empirical"—i.e., scientific—observations about the psyche. This should not be surprising: Assagioli was a long-time student of the esoteric tradition, and in his early years was a close associate of the Theosophist Alice Bailey.

Alice Bailey was born in England in 1880 and, like Madame Blavatsky, claimed that she had been in contact with a "master" since her teens. By 1915, in her thirties, she had moved to the United States, where she joined the Theosophical Society. After a clash with Annie Besant, she left in 1920. She had by this time started receiving channeled messages from one of Blavatsky's minor Masters, Djwal Khul, "the Tibetan," who told her that she was in service to a spiritual hierarchy and that she was given a secret mission to work for the benefit of mankind in its spiritual evolution. In 1923, Bailey founded the Arcane School, and her messages from Djwal Kuhl began to mount up. Her enormous output centers around a vision of mankind's spiritual development culminating in a global federation embodying a universal brotherhood. Bailey too spoke of a coming age of Aquarius and believed that its messiah, the Buddha Maitreya, was about to return.

SPIRITUAL SUMMER SCHOOLS

Assagioli was born in Venice in 1888 into a cultured family and became involved in Theosophy through his mother. Jewish, he was also deeply influenced by the esoteric elements of his religion.[17] He had a genius for language, and by his teens was fluent in German, French, English, Russian, Greek, Latin, and Sanskrit. Art, music, poetry, and the higher pursuits influenced him deeply. Assagioli's interest in culture, idealism, and spirituality led to his break with Freud, and by the late 1920s, he had become Bailey's representative in Italy.[18]

They met in 1930 in Ascona (Chapter Eleven) while lecturing at the Spiritual Summer School held in the socialite Olga Fröbe-Kapteyn's Casa Gabriella. Fröbe-Kapteyn had deep spiritual interests, and in 1927, after the death of her father, she received a large inheritance, part of which was Casa Gabriella on the shores of Lago Maggiore.[19] She used her inheritance to pursue her spiritual path, traveling in search of wisdom and in order to make contact with like-minded people. She was a visitor to Monte Verità, but did not care for its bohemian ambience. She had an interest in the occult and eastern religion, but had no idea what to do with her life. Before becoming hostess to the Eranos Conferences, she had spent seven years in isolation, speaking to no one but her servants.

At the end of this seclusion, suffering a neurosis, she sought out Jung's help; he advised her to find other people like herself, deeply committed to the spiritual life. It was at this point that on a sudden impulse, she had an auditorium built. When it was finished, she had no idea what to do with it. It was Jung who, in 1928, supposedly suggested that she use it as a center, like Hermann Keyserling's in Darmstadt, for bringing together the East and the West.[20]

Fröbe-Kapteyn had by this time become a follower of Alice Bailey, and she offered her auditorium for Bailey's use. The result was the Spiritual Summer School held there in 1930. Among the teachers were Bailey; Alexandra David-Neel, author of the remarkable *Magic and Mystery in Tibet* (1929) and the first European woman to enter the Forbidden City of Lhasa; and Assagioli.[21] More summer schools took place, but by 1932, Bailey grew disenchanted with the project and, as mentioned, told Fröbe-Kapteyn that in ancient times the area was associated with black magic.

A more immediate reason for her change of heart was the nearby presence of bohemian Ascona, whose residents she found objectionable and a continuous temptation to her daughters.[22] Bailey also said that she had recently received an "epoch-making" communication from her master, and she had to devote her attention to starting her "New Groups of World Servers," who would usher in the expected new age.[23] Bailey left Lago Maggiore, and Fröbe-Kapteyn had an empty auditorium on her hands. Fröbe-Kapteyn remembered Jung's suggestion and the idea of Eranos— Greek for "banquet" although "pot luck" might be more apt—took hold.

In 1933, the first Eranos Conference was held, its opening segueing nicely with the closure of Keyserling's School of Wisdom as the Nazis swept into power. Fröbe-Kapteyn had asked Jung to speak at the opening conference, but he declined because of her association with Bailey—he found Theosophists particularly annoying—and Assagioli. This was odd, as the two were thought to be friendly. Jung had earlier turned down taking part in the Spiritual Summer Schools for the same reason. But when he saw that the Hindu scholar Heinrich Zimmer and other noted savants would be opening the Eranos Conference, Jung changed his mind.[24]

PSYCHOSYNTHESIS

Assagioli had worked as a director of the Theosophical journal *Ultra*, one of whose contributors was the controversial Italian esotericist Julius Evola.[25] In the late 1920s, Evola's UR Group, based in Rome, conducted magical and hermetic research, and produced the important esoteric journals, *Ur* and *Krur*. Evola wrote extensively on alchemy, tantra, Buddhism, and other esoteric subjects, from the point of view of a highly race-oriented Traditionalism, whose far-right political associations maintain Evola's status as, in Hermann Hesse's words, a "dangerous author."[26]

Assagioli's views were more tolerant and less belligerent than Evola's, and he would in fact suffer from the new racial laws Mussolini introduced in 1938, which were influenced by Evola's *Three Aspects of the Jewish Problem* (1936), whose diatribes against the "Jewish soul" owe much to the troubled Austrian philosopher Otto Weininger.[27] Assagioli opened his Institute for Psychosynthesis in 1926 in Florence, but in 1938, Mussolini's Fascists forced him to close it and he himself was arrested and imprisoned for a month in solitary confinement. During this time, he developed many important ideas and was able to transform the imprisonment into a spiritual retreat by practicing exercises developing his will and imagination, two central elements of psychosynthesis. Assagioli's staunch internationalism also got him into trouble: during World War II, Assagioli and his family had to go underground.

Assagioli's central idea is the irreducible reality of the Self, a belief he shares with Jung, Maslow, and Rudolf Steiner; and his psychology is aimed at stimulating an experience of that reality through the use of imagination and the will, two necessary ingredients, we remember, for the practicing magician. One of Assagioli's most important ideas—and one that distinguishes his work from Jung's—is his belief in what he calls the "higher unconscious," or, perhaps more apt, the "superconscious."

In his foreword to F. W. H. Myers's *Human Personality and Its Survival of Bodily Death*, Aldous Huxley asked whether the "house of the soul" was a "mere bungalow with a cellar," as Freud's view would have it, or if it had also a "roofless attic . . . open to the sky."[28] Assagioli believed it did, and his "superconsciouness" is the soul's open-topped attic.

Through the discovery and development of the will, Assagioli believed we could harmonize the dark elements of the "lower unconscious" (Freud's basement filled with the "vermin" and "garbage" of our repressed complexes, in Huxley's words) with the "middle unconscious," a subconscious "labor-saving" device that takes over skills we have learned with the conscious mind, freeing it for new activities. (When I first learned to type, it was a painful, laborious effort that I had to consciously go through step by step. Now, my "middle unconscious" does it much more smoothly for me, allowing me to think about *what* I want to write.) Harmonizing these parts of our psyche constitutes our "personal psychosynthesis." It is by bringing in the "superconsciousness," or upper floors of the mind, that we engage in "transpersonal psychosynthesis," the unifying of our own personal egos with the spiritual realities that lie beyond it, rather as Jung's active imagination can introduce us to the "objective psyche." Assagioli even speaks of creating a kind of inner "elevator" that will allow us access to all the levels of our personality.[29]

Much of Assagioli's work involved visualization and other exercises to strengthen the imagination, and it should be no surprise that he often draws on Dante, an important influence on his work. In one of his meditations, we are asked to use our imagination to visualize Dante's descent into Hell and then his ascent through Purgatory to Paradise. Through intensifying our imagination with our will, we can *experience* Dante's inner journey as if we ourselves are participating in it. In other words, through our active imagination we can, like Suhrawardi and others, embark on an inner voyage and enter the world of the Imaginal, the insights and meanings of which come to us through the superconscious.

AQUARIAN CONSPIRACIES

Assagioli's ideas were part of the repertoire of self-transformational disciplines that informed places like Esalen; Michael Murphy made a trip to Florence especially to meet Assagioli, who died in 1974, and said he was the "truest sage" he ever met. By the late seventies, "human potential," transpersonal psychology, eastern forms of spirituality, parapsychology, the "new physics"—quantum mechanics having done away with Newton's old clockwork universe—ideas of higher consciousness and other alternative pursuits seemed to be sending out shoots around the globe and the sense that *something* was happening was palpable. On his "search for the miraculous," Ouspensky had met people "who were interested in the same ideas that interested me, that spoke the same language as I spoke, people between whom and myself there was instantly set up an entirely distinctive understanding," and Ouspensky believed this was the beginning of a "secret society" of people "closely connected by a community of ideas and of language."[30] By 1980, the same feeling was prevalent and a book that came out that year confirmed it.

The Aquarian Conspiracy by Marilyn Ferguson argued that something like Ouspensky's "secret society" was happening, and provided plenty of evidence to prove it. Ferguson, a freelance journalist, was deeply involved in humanistic psychology, as well as in developments in the "new physics" and neuroscience that rejected the dominant reductionist approach. She also edited the influential *Brain/Mind Bulletin*, a newsletter spreading the word about the latest research in these fields. Like Samuel Hartlib, Ferguson was an "intelligencer," and in the years before the Internet, the *Brain/Mind Bullentin*, a kind of 1970s version of Orage's *New Age*, was the means through which many people in disparate but related fields kept up-to-date on what was happening on the "cutting edge."

One of the most exciting topics was the work in "split-brain theory," and Ferguson's bulletin was crucial in communicating new ideas about consciousness to a wide and diverse readership, from philosophers and psychologists to schoolteachers and shopkeepers. Readers of the *Brain/*

Mind Bulletin included, among others, the physicists Fritjof Capra and David Bohm, the neuroscientist Karl Pribram, and the parapsychologist Jean Houston.

Ferguson began to see something like a "movement without a name" emerging from all this, rather like Ouspensky's "secret society" and the "invisible church" of Karl von Eckartshausen. It was formed by a variety of people from different walks of life who all shared a desire to effect some lasting positive change in society and themselves, much like the desire to effect a "universal reformation" that informed the Rosicrucians. Maslow's ideas were prevalent, as were Jung's. Central to Ferguson's vision was the work of the French Catholic philosopher and paleontologist Pierre Teilhard de Chardin, whose influential book, *The Phenomenon of Man* (1959), argued that evolution was not a mindless, mechanical process but, as Henri Bergson had said, was informed and guided by an "evolutionary drive" aiming at greater complexity and freedom. Evolution, Teilhard de Chardin believed, was working through human beings to create what he called the "noosphere," a new dimension of reality produced by the human mind ("noosphere" comes from the Greek *nous*, "mind," and is a "mental sphere" as the atmosphere is one of air).

Teilhard de Chardin's ideas agreed with a remark of H. G. Wells, that as birds are creatures of the air and fish creatures of the sea, we—mankind—are creatures of the mind, an insight with which Plato, Plotinus, and other secret teachers would readily agree. Through the *Brain/Mind Bulletin* and other means, these "creatures of the mind" were linking up, exchanging ideas, making connections, and trying to become conscious agents of evolution's purpose.

It was in fact from Wells—a central figure of the positive fin-de-siècle—that Ferguson borrowed the idea of an "open conspiracy," a "leaderless movement" whose members were recognized by their desire to build a vision of mankind and the world that went beyond the still dominant reductionist paradigm.

In *The Open Conspiracy* (1928), Wells had written that "The world is undergoing immense changes. Never before have the conditions of life changed so swiftly and enormously as they have for mankind in the last fifty years," a remark that is truer today than when Wells wrote it.[31] Wells's "open conspiracy" called for men and women of intelligence, will, and creativity to embrace these developments, take charge of their lives, and liberate themselves from the muddle of old, worn-out traditions, much as the progressive thinkers of the positive fin-de-siècle sought out new, experimental ways of living. Wells's "open conspirators" would help awaken mankind "from an infantile nightmare, of the struggle for existence and the inevitability of war."[32] Ferguson's "Aquarian conspirators" had a similar goal: to liberate mankind from the trammels of a reductionist, mechanistic vision and promote one that encouraged creativity, spirituality, humanistic values, altruism, and the cooperative labor of making a better world.

Although not occult, Ferguson borrowed the idea of a coming age of Aquarius because of its popularity and positive message. She told her readers that they were moving out of a dark time into one of light and that this was happening through their own efforts and those of people like them. Many agreed with her. *The Aquarian Conspiracy* became a best seller, was translated into many languages, and received plaudits from *The New York Times, Time* magazine, and other mainstream periodicals. Ferguson lectured about her ideas around the world. One of her readers was Al Gore, who during his vice presidency invited Ferguson to the White House.

CHANNELS, CRYSTALS, AND OTHER ACCESSORIES

It was inevitable that when the interest in the variety of alternative ideas that Ferguson wrote about became widespread and self-conscious, the "movement without a name" would begin to call itself something. Or at least some members of it would. Absolute beginnings are the bête noir of historians, and exactly when our contemporary usage of "New Age" began is debatable, but at some point in the early 1980s, elements of Ferguson's Aquarian conspiracy became more mystical. "Channeling," a late twentieth-century version of gaslight spiritualism, came to the fore, with a variety of spiritual beings—not the dead this time—communicating important messages and metaphysical teachings for mankind through selected individuals.

Mankind had been receiving similar messages for at least the last century, but the new round of revelations caught on. "Seth," "Ramtha," "Orin," and other similar entities had important things to tell us, and as with UFO sightings, suddenly many people began to discover that they were involved in something extraordinary. Like the messages of their nineteenth-century counterpoints, the quality of these occult communiqués varied, with most expressing hopeful, positive, but frustratingly vague injunctions about our spiritual development. (As with Jung's and Crowley's inspired texts, the style of these communications tended to be heavy on rhetoric.)

Along with these portentous announcements, the sanction of some celebrities spread the word to a yet wider sphere, beyond the members of the Aquarian conspiracy and its antecedents. If the Beatles clinched the occult's entrée into the counterculture, it was the actress Shirley MacLaine's 1987 television miniseries *Out on a Limb,* based on her earlier book about her spiritual adventures, that did it for the New Age.

Millions of television viewers who learned of MacLaine's past lives and of her quest for spiritual fulfilment identified with her and, quite rightly, wanted to explore these questions for themselves. A fresh, large, and affluent market of middle-class consumers rose up and was able to afford the flood of self-help seminars and mystical accessories inspired by MacLaine's account. Other celebrities got into the act, and spirituality became something famous people liked to exhibit. Crystals, pendulums, incense, Tarot cards, body oils, guided meditations, angels, totem animals, archetypes, assorted therapies, "vision quests," Tibetan bells, singing bowls, spiritual retreats, goddess worship, sweat lodges, and many other items deemed necessary to explore one's inner world and follow one's "higher self" found an eager audience, inaugurating a kind of "spiritual consumerism" that continues today.

Echoes of the Me Generation sounded when the idea that we all house hidden potentials we seldom realize was transmuted into the belief that we are all entitled to instant actualization, and the search for wisdom often became the hunt for a spiritual practice that fit into our busy schedules. Parallel to this was the notion, advanced by many therapies, that, as we are—that is, without the need for any discipline or struggle—we are already spiritual, creative, magical beings and should be honored as such, a psychological egalitarianism and "feel-good factor" that led many to celebrate themselves in often ostentatious ways.

To mention this is not to say that all of it was bad. Much good came and continues to come from this popular movement, and the wide dissemination of ideas invariably leads to their dilution.[33] But soon even some of the spiritual teachers involved in this marketable metaphysics saw the danger of losing the essence of the thing in the paraphernalia that speedily accreted around it. The hunger for personal experience and knowledge of spiritual reality that drives the spiritual marketplace is in most cases authentic, and remains a genuine appetite in human beings. How that hunger is fed is another thing. Physical hunger can be met by junk food or a decent meal. Spiritual hunger is no different.

I should mention that some channeling led to solid, concrete results in the more scholarly aspect of the New Age. David Spangler, one of the earliest channelers, was involved with the Findhorn community of Scotland, famous for its remarkable results with farming, its fruits and vegetables known to grow to extraordinary sizes. In 1972, with the cultural historian William Irwin Thompson—one of the more respected and rigorous intellectuals associated with the New Age—Spangler helped found the Lindisfarne Association, named after the holy island of Celtic Christianity. The Lindisfarne Association was a kind of New Age Eranos—it ended in 2012—that promoted, as did Count Keyserling, a "planetary culture." Included among its members were many serious scholars, poets, writers, musicians, economists, and spiritual leaders, such as Gregory Bateson, James Lovelock, Elaine Pagels, E. F. Schumacher, Paul Winter, Wendell Berry, and Kathleen Raine. In 1990, Raine herself started the Temenos Academy in London, an alternative educational program that looks at philosophy and the arts through the lens of the perennial philosophy. *Temenos* is a Greek word meaning "sanctuary" or "holy ground," and the academy was an outgrowth of the *Temenos* journal started by Raine in 1980.

ON THE WAY TO 2012

As in the late sixties, the feeling that some event was needed to mark the felt "planetary shift" arose again, and 1987 also saw the rise of what was known as the "Harmonic Convergence." This was an occult watershed the significance of which was supposed to become clear twenty-five years later, in 2012, when the process then started would culminate in a radical change in the conditions of life—or so its proponents argued. To help the process along, thousands of people around the world gathered at sacred sites and "power spots"—Mount Shasta in California; Sedona, Arizona; Stonehenge in England—to achieve a unified, global meditation needed to ensure that the transition to the "new time" would go smoothly. If what we can call "esotourism," "sacred travel," and the "metaphysical holiday industry" didn't start then—after all, we've seen how travel in search of knowledge is a mainstay of the esoteric tradition—they certainly got a major boost at the time and have remained central parts of postmodern spirituality, as the many spiritual seminars, shamanic weekends, and vision quests available today show.

The idea of the Harmonic Convergence was the brainchild of the art historian and New Age philosopher José Argüelles and the psychedelic guru Terence McKenna. Via different routes, both had arrived at the idea that 2012 would mark a kind of ontological breakthrough and that the process leading up to it would start in 1987, on the weekend of August 16–17 to be exact. (Oddly enough, nearly twenty years earlier the Woodstock Festival took place over the same weekend.) Argüelles got there through a reading—some would say misreading—of the ancient Mayan calendar, a journey he communicated in his best-selling book *The Mayan Factor* (1987). McKenna, who had inherited the mantle of drug guru from Timothy Leary, was a guiding figure of the "rave generation"—a reprise of sixties psychedelia—and had cottoned on to the importance of 2012 via a study of the *I Ching* and a liberal use of magic mushrooms. One result of this suggestive combination was McKenna's book *The Invisible Landscape* (1975). Argüelles's grasp of the meaning of the Mayan calendar and its supposed predictions of global disruption for the year 2012 have been subject to much criticism, and Dennis McKenna, Terence's brother and colleague in psilo-cybin research, has gone on record saying that Terence got it wrong.[34]

Both Argüelles and McKenna argued that a "singularity" would take place in 2012, an event of such fundamental significance that existence itself would radically alter. As the term should suggest, "singularities" don't occur that often. Physicists use the term to refer to the conditions prior to the supposed Big Bang and to the anomalous properties of black holes. Yet many agreed with the prophets and some looked forward to 2012 as a time when the ancient god Quetzalcoatl would return. Prior to that portentous year, books, seminars, workshops, DVDs, lectures, and other essential items fed a hungry market, eager to help the new epoch along. Many also believed that, as actually happened, 2012 would be a year like most others.[35]

MY PART IN ALL THIS

I was not among those meditating on Mount Shasta or promoting good vibes in Sedona, but during the Harmonic Convergence I was, it seems, in one of the most auspicious places on the planet, at least according to the true believers who told me so. At the time I was working in a well-known metaphysical bookshop in Los Angeles and I saw at first hand the rise of the New Age from a concern of a modest group on the cutting edge or lunatic fringe—the difference between the two is often hard to distinguish—to a cultural trend of wide and at times almost manic popu-larity. The bookshop was a favorite with Aquarian conspirators, but after Shirley MacLaine, it opened its doors to a much larger clientele.

I had got there by a circuitous route, which started some twelve years earlier. My introduction to the occult, the esoteric, and the Hermetic hap-pened in 1975, when I was living on New York's Bowery and playing in a rock-and-roll band.[36] Remnants from the sixties generation were still vis-ible amid what would soon be called "punk," and a book I read at the time changed my life. It was Colin Wilson's *The Occult*. Soon after reading it, I developed an enthusiasm for its subject matter that has lasted ever since.

In the years that followed, I studied and practiced magic (Crowley's variety), was for some years involved in the Gurdjieff work, and went on a mini "search for the miraculous" that had me in Chartres Cathedral, Stonehenge, and at the site of Gurdjieff's institute in Fontainebleau, as well as other places. (Later adventures had me visiting Monte Verità and Casa Gabriella, site of the Eranos Conferences.) I also read a great deal. While working at the bookshop—and earning a degree in philosophy—I started writing book reviews and articles for magazines like *Gnosis, Quest, ReVision,* and others, all in some way dedicated to the western inner tradition. By 1996, I had left the bookshop and, after an aborted career in academia, had moved to London, where I became a full-time writer. My first book, *Turn Off Your Mind,* a "revisionist" look at the occult revival of the 1960s, came out in 2001, and I have been writing books ever since.

Along the way, I met and spoke with several people mentioned in this book. I say this not to blow my own horn, but to show that what began as a naïve enthusiasm some forty years ago developed—slowly, and with many detours—into what I hope is a serious study of our "rejected knowledge" and an engagement with some of the people pursuing it today. My point in mentioning this is to provide my credentials for some of the remarks that follow.

ESOTERIC INTERNET

Throughout most of our history, the urgent desire for personal knowledge and experience of the spiritual, the esoteric, the occult, or the inner was for the most part limited to a small number of people. A variety of factors made this so. One was simply that throughout most of our history, only a small number of people were interested enough in these matters to seek them out and submit to the rigors necessary to understand them. Another was the availability of the material itself. For ages, most teaching was done orally, and even when written material existed, it was available only to the few who could read and could gain access to it. It seems obvious, but we should pause to consider what a miracle the invention of the printing press was—all concern for its deleterious effects, as Leonard Shlain has pointed out, notwithstanding. Suddenly what had been in the hands of only the few could now be dispersed to the many.

A similar growth in the power of dissemination occurred with the rise of the popular press, radio, and television. And now these, along with the print media, have been superseded by the Internet, which has made possible the kind of "planetary culture" and "global village" visionaries like Count Keyserling and Marshall McLuhan dreamed of. Today, more times than not, we can communicate with someone on the other side of the planet more easily than we can with our neighbors, and we have practically instantaneous access to a bewildering amount of information coming from a dizzying number of sources.

Yet celebrations of the "information highway" have become somewhat muted in recent times. This is due in part to use and familiarity. My children take the Internet absolutely for granted and can't conceive of a time when computers, cell phones, and other electronic devices were not standard issue. Many of us who bridge the generation gap between pre- and post-Internet feel much the same. But we have also learned that not everything on the information highway is worthy of attention. The first flush of excitement has passed and we recognize that, as in all things, discrimination is key. Early television viewers were amazed to see anything on what was soon dubbed "the idiot box," just as the first cinemagoers were startled by what they saw on the screen. By now, the "wow" factor of the Internet has dwindled and it is not unusual to hear complaints about the amount of "noise" one has to wade through—blogs, Web sites, chat lines, misinformation, advertising—before reaching a "signal."

Similar grumbles were heard in the early twentieth century, when the rise of mass literacy led to the growth of a popular literature whose quality was questionable but which fed the voracious appetite for entertaining reading material. In the nineteenth century, humanists like Matthew Arnold believed that through mass education, the cultural level of the average person would be raised so that they could learn to appreciate great works of art and literature, previously available only to the wealthy and privileged, thereby enriching their lives. Arnold, I think, would be dismayed to see that what actually happened is that the taste of the masses won out, and that the great works of literature, though readily available, still remain the concern of the few. This is true even in the universities, once the bastions of "high culture." There the idea of a "great work" is discredited and the ascendancy of popular culture, if not complete, is surely on its way to being so.[37]

What does this mean in terms of the western esoteric tradition? It suggests to me that, in a very real sense, it is no longer esoteric, or at least not so much as it used to be. Which is to say it is no longer secret. This does not mean, of course, that the content of the esoteric tradition has changed. Hermeticism is still Hermetic and Gnosticism still gnostic, and the challenges facing someone trying to understand them and other elements of the esoteric tradition remain. But these teachings are no longer "hidden" in the way they once were.

When I first became interested in these ideas forty years ago, one still had to make a considerable effort to find them, although the wide distribution of esoteric, spiritual, and occult literature that would soon explode in the New Age had begun. I can't complain about this. After my first exposure to the occult, I was happy to find cheap reprints of occult classics in the remainder bins of many bookshops, and my own introduction to this tradition came through a paperback, not the emissary of a secret society. Still, places like Weiser's Bookshop and Magickal Childe in New York, and Gilbert's and the Bodhi Tree (where I worked) in Los Angeles were special, and their clientele went out of their way to get to them. Of course, a certain amount of nostalgia informs my view of them, but I don't think I am romanticizing too much. More was available in the 1970s than was around in, say, the 1940s or 1950s. But it was nothing like the tidal wave of material available now at little more than the click of a mouse.

In pointing this out I am not saying things were better back then. From the point of view of a writer researching material, the fact that I can find much literature online that earlier I would have had to hunt down in a library—assuming it had it—is in many ways a blessing. What I am trying to convey is that the often instant availability of much esoteric material today has, whether we like it or not, changed its character. This is true not only of occult or esoteric literature. People interested in yoga, meditation, Tarot, alchemy, or any number of other hitherto arcane pursuits can now, more times than not, find access to these things and more easily. This was not always the case and it can only be a good thing that these and other once "mysterious" interests are fairly common. But as mentioned earlier when talking about the New Age, a certain amount of watering down is inevitable, a certain amount of leveling off, of dilution, is unavoidable.

Another factor impacting the esoteric today is its association with political and sociological concerns centering around what has come to be known as "identity politics." This focuses, more or less, on the demands of certain "subcultures" to be recognized as of equal value and importance within an increasingly diverse and multicultural society. So people who consider themselves "pagans" or Wiccans, or some other formerly unrecognized group devoted to an occult or spiritual practice now want to receive the same recognition and representation traditionally reserved for more mainstream beliefs.

Likewise, the New Age focus on "saving the planet" has led to an at times tangled, not to say confused, association of spiritual, esoteric, and environmental concerns. (Gnostics, for example, are not concerned with saving the planet, while many nature-oriented people deny that we are anything more than clever animals.) While these interests are in many ways valid and worthy of attention, they can obscure the more inward necessities of "pure" esotericism. This is something Rudolf Steiner discovered when in his last years he expressed concern that the more practical application of his ideas in education, agriculture, medicine, and other fields was shifting attention away from the "supersensible perception" that was his central aim. Although an enormous task, saving the planet can often seem easier than confronting difficult epistemological questions.

Earlier I mentioned the idea that before the outbreak of spiritualism in the nineteenth century, a conference of esoteric masters convened to discuss the question whether occult knowledge, hitherto held secret, should be released, in order to circumvent the complete triumph of scientific materialism. The decision then was to release the knowledge, but as later esotericists like Madame Blavatsky and Rudolf Steiner believed, the attempt was a failure. I am not suggesting that a similar conference argued about the pros and cons of the New Age and its global dissemination through the Internet. I am pointing out that the problem is a perennial one: whether it is better to err on the side of the conservative view, and retain a teaching's purity by restricting its availability—hence leaving it less effective in the wider world—or on the side of the liberal view, gaining wide distribution at the expense of quality.

It would seem that whether we like it or not, technology has forced the issue, and the liberal view has won out. The secret is no longer secret and the esoteric cat is out of the bag. As Joscelyn Godwin writes: "The secrets once imparted only to initiates are there on the bookshelves."[38] Or as Antoine Faivre said to me many years ago, "When I first starting reading this sort of literature [in the 1950s] names like Crowley, the Golden Dawn, and Gurdjieff sounded mysterious. Now they're no longer mysterious. They ceased to be so as early as the 1970s."[39]

MEDITATIONS ON THE TAROT

Yet is it really true that esoteric work no longer goes on? Perhaps not. One of the most esoteric works of modern times did not appear in an English translation until 1985, and then anonymously, making it truly the work of a secret teacher. I am referring to the remarkable *Meditations on the Tarot,* which is now known to have been written in the late 1960s by the Estonian-Russian polyglot and Christian esotericist Valentin Tomberg. Tomberg was then living in England and it is not clear whether he was aware of the occult revival taking place at the time. He stipulated that his *magnum opus*—the *Meditations* number some 600-plus densely packed pages—would not be published until after his death, and then only anonymously. Tomberg died of a stroke in Majorca in 1973, but it would be more than a decade before a full edition of his masterpiece was made available to the public.

Tomberg was born in 1900 in St. Petersburg, and in his late teens he became interested in Theosophy and the spiritual philosophy of Vladimir Soloviev and the Russian Orthodox Church. He left the Theosophical Society soon after joining it and turned his attention to Steiner's Anthroposophy: in the early 1900s, Steiner had made a powerful impact on the generation of Russia's "God Seekers." Tomberg's family was devastated by the revolution—he lost both parents and a brother—and in 1920, he left Russia and went to Tallinn, Estonia. He later tried to make contact with Steiner, hoping to become his student, but his letters went unanswered. It is unclear if Steiner ever received them; in the last months of his life, he was too ill to keep up correspondence and may simply have been unable to reply.

Tomberg joined the Estonian branch of the Anthroposophical Society in 1925, eventually becoming its secretary general. But his independent mind soon led to friction with the Anthroposophical establishment. Throughout the 1930s, Tomberg wrote many articles for Anthroposophical journals on a variety of esoteric subjects, many having to do with the esoteric interpretation of the Bible, the "return of Christ in the etheric," and the "mission" of different nationalities. These articles were informed by a mystical experience Tomberg had in 1931, in which he said he had been put in contact with the "angelic world." Increasingly his ideas seemed counter to Anthroposophical doctrine, and by the end of the decade, he was asked to leave the society. Tomberg had already sought to find a place for himself at Steiner's Goetheanum in Dornach, Switzerland, but was refused by Steiner's widow.

In 1938, Tomberg moved to Holland, where he became involved in the Dutch Resistance following the Nazi invasion in 1940. He had become involved in the Anthroposophical Society there too, but soon the same frictions occurred and he was again asked to leave. (The essence of these frictions seemed to have been that Tomberg's esotericism was even more Christ-centered than Steiner's.) After the war, he went to Cologne, where he earned a degree in jurisprudence and became deeply involved in Roman Catholicism, leaving the Russian Orthodox Church because its leadership had seemed sympathetic to the Nazis. It is unclear if Tomberg actually converted—accounts differ on this point—but the church clearly became central to his spiritual life.

In 1948, Tomberg moved to England, where friends helped him find work with the BBC as a translator; like Roberto Assagioli, he had a talent for languages (the *Meditations* were originally written in French). Part of his work involved monitoring Soviet broadcasts. He retired in 1960 and devoted the rest of his life to study and to writing. Aside from his early

Anthroposophical articles, the majority of his work appeared only after his death.

The *Meditations on the Tarot* were written, Tomberg said, from the point of view of a voice reaching readers from "beyond the grave," and their aim is to immerse the reader in the current of "thought, effort, and revelation" that constitutes the "millennium-old" Hermetic tradition.[40] The book's subtitle, *A Journey into Christian Hermeticism,* may give contemporary readers some pause, but Tomberg is writing in the French Hermetic tradition which, from Eliphas Levi on, has always been at least a fellow traveler with the church. Tomberg himself says that the book's roots lie in the "pre-Christian Christianity" of ancient Egypt, by which he means the teachings of Hermes Trismegistus. Some readers may be put off by this, but they would be mistaken. The Christian elements in the work are in essence esoteric, and the claims made for the Roman Catholic Church as an insuperable repository of Hermetic wisdom can be taken with the necessary grains of salt. What comes through is that Tomberg has thought hard and deeply and that his wide reading in philosophy, psychology, literature, as well as esotericism—Jung, Gurdjieff, Steiner, Teilhard de Chardin, and Bergson are among his many references—informs his vital intuitive grasp of the Tarot's symbolism.

The *Meditations* are written in the form of letters to an "unknown friend"—the reader—and are essentially allusive, discursive essays on the twenty-two Tarot trumps. Space does not allow me to do more than touch on Tomberg's aim in writing them. Although in the context of Christian teaching, Tomberg's basic aim is to get the reader to think Hermetically, to let the rich symbolism of the trumps reach into our imagination and trigger our faculty for seeing connections, analogies, the subtle correspondences linking everything with everything else—for, that is, a right-brain form of thought.

The trumps are, he says, *arcana* which, in true esoteric fashion, "conceal and reveal their sense at one and the same time according to the depth of meditation."[41] They are not allegories or secrets—or tools for fortune-telling—but a kind of "enzyme" that is essential in order "to be fruitful in a given spiritual domain." These "enzymes" "ferment" the knowledge necessary for spiritual experience, and each trump presents a "spiritual exercise" necessary in order to render us capable of "making new discoveries" and "engendering new ideas." They in a sense help us to live creatively. Such creative living can lead us to what Tomberg calls the "mysteries," spiritual events that alter our consciousness. The Hermeticist engaged in this work is, Tomberg tells his unknown friends, "at one and the same time a mystic, gnostic, magician and philosopher" who brings together and synthesizes "the diverse planes of the macrocosm and the microcosm" and "aspires to conscious participation with the constructive forces of the world."[42]

GEBSER'S BREAKDOWN

It would seem, then, that even as late as the 1960s, work of a truly esoteric character was still being produced. Yet the dense, erudite, and challenging pages of *Meditations on the Tarot* seem something of an exception amid the more "reader friendly" texts informing the high-profile popular spirituality of our time.

Where, then, are we today?

Throughout this book I have mentioned the philosopher Jean Gebser's idea that since Petrarch made his perilous ascent of Mount Ventoux, the western mind has been involved in what Gebser calls the "deficient mode of the mental-rational consciousness structure." By the "deficient mode," Gebser means a time when a particular consciousness structure has exhausted its possibilities, has actualized its capacities, and has reached the end of its development. At this point it can go no further, and like an overripe fruit, it starts to go bad. Its advantages become liabilities and, in a way reminiscent of Gurdjieff's "law of seven" or Jung's *enantiodromia*, it starts to turn against itself.

I have suggested that with the all-out attack on the Hermetic tradition launched by Merin Mersenne in 1623, the deficient mode of the mental-rational consciousness structure entered a particularly heightened state—if we can speak meaningfully of a "heightened deficiency." Like the Gnostic demiurge and Iain McGilchrist's overconfident left brain, it believed it was self-sufficient and ignored any idea that its perspective was only partial, and that, no matter how much it denied it, it was inextricably linked to another perspective, radically other than its own but equally necessary. By the nineteenth century and the triumph of scientific materialism, this deficient mode could lay claim to more or less dominance, with the church ceding more and more ground and with Romantic poets noisily but ineffectively sounding warnings about its debilitating effect on the soul.

It was at this point that spiritualism appeared on the scene. If its appearance was, as some have suggested, aimed at retarding the advance of materialism, we may agree with Madame Blavatsky and Rudolf Steiner that it failed in its mission. Yet that may be too critical a judgment. Blavatsky and Steiner had harsh words about spiritualism. Steiner even said that the spiritualists were the worst materialists of all; with their attempts to "prove" the existence of the spiritual world by photographing spirits or using other scientific means of establishing their reality, they were in effect denying the essence of the spiritual, i.e., that it is not physical. We can understand Steiner's point while at the same time appreciating the work of Frederic Myers, William James, and others. If spiritualism did not stop the spread of materialism, it did introduce many people to the reality of something beyond the physical world, and as we've seen, during the positive fin-de-siècle, it led many of the best minds of the time to a recognition that materialist science, adequate and triumphant in its own realm, was insufficient as a complete vision of the universe.

This was something that science itself would soon recognize. By the late nineteenth century, the mechanical view of the universe was so well established and so confident in its ability to explain everything that scientists believed that if they knew the position and speed of all the particles in the universe, they could accurately predict the future behavior of these particles. In other words, they believed that the future was absolutely determined by the state of things in the present, which was itself determined by the past. Nothing, they believed, fell outside this web of total determinism. This meant that free will was an illusion, given that we ourselves are nothing more than collections of particles, subject to the same inescapable mechanical laws as the rest of the universe.

This view gave man a remarkable predictive power, but it also reduced him to being a cogwheel in an invariable cosmic clockwork. Man had risen to a mastery of the physical world, but at the expense of accepting his slavery to it, and of recognizing himself as only an infinitesimal speck trapped in a universe oblivious to his existence. That such a vision undermined the very vital drive that led to it—that it reduced man's questing spirit and will to truth to fairy tales, since neither spirit nor will were real—was an unfortunate but unavoidable consequence of the facts. These were unpleasant facts, to be sure, but facts nonetheless, and had to be faced stoically. Yet not all were happy with this state of things, and the mindless mechanical existence it affirmed led some sensitive souls to some rather extreme expressions of their disapproval.

The Russian novelist Fyodor Dostoyevsky summed up many people's feeling of rejection when he wrote in *Notes from Underground* (1864) that if everything can be reduced to mathematical formulae, then "man will go insane on purpose" in order to prove that "he is a man and not a cogwheel." With many others, Dostoyevsky recognized that what we crave most is our sense of freedom, and that in a universe in which everything is explained, everything accounted for in an unbreakable chain of cause and effect, that sense withers and dies. Men like Dostoyevsky would rather bring such a universe crashing down and embrace chaos and madness than accept the consequences of a world without freedom.

A WORLD GONE MAD?

The universe may have heard Dostoyevsky. What seemed to have happened in the early twentieth century is that the universe itself—at least its particles—began to act rather strangely, at least from the perspective of mechanical determinism. It would not be too exaggerated to say that it seemed to have gone positively crazy. The quantum mechanics that arose in the early twentieth century with Max Planck presented a universe rather different from the nineteenth-century mechanical one. At the macro level—the level of airplanes, planets, and baseballs—the predictive power of the mechanical view still worked. But at the micro level, that of the particles making up baseballs and everything else, it was running into some problems.

The essence of this shift from a stable, predictable universe to one that suddenly seemed much stranger can be expressed in the "uncertainty principle" of Werner Heisenberg, mentioned earlier. According to this, we cannot predict what the particles making up the universe will be doing in the future, because we can't determine with any accuracy what they are doing now. We can, according to Heisenberg, know their position or their speed, but not both simultaneously. Without knowing both, our predictions become guesses. The particles themselves are now no longer really particles but are thought of as "wave functions" which give the probability, higher or lower, that the particle associated with them will be located in one patch of space or another. We can't say for sure in the way that the nineteenth-century model thought it could.

Further developments led to even more unusual discoveries, and by now readers of popular books on the "new" physics are familiar with a whole host of new elementary particles that the nineteenth-century mechanistic view could not even imagine existed. Some particles are thought to move backward in time. Some can act as a particle, or as a wave, or both. Some come in and out of existence. Particles making up an atom change position without traversing space, the famous "quantum leap," rather as if you got out of bed and found yourself in your office, without having traveled across town to get there. Particles act "nonlocally," reacting to each other's movements without any medium carrying information between them. And every particle in the universe seems in some strange way to be connected to every other particle so that, in some way we can't yet understand, what happens to one affects all the others. In "The Love Song of J. Alfred Prufrock," T. S. Eliot asked the existential question: "Do I dare disturb the universe?" According to quantum physics, we are doing it all the time.

The nineteenth-century model saw particles as billiard balls, bumping into each other, their predictable impact moving the clockwork universe along. Now we have to think of billiard balls that disappear and reappear, that suddenly turn into waves of energy flowing across the billiard table, that move *before* being hit by the cue ball, or that pop out of the table's pockets.

The crazy behavior associated with quantum physics troubled Einstein—whose own ideas about "curved space" fundamentally altered our ideas about space and time—and led him to assert that "God does not play dice with the universe." Later physicists like David Bohm agreed with Einstein and tried to locate the "hidden variables" that Einstein believed could account for the crazy behavior of the quantum world. Yet further developments have not borne Einstein out, and for good or bad, God seems to be, in Stephen Hawking's words, "an inveterate gambler, who throws the dice on every possible occasion."[43] Later developments such as "chaos theory" suggest that even at the macro level, events are not as predictable as we would like, with innocuous butterflies in China causing tornadoes in the Midwest—not to mention wreaking havoc with our weather reports.

A DIFFERENT PERSPECTIVE

In *The Ever-Present Origin,* Gebser charted these developments, as well as parallel ones in philosophy, literature, psychology, history, and many other disciplines, in order to show that, as a consequence of the breakdown of the mental-rational structure of consciousness, the once unassailable mechanical view of existence was falling apart. The "perspective" that arose from Petrarch gazing out from atop Mount Ventoux, and that established ourselves as detached beings confronting a world separate from ourselves, was being dismantled, evidence for which Gebser saw in the "aperspectival" paintings produced by Picasso, Braque, and other members of the Cubist school.

A similar disruption of the linearity associated with perspective and the clean lines of rational thought was emerging in literature too: the great novels of Joyce, Proust, Mann, Musil, and others all take liberties with our usual sense of linear time and stable place. Arnold Schoenberg's difficult "twelve tone" system of music broke up traditional notions of musical form and introduced a strange, alien-sounding "atonal" world. In philosophy, Martin Heidegger's belief that we took a wrong turn at Plato led to his attempt at a "deconstruction" of western philosophy, which he hoped would enable us to once again encounter the mystery of being, free of the constraints placed upon it by our drive to "explain" reality rationally.

In more recent times, Heidegger's insight has been taken up by a host of postmodern thinkers, busily "deconstructing" the western mind's view of reality, rather like the ancient image of the ouroboros snake eating its own tail. In this process, widely diverging views can meet in some unlikely encounters. In an unexpected union, both postmodern and New Age thinking, otherwise rather opposed, suggest, in different ways, that reality is more or less up for grabs, that it is ultimately, as Keats said of beauty, "in the eye of the beholder"—i.e., subjective—and both present a somewhat cavalier attitude in the face of this. And so the idea of some hard, objective reality "out there," which is the heart of the old materialist view, is, it seems, really passé.

The upshot of these and other developments—here I have only touched the surface of Gebser's monumental analysis—is that the once-stable worldview of western consciousness has for some time now been loosening at the seams. In one sense this isn't news. We've already seen that "degeneration" was a popular theme in the fin-de-siècle—popular enough for Max Nordau to write a best-selling book about it. Another best seller on a similar theme, Oswald Spengler's *The Decline of the West*, appeared in Europe after World War I. Spengler argued that, like living organisms, civilizations are born, grow to maturity, and die, and he believed ours was on its way out.

Since then dozens—hundreds—of books have appeared that, in one way or another, support Gebser's thesis. In recent times we have been treated to the "end" of quite a few things. In *The Order of Things* (1966), the philosopher Michel Foucault spoke of the "end of man," meaning the end of the Enlightenment humanism rooted in the philosophy of Kant. The political scientist Francis Fukuyama wrote *The End of History and the Last Man* (1992), which argued that the global spread of liberal democracy and the free market marked the triumph and culmination of western civilization. John Horgan's *The End of Science* (1996) was subtitled *Facing the Limits of Knowledge in the Twilight of the Scientific Age*. In *Grammars of Creation* (2001), George Steiner, one of the last European cultural mandarins, laments that "We have no more beginnings" and concludes that there is "in the climate of spirit at the end of the twentieth century, a core tiredness." "We are, or feel ourselves to be, latecomers."[44] And in *From Dawn to Decadence* (2001), an account of the last five hundred years, the historian

Jacques Barzun—who died in 2012 at the age of 104—presents a picture of early twenty-first-century man undergoing what he calls the "Great Undoing," the West's self-immolation at the hands of chat shows, gangsta rap, and fashionable deconstructionism. The great themes that fueled the West from the Renaissance to today, Barzun argues, have become knotted up in a tangled skein of competing and contradictory "goods" that we have no hope of unraveling. (For example, in order to secure "individual rights and freedom," governments have to introduce more and more laws, thus creating more restrictions and less freedom.)

We live today in a state of what the sociologist Zygmunt Bauman calls "liquid modernity," a flux of rapid change and instability, a sort of social shape-shifting that produces unease and insecurity, yet without providing a clear focus of their source. As the philosopher Leszek Kolakowski remarked, "It seems as though we live with the feeling of an all-encompassing crisis without being able to identify its causes clearly."[45]

A LAST STAND

And at the same time as the worldview of the mental-rational structure of consciousness seems to be petering out, in many ways it also seems that it is expressing itself in more and more radical and dogmatic ways, as if in its death throes it is making one last bid to secure its dominance. So the physicist Steven Weinberg tells us that the more we understand the universe, the more pointless it appears; rabid atheists like Richard Dawkins employ transport advertising to convince us that God doesn't exist; neuroscientists and philosophers of mind like Nicholas Humphrey and Daniel Dennett go to great lengths to "explain" consciousness as an effect of purely physical causes; and advocates of the new "genetic behaviorism" assure us that free will is an illusion and we are really helpless captives of our genes, determined by them at every step.[46]

The list could go on. If all Gebser did was to add his voice to the many speaking darkly of these developments, he would only have presented a remarkably eloquent and richly researched jeremiad about the last days— no small feat, indeed, but not unique. But for Gebser, the breakdown of one consciousness structure is necessary in order to clear ground for the emergence of a new one. Gebser argues that the unraveling of the western rational mind-set that has been taking place throughout the last century and into our own is the prelude and necessary precondition for the appearance of what, as mentioned, Gebser called the "integral structure of consciousness." This is a structure that integrates and transcends the previous structures, a mutation as shattering as the ones that came before. The shift from one consciousness structure to another is no picnic; in a very real sense, whole worlds change in the process. Alfred North Whitehead once remarked that "the major advances in civilization are processes which all but wreck the societies in which they occur."[47] Gebser would agree and would add that out of that wreckage something new and necessary can—must—emerge.

THE NEW CONSCIOUSNESS

I am suggesting that the widespread popular spirituality and interest in the occult that we conveniently speak of as the New Age is another symptom and indication of the breakdown of the mental-rational consciousness structure. It is a grassroots recognition that the explanations and answers the departing consciousness structure provides are no longer completely adequate for our needs, if indeed they ever were. The negative side of this is the "flight from reason" that much of this embodies, the unthinking rejection of the mind, intellect, and critical reasoning that informs a great deal of New Age philosophy. In a way, we can see this as a kind of right-brain guerrilla tactic, a running commando raid on the left-brain's supply lines. It is not enough to inflict serious damage, but it is a persistent annoyance. Yet history's pendulum swings are never precise, and while the plunge into the occult that began in the 1960s can be seen as a necessary compensation for the increasing "scientification" of the modern world, it too presents problems of its own, and I have spelled some of them out in *Turn Off Your Mind*.

We have already seen that Maslow, one of the founders of the human potential movement and an astute critic of reductionist science—as his classic *The Psychology of Science* (1966) makes clear—was wary of the anti-intellectualism popular at places like Esalen. The danger here is to throw the rational baby out with the hyperrational bathwater. The kind of "turn off your mind" and "go with the flow" sensibility informing this anti-intellectualism can too easily succumb to a dangerous irrationalism, to the kind of forced spontaneity and unreflective action that characterized much of the 1960s counterculture and also its equivalent in Europe in the years leading up to World War II. As in the positive fin-de-siècle, many of the interests and pursuits we associate with our own occult revival were popular then too, and more than one historian has made the sobering observation that the embrace of myth, intuition, "the soul," and the unconscious springs of life and vitality that informed the rejection of dry-as-dust intellect in the 1920s and '30s also provided the soil in which dangerous developments like Nazism and Fascism—both of which rejected the critical mind in favor of myth—grew. This is not to say, as some critics have, that a concern with myth and the soul at the expense of the critical intellect necessarily leads to some form of fascism, but that the potential for it doing so is real.

The positive side of our current spiritual revival is that it may contain within it signs of the new consciousness structure Gebser saw on the rise. Again, this is not to say that the New Age is evidence or proof of the new, integral structure of consciousness; merely that within it, mixed in with much that is merely fashionable and downright silly, there may be indications of the kind of shift Gebser had in mind. Gebser was aware of the rising popular interest in new forms of consciousness. In a preface to a new edition of *The Ever-Present Origin,* written just a few months before his death in 1973, Gebser wrote that "The principle subject of the book, proceeding from man's altered relationship to time, is the new consciousness, and to this those of the younger generation are keenly attuned."[48]

Yet Gebser was also aware of the dangers of a too precipitous plunge into the deep waters of the "magical structure of consciousness," whose characteristic form of "group consciousness"—which played a central role in the sixties psychedelic counterculture and continues to do so in the New Age—Gebser had firsthand acquaintance with, witnessing the Nazi rallies in Munich in the 1920s.[49] As with so many things, a fine balance is required here, that "just right" of the "Goldilocks moment," when two extremes come together into a new development, transcending both. That such a critical fine-tuning is required now is the central idea of this book. The pendulum swings from one side to the other really get us nowhere.

Gebser's first hint that a new form of consciousness seemed to be awakening in western man came to him in 1932, through a study of the poetry of Rilke. Like Owen Barfield, Gebser saw that language reflected changes in consciousness, and in studying Rilke's poetry, Gebser experienced a "lightning-like inspiration" that he spent the rest of his life unpacking: the intuition that western consciousness was mutating into some new form, one, as we've seen, that he believed was essentially characterized by a marked change in our appreciation of time. We have seen some of the developments Gebser believed offered proof of this: the breakdown of linear, step-by-step sequential thinking in favor of the simultaneity in the paintings of Picasso; the novels of Joyce, Proust, and others; and the alterations to our understanding of space and time provided by Einstein's relativity theory and quantum physics.

My own belief is that if Gebser was around to witness it, he would have seen confirmation of his ideas in the rise of the Internet and the triumph over time and space offered by popular technological developments like TiVo and podcasts, which allow us to watch or listen to a television or radio program when and where we want, without having to be at a particular place at a particular time. These offer rather banal evidence for Gebser's insight, to be sure, and I am not suggesting that they themselves are some important evolutionary advance. But their sheer triviality seems to suggest a stronger support than some more "mystical" proof. The "irruption of time" that Gebser saw on its way would not necessarily emerge in exciting, romantic ways, as the idea of a radical "singularity" might suggest. When our small, commonplace ways of life are affected, it is clear that some change has occurred.

THE INTEGRAL BRAIN

Gebser's descriptions of the new, integral structure of consciousness offer some of the most difficult passages in *The Ever-Present Origin.* This should not be surprising. From Plato on, throughout this book we have encountered the difficulties of trying to speak of the unsayable. Yet if we are not to rest content with the silence of the *via negativa,* an attempt must be made. And we have seen that, although never completely successful—the meanings we are trying to capture always exceed explicit statement—such attempts are worth the effort. As Owen Barfield, Gebser, Ouspensky, and many others knew, with each new word or expression, some new side of reality is grasped, its precincts are extended by that much, and our own consciousness is likewise enlarged. Language is one of our greatest tools in exploring consciousness, perhaps the most important one. It is our way of mapping reality. Yet it is a strange kind of map: its use increases the area it covers, as if the more you understand the map, the more map there is to understand.

In the case of the integral structure of consciousness, we have to admit, we have a difficult map. Gebser faces the challenge of using the language of one consciousness structure to speak of a very different consciousness structure, one that transcends the basis of the language used to describe it. This is why Gebser's lexicon contains many words beginning with the prefix "a": "aperspectival," "atemporal," "acausality," "amensionality," and others. As with Dionysius the Areopagite and other followers of the *via negativa,* Gebser must resort to saying what the integral structure of consciousness is *not* like, in order to convey some sense of it. And what it is not like is our mental-rational structure, which sees things in terms of perspective, time, causality, the dimensions of space, sequence, and the necessities of Aristotelian logic.

Gebser's more positive coinages—"concretion," "waring," "verition," "diaphaneity"—offer their own difficulties. "Concretion" refers to the "concretizing of the spiritual" that accompanies the integral structure; "waring" reveals the "itself" of ourselves and others; with "verition," the world becomes "pure statement," its being and presence "self-evident"; and "diaphaneity" is the "shining-through" of "Origin," which will become "present" in the new consciousness structure. These are not easy sayings, and to grasp the insight of only one of them requires considerable effort and in effect brings about a change in consciousness itself. In a sense we can say that we can only understand the integral structure of consciousness by experiencing it, and we can experience it by trying to understand it.

Yet in many ways, Gebser's descriptions of the integral structure of consciousness are very similar to the kind of consciousness that throughout this book we have associated with a thinking more informed by a right-brain perspective. This too should not be surprising; as we have seen, Gebser's "mental-rational" consciousness structure is practically identical to the view Iain McGilchrist has associated with a left-brain-dominant consciousness. This suggests that a consciousness that goes beyond the mental-rational structure would be similar to one that went beyond a left-brain dominant view. Such a consciousness would be one that emerged from bringing the two sides of the brain together, from, that is, integrating them, and, via the transcendent function, producing something new. That Gebser calls the new structure of consciousness "integral" suggests something similar. We seem to speaking of an "integral brain," one whose hemispheric fusion "completes the partial mind" and provides access to a more complete reality.

Gebser speaks of such a consciousness as being "ego-free," which he insists does not mean "ego-less." Gebser is not speaking of a return to the whole, a blending of our consciousness with that of the All, as some mystical paths suggest. In "ego-freedom," as I understand it, we are aware of the whole and our relation to it, while retaining our clear awareness of our independent self. We are "ego-free" insofar as we transcend the limited perspective of the ego, the small self, aware of little more than its appetites and complaints, and gain a "bird's-eye view" of the larger world beyond ourselves. It is a more objective view, an embrace of the *impersonal*. We "step back" from the ego, our usual sense of ourselves associated with the left brain, and perceive a larger reality, seeing things "aperspectivally," not from only one "point of view," but many. Such is the case when, as McGilchrist tells us, the left brain relaxes its dominance and allows the right to make its contribution. We are not then ego-less—we still feel ourselves to be an "I," in fact, a much larger one—but we are free of the limited perspective of the left brain, and through the right brain are aware of the "network of connections linking everything to everything else."

COMPLETING THE PARTIAL MIND

As we've seen, Jung believed that the coming shift in the "psychic dominants" would "constellate the problem of the union of opposites." The opposites here in question are the two sides of our brain, and the two modes of consciousness associated with them. (And I point out once again, that even if it turns out that everything said about the left and right brain is wrong, our two modes of consciousness remain and are the important thing, wherever they are located.)

McGilchrist argues that throughout history, there have been brief but significant moments when these two rivals worked together, and the results were transformative: Greek philosophy, Renaissance genius, and Romantic vision were some of them. If, as I have argued, the dismissal of the esoteric, Hermetic, occult tradition and its relegation to the status of "rejected knowledge" four hundred years ago was the result of a coup d'état on the part of the left brain against the right, it seems reasonable to ask what the resurgence of this "rejected knowledge" in the last half century or so means? It can of course mean nothing at all, or merely that what seemed mystic eccentricities in the 1970s have been absorbed into our culture, much like other once-exotic practices have.

In many ways, I would not argue with this. While it is good and pleasant to have yoga centers, spiritual seminars, and New Age best sellers, they in themselves do not guarantee a change in consciousness. A more generous assessment, however, would, I think, wonder if the prevalence of these and similar developments does not suggest that we may be approaching one of those junctures in history when the two rivals inside our heads may join forces again, or at least find themselves in a good position to do so.

The need for such a partnership seems clear. Gebser believed that if we did not participate in the transition from the old consciousness structure to the new one freely—that is, by undergoing it purposefully in our own consciousness—we would most likely go smash and experience the transition as a catastrophe, if we are not doing so already. McGilchrist suggests that the crisis produced by dominance of the left brain, which has led to our disenchanted, soulless, mechanized world, would trigger the return of the right.

My own feeling is that at least some of the conditions that seemed to be associated with past creative partnerships between our two modes of consciousness are present today. One obvious one is the juxtaposition of the old and the new, the past and the future. The historian Arnold Toynbee said that when a civilization goes through what he called its "time of troubles," it seems to react in one of two ways: what he called the "archaist" and the "futurist." It can seek to overcome its present difficulties by returning to the past, by trying to revive some ancient golden age. Or it can try to overcome its challenges by leaping into some bright, dazzling future. Both options seem open to us today. Proponents of an "archaic revival" see our salvation in embracing the wisdom of indigenous, non-western people, at home in nature and untouched by modernity's ills, while advocates of "transhumanism" see our hope in a man-machine merger that would have our minds digitized and downloaded onto computers. It is not too difficult to see the archaist choice as more right brain and the futurist one as more left.

In this scenario, both extremes move away from each other, yet what we are looking for is their closer proximity. It was, we remember, the fusion of old and new that characterized the Renaissance, and we seek a similar "Goldilocks moment," when the balance between the two will be "just right." And while I am not suggesting that we are definitely on the cusp of a similarly creative time—I make no prophecy of yet another new age—there is no reason to believe such an outcome is impossible. Making it possible is up to us. Any lasting change must first take place in the individual. Future historians will have to determine the outcome and what, if anything, we today have learned from the secret teachers of the western world.

ACKNOWLEDGMENTS

Many people helped to make this book possible. Once again I want to thank the staff of the British Library. I would like to thank my editor, Mitch Horowitz, for his patience and understanding and for turning a blind eye to the growing word count. James Hamilton once again allowed me to burden him with endless summaries of the book in progress. Very special thanks go to Anja Flode Bjorlo, who thought of the idea and provided the title. Her insightful comments and encouragement proved indispensable; without these, the book could not have been written. My sons, Joshua and Maximilian, were once again an inspiration, as was their mother, Ruth Jones, whose many questions helped to put things in perspective. I would like to thank Iain McGilchrist for his brilliant book; needless to say, he is not responsible for the use I make of it and I apologize in advance for any misrepresentation of his ideas.

NOTES

INTRODUCTION: REJECTED KNOWLEDGE

1. Iain McGilchrist, *The Master and His Emissary* (London: Yale University Press, 2010), p. 16.
2. Colin Wilson, *Frankenstein's Castle* (Sevenoaks, U.K.: Ashgrove Press, 1980), p. 21.
3. For a recent look at split-brain patients, see David Wolman, "Split-Brain: A Tale of Two Halves," in *Nature* (March 14, 2012); http://www.nature.com/news/the-split-brain-a-tale-of-two-halves-1.10213. See also Colin Wilson, *Access to Inner Worlds* (London: Rider and Co., 1983), in which Wilson discusses the strange case of Brad Absetz. Absetz was not a split-brain patient, but he had developed a method of allowing his right brain to communicate with him directly, and he experienced some of the conflict between the two brains common to split-brain patients.
4. An interesting experiment would be to try to remember what kinds of *images* are in our minds when we experience this, as the right brain communicates through them. I recently tried to remember the name of a musician but for the life of me could not. While I was racking my left brain for clues, an image of a bird came to me and I had a strong sense that this had something to do with the name. A few minutes later it came to me: it was Gil Scott-Heron. A related phenomenon was recognized by the psychologist Anthony Storr in his book *Music and the Mind* (London: HarperCollins, 1992). Storr writes about how, in some situations, we find that a tune is running through our head. We may think that it is random, but it is not; Storr discovered that it often has a clear association with the situation we find ourselves in, that is, in fact, a commentary on it. As the right brain is associated with our appreciation of music, we may see in this a way in which it makes a nonverbal contribution to our experience. A related phenomena would be the "self-symbolic" character of hypnagogic imagery. See Lachman, *A Secret History of Consciousness* (Great Barrington, Mass.: Lindisfarne, 2003), pp. 85–94.
5. "The brain isn't like a computer, with specific sections of hardware charged with specific tasks. It's more like a network of computers connected by very big, busy broadband cables." Wolman, 2012 above.
6. Readers may be interested in my review of *The Master and His Emissary*, which can be found at the *Los Angeles Review of Books;* see "Oppositional Thinking," February 9, 2012; https://lareviewof books.org/review/oppositional-thinking.
7. McGilchrist, p. 3.
8. Michael Polanyi, *The Tacit Dimension* (New York: Anchor Books, 1967), p. 4.
9. This division of labor can be seen in nonhuman species as well, McGilchrist argues, and he evidences birds. In order to eat, they need to be able to detect bits of food amid inedible items, and this requires left-brain accuracy. But they also need to be aware of their overall surroundings so that they don't become food themselves, and here right-brain wide awareness comes in. This double duty, McGilchrist argues, is linked to an asymmetry in avian brains, which blossoms more fully in our own cerebral hemispheres.
10. Steven Weinberg, *The First Three Minutes* (New York: Basic Books, 1993), p. 154.
11. Leonard Shlain, *The Alphabet Versus the Goddess* (New York: Penguin Group, 1999), p. 23.
12. Ibid., p. 21.
13. Lachman 2003, pp. 271–73.
14. Antoine Faivre, *Access to Western Esotericism* (Albany, N.Y.: SUNY Press, 1994), pp. 12–13.
15. Gary Lachman, *The Quest for Hermes Trismegistus: From Ancient Egypt to the Modern World* (Edinburgh: Floris Books, 2011), pp. 188–89.
16. Lachman 2003, pp. 217–67.
17. Jean Gebser, *The Ever-Present Origin*, Noel Barstad and Algis Mickunas, trans. (Athens: Ohio University Press, 1985), p. 1.

18. Ibid., p. 221.
19. Georg Feuerstein, *Structures of Consciousness* (Lower Lake, Calif.: Integral Publishing, 1987), p. 217.
20. Ibid, p. 99.
21. Gebser 1985, pp. 12–15.
22. Frances Yates, *Giordano Bruno and the Hermetic Tradition* (London: Routledge, 1971), p. 13.
23. Ibid., p. 42.
24. For the influence of Hermeticism on modern astronomy and "the occult origins of science," see Lynn Picknett and Clive Prince, *The Forbidden Universe* (London: Constable, 2011).
25. Both Gebser and Julian Jaynes provide examples of a similar "clash of consciousness." In Jaynes's case, it was between "bicameral" and "unicameral" man, exemplified by the fateful encounter between the Incas and the Spanish; for Gebser it was the meeting of a "magical-mythical" consciousness and a "mental-rational" one, when the Aztecs fell prey to their European conquerors. See Julian Jaynes, *The Origin of Consciousness in the Breakdown of the Bicameral Mind* (Princeton, N.J.: Princeton University Press, 1976), p. 160; and Gebser 1985, pp. 4–5. I should also mention that Freud, whose reductive, materialist approach to the psyche seems more left brain than right, spoke of himself as a *conquistador* in his attitude to the unconscious. The right brain, while not identical to the unconscious, certainly seems more open to it and seems to be a way of making contact with it.
26. For more on Mersenne, see Lachman 2011, pp. 181–89.
27. Yates 1971, p. 435.
28. Joscelyn Godwin, *Robert Fludd* (London: Thames and Hudson, 1979), p. 5.
29. Yates 1971, p. 402.
30. Richard Tarnas, *The Passion of the Western Mind* (New York: Ballantine Books, 1991), pp. 400–2
31. Ibid., 376, 363.
32. McGilchrist 2010, p. 439.
33. P. D. Ouspensky, *In Search of the Miraculous* (New York: Harcourt, Brace & Co., 1949), p. 77.
34. Gary Lachman, *Jung the Mystic* (New York: Tarcher/Penguin, 2010), pp. 115–17.
35. Stan Gooch, *The Double Helix of the Mind* (London: Wildwood House, 1980), pp. 128–57.
36. Quoted ibid., pp. 136–37.
37. Owen Barfield, *Romanticism Comes of Age* (Middleton, Conn.: Wesleyan University Press, 1986), p. 153.
38. Arthur Koestler, *Janus: A Summing Up* (London: Pan Books, 1979), p. 57.
39. Tarnas 1991, pp. 302, 376.
40. Lachman 2010, pp. 115–22.
41. I should make clear that I am not suggesting that the western esoteric tradition is synonymous with or has a monopoly on "right-brain consciousness." Art, poetry, music, love, and a variety of other human pursuits are also more "right brain" than others. I am suggesting that the western esoteric tradition is a body of knowledge informed by a right-brain awareness and openness, and that it has acted as a repository of this mode of consciousness as well as a means of initiating it.
42. Arthur Versluis, "Western Esotercism and Consciousness," *Journal of Consciousness Studies* 7, no. 6 (2000), 20–33.
43. Ibid., pp. 21, 26.

CHAPTER 1: AN ANCIENT WISDOM

1. See Lachman 2011, pp. 11–12.
2. Yates 1971, p. 5.
3. Christopher McIntosh, *The Rosicrucians* (Wellingborough, U.K.: Crucible, 1987), p. 30.
4. Eliphas Levi, *Transcendental Magic* (York Beach, Me.: Weiser, 1970), p. 1.
5. Arthur Versluis, *Magic and Mysticism: An Introduction to Western Esotericism* (Lanham, Md.: Rowman & Littlefield, 2007), p. 35.
6. Wouter Hanegraaff, *Western Esotericism: A Guide for the Perplexed* (London: Bloomsbury, 2013), pp. 3–5.
7. Ludwig Wittgenstein, *Culture and Value* (Chicago: University of Chicago Press, 1984), p. 14.
8. The evaporating power of seeking an explicit definition of an implicit meaning is a common experience with many of our most fundamental ideas. When asked the meaning of "time," St. Augustine famously remarked that "if you do not ask the question, I know the answer." This is true of practically all our basic concepts. As Leonard Shlain writes, "The things one loves, lives, and dies for cannot easily be expressed in words" (Shlain 1999, p. 19). This, of course, does not mean that they do not exist. Socrates, whom we may see as a "founding father" of left-brain rationality, exasperated his interlocutors by insisting that they define for him certain ideas the meaning of which they felt

sure they understood. See the early dialogue *Euthyphro* in W. K. C. Guthrie, trans., *Plato: Collected Dialogues* (Princeton, N.J.: Bollingen Series, 1961). This is not to put esotericism on an equal par with love, art, philosophy, or being; but it does share with these a resistance to exact definition.

9. Throughout this book I will use a "loose" meaning of the "esoteric" that will include related but different ideas such as "the occult," and "Hermetic," and also "mystery" and "inner tradition."

10. Joscelyn Godwin, *The Golden Thread* (Wheaton, Ill.: Quest Books, 2007), p. xi.

11. Lachman 2011, pp. 23–49.

12. Versluis 2007, p. 2.

13. Gary Lachman, *Madame Blavatsky: The Mother of Modern Spirituality* (New York: Tarcher/Penguin, 2012), pp. 129, 134.

14. Mark Sedgwick, *Against the Modern World* (Oxford, U.K.: Oxford University Press, 2004), p. 24.

15. James Moore, *Gurdjieff: The Anatomy of a Myth* (Shaftesbury, U.K.: Element Books, 1991), pp. 28–29.

16. G. I. Gurdjieff, *Meetings with Remarkable Men* (London: Penguin Classics, 2015). This new edition includes an Introduction by me.

17. In *A Secret History of Consciousness*, I write about hypnagogia, the strange state of consciousness in between sleeping and waking. This is characterized by vivid hallucinations and symbolic "half-dreams." I discuss the work of Andreas Mavromatis, whose book *Hypnagogia* is an exhaustive account of the subject. One of Mavromatis's arguments is that hypnagogia—which I relate to Rudolf Steiner's ideas about the evolution of consciousness—is linked to the older, subcortical parts of the brain, such as the hippocampus, medulla oblongata, and thalamus. Mavromatis suggests that hypnagogia, which is associated with a kind of "pre-logical thought" involving images, symbols, and analogy, as opposed to the clear, logical thinking associated with the younger cerebral cortex, can be seen as an "older" form of consciousness, much as McGilchrist argues is the case with the right brain.

18. See Lachman 2003, pp. 153–78.

19. "Through the direction and nature of our attention, we prove ourselves to be partners in creation, both of the world and of ourselves," and "the kind of attention we bring to bear on the world changes the nature of the world we attend to," McGilchrist 2010, p. 28.

20. See my article "Rudolf Steiner, Jean Gebser and the Evolution of Consciousness" in *Journal for Anthroposophy* 61 (Fall 1995), pp. 80–93.

21. Arthur Koestler provides some support for Steiner's ideas about a "picture thinking." In *The Act of Creation* (New York: Macmillan, 1964), p. 173, Koestler writes that *"as vehicles of thought,* pictorial and other nonverbal representations are indeed earlier, both phylogenetically and ontogenetically older forms of ideation, than verbal thinking" (italics in original).

22. Stewart Easton, *Man and World in the Light of Anthroposophy* (New York: Steiner Books, 1982), p. 39.

23. Gary Lachman, *Politics and the Occult* (Wheaton, Ill.: Quest Books, 2008), p. 185.

24. In *Meetings With Remarkable Men* Gurdjieff mentions coming across a map of "pre-sand Egypt" traced on an ancient parchment. He fails to go into further detail about it, but in *A New Model of the Universe* (New York: Knopf, 1969), p. 320, Ouspensky remarks that "the Sphinx is older than historical Egypt" and is the work of an "ancient culture, which was possessed of knowledge far greater than our own." Ouspensky does not tell us how he knows this, but in *In Search of the Miraculous* (New York: Harcourt, Brace, 1949), p. 27, Ouspensky tells us that Gurdjieff said the Sphinx was a work of "objective art," that is, it is designed to have a specific effect on its audience. One suspects Ouspensky's ideas about the age of the Sphinx were based on information given to him by Gurdjieff.

25. The "precession of the equinoxes" is an astronomical phenomena caused by a wobble in the Earth's axis. It is responsible for the apparent backward movement of the sun through the signs of the zodiac. A complete cycle takes approximately twenty-six thousand years, and by acting as a backdrop to sunrise at the vernal equinox, each sign gives its name to an "age"—also known as a "Platonic month"—which lasts roughly 2,150 years. We are supposed to be on the verge of entering the age of Aquarius, and exiting the age of Pisces. Before Pisces, it was the age of Aries, then the age of Taurus, and so on. As many have pointed out, fish symbolism surrounds Christ because Christ was the central symbol of the age of Pisces, the astrological sign of the fish. Ram and bull symbolism were prevalent in the previous ages. Much occult and esoteric significance is attached to these ages, which are real phenomena. Needless to say, official science recognizes the phenomena, but not the significance.

26. In the 1970s, a Japanese firm hired by Nissan tried to construct a replica of the Great Pyramid, but on a smaller scale. They originally aimed to use the same techniques as orthodox Egyptologists maintain would have been available to the original builders, but this proved impossible. Even after making several attempts using "state of the art" technology, the effort failed and the project was abandoned; http://www.world-mysteries.com/mpl_wh2.htm.

27. Colin Wilson, *From Atlantis to the Sphinx* (London: Virgin Books, 1996), p. 62.

28. See Graham Hancock and Robert Bauval, *The Message of the Sphinx* (New York: Broadway Books, 1997), pp. 23–57.

29. See http://imagine.gsfc.nasa.gov/docs/science/mysteries_12/lumpy.html.
30. René Schwaller de Lubicz, *The Temples of Karnak* (Rochester, Vt.: Inner Traditions, 1999), p. 15.
31. René Schwaller de Lubicz, *Esotericism and Symbol* (New York: Inner Traditions, 1985), p. 49.
32. René Schwaller de Lubicz, *Nature Word* (West Stockbridge, Mass.: Lindisfarne Press, 1982), p. 135.
33. Ian Marshall and Dana Zohar, *Who's Afraid of Schrödinger's Cat?* (London: Bloomsbury, 1997), pp. 101–2, 384–87.
34. See, for example, Gilles Deleuze, *Bergsonism* (New York: Zone Books, 1990).
35. Aldous Huxley, *The Doors of Perception* (London: Grafton Books, 1987), p. 20.
36. Ibid., p. 15.
37. Ibid.
38. Henri Bergson, *Introduction to Metaphysics* (New York: G. P. Putnam Sons, 1912), p. 7.
39. Robert Lawlor, "Introduction" to René Schwaller de Lubicz, *Symbol and the Symbolic* (Brookline, Mass.: Autumn Press, 1978), p. 8.
40. Much has been written in recent years about the Maya (300 B.C.–900 A.D.) and their supposed prediction of a cataclysmic event in the year 2012. Whatever we may think of this prediction, the Maya do seem to have possessed a remarkable astronomical and mathematical knowledge, and they also seem to have been obsessed with time, calculating no less than four calendars: one for the sun, one for the moon, a sacred calendar used for ritual purposes, and also what they called the "Long Count," dealing with very longs periods of time. They were aware of the existence of Uranus and Neptune, although these were not discovered by Europeans until the mid-nineteenth century, and they also calculated a yearly cycle according to the orbits of Venus, Jupiter, and Saturn. Whatever we may think of the supposed cataclysm of 2012, NASA scientists have informed us that in July 2012, the Earth just missed being hit with a "catastrophic" solar storm. The Maya were especially interested in sun-spot activity, and the dire events predicted for 2012 had to do with this; http://science.nasa.gov/science-news/science-at-nasa/2014/23jul_superstorm/. The Maya, however, did not develop this knowledge on their own. For all their astronomical awareness, they did not discover the wheel, so it is likely they received their knowledge of the heavens from elsewhere and merely maintained a tradition that was taught to them.
41. Colin Wilson, *Beyond the Occult* (London: Bantam Press, 1988), p. 25.
42. Colin Wilson, *Atlantis and the Kingdom of the Neanderthals* (Rochester, Vt.: Bear & Co., 2006), p. 35.
43. Ibid.
44. Lachman 2003, pp. 122–25.
45. Mary Leakey, *Disclosing the Past* (London: Weidenfeld and Nicholson, 1984), p. 177.
46. See http://news.discovery.com/human/evolution/how-neanderthal-dna-changed-humans-140129.htm.
47. A morbid though reasonable thought: Gooch died in 2010, and one wonders if anyone thought to look at his cerebellum to see if it corroborated his theory.
48. Gary Lachman, *Swedenborg: An Introduction to His Life and Ideas* (New York: Tarcher/Penguin, 2012), p. 55.
49. Stan Gooch, *The Paranormal* (London: Fontana, 1979), p. 242.
50. Gooch 1980, pp. 41–65.
51. In one sense, whether it is left brain versus right, or cerebrum versus cerebellum is irrelevant, because what is fundamentally important is the tension between *two modes of consciousness*, whatever their neurological location, if any.
52. Wilson 1996, pp. 266–72.
53. Stan Gooch, *Guardians of the Ancient Wisdom* (London: Fontana, 1980), p. 13.
54. Some paleontologists suggest that the spheres were used as part of a bola, a three-corded weapon used to trap animals, but as one Web site devoted to Paleolithic studies remarks, there is no evidence of bola use in Europe at that time, and the spheres remain an "enigma"; http://donsmaps.com/laquina.html.
55. Richard Rudgley, *Lost Civilizations of the Stone Age* (London: Century, 1998), p. 100.
56. See http://scribol.com/science/the-oldest-lunar-calendar-on-earth.
57. Gooch 1980, p. 101.
58. Aleister Crowley, *The Confessions of Aleister Crowley* (New York: Hill & Wang, 1969), p. 175.
59. Gebser 1985, p. 49.
60. The island of Santorini in the Mediterranean was obliterated by a massive volcanic eruption sometime between 1470 and 1170 B.C. The blast was supposed to have been greater than a nuclear explosion, and Santorini has been proposed as the "real life" basis for the myth of Atlantis. The Sea People were a confederacy of pirates, more or less, that attacked coastal towns and cities of the Mediterranean circa 1276–1178 B.C. No one knows exactly who they were or what land they originated from; http://www.ancient.eu/Sea_Peoples/.

61. Jaynes 1976, p. 75.
62. Lachman 2003, pp. 143–44.
63. Shlain 1998, p. 69.
64. Jaynes 1976, p. 214.
65. Colin Wilson, *A Criminal History of Mankind* (New York: G. P. Putnam Sons, 1984), pp. 4, 5, 158.
66. Friedrich Nietzsche, *Twilight of the Idols and The Antichrist*, R. J. Hollingdale, trans. (Harmondsworth, U.K.: Penguin Classics, 1977) p. 115.

CHAPTER 2: OUT OF THE MYSTERIES

1. Karl Jaspers, *Way to Wisdom*, Ralph Manheim trans. (London: Victor Gollancz, 1951), p. 99.
2. Ibid.
3. Ibid., p. 98.
4. Ibid., pp. 100–101.
5. George Steiner, *Has Truth a Future?* (London: BBC Publications, 1978), pp. 16–17.
6. John Shand, *Philosophy and Philosophers* (London: Penguin Books, 1994), p. 6.
7. Martin Heidegger, *Early Greek Thinking* (New York: Harper & Row, 1984).
8. Tarnas 1991, p. 19.
9. Hermes and Orpheus are considered legendary, not actual, characters. Zoroaster's status is uncertain. There is no consensus about when he lived or if there was more than one individual referred to as "Zoroaster." Classical sources have Zoroaster flourishing in the Neolithic period, c. 6000 B.C. Other sources date Zoroaster anywhere from the eighteenth to sixth centuries B.C. Jaspers places him in his axial age, and for the purposes of this book, I have followed him.
10. David Fideler, ed., *The Pythagorean Sourcebook* (Grand Rapids, Mich.: Phanes Press, 1987), p. 21. Hyperborea was a land of eternal spring that the Greeks believed lay "beyond the north wind"— i.e., somewhere in the Arctic Circle—and which esotericists like Julius Evola believed truly existed in prehistoric times; see Evola, *Revolt Against the Modern World* (Rochester, Vt.: Inner Traditions, 1995). It was the birthplace of the god Apollo's mother, Leto, and every autumn, Apollo left Greece for a visit to his mother's homeland.
11. Fideler 1987, p. 28.
12. See Ernest G. McClain, *The Myth of Invariance: The Origins of the Gods, Mathematics and Music from the Rig Veda to Plato* (New York: Nicholas Hay, 1976).
13. Arthur Koestler, *The Sleepwalkers* (Harmondsworth, U.K.: Penguin Books, 1979), p. 26.
14. Fideler 1987, p. 20.
15. Ibid.
16. Joscelyn Godwin, "Introduction" to Fideler 1987, p. 13. I should perhaps note that the doctrine of the transmigration of souls differs from reincarnation in that it proposes that human souls can enter the physical forms of lower creatures. To simplify, if you act badly in this life, you may come back in your next as a dog or even a vegetable. That some people achieve this last transmigration in their own lifetime is another issue.
17. Koestler 1979, p. 26.
18. George Steiner, *Lessons of the Masters* (Cambridge, Mass.: Harvard University Press, 2003), p. 9.
19. René Guénon, *The Reign of Quantity and The Signs of the Times* (Harmondsworth, U.K.: Penguin Books, 1972).
20. Fideler 1987, p. 21.
21. Ibid.
22. Make a dot which will stand for 1. Then on the diagonal from your dot, make another and on either side of this dot and equidistant from the first dot, make two more. This stands for 3. Make another dot on the diagonal, and again on either side of this add two more, making 5. If you start with two dots for 2, and add two more, you will see the difference.
23. Godwin 2007, p. 32; and Ouspensky 1949, p. 297.
24. Fideler 1987, p. 35.
25. Christopher Bamford, in *Rediscovering Sacred Science,* Chistopher Bamford ed. (Edinburgh: Floris Books, 1994), p. 29.
26. Quoted in Amanda Fielding, ed., *Hofmann's Elixir: LSD and the New Eleusis* (London: Strange Attractor, 2008), p. 28.
27. In 325 B.C., the Roman Emperor Constantine—the first Christian emperor—convened a council of Christian bishops at Nicaea, in what is now Anatolia, in order to arrive at some consensus about the tenets of Christianity. One main point to emerge was the rejection of what is known as the "Arian heresy," the belief that Christ was of a different nature and lower rank than God.
28. Joscelyn Godwin, *Mystery Religions in the Ancient World* (London: Routledge, 1981), p. 33.

29. R. G. Wasson et al., *The Road to Eleusis* (Berkeley, Calif.: North Atlantic Books, 2008).
30. D. C. A. Hillman, *The Chemical Muse: Drug Use and the Roots of Western Civilization* (New York: St. Martin's Press, 2008), pp. 161–80.
31. Albert Hofmann, in Fielding 2008, p. 33.
32. Bamford 1994, p. 17.
33. Frances Cornford, *From Religion to Philosophy* (Princeton, N.J.: Princeton University Press, 1991), p. xiv.
34. See Peter Kingsley, *Ancient Philosophy, Mystery and Magic* (Oxford, U.K.: Clarendon Press, 1995), and *In the Dark Places of Wisdom* (Inverness, Calif.: Golden Sufi Center, 1999).
35. Cornford 1991, p. xiv. Cornford seems to have anticipated some of Iain McGilchrist's findings regarding the left and right brain: "Driven by a deep-lying need to master the world by understanding it, science works steadily toward its goal—a perfectly clear conceptual model of reality, adapted to explain all phenomena by the simplest formula that can be found . . . When we contemplate the finished result, we see that in banishing 'the vague,' it has swept away everything in which another type of mind finds all the value and significance of the world."
36. Bamford 1994, p. 29; Fideler 1987, p. 13.
37. "The safest general characterization of the European philosophical tradition is that it consists of a series of footnotes to Plato," in Alfred North Whitehead, *Process and Reality* (New York: Free Press, 1979), p. 39.
38. Hanegraaff 2013, p. 18.
39. See Tom Harpur, *The Pagan Christ* (Markham, Canada: Thomas Allen Publishers, 2004).
40. C. S. Lewis, *Surprised by Joy*, in *The Essential C. S. Lewis* (New York: Collier Books, 1988), p. 48.
41. In the *Meno*, Socrates is compared to a stingray that numbs all who have contact with it. *Meno* (80b), *Plato* 1985, p. 363.
42. W. B. Yeats, "Sailing to Byzantium."
43. As with Pythagoras, mathematics provided Plato with an example of "absolute knowledge." 2+2=4, now or in ancient Greece or, as far as we know, on another planet, just as a triangle by definition must have three sides, whether any triangles exist in the physical world or not. These truths are self-evident; we do not arrive at them through observation.
44. Gary Lachman, *The Caretakers of the Cosmos* (Edinburgh: Floris Books, 2013), pp. 118–20, for a discussion of Max Scheler's "hierarchy of values" and philosophy's place in it.
45. This is also true of what we suppose is the most physical thing of all, matter. Yet we never see matter but only so-called material things. We only see matter in some shape or form—a stone, a tree, a cloud—never matter itself. We never encounter a lump of matter in the same way that we encounter a lump of, say, iron. Matter is an abstraction, which is to say that it is fundamentally an idea— something that is not material at all.
46. Alfred North Whitehead, *Modes of Thought* (New York: Free Press, 1968), p. 18.
47. Readers will be quick to note the echoes of Plato's cave in the films of *The Matrix* series.
48. Plato 1985, pp. 437–38.
49. *The Way of Hermes*, Clement Salaman, trans. (London: Duckworth, 2001), p. 48.
50. Thomas Taylor, quoted in Manly P. Hall, *The Secret Teachings of All Ages* (New York: Tarcher/Penguin, 2003), p. 162.
51. See, for example, Mircea Eliade, *Shamanism: Archaic Techniques of Ecstasy* (London: Arkana, 1989), and note 38 above.
52. See Lachman 2011, pp. 60–64.
53. Jeremy Naydler, *Plato, Shamanism and Ancient Egypt* (Oxford, U.K.: Abzu Press, 2005), p. 22.
54. Ouspensky 1969, pp. 250–51.

CHAPTER 3: THE SECRET *GNOSIS*

1. It is true that the right side of the body is controlled by the left brain and vice versa, so technically if we want to see their placement in Raphael's fresco as symbolic of their different allegiances, we have a problem. But if we limit the symbolism to a simple contrast between left and right, the analogy, I believe, can stand.
2. Tarnas 1991, p. 68.
3. Faivre 1994, p. 10.
4. Readers looking for a good discussion of the differences between "either/or" and "both/and" kinds of thought should look again to Arthur Koestler's classic, *The Act of Creation*, especially its early sections dealing with humor. Koestler does not use the terms "either/or" or "both/and," but his notion of "bissociation" includes them implicitly.
5. *Timaeus*, in Plato 1961, p. 1157.

6. Versluis 2007, pp. 12–13.
7. Godwin 1981, p. 26.
8. The Thugge was a cult whose members ritually murdered in honor of the Indian goddess Kali. Our word "thug" comes from them.
9. Hall 2003, pp. 48–52.
10. Colin Wilson, *The Occult* (New York: Random House, 1971), p. 199.
11. Much of Freke and Gandy's argument can be found in an obscure book, *Pagan Christs* (1911) by John M. Robertson, a humanist, journalist, and member of the U.K. Parliament; online text at http://sacred-texts.com/bib/cv/pch/index.htm.
12. Timothy Freke and Peter Gandy, *The Jesus Mysteries* (London: Thorsons, 1999), p. 5.
13. For Jesus not dying on the cross, see Hugh Schonfield's classic *The Passover Plot* (1965); and *Holy Blood, Holy Grail* (1982) by Michael Baigent, Richard Leigh, and Henry Lincoln. For Jesus being a mushroom, see John M. Allegro, *The Sacred Mushroom and the Cross* (1970), in which it is argued that Jesus was really a code name for the hallucinogenic mushroom *Amanita muscaria*. Fictional treatments of the "surviving Jesus" theme can be found in D. H. Lawrence, *The Man Who Died* (1929) (also known as *The Escaped Cock*); and Nikos Kazantzakis, *The Last Temptation of Christ* (1953).
14. Morton Smith, *The Secret Gospel: The Discovery and Interpretation of the Secret Gospel According to Mark* (New York: Harper & Row, 1973), pp. 14–17.
15. Richard Smoley, *Inner Christianity* (Boulder, Colo.: Shambhala, 2000), p. 14. I am indebted to this excellent work for much of this section.
16. Ibid, p. 15.
17. Elaine Pagels, *The Gnostic Gospels* (London: Penguin Books, 1990), p. 14.
18. Ibid., p. 15.
19. James M. Robinson, ed., *The Gospel of Truth* in *The Nag Hammadi Library in English* (New York: HarperCollins, 1990), p. 159.
20. Ibid., p. 16.
21. I should point out that "gnostic" has become a kind of catchall term in recent years, having so wide an application in occult, esoteric, spiritual, and other contexts that, like "romantic" or "existential," it has become almost devoid of any concrete meaning. Here I will use "Gnostic" when speaking of the actual sects of the early Christian period, and "gnostic" in a more general sense when indicating either the pursuit of spiritual knowledge or the attitude that is skeptical of dogma or the conventionally accepted view of reality. "Know thyself" is a gnostic injunction, but not necessarily a Gnostic one.
22. Richard Smoley, *Forbidden Faith: The Gnostic Legacy* (New York: HarperCollins, 2006), pp. 13–14.
23. Sean Martin, *The Gnostics* (Harpenden, U.K.: Pocket Essentials, 2006), p. 17.
24. Pagels 1990, p. 97.
25. Ibid., p. 17; Smoley 2006, p. 25.
26. Stephan Hoeller, *The Gnostic Jung and the Seven Sermons to the Dead* (Wheaton, Ill.: Quest Books, 1982), p. 18.
27. The creation versus emanation debate runs throughout western consciousness. Both sides have advantages and drawbacks. Just as the sun cannot help emanating light and heat—it does not choose to do so but must because of its own nature—in the emanationist view, God does not choose to create the cosmos; he or she can't help it, as it is part of God's nature. This puts limits on God—he or she can't avoid emanating—but it lets creation share in God's fullness, rather than be a kind of metaphysical afterthought. To some extent in the emanationist view, God and creation are "one." The Creationist view sees it differently. For it, God was under no constraint regarding creation. There was no necessity for God to create the world. It is something apart from him and he could have *not* created it, if he so chose. This view maintains a God that is beyond any necessity, any compulsion, an absolutely "free" God, not limited by anything, not even his own nature. While this view secures God's freedom, it does suggest an at best "second-class" status for creation. It does not share in God's nature, just as a craftsman's work does not share in his nature. It is something separate from him.
28. Hans Jonas, *The Gnostic Religion: The Message of the Alien God and the Beginnings of Christianity* (Boston: Beacon Press, 1958).
29. Ouspensky 1949, p. 30.
30. Martin 2006, p. 50.
31. Stephan Hoeller, "The Quest for Spiritual Freedom: The Gnostic Worldview," in Jay Kinney, ed., *The Inner West: An Introduction to the Hidden Wisdom of the West* (New York: Tarcher/Penguin, 2004), pp. 49, 52.
32. Ibid., p. 52; Martin 2006, p. 48.
33. Crowley's "sex magic" involved ingesting male and female sexual fluids, and part of his Gnostic Mass included eating a communion wafer spiked with menstrual blood; see Gary Lachman, *Aleister*

Crowley: Magick, Rock and Roll, and the Wickedest Man in the World (New York: Tarcher/Penguin 2014), pp. 187–88.

34. Smoley 2006, p. 20.
35. See Gershom Scholem, *Jewish Gnosticism, Merkabah Mysticism, and Talmudic Tradition* (New York: The Jewish Theological Seminary of America, 1960).
36. Wilson 1971, p. 201.
37. Ibid.
38. Mary Boyce, *Zoroastrians: Their Religious Beliefs and Practices* (London: Routledge, 1979), p. 29.
39. Arthur Darby Nock, quoted in Pagels 1990, p. 27.

CHAPTER 4: FROM THE ONE TO THE ONE

1. Alexander founded several such cities but none rose to such prominence as did the Alexandria in question.
2. Justin Pollard and Howard Reid, *The Rise and Fall of Alexandria: Birthplace of the Modern World* (New York: Penguin Books, 2007), pp. 2–3.
3. See http://www.dailymail.co.uk/sciencetech/article-2779171/What-chamber-hold-Archaeologists -release-images-deeper-inside-Alexander-Great-era-tomb.html.
4. Quoted in Florian Ebeling, *The Secret History of Hermes Trismegistus* (Ithaca, N.Y.: Cornell University Press, 2007), p. 29.
5. Pollard and Reid 2007, p. xvii.
6. Alberto Manguel, *The Library at Night* (London: Yale University Press, 2006), p. 22.
7. Ibid., p. 25.
8. Smoley 2006, p. 38.
9. Pollard and Reid 2007, p. 197.
10. There is some scholarly debate over whether Origen actually did castrate himself, or if this was a story put around by his detractors. The benefit of the doubt seems to fall with those who think he did.
11. Quoted in Smoley 2002, p. 20.
12. Ibid., p. 46.
13. Lachman 2011, pp. 34–41.
14. Ibid., p. 83–84.
15. Ibid.
16. Robert M. Place, *The Tarot: History, Symbolism, and Divination* (New York: Tarcher/Penguin, 2005), p. 29.
17. Eliphas Levi, *The History of Magic* (York Beach, Me.: Weiser, 2000), p. 79.
18. The *Corpus Hermeticum* is believed to be a portion of a larger collection of writings, the *Hermetica*, also attributed to Hermes Trismegistus. Most of the *Hermetica* is lost, but from references in other writings, we can assume that the *Hermetica* consisted of many more works than those that have come down to us today.
19. See Gilles Quispel, "Preface," Salaman 2001, pp. 12–13. See also Quispel's essay "The *Asclepius*: From the Hermetic Lodge in Alexandria to the Greek Eucharist and the Roman Mass," in Roelof van den Broeck and Wouter J. Hanegraaff, eds., *Gnosis and Hermeticism: From Antiquity to Modern Times* (Albany, N.Y.: SUNY Press, 1998), pp. 69–77.
20. I use "Hermetist" to refer to the original Alexandrian followers of Hermes Trismegistus and "Hermeticist" to refer to later devotees of "Hermetic philosophy."
21. Clement Salaman, trans., *Asclepius: The Perfect Discourse of Hermes Trismegistus* (London: Duckworth, 2007), pp. 78–81. The idea of Egypt being an "image of heaven" is of course the central theme of Robert Bauval's ideas about the Giza pyramids and the Nile, mentioned in Chapter One.
22. G. R. S. Mead, *Gnosis of the Mind* (Benares, India: Theosophical Publishing Society, 1906), p. 10.
23. Stephan Hoeller, "Introduction," G. R. S. Mead, *Hymns to Hermes* (Boston: Weiser, 2006), p. 15.
24. Anonymous, *Meditations on the Tarot: A Journey into Christian Hermeticism* (New York: Tarcher/Penguin, 2002). Although published anonymously, it is generally recognized that the author of this work is the Estonian-Russian Valentin Tomberg (1900–1973).
25. See Lachman 2011, pp. 34–49.
26. Salaman 2001, p. 70.
27. Mead 2006, p. 18.
28. Salaman 2001, p. 84.
29. John Gregory, *The Neoplatonists: A Reader* (London: Routledge, 1999), p. 3.
30. Pollard and Reid 2007, p. 247.
31. Rudolf Steiner, *Anthroposophical Leading Thoughts* (London: Rudolf Steiner Press, 1973). Text available at http://wn.rsarchive.org/Books/GA026/English/RSP1973/GA026_c29.html.

32. Gregory 1999, p. 96.
33. Luke 10:42.
34. Andrew Smith, *Philosophy in Late Antiquity* (London: Routledge, 2004), p. 77.
35. Iamblichus, "On the Mysteries of Egypt," in Gregory 1999, p. 149.
36. Ibid.
37. Ibid., p. 151.
38. Smith 2004, p. 83.

1. Hall 2003, p. 650.
2. See http://www.ccel.org/ccel/cyril.
3. We can see parallels with Dionysius's hierarchy in the seven ancient planets and eighth and ninth "spheres" of the Hermetic system, as well as in the *sephiroth* of Kabbalah. Later parallels can be found in Rudolf Steiner's system of cosmic evolution and Gurdjieff's "Ray of Creation."
4. William Anderson, *The Rise of the Gothic* (London: Hutchinson, 1985), p. 12.
5. Ibid., p. 13.
6. Versluis 2007, p. 42; Godwin 2007, p. 67.
7. Julius Evola, *The Doctrine of Awakening*, H. E. Musson, trans. (Rochester, Vt.: Inner Traditions, 1996), p. 24.
8. Dionysius the Areopagite, *Mystical Theology and Celestial Hierarchies* (Brook, Surrey, U.K.: Shrine of Wisdom, 1965), p. 10.
9. This contrast between the *via negativa* and the *via positiva* can be compared with that between Theravada and Mahayana Buddhism, but also between Protestantism, with its rejection of imagery, ritual, and any intermediaries between the worshiper and God, and Catholicism, with its use of imagery, ritual, and pantheon of saints, as well as ecclesiastical hierarchy. Both approaches are deeply rooted in what seem to be two contradictory but also complementary needs of the human psyche: the idea of a God or divine that exceeds the "merely human"—the austere "wholly other" God of the theologian Rudolf Otto—and the need for a God that can be approached through prayer, ritual, imagery, a God that is more than but not entirely beyond the human. We seem to want a God that is both transcendent and immanent.
10. Rodney Collin, *The Theory of Celestial Influence* (London: Watkins Books, 1980), p. 255.
11. Tarnas 1991, p. 476.
12. Anderson 1985, p. 17.
13. Space does not allow me to do more than mention the Celtic church in this survey. Readers interested in a passionate account of its importance in the western spiritual tradition should read Christopher Bamford's essay, "The Mystery of Celtic Christianity," in Christopher Bamford, ed., *An Endless Trace: The Passionate Pursuit of Wisdom in the West* (New Paltz, N.Y.: Codhill Press, 2003).
14. Collin 1980, p. 255.
15. Science fiction is rife with visions of a future dark age. Perhaps the best known is *A Canticle for Leibowitz* (1960) by Walter Miller, in which a future monastic order preserves the knowledge of the past following a nuclear holocaust. Strangely, the inspiration for the book came from the author's participation in the Allied bombing of Monte Cassino during World War II.
16. Anderson 1985, p. 129.
17. Schwaller de Lubicz believed that alchemy stems from the Arabic *al-kemi*. See André VandenBroeck, *Al-Kemi: A Memoir: Hermetic, Occult, Political, and Private Aspects of R. A. Schwaller de Lubicz* (Hudson, N.Y.: Lindisfarne Press, 1987), p. 5.
18. See Lachman 2011, pp. 102–3.
19. Ibid., pp. 106–9.
20. Ebeling 2007, p. 70.
21. It is unlikely, though not impossible, that Jabir had access to the *Corpus Hermeticum*, and his reference to Agathodaimon may have come through the work of Zosimos.
22. For more on Harran, see Lachman 2011, pp. 109–11.
23. Walter Scott, "Introduction," Walter Scott ed., *Hermetica* (Boston: Shambhala, 2001), pp. 98–101.
24. Joscelyn Godwin, *Music, Mysticism and Magic: A Sourcebook* (London: Arkana, 1987), p. 68.
25. Scott 2001, p. 105.
26. Ibid.
27. John Walbridge, *The Leaven of the Ancients: Suhrawardi and the Heritage of the Greeks* (Albany, N.Y.: SUNY Press, 2000), pp. 13–14.
28. Quoted in Henry Corbin, *The Voyage and the Messenger: Iran and Philosophy* (Berkeley, Calif.: North Atlantic Books, 1998), p. xlvii.

29. When Justinian closed the Platonic Academy in 529, one of Damascius's students, Simplicius, accepted the hospitality of King Chosroes of Persia, known as "the philosopher king" because of his love of learning and culture. Simplicius spent three years in the Persian court before being allowed to return to Athens. It may be that during his Persian exile, Simplicius and the Neoplatonists who accompanied him transplanted the Platonic ideas that would later reemerge in Suhrawardi.
30. Corbin 1998, p. xlv.
31. Ibid., p. xlvi.
32. Walbridge 2000, p.14.
33. Henry Corbin, *Mundus Imaginalis, or The Imaginary and the Imaginal* (Ipswich, U.K.: Golgonooza Press, 1976), pp. 3, 10.
34. Think of a work of art. There is the *idea* of it, what the artist wants to express. And there is the finished product, the painting or statue. In between, there is the artist's *image* of it, his "picture" of it in his mind. This picture is something more than the concept, as it has taken on a form. Yet it is not a physical form, but a mental or spiritual one. Or think of a book. There is the idea that the author wants to express and there is the physical book in which he expresses it, the paper and ink. But the true "reality" of the book is your inner experience of it while reading it, and this takes place in your imagination, just as the author's experience of writing it takes place in his. The author and reader share this imaginal realm.
35. Corbin 1976, p. 9.
36. Huxley 1987, pp. 69–70. Our outer world may no longer have a "darkest Africa" or "unmapped Borneos and Amazonian basins," but that such places still exist in our inner world remains true. I should point out that the titles of Huxley's essays come from William Blake and Swedenborg, two well-seasoned inner travelers.
37. Suhrawardi had an older western contemporary in the Christian mystic, philosopher, composer, and polymath Hildegard of Bingen (1098–1180). She was subject to visions from childhood, but it was not until 1142, when she was forty-three, that Hildegard first recorded her visionary experiences. *Scivias* (1142–1151), the first of three volumes of "visionary theology," is an extraordinary work. Also known as "Know the Ways of the Lord," *Scivias* is an illustrated text describing twenty-six visions concerning the Creation, the Fall, salvation, the sacraments, and the coming Kingdom of God. Unlike the negative theology of Meister Eckhart and the Rhineland mystics, Hildegard's path was the *via positiva*. Hildegard began the work after receiving a message from God telling her to do so, much as the later religious visionary Emanuel Swedenborg began recording his own visionary experiences after a visitation from Christ.
38. Corbin 1976, p. 4.
39. See http://phys.org/news/2013-09-scientists-never-before-seen.html.
40. Corbin 1998, p. 140.
41. Corbin 1976, p. 7. Corbin started his career as a philosopher in the phenomenological tradition of Husserl and Heidegger. Readers familiar with this tradition will note a similarity between his description of what takes place "beyond the Ninth Sphere" and what Husserl called "bracketing the natural standpoint," the unquestioned acceptance of the "world" as I "normally" experience it, that is, as *outside* my consciousness. A similar state was also described by P. D. Ouspensky in his essay "Experimental Mysticism," where he writes that in the altered state of consciousness he was exploring, "the objective and subjective could change places. The one could become the other"; Ouspensky 1969, p. 279.
42. Lachman 2013, pp. 75–76.
43. Corbin 1976, p. 19.
44. As there are ten "primal numbers" in the *Sefer Yetzirah*, one wonders if there was a Pythagorean influence on the work.
45. Pinchas Giller, "Kabbalah in Jewish Mysticism" in Kinney 2004, p. 65.
46. Versluis 2007, p. 65.
47. There are variations on the names of the *sephiroth*, but these seem the most common.
48. In *The Caretakers of the Cosmos*, I look at the ideas of Isaac Luria, the sixteenth-century Kabbalist of Safed, who is considered the "father of contemporary Kabbalah." Luria introduced certain revisions into Kabbalistic theory, one of which is the notion of *tikkun*, or "repair"; see Lachman 2013, pp. 29–34.
49. To pass beyond the Abyss is a dangerous objective, although some intrepid souls have made the attempt; see Lachman, 2014, pp. 131–36.
50. Tarnas 1991, p. 195.
51. Versluis 2007, p. 50.
52. Sadly, it was to last less than a century. In 1225, Pope Honorius II condemned Eriugena's work and called for it to be burned.

53. In 1983, during a mini "search for the miraculous," I had the opportunity to spend a day at Chartres, walking the labyrinth and resting in the peculiar light emanating through the rose window. The feeling I had then of entering a space that was *larger* than outdoors remains. A similar though not as pronounced effect occurred during my visits to Notre Dame de Paris, then and in subsequent years.
54. Godwin 2007, p. 81.
55. Anderson 1996, p. 66.
56. Ibid., p. 315.
57. Jean Gimpel, *The Medieval Machine: The Industrial Revolution of the Middle Ages* (London: Penguin Books, 1977), pp. 69–70.
58. Who Fulcanelli was, if he ever existed, has never been satisfactorily determined. Schwaller de Lubicz claimed to have met him in a Montparnasse café in 1918, and that the two worked together on discovering the secret of "alchemical stained glass." But other accounts say that "Fulcanelli" was the code name of a group of French alchemists. See VandenBroeck, *Al-Kemi* 1987; and Geneviève Dubois, *Fulcanelli and the Alchemical Revival* (Rochester, Vt.: Destiny Books, 2006).
59. Fulcanelli, *Le Mystère des Cathédrals* (Las Vegas, Nev.: Brotherhood of Life, 2005), p. 42.
60. Ouspensky 1969, p. 306.
61. See Ean Begg, *The Cult of the Black Virgin* (London: Arkana, 1989).
62. Anderson 1996, p. 67.
63. Quoted in Anderson 1985, p. 126.
64. Colin Wilson, *The Musician as Outsider* (Nottingham, U.K.: Pauper's Press, 1987), p. 12.
65. Ibid.
66. Denis De Rougemont, *Love in the Western World* (Princeton, N.J.: Princeton University Press, 1983), p. 76.
67. Ibid.
68. Ibid., p. 103.

CHAPTER 6: SPIRITUAL LOVE IN THE WESTERN WORLD

1. Smoley 2006, p. 68.
2. But see Yuri Stoyanov, *The Hidden Tradition in Europe* (London: Arkana, 1994).
3. In 1996, during a trip to Eastern Europe, I visited what I was told were some ancient Bogomil sites outside of Tuzla, Bosnia. There I was shown what my guides told me were "Bogomil stones"—long, gravestone-like slabs decorated in stars, spirals, six-pointed crosses, lozenges, and other fluid shapes.
4. De Rougemont 1983, p. 107.
5. Martin 2006, p. 114.
6. Godwin 2007, pp. 59–60.
7. I am especially indebted to Richard Smoley's account of the ritual of the *consolamentum* for this section (Smoley 2006, pp. 74–75).
8. Ibid., p. 75.
9. J. G. Bennett, *Gurdjieff: Making a New World* (New York: Harper & Row, 1973), p. 31. In his autobiography *Witness* (Tucson, Ariz.: Omen Press, 1974; pp. 115–18), Bennett tells of his experience at Gurdjieff's *Prieuré* in Fontainebleau, when he received an "influx of immense power" from Gurdjieff.
10. Henri Bergson made the difference between "dynamic" and "static" religion the central theme of one of his last books, *The Two Sources of Morality and Religion* (New York: Henry Holt, 1932).
11. 2 Corinthians 3:6: "For the letter kills, but the spirit gives life."
12. This does not mean "induce an erection," as a politically correct editor of mine once wondered, although Goethe, I'm sure, would have been amused.
13. Czeslaw Milosz, "Foreword," O. V. de Lubicz Milosz, *Amorous Initiation* (Rochester, Vt.: Inner Traditions, 1994), p. vi. For more on O. V. de Lubicz Milosz, see Gary Lachman, *A Dark Muse: A History of the Occult* (New York: Thunder's Mouth Press, 2005), pp. 245–53.
14. See Lachman 2013, pp. 108–11.
15. Julius Evola, *The Mystery of the Grail* (Rochester, Vt.: Inner Traditions, 1997), p. 138.
16. Ibid., pp. 139, 145.
17. Ibid., pp. 145–46.
18. Ibid., p. 139.
19. Dante, *La Vita Nuova*, Barbara Reynolds trans. (Harmondsworth, U.K.: Penguin Books, 1969), II: 29–30, XI:41.
20. For more on Poe and Novalis, see Lachman 2005, pp. 84–88 and 73–78.
21. William Anderson, *Dante the Maker* (London: Routledge, 1980), p. 83; Evola 1997, p. 145.
22. Anderson 1980, pp. 86, 85, 413.

23. See Lachman 2008, pp. 44–45.
24. See http://www.grahamhancock.com/forum/BlackJ2.php.
25. Evola 1997, p. 145.
26. Anderson 1980, p. 279.
27. Robert Richardson, "The Hidden Sages and the Knights Templar," in Kinney 2004, p. 184.
28. Anderson 1980, p. 85.
29. Henry Corbin, *Creative Imagination in the Sufism of Ibn 'Arabi* (Princeton, N.J.: Princeton University Press, 1969), p. 52.
30. Ibid., p. 100.
31. Surface beauty, to be sure, is not enough, and warnings abound about various "femmes fatales," from the Sirens on, who lead men not to their souls but to perdition.
32. Corbin 1969, p. 100.
33. Ibid., p. 110.
34. Ibid.
35. William Anderson, *The Face of Glory* (London: Bloomsbury, 1996), p. 279.
36. Kathleen Raine, *The Inner Journey of the Poet* (New York: George Braziller, 1982), p. 27.
37. Quoted in Anderson 1996, p. 406: "We perceive many things by the intellect for which language has no terms—a fact which Plato indicates plainly enough in his books by his employment of metaphors."
38. Dante, *Il Paradiso*, Canto XVIII:131, Dorothy Sayers, trans. (London: Penguin Books, 1962), p. 304.
39. Ibid., Canto XXXIII:70–72.
40. Ibid., 64.
41. R. M. Bucke, *Cosmic Consciousness* (New York: E. P. Dutton, 1966), p. 137.
42. Anderson 1980, p. 296.
43. P. D. Ouspensky 1969, p. 278.
44. Anderson 1980, p. 410.
45. Lachman 2010, pp. 124–26.
46. In his own mystical experience, Ouspensky also saw a rose "the petals of which were continually unfolding from the middle . . . In this flower there was an incredible quantity of light, movement, color, music, emotion, agitation, knowledge, intelligence, mathematics, and continuous unceasing growth"; Ouspensky 1969, p. 290.
47. Richard Woods, *Meister Eckhart: Master of Mystics* (London: Continuum International Publishing Group, 2011), p. viii.
48. Walter T. Stace, *The Teachings of the Mystics* (New York: Mentor Books, 1960), p. 139.
49. Evelyn Underhill, *Mysticism* (New York: E. P. Dutton, 1961), p. 463.
50. Woods 2011, p. 2.
51. Ibid., p. 3.
52. Ibid., p. 34.
53. Underhill 1961, pp. 419–20.
54. Evelyn Underhill, *The Essentials of Mysticism* (New York: Cosimo Classics, 2007), p. 130.
55. Stace 1961, p. 139.
56. Ira Progoff, "Introductory Commentary," *The Cloud of Unknowing* (London: Rider, 1959), p. 27.
57. Ibid.
58. Ibid., p. 29.
59. Alfred North Whitehead, *Religion in the Making* (Cambridge, U.K.: Cambridge University Press, 1926), p. 6.
60. Woods 2011, p. 39.
61. Henry Miller, *Tropic of Cancer* (New York: Grove Press, 1961), p. 1.

CHAPTER 7: AN ESOTERIC RENAISSANCE

1. Laura's identity remains obscure and, as in the case of Beatrice, many have wondered if she existed at all and was not really a symbol of the poet's aspirations. See Mark Musa, "Introduction," Petrarch, *The Canzoniere and Other Works* (Oxford, U.K.: Oxford University Press, 1985), p. xvii.
2. Tarnas 1991, pp. 209–11.
3. Petrarch 1985, p. 11.
4. Lachman 2013, p. 144; Hans Blumenberg, *The Legitimacy of the Modern Age* (Cambridge, Mass.: MIT Press, 1983), p. 342.
5. Mary Wollstonecraft, author of *A Vindication of the Rights of Women* (1792), predated Wordsworth and Coleridge by two years in extolling the aesthetic virtues of nature. In *Letters Written During a Short Residence in Sweden, Norway, and Denmark* (1796), Wollstonecraft speaks of the "spontaneous

pleasure . . . dilating the emotions" as she contemplated the Scandinavian coastline, with "sunbeams that played upon the ocean" in contrast with the "huge dark rocks, that looked like the rude materials of creation." Wollstonecraft spoke of the feeling of the "sublime" that came to her while she gazed upon the rugged coast. Wollstonecraft (Harmondsworth, U.K.: Penguin, 1987), p. 68. Title given in note.

6. Petrarch 1985, pp. 15, 17.
7. Ibid., pp. 17, 15. Space allows me to only mention the remarkable synchronicity Petrarch experienced when he opened his pocket copy of Augustine's *Confessions;* for more, see Lachman 2003, pp. 219-20; and Lachman 2011, pp. 125, 226, n. 9.
8. Ibid.
9. Jacob Burckhardt, *The Civilization of the Renaissance in Italy* (London: Phaidon Press, 1944), p. 179.
10. Ernst Cassirer, *The Individual and the Cosmos in Renaissance Philosophy* (Philadelphia: University of Pennsylvania Press, 1972), pp. 141–44.
11. Blumenberg 1983, p. 341.
12. James Hillman, *Re-Visioning Psychology* (New York: Harper Colophon Books, 1977), pp. 196–97.
13. Johann Wolfgang von Goethe, *Faust*, Walter Kaufmann, trans. (New York: Anchor Books, 1961), p. 121.
14. Gebser 1985, p. 12.
15. All painting is two-dimensional, as it exists on the flat surface of a canvas. The trick with perspective painting is to render figures and landscape "realistically," i.e., approximating to how we "really" see things. So a church in the distance is smaller than figures in the foreground, because that is how we would see it, not larger because of its place in the spiritual hierarchy. We can see the same kind of relation to the world that medieval tapestry depicts in Egyptian wall painting as well.
16. Owen Barfield, *Saving the Appearances* (New York: Harcourt, Brace & World, 1957), pp. 76–77.
17. Russell Kirk, "Introduction," Giovanni Pico della Mirandola, *Oration on the Dignity of Man* (Chicago: Gateway Editions, 1956), p. xiii.
18. Tarnas 1991, p. 209.
19. Ficino did not meet Plethon. He made this remark in dedicating his translation of Plotinus's *Enneads* to his patron, Lorenzo de' Medici. Quote in Wouter J. Hanegraaff, "The Pagan Who Came from the East: George Gemistos Plethon and Platonic Orientalism," in Hanegraaff and Pijnenburg, eds., *Hermes in the Academy* (Amsterdam, The Netherlands: Amsterdam University Press, 2009), p. 33.
20. See http://www.newadvent.org/cathen/12166a.htm.
21. Joscelyn Godwin, *The Pagan Dream of the Renaissance* (York Beach, Me.: Weiser, 2005), p. 11.
22. Plethon collected his arguments about the differences between Artistotle and Plato in *De Differentiis*, which he wrote during his stay in Florence; see https://www.bu.edu/wcp/Papers/Medi/Medi Debo.htm.
23. See http://www.newadvent.org/cathen/12166a.htm.
24. Hanegraaff, in Hanegraaff and Pijnenburg 2009, p. 37.
25. Godwin 2007, p. 8.
26. Hanegraaff, in Hanegraaff and Pijnnburg 2009, p. 39.
27. Henry Corbin also believed that Plethon shared much with Suhrawardi; see Corbin 1969, pp. 20–21.
28. Hanegraaff, in Hanegraaff and Pijnenburg 2009, p. 40; George of Trebizond's *Comparatio Aristotelis et Platonis* was countered by *In Calumniatorem Platonis* by Plethon's student, Basilios Bessarion.
29. Plethon brought more than Plato to Florence. He also brought the work of the Greek geographer Strabo (64 B.C.–A.D. 24), who until then had been unknown in western Europe. One who profited by Strabo's appearance was Christopher Columbus, who used Strabo's work in his voyage to the New World. We might say that in a sense, we owe the discovery of America to a Byzantine Platonist.
30. Marsilio Ficino, *Letters, vol. I*, translated by the Language Department of the School of Economic Science (London: Shepard-Walwyn, 1975), p. 19.
31. Hillman 1977, p. 201.
32. See Lachman 2011, pp. 14–16.
33. Plethon himself did not include Hermes Trismegistus in his list of ancient sages. As Wouter J. Hanegraaff argues, this was most likely because he saw Hermes as conscripted by Christianity; in Chapter Four, we saw that church fathers like Lactantius believed Hermes Trismegistus was a precursor of Christ. Plethon advocated a pagan revival free of any Christian taint; hence the "thrice great one" was guilty by association; see Hanegraaff, in Hanegraaff and Pijnenburg 2009, p. 40.
34. Yates 1971, p. 13.
35. Charles Boer, "Introduction," Marsilio Ficino, *The Book of Life*, Charles Boer, trans. (Woodstock, Conn.: Spring Publications, 1996), p. xv.
36. Yates 1971, p. 54.

37. Hillman 1977, p. 200–201. Hillman's Ficinian ideas about the soul were popularized through the writings of the ex-monk and psychotherapist Thomas Moore, particularly the best-selling *Care of the Soul* (1992).

38. Proclus had written his own *Platonic Theology,* which Ficino knew well and admired but which in the end was anti-Christian. Ficino's desire to wed Plato and Christ led him to, as it were, redo Proclus's work, but with a pro-Christian ending.

39. On the idea of "repairing" the world, see Lachman 2013.

40. Yates 1971, p. 104.

41. Ibid., p. 77; see also Ficino 1975, p. 20.

42. Pico della Mirandola 1956, p. xii.

43. Russell Kirk, "Introduction," Pico della Mirandola 1956, p. xiii.

44. Wilson 1971, p. 321.

45. Pico della Mirandola 1956, pp. 6–7.

46. Ibid.

47. Ibid.

48. Ibid.

49. Guénon 1972, p. 232; Charlene Spretnak, *States of Grace: The Recovery of Meaning in the Postmodern Age* (San Francisco: HarperSanFrancisco, 1991), pp. 197, 202.

50. Yates 1971, p. 116.

51. Picknett and Prince 2011, p. 12. This book makes clear that the standard history of the battle between religion and science is slanted, as might be expected, in science's favor, and paints an often inaccurate picture. The church often went to great lengths to accommodate the new discoveries that were literally "rocking" the world. What becomes clear is that the real struggle was not between dogma and reason, but between the strong-willed and often stubborn individuals on either side of the debate. In this context, see also Koestler 1979.

52. For more on Rudolph II, see Peter Marshall, *The Theatre of the World* (London: Harvill Secker, 2006).

53. See http://www.vaticanobservatory.org.

54. After saving his life by recanting the belief that the Earth moves around the sun, Galileo is said to have muttered to himself "*Eppur si muove*" ("And yet it moves"), meaning that regardless of what he or his inquisitors may say, the Earth still revolves around the sun. There is debate about the truth of this and many historians consider the story apocryphal.

55. Godwin 2005, p. 162.

56. Antoine Faivre, *The Eternal Hermes* (Grand Rapids, Mich.: Phanes Press, 1995), p. 100.

57. Versluis 2007, p. 80.

58. Ibid.

59. Letter from Trithemius to Johann Virdung quoted in Hans Christoph Binswanger, *Money and Magic: A Critique of the Modern Economy in Light of Goethe's Faust* (Chicago: University of Chicago Press, 1994), pp. 1–2. See also Lachman 2005, pp. 67–68.

60. Both Trithemius and Dee's Enochian would play central roles in the history of the Hermetic Order of the Golden Dawn, the most important magical society of the late nineteenth and early twentieth centuries. The "cipher manuscript" involved in the society's origin was written in a code devised by Trithemius, and Dee's "Enochian" was used in its rituals. See Lachman 2014, p. 61; and Francis King, *Megatherion: The Magical World of Aleister Crowley* (Creation Books, 2011), p. 56.

61. Magic and science were early on associated through the fascination with "mechanical marvels" that was part of the Renaissance pagan revival. Many Renaissance gardens, like those at the Villa d'Este in Tivoli, contained statues or figures that were animated through the use of steam or water. To many, these seemed no different than the demonically "animated" statues spoken of in the *Asclepius*; see Lachman 2011, pp. 160–62.

62. Benjamin Wooley, *The Queen's Conjurer* (London: HarperCollins, 2001), p. 12.

63. Ibid., pp. 54–55.

64. D. P. Walker, *Spiritual and Demonic Magic: From Ficino to Campanella* (Stroud, U.K.: Sutton Publishing, 2000), p. 36.

65. Lachman 2011, p. 161.

66. A fuller account of this can be found in Lachman 2011, pp. 166–70.

67. Ibid., pp. 84–86.

68. See Introduction, note 14.

69. Lachman 2011, pp. 157–60.

70. Yates 1971, p. 163.

CHAPTER 8: ESOTERIC UNDERWORLD

1. Among these were Ralph Cudworth and Henry More, important members of the Cambridge Platonists, a group of theologians and philosophers who adhered to Agostino Steuco's notion of a *philosophia perennis*, and Tommaso Campanella, an Italian philosopher and magician in the Bruno tradition who, like Bruno and Plethon, envisioned a pagan revival. His utopia designs were set out in his *City of the Sun* (1623). See Lachman 2011, pp. 170–73.
2. Hall 2003, p. 441.
3. McIntosh 1987, p. 48. McIntosh suggests that the roots of the Rosicrucians may lie in what he dubbed the "Tubingen circle," a group of devout Lutheran intellectuals with socialist and esoteric leanings.
4. The largest and most well known of these is the Ancient Mystical Order of Rosae Crucis (or AMORC, as it is usually called), founded by H. Spencer Lewis in 1915. AMORC traces its roots back to ancient Egypt, somewhat earlier than the seventeenth-century Rosicrucians who concern us here. The link between AMORC, the Rosicrucian Order of Max Heindel—onetime student of Rudolf Steiner, who called his own spiritual approach Rosicrucian—and other modern Rosicrucian groups such as Jan van Rijckenborgh's Lectorium Rosicrucianum—an offshoot of Heindel's group—and the Rosicrucians of 1614 is unclear.
5. Frances Yates, *The Rosicrucian Enlightenment* (Boulder, Colo.: Shambhala, 1978), p. 57.
6. Lachman 2008, p. 5. In the book containing Christian Rosenkreutz's wisdom, the discoverers of his tomb found the inscription "We are born of God, we die in Jesus, we live again through the Holy Spirit." This is in line with Joachim's three ages.
7. McIntosh 1987, pp. 36, 32.
8. Frances Yates's account of the political machinations leading up to Frederick V's defeat is too detailed to précis here and the reader is advised to go to the source. A summary of it can be found in Lachman 2008, pp. 13–18.
9. Quoted in Yates 1978, p. 47.
10. Ibid., p. 253.
11. See note 1 above.
12. Quoted in Wilson 1971, p. 232.
13. Sean Martin, *Alchemy and Alchemists* (Harpenden, U.K.: Pocket Essentials, 2006), p. 53.
14. Quoted in Yates 1978, p. 161.
15. Godwin 1979, p. 5.
16. Peter Marshall, *The Philosopher's Stone: A Quest for the Secrets of Alchemy* (London: Macmillan, 2001), p. 279; Corbin 1969, p. 20.
17. Martin 2006, p. 55.
18. Marshall 2001, p. 280.
19. Marie-Louise von Franz, *Alchemy: An Introduction to the Symbolism and the Psychology* (Toronto: Inner City Books, 1980), pp. 179–82.
20. See Henri Ellenberger's classic work, *The Discovery of the Unconscious* (London: Fontana, 1994).
21. Martin 2006, p. 59.
22. Titus Burckhardt, *Alchemy* (Longmead, U.K.: Elemental Books, 1986), p. 9.
23. See Jung's late work *Mysterium Coniunctionis*, in C. G. Jung, *The Collected Works of Jung, Vol. 14* (Princeton, N.J.: Princeton University Press, 1977).
24. Burckhardt 1986, p. 9.
25. Ibid.
26. For this account I am indebted to Colin Wilson, *Mysteries* (London: Watkins Publishing, 2006), pp. 405–7; and Martin 2006, pp. 64–66.
27. See Janet Gleeson, *The Arcanum: The Extraordinary True Story* (New York: Grand Central Publishing, 1999).
28. Nicholas Goodrick-Clarke, "Introduction," Goodrick-Clarke, ed., *Paracelsus: Essential Readings* (Wellingborough, U.K.: Crucible, 1990), p. 13.
29. Philip Ball, *The Devil's Doctor* (London: Heinemann, 2006), p. 18. "Bombast" was an old Swabian name. "Bombast" as puffed-up rhetoric derives from *bombax*, medieval Latin for silkworm, which also came to mean "padding" in the sixteenth century.
30. Ibid., pp. 211–12.
31. Marshall 2001, pp. 354–55.
32. Goodrick-Clarke 1990, p. 23.
33. Ibid.
34. Ibid.
35. Jeremy Narby, *The Cosmic Serpent* (London: Phoenix Books, 1999), pp. 1–9.

36. Shlain 1998, pp. 54–55.
37. Ball 2006, pp. 187-89. Opium's effects, however, are not the same as psychedelics, and certainly not the same as ayahuasca. It is generally classified as a narcotic and not as a hallucinogen.
38. Quoted in Wilson 1971, p. 243.
39. Ibid., p. 239.
40. See http://www.independent.co.uk/life-style/health-and-families/healthy-living/how-moods-aff ect-our-health-764289.html.
41. Quoted in Wilson 1971, p. 239.
42. John Cowper Powys, *Autobiography* (London: Picador, 1982), p. 408.
43. Barfield (1957), p. 145.
44. W. B. Yeats, *The Collected Letters of W. B. Yeats,* vol. III (Oxford, U.K.: Oxford University Press, 1994), p. 40.
45. Corbin 1969, p. 179.
46. Ibid.
47. Ibid.
48. Wilson 1971, p. 244.
49. A fragment of it remains, and from what there is, it seems that Thomas South was a devotee of the *prisca theologia*; see http://www.levity.com/alchemy/t_south.html.
50. Wilson 2006, p. 403.
51. The complete text is available at https://archive.org/stream/suggestiveinquir00atwo#page/68/mode/2up.
52. Mary Anne South, *A Suggestive Inquiry into the Hermetic Mystery with a Dissertation on the More Celebrated of the Alchemical Philosophers* (London: Trelawney Saunders, 1850), p. 135.
53. Ibid., p. 69.
54. Ibid., p. 192.
55. Ibid., p. 334.
56. Ibid., p. 136.
57. Jacob Boehme, *Genius of the Transcendent: Mystical Writings of Jacob Boehme,* Michael L. Birkel and Jeff Bach, eds. (Boston & London: Shambhala, 2010), p. 37.
58. Basarab Nicolescu, *Science, Meaning, & Evolution: The Cosmology of Jacob Boehme* (New York: Parabola, 1991).
59. Yates 1978, p. 99.
60. Colin Wilson, *Religion and the Rebel* (Boston: Houghton Mifflin, 1957), p. 153.
61. Abraham von Franckenberg, *The Life and Death of Jacob Boehme,* at http://www.jacobboehmeonline .com/frankenberg.
62. Quoted in Wilson 1957, p. 154.
63. Bucke 1966, p. 184.
64. Boehme 2010, pp. 2–3.
65. George Steiner, *After Babel* (Oxford, U.K.: Oxford University Press, 1976), p. 62.
66. Nikolai Berdyaev, "Introduction," Jacob Boehme, *Six Theosophic Points* (Ann Arbor: University of Michigan Press, 1958), p. v.
67. Boehme 2010, p. 1.
68. Versluis 2007, p. 109.
69. For more on Saint-Martin and Eckartshausen, see Lachman 2005, pp. 30–37; for Crowley and Eckartshausen, see Lachman 2014, pp. 51–52.
70. Boehme 1958, p. xxv.
71. J. G. Bennett, *The Dramatic Universe* (London: Hodder & Stoughton, 1956).

CHAPTER 9: THIS IS THE MODERN WORLD

1. Versluis 2007, p. 92. Full text available at http://www.levity.com/alchemy/secret_s.html.
2. Examples of these illustrations can be found at https://www.google.co.uk/search?q=Theosophische +Werke+Boehme&espv=2&tbm=isch&tbo=u&source=univ&sa=X&ei=L9TcVPKGOMyqPLu7g dgD&ved=0CEAQsAQ&biw=1366&bih=643.
3. Boehme 2010, p. 6.
4. Picknett and Prince 2011, p. 150.
5. Ibid., p. 151.
6. Margery Purver, *Royal Society: Concept and Creation* (London: Routledge, 1967), pp. 198–99.
7. Paolo Rossi, *Francis Bacon: From Magic to Science* (London: Routledge, 1968), pp. 13–14.
8. The celebration was to be held in 1942, but World War II interfered with the plans. It took place in Cambridge in July 1946. Keynes had died in April of that year and his brother Geoffrey read his

address. The text of Keynes's lecture is available at http://www-history.mcs.st-and.ac.uk/Extras/Keynes_Newton.html.

9. See http://content.time.com/time/magazine/article/0,9171,36508,00.html.

10. Christopher Hitchens, *God Is Not Great* (New York: Atlantic Books, 2007), p. 65.

11. Anthony Storr, *Solitude: A Return to the Self* (New York: Ballantine Books, 1988), p. 165.

12. Ibid.

13. Ibid.

14. Selig Brodetsky, *Sir Isaac Newton* (London: Methuen & Co., 1927), p. 89.

15. See http://io9.com/5877660/was-robert-hooke-really-sciences-greatest-asshole.

16. Marshall 2001, p. 401.

17. Jasper Ridley, *The Freemasons* (London: Robinson, 2000), p. 21.

18. Ibid.

19. Marshall 2001, p. 402.

20. Sadly space does not allow me to do more than mention Ramon Lull (1232–1315), a Majorcan philosopher, Franciscan monk, and early troubadour, who developed what has been seen as an early form of computation. "Lullian Art" is a supposed universal system of knowledge using geometrical figures, symbols, and letters, which Lull arranged in a system of revolving concentric circles. By turning the circles, one could arrive at a combination of "dignities" that revealed truths about the universe. Lull is credited with writing many alchemical texts, but it is doubtful he is their true author. Basil Valentine is credited with many alchemical works of the sixteenth century. Most scholars accept that the name is a pseudonym and there is debate whether it refers to one person or a group.

21. Marshall 2001, pp. 403–4.

22. Newton's translation of the *Emerald Tablet* can be found at http://www.sacred-texts.com/alc/emerald.htm.

23. Colin Wilson, *Starseekers* (London: Hodder & Stoughton, 1980), p. 148.

24. Picknett and Prince 2011, pp. 169–72. Picknett and Prince mention specifically the research of J. Edward McGuire and Piyo M. Rattansi in their paper "Newton and the Pipes of Pan," published in the *Notes and Records of the Royal Society* (December 1966); the historian of science Richard S. Westfall's paper, "Newton and the Hermetic Tradition" in *Science, Medicine and Society in the Renaissance*, ed. Allen G. Debus (New York: Science History Publications, 1972); and Betty Jo Teeter Dobbs's books *The Foundations of Newton's Alchemy* (Cambridge, U.K.: Cambridge University Press, 1975) and *The Janus Face of Genius: The Role of Alchemy in Newton's Thought* (Cambridge, U.K.: Cambridge University Press, 1991).

25. Picknett and Prince p. 172.

26. Marshall 2001, pp. 408–9.

27. Picknett and Prince 2011, p. 169.

28. Ridley 2000, p. 22.

29. Ibid., pp. 21–22.

30. Quoted in Yates 1978, p. 211.

31. Ibid.

32. Thomas De Quincey, "Historico-Critical Inquiry into the Origins of the Rosicrucians and the Freemasons," originally published in the *London Magazine*, January 1824; text at http://www.freemasons-freemasonry.com/dequincey_rosicrucians_freemasons.html.

33. Smoley 2006, p. 141.

34. See Christopher Knight and Robert Lomas, *The Hiram Key* (Minneapolis, Minn.: Fair Winds Press, 2001); *The Second Messiah* (Minneapolis, Minn.: Fair Winds Press, 2001); and *Uriel's Machine* (Minneapolis, Minn.: Fair Winds Press, 2001); Graham Hancock, *The Sign and the Seal* (New York: Touchstone, 1992); and Lynn Picknett and Clive Prince, *The Templar Revelation* (New York: Touchstone, 1998).

35. Manly P. Hall, *The Lost Keys of Freemasonry* (Los Angeles: Philosophical Research Society, 1923), pp. xxi–xxii; Hall 2003, pp. 282, 283, 658.

36. See David Ovason, *The Secret Zodiacs of Washington, D.C.* (New York: Century, 1999); and Robert Hieronimus, *Founding Fathers, Secret Societies: Freemasons, Illuminati, Rosicrucians, and the Decoding of the Great Seal*.

37. Ridley 2000, pp. 26–27.

38. Jay Kinney, *The Masonic Myth* (New York: HarperCollins, 2009), p. 9.

39. Ibid., p. 10.

40. Ridley 2000, p. 1.

41. Jean Gimpel, *The Cathedral Builders* (London: Michael Russell, 1983), pp 68–69.

42. Ridley 2000, p. 5.

43. Ibid., p. 17.

44. It is true that Hermetic science also believed that knowledge of God could be had through observing his creation, but for it, nature was a living being, not a machine.

45. See Blake's "There is No Natural Religion."

46. Michael Baigent and Richard Leigh, *The Temple and the Lodge* (London: Arrow Books, 1998), p. 295.

47. Ibid., p. 244.

48. Marsha Keith Schuchard, *Why Mrs. Blake Cried* (London: Century, 2006).

49. Lars Berquist, *Swedenborg's Secret* (London: Swedenborg Society, 2005), p. 170.

50. Sadly, these inventions didn't get beyond the drawing board, and Swedenborg's father is said to have discarded his designs. For more on Swedenborg's inventions and his life in general, see Lachman 2012.

51. Emanuel Swedenborg, *The Principia*, quoted in Steve Koke, "The Search for a Religious Cosmology" in *Emanuel Swedenborg: A Continuing Vision*, Stephen Larsen ed. (New York: Swedenborg Foundation, 1988), p. 459.

52. *The Principia* is the third part of Swedenborg's three-volume *The Mineral Kingdom* (1734); Parts 1 and 2 deal with technical issues concerning mines and mineralogy.

53. See David Bohm, *Wholeness and the Implicate Order* (London: Routledge, 1980); and Lachman 2012, pp. 28–29.

54. See http://www.newchurchhistory.org/articles/glb2007/baker.pdf.

55. See http://blogs.scientificamerican.com/life-unbounded/2012/10/15/the-panspermia-paradox/.

56. For a list of Swedenborg's astronomical insights, see Lachman 2012, pp. 48–50.

57. Ibid., pp. 54–55.

58. For more on Count Zinzendorf and the Moravians, see Lachman 2008, pp. 53–62.

59. It was *Ecce Homo* by the Baroque artist Domenico Feti.

60. Berquist 2005, p. 204.

61. Joscelyn Godwin, *The Theosophical Enlightenment* (Albany, N.Y.: SUNY Press, 1994), p. 223.

62. For more on hypnagogia, see Lachman 2003, pp. 85–94.

63. It is no surprise that of western visionaries, the one Corbin occupied himself with most was Swedenborg. See Henry Corbin, *Swedenborg and Esoteric Islam* (Chester, Penn.: Swedenborg Foundation, 1999).

64. An incisive and entertaining depiction of a Swedenborgian heaven and hell can be found in Bernard Shaw's philosophical comedy, "Don Juan in Hell," the third act of his creative evolutionist play, *Man and Superman*.

65. Ralph Waldo Emerson, *Swedenborg: Introducing the Mystic* (London: Swedenborg Society, 2009), p. 40.

66. Emanuel Swedenborg, *Heaven and Hell*, J. C. Ager, trans. (London: Swedenborg Society, 1958), pp. 44–45.

67. Czeslaw Milosz, "Introduction," *The Noble Traveler: The Life and Writings of O. V. de L. Milosz* (West Stockbridge, Mass.: Lindisfarne Books, 1985), p. 33.

68. Other artists who used synesthesia include the painter Wassily Kandisky (a Theosophist); the composers Olivier Messiaen and Alexandre Scriabin (also a Theosophist); the playwright August Strindberg; and the novelist Vladimir Nabokov.

69. Readers interested in how Baudelaire arrived at Symbolism might consult my essay "The Spiritual Detective: How Baudelaire Invented Symbolism, by Way of Swedenborg, E. T. A. Hoffmann and Edgar Allan Poe," in *Philosophy, Literature, Mysticism: An Anthology of Essays on the Thought and Influence of Emanuel Swedenborg* (London: Swedenborg Society, 2013), pp. 217–32.

CHAPTER 10: THE ROMANTIC CENTURY

1. Robert Darnton, *Mesmerism and the End of the Enlightenment* (Cambridge, Mass.: Harvard University Press, 1969), p. 34.

2. Ibid.

3. Place 2005, pp. 108–11.

4. Wilson, *Frankenstein's Castle* 1980, pp. 70–84.

5. Brian Inglis, *Natural and Supernatural* (Bridgeport, UK: Prism Press, 1992) p. 142.

6. Although some, like the frenetic Abbé Barruel, believed that Masons—specifically the Illuminati—were responsible for the French Revolution, as in the case with the American Revolution, Masons found themselves on both sides of the guillotine. See Lachman 2008, p. 69.

7. For more on *tikkun*, see Lachman 2013, pp. 34–35.

8. Ibid., p. 20.

9. Ibid., p. 21.

10. Quoted in Wilson 1971, pp. 321–22.

11. S. Foster Damon, *A Blake Dictionary* (Boulder, Colo.: Shambhala, 1979), p. 419.
12. William Blake, *The Complete Poetry and Prose of William Blake*, David V. Erdman, ed. (Berkeley: University of California Press, 1982), pp. 565, 555.
13. Quoted in Paul Davies, *Romanticism and Esoteric Tradition* (Hudson, N.Y.: Lindisfarne Books, 1998), p. 80.
14. For more on Coleridge's philosophy, see Owen Barfield, "The Philosophy of Samuel Taylor Coleridge" in Barfield 1986.
15. Godwin 1994, p. 234.
16. John Livingston Lowes, *The Road to Xanadu* (London: Pan Books, 1978), p. 211.
17. Thomas Taylor, *Eleusinian and Bacchic Mysteries*, "Introduction," quoted in Kathleen Raine, *Golgonooza, City of Imagination* (Hudson, N.Y.: Lindisfarne Books, 1991), p. 3.
18. See http://www.academia.edu/1264783/A_Vindication_of_the_Rights_of_Brutes.
19. Lowes 1978, p. 211.
20. S. Damon Foster 1979, p. 396.
21. The difference between Goethe and Blake can be seen in an anecdote about Goethe and Beethoven, another "thundering" Romantic, recorded by their mutual friend Bettina von Arnim. Once, while together, Goethe and Beethoven encountered royalty walking toward them. Goethe was polite and, doffing his hat, gracefully made way. Beethoven, who acknowledged no aristocracy but genius, refused and, hands in pockets, marched through the dukes and duchesses with a scowl. Beethoven's esoteric interests, as well as those of other composers, can be found in my essay "Concerto for Magic and Mysticism: Esotericism and Western Music" at https://www.theosophical.org/publications/1289.
22. John Armstrong, *Love, Life, Goethe* (London: Penguin Allen Lane, 2006), p. 291.
23. For more on Goethe's ideas about color, see Arthur Zajonc, *Catching the Light* (New York: Bantam, 1993). For "Goethean science," see Henri Bortoft, *The Wholeness of Nature* (Great Barrington, Mass.: Lindisfarne Books, 1996).
24. Peter Watson, *The German Genius* (London: Simon & Schuster, 2010), p. 205; James Gleick, *Chaos* (New York: Penguin, 1988), pp. 163–65.
25. See Ronald D. Gray, *Goethe the Alchemist* (Cambridge, U.K.: Cambridge University Press, 1952).
26. Johann Wolfgang von Goethe, *Autobiography* (Chicago: University of Chicago Press, 1974), p. 371.
27. Arthur Koestler, *The Ghost in the Machine* (New York: Macmillan, 1967), p. 138.
28. Johann Wolfgang von Goethe, *Italian Journey* (New York: Schocken Books, 1968), p. 241.
29. Johann Wolfgang von Goethe, *Maxims and Reflections* (Harmondsworth, U.K.: Penguin Books, 1998), p. 155.
30. Quoted in Erich Heller, *The Disinherited Mind* (New York: Farrar, Strauss and Cudahy, 1957), p. 31.
31. Ibid.
32. Novalis, *Pollen and Fragments*, Arthur Versluis, trans. (Grand Rapids, Mich.: Phanes Press, 1989), p. 50.
33. Ibid., pp. 71, 26.
34. Ibid., p. 115.
35. Ibid., p. 15.
36. Watson 2010, p. 201.
37. Faivre 1994, p. 83.
38. Quoted in Koestler 1967, p. 138.
39. Colin Wilson, *Poltergeist!* (London: New English Library, 1981), pp. 250–53.
40. See http://blogs.forteana.org/node/143. Crowe suffered a kind of breakdown a few years after *The Night-Side of Nature* appeared and was said to be seen running naked through the streets of Edinburgh, advised by spirits that she would be invisible. Debate remains over the truth of the story.
41. Catherine Crowe, *The Night-Side of Nature* (Wellingborough, U.K.: Aquarian Press, 1986), p. 30.
42. Ibid., p. 48.
43. Darnton 1969, p. 88.
44. Mitch Horowitz, *Occult America* (New York: Bantam Books, 2009), p. 49; Versluis 2007, p. 149.
45. Bulwer-Lytton is an important figure and deserves more recognition. For more, see Lachman 2006, pp. 99–105.
46. Horowitz 2009, p. 37.
47. See Sir Patrick Moore, "Foreword," Edgar Allan Poe, *Eureka* (London: Hesperus Press, 2002), pp. vii–ix, where he speaks of Poe's insights being confirmed in the twentieth century.
48. Lachman 2008, pp. 111–15.
49. In his book on Home, *The First Psychic* (London: Abacus, 2006), the skeptical psychic investigator and stage magician Peter Lamont admits that Home was never "found out," as he argues all of the other famous Victorian psychics were—a highly debatable claim. He also admits that he can see no "normal" way in which Home could have performed the feats he did.

50. Wilson 1981, p. 265.
51. See C. G. Harrison, *The Transcendental Universe* (London: Temple Lodge, 1993); and Rudolf Steiner, *The Occult Movement in the Nineteenth Century* (London: Rudolf Steiner Press, 1973).
52. Levi 1970, p. 10.
53. Some accounts put the Pantheon on Regent Street, but according to *Pocket Britain*, it was on Oxford Street; see http://www.pocketbritain.com/OxfordStreet.html.
54. Place 2005, pp. 70–73.
55. A few years ago I appeared in an episode of the television program *Myth Hunters* dedicated to the *Book of Thoth*, or, as the producer of the show called it, "the *Book of Spells*." I explained several times during my interview that no one "*Book of Thoth*" existed. Not surprisingly, my explanations reached the cutting room floor. The result can be seen here: https://www.youtube.com/watch?v=De2X-e5IOW0.
56. See https://www.etsy.com/listing/189145471/pentagram-bikini-666-baphomet-swimsuit?ref=market.
57. Christopher Bamford, "Introduction," Harrison 1993, p. 8.
58. Readers interested in some idea of Blavatsky's life can find out more in my *Madame Blavatsky: The Mother of Modern Spirituality* (New York: Tarcher/Penguin, 2012).
59. For the Orphic Circle, Hermetic Brotherhood of Luxor, and the "hidden hand" theory of spiritualism, see Lachman 2012, pp. 104–31.
60. Colonel Olcott took to Buddhism with typical energy and efficiency, writing a *Buddhist Catechism* that became hugely popular and which introduced the religion to many Buddhists who were ignorant of its teachings. He remains a national hero in Sri Lanka, where a stamp bears his image, a statue of him stands in Colombo Fort Railway Station, and streets are named after him.
61. For a fuller account of the Coulombe-Hodgson affair, see Lachman 2012, pp. 201–31.

CHAPTER II: TOWARD THE NEW AGE

1. James Webb, *The Occult Establishment* (La Salle, Ill.: Open Court, 1976), p. 8.
2. See my essay "New Age *Fin-de-Siècle*" in *The Fin-de-Siècle World*, Michael Saler, ed. (New York: Routledge, 2015), pp. 611–22.
3. See my essay "Kandinsky's Thought Forms: The Occult Roots of Modern Art" at https://www.theosophical.org/publications/1405.
4. The question of who made the first "abstract painting," and indeed what abstract painting itself is, remains controversial. In recent years I have lectured on the work of the little-known Swedish painter Hilma af Klint, a spiritualist and follower of Theosophy and Rudolf Steiner, who died in 1944. Hilma af Klint's early efforts in "automatic painting"—in which the artist acts as a medium for spiritual forces—were done in 1906 and are increasingly seen as predating Kandinsky's abstract works of 1911. See http://www.tate.org.uk/context-comment/articles/first-abstract-artist-and-its-not-kandinsky.
5. Kandinsky and Mondrian were by no means the only modern artists with an interest in the esoteric or Theosophy, as was made clear in 1986 at the groundbreaking exhibition "The Spiritual in Art: Abstract Painting 1890–1985," held at the Los Angeles County Museum of Art and which I had the good fortune to attend; see Maurice Tuchman, *The Spiritual in Art: Abstract Painting 1890–1985* (New York: Abbeville Press, 1986).
6. Ralph Freedman, *Hermann Hesse: Pilgrim of Crisis* (New York: Pantheon Books, 1978), pp. 136–37.
7. Thomas Halk, *Eranos* (Sheffield, U.K.: Equinox Publishing, 2013), p. 7.
8. Deborah Blum, *Ghosthunters* (London: Century, 2007), p. 41.
9. Ibid., p. 43.
10. William James, *The Varieties of Religious Experience* (New York: Collier Books, 1977), p. 305.
11. Ibid., pp. 89–91.
12. See Lachman 2014 for more on Crowley's tenure with the Golden Dawn and the activities of the *Argentium Astrum*.
13. Marco Pasi, *Aleister Crowley and the Temptation of Politics* (Durham, U.K.: Acumen Publishing, 2014), p. 175–76, n. 107.
14. Norman and Jeanne MacKenzie, *The Fabians* (New York: Simon & Schuster, 1977), p. 344.
15. A. R. Orage, *Consciousness: Animal, Human and Superman* (New York: Samuel Weiser, 1974), p. 51.
16. Ibid., p. 68.
17. Lachman 2003, p. 35.
18. For more on Krishnamurti, see Gary Lachman, *Turn Off Your Mind: The Mystic Sixties and the Dark Side of the Age of Aquarius* (New York: Disinformation Company, 2003), pp. 81–86.
19. Steven Phillips, *Extra-sensory Perception of Quarks* (Adyar, India: Theosophical Publishing House, 1995).

20. Ibid., pp. 161–62.
21. For more on Bely and Bryusov, see Lachman 2005. See also my "Afterword" to Bryusov, *The Fiery Angel* (Sawtry, U.K.: Dedalus Books, 2005).
22. I look at Steiner's system of "planetary evolution" in more detail in Lachman 2007, pp. 125–51.
23. See https://archive.org/details/warthatwillendwa00welluoft.
24. Ouspensky 1949, p. 4.
25. Ibid., pp. 6–7.
26. Ibid., p. 19.
27. Gurdjieff and Heidegger also agreed that one way of remembering our being is through a vivid awareness of the reality of our death. Both believed that a vivid grasp of the truth that we shall one day die—what Heidegger called our "finitude"—can shake us out of our forgetfulness. An exploration of the similarities between Gurdjieff and Heidegger would, I believe, prove fruitful.
28. http://poetry.about.com/od/poemsbytitleu/l/blyeatsunderbenbulben.htm.
29. Ouspensky 1949, p. 82.
30. See Lachman 2013, pp. 167–70.
31. Ouspensky 1949, p. 85.
32. Ibid., p. 122.
33. Ibid., p. 77.
34. Bennett 1973.
35. For a full account of Ouspensky's "escape," see Lachman 2006, pp. 177–89.
36. For more on Ouspensky's influence on Eliot, Huxley, and other British writers, see my essay "Ouspensky in London" in Gary Lachman, *Revolutionaries of the Soul* (Wheaton, Ill.: Quest, 2014), pp. 151–61.
37. Lachman 2010, pp. 186–89.
38. C. G. Jung, *Memories, Dreams, Reflections* (London: Fontana Paperbacks, 1989), p. 207.
39. Hoeller 1982, p. 26.
40. Jung 1989, p. 210.
41. See Silberer's 1909 paper, which Jung knew, "Report on a Method of Eliciting and Observing Certain Symbolic Hallucination-Phenomena" in David Rapaport, ed., *Organisation and Pathology of Thought* (New York: Columbia University Press, 1951). Silberer's interest in the "anagogic"— spiritual—aspect of dreams cost him Freud's favor, and led to his suicide; see also Lachman 2010, pp. 119–20.
42. See http://www.schoolofwisdom.com/history/founders/count-hermann-keyserling/.
43. See Lachman 2007, pp. 177–83.
44. See Lachman 2014, pp. 218–49.
45. See http://www.npg.org.uk/collections/search/person/mp64137/edward-alexander-aleister-crowley ?search=sas&sText=Aleister+Crowley.
46. Ouspensky's original title for this was *Fragments of an Unknown Teaching*, but he rejected this because it was too close to G. R. S. Mead's *Fragments of a Faith Forgotten*. After his death, Ouspensky's publishers chose *In Search of the Miraculous*, a title from a chapter in *A New Model of the Universe*.
47. See P. D. Ouspensky, *A Record of Meetings* (London: Penguin/Arkana 1992).
48. See William Patrick Patterson's interesting work, *Voices in the Dark: Esoteric, Occult and Secular Voices in Nazi-Occupied Paris, 1940–44* (Fairfax, Calif.: Arete Communications, 2000) for Gurdjieff's context in occupied Paris.

CHAPTER 12: THE NEXT STEP BEYOND

1. C. G. Jung, *Letters, Vol. I: 1906–1950*, Gerhard Adler, ed. (London: Routledge, 1973), p. 285.
2. Carpenter wrote an essay, "The Symbolism of the Equinox," that was based on the work of the poet and spiritualist Gerald Massey, whose *Lectures* (1900) talk about the transition from the age of Fishes (Pisces) to that of the Water Bearer (Aquarius).
3. C. G. Jung, *Aion* (Princeton, N.J.: Princeton University Press, 1979), p. 87.
4. C. G. Jung, *Flying Saucers: A Modern Myth of Things Seen in the Sky*, in Jung, *Collected Works*, vol. 10 (London: Routledge, 1964), p. 311.
5. See Lachman 2003, pp. 337–40.
6. Albert Hofmann, *LSD: My Problem Child* (Los Angeles: J. P. Tarcher, 1983), p. 15.
7. Although the most widely known, Huxley's drug experience was preceded by similar experiments carried out by the German writers Walter Benjamin and Ernst Jünger. Jünger and Hofmann took several celebrated "trips" together.
8. Michael Hollingshead, *The Man Who Turned On the World* (London: Blond and Briggs, 1973), p. 8.

9. At the time Anaïs Nin and her lover, Henry Miller, said that they had met Crowley, he had been deported from France and was not allowed back in; see Paul Newman, *The Tregerthen Horror* (London: Abraxas Editions, 2005), p. 54.

10. See http://www.beatlesinterviews.org/db1980.jlpb.beatles.html; and *Hit Parade,* October 1976 (14), and *Musicians Special Collector's Edition,* 1988, p. 12.

11. Timothy Leary, *Confessions of a Hope Fiend* (New York: Bantam Books, 1973), p. 288; and http://www.youtube.com/watch?v+2gY3dSqs68A.

12. See Norman Mailer, *The Armies of the Night* (Harmondsworth, U.K.: Penguin, 1968) for a full account of the "occult" aspects of the peace march.

13. Lachman 2003, p. 191.

14. Kurt Vonnegut, "The Mysterious Madame Blavatsky," *McCall's,* March 1970.

15. See Edward Hoffmann, *The Right to be Human: A Biography of Abraham Maslow* (Los Angeles: J. P. Tarcher, 1988), pp. 287–90.

16. Abraham Maslow, *Future Visions: The Unpublished Papers of Abraham Maslow* (Thousand Oaks, Calif.: Sage Publications, 1996), pp. 129–31.

17. Hans Thomas Hakl, *Eranos: An Intellectual History of the Twentieth Century,* Christopher McIntosh, trans. (Sheffield, U.K.: Equinox, 2013), p. 29.

18. Ibid.

19. Ibid., p. 16.

20. Ibid., p. 25.

21. For more on Alexandra David-Neel, see *Magic and Mystery in Tibet* (New York: Dover Books, 1971), and *My Journey to Lhasa* (London: Virago Press, 1988). She was in many ways a remarkable woman whose life parallels that of Madame Blavatsky. Among her other accomplishments, she lived to be one hundred years old—born in 1868, she died in 1969.

22. Hakl 2013 p. 31.

23. Ibid., p. 30.

24. Ibid., p. 45.

25. Ibid., p. 29.

26. For more on Evola, see my essay "Mussolini's Mystic," in Lachman, *Revolutionaries,* 2014, pp. 123–35.

27. For more on Weininger, see Gary Lachman, *The Dedalus Book of Literary Sucides: Dead Letters* (Sawtry, U.K.: Dedalus Books, 2009), pp. 192–99.

28. Aldous Huxley, "Foreword," F. W. H. Myers, *Human Personality and Its Survival of Bodily Death* (New York: Dover Books, 2005), p. 7.

29. Interview with Sam Keen, "The Golden Mean of Roberto Assagioli" in *Psychology Today* (December 1974).

30. Ouspensky 1969, pp. 9–10.

31. H. G. Wells, *The Open Conspiracy* (Thirsk, U.K.: House of Stratus, 2002), p. 1.

32. Ibid., p. 161.

33. This is true not only of "occult" or "spiritual" ideas. The philosopher Allan Bloom's controversial book, *The Closing of the American Mind* (1987), appeared at the same time as Shirley MacLaine's television miniseries. In it, Bloom attacks the easy and unthinking "relativism" he found rampant on universities, spread by the popularizing of postmodern ideologies like "deconstructionism." Although on opposite poles, both New Age philosophy and postmodernism share a similar disregard for objective "reality" and "truth," leaving both very much up to the subjectivity of the individual. Each arrives at its own version of "anything goes," a conclusion that Bloom, a Platonist, could not accept.

34. See Dennis McKenna, "Reflections in a Rear-View Mirror: Speculations on Novelty Theory and the End Times," in *The Divine Spark: Psychdeliccs, Consciousness and the Birth of Civilization,* Graham Hancock, ed. (London: Hay House, 2015), pp. 40–50.

35. For my own take on the 2012 phenomenon, see my essay "2013: Or What to Do When the Apocalypse Doesn't Arrive," at http://disinfo.com/2009/10/2013-or-what-to-do-when-the-apocalypse-doesn%E2%80%99t-arrive/.

36. See my *New York Rocker: My Life in the Blank Generation with Blondie, Iggy Pop and Others 1974–1981* (New York: Thunders Mouth Press, 2006), written under my stage name "Gary Valentine."

37. In recent times, "great works" have also been explained as purely products of our brains' neural activity; see http://m.chronicle.com/article/Neuroscience-Is-Ruining-the/150141/.

38. Godwin 2007, p. xii.

39. Gary Lachman, "Access to a Western Esotericist," at https://www.theosophical.org/publications/1487.

40. Valentin Tomberg, *Meditations on the Tarot* (New York: Tarcher/Putman, 2002), pp. ix–x.

41. Ibid., p. 4.
42. Ibid., pp. 48, 89, 90.
43. See http://www.hawking.org.uk/does-god-play-dice.html.
44. George Steiner, *Grammars of Creation* (London: Faber and Faber, 2001), pp. 1–2.
45. Leszek Kolakowski, *Modernity on Endless Trial* (Chicago: University of Chicago Press, 1990), p. 12.
46. See https://humanism.org.uk/about/atheist-bus-campaign/.
47. Alfred North Whitehead, *Symbolism, Its Meaning and Effect* (New York: G. P. Putnam, 1959), p. 88.
48. Gebser 1985, p. xxx.
49. Ibid., p. 49.

SELECTED BIBLIOGRAPHY

Anderson, William (1980). *Dante the Maker*. London: Routledge and Kegan Paul.
——— (1985). *The Rise of the Gothic*. London: Hutchinson.
——— (1996). *The Face of Glory*. London: Bloomsbury.
Anonymous (2002). *Meditations on the Tarot: A Journey into Christian Hermeticism*. New York: Tarcher/Penguin.
Armstrong, John (2006). *Love, Life, Goethe*. London: Penguin Allen Lane.
Baigent, Michael, and Leigh, Richard (1998). *The Temple and the Lodge*. London: Arrow Books.
Ball, Philip (2006). *The Devil's Doctor*. London: Heinemann.
Bamford, Christopher, ed. (1994). *Rediscovering Sacred Science*. Edinburgh: Floris Books.
——— (2003). *An Endless Trace: The Passionate Pursuit of Wisdom in the West*. New Paltz, N.Y.: Codhill Press.
Barfield, Owen (1957). *Saving the Appearances*. New York: Harcourt, Brace.
——— (1985). *History in English Words*. West Stockbridge, Mass.: Lindisfarne Press.
——— (1986). *Romanticism Comes of Age*. Middleton, Conn.: Wesleyan University Press.
Barzun, Jacques (2001). *From Dawn to Decadence*. New York: HarperCollins.
Begg, Ean (1989). *The Cult of the Black Virgin*. London: Arkana.
Bennett, J. G. (1956). *The Dramatic Universe*. London: Hodder & Stoughton.
——— (1973). *Gurdjieff: Making a New World*. New York: Harper & Row.
——— (1974). *Witness*. Tuscon, Ariz.: Omen Press.
Bergson, Henri (1911). *Creative Evolution*. London: The Macmillan Company.
——— (1912). *Introduction to Metaphysics*. New York: G. P. Putnam.
——— (1935). *The Two Sources of Morality and Religion*. New York: Henry Holt.
Berquist, Lars (2005). *Swedenborg's Secret*. London: Swedenborg Society.
Binswanger, Hans Christoph (1994). *Money and Magic: A Critique of the Modern Economy in Light of Goethe's Faust*. Chicago: University of Chicago Press.
Blake, William (1982). David K. Erdman, ed. *The Complete Poetry and Prose of William Blake*. Berkeley: University of California Press.
Blum, Deborah (2007). *Ghosthunters*. London: Century.
Blumenberg, Hans (1983). *The Legitimacy of the Modern Age*. Cambridge, Mass.: MIT Press.
Boehme, Jacob (1958). *Six Theosophic Points*. Ann Arbor: University of Michigan Press.
——— (2010). Michael L. Birkel and Jeff Bach, eds. *Genius of the Transcendent: Mystical Writings of Jacob Boehme*. Boston & London: Shambhala.
Bohm, David (1980). *Wholeness and the Implicate Order*. London: Routledge.
Boyce, Mary (1979). *Zoroastrians: Their Religious Beliefs and Practices*. London: Routledge.
Brodetsky, Selig (1927). *Sir Isaac Newton*. London: Methuen & Co.
Bucke, R. M. (1966). *Cosmic Consciousness*. New York: E. P. Dutton.
Burckhardt, Jacob (1944). *The Civilization of the Renaissance in Italy*. London: Phaidon Press.
Burckhardt, Titus (1986). *Alchemy*. Longmead, U.K.: Elemental Books.
Cassirer, Ernst (1972). *The Individual and the Cosmos in Renaissance Philosophy*. Philadelphia: University of Pennsylvania Press.
Collin, Rodney (1980). *The Theory of Celestial Influence*. London: Watkins Books.
Corbin, Henry (1969). *Creative Imagination in the Sufism of Ibn 'Arabi*. Princeton, N.J.: Princeton University Press.
——— (1976). *Mundus Imaginalis, or The Imaginary and the Imaginal*. Ipswich, U.K.: Golgonooza Press.
——— (1998). *The Voyage and the Messenger: Iran and Philosophy*. Berkeley, Calif.: North Atlantic Books.
——— (1999). *Swedenborg and Esoteric Islam*. Chester, Penn.: Swedenborg Foundation.

Cornford, Frances (1991). *From Religion to Philosophy.* Princeton, N.J.: Princeton University Press.
Crowe, Catherine (1986). *The Night-Side of Nature.* Wellingborough, U.K.: Aquarian Press.
Crowley, Aleister (1969). *The Confessions of Aleister Crowley.* New York: Hill & Wang.
Damon, S. Foster (1979). *A Blake Dictionary.* Boulder, Colo.: Shambhala.
Dante Alighieri (1962). Dorothy Sayers trans. *Il Paradiso.* London: Penguin Books.
——— (1969). Barbara Reynolds trans. *La Vita Nuova.* Harmondsworth, U.K.: Penguin Books.
Darnton, Robert (1969). *Mesmerism and the End of the Enlightenment.* Cambridge, Mass.: Harvard University Press.
Davies, Paul (1998). *Romanticism and Esoteric Tradition.* Hudson, N.Y.: Lindisfarne Books.
de Rougemont, Denis (1983). *Love in the Western World.* Princeton, N.J.: Princeton University Press.
Deleuze, Gilles (1990). *Bergsonism.* New York: Zone Books.
Dionysius the Areopagite (1965). *Mystical Theology and Celestial Hierarchies.* Brook, Surrey, U.K.: Shrine of Wisdom.
Dubois, Geneviève (2006). *Fulcanelli and the Alchemical Revival.* Rochester, Vt.: Destiny Books.
Easton, Stewart (1982). *Man and World in the Light of Anthroposophy.* New York: Steiner Books.
Ebeling, Florian (2007). *The Secret History of Hermes Trismegistus.* Ithaca, N.Y.: Cornell University Press.
Eliade, Mircea (1989). *Shamanism: Archaic Techniques of Ecstasy.* London: Arkana.
Ellenberger, Henri (1994). *The Discovery of the Unconscious.* London: Fontana.
Evola, Julius (1995). *Revolt Against the Modern World.* Rochester, Vt.: Inner Traditions.
——— (1996). H. E. Musson trans. *The Doctrine of Awakening.* Rochester, Vt.: Inner Traditions.
——— (1997). *The Mystery of the Grail.* Rochester, Vt.: Inner Traditions.
Faivre, Antoine (1994). *Access to Western Esotericism.* Albany, N.Y.: SUNY Press.
——— (1995). *The Eternal Hermes.* Grand Rapids, Mich.: Phanes Press.
Feuerstein, Georg (1987). *Structures of Consciousness.* Lower Lake, Calif.: Integral Publishing.
Ficino, Marsilio (1975). *Letters,* vol. I. London: Shepard-Walwyn.
——— (1996). Charles Boer trans. *The Book of Life.* Woodstock, Conn.: Spring Publications.
Fideler, David, ed. (1987). *The Pythagorean Sourcebook.* Grand Rapids, Mich.: Phanes Press.
Fielding, Amanda, ed. (2008). *Hofmann's Elixir: LSD and the New Eleusis.* London: Strange Attractor.
Freedman, Ralph (1978). *Hermann Hesse: Pilgrim of Crisis.* New York: Pantheon Books.
Freke, Timothy, and Gandy, Peter (1999). *The Jesus Mysteries.* London: Thorsons.
Fulcanelli (2005). *Le Mystère des Cathédrals.* Las Vegas, Nev.: Brotherhood of Life.
Gebser, Jean (1985). Noel Barstad and Algis Mickunas trans. *The Ever-Present Origin.* Athens: Ohio University Press.
Gimpel, Jean (1977). *The Medieval Machine: The Industrial Revolution of the Middle Ages.* London: Penguin Books.
——— (1983). *The Cathedral Builders.* London: Michael Russell, 1983.
Gleeson, Janet (1999). *The Arcanum: The Extraordinary True Story.* New York: Grand Central Publishing.
Gleick, James (1988). *Chaos.* New York: Penguin.
Godwin, Joscelyn (1979). *Robert Fludd.* London: Thames and Hudson.
——— (1981). *Mystery Religions in the Ancient World.* London: Routledge.
——— (1987). *Music, Mysticism and Magic: A Sourcebook.* London: Arkana.
——— (1994). *The Theosophical Enlightenment.* Albany, N.Y.: SUNY Press.
——— (2005). *The Pagan Dream of the Renaissance.* York Beach, Me.: Weiser.
——— (2007). *The Golden Thread.* Wheaton, Ill.: Quest Books.
Goethe, Johann Wolfgang von (1961). Walter Kaufmann trans. *Faust.* New York: Anchor Books.
——— (1968). *Italian Journey.* New York: Schocken Books.
——— (1974). *Autobiography.* Chicago: University of Chicago Press.
——— (1998). *Maxims and Reflections.* Harmondsworth, U.K.: Penguin Books.
Gooch, Stan (1980). *The Double Helix of the Mind.* London: Wildwood House.
——— (1979). *The Paranormal.* London: Fontana.
——— (1980). *Guardians of the Ancient Wisdom.* London: Fontana.
Goodrick-Clarke, Nicholas, ed. (1990). *Paracelsus: Essential Readings.* Wellingborough, U.K.: Crucible.
Gregory, John (1999). *The Neoplatonists: A Reader.* London: Routledge.
Guénon, René (1972). *The Reign of Quantity and the Signs of the Times.* Harmondsworth, U.K.: Penguin Books.
Gurdjieff, G. I. (2015). *Meetings with Remarkable Men.* London: Penguin Classics.
Hakl, Thomas (2013). *Eranos.* Sheffield, U.K.: Equinox Publishing.
Hall, Manly P. (1923). *The Lost Keys of Freemasonry.* Los Angeles: Philosophical Research Society.
——— (2003). *The Secret Teachings of All Ages.* New York: Tarcher/Penguin.
Hancock, Graham, and Bauval, Robert (1997). *The Message of the Sphinx.* New York: Broadway Books.

Hanegraaff, Wouter (2013). *Western Esotericism: A Guide for the Perplexed.* London: Bloomsbury.
Hanegraaff, Wouter, and Pijnenburg, Joyce, eds. (2009). *Hermes in the Academy.* Amsterdam, the Netherlands: Amsterdam University Press.
Harpur, Tom (2004). *The Pagan Christ.* Markham, Canada: Thomas Allen Publishers.
Harrison, C. G. (1993). *The Transcendental Universe.* London: Temple Lodge.
Heidegger, Martin (1984). *Early Greek Thinking.* New York: Harper & Row.
Heller, Erich (1957). *The Disinherited Mind.* New York: Farrar, Strauss and Cudahy.
——— (1984). *In the Age of Prose.* Cambridge, U.K.: Cambridge University Press.
Hillman, D. C. A. (2008). *The Chemical Muse: Drug Use and the Roots of Western Civilization.* New York: St. Martin's Press.
Hillman, James (1977). *Re-Visioning Psychology.* New York: Harper Colophon Books.
Hitchens, Christopher (2007). *God Is Not Great.* New York: Atlantic Books.
Hoeller, Stephan (1982). *The Gnostic Jung and the Seven Sermons to the Dead.* Wheaton, Ill.: Quest Books.
Hoffmann, Edward (1988). *The Right to Be Human: A Biography of Abraham Maslow.* Los Angeles: J. P. Tarcher.
Hofmann, Albert (1983). *LSD: My Problem Child.* Los Angeles: J. P. Tarcher.
Hollingshead, Michael (1973). *The Man Who Turned On the World.* London: Blond and Briggs.
Horowitz, Mitch (2009). *Occult America.* New York: Bantam Books.
Huxley, Aldous (1987). *The Doors of Perception.* London: Grafton Books.
James, William (1977). *The Varieties of Religious Experience.* New York: Collier Books.
Jaspers, Karl (1951). Ralph Manheim trans. *Way to Wisdom.* London: Victor Gollancz.
Jaynes, Julian (1976). *The Origin of Consciousness in the Breakdown of the Bicameral Mind.* Princeton, N.J.: Princeton University Press.
Jonas, Hans (1958). *The Gnostic Religion: The Message of the Alien God and the Beginnings of Christianity.* Boston: Beacon Press.
Jung, Carl Gustav (1964). *Collected Works,* vol. 10. London: Routledge.
——— (1973). Gerhard Adler ed. *Letters, Vol. I: 1906–1950.* London: Routledge.
——— (1977). *The Collected Works of Jung,* vol. 14. Princeton, N.J.: Princeton University Press.
——— (1979). *Aion.* Princeton, N.J.: Princeton University Press.
——— (1989). *Memories, Dreams, Reflections.* London: Fontana Paperbacks.
King, Francis (2011). *Megatherion: The Magical World of Aleister Crowley.* Creation Books.
Kingsley, Peter (1995). *Ancient Philosophy, Mystery and Magic.* Oxford, U.K.: Clarendon Press.
——— (1999). *In the Dark Places of Wisdom.* Inverness, Calif.: Golden Sufi Center.
Kinney, Jay, ed. (2004). *The Inner West: An Introduction to the Hidden Wisdom of the West.* New York: Tarcher/Penguin.
——— (2009) *The Masonic Myth.* New York: HarperCollins.
Koestler, Arthur (1964). *The Act of Creation.* New York: Macmillan.
——— (1967). *The Ghost in the Machine.* New York: Macmillan.
——— (1979). *Janus: A Summing Up.* London: Pan Books.
——— (1979) *The Sleepwalkers.* Harmondsworth, U.K.: Penguin Books.
Lachman, Gary (2003). *Turn Off Your Mind: The Mystic Sixties and the Dark Side of the Age of Aquarius.* New York: Disinformation Company.
——— (2003). *A Secret History of Consciousness.* Great Barrington, Mass.: Lindisfarne.
——— (2005). *A Dark Muse: A History of the Occult.* New York: Thunder's Mouth Press.
——— (2007). *Rudolf Steiner: An Introduction to His Life and Work.* New York: Tarcher/Penguin.
——— (2008). *Politics and the Occult.* Wheaton, Ill.: Quest Books.
——— (2009). *The Dedalus Book of Literary Sucides: Dead Letters.* Sawtry, U.K.: Dedalus Books.
——— (2010). *Jung the Mystic.* New York: Tarcher/Penguin.
——— (2011). *The Quest for Hermes Trismegistus: From Ancient Egypt to the Modern World.* Edinburgh: Floris.
——— (2012). *Madame Blavatsky: The Mother of Modern Spirituality.* New York: Tarcher/Penguin.
——— (2012). *Swedenborg: An Introduction to His Life and Ideas.* New York: Tarcher/Penguin.
——— (2013). *The Caretakers of the Cosmos.* Edinburgh: Floris Books.
——— (2014). *Aleister Crowley: Magick, Rock and Roll, and the Wickedest Man in the World.* New York: Tarcher/Penguin.
——— (2014). *Revolutionaries of the Soul.* Wheaton: Quest.
Larsen, Stephen, ed. (1988). *Emanuel Swedenborg: A Continuing Vision.* New York: Swedenborg Foundation.
Leakey, Mary (1984). *Disclosing the Past.* London: Weidenfeld and Nicholson.
Leary, Timothy (1973). *Confessions of a Hope Fiend.* New York: Bantam Books.
Levi, Eliphas (1970). *Transcendental Magic.* York Beach, Me.: Weiser.

———— (2000). *The History of Magic*. York Beach, Me.: Weiser.

Lewis, C. S. (1988). *The Essential C. S. Lewis*. New York: Collier Books.

Lowes, John Livingston (1978). *The Road to Xanadu*. London: Pan Books.

McClain, Ernest G. (1976). *The Myth of Invariance: The Origins of the Gods, Mathematics and Music from the Rig Veda to Plato*. New York: Nicholas Hay.

McGilchrist, Iain (2010). *The Master and His Emissary*. London: Yale University Press.

McIntosh, Christopher (1987). *The Rosicrucians*. Wellingborough, U.K.: Crucible.

MacKenzie, Norman and Jeanne (1977). *The Fabians*. New York: Simon & Schuster.

Manguel, Alberto (2006). *The Library at Night*. London: Yale University Press.

Marshall, Ian, and Zohar, Dana (1997). *Who's Afraid of Schrödinger's Cat?* London: Bloomsbury.

Marshall, Peter (2001). *The Philosopher's Stone: A Quest for the Secrets of Alchemy*. London: Macmillan.

———— (2006). *The Theatre of the World*. London: Harvill Secker.

Martin, Sean (2006). *The Gnostics*. Harpenden, U.K.: Pocket Essentials.

———— (2006). *Alchemy and Alchemists*. Harpenden, U.K.: Pocket Essentials.

Maslow, Abraham (1996). *Future Visions: The Unpublished Papers of Abraham Maslow*. Thousand Oaks, Calif.: Sage Publications.

Mavromatis, Andreas (1987). *Hypnagogia*. London: Routledge.

Mead, G. R. S. (1906). *Gnosis of the Mind*. Benares, India: Theosophical Publishing Society.

———— (2006) *Hymns to Hermes*. Boston: Weiser.

Miller, Henry (1961). *Tropic of Cancer*. New York: Grove Press.

Milosz, O. V. de Lubicz (1985). *The Noble Traveler: The Life and Writings of O. V. de L. Milosz*. West Stockbridge, Mass.: Lindisfarne Books.

———— (1994). *Amorous Initiation*. Rochester, Vt.: Inner Traditions.

Moore, James (1991). *Gurdjieff: The Anatomy of a Myth*. Shaftsbury, U.K.: Element Books.

Myers, F. W. H. (2005). *Human Personality and Its Survival of Bodily Death*. New York: Dover Books.

Narby, Jeremy (1999). *The Cosmic Serpent*. London: Phoenix Books.

Naydler, Jeremy (2005). *Plato, Shamanism and Ancient Egypt*. Oxford, U.K.: Abzu Press.

Nicolescu, Basarab (1991). *Science, Meaning, & Evolution: The Cosmology of Jacob Boehme*. New York: Parabola.

Nietzsche, Friedrich (1977). R. J. Hollingdale trans. *Twilight of the Idols and The Antichrist*. Harmondsworth, U.K.: Penguin Classics.

Novalis (1989). Arthur Versluis, trans. *Pollen and Fragments*. Grand Rapids, Mich.: Phanes Press.

Orage, A. R. (1974). *Consciousness: Animal, Human and Superman*. New York: Samuel Weiser.

Ouspensky, P. D. (1949). *In Search of the Miraculous*. New York: Harcourt, Brace.

———— (1969). *A New Model of the Universe*. New York: Alfred A. Knopf.

———— (1981). *Tertium Organum*. New York: Alfred A. Knopf.

Pagels, Elaine (1990). *The Gnostic Gospels*. London: Penguin Books.

Pasi, Marco (2014). *Aleister Crowley and the Temptation of Politics*. Durham, U.K.; Acumen Publishing.

Petrarch (1985). *The Canzoniere and Other Works*. Oxford, U.K.: Oxford University Press.

Phillips, Steven (1995). *Extra-sensory Perception of Quarks*. Adyar, India: Theosophical Publishing House.

Picknett, Lynn, and Prince, Clive (2011). *The Forbidden Universe*. London: Constable.

Pico della Mirandola, Giovanni (1956). *Oration on the Dignity of Man*. Chicago: Gateway Editions.

Place, Robert M. (2005). *The Tarot: History, Symbolism, and Divination*. New York: Tarcher/Penguin.

Plato (1961). W. K. C. Guthrie trans. *Collected Dialogues*. Princeton, N.J.: Bollingen Series.

Poe, Edgar Allan (2002). *Eureka*. London: Hesperus Press.

Polanyi, Michael (1967). *The Tacit Dimension*. New York: Anchor Books.

Pollard, Justin, and Reid, Howard (2007). *The Rise and Fall of Alexandria: Birthplace of the Modern World*. New York: Penguin Books.

Powys, John Cowper (1982). *Autobiography*. London: Picador.

Purver, Margery (1967). *The Royal Society: Concept and Creation*. London: Routledge.

Raine, Kathleen (1982). *The Inner Journey of the Poet*. New York: George Braziller.

———— (1991). *Golgonooza, City of Imagination*. Hudson, N.Y.: Lindisfarne Books.

Ridley, Jasper (2000). *The Freemasons*. London: Robinson.

Robinson, James M., ed. (1990). *The Nag Hammadi Library in English*. New York: HarperCollins.

Rossi, Paolo (1968). *Francis Bacon: From Magic to Science*. London: Routledge.

Rudgley, Richard (1998). *Lost Civilizations of the Stone Age*. London: Century.

Salaman, Clement, trans. (2001). *The Way of Hermes*. London: Duckworth.

———— (2007). *Asclepius: The Perfect Discourse of Hermes Trismegistus*. London: Duckworth.

Saler, Michael, ed. (2015). *The Fin-De-Siècle World*. New York: Routledge.

Scholem, Gershom (1960). *Jewish Gnosticism, Merkabah Mysticism, and Talmudic Tradition*. New York: The Jewish Theological Seminary of America.

Schuchard, Marsha Keith (2006). *Why Mrs. Blake Cried*. London: Century.

Schwaller de Lubicz , René (1978). *Symbol and the Symbolic*. Brookline, Mass.: Autumn Press.

—— (1982). *Nature Word*. West Stockbridge, Mass.: Lindisfarne Press.

—— (1985). *Esotericism and Symbol*. New York: Inner Traditions.

—— (1999). *The Temples of Karnak*. Rochester, Vt.: Inner Traditions.

Scott, Walter, ed. (2001). *Hermetica*. Boston: Shambhala.

Sedgwick, Mark (2004). *Against the Modern World*. Oxford, U.K.: Oxford University Press.

Shand, John (1994). *Philosophy and Philosophers*. London: Penguin Books.

Shlain, Leonard (1999). *The Alphabet Versus the Goddess*. New York: Penguin.

Smith, Andrew (2004). *Philosophy in Late Antiquity*. London: Routledge.

Smith, Morton (1973). *The Secret Gospel: The Discovery and Interpretation of the Secret Gospel According to Mark*. New York: Harper & Row.

Smoley, Richard (2000). *Inner Christianity*. Boulder, Colo.: Shambhala.

—— (2006). *Forbidden Faith: The Gnostic Legacy*. New York: HarperCollins.

South, Mary Anne (1850). *A Suggestive Inquiry into the Hermetic Mystery with a Dissertation on the More Celebrated of the Alchemical Philosophers*. London: Trelawney Saunders.

Spretnak, Charlene (1991). *States of Grace: The Recovery of Meaning in the Postmodern Age*. San Francisco: HarperSanFrancisco.

Stace, Walter T. (1960). *The Teachings of the Mystics*. New York: Mentor Books.

Steiner, George (1976). *After Babel*. Oxford, U.K.: Oxford University Press.

—— (1978). *Has Truth a Future?* London: BBC Publications.

—— (2001). *Grammars of Creation*. London: Faber and Faber.

—— (2003). *Lessons of the Masters*. Cambridge, Mass.: Harvard University Press.

Steiner, Rudolf (1973). *Anthroposophical Leading Thoughts*. London: Rudolf Steiner Press.

—— (1973). *The Occult Movement in the Nineteenth Century*. London: Rudolf Steiner Press.

—— (1995). *Intuitive Thinking as a Spiritual Path: A Philosophy of Freedom*. New York: Anthroposophical Press.

—— (1997). *Outline of Esoteric Science*. New York: Anthroposophical Press.

Storr, Anthony (1988). *Solitude: A Return to the Self*. New York: Ballantine Books.

—— (1992). *Music and the Mind*. London: HarperCollins.

Stoyanov, Yuri (1994). *The Hidden Tradition in Europe*. London: Arkana.

Swedenborg, Emanuel (1958). J. C. Ager trans. *Heaven and Hell*. London: Swedenborg Society.

Tarnas, Richard (1991). *The Passion of the Western Mind*. New York: Ballantine Books.

Underhill, Evelyn (1961). *Mysticism*. New York: E. P. Dutton.

—— (2007). *The Essentials of Mysticism*. New York: Cosimo Classics.

VandenBroeck, André (1987). *Al-Kemi: A Memoir: Hermetic, Occult, Political, and Private Aspects of R. A. Schwaller de Lubicz*. Hudson, N.Y.: Lindisfarne Press.

van den Broeck, Roelof, and Hanegraaff, Wouter J., eds. (1998). *Gnosis and Hermeticism: From Antiquity to Modern Times*. Albany, N.Y.: SUNY Press.

Versluis, Arthur (2007). *Magic and Mysticism: An Introduction to Western Esotericism*. Lanham, Md.: Rowman & Littlefield.

von Franz, Marie-Louise (1980). *Alchemy: An Introduction to the Symbolism and the Psychology*. Toronto: Inner City Books.

Walbridge, John (2000). *The Leaven of the Ancients: Suhrawardi and the Heritage of the Greeks*. Albany, N.Y.: SUNY Press.

Walker, D. P. (2006). *Spiritual and Demonic Magic from Ficino to Campanella*. Stroud, U.K.: Sutton Publishing.

Wasson, R. Gordon, et al. (2008). *The Road to Eleusis*. Berkeley, Calif.: North Atlantic Books.

Watson, Peter (2010). *The German Genius*. London: Simon & Schuster.

Webb, James (1976). *The Occult Establishment*. La Salle, Ill.: Open Court.

Weinberg, Steven (1993). *The First Three Minutes*. New York: Basic Books.

Whitehead, Alfred North (1926). *Religion in the Making*. Cambridge, U.K.: Cambridge University Press.

—— (1955). *Symbolism: Its Meaning and Effect*. New York: G. P. Putnam Sons.

—— (1968). *Modes of Thought*. New York: Free Press.

—— (1979). *Process and Reality*. New York: Free Press.

Wilson, Colin (1957). *Religion and the Rebel*. Boston: Houghton Mifflin.

—— (1971). *The Occult*. New York: Random House.

—— (1980). *Starseekers*. London: Hodder & Stoughton.

—— (1980). *Frankenstein's Castle*. Sevenoaks, U.K.: Ashgrove Press.

—— (1981). *Poltergeist!* London: New English Library.

———— (1983). *Access to Inner Worlds.* London: Rider and Co.

———— (1984). *A Criminal History of Mankind.* New York: G. P. Putnam Sons.

———— (1987). *The Musician as Outsider.* Nottingham, U.K.: Pauper's Press.

———— (1988). *Beyond the Occult.* London: Bantam Press.

———— (1996). *From Atlantis to the Sphinx.* London: Virgin Books.

———— (2006). *Atlantis and the Kingdom of the Neanderthals.* Rochester, Vt.: Bear & Co.

———— (2006). *Mysteries.* London: Watkins Publishing.

Wittgenstein, Ludwig (1984). *Culture and Value.* Chicago: University of Chicago Press.

Woods, Richard (2011). *Meister Eckhart: Master of Mystics.* London: Continuum International Publishing Group.

Wooley, Benjamin (2001). *The Queen's Conjurer.* London: HarperCollins.

Yates, Frances (1971). *Giordano Bruno and the Hermetic Tradition.* London: Routledge & Kegan Paul.

———— (1978). *The Rosicrucian Enlightenment.* Boulder, Colo.: Shambhala.

Yeats, W. B. (1994). *The Collected Letters of W. B. Yeats,* vol. III. Oxford, U.K.: Oxford University Press.

INDEX

ABOUT THE AUTHOR

GARY LACHMAN is the author of many books on consciousness, culture, and the western esoteric tradition, including *Rudolf Steiner: An Introduction to His Life and Work*; *In Search of P. D. Ouspensky*; *A Secret History of Consciousness*; *Politics and the Occult*; and *The Quest for Hermes Trismegistus*. He writes for several journals in the United States and the UK and lectures on his work in the United States, the UK, and Europe. His books have been translated into more than a dozen languages and he has appeared in several radio and television documentaries. He is assistant professor in the Evolution of Consciousness at the California Institute of Integral Studies. A founding member of the rock group Blondie, he was inducted into the Rock and Roll Hall of Fame in 2006. He can be reached at www.garylachman.co.uk.